A

CRITICAL AND HISTORICAL INTRODUCTION

TO THE

CANONICAL SCRIPTURES

OF THE

OLD TESTAMENT.

From the German

OF

WILHELM MARTIN LEBERECHT DE WETTE.

TRANSLATED AND ENLARGED

BY

THEODORE PARKER,

MINISTER OF THE SECOND CHURCH IN ROXBURY

Πάταξον μὲν, ἄκουσον δέ.

IN TWO VOLUMES

VOL. II.

FOURTH EDITION.

NEW YORK:

D. APPLETON AND COMPANY.

BOSTON: T. O. H. P. BURNHAM.

1864.

PART III.

PARTICULAR INTRODUCTION TO THE CANONICAL BOOKS OF THE OLD TESTAMENT.

---

§ 125.

A SURVEY AND CLASSIFICATION OF THE BOOKS OF THE OLD TESTAMENT.

THE classification of the literary productions of a nation must be made in the spirit of that nation's history, and in accordance with an accurate conception of that history. Just, though not perfectly clear and pure ideas of classification may be found in the Jewish division into the *Law*, *Prophets*, and *Other Writings*.

According to the most accurate principles, it seems the two first divisions — the *Law* and the *Prophets* — must be put together, for they contain a cyclus of *theocratic* writings. In this cyclus it is easy to separate the *theocratic-historical* from the *theocratic-inspired* writings. To the former belong the *Law*, the *first Prophets*, as they are called, that is, the *historical books;* and from the third miscellaneous division, the books of *Ezra*, *Nehemiah*, *Ruth*, *Esther*, and *Chronicles*, are added as appendices and a supplement. To the latter belong the *later Prophets*, as they are called, and, from the third division, the later prophetical production, the book of *Daniel*.

There then remain, as a third class, the poetic books, that is, the *lyric* and *gnomologic* (or sententious) writings, namely, the *Psalms*, *Job*, the *Salomonic writings*, and the *Lamentations*. All of these—with the exception of *Solomon's Song*, which was probably explained in an allegorical manner, to judge from its reception into the canon—have a religious, but not a theocratical character.

§ 126.

VARIOUS STYLES, POETIC AND PROSAIC.

Since every peculiar subject brings with it a peculiar form, the above classification must be confirmed by a difference in the style of the several divisions. The Hebrews, like other nations, have their poetic and prosaic style, which differ from one another in the substance of the discourse; that is, in the use of more choice and flowing language, (§ 34,) and in the form of the movement. The former has a quiet and irregular motion; the latter a dancing and measured movement,—a rhythm.

The quiet form of prose is suited to the quiet, simple narration of historical events; therefore the historical books, with the exception of single passages, are written in prose. But since, in the quiet movement of the style, the law of euphony and harmony is not at all inadmissible, in many historical passages,—for example, Gen. i. xxiii., Ex. vii.—x., Num. xxii.—xxiv.,—there is not only a certain *numerus*, [or measure,] but likewise an attempt at a rhythmical movement, and a division into strophes. This kind of prose may be called the *epic*, and the other the *common*.

§ 127.

RHYTHMICAL BOOKS.

Soon as the Hebrew began to write with a higher inspiration, and rose above a simple narrative of events, and drew out of his own soul, rhythm came to him spontaneously. For this reason, the *theocratical-inspired* and *poetic* books are written in a rhythmical style. But they are written in various degrees of rhythm, according as the writer was more or less inspired. Some passages in the Prophets and Ecclesiastes rise little, or not at all, above prose, or soon sink back into it. This transition from prose to rhythm, and the reverse, constitutes a peculiar beauty of Hebrew poetry; but it is only obtained by the remarkable irregularity of its rhythm.

§ 128.

SYMMETRY OF THE MEMBERS.

The Hebrews neglect the rhythm of syllables, and, in this respect, recognize only an irregular measure, (*numerus*,) which sometimes has a uniform movement.[a] But the proportion of the members in the sentence is deter-

---

[a] Since, in Hebrew, all the syllables have the same duration, or, according to the *systema morarum*, three moments of time,—for example, קָ, מַל, —therefore the change of the tone (*Wechsel der Rede*) is produced by the accent, which gives the tone-syllable greater emphasis; for example, קָטַל. This law once admitted, there would generally be found a free mixture of iambuses, (עַמִּיר, מַלְכָּה,) trochees, (מֶלֶךְ, אֵלֶּה,) amphibrachs, (קָטַלְתָּ,) anapests, (יִשְׂרָאֵל,) &c.

Sometimes there would be a predominance of iambic, trochaic, or anapostic movement; for example,

mined by the law of symmetry,—*parallelismus membrorum*,—the fundamental law of all rhythmical movement, which always consists in a certain uniform return. The Samaritan and Æthiopian languages have merely a measure of lines, without any measure of syllables. In Hebrew poetry, this return is given in its simplest form, in the succession of two corresponding members, as it were the pulse-beat of the discourse, by which the swelling heart expresses its emotions.

"The Hebrew soul," says a writer, "is the silent, yet still unfathomed deep of the divine in man. It is not the ocean over which the winds are sweeping, and in which all the floods rush together; but it is the lowest, the living deep and fountain, which only discloses itself in a soft and gentle stream, scarcely perceptible to mortal ear. Hence there is the simple parallelism, which continually recurs, and the unconfined and unadorned heart of poetry, with its uniform beat."[a]

הַלְלוּ עַבְדֵי יְהוָה הַלְלוּ אֶת־שֵׁם יְהוָה׃

יֹאבַד יוֹם אִוָּלֶד בּוֹ וְהַלַּיְלָה אָמַר הֹרָה גָבֶר׃

בְּצֵאת יִשְׂרָאֵל מִמִּצְרָיִם בֵּית יַעֲקֹב מֵעַם לֹעֵז׃

הָיְתָה יְהוּדָה לְקָדְשׁוֹ יִשְׂרָאֵל מַמְשְׁלוֹתָיו

הַהֹפְכִי הַצּוּר אֲגַם־מָיִם חַלָּמִישׁ לְמַעְיְנוֹ־מָיִם׃

For this discovery we are indebted to *Bellermann*, Versuch. üb. d. Metrik d. Hebräer; Berl. 1813. But he goes too far when he attempts to prove there is actual versification in the Hebrew poetry. To this it may be added that, perhaps, the *shevas* when a consonant is closely connected with them, and the composite *shevas*, form half a short syllable, so that in the last example we must scan thus: אֲגַם־מָיִם. *Leutwein*, also, has referred to the *numerus*, Biblische Verskunst; Tüb. 1795.

[a] "Rhythm — which is a fundamental law of the voice — can never be entirely wanting in any human discourse. But it appears the more distinctly

At the same time, this form helps to overcome the peculiarity of the language, and the constant use of, and even fondness for, tautology and synonymes, which is characteristic of the Hebrew, when not overruled by inspiration, and filled with the subject. This instinct, which makes divisions or cæsuras between the larger members of the discourse, brings with it a symmetry, and demands also cæsuras and symmetry within the members or half-verses thus divided and arranged one after the other; and these subordinate passages or subdivisions of the rhythm become the more frequent as the discourse is more rich in thought and takes a wider compass. Thus there are verses of a single member, at the beginning of a psalm, (Ps. xviii. 2, xxiii. 1,) like the preliminary beating time, but rarely in the middle of the ode. (Ps. xlii. 9.)

§ 129.

DIFFERENT KINDS OF SYMMETRY OF MEMBERS.

1. Symmetry of Words.

Since the Hebrews have no measure of syllables, they cannot mark the symmetry by using an equal number of syllables. Their poetry consists chiefly in the thought, and, therefore, it has a rhythm of thoughts. But since the thought is expressed in words, the original

as the waves of voice swell higher with the increasing elevation of feeling, and the mass and power of the rhythmical movement increases in proportion; consequently the effort to preserve an equilibrium is more decided, and the successive risings and fallings extend farther. This takes place the most perfectly in poetry — when the soul, tuned in harmony with the gently-swelling wave of life, pours out her thought in symmetrical ranks, which are sometimes merely internal, expressed only in the *thoughts*, — as in the Hebrew parallelism, and the poetry of the people in general, — and sometimes

and simplest form of symmetry is that shown by an equal number of words in the corresponding members of the sentence.[a]

But here a word must often be repeated in thought.

A similar sound, or rhyme, is sometimes found at the end of the lines.[b]

For the sake of this rhyme, suitable grammatical forms are sometimes designedly selected, and even sought for.[c]

§ 130.

2. Symmetry of Thoughts.

A. *With similar Members.*

The Hebrews seldom seek for similarity between the words in the different members of a sentence, or they follow this rule with great looseness. The symmetry is rather expressed in the thoughts —

---

they are also external, expressed in the particular *sounds*, — as in the poetry of the Greeks and other nations, which is measured by syllables."

Hupfeld, in Studien und Kritiken, for 1837, p. 869, sq. See *Ewald*, Poet. Buch. der A. T. vol. i. p. 57, sq., 92, sq. *Gügler*, Die heilige Kunst; Lands. 1815.

[a] Job vi. 5.

הֲיִנְהַק פֶּרֶא עֲלֵי דֶשֶׁא
אִם יִגְעֶה־שּׁוֹר עַל־בְּלִילוֹ׃

Ps. xx. 9. Prov. x. 15. Ps. xix. 8. *Ewald*, l. c. vol. i. p. 65. See § 132.

[b] Gen. iv. 23.

עָדָה וְצִלָּה שְׁמַעַן קוֹלִי
נְשֵׁי לֶמֶךְ הַאְזֵנָּה אִמְרָתִי
כִּי אִישׁ הָרַגְתִּי לְפִצְעִי
וְיֶלֶד -- לְחַבֻּרָתִי׃

[c] Job xvi. 12.

שָׁלֵו הָיִיתִי וַיְפַרְפְּרֵנִי
וְאָחַז בְּעָרְפִּי וַיְפַצְפְּצֵנִי

Job xxxvii. 16. Amos v. 26.

1. Sometimes by *synonymes.*

Psalm viii. 4.

"When I consider thy heavens, the work of thy fingers,
The moon and stars which thou hast made,
What is man, that thou art mindful of him?
And the son of man, that thou visitest him?"

Psalm viii. 7.

"Thou hast given him dominion over the works of thy hands.
All thou hast put under his feet."

Ps. lx. 2, 9, 10, and many other places.

2. Sometimes by *antithesis.*

Proverbs x. 3, 4.

"Jehovah will not suffer the soul of the righteous to famish,
But will scatter the substance of the wicked.
A slack hand makes poor.
A diligent hand makes rich."

Also, 6, 8, 9, 11, and many others.

3. Sometimes by *synthesis.*

Psalm i. 6.

"For the Lord knoweth the way of the righteous,
But the way of the wicked shall perish."

Psalm iii. 3.

"Many say of my soul,
'No help for it in Elohim.'"

See, also, 5, 7, 9, iv. 4, 5, et al.

4. By *an identical expression;* that is, by repeating in fuller and stronger form.

Job xviii. 13.

"It shall devour the strength of his body.
The first-born of death shall devour his strength."

Hos. ix. 14. Ps. xxi. 5, lvii. 4.[a]

---

[a] Compare *Lowth,* De sac. Poesi Heb. Prælect. xix. p. 365, ed. *Michaelis*

In these simple couplets or distichs, besides the chief cæsura in the middle of the verse, we find always smaller cæsuras, the most distinctly marked in the second half-verse, towards the end, in order to preserve the cadence.

Psalm viii. 4.

כִּי־אֶרְאֶה שָׁמֶיךָ | מַעֲשֵׂה אֶצְבְּעֹתֶיךָ
יָרֵחַ וְכוֹכָבִים | אֲשֶׁר כּוֹנָנְתָּה

"I look at thy heavens, | the work of thy fingers;
The moon and the stars, | which thou hast created."

§ 131.

B. *Symmetry with dissimilar Members.*

By the internal force of the thought also, members that are disproportionate, and dissimilar in expression, are brought under a rhythmical symmetry, and often with fine effect.

Hosea iv. 17.

"Ephraim is joined unto idols:
Let him alone." [a]

Two or more passages, parallel among themselves, may individually be so opposed to one another, that larger rhythmical periods will be produced, and with fine effect.

Psalm xxxvi. 7.

"Thy righteousness is like the great mountains;
Thy judgments are a great deep;
Man and beast thou preservest, Jehovah." [b]

---

[a] חֲבוּר עֲצַבִּים אֶפְרָיִם
הַנַּח לוֹ׃ Ps. xxxvii. 13, xlviii. 5, lxviii. 33. Job xiv. 14.

[b] Ps. cxii. 10. Job iii. 5, vii. 11, x. 1, 15, 17, xx. 26. Ps. xv. 4, xlix. 11, xxii. 25, xl. 10, xci. 7, i. 3, lxv. 10. Am. iv. 13.

Sometimes one member has merely an echo of itself in the next.

Psalm v. 3.

"Hearken to the voice of my supplication, my King and my God,
For unto thee will I pray."

Ps. xxiii. 3, xxvii. 11, 12.

In all these forms the above logical distinction is repeated.

§ 132.

C. *With double Members.*

When there is a richer fulness of thoughts and images, both members are doubled. Then, either each member has its own sub-parallelism, or it overleaps and disregards the parallelism. Here, likewise, the same logical distinctions are repeated.

Psalm xxxi. 11.

"For my life is consumed in affliction,
And my years in sighing;
My strength fails because of my sin,
And my bones decay."[a]

A passage may be contrasted with such a double member three or more times. By this arrangement, the greatest compass is given to rhythmical periods. The prophets, in particular, are fond of this more extended form.

Habakkuk iii. 17.

"Though the fig-tree bear not fruit,
And there is no increase of the vines;
Though the fruit of the olive fail,
And the fields do not furnish food,

---

[a] Ps. xl. 17, xxxv. 26, xxxvii. 14, lxxix. 2. Cant. v. 3. Mich. i. 4. Ps. xxx. 6, lv. 22, xliv. 3. Cant. ii. 3.

The flock fail from the fold,
And there is no herd in the stalls," &c.

Amos ii. 9, v. 5, vii. 17. Mich. ii. 13, vii. 3.

Ewald distinguishes what he calls an *extended rhythm*, which is the extension of a couplet into a period of ten or eleven syllables, in Psalm ii. 12, xxxii. 4, 6, xxxix. 2, lxii. 4, 5, 10, 11. But here I find only connected members, where there is no symmetry of thought, like that described in the next section.

§ 133.

3. Rhythmical Symmetry.

As, among us, a short syllable may be made long, by the tone, (*tact*,) so the Hebrews have sometimes a symmetry of the members of a sentence, which is not founded in the sense of the passage, but is only continued by the rhythmical movement, when once it is begun. This contrivance introduces variety into the style, which would otherwise be stiff and uniform.

This rhythmical symmetry consists in having the same number of words in each member, (as, for example, in Ps. xix. 12,) or in having a great difference in the number of words in the two members, (for example, Ps. xiv. 7, xxx. 3.) The parallelism also may be double.

Psalm xxxi. 23.

" And I said in my haste,
'I am cut off from before thine eyes;'
But yet thou didst hear the voice of my prayer,
In my crying unto thee."

In the use of this form there is sometimes a transition to an unmeasured style.

Malachi i. 6.

"A son honoreth his father,
And a servant his master:
If I, then, be a father, where is my honor?
And if I be a master, where is the fear of me?
Saith Jehovah of hosts to you, priests that despise my name.'

Zech. xiii. 3. It often occurs in Jeremiah.

Sometimes the course of the rhythmical periods differs from the logical order of thought.

Psalm cii. 8.

"I watch, and am
Like a solitary sparrow on the house-top."

Job xxxvii. 12. Zeph. iii. 18.

§ 134, *a*.

RHYTHM INDICATED BY THE ACCENT.

The symmetry, and the other rhythmical relations, of the members, are denoted by the accents.[a] But the distinction between the prosaic and the poetic accentuation of the books of Job, Proverbs, and the Psalms, is of no great importance.[b] In the former, *silluk* with *soph-pasuk* marks the end; in the former, *athnah*, (—֑—,) and in the latter *merka-mahpak*, (—֥֤—,) designate the main

[a] Among the Jews, recitation degenerated into cantillation; and so the accents acquired a musical signification, and are called *neginoth*, (נְגִינוֹת.) A scheme of this cantillation according to the accents is called *Sarka*, and may be found in *Jablonski's* Preface to his Hebrew Bible. This use of the accents has erroneously been looked upon as their original use. Christian scholars first discovered the logical, rhythmical nature of the accents. *Bohle*, Santin. sac. s. ex Accentibus; 1636. *Wasmuth*, Instit. Accentuat. Heb.; 1664. *Jo. Frank*, Diacrit. Sac.; 1710. *J. F. Hirt*. Syst. Accent. Heb.; 1752. *C. B. Spitzner*, Instit. ad Analyt. s. Text. Heb. V. T. ex Accentibus; 1786. *Hupfeld* (l. c. p. 826) arrives at some new conclusions.

[b] *Ewald*, Gram. 2d ed. p. 89. The poetical has shorter and easier propositions, and more manifold and subtile distinctions.

division of the verses. But, in the smaller verses, this is effected by means of the lesser distinctive accents, which are commonly used to mark the subdivisions. But, although the observance of the accents is useful in determining the rhythmical proportion, yet we are not to follow them in a servile spirit; for, in general, it is doubtful that the authors of the accentuation were clearly conscious of the nature of rhythm. In two psalms (cxi. cxii.) the half-verses are indicated by the initial letters, which follow the order of the alphabet.[a]

§ 134, *b*.

STROPHES, OR SYMMETRY OF VERSES.

It would be a very natural occurrence if this same symmetry extended to the larger divisions, to the periods and sections, and formed strophes. Even in prose there is a similar proportion, either more or less distinct.[b]

It has long been known that rhythmical stropnes (or such as have definite outward forms) could be found, namely

1. In the alphabetic poems, where single verses are sometimes connected so as to correspond with one another.

Psalm xxv.[c]

1 "To thee, O Lord, do I lift up my soul!
2 O my God, I trust in thee! Let me not be put to shame!
Let not my enemies triumph over me!
3 Yea, none that hope in thee shall be put to shame;
They shall be put to shame who wickedly forsake thee.

---

[a] On this whole subject, see *De Wette*, in Bib. Repository, vol. iii. p. 470, sqq., [*Nordheimer*, Heb. Gram. § 1120—1158,] and *Carpzov*, Int. ii. p. 3, sqq.

[b] See *Köster*, on the Strophes, or Parallelism of the Heb. Poetry, in Theol. St. and Kr., (1831,) p. 40, and his work das B. Hiob u. d. Pred. Salom., &c. Schlesw. 1831. The author goes too far.

[c] Noyes's Translation.

4 Show me thy ways, O Lord,
Teach me thy paths!
5 Lead me in thy truth, and teach me;
For thou art the God, from whom cometh my help;
In thee do I trust at all times!
6 Remember thy kindness, O Lord, and thy mercy,
Which thou hast exercised of old!
7 Remember not the faults and transgressions of my youth;
According to thy mercy remember thou me,
For thy goodness' sake, O Lord!
8 "Good and righteous is Jehovah;
Therefore showeth he to sinners the way;
9 The humble he guideth in his statutes,
And the humble he teacheth his way.
10 All the doings of Jehovah are mercy and truth,
To those who keep his covenant and his precepts.
11 For thy name's sake, O Jehovah,
Pardon my iniquity, for it is great!"

Ps. xxxiv. cxlv. Prov. xxxi. 10, sqq. Lam. i. ii. iv.

Sometimes two or more verses are connected in greater strophes; for example, Ps. xxxvii. cxix.

2. Strophes occur distinguished by the *refrain*, (or "*burden*,") or something similar.

Isaiah ix. 8—x. 4.[a]

1.

8 "The Lord sendeth a word against Jacob;
It cometh down to Israel.
9 His whole people shall feel it;
Ephraim, and the inhabitants of Samaria,
Who say, in pride and arrogance of heart,
10 'The bricks are fallen down, but we will build with hewn stones;
The sycamores are cut down, but we will replace them with cedars.'
11 Jehovah raiseth up the enemies of Rezin against you,
And armeth your adversaries;
12 The Syrians before, the Philistines behind,

[a] Noyes's Translation.

Who shall devour Israel with full jaws.
For all this his anger is not turned away,
But his hand is stretched out still.

2.

13 "The people turneth not to him that smiteth them;
Neither do they seek Jehovah of hosts.
14 Therefore shall Jehovah cut off from Israel the head and the tail
The palm-branch, and the rush, in one day;
15 [The aged and the honorable are the head,
And the prophet, that speaketh falsehood, is the tail.]
16 For the leaders of this people lead them astray,
And they that are led by them go to destruction.
17 Therefore shall Jehovah have no joy in their young men,
And on their orphans and widows he shall have no compassion;
For they are all profane, and evil-doers;
Every mouth speaketh folly.
For all this his anger is not turned away,
But his hand is stretched out still.

3.

18 "For wickedness burneth like a fire;
It consumeth the briers and thorns,
And it kindleth the thicket of the forest,
So that it goeth up in columns of smoke.
19 Through the wrath of Jehovah of hosts is the land burned,
And the people are food for the fire;
No one spareth another.
20 They consume on the right hand, and yet are hungry;
They devour on the left, and are not satisfied;
Every one devoureth the flesh of his arm.
21 Manasseh is against Ephraim, and Ephraim against Manasseh,
And both together against Judah.
For all this his anger is not turned away,
But his hand is stretched out still.

4.

1 "Woe to them that make unrighteous decrees,
That write oppressive decisions!
2 To turn away the needy from judgment,
And rob the poor of my people of their right.

3 What will ye do in the day of visitation,
And in the desolation which cometh from afar?
To whom will ye flee for help,
And where will ye deposit your glory?
4 Forsaken by me, they shall sink down among the bound,
And fall among the slain.
For all this his anger is not turned away,
But his hand is stretched out still."

Ps. xlii. xliii. xlvi. Isa. ix. 7, x. 4. Am. i. 2—ii. 16. Ps. cvii. xlix. lix.

But there are so few logical strophes,[a] that we cannot consider them any thing more than the work of unconscious instinct.

---

[a] Ps. i. ii. iii. iv. vi. vii. xi. and Job viii.

BOOK I.

THEOCRATICAL-HISTORICAL BOOKS.[a]

---

§ 135.

A VIEW OF THESE BOOKS, AND A CLASSIFICATION OF THEM

They contain the history of the theocracy; and,

I. The *books of Moses* and *Joshua* contain the history of its establishment, together with the theocratic laws.

---

[a] LIST OF THE BEST AND MOST VALUABLE EXEGETICAL WORKS ON THE BOOKS OF THE OLD TESTAMENT.

I. RABBINICAL COMMENTARIES.

R. Salomo Jarchi, (or R. Salomo Isaac, commonly abbreviated רשי, Raschi,) Commentary on the whole Bible, in *Buxtorf's* Rabb. Bible; Lat., with notes, ed. by *Breithaupt;* Gotha, 1710—1714, 3 vols. 4to.

Aben Esra, (or Abraham Ben Meir A. E.,) Commentary upon most of the Books of the O. T., in *Buxtorf's* Rabb. Bible, wherein, also, is *David Kimchi's* Comment. on the early and later Prophets and the Chronicles, and *R. Levi Ben Gerson's* Explanation of the first Prophets, the Proverbs of Solomon and Job.

Isaak Abarbanel, Comment. on the Pentateuch; Lat., by *Henr. van Bashuisen;* Hannov. 1710, fol. On the historical books, by *Aug. Pfeiffer;* Leipz. 1686, fol. On the later Prophets; Amst. 1641, fol. On Isaiah; Lat. by *J. H. Majus;* Frcf. a. M. 1711, 4to. On Hosea; Lat. by *Fr. von Hasen;* Leid. 1686. On Nahum, Hebr. and Lat. by *J. D. Sprecher;* Helmst. 1703. On Malachi, with Commentaries of *Aben Esra, Jarchi*, and *Kimchi;* Lat. by *Sam. Bohl;* Rost. 1637, 4to.

R. Salomo Ben Melech, מִכְלַל יוֹפִי; best editions, Const. 1685, fol., with *Abendana's* addition. Ex Michlal Jophi, sive Commentario R. Salom. Ben

II. The (so called) *historic books*, with their appendages, *Chronicles* and the *book of Ruth*, contain the

---

Melech in V. T. Libros . . . . . . particula complectens Prophetiam Jonæ. Vers. Lat. et Indice illustravit, Paraphrasin Chald. Textui Hebr. adposuit atque Præf. præmisit *Ern. Chr. Fabricius;* Gott. 1792, 8vo.

II. Church Fathers.

Origen, Exegetical Remains on the O. T., in *Origenis* Commentaria, ed. *Huetius;* Rothomagi, 1668. Opera, ed. *De la Rue*, vol. ii. iii.

Jo. Chrysostomus, Homilies, Opp. ed. *Montfaucon;* Paris, 1718—1738, 13 vols. fol.

Ephraem the Syrian's Commentary on the O. T., after the Peshito, in his Opp. Syr. et Lat. ed. *Petr. Benedictus;* Rom. 1740, fol.

Theodoreti Quæst. in Pentat., Jos., Jud., Ruth, Sam., Regg., Paralip. Comment. in Psalm., Cant. Cant., Proph., Opp. ed. *Jac. Sirmond;* Par. 1642, 4 tom. fol.; ed. *J. L. Schulz* et *J. A. Nösselt;* Hal. 1769—1774, 5 tom. 8vo.

Procopii Gazaei Comment. in Octateuchum Lat.; Tigur. 1555; in Libros Regg. et Paralipp. Græce et Latine a *Jo. Meursio;* Lug. Bat. 1620, 4to. Variorum in Esaiam Prophetam Commentariorum Epitome Græce et Lat. a *Jo. Curterio;* Paris, 1580.

Σειρὰ ἑνὸς πεντήκοντα ὑπομνηματιστῶν εἰς τὴν 'Οκτάτευχον καὶ τῶν Βασιλειῶν ἤδη πρῶτον τύποις ἐκδοθεῖσα ἐπιμελείᾳ Νικηφόρου; Leipz. 1772, 2 vols. fol. Catena Græcorum P. P. in beatum Job. Collectore *Niceta* ed. et Lat. Vers. Op. et St. *Patricii Junii;* Lond. 1637, fol. Expositio Patrum Græcorum in Psalmos a *Balth. Corderio* ex Codd. concinnata, Latinitate donata; Antwerp, 1643—1646; fol. 3 vols. *Eusebii, Polychronii, Psellii* in Cant. Cant. Expositt. Græce *Jo. Meursius* publicavit; Lug. Bat. 1617, 4to.

Hieronymi Comment. in Prophetas, Eccles. Quæst. Hebr. in Genes. Epist. critt. xviii. Opp. ed. *Martianay;* Par. 1693—1706, 5 vols. fol.;—ed. *Vallarsi;* Veron. 1734—1742, 11 vols. fol.; ed. 2, 1766—1772, 11 vols. 4to.

Augustini Liber de Genesi ad Litteram imperf.; de Genesi ad Litteram LL. xii.; Quæst. in Heptateuchum LL. vii.; Enarrat. in Psalm.; Annotatt. in Job. L. I. Opp. ed. Bened.; Par. 1679—1701, 11 vols. fol.;—ed. 2, Cur. *Clerici;* Antwerp, 1700—1703, 12 vols. fol.

III. Modern Interpreters.

Conr. Pellicani Comm. in Libros V. et N. T.; Tigur. 1532—1539, 9 vols. fol.

Jo. Piscatoris Comm. in omnes Libros V. T.; Herborn. 1646, fol.

Cornel. a Lapide, Comm. in omnes S. S. Libros; Venet. 1688, 16 vols. fol.

Calvini Comm. in his Opp.; Amst. 1671, 9 vols. fol.

subsequent history of the theocracy, its struggle and downfall.

Franc. Vatabli (Vatblé) Annotatt. in V. T. ex ejus Prælectt. collectæ a *Bertino le Comte;* Par. 1545; also at the end of the Vulgate of *Rob. Stephanus;* 1557, 2 vols. fol.

Seb. Münster, Annotatt. in omnes Libros V. T. in his Bibl. Hebr. Lat.; 1535—1546.

Jo. le Mercier, Comm. in Gen.; 1598; in Job., Proverbb., etc.; 1573, fol.; in Prophetas quinque priores inter eos, qui minores vocantur; 1698, 4to.

Jo. Drusii Annotatt. in Loca diffic. Pentateuchi; Frankf. 1617, 4to.; in Loca diffic. Jos., Judd., et Sam.; 1618, 4to. Lectiones in Proph. Nahum, Hab., Sophon., Joel., Jon., Abdiam. In Græcam Editionem Conjectanea, et Interpretum vett. quæ exstant Fragmenta; Leid. 1595. Lect. in Hos., etc.; Leid. 1699. In Amos; Leid. 1600. In Mich., Agg., Zachar., et Malach.; Amst. 1627, 4to. Comm. in Prophetas min., ed. Sixt. Amama; Amst. 1627, 4to. Comm. in Libr. Ruth; 1586, 4to. Annotatt. in L. Esther; Leid. 1586. Scholia in Job.; Amst. 1636. In Cohel.; ib. 1635, 4to.

Grotii Annotatt. in V. T.; Par. 1644, 3 vols. fol.;— ed. *G. J. L. Vogel* et *Döderlein;* Hal. 1775, 1776, 3 vols. 4to.;—with an Auctarium by *Döderlein;* 1779, 4to.

See these and other interpreters in Critt. sacris; Lond. 1660, 9 vols. fol., (by *J.* and *R. Pearson Scattergood,* and *Gouldman,*) reprinted and enlarged; Amst. 1698, 9 vols. fol., ed. by *Gürtler;* Frankf. 1696, 7 vols. fol.; and 2 suppl. vols.; 1700, 1701. *Matth. Poli,* Synopsis Criticorum aliorumque S. S. Interpretum; Lond. 1669, 5 vols. fol.; Frankf. 1712, 5 vols. fol.; ib. 1694, 5 vols. 4to.

Jo. Maldonati Comm. in Præcip. Libr. V. T.; Par. 1643, fol.

Lud. de Dieu, Animadverss. in V. T. Libros omnes; Leid. 1648. Critica sac. sive Animadverss. in Loca quæd. diffic. V. et N. T.; Amst. 1693, fol.

Lud. Cappelli Comm. et Notæ criticæ in V. T., cum *Jac. Cappelli* Observatt. in V. T.; Amst. 1689, fol.

Abrah. Calovii Biblia V. et N. T. illustrata, sive Comm. Locupl. in V. et N. T., præmissis Chronico s., Tractatu de Nummis, Ponderibus, et Mensuris, insertis et refutatis Annotatt. Grotianis universis; Frcf. a. M. 1672—1676, 4 vols. fol.

Seb. Schmidt, Annotatt. super Mosis L. I.; Arg. 1697, 4to. Prælect. in viii. priora c. Jos. in his Comm. in Jes.; Hamb. 1723, 4to. Comm. in Libr. Judd.; Arg. 1706, 4to. Annotatt. in L. Ruth; ib. 1696, 4to. Comm. in Librr. Sam.; ib. 1697, 4to. Annotatt. in Librr. Regg.; ib. 1697. Comm. in Job.; ib. 1705, 2 vols. 4to. In Cohel.; ib. 1704, 4to. Super Prophet. Jes.; Hamb. 1702, 4to. In Jerem.; Frcf. a. M. 1706, 2 vols. 4to. In Proph. min.; Lips. 1698, 4to.

Jo. Clerici Comm. in Pentat.; Amst. 1710. In Libros hist. V. T.; 1708. In Hagiogr.; 1731. In Proph.; 1731, fol.

III. The *books of Ezra, Nehemiah*, and *Esther*, treat of the history of the people of Israel after the exile, that is, of the second temple.

Commentaire littéral sur tous les Livres de l'Ancien et N. T. par *Augustin Calmet*; Paris, 1724—1726, 8 vols. fol.

J. H. Michaelis, Annotatt. in V. T., in his Bib. Heb.; Hal. 1720. Engl. Bibelwerk, deutsch herausgeg. von *Romanus Teller, Baumgarten, Dietelmaier*, and *Brucker*; Leipz. 1749—1770, 19 vols. 4to.

J. D. Michaelis, Uebers des A. T. mit Anmerk. für Ungelehrte, 13 vols.; Gött. 1769—1783, 4to.

Uebers. u. Erkl. der heil. Bücher des A. T. von *Moldenhauer*; Quedlinb. 1774—1787, 10 vols. 4to.

W. F. Hezel, Die Bibel A. und N. T. mit vollst. erklär. Anmerkk.; Lemgo, 1780—1791, 10 vols.

Die heil. Schrift d. A. T. v. *Dm.* v. *Brentano*, 1 pt., fortges. v. *Dereser*, 2 pt. — 4 pt. 3 vols., geend. v. *Scholz*, 4 pt. 4 vol.; 1797—1832.

J. D. Dathe, Pentateuchus Lat. Vers. Notisque philol. et crit. illustr.; Hal. 1781; ed. 2, 1791, 8vo. Libri hist.; 1784. Proph. maj.; 1779; ed. 2, 1785. Proph. min.; 1773; ed. 2, 1779; ed. 3, 1790. Psalmi; 1787; ed. 2, 1794. Job, Prov., Sal., Eccles., Cant. Cant.; 1789.

J. Chr. F. Schulz, Schol. in V. T. inde a iv. tom. contin. a *G. Lor. Bauer*; Norimb. 1783—1798, 10 vols. 8vo.

E. F. C. Rosenmüller, Schol. in V. T. P. I. cont. Gen. et Exod.; Lips. 1788; ed. 2, 1795; ed. 3, 2 vols. 1821, 1822. P. II. Lev., Num., et Deuteron.; 1790; ed. 2, 1798; ed. 3, 1824. Schol. in Pentat. in Compend. redacta; 1828. P. III. sect. 1—2, cont. Jes.; 1790—1793; ed. 2, 3 vols., 1810, 1818, 1820; ed. 3, 1829, vol. i. P. IV. vol. i.—iii. cont. Pss.; 1800—1804; ed. 2, 1821—1823; in comp. red.; 1831. P. V. vol. i. ii., cont. Job.; 1806; ed. 2, 1824. P. VI. vol. i. ii. cont. Ezech.; 1808; ed. 2, 1826. P. VII. vol. i.—iv. cont. Proph. min.; 1812—1816; ed. 2, 1827, 1828. P. VIII. vol. i. ii. cont. Jer., Vatic., et Thren.; 1826, 1827. P. IX. vol. i. ii. cont. Salom. scripta; 1829, 1830. P. X. cont. Dan.; 1832.

Exegetisches Handbuch des A. T.; Leipz. 1797—1800, 9 vols., cont. Jos., Richter, Ruth, Sam., B. der Kön., Jes.

Kurzgefasstes exegetisches Handbuch zum Altes Test. pt. i. die 12 kleinen Proph.; Leipz. 1838, by *Hitzig*; pt. ii. Job; ib. 1839, by *Hirzel*; pt. iii.; ib. 1841, Jeremiah, by *Hitzig*; pt. iv.; 1842, Samuel, &c.

[The Reformer's Bible, (reprinted;) Lond. 1810, 4to. Annotations on all the Books of the Old and New Testament, (the "Assemblies' Annotations;") Lond. 1657, 2 vols. fol.

Poole, Annot. upon the Holy Bible; 1683, 2 vols. fol. The Old and New Testament, with Annotations, &c., by *Samuel Clarke*; Lond. 1690, fol. (A false book was published in the name of *S. Clarke*; 1811, fol.)

Patrick, Lowth, Whitby's and *Arnald's* Commentary on the Bible; Lond.

§ 136, *a*

GENERAL PECULIARITIES OF THESE BOOKS

1. With Reference to their Contents and Style.

The reference to the theocracy (that is, to the inward connection between God and the people of Israel, and to the particular government of God over them and in the midst of them) gives these books two peculiarities; and, to present these in the most forcible manner, the whole history is actively pervaded by a theocratic idea.

1. The whole history is penetrated by a clear and constant plan of the divine government of the world; to which individual circumstances are subordinated, with a greater or less degree of consistency: this is *theocratical pragmatism*, [that is, the reference of all events to God, as the immediate cause.]

2. The divine influence is likewise *immediately* displayed in the history, in *revelations* and *miracles:* this is *theocratical mythology*.

These peculiarities are most evident in those books and chapters which contain the most ancient history of the theocracy, of its establishment, and which treat of the most important points in its development; that is, in the books of Moses, Joshua, Judges, Samuel, 1 Kings xiii.—2 Kings viii. They are the least conspicuous, and, indeed, are scarcely perceptible, in those

---

1727—1760, 7 vols. fol. (reprinted 1809, 1821.) *Henry's* Exposition, 5 vols. fol. *Gill's* Exposition of the Old and New Testament; 1748—1763, 9 vols. fol. Other works, more or less valuable, have been prepared by *Purver, Wesley, Benson, Cruden, Dodd, Goadby, Scott, Wilson, Yonge, Bulkley, Priestley, Trimmer, Burder, Hewlett, D'Oyly* and *Mant*, and *Adam Clarke*.]

which belong to an age destitute of the theocratic spirit; that is, in the historical books of the Hagiographa.

[The application of the term *mythology* to certain narratives and opinions in the Bible need excite no surprise. The Jews had their mythology, as well as the Hindoos, the Goths, and the Greeks. Symbols and myths are necessarily used, by a rude people, to clothe abstract truths. It is evident the ancient Hebrews made use of them as the drapery of religious truth. This appears from the temple ceremonies, the visions and symbolic actions of the prophets; from the figurative expressions relating to the Deity, and the perpetual recurrence of anthropo-morphitic views of him. It is often difficult to determine where the myth begins, and the plain statement ends. But the Hebrew Scriptures have this difficulty in common with all very ancient, and especially Oriental writings. Symbolical language is sometimes used *consciously*, as properly symbolical, and sometimes *unconsciously*, when the writer himself had no clear conception of the subject, but confounded figure and fact.

"A dogma is a creation of the Understanding; a symbol, of the Feelings; and a myth, of Fancy. The first expresses itself in ideas; the second, in æsthetic images; the third, in history. The first is an object of faith; the second, of devout reverence; but the third is, originally, neither the one nor the other; it is a free play of fiction."] [a]

---

[a] We apply the term *mythology* to historical narratives, some of which relate to the supersensuous, and others date back to an ideal antiquity, and both rise above the ordinary laws of historical causality. Such narratives usually originate in legends, whence the name. See *De Wette*, Bio. Dogmatik. § 55. [*Bauer*, Heb. Mythologie, 1802, § 1—7.] *Georgi*, Mythus and Saga; Berlin, 1837. *Tuch*, Genesis, p. 1, sqq. *A myth* is an idea clothed in facts: a *saga* contains facts penetrated and transformed by ideas.

§ 136, *b*.

[CONTINUATION OF THE ABOVE.

"The Jews never reached a high degree of culture, and always preserved a national character so peculiar, that they were in the most striking manner distinguished from the neighboring and contemporary nations. The belief that they were the only favorites of Jehovah, the Creator and Lord of the whole world, is as old as the nation itself; it first received a steady direction from Moses, the founder of the theocratic constitution of the state. They considered that Jehovah was the supreme, invisible Governor of the nation, and that all which befell them, in great and little affairs, was brought about by his immediate command, and by his special contrivance and coöperation. This belief exerted so powerful an influence, that all which had the remotest connection with the body of the people and the state, was referred *immediately* to God. This opinion was supported by the limited knowledge possessed in those times, which referred all events in the lives of individuals to a higher cause, and both together produced the *theocratical-religious pragmatism* of the old Hebrew historians.

"If *pure historical pragmatism* consists in developing every fact from its original cause, then *theocratic-religious pragmatism* consists in referring all historical events to the God Jehovah. Therefore, in the old historical books of the Hebrews, all active persons appear only as instruments of God. Every thing proceeds from the will and express command of God. Whatever thoughts, conclusions, and maxims, arise in the mind, God speaks them. The formula, '*Thus saith the Lord*,' is so common in the old Hebrew historians, that the whole history becomes, as it were, a history of God.

"On account of this, almost every thing has a miraculous coloring. But, in respect to this, a distinction must be made between the general and the particular. The law of theocratic-religious *pragmatism*, in general, refers every thing to one higher cause. But, notwithstanding this, it may be considered as *outwardly* or *actually* following the order and common course of nature. The miracle consists only in this,—that God has done an action perfectly natural in itself, or that it has been done at his bidding. But single events and occurrences form an exception; for they are related as if the order of nature was violated in respect to them. These narratives are called the *miraculous history* of the Old Testament; and they have their foundation partly in the deficiency and narrowness of human knowledge at that time, connected with the religious spirit generally prevalent, and partly in the distance of time between the event itself and the written account of it. Many events were, for a long time, related orally. Now, every legend is enlarged in the mouth of posterity, and as nations were then in a lower stage of civilization than now, such legends must necessarily be wrought up to the miraculous. When this transformation has taken place, they are called *historical myths*. For the Hebrews, as well as others, had their myths, which abound in their histories. And therefore, if any one would penetrate into the spirit of the Hebrew historians, he must not forget that it sometimes assumes a mythical character.

"The dissolution of the Hebrew nation, by the Assyrians and Chaldees, and their dispersions among many other nations, laid the foundation for a change in their historical views. The bond of the theocracy became looser, and when a part of the people assembled again in their old and native land, it could never acquire its former strictness, for the theocracy, in the proper sense, was never restored. The influence of these circumstances, in the historical writings, is very striking, for in the modern historical books of the Old Testament, in Nehemiah and Ezra, the *theocratic-religious pragmatism* no longer prevails, but the narrative is constructed according to the natural laws of things, and approaches pure historical writing.

"The same fact will be observed in the historical books of the Apocrypha; but with this difference,—there the historical and the religious views are intermingled. But this was the result of the spirit of the age and nation, at that time. For, after the exile, the Jews, on account of their outward condition, must mainly have given up their old theocratic ideas. Their religious ideas gradually became more fixed, and this result was not a little hastened by the expansion and increase of their moral ideas, consequent upon their acquaintance with the Babylonians, Persians, and other nations. In consequence of this, *religious pragmatism* appears in the historical books of the Apocrypha. It is not said in them, 'God spake and it was done,' as in the old historical works, which were either written before the exile, or, after it, were compiled from more ancient, written documents, or popular legends. But still, for the most part, events are represented as under the influence and direction of God.

"From these condensed remarks, it must become clear that the historical writings of the Bible are of such a character, that very few of its narratives admit of a *lit-*

eral interpretation, or are to be regarded as purely historical. But they must be considered in part as the results of theocratic-religious, or simply religious *pragmatism*, and partly as mythical histories. Under these circumstances, they will not yield the historian any certain results, until historical criticism is applied to them."][a]

§ 137.

2. In Reference to their Literary Origin.

The greatest part of these books are not the work of one hand, nor do they preserve their primitive form, but have principally arisen from compilation, either by weaving together and connecting different narratives, or by making extracts from larger historical works. In the historical literature of the Hebrews, we must separate the composition of independent history from mere historical compilation. The first is earlier, and belongs to the period when literature flourished in full bloom; while the latter indicates its decaying vigor.

Theocratical historiography probably owes its origin and formation to theocratical men, the prophets and the priests,[b] since many prophets are actually referred to as

---

[a] [*Berger*, Practische Einl. in A. B. vol. ii. p. xiii., sqq. On this subject, see the following works: On the phrase, "*God spake*," in O. T., *Henke's* Mag. vol. ii. p. 333, sqq., vol. iii. p. 1.] *Hezel's* Geist und Phil. der Sprache d. Alten Welt. vol. i. *Gabler*, Journal Theol. Lit. vol. ii. p. 43. *Bertholdt*, Einleit. vol. iii. p. 748, sqq. *Augusti*, § 84.

[b] *Augusti*, l. c. § 87. The Hebrew kings, however, had their annalists, (מַזְכִּירִים.) It is doubtful whether they were prophets. The transcription of the Law was, perhaps, the duty of the priest.

[Some think the school of the prophets performed the office of modern "historical societies," and "academies of science," and that their productions were published anonymously, because they derived their authority

the authors of historical documents. This fact explains the great uniformity of all the historical books, both as to their plan and manner of execution. But their origin from compilation, connected with the one-sided theocratical *pragmatism*, plainly shows why so many chasms are left in the history, and why so many things are related very imperfectly and briefly.

CHAPTER I.

THE BOOKS OF MOSES.[a]

§ 138.

THEIR NAMES.

THE Jews named the entire work from its chief part, *the Law*, (תּוֹרָה, ὁ νόμος,) and, from its original

---

from the whole school, and not from the name of the writer. See *Nachtigal's* essay on this subject, in *Eichhorn's* Allg. Bib. vol. ix. p. 379, sqq.]

[a] *Clerici* Comment. *Rosenmüller*, Schol.

Henr. Ainsworth, Annotations upon the Five Books of Moses; Lond. 1627, fol.

Jac. Bonfrerii Pentat. Mos. comm. illustratus; Antw. 1625, fol.

Jo. Ad. Osiandri Comm. in Pentat.; Tüb. 1675, sqq. 5 vols. fol.

Jo. Markii Comm. in præcipuas quasd. Partes Pentateuchi; Lug. Bat 1721, 4to.

J. S. Vater, Comm. über den Pentateuch, mit Einleitt. z. d. einz. Abschnitten, der eingeschalt. Uebers. von *Dr. Alex. Geddes* merkwürdigeren krit. u. exeg. Anmerkk. u. einer Abhandl. über Moses und die Verfasser des Pentateuchs; Halle, 1802—1805, 3 vols.

Jul. Sterringa, Observatt. phil. sac. in Pentateuchum; Lug. Bat. 1721, 4to.

J. F. Gaab, Beiträge zur Erklär. des 1, 2, u. 4 B. Mose; Tüb. 1796.

Jo. Gerhardi Comm. in Genes.; Jen. 1693, 4to.

Seb. Schmidt, *Jo. Mercer.* Comm. in Gen.

Haitsma, Curæ philol. exeget. in Genes.; Franequ. 1753, 4to. Comm. in Exod.; 1771, 4to.

division[a] into five books, *the five fifths of the Law*, (חֲמִשָּׁה חוּמְשֵׁי הַתּוֹרָה.) The Greeks[b] named it ἡ *Πεντά-τευχος*, that is, *Βίβλος Πεντάτευχος*, and the Latins called it *Pentateuchus*, that is, *liber Pentateuchus.*[c]

The Jews call single books by their initial words, and the Christians name them according to their contents.[d]

§ 139.

CONTENTS OF THESE BOOKS.

1. Genesis. (בְּרֵאשִׁית.)

The history of the establishment of the theocracy is contained in these books, in the following order: Ac-

---

Hensler, Bemerkk. üb. Stellen in d. Psalm. u. d. Gen.; Hamb. 1791, 8vo.

Pentateuchus Hebr. et Gr. c. Annotatione perp. ed. *G. A. Schumann*, vol. i. Gen. compl.; Lips. 1829.

[*Hartmann*, Forschungen üb. die 5 BB. Moses; Rost. 1831.

Diodati, Annotations on the Bible, translated from the Italian; Lond. 1664, fol. *Geddes*, Holy Bible; 1792, sqq. 3 vols. 4to. *Kidder*, Commentary on the Five Books, &c.; 1694, 2 vols. 8vo. *Jamieson*, Critical and Practical Expos. of the Pentateuch; 1748, fol. *Hughes*, Analytical Exposition of the First Book of Moses, &c.; 1672, fol. *Graves*, Lectures, &c.; 1815, 2 vols. 8vo. Other works on the whole or a part of the Pentateuch have been written or compiled by the following authors: *Durell*, *Lightfoot*, (A Handful of Gleanings, &c.,) *Dawson*, *Harwood*, *Franks*, *Dimock*, *Fuller*, *Rudge*, *Hopkins*, &c.]

[a] Josephus recognizes this division, (C. Ap. i. 8;) but it does not appear to be alluded to in 1 Cor. xiv. 19, as Jerome supposes, (Ep. 103 ad Paulinum, tom. iv. pt. 2, p. 572:) Huc usque Pentateuchus, quibus quinque verbis loqui se velle apostolus in ecclesia gloriatur.

[b] *Origen*, xiv. in Joh. p. 218.

[c] See *Tertullian*, Cont. Marc. vol. i. p. 10. Compare, on the other side, *Stange*, Cujus Generis est Pentateuchus? in *Keil's* and *Tzschirner's* Anal. vol. i. 1 pt.

[d] The following names also occur among the Jews: סֵפֶר יְצִירָה נְזִיקִין, (Comp. *Buxtorf*, Lex. Talm. p. 1325,) תּוֹרַת כֹּהֲנִים, or סֵפֶר ;ת' הַקָּרְבָּנוֹת הַמִּסְפָּרִים, or סֵפֶר פִּקּוּדִים; מִשְׁנֵה תוֹרָה, or סֵפֶר תּוֹכָחוֹת. See *Hottinger*, Thes. Phil. p. 456, sqq. above, vol. i. p. 89, sqq.

cording to the opinion of the Hebrews, the theocracy is the centre and object of the whole history of the world, it is therefore related in *Genesis*, that the ground of it was laid immediately after the creation of the world; that the people of God was gradually separated from the other people, and the promise of the holy land, and of the holy constitution, was made to the patriarchs; and that even the fundamental laws of the state were then given.

Beside these principal matters, there are genealogical and ethnographical accounts and fragments of the first history of the human race inserted, as well as family histories of the descendants of Abraham. Among these, those which relate to Abraham, Jacob, and Joseph, are the most conspicuous.[a]

[It has often been asserted that the book of Genesis was designed to serve as an introduction to the Law. Thus, it is supposed, the fact that Adam and Eve were forbidden to eat of a certain tree, is related to sanction the prohibition of certain kinds of food forbidden to the Jews. The sad consequences which followed Adam's transgression were to warn the Jews against a similar offence. The misfortune which befell Lamech after marrying two wives, was "to show the Jews why the Law was not favorable to polygamy." When the sons of God dwelt with the daughters of men, the race became corrupt, and the deluge was sent to punish

---

[a] The following passages are the most important to show the theocratic plan of the book, which has a certain unity in its present form: Gen. ii. 3, ix. 1—17, 20—27, xii. 1—3, xiii. 14—17, xv. xvii. xix. 30—38, xxi. 1—20, xxiii. xxiv. 2—8, xxv. 1—6, 19—34, xxvii. xxviii. xxxv. 9—15, xxxvi. 6, xlvi. 1—7, xlviii. xlix. l. 7—13. See *De Wette*, Kritik der Israelit. Gesch., or Beiträge ins A. T. vol. ii. *Ewald*, Gen. § 17, 18. *Tuch*, l. c. p. xxi.

Long passages, like xiii. 14—17, and xxiii., may be *apologetic*, in the proper sense of the word; i. e. designed to show the Hebrew nation was the favorite of Heaven, and that their customs and laws were very ancient. See *Augusti*, § 108.

them. This was related to warn the Hebrews of the consequences that would ensue if they should marry the women of Canaan.[a] Such assertions are entirely arbitrary. It might with equal truth be said Genesis was designed as an introduction to the Psalms, or to the book of Ecclesiastes. The book simply records the uncertain and mythical history of the Hebrew race, from Adam till the descent to Ægypt. Abraham, therefore, is the most conspicuous character in the book. From him the history goes back in two genealogical lines, —from Seth, before the flood, from Shem, after it. After Abraham, his descendants were the only heroes of the story. Various statements and accounts came in as subsidiary to this general plan. This book was, doubtless, of great value to the Hebrews, as it is to us a priceless relic of olden times.

"Read it as two historical works[b] of the old world," says Eichhorn, "breathe therein the air of its age and country. Forget the age you live in, and the knowledge it affords you; and if you cannot do this, dream not that you can enjoy the book in the spirit of its origin. The youth of the world which it describes demands a spirit that has descended to its deeps. The first rays of the glimmering light of reason do not harmonize with the clear light of broad noon. The shepherd only speaks in the soul of the shepherd; and the primitive Oriental only speaks in the soul of another Oriental. Without an intimate acquaintance with the customs of pastoral life; without an accurate knowledge of the East and its manners; without a close intimacy with the manner of thinking

---

[a] See numerous instances of this character in *Jahn*, vol. ii. § 9.

[b] [Referring to the two documents from which the book is composed. See below, § 150, sqq.]

and speaking in the uncivilized world, (obtained by a knowledge of Greece in its earliest ages, and of the uncultivated nations of modern times,) — you easily become a traitor to the book, when you would be its deliverer and interpreter.

"In particular, its language must not be treated like that of a cultivated and philosophic age. Above all, in this book, it is like the world in its childhood; it is often destitute of comprehensive general expressions, and therefore it must mention the parts of things, to furnish an idea of the whole. It is like a painting, or the language of poetry; like them it represents every thing part by part. And, since the language of our age is so far removed from the original simplicity of language in the ancient world, we must separate the thought from its dress.

"Finally, according to the language of this book, God produces every thing directly, without availing himself of the course of nature and certain intermediate causes. But in this there is nothing peculiar to it. Its conceptions are only like those of the ancient world in general, when it had not been ascertained, by long-continued inquiry, that all events are connected into a series of intermediate causes. Therefore it stops with God, the ultimate cause, as if he were supposed to be the immediate cause. And even for us, who have inquired into the causes of things, the name of God, in these cases, is often a superfluous expletive, and no sign that God has ever interrupted the course of things."][a]

---

[a] [*Eichhorn*, § 423.]

§ 140.

2. Exodus. (וְאֵלֶּה שְׁמוֹת.)

The bonds of this people, which was called to a higher destiny, were knit, in the previous book, by the migration into Ægypt, and were then drawn closer by their servitude; but they were soon loosed by the omnipotence of Jehovah, which was manifested through Moses. The people were brought out of Ægypt amid miracles and punishments; and the long-promised covenant of God was solemnly established with them at Mount Sinai. The civil and religious institutions of the theocracy were established, and God took up his abode among his people.[a]

§ 141.

3. Leviticus. (וַיִּקְרָא.)

This book must be considered as an addition to the legislation at Sinai, — the main features of which were contained in the previous book, — and it contains the chief laws which relate to the offerings, the feasts, and the priests, as well as the ordinances of sacred discipline. It contains only a little historical information, and that relates to the priests, (viii.—x.) The theocratical history advances no farther; it is only filled out, and completed.

---

[a] The following passages belong to this part of the theocratic plan: Ex. iii. iv. vi. 2—8, xii. 1—28, xiii. 1—16, xix. xx. xxiv. xl.

§ 142.

4. Numbers. (במדבר.)

The commencement of this book is likewise supplementary, (i. 1—x. 10.) It contains the important part of the holy *constitution*, the selection of the Levites to the priesthood. Then begins the history of the march through the wilderness, and the conflict between the new constitution and the evil dispositions of the people.

We soon come to the end of this march, when the contest for the possession of the country commences: Moses opens the campaign successfully, and then prepares for his departure from the scene of action.

The passages which are not narrative, but are inserted between the narrations, are of the greatest importance from the political and statistic information which they afford. Chap. xxii.—xxiv. form an episode.[a]

§ 143.

5. Deuteronomy. (אלה הדברים.)

Shortly before his death, Moses appears before the people, and, by reference to their early history, admonishes them to obey God and his laws; he in part repeats the laws previously given, and in part gives new ones. Finally, he gives a solemn sanction to his legislation, appoints Joshua as his successor, and, after giving reminiscences, warnings, and prophecies, in a spirited discourse, and casting a glance into the beloved

---

[a] See *Carpzov*, Int. in V. T. vol. i. p. 46; he also finds an account of the political administration in this book.

land which was shut to him, he mysteriously departs from the scene![a]

§ 144.

PECULIARITIES OF THIS NARRATIVE.

1. In Reference to Completeness.

While the narrative expresses itself fully in many accounts and descriptions, and is even tedious at times,[b] on the other hand we notice important chasms,[c] which cannot be ascribed to the narrator's want of order, but must rather be attributed to his want of documents.

The most important chasms are between Genesis and Exodus, where a period of four hundred years is passed over; and between Numbers xiii., in the *second* year of the Exode, when the camp was at Kadesh-Barnea, and Numbers xx., in the *fortieth* year of the Exode, when the Jews arrive at the wilderness of Zin. Of all this period of thirty-eight years, we know as good as nothing.[d]

---

[a] Notice the parallel between Deut. xxvii. and Ex. xxiv.; Deut. xxviii. and Levit. xxvi.; Deut. xxxi. 14—23, xxxii. 48—52, and Num. xxvii. 12—23; Deut. xxxiii. and Gen. xlix.; besides the repetitions and alterations of the Laws.

[b] Gen. xxiv. xxvii.—xxxiv. xxxvii.—xlv. Ex. v.—xi. xxv.—xxx. xxxvi. —xl. Num. i.—iv. xxii.—xxiv. xxxi., et al.

[c] See *De Wette's* Kritik. der Israelit. Gesch. 169—351. *Goethe*, West-östliche Divan, p. 444, sqq.

[d] Compare Num. xx. 28, sq. with xxxiii. 38, and with Deut. ii. 14.

§ 145.

2. With Reference to Pragmatism[a] and Mythology.

The causes which lay in the divine mind are clearly indicated; but the natural causes, the human motives, and the natural connection of circumstances, are but imperfectly pointed out.[b] This is the reason that so many events contradict the laws of nature, and suppose, not merely higher powers of nature, which are conceivable, but a direct interposition on the part of God. Now, since it is at least doubtful, to a cultivated mind, that *such miracles actually took place*, the question naturally rises, Did they *appear* so to the eye-witnesses, and to such as were actively engaged in the events recorded in this history? or did the writer understand them as natural events, but yet portray them in a poetico-miraculous light?[c] But this must be denied as soon as we examine the narratives somewhat more carefully; for they are entirely destitute of that credulous, poetic turn of mind which is the key to the marvellous. This is plain from the difference between the natural and the miraculous accounts of the same or similar things. Compare the natural account in Ex. xviii. with the miraculous in Ch. xix., and with Num. xi., where both seem to be united; Levit. ix. 10, 13, 14, 17, 20, where the offering is burnt in the common manner, with verse 24, where a fire came out from Jehovah and consumed the burnt-offering; Num. x. 29—32, with ix. 15—23, xvii. 6, where *Moses* gives a natural command, and xvi. 20,

---

[a] [A reference to the *ultimate* as the *immediate* cause.]

[b] Pragmatic passages, like Ex. xxiii. 13, sqq., Num. x. 29, sqq., are rare.

[c] Against *Eichhorn's* erroneous explanation of miracles, see *De Wette*, l. c.

sqq., and xvii. 10, sqq., where *Jehovah* speaks to Moses and Aaron. Ex. xv. 25, (where it is said Jehovah informed Moses of a method to heal the waters at Marah,) is the only passage which can be explained as subjective. But the historical occasion of a miraculous legend may be ascertained with greater or less probability; for example, in Ex. xiv. xvi.

If these considerations favor the natural prejudice that the accounts of these miracles are not contemporary with the alleged events, or derived from contemporary sources; if such sources are not possible in the case of some of the narratives of the most ancient time, and there is a striking affinity between many of them (Gen. vi. 1—4, vi. 5—viii. xi. 1—9, xix.) and the myths of other nations,—then the analogy of all the historical literature of the Hebrews leads us to a clear and just view of the matter; for we find, in fact, that the miraculous in the historical books diminishes just in proportion as they approach historical times, and that it entirely ceases in that period from which we have contemporary accounts. In the earliest times, men have intercourse with God; later, angels appear [as messengers between man and God;] still later, the prophets perform the miraculous; but in the times after the exile, from which we have contemporary history, the miraculous ceases altogether. Miracles appear again only in the book of Daniel and 2 Maccabees, and in the latter, they are confuted by the historical accounts of 1 Maccabees. The Protestants are not consistent in rejecting the miracles of the Apocrypha, because objections might be drawn from them against the credibility of the other books. The Catholics are consistent in placing them in the same line with the miracles of the canonical books.

§ 146.

ORIGIN AND PROGRESS OF THE MOSAIC MYTHOLOGY.

The conclusion that these accounts of miraculous events are entirely forged would be too rash. This may be the case in the later books, as in Daniel and 2 Maccabees, for example; but it can scarcely be so in the books of Moses. Here a genuine historical legend lies at the foundation, which was connected with certain monuments, supported by popular songs, and preserved in the mouth of the people. Thus, for example, the following are connected with certain monuments:—

In Gen. xix. 26, it is said, Lot's wife looked back as she was fleeing, reluctantly, from Sodom, and became a pillar of salt; but, from the Wisdom of Solomon, (x. 7,) it seems a pillar of salt was erected on the spot where she turned back. Josephus says such a pillar was standing in his time.[a] Of this character are the narratives in Gen. xxxiii. 17, where a place is called *Succoth*, (*tents*,) from the temporary huts Jacob made for his cattle; and in xxxv. 8, where a place is named *Allon Bachuth*, (*the oak of weeping*,) because Rebekah's nurse was buried there; and in verse 20. The following passages belong to the same class: Num. xxi. 4—9, which contains the account of the brazen serpent, said to be contrived to cure such as were bitten by real living serpents,—but which appears as an object of idolatrous worship in 2 Kings xviii. 4; xxi. 17, sq., containing the poetic legend of the well; and Josh. x. 12—14, where it is said the sun stood still at the command of Joshua.

To this class belong the etymological myths, especial-

---

[a] *Josephus*, Antiq. i. 11, 4.

ly such as relate to *places;* for example, Gen. xvi. 14, where a place is named *Beer-la-hai-roi, (well of living vision;)* xxi. 31, where the name *Beer-sheba (well of the oath)* is given to a place; xxviii. 10, sqq., in which the old name *Luz (almond-tree)* is changed to *Beth-el, (house of God,)* because Jacob dreamed he saw God in that place; xxxv. 1—8, 9—15, l. 11, and others. But these may, in part, have an artificial origin.[a] In the same manner, the legends of the Arabs are connected with names and proverbs.[b]

But in the popular legend, there came an idealo-poetic element, and mingled itself with the real historical elements. By this means the tradition was transformed, gradually, into the miraculous and the ideal. The popular songs conduced chiefly to bring about this end; for they, in the bold, lyric flight of imagination, represented what was surprising and wonderful in a *supernatural* light, and a people credulous of miracles easily misunderstood the account. Thus the miracle in Josh. x. 14, arose from the lyric hyperbola of the two preceding verses. So, in Ex. xiv. 22, we have the historical statement, "And the children of Israel went into the midst of the sea upon the dry ground, and the waters were a wall unto them, on their right hand and on their left;" and in xv. 8, the lyric exaggeration, "And with the blast of thy nostrils the waters were gathered together, the floods stood upright as a heap, and the depths were congealed in the heart of the sea."

---

[a] See § 147, *a.*

[b] *Pococke,* Spec. Hist. Arab. p. 41, 43, 45, 58, 79, and elsewhere. Num. xxi. 17, 18, 27, sqq.

·6 §

§ 2.

ORIGIN AND ANTIQUITY OF THE SAMARITAN CODEX.

§ 147, *a*.

LATER LITERARY TREATMENT OF THESE LEGENDS.

The analogy of other nations plainly shows us that popular traditions are not reduced to writing until a late period. And, besides, the authors of the Mosaic books actually betray themselves as living at a later date.

1. By using the formula *unto this day*, which they have in common with the other Hebrew historians.[a] (Gen. xix. 58, xxvi. 33, xxxii. 32, xxxv. 20, xlvii. 26. Deut. ii. 22, iii. 14, x. 8, xxix. 4, xxxiv. 6.)

2. By archæological explanations; for example, Ex. xvi. 36, "Now an *omer* [an ancient measure] is the tenth part of an *ephah*," [a modern measure.] Deut. iii. 5, where it is said all these cities [taken a few years previous] had high walls, gates, and bars — a circumstance the men who had taken the cities would not need to have spoken of. Verse 9, where the Sidonian and Amorite names of a town are given, is in the spirit of an antiquary. Verse 11, in which men supposed to live at the time of these events are told Og was the last of the giants, that his bedstead was iron, of unusual size, and was preserved in Rabbath. (xi. 30. Gen. xiv. 2, 7, 8, 17, xxiii. 2, xxxv. 19.)[b]

3. By reference to old authorities, Num. xxi. 14, 16, 27.

---

[a] Compare the same formula in the other historical books, § 170, 175, 180, 185. In the books of Ezra and Nehemiah, it is only used in reference to the old history, Ezra ix. 7.

[b] The opinion of *Eichhorn* and others, that these expressions are glosses, can only be justified after the earlier composition of these books has been made out from other evidence. [One great fault of previous attempts to prove the Pentateuch written by Moses has been in this: The writer *assumes*, without any external evidence, that all those explanatory passages are the additions of commentators, and then uses them to show the text is still more ancient.]

4. By their local position in Palestine, (Gen. l. 10, sq.,) in which the term "beyond Jordan" means, on the east side of that river. Num. xxii. 1; xxxv. 14, (?) Deut. i. 1, 5, iii. 8, iv. 41, 46, 47. Compare iii. 20, 25, xi. 30, where "this side the Jordan" means to the *west* of that river. Compare iii. 20, 25, xi. 30, where "beyond" means to the *east* of the Jordan.[a]

5. By their treatment of the Mosaic history, even its most recent events, as if they had taken place in times long past, as in the whole of Deut. i. — iii., but in particular

Deuteronomy iii. 4—9, 14—20, 29.

"And we took all his cities at that time; there was not a city which we took not from them; threescore cities, all the region of Argob, the kingdom of Og in Bashan. All these cities *were* fenced with high walls, gates, and bars; besides unwalled towns a great many. And we utterly destroyed them, as we did unto Sihon king of Heshbon, utterly destroying the men, women, and children, of every city. But all the cattle, and the spoil of the cities, we took for a prey to ourselves. And we took at that time out of the hand of the two kings of the Amorites the land that was on this side Jordan, from the River of Arnon unto Mount Hermon; (which Hermon the Sidonians call Sirion; and the Amorites call it Shenir.) . . . . . .

"Jair the son of Manasseh took all the country of Argob, unto the coasts of Geshuri, and Maachathi; and called them after his own name, Bashan-havoth-jair, unto this day. And I commanded you at that time, saying, 'The Lord your God hath given you this land to possess it; ye shall pass over armed before your brethren the children of Israel, all that are meet for the war. But your wives, and your little ones, and your cattle, (for I know that ye have much cattle,) shall abide in your cities which I have given you.'

"So we abode in the valley over against Beth-Peor."[b]

---

[a] But the use of בְּעֵבֶר and מֵעֵבֶר varies, at least in Num. xxxii. 19, xxxv. 14, Jos. i. 14, sq., v. 1, xii. 1, 7, xxii. 7, 1 Kings v. 4, 1 Ch. xxvi. 30. See *Maurer*, Com. zur Joshua, ix. 1. Doubtful in Deut. i. 1, 5, et al.

[b] See *Fulda* in *Paulus*, N. Rep. vol. iii. p. 230, sqq. Even *Eichhorn* (§ 434) admits Deut. ii. 10—12, 20—23, iii. 9—11, are later interpolations.

[Such facts as these could not readily escape from the minds of men contemporary with these events; and so the relation of them in a public harangue, as this book pretends to be, supposes that a long time had elapsed since the events took place.]

In reducing these legends to writing, the authors of these books scarcely design to write a history. They were the less inclined to it as this design had exerted so small an influence in preserving the legend. They exercised the rights of the religious imagination natural to their countrymen, and the more freely, as this had formerly been so active in developing and embellishing these same legends, and as the substance of them was so indefinite and fluctuating.

The author of Deuteronomy had read the earlier Mosaic books. Their very language was present in his memory, and yet he departed from those narratives. Even in times still later, when the greatest veneration prevailed for the sacred letter, Josephus allowed himself to take surprising liberties in his treatment of the Mosaic legends; or, if he followed the tradition of his countrymen, others had taken these liberties before him; for example, there is a remarkable difference between the account of Abraham's dissimulation, in respect to his wife, in Josephus,[a] and the account of the same transactions in Gen. xx. The story of Joseph,[b] the account of the oppressions of the Hebrews in Ægypt,[c] the history of Moses,[d] contain statements unknown to the Bible. Josephus explains the passage of the Red Sea as a *natural*, the Bible as a *miraculous*, event.[e] There is a difference, also, between iii. 1—6, and the corresponding parts of Scripture. The same may be said of the additions in the Targums.

---

[a] Antiq. i. 12, 1. [b] ii. 4, 3. [c] ii. 9, 2—7. [d] ii. 11, 1. [e] ii. 16, 3.

§ 147, *b*.

THE EPIC AND PROPHETIC TREATMENT OF THESE LEGENDS.

The history of the primitive time, of the patriarchal and Mosaic age, has been treated according to a religious, poetical, and didactic plan, which discloses itself most clearly in the document Elohim, which lies at the basis of it.[a] In conformity with this plan, the Jews are constantly told of their high destination, — that they are the chosen people of God,—and of the divine origin of their institutions and laws. By this means, an inspiration was kindled in them for their religion and their country, — in a word, for the theocracy.

I. If an historical narrative, written without critical investigation of facts,[b] but treated so as to suit religious and poetical ideas, is an epic composition, then the Pentateuch may be called the theocratical epic poem of the Israelites, without denying that there is an historical basis at the bottom.[c] This epic treatment shows itself,

1. In the poetic form of the narrative, which satisfies the poetic sense, not only by its intuitiveness and spiritedness,[d] but even by the rhythmic elevation of the style.[e]

2. In the subject matter, and, indeed, in the miraculous events, and the supernatural intercourse of man with God; for the epic loves the miraculous. The popular legend had prepared the way for this treatment, and the epic poets—who needed miracles to answer the end they proposed—sometimes developed the miraculous legend still farther, and sometimes invented new

---

[a] § 150. [b] ἱστορία.

[c] *Meyer* (Apol. Gesch. A. T.; 1811) misunderstands my view in Beitr. vol. i.

[d] Anschaulichkeit und Gemüthlichkeit. [e] § 126.

miracles; for they also availed themselves of the right, so frequently used by the poets and prophets, of constructing symbolical poems. The book of Chronicles[a] shows how the miracles were enlarged upon and farther developed. It is probable the author of the Jehovistic fragments has transformed much into the miraculous which was natural and simple in the Elohistic fragment. Passages like Ps. l., Isa. vi., Ezek. i., and Ex. xix., belong to this kind of symbolic poetry. The story of the manna in Ex. xvi. is obviously designed to impress men with the holiness of the Sabbath.

[We can never determine to what extent historical narratives have been altered to suit the theocratical ideas; but the fact of such alteration, or else of the invention of circumstances, is very plain; for example, the following passages seem designed to suit the notion of a *covenant* between Jehovah and the Israelites; that he had miraculous communication with them; had selected them, and rejected all other nations; and had founded the theocracy at an early date: Gen. xv., where it is said Jehovah appears to Abraham, and makes a covenant to give him, or his posterity, all the region from the River of Ægypt to the Euphrates; (the covenant was ratified by a sacrifice, and a miraculous furnace and blazing torch pass between the divided portions of the slaughtered animals;) Gen. xvii., where the same covenant is renewed, the rite of circumcision established, and the birth of Isaac promised; Gen. xxxv. 9—15, where the blessing is confirmed to Jacob; Gen. xlvi. 1—7.

Exodus xiii. 21, 22.

"And the Lord went before them by day in a pillar of a cloud, to lead them the way; and by night in a pillar of fire, to give them

[a] § 190, c.

.ight to go by day and night. He took not away the pillar of the cloud by day, nor the pillar of fire by night, from before the people."

Exodus xl. 34—38.

"Then a cloud covered the tent of the congregation, and the glory of the Lord filled the tabernacle. And Moses was not able to enter into the tent of the congregation, because the cloud abode thereon, and the glory of the Lord filled the tabernacle. And when the cloud was taken up from over the tabernacle, the children of Israel went onward in all their journeys. But if the cloud were not taken up, then they journeyed not till the day that it was taken up. For the cloud of the Lord was upon the tabernacle by day, and fire was on it by night, in the sight of all the house of Israel, throughout all their journeys."

Leviticus ix. 23, 24.

"And Moses and Aaron went into the tabernacle of the congregation, and came out, and blessed the people: and the glory of the Lord appeared unto all the people. And there came a fire out from before the Lord, and consumed upon the altar the burnt-offering and the fat: which when all the people saw, they shouted and fell on their faces."

Numbers ix. 15—23.

"And on the day that the tabernacle was reared up, the cloud covered the tabernacle, namely, the tent of the testimony; and at even there was upon the tabernacle as it were the appearance of fire, until the morning. So it was always: the cloud covered it by day, and the appearance of fire by night. And when the cloud was taken up from the tabernacle, then after that the children of Israel journeyed: and in the place where the cloud abode, there the children of Israel pitched their tents. At the commandment of the Lord the children of Israel journeyed, and at the commandment of the Lord they pitched: as long as the cloud abode upon the tabernacle they rested in their tents. And when the cloud tarried long upon the tabernacle many days, then the children of Israel kept the charge of the Lord, and journeyed not. And so it was, when the cloud was a few days upon the tabernacle; according to the commandment of the Lord they abode in their tents, and according to the commandment of the Lord they journeyed. And so it was, when the cloud abode from even unto the morning, and that the cloud was taken up in the morning, then they journeyed: whether it was by day or by night that the cloud was taken up, they journeyed. Or whether it were two days, or a month, or a year, that the cloud tarried upon the tabernacle, remaining thereon, the children of Israel abode in their tents, and journeyed not: but when it was taken up, they journeyed. At the commandment of the Lord they rested in their tents, and at the commandment of the Lord they journeyed: they kept the charge of the Lord, at the commandment of the Lord by the hand of Moses."

The history of Isaac, contained in Gen. ix. 20—29, xii. 1, xix. 30—38, xxi. 9—21, xxiv. xxv. 19—34, xxvii.; Gen. ii. 3, which mentions the Sabbath; Gen. ix. 4—6, where blood is forbidden; Gen. xvii. 10—14, where the rite of circumcision is enjoined; Gen. xii., containing the alleged trial of Abraham's faith; Gen. xlviii. 13—22, Jacob's blessing on the sons of Joseph; Gen. xlix., his *final* blessing of all his sons; Ex. xii. 1—28, xiii. 1—16, the institution of the Passover.]

II. Since the chief design of the theocratical epic poem was to inspire the people with reverence for their sacred laws and institutions, therefore the author of the document Elohim not only, in conformity with the actual tradition, showed how they proceeded from Moses, the lawgiver, who received divine influence, but he also ascribed to him, and in a manner not historical, many later developments of his laws, and additions which seemed necessary to the writer. Thus he sanctioned many laws and customs by assigning them an origin still more ancient than the time of Moses. Where laws are thus referred back to a more remote antiquity, I have called them *juridical* or *legal myths*. Such a one is found in Gen. ii. 3—"And God blessed the seventh day, and sanctified it, because that in it God had rested from all his work which God created and made;" and Ex. xvi. is certainly of this same character. The mythical origin of the Passover, (Ex. xii.,) and some others, may be contested. But two things are certain — 1. That the author of Deuteronomy ascribes to Moses a body of laws which were obviously modified after his time.[a] 2. That the author of the document Jehovah has referred certain customs and laws to an origin more ancient than their real date. Perhaps the progressive formation of the Mosaic law is acknowledged in

Numbers xv. 23.

"And if ye have erred, and not observed all these commandments which the Lord hath spoken unto Moses, even all that the Lord hath commanded you by the hand of Moses, from the day that the Lord commanded Moses, and henceforward among your generations."

III. In connection with this, a sort of spirit of investigation and combination was also at work. We are indebted to this for the genealogical and ethnographical accounts contained in the Pentateuch. They are designed in sober earnest, and are not without some historical foundation, but are rather the result of fancy and conjecture than of genuine historical investigation. To test the accuracy of the table Gen. x., compare the following passages: —

Genesis.	Genesis.
Chap. x. 23. "And the children of Aram: *Uz*, and *Hul*, and *Gether*, and *Mash*."	Chap. xxii. 21. "*Huz*, his first born, and *Buz*, his brother, and *Kemuel, the father of Aram*." Chap. xxxvi. 28. "The children of Dishan ...... *Uz* and *Aran*."

[a] § 156.

7 "The sons of *Cush*, Seba, and Havilah, and Sabtah, and Raamah, and Sabtecha, and the sons of Raamah: *Sheba* and *Dedan*.
25 And unto Eber were born two sons . . . . . . Peleg . . . . . . and his brother's name was *Joktan*.
28 *Sheba* is the son of Joktan."

Chap. xxv. 2. "*Abraham* took a wife . . . . . . Keturah; and she bare him Zimran and *Jokshan*, Medan, and Midian, and Ishbak, and Shuah; and Jokshan begat *Sheba* and *Dedan*." . . . . . .

The derivation from *Cush*, *Canaan*, *Elam*, and *Ashur*, is opposed by the history of the language.[a]

To test the accuracy of the other table, compare the following passages: —

Genesis.

Chap. xxxvi. 2, 3. "Esau took his wives of the daughters of Canaan; Adah the daughter of Elon the Hittite, and Aholibamah the daughter of Anah the daughter of Zibeon the Hivite; and Bashemath, Ishmael's daughter, sister of Nebajoth."

Chap. xxxvi. 15—30. "These were dukes of the sons of Esau: the sons of Eliphaz, the first-born son of Esau; duke Teman, duke Omar, duke Zepho, duke Kenaz, duke Korah, duke Gatam, and duke Amalek: these are the dukes that came of Eliphaz, in the land of Edom: these were the sons of Adah. And these are the sons of Reuel, Esau's son; duke Nahath, duke Zerah, duke Shammah, duke Mizzah: these are the dukes that came of Reuel, in

Genesis.

Chap. xxvi. 34, 35. "And Esau was forty years old when he took to wife Judith the daughter of Beeri the Hittite, and Bashemath the daughter of Elon the Hittite, which were a grief of mind unto Isaac and to Rebekah."

Chap. xxxvi. 40—43. "And these are the names of the dukes that came of Esau, according to their families, after their places, by their names; duke Timnah, duke Alvah, duke Jetheth, duke Aholibamah, duke Elah, duke Pinon, duke Kenaz, duke Teman, duke Mibzar, duke Magdiel, duke Iram: these be the dukes of Edom, according to their habitations, in the land of their possession; he is Esau the father of the Edomites."

[a] But see *Rosenmüller*, Alt. vol. iii. p. 33, 160, 174.

the land of Edom: these are the sons of Bashemath, Esau's wife.

"And these are the sons of Aholibamah, Esau's wife; duke Jeush, duke Jaalam, duke Korah: these were the dukes that came of Aholibamah the daughter of Anah, Esau's wife. These are the sons of Esau, (who is Edom,) and these are their dukes.

"These are the sons of Seir, the Horite, who inhabited the land; Lotan, and Shobal, and Zibeon, and Anah, and Dishon, and Ezer, and Dishan; these are the dukes of the Horites, the children of Seir in the land of Edom. And the children of Lotan were Hori, and Heman; and Lotan's sister was Timna. And the children of Shobal were these; Alvan, and Manahath, and Ebal, Shepho, and Onam. And these are the children of Zibeon; both Ajah, and Anah; this was that Anah that found the mules in the wilderness, as he fed the asses of Zibeon his father. And the children of Anah were these; Dishon, and Aholibamah the daughter of Anah. And these are the children of Dishon; Hemdan, and Eshban, and Ithran, and Cheran. The children of Ezer are these; Bilhan, and Zaavan, and Akan. The children of Dishan are these; Uz and Aran. These are the dukes that came of the Horites; duke Lotan, duke Shobal, duke Zibeon, duke Anah.

Chap. xiv. 6. "And the Horites in their Mount Seir."

Deuteronomy.

Chap. ii. 12—22. "The Horims also dwelt in Seir beforetime, but the children of Esau succeeded them, when they had destroyed them from before them, and dwelt in their stead; as Israel did unto the land of his possession, which the Lord gave unto them. The children of Esau, which dwelt in Seir, when he destroyed the Horims from before them; and they succeeded them, and dwelt in their stead even unto this day."

duke Dishon, duke Ezer, duke Dishan, these are the dukes that came of Hori, among their dukes in the land of Seir.[a]

We find less seriousness, and more of a religious and poetical spirit of fancy in the etymological myths, where an account is given of the origin of the names of persons and places. Some of these are conformable to tradition; but others, by their artificial character, betray themselves as the productions of later reflection; for example, Gen. xi. 9, "Therefore is the name of it called Babel, because the Lord did there confound the language of all the earth." Gen. xix. 22, "Therefore the name of the city was called *Zoar*."[b]

IV. The religious and didactic design of the writer appears in the didactic myths in their general form, or in the setting forth of religious truths which belong out of the circle of the national and theocratical history; for example, in Gen. i.—iii., and Ex. xxxiii. 12—23.

V. Since the authors of the Pentateuch—who, perhaps, were prophets—found the laws and institutions of the Israelitish nation in the most ancient history, and likewise their rules and forms in the divine plan of the world, they were therefore led, by custom and the necessity of prophetic vision, to throw back into ancient history the prophecy of later events and circumstances, by means of *fictitious predictions*, and thus to establish a closer connection between the present and the past, and at the same time lay a foundation for actual prophecies of the future. Examples of this are as follows:—

---

[a] See *Vater* and *Tuch*, in loc. Comp. Gen. xxxvi. 15, 18, 22, with xxvi. 18, 40, 41.

[b] [*Smallness*, because Lot said, "It is a little one."]

Genesis xxv. 23.

"Two nations are in thy womb, and two manner of people shal be separated from thy bowels, and the one people shall be stronger than the other people, and the elder shall serve the younger."

Genesis xxvii. 28, 29, 39, 40.

"Therefore God give thee of the dew of heaven, and the fatness of the earth, and plenty of corn and wine; let people serve thee, and nations bow down to thee; be lord over thy brethren, and let thy mother's sons bow down to thee; cursed be every one that curseth thee, and blessed be he that blesseth thee.......

"And Isaac his father answered, and said unto him, 'Behold, thy dwelling shall be the fatness of the earth, and of the dew of heaven from above; and by thy sword shalt thou live, and shalt serve thy brother; and it shall come to pass when thou shalt have the dominion, that thou shalt break his yoke from off thy neck.'"

Genesis xlix. Numbers xxiii. 7—10, and

Numbers xxiii. 23, 24.

"Surely there is no enchantment against Jacob, neither is there any divination against Israel: according to this time it shall be said of Jacob and of Israel, 'What hath God wrought!' Behold, the people shall rise up as a great lion, and lift up himself as a young lion; he shall not lie down until he eat of the prey, and drink the blood of the slain."

Num. xxiv. 3—9, 15—24. Levit. xxvi. Deut. xxviii. xxxii. § 159, 257.[a]

§ 148.

ERRORS IN RESPECT TO HISTORICAL TRUTH.

In the course of such a treatment, various errors in regard to historical truth would naturally be made. These betray the later writer.

I. The order in which events follow one another, in the Mosaic history, is not accurately observed.[b]

---

[a] See Asiatic Researches, vol. viii. p. 486.

[b] For an enumeration of all that may be called anachronisms, see *Vater.*

Exodus xvi. 23—30.

"And he said unto them, 'This is that which the Lord hath said, "To-morrow is rest of holy Sabbath unto the Lord: bake that which ye will bake to-day, and seethe that ye will seethe; and that which remaineth over lay up for you to be kept until the morning."' And they laid it up till the morning, as Moses bade: and it did not stink, neither was there any worm therein. And Moses said, 'Eat that to-day; for to-day is Sabbath unto the Lord; to-day ye shall not find it in the field. Six days ye shall gather it; but on the seventh day, which is the Sabbath, in it there shall be none.'

"And it came to pass, that there went out some of the people on the seventh day for to gather, and they found none. And the Lord said unto Moses, 'How long refuse ye to keep my commandments and my laws? See, for that the Lord hath given you the Sabbath, therefore he giveth you on the sixth day the bread of two days: abide ye every man in his place; let no man go out of his place on the seventh day.' So the people rested on the seventh day."

Here the law of the Sabbath is supposed to be well known. But it is not given till after this time. Ex. xx. 9, "Six days shalt thou labor, and do all thy work; but the seventh is Sabbath; in it thou shalt not do any work."

Ex. xix. 22. At the time Moses ascends the mountain, Jehovah commands the *priests* to be sanctified, "lest Jehovah should break out upon them." Verse 24, he permits Aaron, as one peculiarly sanctified, to accompany Moses on the mount. But it is plain there was no *body of priests* at that time; for (xxiv. 5) Moses sent *young men* (not priests, whose office it was) *to sacrifice to Jehovah.* Aaron was not consecrated as high priest at that time, for he and the priests are first appointed by Jehovah, in chap. xxviii. xxix. Again:

---

l. c. p. 631, sqq. *Bertholdt*, vol. iii. p. 771, sqq. *Hartmann*, Hist. Krit. Forschungen, &c. p. 689, sq. But see *Jahn's* defence of them in *Bengel's* Archiv. vol. iii. p. 574, sqq., and *Ch. Fr. Fritzsche*, Prüfung der Gründe, mit welchen neuerlich die Aechtheit, d. B. Mos., bestritten worden; 1814, p. 124, sqq.

Exodus xvi. 32—34.

"And Moses said, 'This is the thing which the Lord commandeth: "Fill an omer of it, to be kept for your generations; that they may see the bread wherewith I have fed you in the wilderness, when I brought you forth from the land of Ægypt."' And Moses said unto Aaron, 'Take a pot, and put an omer full of manna therein, and lay it up before the Lord, to be kept for your generations.' As the Lord commanded Moses, so Aaron laid it up before the testimony, to be kept."

Here the manna is to be laid up before the *ark of the covenant in the holy place of the tabernacle.* But the tabernacle itself does not appear until after this, namely, in

Exodus xxxiii. 7—11.

"And Moses took the tabernacle, and pitched it without the camp, afar off from the camp, and called it the Tabernacle of the Congregation. And it came to pass, that every one which sought the Lord went out unto the Tabernacle of the Congregation, which was without the camp. And it came to pass, when Moses went out unto the tabernacle, that all the people rose up, and stood every man at his tent-door, and looked after Moses, until he was gone into the tabernacle. And it came to pass, as Moses entered into the tabernacle, the cloudy pillar descended, and stood at the door of the tabernacle, and the Lord talked with Moses. And all the people saw the cloudy pillar stand at the tabernacle-door: and all the people rose up and worshipped, every man in his tent-door. And the Lord spake unto Moses face to face, as a man speaketh unto his friend. And he turned again into the camp; but his servant Joshua, the son of Nun, a young man, departed not out of the tabernacle."

In xxxiv. 34, 35, Moses unveils himself on entering this *tabernacle;* and yet a subsequent passage (xxxvi.—xl.) contains an account of the *building of this tabernacle*, according to the instructions given xxv.—xxvii. But this tabernacle is not said to be made to supply the place of an old one.

Leviticus xxv. 32—34.

"Notwithstanding, the cities of the Levites, and the houses of the cities of their possession, may the Levites redeem at any time. And if a man purchase of the Levites, then the house that was sold, and the city of his possession, shall go out in the year of jubilee: for the houses of the cities of the Levites are their possession among the children of Israel. But the field of the suburbs of their cities may not be sold; for it is their perpetual possession."

Here the Levites are supposed to possess landed estates. But the law assigning them cities to dwell in was not enacted till long afterward, namely, in

Numbers xxxv. 1—5.

"And the Lord spake unto Moses in the plains of Moab by Jordan near Jericho, saying, 'Command the children of Israel that they give unto the Levites of the inheritance of their possession cities to dwell in; and ye shall give also unto the Levites suburbs for the cities round about them. And the cities shall they have to dwell in, and the suburbs of them shall be for their cattle, and for their goods, and for all their beasts. And the suburbs of the cities which ye shall give unto the Levites shall reach from the wall of the city and outward, a thousand cubits round about. And ye shall measure from without the city on the east side two thousand cubits, and on the south side two thousand cubits, and on the west side two thousand cubits, and on the north side two thousand cubits; and the city shall be in the midst: this shall be to them the suburbs of the cities.'"

Compare, also, Num. i. 1, sqq., with Ex. xxxviii. 25, and xxx. 11—16. This latter passage is evidently out of place, for it occurs in the midst of instructions respecting the tabernacle. Num. ix. 1, contains the account of a transaction which took place in the *first* month of the second year; while the earlier passage (i. 1, sq.) details a census of the people made in the *second* month of the same year.

II. Later manners, customs, institutions, and opinions, are referred back to ancient times.

Genesis.

Chap. iv. 3, 4. "And in process of time it came to pass, that Cain brought of the fruit of the ground an offering unto the Lord. And Abel, he also brought of the firstlings of his flock, and of the fat thereof."

Leviticus.

Chap. ii. 14. "And if thou offer a meat-offering of thy first-fruits unto the Lord, thou shalt offer for the meat-offering of thy first-fruits, *green ears of corn dried by the fire, even corn beaten out* of full ears."

Chap. iii. 3. "And he shall offer of the sacrifice of the peace-offering, an offering made by fire unto the Lord, the *fat* that covereth the inwards, and all the *fat* that *is* upon the inwards."

Numbers.

Chap. xv. 20. "Ye shall offer up a cake of the first of your dough for a heave-offering: as ye do the heave-offering of the threshing-floor, so shall ye heave it."

Gen. iv. 14, 17, 26, "Then began men to call on the name of Jehovah." Gen. vii. 8, and viii. 20, the division of clean and unclean beasts is made use of as if it were common and well known. Gen. xxxvii. 3, and 23, Joseph has a coat of many colors; compare it with 2 Sam. xiii. 18, where David's daughters are said to wear garments of various colors. See, also, xxv. 22, and xxiv. 22, 30. This passage, (Gen. xlix. 10,) "The sceptre shall not depart from Judah, nor a lawgiver from between his feet, until Shiloh come," belongs to this class, if it relates to the Messiah. The same must be said of xii. 3, and xviii. 18, — "I will bless him that blesseth thee, and curse him that curseth thee, and in thee shall all the tribes of the earth be blessed;" "Abraham shall become a great and mighty nation." Besides, the historical coloring is changed to suit the purpose of the writer, as in Num. xxii.—xxiv., where Balaam is made a *prophet of Jehovah.*

III. Later circumstances and events are alluded to as it appears from the following examples: Gen. xii. 6, "The *Canaanite* was then in the land." Gen. xiii. 7, "The *Canaanite* and the *Perizzite* were then in the land"—a remark no one would naturally make until after these nations were driven out, that is, after the time of Joshua. Levit. xviii. 28, "That the land do not vomit you out, *as it did the nations before you,*" who were still present in the time the book is alleged to have been written.

Deuteronomy ii. 12.

"The Horims also dwelt in Seir beforetime, but the children of Esau succeeded them when they had destroyed them from before them, and dwelt in their stead, as Israel did unto the land of his possession, which the Lord gave unto them."

Ex. xxii. 20, xxiii. 9, "Thou shalt neither vex a stranger nor oppress him, for ye were strangers in the land of Ægypt;" "For ye know the heart of a stranger, since ye were strangers in the land of Ægypt." (Perhaps xii. 45, belongs here.)

Deuteronomy xix. 14.

"Thou shalt not remove thy neighbor's landmark, which they of old time have set in thine inheritance, which thou shalt inherit in the land that the Lord thy God giveth thee to possess it."

Exodus xv. 17.

"Thou shalt bring them in, and plant them in the mountain of thine inheritance, in the place, O Lord, which thou hast made for thee to dwell in, in the sanctuary, O Lord, which thy hands have established." [a]

---

[a] According to *Bleek,* in Stud. und Krit. for 1831, p. 520, sqq., there is no reference to the temple mountain, Moriah, in Gen. xxii. 2, 14.

Here the *temple mountain*,—Mount Moriah, in Jerusalem, where Solomon's temple was erected,—and the *sanctuary*, are referred to. See, also, xxiii. 19.

[Deuteronomy xxxiii. 12.

"Of Benjamin he said,
'The beloved of Jehovah shall dwell in safety with HIM.
HE shall protect him every day,
And shall rest in his borders.'"

Is not here an allusion to the fact that Jerusalem and the temple were within the borders of the tribe of Benjamin?]

Genesis xlviii. 5, 18—20.

"And now thy two sons, Ephraim and Manasseh, which were born unto thee in the land of Ægypt, before I came unto thee into Ægypt, are mine: as Reuben and Simeon, they shall be mine.

"And Joseph said unto his father, 'Not so, my father; for this is the first-born: put thy right hand upon his head.' And his father refused, and said, 'I know it, my son, I know it; he also shall become a people, and he also shall be great; but truly his younger brother shall be greater than he, and his seed shall become a multitude of nations.' And he blessed them that day, saying, 'In thee shall Israel bless, saying, "God make thee as Ephraim and as Manasseh."' And he set Ephraim before Manasseh."

Here the superiority of Ephraim, the chief tribe, is referred to, as a well-known fact.

Genesis xlix. 8—12.

"Judah, thou art he whom thy brethren shall praise; thy hand shall be in the neck of thine enemies: thy father's children shall bow down before thee. Judah is a lion's whelp; from the prey, my son, thou art gone up: he stooped down, he couched as a lion, and as an old lion; who shall rouse him up? The sceptre shall not depart from Judah, nor a lawgiver from between his feet, until Shiloh come; and unto him shall the gathering of the people be; binding his foal unto the vine, and his ass's colt unto the choice vine; he washed his garments in wine, and his clothes in the blood of grapes. His eyes shall be red with wine, and his teeth white with milk."

Here Judah is the royal tribe, and continual prosperity is assigned him. Contrast it with the fate appointed for the descendants of Joseph, that is, the tribe of Ephraim, or the kingdom of the ten tribes.

Genesis xlix. 22—26.

" Joseph is a fruitful bough, even a fruitful bough by a well, whose branches run over the wall. The archers have sorely grieved him, and shot at him, and hated him; but his bow abode in strength, and the arms of his hands were made strong by the hands of the mighty God of Jacob; even by the God of thy father who shall help thee; and by the Almighty, who shall bless thee with blessings of heaven above, blessings of the deep that lieth under, blessings of the breasts and of the wombs; the blessings of thy father have prevailed above the blessings of my progenitors, unto the utmost bound of the everlasting hills; they shall be on the head of Joseph, and on the crown of the head of him that was separate from his brethren."

The song of Moses, (Deut. xxxii., especially 5—33,) and the remark, xxix. 28, presuppose a state of things not possible in the time of Moses. [The curses for disobedience in Levit. xxvi. belong to the same class.

Leviticus xxvi. 33—43.

" And I will scatter you among the heathen, and will draw out a sword after you; and your land shall be desolate, and your cities waste. Then shall the land enjoy her Sabbaths as long as it lieth desolate, and ye be in your enemies' land; even then shall the land rest, and enjoy her Sabbaths. As long as it lieth desolate it shall rest; because it did not rest in your Sabbaths, when ye dwelt upon it. And upon them that are left alive of you, I will send a faintness into their hearts in the lands of their enemies; and the sound of a shaken leaf shall chase them; and they shall flee as fleeing from a sword; and they shall fall when none pursueth. And they shall fall one upon another, as it were before a sword, when none pursueth: and ye shall have no power to stand before your enemies. And ye shall perish among the heathen, and the land of your enemies shall eat you up. And they that are left of you shall pine away in their iniquity in your enemies' lands; and also in the iniquities of their fathers shal they pine away with them. If they shall confess their iniquity, and the iniquity of their fathers, with their trespass which they trespassed against me, and that also they have walked contrary unto me; and that I also have walked contrary unto them, and have brought them into the land of their enemies; if then their uncircumcised hearts be humbled, and they then accept of the punishment of their iniquity; then will I remember my covenant with Jacob, and also my covenant with Isaac, and also my covenant with Abraham will I remember; and I will remember the land. The land also shall be left of them, and shall enjoy her Sabbaths, while she lieth desolate without them: and they shall accept of the punishment of their iniquity; because, even because they despised my judgments, and because their soul abhorred my statutes."

The following passage will perhaps help us to the date of these curses:—

2 Chronicles xxxvi. 20, 21.

"And them that had escaped from the sword carried he away to Babylon, where they were servants to him and his sons, until the reign of the kingdom of Persia; to fulfil the word of the Lord by the mouth of Jeremiah, until the land had enjoyed her Sabbaths; for as long as she lay desolate she kept Sabbath, to fulfil threescore and ten years."

To the same class of curses belong the following:—

Deuteronomy iv. 27.

"And the Lord shall scatter you among the nations, and ye shall be left few in number among the heathen, whither the Lord shall lead you."

Deuteronomy xxviii. 25, 36, 37, 64.

"The Lord shall cause thee to be smitten before thine enemies: thou shalt go out one way against them, and flee seven ways before them; and shalt be removed into all the kingdoms of the earth. . . . . .

"The Lord shall bring thee, and thy king which thou shalt set over thee, unto a nation which neither thou nor thy fathers have known; and there shalt thou serve other gods, wood and stone. And thou shalt become an astonishment, a proverb, and a by-word, among all nations whither the Lord shall lead thee. . . . . .

"And the Lord shall scatter thee among all people, from the on end of the earth even unto the other; and there thou shalt ser other gods, which neither thou nor thy fathers have known, eve wood and stone."

Deuteronomy xxix. 25, sqq.

"Then men shall say, 'Because they have forsaken the covenant of the Lord God of their fathers, which he made with them, when he brought them forth out of the land of Ægypt: for they went and served other gods, and worshipped them, gods whom they knew not, and whom he had not given unto them. And the anger of the Lord was kindled against this land, to bring upon it all the curses that are written in this book: and the Lord rooted them out of their land in anger, and in wrath, and in great indignation, and cast them into another land, as it is this day.'"]

Sometimes later events are only faintly alluded to: Gen. xvii. 6, "And I will make thee exceeding fruitful, and I will make nations of thee; and kings shall come out of thee." Verse 16, "And I will bless her, [Sarah,] and give thee a son also of her: yea, I will bless her, and she shall be a mother of nations; kings of people shall be of her." And the similar passage, xxxv. 11.

In Gen. xxxvi. 31, there is mention of *kings of Israel:* "And these are the kings that reigned in the land of Edom, before there reigned any king over the children of Israel." A similar allusion is made Deut. xxviii. 36.

Gen. xxvii. 40, Jacob, blessing Esau, says, "By thy sword shalt thou live, and shalt serve thy brother. But it shall come to pass when thou shalt have the dominion, that thou shalt break his yoke from off thy neck." Compare the following passages: —

2 Samuel viii. 14.

"And he [David] put garrisons in Edom; throughout all Edom put he garrisons: and all they of Edom became David's servants."

2 Kings viii. 20.

"In his days Edom revolted from under the hand of Judah, and made a king over themselves."

Numbers xxiv. 7.

"He [Jacob] shall pour the water out of his buckets, and his seed shall be in many waters, and his king shall be higher than Agag, and his kingdom shall be exalted."

Numbers xxiv. 17—20.

"I shall see him, but not now; I shall behold him, but not nigh: there shall come a Star out of Jacob, and a Sceptre shall rise out of Israel, and shall smite the corners of Moab, and destroy all the children of Sheth. And Edom shall be a possession; Seir also shall be a possession for his enemies; and Israel shall do valiantly. Out of Jacob shall come he that shall have dominion, and shall destroy him that remaineth of the city. And when he looked on Amalek, he took up his parable, and said, 'Amalek was the first of the nations, but his latter end shall be that he perish forever.'"

Compare 1 Sam. xv., where Saul routs the Amalekites, and Samuel hews Agag, their king, in pieces; xiv. 47, where Saul's conquest of this nation is related; 1 Ch. iv. 43, where their destruction is completed; and 2 Sam. viii. 2, 14.

Num. xxiv. 22. "The Kenite shall be wasted until Ashur shall carry thee away captive." But this is doubtful. Compare the following: —

Deuteronomy xxviii. 68.

"And the Lord shall bring thee into Ægypt again with ships, by the way whereof I spake unto thee, 'Thou shalt see it no more again:' and there ye shall be sold unto your enemies for bond-men and bond-women, and no man shall buy you."

Isaiah xi. 11.

"And it shall come to pass in that day, that the Lord shall set his hand again the second time to recover the remnant of his people, which shall be left, from Assyria, and from Ægypt, and from Pathros, and from Cush, and from Elam, and from Shinar, and from Hamath, and from the islands of the sea."

Zephaniah iii. 10.

"From beyond the rivers of Æthiopia my suppliants, even the daughter of my dispersed, shall bring mine offering."

IV. Names of places and regions, which were first known at a later date, also occur: — *Hebron.* Gen. xiii. 18, "Mamre, which is Hebron," &c. But from Josh. xiv. 15, xv. 13, it appears Hebron was a modern name, probably given in honor of the grandson of Caleb. (1 Ch. ii. 41.) [Formerly it had been called *Kirjath-arba.* It is even called by its ancient name in Neh. xi. 25.]

Dan is mentioned Gen. xiv. 14, and Deut. xxxiv. 1. In the last passage, it is the extreme limit of the land of Gilead. But the place did not come into the possession of Dan until long after Moses, as it appears from Judg. xviii. 29 — "And they called the name of the city Dan, after the name of Dan their father, who was born unto Israel: howbeit, the name of the city was Laish at the first."

Beth-el is mentioned Gen. xii. 8 — "And he [Abram] removed from thence unto a mountain on the east of Beth-el; there he builded an altar." Again, (xxviii. 19,) Jacob comes to the place, where he passes the night, and has a remarkable dream; "And he called the name of that place Beth-el; but the name of the city was Luz at first." Gen. xxxv. 15, as Jacob returns from Padan-aram, Elohim appears to him, "And Jacob called the name of the place where Elohim spake with him Beth-el." But in Josh. xviii. 13, it is still called "Luz, (which is Beth-el.)"

Havoth-jair (the villages of Jair) is mentioned Num. xxxii. 41 — "And Jair the son of Manasseh went and took the small towns thereof, and called them Havoth-jair;" and Deut. iii. 14, "Jair the son of Manasseh took all the country of Argob, unto the coasts of Geshuri, and Maachathi, and called them after his own name, Bashan-havoth-jair, unto this day." But, according to Judges, (x. 3, 4,) the place was named from Jair, who judged Israel long after Moses. "And after him arose Jair, a Gileadite, and judged Israel twenty-and-two years. And he had thirty sons that rode on thirty ass-colts, and they had thirty cities, which are called Havoth-jair unto this day, which are in the land of Gilead."

Ophir, also, is mentioned Gen. x. 29. Compare 1 Kings ix. 28.

In the course of such an unhistorical and arbitrary treatment, it was natural that the same thing should be differently represented, and the various writers should contradict themselves.

Compare Gen. ii. 4—25, with the very different account of the same things in i. 1—ii. 3. Compare, also, the following:—

Genesis.

Chap. vi. 19—21. "And of every living thing of all flesh, two of every sort shalt thou bring into the ark, to keep them alive with thee: they shall be male and female. Of fowls after their kind, and of cattle after their kind, of every creeping thing of the earth after his kind; two of every sort shall come unto thee, to keep them alive. And take thou unto thee of all food that is eaten, and thou shalt gather it to thee; and it shall be for food for thee, and for them."	Chap. vii. 2, 3. "Of every clean beast thou shalt take to thee by sevens, the male and his female; and of beasts that are not clean by two, the male and his female. Of fowls also of the air by sevens, the male and the female; to keep seed alive upon the face of all the earth."
Chap. ix. 8—17. "And God spake unto Noah, and to his	Chap. viii. 20—22. "And Noah builded an altar unto the

sons with him, saying, 'And I, behold, I establish my covenant with you, and with your seed after you; and with every living creature that is with you, of the fowl, of the cattle, and of every beast of the earth with you, from all that go out of the ark, to every beast of the earth. And I will establish my covenant with you; neither shall all flesh be cut off any more by the waters of a flood; neither shall there any more be a flood to destroy the earth.' And God said, 'This is the token of the covenant which I make between me and you, and every living creature that is with you, for perpetual generations. I do set my bow in the cloud, and it shall be for a token of a covenant between me and the earth. And it shall come to pass, when I bring a cloud over the earth, that the bow shall be seen in the cloud: and I will remember my covenant, which is between me and you, and every living creature of all flesh; and the waters shall no more become a flood to destroy all flesh. And the bow shall be in the cloud; and I will look upon it, that I may remember the everlasting covenant between God and every living creature of all flesh that is upon the earth.' And God said unto Noah, 'This is the token of the covenant which I have established between me and all flesh that is upon the earth.'"

Lord, and took of every clean beast, and of every clean fowl, and offered burnt-offerings on the altar. And the Lord smelled a sweet savor; and the Lord said in his heart, 'I will not again curse the ground any more for man's sake; for the imagination of man's heart is evil from his youth: neither will I again smite any more every thing living, as I have done. While the earth remaineth, seed-time and harvest, and cold and heat, and summer and winter, and day and night, shall not cease.'"

Genesis.

[Chap. xi. 26, 32. "And Terah lived seventy years, and begat Abram, Nahor, and Haran.

"And the days of Terah were two hundred and five years: and Terah died in Haran."

Chap. xii. 4. "So Abram departed, as the Lord had spoken unto him; and Lot went with him: and Abram was seventy and five years old when he departed out of Haran."]

Compare the whole of chapter xv. with the repetition of the same thing in xvii. Compare also the following passages: —

Chapter xvii. 17. "Then Abraham fell upon his face, and laughed, and said in his heart, 'Shall a child be born unto him that is a hundred years old? and shall Sarah, that is ninety years old, bear?'"

Chapter xxi. 5, 6. "And Abraham was a hundred years old when his son Isaac was born unto him.

"And Sarah said, 'God hath made me to laugh, so that all that hear will laugh with me.'"

Chap. xviii. 12—15. "Therefore Sarah laughed within herself, saying, 'After I am waxed old, shall I have pleasure, my lord being old also?' And the Lord said unto Abraham, 'Wherefore did Sarah laugh, saying, "Shall I of a surety bear a child, which am old?" Is any thing too hard for the Lord? At the time appointed I will return unto thee, according to the time of life, and Sarah shall have a son.' Then Sarah denied, saying, 'I laughed not;' for she was afraid. And he said, 'Nay; but thou didst laugh.'"

Here the same fact is related *three* times, with only

this difference, that in one passage Abraham, but in both the others Sarah, laughs.

Genesis.

Chap. xxi. 22—32. "And it came to pass at that time, that Abimelech, and Phichol the chief captain of his host, spake unto Abraham, saying, 'God is with thee in all that thou doest. Now, therefore, swear unto me here by God, that thou wilt not deal falsely with me, nor with my son, nor with my son's son: but according to the kindness that I have done unto thee thou shalt do unto me, and to the land wherein thou hast sojourned.' And Abraham said, 'I will swear.' And Abraham reproved Abimelech because of a well of water, which Abimelech's servants had violently taken away. And Abimelech said, 'I wot not who hath done this thing: neither didst thou tell me, neither yet heard I of it but to-day.' And Abraham took sheep and oxen, and gave them unto Abimelech: and both of them made a covenant. And Abraham set seven ewe-lambs of the flock by themselves. And Abimelech said unto Abraham, 'What mean these seven ewe-lambs which thou hast set by themselves?' And he said, 'For these seven ewe-lambs shalt thou take of my hand, that they may be a witness unto me that I have digged this well.' Wherefore he called that place

Chap. xxvi. 26—33. "Then Abimelech went to him from Gerar, and Ahuzzath one of his friends, and Phichol the chief captain of his army. And Isaac said unto them, 'Wherefore come ye to me, seeing ye hate me, and have sent me away from you?' And they said, 'We saw certainly that the Lord was with thee: and we said, "Let there be now an oath betwixt us, even betwixt us and thee, and let us make a covenant with thee; that thou wilt do us no hurt, as we have not touched thee, and as we have done unto thee nothing but good, and have sent thee away in peace: thou art now the blessed of the Lord.'" And he made them a feast, and they did eat and drink. And they rose up betimes in the morning, and sware one to another: and Isaac sent them away, and they departed from him in peace. And it came to pass the same day, that Isaac's servants came and told him concerning the well which they had digged, and said unto him, 'We have found water.' And he called it Shebah; therefore the name of the city is Beer-sheba unto this day."

Beer-sheba, because there they sware both of them. Thus they made a covenant at Beer-sheba: then Abimelech rose up, and Phichol the chief captain of his host, and they returned into the land of the Philistines."

Genesis.

Chap. xxviii. 10—19. "And Jacob went out from Beer-sheba, and went toward Haran. And he lighted upon a certain place, and tarried there all night, because the sun was set: and he took of the stones of that place, and put them for his pillows, and lay down in that place to sleep. And he dreamed, and behold, a ladder set upon the earth, and the top of it reached to heaven: and behold, the angels of God ascending and descending on it. And behold, the Lord stood above it, and said, 'I am the Lord God of Abraham thy father, and the God of Isaac: the land whereon thou liest, to thee will I give it, and to thy seed. And thy seed shall be as the dust of the earth; and thou shalt spread abroad

Chap. xxxv. 1—8. "And God said unto Jacob, 'Arise, go up to Beth-el, and dwell there; and make there an altar unto God, that appeared unto thee when thou fleddest from the face of Esau thy brother.' Then Jacob said unto his household, and to all that were with him, 'Put away the strange gods that are among you, and be clean, and change your garments: and let us arise, and go up to Beth-el: and I will make there an altar unto God, who answered me in the day of my distress, and was with me in the way which I went.' And they gave unto Jacob all the strange gods which were in their hand, and all their ear-rings which were in their ears: and Jacob hid them under the oak which was by Shechem.

Chap. xxxv. 9—15. "And God appeared unto Jacob again, when he came out of Padan-aram, and blessed him. And God said unto him, 'Thy name is Jacob: thy name shall not be called any more Jacob, but Israel shall be thy name. And he called his name Israel. And God said unto him, 'I am God Almighty; be fruitful, and multiply: a nation, and a company of nations, shall be of thee; and kings shall come out of thy loins: and the land which I gave Abraham and Isaac, to thee I will give it, and to thy seed after thee will I give the land.' And God went up from him in the place where he talked with him. And Jacob set up a pillar in the place where he talked with him, even a pillar of stone; and he poured a drink-

to the west, and to the east, and to the north, and to the south: and in thee and in thy seed shall all the families of the earth be blessed. And behold, I am with thee, and will keep thee in all places whither thou goest, and will bring thee again into this land: for I will not leave thee, until I have done that which I have spoken to thee of.'

"And Jacob awaked out of his sleep, and he said, 'Surely the Lord is in this place; and I knew it not.' And he was afraid, and said, 'How dreadful is this place! this is none other but the house of God, and this is the gate of heaven.' And Jacob rose up early in the morning, and took the stone that he had put for his pillows, and set it up for a pillar, and poured oil upon the top of it. And he called the name of that place Beth-el: but the name of that city was called Luz at the first."

And they journeyed: and the terror of God was upon the cities that were round about them, and they did not pursue after the sons of Jacob.

So Jacob came to Luz, which is in the land of Canaan, (that is, Beth-el,) he, and all the people that were with him. And he built there an altar, and called the place El-beth-el; because there God appeared unto him, when he fled from the face of his brother. But Deborah, Rebekah's nurse, died, and she was buried beneath Beth-el under an oak: and the name of it was called Allon-bachuth."

offering thereon, and he poured oil thereon. And Jacob called the name of the place where God spake with him, Beth-el."

Exodus ii. 18.	Exodus iii. 1.
[" And when they came to Reuel their father, he said, 'How is it that ye are come so soon to-day?' "	"Now Moses kept the flock of Jethro his father-in-law, the priest of Midian: and he led the flock to the back side of the desert, and came to the mountain of God, even to Horeb."

Ex. iv. 18, and xviii. 1, sqq.]

Compare, also, Ex. vi. 2—8 with all the corresponding *Jehovistic* passages in Genesis; but especially compare the following:—

Exodus vi. 2—8.	Genesis iv. 26.
"And Elohim spake unto Moses, and said unto him, 'I am Jehovah. And I appeared unto Abraham, unto Isaac, and unto Jacob, as Elshaddai; but by my name JEHOVAH was I not known to them. And I have also established my covenant with them, to give them the land of Canaan, the land of their pilgrimage, wherein they were strangers. And I have also heard the groaning of the children of Israel, whom the Ægyptians keep in bondage; and I have remembered my covenant. Wherefore say unto the children of Israel, "I am Jehovah, and I will bring you out from under the burdens of the Ægyptians, and I will rid you out of their bondage; and I will redeem you with a stretched-out arm, and with great judgments. And I will take you to me for a people, and I will be	"Then men began to call upon the name of Jehovah."

to you Elohim, and ye shall know that I am Jehovah, your God, which bringeth you out from under the burdens of the Ægyptians. And I will bring you in unto the land, concerning the which I did swear to give it to Abraham, to Isaac, and to Jacob, and I will give it you for a heritage; I am Jehovah." ' "

Compare, also, Ex. iv. 21—23, with Gen. v.—xi.; Num. xxii.—xxiv., where *Elohim* and *Jehovah* are *both* used, with Gen. xxxi. 9, 16, and others, where the *latter* is used exclusively.[a]

§ 149.

THE ACCOUNTS PRETENDED TO BE CONTEMPORARY WITH THE EVENTS, OR VERY ANCIENT.

Some historical marks, which betray a certain acquaintance with Ægypt, have been looked upon as proofs that Moses was the author of the Pentateuch;[b] as if the Hebrews could not, at a later time, have ac-

[a] See below, § 154, 156. See *Ewald,* Genesis, p. 176, sqq., 191, sqq.

[b] The following are some of the passages: In Gen. xiii. 10, Ægypt is said to be well watered. Deut. xi. 10, it is implied that Ægypt is a level country, its fields are watered artificially, and that it never is refreshed by rain. Num. xiii. 22, Hebron was built seven years before Zoar in Ægypt. In Gen. xl. 11, 16, an acquaintance with the customs of the Ægyptian court is apparent. Gen. xlii. 9, the unprotected state of Ægypt is alluded to. Gen. xliii. 32, mention is made that the Ægyptians would not sit at table with the Hebrews. Gen. xlvii. 20—26, "And Joseph bought all the land of Ægypt for Pharaoh; for the Ægyptians sold every man his field, because the famine prevailed over them: so the land became Pharaoh's. And as for the people, he removed them to cities from one end of the borders of Ægypt even to the other end thereof. Only the land of the priests bought he not; for the priests had a portion assigned them of Pharaoh, and did eat their portion which Pharaoh gave them; wherefore they sold not their lands. Then Joseph said unto the people, 'Behold, I have bought you this day and your land for Pharaoh: lo, here is seed for you, and ye shall sow the land. And it shall come to pass in the increase, that ye shall give the fifth part unto Pharaoh, and four parts shall be your own, for seed of the field, and for your food, and for them of your households, and for food for your little ones.' And they said, 'Thou

quired such an acquaintance by their political and commercial connection with the Ægyptians.[a]

With still less probability can the accounts of the original inhabitants of Canaan and the neighboring countries be looked upon as proofs of a Mosaic origin; for these accounts are very defective and contradictory.[b] [Some critics have contended that the antiquity of these books was established by the *peculiarities* of some narratives they contain.

Thus, in Gen. xxxvi. 31, sqq., there is a list of eight kings of Edom, all of whom are said to have died, excepting the last, whose death is not mentioned. An easy inference is, that he was not dead at the time of writing the account. But since the title of this list is, "Kings that reigned in the land of Edom before any king reigned over the children of Israel," it is more natural to suppose the last one mentioned was not dead when the first king of Israel came to the throne.]

Such catalogues as those in Num. i. iii. vii. xxvi. and elsewhere, are by no means incontestable con-

---

hast saved our lives; let us find grace in the sight of my lord, and we will be Pharaoh's servants.' And Joseph made it a law over the land of Ægypt unto this day, that Pharaoh should have the fifth part; except the land of the priests only, which became not Pharaoh's." [This probably contains an erroneous explanation of a real fact. See *Von Bohlen*, Alt. Ind. vol. ii. p. 45.] In xlvi. 34, shepherds are said to be an abomination to the Ægyptians. Ex. vii. 19, ix. 27. See *Michaelis*, Einleit. in d. A. T. p. 189. *Eichhorn*, § 439, 435, *a*. De Ægypti Anno mirabili Comment. Reg. Soc. Gott. recent. vol. iv. p. 35. Class. Hist. and Philol.

[a] *Vater*, vol. iii. p. 605. On the intercourse between Palestine and Ægypt, see *Hartmann*, Die Hebräerin am Putztische, vol. i. pp. 212, 460, vol. iii. p. 159, and his Hist. Krit. Forschungen, p. 726. Compare, likewise, Isa. xix. Ezek. xxix. 30. Ex. x. 13, is an untrue account. Comp. *Hasselquist*, Reise, p. 254.

[b] See *Michaelis*, l. c. p. 183. *Vater*, on the other hand, l. c. 600. For the verification of such accounts, compare Gen. xiv. 7, with xxxvi. 12—16, (concerning the Amalekites;) Gen. xxiii. 3, with Num. xiii. 22; Jos. xv. 13, Judges i. 20, and Gen. xiv. 13, (on the inhabitants of Hebron;) Gen. xv 19, with Num. xxxii. 12, (on the Kenezites.) *Vater*, vol. i. p. 136.

temporary records, as Bertholdt maintains;[a] for much may be advanced against their credibility, and it may be proved—at least by such examples as Gen. v. xi. 10—26, 1 Ch. ix. xxiii. xxvii. and Neh. x.—that such passages owe their origin to an uncertain and often arbitrary tradition,[b] as it may also be seen in the comparison of the following parallels:—

Numbers xxi. 10—20.

"And the children of Israel set forward, and pitched in Oboth. And they journeyed from Oboth, and pitched at Ije-abarim, in the wilderness which is before Moab, toward the sunrising. From thence they removed, and pitched in the valley of Zared. From thence they removed, and pitched on the other side of Arnon, which is in the wilderness that cometh out of the coasts of the Amorites; for Arnon is the border of Moab, between Moab and the Amorites. And from the wilderness they went to Mattanah; and from Mattanah to Nahaliel; and from Nahaliel to Bamoth; and from Bamoth in the valley, that is in the country of Moab, to the top of Pisgah, which looketh toward Jeshimon."

Numbers xxxiii. 44—49.

"And they departed from Punon, and pitched in Oboth. And they departed from Oboth, and pitched in Ije-abarim, in the border of Moab. And they departed from Iim, and pitched in Dibon-gad. And they removed from Dibon-gad, and encamped in Almon-diblathaim. And they removed from Almon-diblathaim, and pitched in the mountains of Abarim, before Nebo. And they departed from the mountains of Abarim, and pitched in the plains of Moab, by Jordan near Jericho. And they pitched by Jordan, from Beth-jesimoth even unto Abel-shittim, in the plains of Moab."

Though it may be admitted that, among the Mosaic laws, some may be old and genuine,[c] yet at least the

[a] *Bertholdt*, p. 787. On the other hand, *Vater*, vol. iii. p. 550, sqq. *De Wette*, Beiträge, vol. ii. p. 323, sqq., 377, sqq.

[b] See below, § 162, *d*.

[c] *Bertholdt*, p. 789. *Stäudlin*, Defence of the Laws of Moses, in *Ammon* and *Bertholdt's* Theol. Journal, vol. iii. and iv. *Bleek*, in *Rosenmüller's* Repert. vol. i. p. 7, sqq. Stud. und Krit. for 1831, p. 488, sqq.

proof of their originality, which has been sought for in their relation to the state of the nation while in the wilderness, is uncertain;[a] and the fact is as good as certain that the main part of the laws of Moses has come down to us only in a twofold paraphrase. The two editions —so to say—of the decalogue present this in a striking light.[b]

Exodus xx. 1—17.	Deuteronomy v. 6—21.
"I am the Lord thy God, which brought thee out of the land of Ægypt, out of the house of bondage. Thou shalt have no other gods before me.	"I am the Lord thy God, which brought thee out of the land of Ægypt, out of the house of bondage. Thou shalt have no other gods before me.
"Thou shalt not make unto thee any graven image, or any likeness of any thing that is in heaven above, or that is in the earth beneath, or that is in the water under the earth: thou shalt not bow down thyself to them,	"Thou shalt not make thee any graven image, any likeness of any thing that is in heaven above, or that is in the earth beneath, or that is in the waters under the earth: thou shalt not bow down thyself unto them, nor

[a] It is not so improbable as *Bleek* supposes, that a writer should transfer himself so perfectly into the historical circumstances of the people. The law relative to sacrifices, in Levit. xvii. at least, if we may judge from its style, belongs to the Elohistic document. Of the law in Levit. xvi., the part verse 21—34 was probably not written in the desert. The difficult word לַעֲזָאזֵל was obscure to the writer himself. This fact, and the want of distinctness in respect to the trespass and sin-offerings, (Levit. iv.—vii.,) and respecting Urim and Thummim, (Ex. xxviii. 30,) must be laid to the charge of a writer who was only acquainted with the law of sacrifices through practice, and understood the pontifical mysteries only by hearsay. In Levit. xviii. 28, it is presupposed that the Canaanites were already driven out of the land. Levit. xiv. 33, sqq., and xxv. 29, sqq., relate to dwelling in houses and cities. The law in vi. 5, 6, (12, 13, Eng. trans.) could not be carried out in the desert.

[b] *Fulda*, in *Paulus*, Mem. vol. iii. p. 205. *De Wette*, Beit. vol. ii. p. 253, sq. See *Bleek's* objection to this view, l. c.

nor serve them: for I the Lord thy God am a jealous God, visiting the iniquity of the fathers upon the children even unto the third and fourth generation of them that hate me, and showing mercy unto thousands of them that love me, and keep my commandments.

serve them: for I the Lord thy God am a jealous God, visiting the iniquity of the fathers upon the children unto the third and fourth generation of them that hate me, and showing mercy unto thousands of them that love me, and keep my commandments.

"Thou shalt not take the name of the Lord thy God in vain: for the Lord will not hold him guiltless that taketh his name in vain.

"Thou shalt not take the name of the Lord thy God in vain: for the Lord will not hold him guiltless that taketh his name in vain.

"Remember the Sabbath day, to keep it holy. Six days thou shalt labor, and do all thy work: but the seventh day is the Sabbath of the Lord thy God: in it thou shalt not do any work, thou, nor thy son, nor thy daughter, thy man-servant, nor thy maid-servant, nor thy cattle, nor thy stranger that is within thy gates: for in six days the Lord made heaven and earth, the sea, and all that in them is, and rested the seventh day: wherefore the Lord blessed the Sabbath day, and hallowed it.

"Keep the Sabbath day, to keep it holy, as the Lord thy God hath commanded thee. Six days thou shalt labor, and do all thy work: but the seventh day is the Sabbath of the Lord thy God: in it thou shalt not do any work, thou, nor thy son, nor thy daughter, nor thy man-servant, nor thy maid-servant, nor thine ox, nor thine ass, nor any of thy cattle, nor thy stranger that is within thy gates; that thy man-servant and thy maid-servant may rest as well as thou. And remember that thou wast a servant in the land of Ægypt, and that the Lord thy God brought thee out thence, through a mighty hand, and by a stretched-out arm: therefore the Lord thy God commanded thee to keep the Sabbath day.

"Honor thy father and thy mother: that thy days may be

"Honor thy father and thy mother, as the Lord thy God

long upon the land which the Lord thy God giveth thee.

"Thou shalt not kill.

"Thou shalt not commit adultery.

"Thou shalt not steal.

"Thou shalt not bear false witness against thy neighbor.

"Thou shalt not covet thy neighbor's house, thou shalt not covet thy neighbor's wife, nor his man-servant, nor his maid-servant, nor his ox, nor his ass, nor any thing that is thy neighbor's."

hath commanded thee: that thy days may be long, and that it may go well with thee, in the land which the Lord thy God giveth thee.

"Thou shalt not kill.

"And thou shalt not commit adultery.

"And thou shalt not steal.

"And thou shalt not bear false witness against thy neighbor.

"And thou shalt not covet thy neighbor's wife, neither shalt thou desire thy neighbor's house, his field, or his man-servant, or his maid-servant, his ox, or his ass, or any thing that is thy neighbor's."

The following odes may be referred with certainty to the age of Moses: —

Numbers xxi. 17, 18, and 27—30.

"Spring up, O well!
A well! princes dug it.
Chiefs of the people hollowed it out, with the sceptre
and their staves!"

"Come unto Heshbon!
Let the city of Sihon be built, and made strong;
For fire went out from Heshbon,
A flame from the city of Sihon.
It eat up Ar of Moab,

The dwellers on Arnon's heights.
Alas for thee, Moab!
Thou art lost, O people of Chemosh:
He (Chemosh) gave his sons as fugitives,
His daughters for captives to Sihon, king of the Amorites.
But we shot at them!
Heshbon is lost as far as Dibon;
We have laid waste to Nophah,
With fire to Medeba." [a]

It is probable, however, that these poetical pieces were preserved by oral tradition, and subsequently found a place in some collection, from which the author of this chapter received them.

§ 150.

3. The various Fragments which compose these Books.

A. *Genesis.*

It has been proved by the observations and inquiries of numerous critics, and confirmed and defended against the opposition of such as maintain the original unity of the book,[b] that there are several different fragments united together in the book of Genesis.[c] At the first

---

[a] [In the last line I have followed the reading of the LXX., Copt., and Vulg., אֵשׁ, instead of אֲשֶׁר, which is in the printed text, though marked as suspicious by the Masorites.]

[b] *Hasse*, Entdeckungen, &c.; 1805, vol. ii. p. 196. *Sack*, De Usu Nom. Dei in Genes. in his Commentatt.; 1821. *Rink*, Einleit. d. Mos. Schöpfungs-Berichte; 1822. *Ewald*, Compos. der Genes. *Ranke*, Ub. Pentateuch; 1834, p. 157, sqq. *Hengstenberg*, Authentie der Pent.; 1836, vol. i. p. 180, sqq. *Drechsler*, Einleit. und Æchtheit d. Gen.; 1838. *Hävernik*, l. c. vol. ii. pt. i. p. 205, sqq. [See *Turner*, Companion to Genesis; New York, 1841.]

[c] *Astruc*, Conjectures sur les Memoires origénaux, dont il paroit que

glance, they betray themselves by the different names applied to the Supreme Being—ELOHIM and JEHOVAH. But in this, however, the use of Elohim as an appellative, or otherwise peculiar word, must not be enumerated.[a] On a closer examination, these are found to be distinguished by other peculiar characteristic marks.

There are several different hypotheses which have been based on this phenomenon. The theory of Astruc, Eichhorn, Illgen, and Gramberg, which supposes there were two or more documents that extend throughout the whole book, falls to pieces of itself. But the other theory, which assumes that there were only several fragments of various authors, will appear to be limited to a small extent by the fact that the Elohistic fragments form a whole, which can be restored in a form almost perfect, while the Jehovistic passages cannot be thus united together.[b]

In the following pages I have put together those portions of the document Elohim, which, by the characteristics of language and contents, were easily arranged in a certain order; and, likewise, I have placed opposite them parallel or opposing passages.

Moÿse s'est sérvi pour composer le Livre de Genese; Bruxelles, 1753. [See the substance of the book translated in the Scriptural Interpreter, vol. vi. and vii.; Boston, 1836.] *Eichhorn*, Repert. vol. iv. p. 173, sqq. *Möller*, Uber d. Verschiedenheit der Styls...... Gen.; 1792. *Illgen*, Urkunden de Jerusalem. Tempelarchivs in ihrer Urgestalt; 1798. *Vater*, l. c. vol. iii. p. 412, sqq., 696, sqq. *Gramberg*, Libri Gen. secundum Fontes rite dignoscendos Adumbratio nova; 1828. *Stähelin*, Krit. Untersch. üb. Gen.; 1830. *Hartmann*, Hist. Krit. Forschungen ub. d. 5 Büch. Mosis; 1831. *Ewald*, in Stud. und Krit. for 1831, pt. iii. *Von Bohlen*, Genesis. *Tuch*, Genesis.

[a] As in vi. 2, xxviii. 21, iii. 1, 3, 5, ix. 27.

[b] [This fact will be shown below. The *Elohistic* passages are such as belong to the document where *Elohim* is used for God, the *Jehovistic* to that where God is called *Jehovah*.]

Document "Elohim."

I. Gen. i.—ii. 3. *Creation of the World.*

"In the beginning, Elohim created the heaven and the earth. And the earth was without form, and void; and darkness was upon the face of the deep; and the Spirit of Elohim moved upon the face of the waters. And Elohim said, 'Let there be light:' and there was light. And Elohim saw the light, that it was good: and Elohim divided the light from the darkness. And Elohim called the light Day, and the darkness he called Night: and the evening and the morning were the first day.

"And Elohim said, 'Let there be a firmament in the midst of the waters, and let it divide the waters from the waters.' And Elohim made the firmament, and divided the waters which were under the firmament from the waters which were above the firmament: and it was so. And Elohim called the firmament Heaven: and the evening and the morning were the second day.

"And Elohim said, 'Let the waters under the heaven be gathered together unto one place, and let the dry land appear:' and it was so. And Elohim called the dry land Earth: and the gathering together of the waters called he Seas: and Elohim saw that it was good. And Elohim said, 'Let the earth

Parallels, Additions, and Interpolations, with the Name "Jehovah."

Gen. ii. 4—iii. 24. *Creation of the World, Original History of Man, and the Origin of Evil.* (*Jehovah Elohim.*)

"These are the generations of the heavens and of the earth when they were created, in the day that Jehovah Elohim made the earth and the heavens, and every plant of the field before it was in the earth, and every herb of the field before it grew: for Jehovah Elohim had not caused it to rain upon the earth, and there was not a man to till the ground. But there went up a mist from the earth, and watered the whole face of the ground. And Jehovah Elohim formed man of the dust of the ground, and breathed into his nostrils the breath of life; and man became a living soul.

"And Jehovah Elohim planted a garden eastward in Eden; and there he put the man whom he had formed. And out of the ground made Jehovah Elohim to grow every tree that is pleasant to the sight, and good for food; the tree of life also in the midst of the garden, and the tree of knowledge of good and evil. And a river went out of Eden to water the garden: and from thence it was parted, and became into four heads. The name of the first is Pison: that is it

DOCUMENT "ELOHIM."

bring forth grass, the herb yielding seed, and the fruit-tree yielding fruit after his kind, whose seed is in itself, upon the earth:' and it was so. And the earth brought forth grass, and herb yielding seed after his kind, and the tree yielding fruit, whose seed was in itself, after his kind: and Elohim saw that it was good. And the evening and the morning were the third day.

" And Elohim said, 'Let there be lights in the firmament of the heaven, to divide the day from the night; and let them be for signs and for seasons, and for days and years. And let them be for lights in the firmament of the heaven to give light upon the earth:' and it was so. And Elohim made two great lights, the greater light to rule the day, and the lesser light to rule the night: he made the stars also. And Elohim set them in the firmament of the heaven to give light upon the earth, and to rule over the day, and over the night, and to divide the light from the darkness: and Elohim saw that it was good. And the evening and the morning were the fourth day. And Elohim said, 'Let the waters bring forth abundantly the moving creature that hath life, and fowl that may fly above the earth in the open firmament of heaven.' And Elohim created great whales, and every living creature that moveth, which

DOCUMENT "JEHOVAH."

which compasseth the whole land of Havilah, where there is gold; and the gold of that land is good: there is bdellium, and the onyx-stone. And the name of the second river is Gihon: the same is it that compasseth the whole land of Æthiopia. And the name of the third river is Hiddekel: that is it which goeth toward the east of Assyria. And the fourth river is Euphrates. And Jehovah Elohim took the man, and put him into the garden of Eden, to dress it, and to keep it. And Jehovah Elohim commanded the man, saying, 'Of every tree of the garden thou mayest freely eat. but of the tree of the knowledge of good and evil, thou shalt not eat of it: for in the day that thou eatest thereof thou shalt surely die.'

" And Jehovah Elohim said, 'It is not good that the man should be alone: I will make him a help meet for him.' And out of the ground Jehovah Elohim formed every beast of the field, and every fowl of the air, and brought them unto Adam to see what he would call them; and whatsoever Adam called every living creature, that was the name thereof. And Adam gave names to all cattle, and to the fowl of the air, and to every beast of the field: but for Adam there was not found a help meet for him. And Jehovah Elohim caused a deep sleep to fall upon

DOCUMENT "ELOHIM."

the waters brought forth abundantly after their kind, and every winged fowl after his kind: and Elohim saw that it was good. And Elohim blessed them, saying, 'Be fruitful, and multiply, and fill the waters in the seas, and let fowl multiply in the earth.' And the evening and the morning were the fifth day. And Elohim said, 'Let the earth bring forth the living creature after his kind, cattle and creeping thing, and beast of the earth after his kind:' and it was so. And Elohim made the beast of the earth after his kind, and cattle after their kind, and every thing that creepeth upon the earth after his kind: and Elohim saw that it was good.

"And Elohim said, 'Let us make man in our image, after our likeness; and let them have dominion over the fish of the sea, and over the fowl of the air, and over the cattle, and over all the earth, and over every creeping thing that creepeth upon the earth.' So Elohim created man in his own image, in the image of Elohim created he him; male and female created he them. And Elohim blessed them, and Elohim said unto them, 'Be fruitful, and multiply, and replenish the earth, and subdue it: and have dominion over the fish of the sea, and over the fowl of the air, and over every living thing that moveth upon the earth.'

DOCUMENT "JEHOVAH."

Adam, and he slept; and he took one of his ribs, and closed up the flesh instead thereof: and the rib, which Jehovah Elohim had taken from man, made he a woman, and brought her unto the man. And Adam said, 'This is now bone of my bones, and flesh of my flesh: she shall be called Woman, because she was taken out of man. Therefore shall a man leave his father and his mother, and shall cleave unto his wife: and they shall be one flesh.' And they were both naked, the man and his wife, and were not ashamed.

"Now the serpent was more subtle than any beast of the field which Jehovah Elohim had made: and he said unto the woman, 'Yea, hath Elohim said, "Ye shall not eat of every tree of the garden?"' And the woman said unto the serpent, 'We may eat of the fruit of the trees of the garden: but of the fruit of the tree which is in the midst of the garden, Elohim hath said, "Ye shall not eat of it, neither shall ye touch it, lest ye die."' And the serpent said unto the woman, 'Ye shall not surely die: for Elohim doth know, that in the day ye eat thereof, then your eyes shall be opened; and ye shall be as gods, knowing good and evil.' And when the woman saw that the tree was good for food, and that it was pleasant to the eyes, and a

DOCUMENT "ELOHIM."

"And Elohim said, 'Behold, I have given you every herb bearing seed, which is upon the face of all the earth, and every tree, in the which is the fruit of a tree yielding seed; to you it shall be for meat. And to every beast of the earth, and to every fowl of the air, and to every thing that creepeth upon the earth, wherein there is life, I have given every green herb for meat:' and it was so. And Elohim saw every thing that he had made, and behold, it was very good. And the evening and the morning were the sixth day.

"Thus the heavens and the earth were finished, and all the host of them. And on the seventh day Elohim ended his work which he had made, and he rested on the seventh day from all his work which he had made. And Elohim blessed the seventh day, and sanctified it; because that in it he had rested from all his work which Elohim created and made."

DOCUMENT "JEHOVAH."

tree to be desired to make one wise, she took of the fruit thereof, and did eat; and gave also unto her husband with her, and he did eat. And the eyes of them both were opened, and they knew that they were naked: and they sewed fig-leaves together, and made themselves aprons. And they heard the voice of Jehovah Elohim walking in the garden in the cool of the day: and Adam and his wife hid themselves from the presence of Jehovah Elohim amongst the trees of the garden. And Jehovah Elohim called unto Adam, and said unto him, 'Where art thou?' And he said, 'I heard thy voice in the garden: and I was afraid because I was naked; and I hid myself.' And he said, 'Who told thee that thou wast naked? Hast thou eaten of the tree whereof I commanded thee, that thou shouldest not eat?' And the man said, 'The woman whom thou gavest to be with me, she gave me of the tree, and I did eat.' And Jehovah Elohim said unto the woman, 'What is this that thou hast done?' And the woman said, 'The serpent beguiled me, and I did eat.' And Jehovah Elohim said unto the serpent, 'Because thou hast done this, thou art cursed above all cattle, and above every beast of the field: upon thy belly shalt thou go, and dust shalt thou eat all the days of thy life:

DOCUMENT "JEHOVAH."

and I will put enmity between thee and the woman, and between thy seed and her seed: it shall bruise thy head, and thou shalt bruise his heel.' Unto the woman he said, 'I will greatly multiply thy sorrow and thy conception; in sorrow thou shalt bring forth children: and thy desire shall be to thy husband, and he shall rule over thee.' And unto Adam he said, 'Because thou hast hearkened unto the voice of thy wife, and hast eaten of the tree of which I commanded thee, saying, "Thou shalt not eat of it;" cursed is the ground for thy sake; in sorrow shalt thou eat of it all the days of thy life; thorns also and thistles shall it bring forth to thee; and thou shalt eat the herb of the field. In the sweat of thy face shalt thou eat bread, till thou return unto the ground; for out of it wast thou taken: for dust thou art, and unto dust shalt thou return.' And Adam called his wife's name Eve, because she was the mother of all living. Unto Adam also and to his wife did Jehovah Elohim make coats of skins, and clothed them.

"And Jehovah Elohim said, 'Behold, the man is become as one of us, to know good and evil. And now, lest he put forth his hand, and take also of the tree of life, and eat, and live forever:' therefore Jehovah Elohim sent him forth from the garden of Eden, to till the ground from whence he was taken. So he drove out the man: and he placed at the east of the garden of Eden cherubims, and a flaming sword, which turned every way, to keep the way of the tree of life."[a]

DOCUMENT "ELOHIM."

II. Gen. v. 1—32. *Genealogical Table till the Time of Noah.* (Verse 1—3 connects with i. 26; verse 29 is interpolated.)

"This is the book of the generations of Adam: In the day that Elohim created man, in the likeness of Elohim made he him. Male

DOCUMENT "JEHOVAH."

Gen. iv. 1—26. *Family History of Adam, with a parallel Genealogy. Increase of Evil.*

"And Adam knew Eve his wife; and she conceived, and bare Cain, and said, 'I have gotten a man from Jehovah.' And she again bare his broth-

[a] [These two documents, i.—ii. 3, and ii. 14—24, contain an account of the same event. The inscription, "These are the generations of the heavens and the earth when they were created," plainly marks the point when the two separate. But the difference between them is remarkable in many passages, but most striking between i. 26, 27, and ii. 7, and 21, 22. *Eichhorn* thinks the above Jehovistic passage, ii. 4—iii. 24, is a whole by itself, and does not belong to the document "Jehovah," because God is called *Jehovah Elohim.*]

DOCUMENT "ELOHIM."

and female created he them; and blessed them, and called their name Adam, in the day when they were created.

"And Adam lived a hundred and thirty years, and begat a son in his own likeness, after his image; and called his name Seth: and the days of Adam after he had begotten Seth were eight hundred years: and he begat sons and daughters: and all the days that Adam lived were nine hundred and thirty years; and he died.

"And Seth lived a hundred and five years, and begat Enos: and Seth lived after he begat Enos eight hundred and seven years, and begat sons and daughters: and all the days of Seth were nine hundred and twelve years; and he died.

"And Enos lived ninety years, and begat Cainan:[a] and Enos lived after he begat Cainan eight hundred and fifteen years, and

DOCUMENT "JEHOVAH."

er Abel. And Abel was a keeper of sheep, but Cain was a tiller of the ground. And in process of time it came to pass, that Cain brought of the fruit of the ground an offering unto Jehovah. And Abel, he also brought of the firstlings of his flock, and of the fat thereof. And Jehovah had respect unto Abel, and to his offering: but unto Cain, and to his offering, he had not respect. And Cain was very wroth, and his countenance fell. And Jehovah said unto Cain, 'Why art thou wroth? and why is thy countenance fallen? If thou doest well, shalt thou not be accepted? and if thou doest not well, sin lieth at the door. And unto thee shall be his desire, and thou shalt rule over him.' And Cain talked with Abel his brother: and it came to pass when they were in the field, that Cain rose up against Abel his brother, and slew him.

---

[a] [There is a striking similarity in the names of the alleged descendants of *Adam* and *Enos*. They are essentially the same. Here follows a list of the descendants of each. It is to be remembered that both names signify *man*.

I.		II.	
ADAM, ...	אדם.	ENOS, ...	אנוש.
Cain, ...	קין.	*Cainan*, ...	קינן.
Enoch, ...	חנוך.	*Enoch*, ...	חנוך.
Irad, ...	עירד.	*Jared*, ...	ירד.
Mehujael, . . .	מחויאל.	*Mahalaleel*, . .	מהללאל.
Methusael, . . .	מתושאל.	*Methuselah*, . .	מתושלח.
Lamech, ...	למך.	*Lamech*, ...	למך.

The reader will draw his own inferences from this, or may see those of *Buttmann*, in his Mythologus, vol. i. ch. vii. p. 171.]

DOCUMENT "ELOHIM."

begat sons and daughters. and all the days of Enos were nine hundred and five years; and he died.

"And Cainan lived seventy years, and begat Mahalaleel: and Cainan lived after he begat Mahalaleel eight hundred and forty years, and begat sons and daughters: and all the days of Cainan were nine hundred and ten years; and he died.

"And Mahalaleel lived sixty and five years, and begat Jared: and Mahalaleel lived after he begat Jared eight hundred and thirty years, and begat sons and daughters: and all the days of Mahalaleel were eight hundred ninety and five years; and he died.

"And Jared lived a hundred sixty and two years, and he begat Enoch: and Jared lived after he begat Enoch eight hundred years, and begat sons and daughters: and all the days of Jared were nine hundred sixty and two years; and he died.

"And Enoch lived sixty and five years, and begat Methuselah: and Enoch walked with Elohim after he begat Methuselah three hundred years, and begat sons and daughters: and all the days of Enoch were three hundred sixty and five years: and Enoch walked with Elohim, and he was not: for Elohim took him.

"And Methuselah lived a hundred eighty and seven years, and begat Lamech: and Methuselah

DOCUMENT "JEHOVAH."

"And Jehovah said unto Cain, 'Where is Abel thy brother?' And he said, 'I know not: am I my brother's keeper?' And he said, 'What hast thou done? the voice of thy brother's blood crieth unto me from the ground. And now art thou cursed from the earth, which hath opened her mouth to receive thy brother's blood from thy hand: When thou tillest the ground, it shall not henceforth yield unto thee her strength. A fugitive and a vagabond shalt thou be in the earth.' And Cain said unto Jehovah, 'My punishment is greater than I can bear. Behold, thou hast driven me out this day from the face of the earth; and from thy face shall I be hid; and I shall be a fugitive and a vagabond in the earth; and it shall come to pass, that every one that findeth me shall slay me.' And Jehovah said unto him, 'Therefore whosoever slayeth Cain, vengeance shall be taken on him seven-fold.' And Jehovah set a mark upon Cain, lest any finding him should kill him.

"And Cain went out from the presence of Jehovah, and dwelt in the land of Nod, on the east of Eden. And Cain knew his wife, and she conceived, and bare Enoch: and he builded a city, and called the name of the city after the name of his son Enoch. And unto Enoch was born Irad: and Irad begat Mehujael; and

DOCUMENT "ELOHIM."

lived after he begat Lamech seven hundred eighty and two years, and begat sons and daughters: and all the days of Methuselah were nine hundred sixty and nine years; and he died.

"And Lamech lived a hundred eighty and two years, and begat a son: and he called his name Noah.[a] And Lamech lived after he begat Noah five hundred ninety and five years, and begat sons and daughters: and all the days of Lamech were seven hundred seventy and seven years: and he died. And Noah was five hundred years old; and Noah begat Shem, Ham, and Japheth."

DOCUMENT "JEHOVAH."

Mehujael begat Methusael; and Methusael begat Lamech.

"And Lamech took unto him two wives: the name of the one was Adah, and the name of the other Zillah. And Adah bare Jabal: he was the father of such as dwell in tents, and of such as have cattle. And his brother's name was Jubal: he was the father of all such as handle the harp and organ. And Zillah, she also bare Tubal-cain, an instructor of every artificer in brass and iron: and the sister of Tubal-cain was Naamah. And Lamech said unto his wives, Adah and Zillah, 'Hear my voice, ye wives of Lamech, hearken unto my speech: for I have slain a man to my wounding, and a young man to my hurt.[b] If Cain shall be avenged seven-fold, truly Lamech seventy and seven-fold.'

"And Adam knew his wife again, and she bare a son, and called his name Seth: 'For Jehovah,'[c] said she, 'hath appoint-

---

[a] [Verse 29 contains an etymology of the word *Noah* — "He shall comfort us for our work and the toil of our hands, because of the ground which *Jehovah* has cursed." It is evidently an interpolation.]

[b] [Chap. iv. 23. This is, perhaps, a better translation of this song: —

> "Ye wives of Lamech, hear my voice,
> Listen to my words:
> I have killed a man for wounding me,
> A young man for striking me.
> If Cain shall be avenged seven-fold,
> So Lamech seventy and seven-fold."

Here he alludes to his power of defending himself with the sword recently invented by his son, Tubal-cain. See *Herder*, Geist Eb. Poes, vol. i. p. 319.]

[c] [Chap. iv. 25, *Elohim* occurs instead of *Jehovah*. Some have conjectured the true reading was *Jehovah*, which I have followed.]

DOCUMENT "JEHOVAH."

ed me another seed instead of Abel, whom Cain slew.' And to Seth, to him also there was born a son; and he called his name Enos. then began men to call upon the name of Jehovah."

DOCUMENT "ELOHIM."

III. Gen. vi. 9—22. *History of the Deluge and of Noah.* (Verse 9 refers to v. 22, 24; verse 29 to i. 24.)

(1.) "These are the generations of Noah: Noah was a just man, and perfect in his generations, and Noah walked with Elohim. And Noah begat three sons, Shem, Ham, and Japheth. The earth also was corrupt before Elohim; and the earth was filled with violence. And Elohim looked upon the earth, and behold, it was corrupt: for all flesh had corrupted his way upon the earth. And Elohim said unto Noah, 'The end of all flesh is come before me; for the earth is filled with violence through them: and behold, I will destroy them with the earth.

"'Make thee an ark of gopher-wood: rooms shalt thou make in the ark, and shalt pitch it within and without with pitch. And this is the fashion which thou shalt make it of: The length of the ark shall be three hundred cubits, the breadth of it fifty cubits, and the height of it thirty cubits. A window shalt thou make to the ark,

DOCUMENT "JEHOVAH."

Chap. vi. 1—8, vii. 1—5. *History of the Deluge, and of Noah.*

"And it came to pass, when men began to multiply on the face of the earth, and daughters were born unto them, that the sons of Elohim saw the daughters of men that they were fair; and they took them wives of all which they chose. And Jehovah said, 'My Spirit shall not always strive with man, for that he also is flesh: yet his days shall be a hundred and twenty years.' There were giants in the earth in those days; and also after that, when the sons of Elohim came in unto the daughters of men, and they bare children to them, the same became mighty men, which were, of old, men of renown.

"And Jehovah[a] saw that the wickedness of man was great in the earth, and that every imagination of the thoughts of his heart was only evil continually. And it repented Jehovah that he had made man on the earth, and it grieved him at his heart. And Jehovah said, 'I will destroy man whom I have created from the face of the earth, both man and

---

[a] [Chap. vi. 5. The common English version has *God*, as if it were *Elohim*, in the text, but the Hebrew reads *Jehovah.*]

DOCUMENT "ELOHIM."

and in a cubit shalt thou finish it above; and the door of the ark shalt thou set in the side thereof: with lower, second, and third stories shalt thou make it. And behold, I, even I, do bring a flood of waters upon the earth, to destroy all flesh, wherein is the breath of life, from under heaven: and every thing that is in the earth shall die. But with thee will I establish my covenant: and thou shalt come into the ark, thou, and thy sons, and thy wife, and thy sons' wives with thee. And of every living thing of all flesh, two of every sort shalt thou bring into the ark, to keep them alive with thee: they shall be male and female. Of fowls after their kind, and of cattle after their kind, of every creeping thing of the earth after his kind; two of every sort shall come unto thee, to keep them alive. And take thou unto thee of all food that is eaten, and thou shalt gather it to thee; and it shall be for food for thee, and for them.' Thus did Noah; according to all that Elohim commanded him, so did he."

(2.) Chap. vii. 11—16. "In the six hundredth year of Noah's life, in the second month, the seventeenth day of the month, the same day were all the fountains of the great deep broken up, and the windows of heaven were opened. And the rain was upon the earth forty days and forty nights. In the self-same

DOCUMENT "JEHOVAH."

beast, and the creeping thing, and the fowls of the air: for it repenteth me that I have made them.' But Noah found grace in the eyes of Jehovah.

"And Jehovah said unto Noah, 'Come thou and all thy house into the ark: for thee have I seen righteous before me in this generation. Of every clean beast thou shalt take to thee by sevens, the male and his female; and of beasts that are not clean by two, the male and his female; of fowls also of the air by sevens, the male and the female; to keep seed alive upon the face of all the earth. For yet seven days, and I will cause it to rain upon the earth forty days and forty nights: and every living substance that I have made will I destroy from off the face of the earth.' And Noah did according unto all that Jehovah commanded him. And Noah was six hundred years old when the flood of waters was upon the earth."

Chap. vii. 7—10. "And Noah went in, and his sons, and his wife, and his sons' wives with him, into the ark, because of the waters of the flood. Of clean beasts, and of beasts that are not clean, and of fowls, and of every thing that creepeth upon the earth, there went in two and two unto Noah

DOCUMENT "ELOHIM."

day entered Noah, and Shem, and Ham, and Japheth, the sons of Noah, and Noah's wife, and the three wives of his sons with them, into the ark: they, and every beast after his kind, and all the cattle after their kind, and every creeping thing that creepeth upon the earth after his kind, and every fowl after his kind, every bird of every sort.[a] And they went in unto Noah into the ark, two and two of all flesh, wherein is the breath of life."

(3.) Gen. vii. 18—22. "And the waters prevailed, and were increased greatly upon the earth: and the ark went upon the face of the waters. And the waters prevailed exceedingly upon the earth; and all the high hills that were under the whole heaven were covered. Fifteen cubits upward did the waters prevail: and the mountains were covered.[b] And all flesh died that moved upon the earth, both of fowl, and of cattle, and of beast, and of every creeping thing that creepeth upon the earth, and every man: all in

DOCUMENT "JEHOVAH."

into the ark, the male and the female, as Jehovah[c] had commanded Noah. And it came to pass, after seven days, that the waters of the flood were upon the earth."

Chap. vii. 17, 23. "And the flood was forty days upon the earth; and the waters increased, and bare up the ark, and it was lifted up above the earth. And every living substance was destroyed which was upon the face of the ground, both man, and cattle, and the creeping things, and the fowl of heaven; and they were destroyed from the earth; and Noah only remained alive, and they that were with him in the ark."

---

[a] Chap. vii. 14, sqq.; compare with vi. 19, sqq. Noah is commanded to take two of each sort, in one passage; in the other they enter the ark of their own accord. Ver. 16—"And they that went in, went in male and female of all flesh, as Elohim had commanded him, and Jehovah shut him in"—is an interpolation.

[b] Chap. vii. 21. A comparison with vi. 17, shows that both verses belong to the same document.

[c] [Chap. vii. 9. *Elohim* occurs again in the Jehovistic document. But the Samaritan and one Heb. MS. have *Jehovah;* so the Chaldee Paraphrase, and the Vulgate, and even Luther, who had no critical hypothesis to support thereby. I have followed their authority.]

DOCUMENT "ELOHIM."

whose nostrils was the breath of life, of all that was in the dry land, died. And the waters prevailed upon the earth a hundred and fifty days."

(4.) Gen. viii. 1—19. "And Elohim remembered Noah, and every living thing, and all the cattle that was with him in the ark: and Elohim made a wind to pass over the earth, and the waters assuaged; the fountains also of the deep, and the windows of heaven were stopped, and the rain from heaven was restrained; and the waters returned from off the earth continually: and after the end of the hundred and fifty days, the waters were abated.

"And the ark rested in the seventh month, on the seventeenth day of the month, upon the mountains of Ararat. And the waters decreased continually, until the tenth month: in the tenth month, on the first day of the month, were the tops of the mountains seen.

"And it came to pass at the end of forty days, that Noah opened the window of the ark which he had made: and he sent forth a raven, which went forth to and fro, until the waters were dried up from off the earth. Also he sent forth a dove from him, to see if the waters were abated from off the face of the ground; but the dove found no rest for the sole of her foot, and she returned unto him into the ark; for the waters were on the face of the whole earth. Then he put forth his hand, and took her, and pulled her in unto him into the ark. And he staid yet other seven days, and again he sent forth the dove out of the ark; and the dove came in to him in the evening, and lo, in her mouth was an olive leaf plucked off. So Noah knew that the waters were abated from off the earth. And he staid yet other seven days, and sent forth the dove; which returned not again unto him any more.

"And it came to pass in the six hundredth and first year, in the first month, the first day of the month, the waters were dried up from off the earth: and Noah removed the covering of the ark, and looked, and behold, the face of the ground was dry. And in the second month, on the seven and twentieth day of the month, was the earth dried.

"And Elohim spake unto Noah, saying, 'Go forth of the ark, thou, and thy wife, and thy sons, and thy sons' wives with thee.[a] Bring forth with thee every living thing that is with thee, of all flesh, both of fowl, and of cattle, and of every creeping thing that creepeth upon the earth; that they may breed abundantly in the earth, and be fruitful, and multiply upon the earth.' And Noah went forth, and his sons, and his wife, and his sons' wives with him: every beast, every

[a] Comp. vii. 13.

DOCUMENT "ELOHIM."

creeping thing, and every fowl, and whatsoever creepeth upon the earth, after their kinds, went forth out of the ark."[a]

DOCUMENT "ELOHIM."

(5.) Chap. ix. 1—17. *Covenant of Elohim with Noah.*

"And Elohim blessed Noah and his sons, and said unto them, 'Be fruitful and multiply, and replenish the earth.[b] And the fear of you, and the dread of you, shall be upon every beast of the earth, and upon every fowl of the air, upon all that moveth upon the earth, and upon all the fishes of the sea; into your hand are they delivered. Every moving thing that liveth shall be meat for you; even as the green herb have I given you all things:[c] but flesh, with the life thereof, which is the blood thereof, shall ye not eat. And surely your blood of your lives will I require: at the hand of every beast will I require it, and at the hand of man: at the hand of every man's brother will I require the life of man. Whoso sheddeth man's blood, by man shall his blood be shed; for in the image of Elohim made he man.[d] And you, be ye fruitful, and multiply: bring forth abundantly in the earth, and multiply therein.'

"And Elohim spake unto Noah, and to his sons with him, saying, 'And I, behold, I establish my covenant with you, and with your seed after you;[e] and with ev-

DOCUMENT "JEHOVAH."

Chap. viii. 20—22. *Reconciliation of Jehovah by an Offering. His Promise that a Deluge shall not again return.*

"And Noah builded an altar unto Jehovah, and took of every clean beast, and of every clean fowl, and offered burnt-offerings on the altar. And Jehovah smelled a sweet savor; and Jehovah said in his heart, 'I will not again curse the ground any more for man's sake; for the imagination of man's heart is evil from his youth: neither will I again smite any more every thing living, as I have done. While the earth remaineth, seed-time and harvest, and cold and heat, and summer and winter, and day and night, shall not cease.'"

---

[a] Comp. verse 17 with i. 28. [b] Comp. 1 and 7 with i. 28.
[c] Comp. i. 29. [d] Comp. i. 26. [e] Comp. vi. 18.

DOCUMENT "ELOHIM."

ery living creature that is with you, of the fowl, of the cattle, and of every beast of the earth with you, from all that go out of the ark to every beast of the earth. And I will establish my covenant with you; neither shall all flesh be cut off any more by the waters of a flood; neither shall there any more be a flood to destroy the earth.' And Elohim said, 'This is the token of the covenant which I make between me and you, and every living creature that is with you, for perpetual generations. I do set my bow in the cloud, and it shall be for a token of a covenant between me and the earth. And it shall come to pass, when I bring a cloud over the earth, that the bow shall be seen in the cloud: and I will remember my covenant, which is between me and you, and every living creature of all flesh; and the waters shall no more become a flood to destroy all flesh. And the bow shall be in the cloud; and I will look upon it, that I may remember the everlasting covenant between Elohim and every living creature of all flesh that is upon the earth.' And Elohim said unto Noah, 'This is the token of the covenant which I have established between me and all flesh that is upon the earth.'"

DOCUMENT "ELOHIM."

(6.) Chap. ix. 28. "And Noah lived after the flood three hundred and fifty years, and all the years of Noah were nine hundred and fifty years, and he died."

DOCUMENT "JEHOVAH."

Chap. ix. 20—27. "And Noah began to be a husbandman, and he planted a vineyard: and he drank of the wine, and was drunken; and he was uncovered within his tent. And Ham, the father of Canaan, saw the nakedness of his father, and told his two brethren without. And Shem and Japheth took a garment, and laid it upon both their shoulders, and went backward, and covered the nakedness of their father: and their faces were backward, and they saw not their father's nakedness. And Noah awoke from his wine, and knew what his younger son had done unto him. And he said, 'Cursed be Canaan; a servant of

DOCUMENT "JEHOVAH."

servants shall he be unto his brethren." And he said, 'Blessed be Jehovah Elohim of Shem; and Canaan shall be his servant. Elohim shall enlarge Japheth, and he shall dwell in the tents of Shem; and Canaan shall be his servant.'"[a]

DOCUMENT "ELOHIM."	DOCUMENT "JEHOVAH."
IV. Chap. xi. 10—26.[b] Genealogical register till Abraham.	Chap. x. Register of the nations, with parallel genealogies.

V. Chap. xi. 27—32 is decidedly Elohistic. The passage xii.—xiv.—containing Abraham's migration to Canaan and Ægypt, his separation from Lot, his military expedition—is chiefly Jehovistic, but, perhaps, contains some Elohistic verses, as in xii. 5, 6, and elsewhere.[c]

VI. Chap. xvii. God's covenant with Abraham.[d]	Chap. xv. A covenant also, but without the institution of circumcision, and the promise of Isaac, which is related in chap. xviii.
VII. Chap. xix. 29. Destruction of Sodom, and delivery of Lot.	Chap. xix. 1—28. The same. Verses 30—38. Lot's incest.
VIII. Chap. xx. Abraham's residence at *Gerar*, and seizure of *Sarah*.[e]	Chap. xii. 10—19. A similar adventure in *Ægypt*. Chap. xxvi. 1—11. A similar adventure befalls *Rebekah*.

DOCUMENT "ELOHIM."	DOCUMENT "JEHOVAH."	
Seizure of Sarah in Gerar.	*Seizure of Sarah in Ægypt.*	*Seizure of Rebekah.*
"And Abraham journeyed from thence toward the south country, and dwelled	"And there was a famine in the land: and Abram went down into Ægypt to	"And there was a famine in the land, besides the first famine that was in the days of Abraham.

[a] [Perhaps verses 18, 19, likewise belong here.]

[b] Comp. chap. v.

[c] See *Tuch*, l. c. p. 4.

[d] Comp. the passage ix. 1—17, which is closely allied to this.

[e] Verse 18 is interpolated.

DOCUMENT "ELOHIM."

between Kadesh and Shur, and sojourned in Gerar. And Abraham said of Sarah his wife, 'She is my sister:' and Abimelech king of Gerar sent and took Sarah. But Elohim came to Abimelech in a dream by night, and said to him, 'Behold, thou art but a dead man, for the woman which thou hast taken: for she is a man's wife.' But Abimelech had not come near her; and he said, 'Lord, wilt thou slay also a righteous nation? Said he not unto me, "She is my sister?" and she, even she herself, said, "He is my brother:" in the integrity of my heart, and innocency of my hands, have I done this.' And Elohim said unto him in a dream, 'Yea, I know that thou didst this in the integrity of thy heart; for I also withheld thee from sinning against me: therefore suffered I thee not to touch her.

DOCUMENT "JEHOVAH."

sojourn there; for the famine was grievous in the land. And it came to pass, when he was come near to enter into Ægypt, that he said unto Sarai his wife, 'Behold now, I know that thou art a fair woman to look upon: therefore it shall come to pass, when the Ægyptians shall see thee, that they shall say, "This is his wife;" and they will kill me, but they will save thee alive. Say, I pray thee, thou art my sister; that it may be well with me for thy sake; and my soul shall live because of thee.'

"And it came to pass, that when Abram was come into Ægypt, the Ægyptians beheld the woman that she was very fair. The princes also of Pharaoh saw her, and commended her before Pharaoh: and the woman was taken into Pharaoh's house. And he entreated Abram well for her sake: and he had

And Isaac went unto Abimelech king of the Philistines unto Gerar. And Jehovah appeared unto him, and said, 'Go not down into Ægypt: dwell in the land which I shall tell thee of. Sojourn in this land, and I will be with thee, and will bless thee: for unto thee and unto thy seed I will give all these countries, and I will perform the oath which I sware unto Abraham thy father: and I will make thy seed to multiply as the stars of heaven, and will give unto thy seed all these countries: and in thy seed shall all the nations of the earth be blessed: because that Abraham obeyed my voice, and kept my charge, my commandments, my statutes, and my laws.'

"And Isaac dwelt in Gerar: and the men of the place asked him of his wife; and he said, 'She is my sister:' for he feared

DOCUMENT "ELOHIM."

Now, therefore, restore the man his wife; for he is a prophet, and he shall pray for thee, and thou shalt live: and if thou restore her not, know thou that thou shalt surely die, thou, and all that are thine.'

"Therefore Abimelech rose early in the morning, and called all his servants, and told all these things in their ears: and the men were sore afraid. Then Abimelech called Abraham, and said unto him, 'What hast thou done unto us? and what have I offended thee, that thou hast brought on me, and on my kingdom, a great sin? Thou hast done deeds unto me that ought not to be done.' And Abimelech said unto Abraham, 'What sawest thou, that thou hast done this thing?' And Abraham said, 'Because I thought, "Surely the fear of Elohim is not in this

DOCUMENT "JEHOVAH."

sheep, and oxen, and he-asses, and men-servants, and maid-servants, and she-asses, and camels.

"And Jehovah plagued Pharaoh and his house with great plagues because of Sarai, Abram's wife. And Pharaoh called Abram, and said, 'What is this that thou hast done unto me? Why didst thou not tell me that she was thy wife? Why saidst thou, "She is my sister"? so I might have taken her to me to wife: now, therefore, behold thy wife; take her and go thy way.' And Pharaoh commanded his men concerning him: and they sent him away, and his wife, and all that he had."

to say, 'She is my wife;' 'lest,' said he, 'the men of the place should kill me for Rebekah;' because she was fair to look upon. And it came to pass when he had been there a long time, that Abimelech king of the Philistines looked out at a window, and saw, and behold, Isaac was sporting with Rebekah his wife. And Abimelech called Isaac, and said, 'Behold, of a surety, she is thy wife; and how saidst thou, "She is my sister"?' And Isaac said unto him, 'Because I said, "Lest I die for her."' And Abimelech said, 'What is this thou hast done unto us? One of the people might lightly have lien with thy wife, and thou shouldest have brought guiltiness upon us.' And Abimelech charged all his people, saying, 'He that toucheth this man or his wife, shall surely be put to death."

DOCUMENT "ELOHIM."

place; and they will slay me for my wife's sake." And yet indeed she is my sister; she is the daughter of my father, but not the daughter of my mother: and she became my wife. And it came to pass, when Elohim caused me to wander from my father's house, that I said unto her, "This is thy kindness which thou shalt show unto me; at every place whither we shall come, say of me, 'He is my brother.'"'

"And Abimelech took sheep, and oxen, and men-servants, and women-servants, and gave them unto Abraham, and restored him Sarah his wife. And Abimelech said, 'Behold, my land is before thee: dwell where it pleaseth thee.' And unto Sarah he said, 'Behold, I have given thy brother a thousand pieces of silver; behold, he is to thee a covering of the eyes unto all that are with thee, and with all other:' thus she was reproved.

"So Abraham prayed unto Elohim; and Elohim healed Abimelech, and his wife, and his maid-servants; and they bare children."

DOCUMENT "ELOHIM."

IX. Chap. xxi. 1—21.[a] *Birth of Isaac, and Expulsion of Ishmael.*

"Sarah conceived, and bare Abraham a son in his old age, at the set time of which Elohim had spoken to him. And Abraham called the name of his son that was born unto him, whom Sarah bare to him, Isaac. And Abraham circumcised his son Isaac, being eight days old, as Elohim had commanded him. And Abraham was a hundred years old when his son Isaac was born unto him.

"And Sarah said, 'Elohim hath made me to laugh, so that all that hear will laugh with me.' And she said, 'Who would have said

DOCUMENT "JEHOVAH."

Chap. xvi. *Similar Events.*

"Now Sarai, Abram's wife, bare him no children: and she had a handmaid, an Ægyptian, whose name was Hagar. And Sarai said unto Abram, 'Behold, now, Jehovah hath restrained me from bearing: I pray thee, go in unto my maid; it may be that I may obtain children by her.' And Abram hearkened to the voice of Sarai. And Sarai, Abram's wife, took Hagar her maid the Ægyptian, after Abram had dwelt ten years in the land of Canaan, and gave her to her husband Abram to be his wife.

"And he went in unto Hagar, and she conceived: and when she

[a] Comp. verses 2—4 with xvii. 21, 10—14; verse 13 with xvii. 20. Verse 1 is interpolated.

DOCUMENT "ELOHIM."

unto Abraham that Sarah should have given children suck? for I have borne him a son in his old age.' And the child grew, and was weaned: and Abraham made a great feast the same day that Isaac was weaned.

"And Sarah saw the son of Hagar the Ægyptian, which she had borne unto Abraham, mocking. Wherefore she said unto Abraham, 'Cast out this bond-woman and her son: for the son of this bond-woman shall not be heir with my son, even with Isaac.' And the thing was very grievous in Abraham's sight, because of his son.

"And Elohim said unto Abraham, 'Let it not be grievous in thy sight, because of the lad, and because of thy bond-woman; in all that Sarah hath said unto thee, hearken unto her voice: for in Isaac shall thy seed be called. And also of the son of the bond-woman will I make a nation, because he is thy seed.' And Abraham rose up early in the morning, and took bread and a bottle of water, and gave it unto Hagar (putting it on her shoulder) and the child, and sent her away: and she departed, and wandered in the wilderness of Beer-sheba. And the water was spent in the bottle, and she cast the child under one of the shrubs. And she went, and sat her down over

DOCUMENT "JEHOVAH."

saw that she had conceived, her mistress was despised in her eyes. And Sarai said unto Abram, 'My wrong be upon thee: I have given my maid into thy bosom; and when she saw that she had conceived, I was despised in her eyes: Jehovah judge between me and thee.' But Abram said unto Sarai, 'Behold, thy maid is in thy hand; do to her as it pleaseth thee.' And when Sarai dealt hardly with her, she fled from her face.

"And the angel of Jehovah found her by a fountain of water in the wilderness, by the fountain in the way to Shur. And he said, 'Hagar, Sarai's maid, whence camest thou? and whither wilt thou go?' And she said, 'I flee from the face of my mistress Sarai.' And the angel of Jehovah said unto her, 'Return to thy mistress, and submit thyself under her hands.' And the angel of Jehovah said unto her, 'I will multiply thy seed exceedingly, that it shall not be numbered for multitude.' And the angel of Jehovah said unto her, 'Behold, thou art with child, and shalt bear a son, and shalt call his name Ishmael; because Jehovah hath heard thy affliction. And he will be a wild man: his hand will be against every man, and every man's hand against him; and he shall dwell in the presence of all his brethren

DOCUMENT "ELOHIM."

against him, a good way off, as it were a bow-shot: for she said, 'Let me not see the death of the child.' And she sat over against him, and lifted up her voice, and wept. And Elohim heard the voice of the lad: and the angel of Elohim called to Hagar out of heaven, and said unto her, 'What aileth thee, Hagar? Fear not; for Elohim hath heard the voice of the lad where he is. Arise, lift up the lad, and hold him in thine hand: for I will make him a great nation.'

"And Elohim opened her eyes, and she saw a well of water: and she went, and filled the bottle with water, and gave the lad drink. And Elohim was with the lad; and he grew, and dwelt in the wilderness, and became an archer. And he dwelt in the wilderness of Paran: and his mother took him a wife out of the land of Ægypt."

DOCUMENT "JEHOVAH."

And she called the name of Jehovah that spake unto her, 'THOU GOD OF VISION:'[a] for she said, 'Have I also here looked after him that seeth me?' Wherefore the well was called Beer-lahai-roi, [*well of living vision;*] behold, it is between Kadesh and Bered.

"And Hagar bare Abram a son: and Abram called his son's name, which Hagar bare, Ishmael.

"And Abram was fourscore and six years old, when Hagar bare Ishmael to Abram"

X. Chap. xxi. 22—34. *Abraham's Covenant with Abimelech.*[b]

"And it came to pass at that time, that Abimelech and Phichol the chief captain of his host spake unto Abraham, saying, 'Elohim is with thee in all that thou doest:

Chap. xxvi. 26—33. *A similar Event in the History of Isaac.*

"Then Abimelech went to him from Gerar, and Ahuzzath one of his friends, and Phichol the chief captain of his army. And Isaac said unto them, 'Wherefore come ye to me, seeing ye hate

[a] [I have departed in this from the common version.]

[b] Verses 33 and 34 are interpolated.

DOCUMENT "ELOHIM."

now, therefore, swear unto me here by Elohim that thou wilt not deal falsely with me, nor with my son, nor with my son's son; but, according to the kindness that I have done unto thee, thou shalt do unto me, and to the land wherein thou hast sojourned.' And Abraham said, 'I will swear.' And Abraham reproved Abimelech because of a well of water, which Abimelech's servants had violently taken away. And Abimelech said, 'I wot not who hath done this thing: neither didst thou tell me, neither yet heard I of it, but to-day.' And Abraham took sheep and oxen, and gave them unto Abimelech: and both of them made a covenant. And Abraham set seven ewe-lambs of the flock by themselves. And Abimelech said unto Abraham, 'What mean these seven ewe-lambs, which thou hast set by themselves?' And he said, 'For these seven ewe-lambs shalt thou take of my hand, that they may be a witness unto me that I have digged this well. Wherefore he called that place Beer-sheba: because there they sware both of them. Thus they made a covenant at Beer-sheba: then Abimelech rose up, and Phichol the chief captain of his host, and they returned into the land of the Philistines"

DOCUMENT "JEHOVAH."

me, and have sent me away from you?' And they said, 'We saw certainly that Jehovah was with thee: and we said, "Let there be now an oath betwixt us, even betwixt us and thee, and let us make a covenant with thee; that thou wilt do us no hurt, as we have not touched thee, and as we have done unto thee nothing but good, and have sent thee away in peace; thou art now the blessed of Jehovah."' And he made them a feast, and they did eat and drink. And they rose up betimes in the morning, and sware one to another: and Isaac sent them away, and they departed from him in peace. And it came to pass the same day, that Isaac's servants came and told him concerning the well which they had digged, and said unto him, 'We have found water.' And he called it Shebah: therefore the name of the city is Beer-sheba unto this day."

DOCUMENT "ELOHIM."

XI. Chap. xxii. 1—13, and verse 19. *God tempts Abraham.*[a]

"And it came to pass after these things, that Elohim did tempt Abraham, and said unto him, 'Abraham:' and he said, 'Behold, here I am.' And he said, 'Take now thy son, thine only son Isaac, whom thou lovest, and get thee into the land of Moriah; and offer him there for a burnt-offering upon one of the mountains which I will tell thee of.'

"And Abraham rose up early in the morning, and saddled his ass, and took two of his young men with him, and Isaac his son, and clave the wood for the burnt-offering, and rose up, and went unto the place of which Elohim had told him. Then on the third day Abraham lifted up his eyes, and saw the place afar off. And Abraham said unto his young men, 'Abide ye here with the ass, and I and the lad will go yonder and worship, and come again to you.' And Abraham took the wood of the burnt-offering, and laid it upon Isaac his son; and he took the fire in his hand and a knife: and they went both of them together. And Isaac spake unto Abraham his father, and said, 'My father:' and he said, 'Here am I, my son.' And he said, 'Behold the fire and the

DOCUMENT "JEHOVAH."

Chap. xxii. 14—18. *God tempts Abraham.*

"And Abraham called the name of that place Jehovah-jireh: as it is said to this day, 'In the mount of Jehovah it shall be seen.'

"And the angel of Jehovah called unto Abraham out of heaven the second time, and said, 'By myself have I sworn, saith Jehovah, — for because thou hast done this thing, and hast not withheld thy son, thine only son,— that in blessing I will bless thee, and in multiplying I will multiply thy seed as the stars of the heaven, and as the sand which is upon the sea-shore; and thy seed shall possess the gate of his enemies; and in thy seed shall all the nations of the earth be blessed; because thou hast obeyed my voice."

[a] Verse 11 is interpolated.

DOCUMENT "ELOHIM."

wood: but where is the lamb for a burnt-offering?' And Abraham said, 'My son, Elohim will provide himself a lamb for a burnt-offering:' so they went both of them together. And they came to the place which Elohim had told him of: and Abraham built an altar there, and laid the wood in order; and bound Isaac his son, and laid him on the altar upon the wood. And Abraham stretched forth his hand, and took the knife to slay his son. And the angel of Jehovah called unto him out of heaven, and said, 'Abraham, Abraham.' And he said, 'Here am I.' And he said, 'Lay not thine hand upon the lad, neither do thou any thing unto him: for now I know that thou fearest Elohim, seeing thou hast not withheld thy son, thine only son, from me.' And Abraham lifted up his eyes, and looked, and behold, behind him a ram caught in a thicket by his horns: and Abraham went and took the ram, and offered him up for a burnt-offering in the stead of his son.

"So Abraham returned unto his young men, and they rose up, and went together to Beer-sheba; and Abraham dwelt at Beer-sheba."

DOCUMENT "ELOHIM."	DOCUMENT "JEHOVAH."
XII. Chap. xxiii. Purchase of the cave at Macpelah.	
XIII. (1.) Chap. xxv. 1—11. Abraham's second marriage, and death.[a]	
(2.) Chap. xxv. 12—18. Ishmael's genealogy.	
(3.) Chap. xxv. 19—21,[b] 24—26. Isaac's marriage and sons.	Chap. xxiv. A detailed account of Isaac's marriage. Chap. xxv. 22, 23. Prophecy respecting his sons.
(4.) Chap. xxv. 27—35. Esau sells his birthright.[c]	Chap. xxvii. 1—40. Jacob deceives Esau to obtain his father's blessing.
(5.) Chap. xxvi. 34, 35. Esau's wives.	Chap. xxvi. 1—33. Isaac's residence at Gerar.

[a] Comp. verses 9, 10, with xxiii.

[b] Verse 21 is an interpolation.

[c] *Astruc*, *Stähelin*, and others, place it differently.

DOCUMENT "ELOHIM."

XIV. Chap. xxvii. 46—xxviii. 9. *Jacob sent to Mesopotamia to procure a Wife.*[a]

"And Rebekah said to Isaac, 'I am weary of my life, because of the daughters of Heth: if Jacob take a wife of the daughters of Heth, such as these which are of the daughters of the land, what good shall my life do me?'

"And Isaac called Jacob, and blessed him, and charged him, and said unto him, 'Thou shalt not take a wife of the daughters of Canaan. Arise, go to Padan-aram, to the house of Bethuel thy mother's father; and take thee a wife from thence of the daughters of Laban thy mother's brother. And Elohim Almighty bless thee, and make thee fruitful, and multiply thee, that thou mayest be a multitude of people; and give thee the blessing of Abraham, to thee, and to thy seed with thee; that thou mayest inherit the land wherein thou art a stranger, which Elohim gave unto Abraham.' And Isaac sent away Jacob: and he went to Padan-aram unto Laban, son of Bethuel the Syrian, the brother of Rebekah, Jacob's and Esau's mother.

"When Esau saw that Isaac had blessed Jacob, and sent him away to Padan-aram, to take him a wife from thence; and that as he blessed him, he gave him a

DOCUMENT "JEHOVAH."

Chap. xxvii. 41—45. *Jacob flees to Mesopotamia.*

"And Esau hated Jacob because of the blessing wherewith his father blessed him: and Esau said in his heart, 'The days of mourning for my father are at hand; then will I slay my brother Jacob.' And these words of Esau her elder son were told to Rebekah: and she sent and called Jacob her younger son, and said unto him, 'Behold, thy brother Esau, as touching thee, doth comfort himself, purposing to kill thee. Now, therefore, my son, obey my voice; and arise, flee thou to Laban my brother to Haran; and tarry with him a few days, until thy brother's fury turn away; until thy brother's anger turn away from thee, and he forget that which thou hast done to him: then I will send and fetch thee from thence. Why should I be deprived also of you both in one day?'"

[a] Comp. xxviii. 3, 4, with xvii. 1, 8, 20.

DOCUMENT "ELOHIM."

charge, saying, 'Thou shalt not take a wife of the daughters of Canaan;' and that Jacob obeyed his father, and his mother, and was gone to Padan-aram; and Esau seeing that the daughters of Canaan pleased not Isaac his father; then went Esau unto Ishmael, and took unto the wives which he had, Mahalath the daughter of Ishmael, Abraham's son, the sister of Nebajoth, to be his wife."

DOCUMENT "ELOHIM."	DOCUMENT "JEHOVAH."
XV. Chap. xxviii. 10—12, 17, 20—22.[a] Jacob's dream and vow at Beth-el.	Chap. xxviii. 13—16. Jehovah's promise to Jacob at Beth-el. Verses 18, 19. Anticipation of the consecration of Beth-el. Compare xxxv. 14.[e]
XVI. Chap. xxix.[b] xxx. 1—13, 17—23,[c] part of 24. Jacob's arrival in Mesopotamia, marriage, and children.	Chap. xxx. 14—16. Reuben's mandrakes. Chap. xxx. 24. Another etymology of *Joseph*.
XVII. (1.) Chap. xxxi. 4—16. Jacob resolves to flee. (2.) Chap. xxxi. 17—xxxii. 4. Flight, and covenant with Laban.[d]	Chap. xxx. 25—42. Different account to show how Jacob acquired wealth by deceit

XVIII. Jacob meets Esau. Chap. xxxii. 4—xxxiii. 16, is referred to the document "Jehovah" by Gramberg, to "Elohim" by Tuch, with the exception of xxxii. 10—12: xxxiii. 1—16, unquestionably belongs here. But Esau's residence in Edom (xxxii. 4) contradicts the Elohistic account, (xxxvi. 6, sqq.,) that he went there after Jacob's arrival. The supposition of enmity between Jacob and Esau (xxxii. 21) belongs to the Jehovistic document. The change of Jacob's name (xxxii. 23, sq.) cannot be Elohistic,[f] since this first occurs xxxv. 10, and is observed by the narrator himself in verse 21.

DOCUMENT "ELOHIM."	DOCUMENT "JEHOVAH."
XIX. Chap. xxxiii. 17—20. Jacob's arrival in Canaan.	

[a] Verse 21 is interpolated.

[b] Verses 31—35 are interpolated.

[c] *Stähelin* differently.

[d] Chap. xxxi. 49, interpolated.

[e] *Tuch* arranges differently.

[f] The name *Elohim* (verses 29, 31) proves nothing.

DOCUMENT "ELOHIM."

XX. Chap. xxxiv. Violation of Dinah.[a]

XXI. Chap. xxxv. Jacob's journey to Beth-el. God's promises to him. Change of Jacob's name. Consecration of Beth-el. Death of Isaac.[b] Verse 10, "Thy name is Jacob," (*Heel-catcher;*) "thy name shall not be called Jacob any more, but thy name shall be Israel," (*Soldier-of-God.*)

XXII. Chap. xxxvi.[c] Esau's family register.

XXIII. Chap. xxxvii. Joseph is sold into Ægypt. But the narrative (23—30) does not agree together.[d]

DOCUMENT "JEHOVAH."

Chap. xxviii. 18, 19. Earlier consecration of Beth-el.

Chap. xxxii. 22—32. Another account of the change of Jacob's name; 24—29. "And Jacob was left alone: and there wrestled a man with him until the breaking of the day. And when he saw that he prevailed not against him, he touched the hollow of his thigh; and the hollow of Jacob's thigh was out of joint as he wrestled with him. And he said, 'Let me go, for the day breaketh.' And he said, 'I will not let thee go, except thou bless me.' And he said unto him, 'What is thy name?' And he said, 'Jacob.' And he said, 'Thy name shall be called no more Jacob, but Israel: for as a prince hast thou power with Elohim and with men, and hast prevailed.' And Jacob asked him, and said, 'Tell me, I pray thee, thy name.' And he said, 'Wherefore is it that thou dost ask after my name?' And he blessed him there."

Chap. xxxviii. Judah's incest with Tamar.

---

[a] The mention of circumcision shows this belongs to the Elohistic document. Comp. xvii. Comp., also, verse 1 with xvii. 12; verse 2 with xvii. 20, xxiii. 6, xxv. 16.

[b] The Jehovist differs from verses 1, 7, and perhaps other passages; for Deborah (verse 8) could scarcely be, at that time, in the camp of Jacob.

[c] Comp. verses 6—8 with xvii. 8, xxviii. 4.

[d] See the remarks of *Ranke*, *Drechsler*, and *Tuch*. Comp. verse 28 with 25. See *Gramberg* and *Stähelin*.

DOCUMENT "ELOHIM."	DOCUMENT "JEHOVAH."
XXIV. Chap. xxxix. 6—20. Joseph favored by his master, but at length cast into prison.	Chap. xxxix. 1—5. Jehovah's blessing is with Joseph, (21—23,) who gains the jailer's favor.

XXV. Joseph comes to high honors by interpreting dreams; xl.—xli. Gramberg and Stähelin find the document "Jehovah" in this.

XXVI. The two journeys of Joseph's brothers (xlii.—xlv.) are likewise Elohistic. There is a disagreement between xlii. 27, 28, xliii. 21, and xlii. 35; between xliii. 3—13, xliv. 19—23, and xlii. 9—20, 30—34. Gramberg and others refer this disagreement to the two sources of the document; but perhaps it is, as Tuch supposes, to be referred to the inaccuracy of the narrator.

XXVII. Jacob's journey to Ægypt, and settlement in Goshen Chap. xlvi. xlvii. 1—7, is characteristic. (Compare xxxv. 9—15, xvii.) The passages xlvi. 31—xlvii. 6, do not seem to agree with xlvi. 17—20; but this disagreement is, perhaps, to be referred to the carelessness of the author.[a]

XXVIII. Jacob's blessing and last will, xlix. 29, 32, refer to xxiii.; verses 3—5, to xxxiv. xxxv. 22. The blessing, verses 1—27, is either interpolated by the Elohist,[b] or written by him, and verse 18 interpolated by the Jehovist.[c]

XXIX. Jacob's burial. Joseph's death.[d]

---

[a] *De Wette*, Beit. vol. ii. p. 152, sqq. *Stähelin*, p. 83.

[b] See *Tuch*, p. 554, sqq. [c] See *Bleek*.

[d] Comp. verse 5 with xlvii. 30, 31; verses 12, 13, with xlix. 29, sqq.; verse 20 with xlv. 5, 7.

The chief characteristics of the document "Elohim" are as follows: —

1. In the style, beside the use of *Elohim*, *El-shaddai* (אל־שדי) is used for God; xvii. 1, xxviii. 3, xxxv. 11, xliii. 14, xlviii. 3, 28. Mesopotamia is called *Padan-aram*, פדן ארם; xxv. 20, xxviii. 2, xxxi. 19, xxxiii. 18, xxxv. 9, 26, xlviii. 7. *Male and female*, זכר ונקבה; i. 27, v. 2, vi. 19, vii. 16. *Be fruitful and multiply*, פרה ורבה, (used also in Hiphil;) i. 22, 28, viii. 17, ix. 1, 7, xvii. 20, xxviii. 3, xxxv. 11, xlvii. 27, xlviii. 4. *After his kind* or *their kind*, למינהו, or למינהם; i. 11, 12, 21, vi. 20, vii. 14. *That self-same day*, בעצם היום הזה; vii. 23, xvii. 23, 26. *In their generations*, לדרתם; xvii. 7, 12; comp. ix 12, xxv. 16, xxxvi. 40, 43. *Land of strangers*, ארץ מגרים; xvii. 8,

§ 151.

B. *Exodus.*

It has been remarked by Eichhorn, and in former editions of this work, that the document "Elohim" ex-

---

xxviii. 4, xxxvi. 7, xxxvii. 1; comp. xlvii. 9. *For a possession*, אחזה; xvii. 8, xxiii. 4, 9, 20, xxxvi. 43, xlvii. 11, xlix. 30, l. 13. *Establish a covenant*, הקים ברית, or נתן ברית; vi. 18, ix. 8, 11, 12, xvii. 2, 7, 19, &c. It is distinguished by diffuseness, circumstantiality, and repetitions. Comp. i. 11, 12, 20, 21, 24, 25, 29, vi. 20, vii. 14, 21—23, viii. 17, ix. 2, xvii. 10—14, 23—27, xxiii. 17, xxv. 9, 10, xlix. 29, sqq., l. 13.

2. *In the ideas, views, and plan.* God is not recognized as Jehovah, (Ex. vi. 2;) therefore the name does not occur. There is no Jehovah worship, (none after the Mosaic form,) but there is a more free worship. There is no distinction of clean and unclean beasts. There seems to be a worship of *sacred stones*, (xxviii. 18, 19, (?) xxxv. 14, 15.) Yet the ground of the theocracy was laid by the selection and separation of Abraham, Isaac, and Jacob, which is confirmed by genealogies carried out with reference to a plan. There is also a ground for some theocratical institutions, (ii. 2, ix. 6, xvii. 10, sqq.)

In general, the *Elohist* knows well how to transfer himself to the primitive times, and to describe them in respect to morals, (i. 31, v. 22, 24, vi. 9; comp. vi. 11,) and physical circumstances, (v. 5, sqq., xi. 10, sqq.; comp. xlvii. 9.) He does this more perfectly and simply than the other; (comp. i. 31, with ix. 3.) He describes also the customs of the patriarchs.

On the other hand, the *Jehovist* makes the worship of Jehovah begin and continue even under the patriarchs, (iv. 26, xii. 8, xiii. 4, xxi. 33, xxvi. 25.) Hence he puts the name *Jehovah* even in the mouth of the heathen, (xxvi. 28, 29.) He refers to the ancient time the *Levitical sacrifices*, (iv. 3, 4, viii. 20;) the *oracle of Jehovah*, (xxv. 22;) a *positive legislation*, (xxvi. 5;) the *levirate marriage*, (chap. xxxviii.;) *vengeance of blood*, (iv. 14;) as well as later civilization and luxury, (iv. 17, 20, 22, ix. 20, xi. 3, 4, xiii. 2, xxiv. 22, 30, 47, 53.) The mythology, which in the *Elohist* is simple, here becomes more fantastic, (iii. 1, sqq., 24, xix. 17, 26, iii. 8, 9, xi. 7, xviii. 1—8, xix. 1, sqq., xv. 17, vi. 1, sqq.)

In respect *of style.* He calls Mesopotamia "*Syria of the two rivers*," ארם נהרים; xxiv. 10. He says, "*man and his woman*," instead of male and female, איש ואשתו, for זכר ונקבר; vii. 2. עתר, for התפלל; xxv. 21. בגלל; xii. 13, xxx. 27, xxxix. 5. כָּרַת בְּרִית, xv. 18, xxvi. 28. ככוכבי השמים; xxii. 17, xxvi. 4. (Comp. xv. 5, and other places. See *Tuch*, l. c. p. lix., sqq. *Stähelin*, p. 87, sqq.) He inserts odes and proverbs, (iv. 23, x. 9, xxii. 14, xxv. 23,) and poetical discourses, (ix. 26, 27, xiv. 19, 20, xxvii. 23, sqq., 37,

tends also to this book, as it was required by the author's plan to go farther than Genesis. Yet this subject has not been investigated on all sides, and the present views are not so perfectly established as it is desirable. However, the following distinction of the Elohistic and Jehovistic fragments, made according to Stähelin's plan, is, as a whole, certainly correct.[a]

DOCUMENT "ELOHIM."	DOCUMENT "JEHOVAH."
I. Chap. i. 1—7, perhaps, also, verse 8—22. Increase of the Israelites in Ægypt. Elohim occurs xvii. 20, 21.[b]	
II. Chap. ii. 23—25.[c] God remembers the Israelites.	Chap. ii. Birth of Moses, &c. This is considered Jehovistic, from the motive given for the name of Moses,[d] and the scene at the Well.[e] The name *Raguel* favors the Elohistic, for the Jehovistic has *Jethro;* iii. 1. Chap. iii. 1—iv. 17. Mission of Moses. Chap. iii. 14, containing the explanation of the name *Jehovah,* is decidedly Jehovistic. But elsewhere the name *Elohim* occurs seven times; ii. 4, 6, 11—15.

sqq.,) and displays greater skill, and better arrangement, with less diffuseness. See *Tuch*, p. lix., sqq. *Stähelin*, p. 87, sq.

[a] *Stähelin's* contributions to the critical investigation of the Pentateuch, and the books of Joshua and Judges, in the Stud. und Krit. for 1835, p. 461, sqq., and a MS., communicated to the author, from which, however, he sometimes ventures to differ.

[It will be seen, from what follows, that the two documents are not to be separated in Exodus with the same certainty as in Genesis, because one of the chief characteristics of distinction ceases to be such after chap. iii.]

[b] The word פרך, verse 13, 14. Comp. Levit. xxv. 43, 46, 53.

[c] Comp. verse 24 with Gen. xvii. &c., and Ex. vi. 5.

[d] But comp. Gen. xxx. 1—13, 17—24.

[e] But comp. Gen. xxix.

DOCUMENT "ELOHIM."

III. Chap. vi. 2—vii. 7. God, as Jehovah, declares to the people, through Moses, his intention to deliver them. Genealogy of Moses. Aaron appointed as Moses' spokesman.

Chap. vi. 9. "But they *hearkened not unto Moses*, for anguish of spirit, and for cruel bondage."

Chap. vi. 30, vii. 1, 2. "And Moses said before Jehovah, 'Behold, I am of uncircumcised lips, and how shall Pharaoh hearken unto me?'

"And Jehovah said unto Moses, 'See, I have made thee a god to Pharaoh: and Aaron thy brother shall be thy prophet. Thou shalt speak all that I command thee: and Aaron thy brother shall speak unto Pharaoh, that he send the children of Israel out of his land.'"

The genealogy (vi. 14—27) corresponds to the genealogies of document "Elohim;" but vii. 3, is probably Jehovistic. Compare ix. 12, and xiv. 4—17.

DOCUMENT "JEHOVAH."

Chap. iv. 18—31. Moses' journey. Arrival in Ægypt. Confirmed before the people. Compare verse 20 with iv. 2; verse 21, 28, 30, with iv. 1—9.

In chap. iv. 31, there is a striking antithesis to vi. 9. "*And the people believed;* and when they heard that Jehovah had visited the children of Israel, then they bowed their heads and worshipped."

Chap. iv. 10—16. "And Moses said unto Jehovah, 'O my Lord, I am not eloquent, neither heretofore, nor since thou hast spoken unto thy servant: but I am slow of speech, and of a slow tongue.' And Jehovah said unto him, 'Who hath made man's mouth? or who maketh the dumb, or deaf, or the seeing, or the blind? Have not I Jehovah? Now, therefore, go, and I will be with thy mouth, and teach thee what thou shalt say.' And he said, 'O my Lord, send, I pray thee, by the hand of him whom thou wilt send.' And the anger of Jehovah was kindled against Moses, and he said, 'Is not Aaron the Levite thy brother? I know that he can speak well. And also, behold, he cometh forth to meet thee; and when he seeth thee, he will be glad in his heart. And thou shalt speak unto him, and put words in his mouth; and

DOCUMENT "JEHOVAH."

I will be with thy mouth, and with his mouth, and will teach you what ye shall do. And he shall be thy spokesman unto the people: and he shall be, even he shall be to thee instead of a mouth, and thou shalt be to him instead of God.'"

DOCUMENT "ELOHIM."	DOCUMENT "JEHOVAH."
	Chap. v. 1—vi. 1. Moses and Aaron's first unlucky visit to Pharaoh. Compare ver. 3 with iii. 18. Chap. vii. 8—xi. 10. Moses' miracles in Ægypt. Chap. vii. 8, sq., refers to iv. 1 sqq. All agree together; the inconsistent passage, xi. 1—3, refers back to iii. 21, 22.
IV. Chap. xii. 1—28, 37—51. Institution of the passover. Exode of the Israelites. The consecration of the first-born is perhaps Elohistic; xiii. 1. Chap. xii. 16 is opposed to xiii. 6.	Chap. xii. 29—36. Plague of the first-born. Expulsion of the Israelites. Chap. xiii. 2—16. Another law of the passover and the first-born.
V. Chap. xiii. 17—20. March to Etham.	Chap. xiii. 21, 22. Pillar of fire and cloud. Comp. Num. x. 11–28. Chap. xiv. 1—xv. 21. Passage of the Red Sea, and song of triumph. Compare xiv. 19, sqq., with xiii. 21. Chap. xv. 22—27. March to Mara. Verse 26 refers to ix. 1—12.
VI. Chap. xvi. *Gift of Manna, and the Quails. The Sabbath.*[a]	Num. xi. *A similar Account of the Gift of Quails.*
"And the whole congregation of the children of Israel murmured against Moses and Aaron	"And the mixed multitude that was among them fell a lusting; and the children of Israel also

[a] This is known to be *Elohistic*, from the accurate date (verse 1) and the consecration of the Sabbath.

DOCUMENT "ELOHIM."

in the wilderness. And the children of Israel said unto them, 'Would to God we had died by the hand of Jehovah in the land of Ægypt, when we sat by the flesh-pots, and when we did eat bread to the full; for ye have brought us forth into this wilderness, to kill this whole assembly with hunger.'

"Then said Jehovah unto Moses, 'Behold, I will rain bread from heaven for you; and the people shall go out and gather a certain rate every day, that I may prove them, whether they will walk in my law, or no.'

"And Jehovah spake unto Moses, saying, 'I have heard the murmurings of the children of Israel; speak unto them, saying, "At even ye shall eat flesh, and in the morning ye shall be filled with bread; and ye shall know that I am Jehovah your God."' And it came to pass, that at even the quails came up, and covered the camp; and in the morning the dew lay round about the host. And when the dew that lay was gone up, behold, upon the face of the wilderness there lay a small round thing, as small as the hoar frost on the ground. And when the children of Israel saw it, they said one to another, 'It is manna;' for they wist not what it was. And Moses said unto them, 'This is the bread which Jehovah hath given you to eat.'"

DOCUMENT "JEHOVAH."

wept again, and said, 'Who shall give us flesh to eat? We remember the fish which we did eat in Ægypt freely; the cucumbers, and the melons, and the leeks, and the onions, and the garlic. But now our soul is dried away; there is nothing at all, besides this manna, before our eyes.'

"And the manna was as coriander-seed, and the color thereof as the color of bdellium. And the people went about, and gathered it, and ground it in mills, or beat it in a mortar, and baked it in pans, and made cakes of it; and the taste of it was as the taste of fresh oil. And when the dew fell upon the camp in the night, the manna fell upon it.

"Then Moses heard the people weep throughout their families, every man in the door of his tent; and the anger of Jehovah was kindled greatly; Moses also was displeased. And Moses said unto Jehovah, 'Wherefore hast thou afflicted thy servant? and wherefore have I not found favor in thy sight, that thou layest the burden of all this people upon me? Have I conceived all this people? have I begotten them, that thou shouldest say unto me, "Carry them in thy bosom (as a nursing-father beareth the suckling child) unto the land which thou swarest unto their fathers." Whence should I have flesh to give unto all this

DOCUMENT "JEHOVAH."

people? For they weep unto me, saying, "Give us flesh, that we may eat." I am not able to bear all this people alone, because it is too heavy for me. And if thou deal thus with me, kill me, I pray thee, out of hand, if I have found favor in thy sight; and let me not see my wretchedness.'

"And Jehovah said unto Moses, 'Gather unto me seventy men of the elders of Israel, whom thou knowest to be the elders of the people, and officers over them; and bring them unto the tabernacle of the congregation, that they may stand there with thee. And I will come down, and talk with thee there; and I will take off the spirit which is upon thee, and will put it upon them; and they shall bear the burden of the people with thee, that thou bear it not thyself alone. And say thou unto the people, "Sanctify yourselves against to-morrow, and ye shall eat flesh; (for ye have wept in the ears of Jehovah, saying, 'Who shall give us flesh to eat? for it was well with us in Ægypt;') therefore Jehovah will give you flesh, and ye shall eat. Ye shall not eat one day, nor two days, nor five days, neither ten days, nor twenty days; but even a whole month, until it come out at your nostrils, and it be loathsome unto you; because that ye have despised Jehovah, which is among you, and have wept before him, saying, 'Why came we forth out of Ægypt?'"' And Moses said, 'The people among whom I am are six hundred thousand footmen; and thou hast said, "I will give them flesh, that they may eat a whole month." Shall the flocks and the herds be slain for them, to suffice them? or shall all the fish of the sea be gathered together for them, to suffice them?' And Jehovah said unto Moses, 'Is Jehovah's hand waxed short? Thou shalt see now whether my word shall come to pass unto thee, or not.' And Moses gat him into the camp, he and the elders of Israel.

"And there went forth a wind from Jehovah, and brought quails from the sea, and let them fall by the camp as it were a day's journey on this side, and as it were a day's journey on the other side, round about the camp, and as it were two cubits high upon the face of the earth."

Chap. xvii. 1—15. Water from the rock. Victory over Amalek. Compare verse 5 with vii. 20.

Chap. xviii. 1—12. Jethro's visit to Moses, as Stähelin thinks, is Jehovistic, from a comparison of verses 2—4 with ii. 22, iv. 20, 21,—though there is rather a contradiction between them,—and on account of the phrase *Mount of Elohim*, (verse 5, compared with iii. 3,) the phrase *delivered out of the hand of*, (compare iii. 8,) and, in general, on account of the reference to the *plagues of Ægypt*. (Compare verse 9 with Num. xx. 15.) On the other hand, 13—17 is Elohistic.

Chap. xix. Legislation on Mount Sinai. This is Jehovistic, according to Stähelin, because verse 2 does not connect with verse 1, but with xvii.; (but compare Num. xxxiii. 11—15;) on account of Jehovah's descent and appearance, as in other Jehovistic passages, (xvii. 6, iii. 1, sqq., and Gen. xi. 7;) because the existence of the priests is presupposed, (verse 22, and elsewhere.) But, on the other hand, Elohim occurs verses 17, 19; and the necessity for the appearance of God on this occasion, leads us to suppose the two accounts are united.

VII. Chap. xx. 1—13. The ten commandments. This is Elohistic. (Compare verse 11 with Gen. ii. 2, 3.) Stähelin thinks differently.

Chap. xx. 14—23. This is in part Jehovistic. Verses 14—18 refer to chap. xix., (but verses 16—18 are Elohistic.) Part is uncertain, but Stähelin calls the whole Jehovistic.

Chap. xxi.—xxiii. Ewald[a] considers this an older writing, that has been inserted; and the repetition (xxiv. 11, sqq) favors the supposition.[b] Stähelin considers it Jehovistic, because *Abib* occurs, xxiii. 15, as in xiii. 4; an *angel*, verse 20, as in xxxii. 34, and xiv. 19; the *Canaanites* are mentioned, verses 23, 28, ás in iii. 18, xiii. 5, Gen. xv. 19; and the *Euphrates*, verse 31, as *the limit of the land*, as in Gen. xv. 18. Compare, also, verse 20 with xv. 17.[c]

---

[a] Studien und Kritiken for 1831, p. 603.

[b] See Studien und Kritiken for 1837, p. 955.

[c] [The difficulty is easily solved by the hypothesis that xxi. 1—xxiii. 17, is an independent document, neither Elohistic nor Jehovistic. The latter part of verse 15, telling how and why the feast is kept, looks like an interpolation by the *Jehovistic* writer. The rest (18—33) has all the marks of the *Jehovistic* fragment. The former fragment is unique in its character, and contains laws not elsewhere alluded to. Chap. xxi. 1, seems prefixed merely to connect it in some manner with the preceding account; but still the connection is very loose.]

DOCUMENT "JEHOVAH."

Chap. xxiv. is Jehovistic, according to Stähelin. It corresponds to chap. xix. There is a covenant and sacrifice, as in Gen. xv. 18. The sacrificial feast (?) occurs verse 9, sqq. [Here, also, it seems to me a different arrangement may be made. Chap. xxiv. 1—8, xii. 15—18, seems entirely Jehovistic. The passage 9—11, and 13, 14, are Elohistic, and parallel with xxxiii. 12, sqq.

DOCUMENT "ELOHIM."

Chap. xxiv. 9–11,13,14. "Then went up Moses and Aaron, Nadab, and Abihu, and seventy of the elders of Israel; and they saw the Elohim of Israel; and there was under his feet as it were a paved work of a sapphire-stone, and as it were the body of heaven in his clearness. And upon the nobles of the children of Israel he laid not his hand; also, they saw Elohim, and did eat and drink. And Moses rose up, and his minister Joshua; and Moses went up into the Mount of Elohim. And he said unto the elders, 'Tarry ye here for us, until we come again unto you; and behold, Aaron and Hur are with you; if any man have any matters to do, let him come unto them.'"

DOCUMENT "JEHOVAH."

Chap. xxxiii. 12—22. "And Moses said unto Jehovah, 'See, thou sayest unto me, "Bring up this people;" and thou hast not let me know whom thou wilt send with me. Yet thou hast said, "I know thee by name, and thou hast also found grace in my sight." Now, therefore, I pray thee, if I have found grace in thy sight, show me now thy way, that I may know thee, that I may find grace in thy sight; and consider that this nation is thy people.' And he said, 'My presence shall go with thee, and I will give thee rest.' And he said unto him, 'If thy presence go not with me, carry us not up hence. For wherein shall it be known here that I and thy people have found grace in thy sight? Is it not in that thou goest with us? So shall we be separated, I and thy people, from all the people that are upon the face of the earth.' And Jehovah said unto Moses, 'I will do this thing, also, that thou hast spoken; for thou hast found grace in my sight, and I know thee by name.' And he said, 'I

DOCUMENT "JEHOVAH."

beseech thee, show me thy glory.' And he said, 'I will make all my goodness pass before thee, and I will proclaim the name of Jehovah before thee; and will be gracious to whom I will be gracious, and will show mercy on whom I will show mercy.' And he said, 'Thou canst not see my face, for there shall no man see me and live.' And Jehovah said, 'Behold, there is a place by me, and thou shalt stand upon a rock: and it shall come to pass, while my glory passeth by, that I will put thee in a cleft of the rock, and will cover thee with my hand while I pass by: and I will take away my hand, and thou shalt see my back parts: but my face shall not be seen.'"]

DOCUMENT "ELOHIM."

VIII. Chap. xxv. 1—xxxi. 17. Command to erect the tabernacle; all from the same hand. This is Elohistic, if we are to judge from the repetitions, and the resemblance to Gen. vi. 13—22. There are several Elohistic formulas, such as, *I will be their God;* xxix. 45, 46, as in vi. 7, xxxi. 12—17, and xx. 11.[a]

DOCUMENT "JEHOVAH."

Chap. xxxi. 18, connects with chap. xxiv.

Chap. xxxii.—xxxiv. The story of the golden calf. This is Jehovistic, as it appears from xxxiv. 11, as compared with xxiii. 20, sqq.,—for the *Hivites*, &c., are mentioned in both,—and from the erection of the tabernacle, ch. xxxiii. 7, sqq.; see xl. 17, sqq.[b]

---

[a] [I would rather consider the whole passage as *Jehovistic*, except xxix. 45, 46, and xxxi. 18, (which are decidedly *Elohistic*,) both of which seem torn from their connection, and much misplaced in their present position. The sanguinary command, xxxi. 15, savors of the *Jehovistic*.]

[b] The *characteristics* reappear: עתר; viii. 4, 24, 25, 26, ix. 28, x. 17, 18. *Stars of heaven;* xxxii. 13. *Canaanites;* iii. 8, 17, xiii. 5, xxiii. 23, 28, xxxiii. 2, xxxiv. 11, Gen. xv. 19, sqq. *Euphrates as a limit;* xxxiii. 31; comp. Gen. xv. 18. *Flowing with milk and honey* is new; iii. 8, 17, xiii.

DOCUMENT "ELOHIM."	DOCUMENT "JEHOVAH."
IX. Chap. xxxv.—xl.[a] Execution of the command respecting the erection of the tabernacle.	

5, xxxiii. 3. נקרה, in the sense of *to meet with;* iii. 18, iv. 5, v. 3. *A strong hand,* (יד חזקה;) iii. 19, vi. 1, xiii. 9, xxii. 11. *Hardened the heart,* (חזק את לב,) and the like; ix. 12, xiv. 4, vii. 3; comp. vii. 13, 22, viii. 15, viii. 11, ix. 34, ix. 7. *Staff of God,* or *Moses;* iv. 2, 20, vii. 19, viii. 1, xiv. 6, xvii. 5. *Signs;* iv. 8, 17, 30, vii. 9, viii. 23, xi. 10; comp. iv. 15. *Angel of Jehovah,* confounded with Jehovah himself. *Pillar of cloud;* iii. 2, 4, xiv. 4, xxiii. 20, xxxii. 34; see Gen. xviii. 19, xxii. 11. *Sensual appearances of God; Descent of God; Moses' conversation with Jehovah face to face;* iii. 2, (see Gen. xv. 17,) xvii. 6, chap. xix. xxiv. xxxiii. 11, xxxiv. 11. *The tent out of the camp;* xxxiii. 7, sqq. *Joshua the servant of Moses;* xxiv. 13, xxxiii. 11.

[a] The characteristic marks recur. *El-shaddai;* vi. 3. *Increase and multiply;* i. 7. *In that self-same day;* xii. 17, 41. *Your generations,* and the like; xii. 14, 17, xvi. 32, 33, xxvii. 21, xxix. 42, xxx. 8, 21, xxxi. 13, 16, xl. 15. *Land of strangers;* vi. 4. *Establish a covenant,* הקים ב"; vi. 4. The threat, (Gen. xvii. 14,) *soul shall be cut off,* recurs, xii. 15, 19, xxx. 33, 38, xxxi. 14. —The *diffuse style and repetitions:* a *statute forever* (חקת עולם) is a new phrase; xii. 14, 17, xxvii. 21, xxviii. 43, xxix. 9, 28, xxx. 21; see xxx. 16. *Sabaoth,* applied to Israel; vi. 26, vii. 4, xii. 17, 41, 51. *Appearance of the splendor of Jehovah in a cloud;* xvi. 10, xl. 34. *Jehovah's interview with Moses in the tabernacle;* xxv. 22, xxix. 42, 43, xxx. 6, 36.

[I can see no sufficient reason for separating this passage from the preceding. To me it seems *Jehovistic* throughout, like xxxii.—xxxiv., above; xxxv. 1—3, seems misplaced, and so does xl. 36—38, which does not profess to be contemporary with the erection of the tabernacle. These accounts of the tabernacle present some important peculiarities. In Ex. xxv. Moses is commanded to make the tabernacle and its furniture after a certain pattern. A minute description is given of the furniture to be made for it, of the dresses of the priests, and the form of consecration, and two men are said to be inspired to perform the work. Next, (xxxiii. 7, sq.,) it seems, the tabernacle is finished. It is named the "tabernacle of assembly." The people flock to it to seek Jehovah. Moses entered, and a cloud stood at the door of it. But *after this,* (chap. xxxv. sq.,) Moses requests contributions for building the tabernacle. They were brought; the tabernacle is made; it is called the "tabernacle of the assembly," and the cloud descends upon it. But Moses was not able to enter it.]

§ 152, *a.*

C. *Leviticus.*

Here the style is marked by the Elohistic peculiarities,[a] with only a few exceptions which may surprise us.[b]

---

[a] The following are some of the Elohistic peculiarities: —

1. *Increase and multiply*, הרפה והרבה; xxvi. 9.

2. *Male and female*, זכר ונקבר; iii. 6, xii. 7: (xxvii. 3, sqq., does not seem to be in point.)

3. *In your generations*, לדרתיכם; iii. 17, vi. 11, 36, x. 9, xvii. 7, xxii. 3, xxiii. 14, 21, 31, 41, xxiv. 3.

4. *A statute forever*, חקת עולם; iii. 17, vi. 11, vii. 36, x. 9, 15, xvi. 29, 31, 34, xvii. 7, xxiii. 14, 21, 31, 41, xxiv. 3, 9.

5. *That self-same day;* xxiii. 14.

6. *A possession*, אחזה; xiv. 34, xxv. 10, 13, 24, 25, 27, 28, 32, sq., 41, 45, 46, xxvii. 16, 21, 22, 24, 28.

7. The threat, *That soul shall be cut off;* vii. 20, 21, 27, xvii. 4—10, xviii. 29, xix. 8, xx. 18, xxiii. 29. See xxii. 3.

8. *To oppress*, פרך; xxv. 43, 46, 53, as in Ex. i. 13.

9. *To make a difference between ...... and between .....*, לחבדיל בין "ובין; x. 10, xi. 47, xx. 25, as in Gen. i. 18.

10. *A citizen, or a stranger*, האזרח והגר; xvi. 29, xvii. 15, xviii. 26, xix. 34, xxiv. 16, and 22. See Ex. xii. 49.

11. *He shall bring ...... unto the door of the tabernacle of assembly*, expressed in the form פתה אהל מועד (לפני or) ־אל (הביאר or) חקריב; iv. 4, 14, ix. 5, xii. 6, xvii. 4, 5, as in Ex. xxix. 4, 10, xl. 12. The same form, to *bring a gift*, קרבן (הביא or) הקריב; i. 2, ii. 1, 12, iii. 7, 14;—קרבן, *a gift;* ii. 4, 13, vi. 13, vii. 14, 38, ix. 7, xvii. 4, xxiii. 14, xxvii. 9, 11.

Other marks are the appearance of the *glory of Jehovah*, (ix. 23;) the *appearance of Jehovah in the cloud over the mercy-seat*, (xvi. 2, as in Ex. xxv. 22, and elsewhere;) *two festal days* at the chief feasts, (xxiii. 7, 8, 35, 36, 39, as in Ex. xii. 16.) There is an opposition between xxv. 39, sq., and Ex. xxi. 1, sqq. In Exodus it is permitted to buy a Hebrew slave; in Leviticus it is forbidden.

[b] Chap. xviii. 3, 24—28, xx. 22, 23. The reference to the Canaanites seems surprising, xx. 9—11, 13, 16. The formula, *dying thou shalt die*, מות יומת, verse 9—13, 16, 27. *His blood upon him*, (דמיו בו,) &c. *The punishment of stoning*, in verse 2. *Flowing with milk and honey*, (xx.

The single pieces, which seem insulated and removed from their connection, refer back to one another, and to the earlier Elohistic passages.[a] For example, xxiv. 1—23, xxvi., and xix., are a compilation of different laws, some of which are repeated elsewhere in the Elohistic pieces; thus blood is prohibited, xix. 26, and also in xvii. 10, sqq., iii. 17, vii. 26; gleaning fields is prohibited, and something is commanded to be left for the poor, xxiii. 22, and xix. 9. The regulations respecting the lamps, in xxiv. 1—4, agree with Ex. xxvii. 20, 21.

DOCUMENT "ELOHIM."	DOCUMENT "JEHOVAH."
Chap. xi. 39, 40. "If any beast die, ... he that eateth the carcass of it shall wash his clothes, and be unclean until the even."	Chap. xvii. 15. "And every soul that eateth that which died of itself, ... shall both wash his clothes and bathe in water, and be unclean until the even."
Chap. xxiv. 1, 2. "Command the children of Israel that they bring unto thee pure olive-oil, beaten for the light, to supply the lamps continually."	Ex. xxvii. 20, sq. The very same words occur.

24,) is *Jehovistic;* but the *Elohistic* phrase that occurs in verse 8, and verses 3, 6, are like xvii. 10, xxvi. 17. The formula, *I am Jehovah which sanctify you,* recurs verse 8, and afterwards in xxi. 8, 15, 23, xxii. 9, 16, 32, and has its parallel in xi. 44, 45, [both of which verses have the air of an interpolation, as they disturb the unity of the passage, and introduce a phrase apparently foreign to the context.] The formulas, *I am Jehovah your God, I am Jehovah,* first appear, xviii. 2, 4—6, 21, 30; but frequently after that, xix. 3, 4, 10, 12, 14, 16, 18, 25, 28, 31, 33, 36, 37, xxii. 2, 3, 8, 30—33, xxiii. 22, 43, xxvi. 1, 2, and appear to belong to the same author. [See § 152, *b*.]

[a] Chap. vii. 34—36, with Ex. xxix. 27, 28; viii. ix. with Ex. xxviii. xxix; xii. 3, with Gen. xvii. 11, 12; xiv. 21, with v. 7, 11; xiv. 23—29, with viii. 23, 24, and Ex. xxix. 20; xv. 13, 19, 29, 30, with xiv. 21, 31; xv. 5—10, 19—24, 27, 28, with xi. 32, 39, 40; xvi. with Ex. xxx. 10; xvi. 1, with x. 1, sqq.; xvi. 14, with iv. 6, 17; xvi. 27, 28, with iv. 12, 21; xvii. 15, with xi. 40; xix. 6—8, with vii. 16—18; xix. 21, 22, with iv. 26, 31, 35; xx. 27, with xix. 31; xxii. 29, with vii. 15; xxiii. 5—8, with Ex. xii. 1—20; xxiii. 26—32, with xvi.;

In xxiv. 5—9, is a minute account of the show-bread, which was commanded to be made, (Ex. xxv. 30.)

The formula of concluding a statute is characteristic—*This is the law*, &c. (Chap. vii. 37, 38, xi. 46, 47, xiv. 57, xv. 32, 33.)

From these considerations it appears that almost the whole book is a part of the Elohistic document, which seems to be chiefly devoted to the laws.

§ 152, *b.*

Same Subject continued.

[I cannot entirely agree with the author, that Leviticus is derived, as a whole, from the single document "Elohim." It seems more probable that it was compiled by some Levitical writer, from several legal documents before him; he may have added the introductory and concluding formulas, and perhaps have changed the phraseology in some few instances. On this hypothesis we can explain the difficult phenomena of the book, such as the technical phraseology of the Elohist,—which certainly pervades the greater part of it,—the different phrases which occur in its different sections, the frequent repetitions and occasional contradictions in the book. Leviticus is divided into three main portions, namely, chap. i.—xvii., xviii.—xxvi., with an appendix, chap. xxvii.

I. Levit. i.—iii. has, perhaps, no peculiarities to distinguish it from the other Elohistic pieces. But the next passage (iv.—vi. 7) is characterized by three

xxiv. 1—4, with Ex. xxvii. 20, 21; xxiv. 5—9, with Ex. xxv. 30; xxv. 9, with xvi. Chap. xxv. 39, sqq., contradicts Ex. xxi. 1—11. Chap. xxvi. 2, and xix. 30, are the same. Comp. xxvi. 42, 45, with Ex. ii. 24; xxvii. 24, with xxv.

distinct expressions, namely, 1. *It shall be forgiven them*,[a] (iv. 20, 26, 31, 35, v. 10, 13, 16, 18, vi. 7.) The same occurs in Num. xv. 25, 26, 28, and but once more in the whole Bible, (Levit. xix. 22,) where it may be naturally accounted for. 2. *He is guilty*, or *they are guilty*,[b] (iv. 13, 22, 27, v. 2—4, 5, 17.) 3. *It is a sin-offering*, or *trespass-offering*,[c] (iv. 24, v. 9, 11, 12, 19.)

The next section is vi. 8—x., distinguished by the phrase *it is most holy*, (vi. 25, 29, (18, 22,) vii. 1, 6, x. 12, 17,)[d] and *as Jehovah commanded*,[e] (viii. 4, 9, 13, 17, 21, 29, ix. 7, 10, 15; compare Gen. vii. 5, Ex. vii. 6.) The next is xi.—xiv., the law of uncleanness and leprosy. It has the usual Elohistic marks. The formula *This is the law*[f] often occurs, (xi. 46, xiii. 59, xiv. 2, 32, 57, xv. 32.) The next, xvi.—xvii., has only this characteristic,—*a perpetual statute*, (xvi. 31, 34, xvii. 7,)—a common Elohistic phrase, which does not occur in the last section.

II. Chap. xviii.—xxvi. This part is distinguished by the frequent recurrence of the phrase *I am Jehovah your God*,[g] *I am Jehovah*, and *I Jehovah, your God, am holy*,[h] which occur very frequently. This use of the phrase *I am Jehovah*, &c., is peculiar to this section; for xi. 44, 45, the only passage where it has occurred before, has the appearance of an interpolation. Several Elohistic marks, however, occur throughout this passage, such as, *that soul shall be cut off*, (xviii. 29, xix. 8, xx. 18, xxii. 3, xxiii. 29,) *floweth with milk and honey*, (xx. 24,)

---

[a] נסלח להם.

[b] אשם, or אשמו.

[c] חטאת הוא.

[d] קדש קדשים הוא.

[e] כאשר צוה יהוה.

[f] זאת תורת.

[g] אני יהוה אלהיכם.

[h] קדוש אני יהוה.

everlasting covenant, or *statute*,[a] (xxiv. 8, 9,) and others. Chap. xix. has some resemblance to that striking passage, Ex. xxi.—xxiii.; there is the same apothegmatic character, the same reference *to Ægypt*, which is elsewhere in Leviticus so unusual.[b] The same apothegmatic and simple character distinguishes both. Separate laws are put together, like the maxims in Proverbs. The short section, xx. 9—17, and verse 27, have the peculiar phrase *his blood shall be upon him*,[c] (verses 9, 11, 12, 13, 16.) Perhaps this whole passage was originally composed out of several distinct legal documents, of different periods, which were brought into their present form by some one who gave them their enacting clause, *And Jehovah said to Moses*,[d] and modified the language in some respects, while he retained some of their peculiar phrases, though without always taking care to avoid repetitions and contradictions. Chap. xvii. 10, sqq., blood is forbidden, and the prohibition is repeated, xix. 26. The same had been given before, in iii. 17, and vii. 26. Compare xix. 31, with xx. 27, and the following:—

Chap. xix. 9. "When ye reap the harvest of your land, thou shalt not wholly reap the corners of thy field, neither shalt thou gather the gleanings of thy harvest."	Chap. xxiii. 22. "When ye reap the harvest of your land, thou shalt not wholly reap the corners of thy field, neither shalt thou gather the gleanings of thy harvest."

Compare xxiv. 17, sqq., with Ex. xxi. 23—27. Any attempt, however, to separate the original documents

---

a ברית עולם, or חק.

b Comp. Ex. xxii. 21, and xxiii. 9, with Levit. xix. 34, 36, and xxii. 33, xxiii. 43, xxv. 38, 42, 55, xxvi. 13, 45.

c דמיו בו.

d וידבר יהוה, &c..

from the additions of the compiler, must be arbitrary and uncertain, though the different age of some of the laws is quite obvious. The historical paragraph, xxiv. 10—16, and 23, has a foreign aspect in this book; and, besides, has no connection with the rest.

III. The appendix, chap. xxvii. It is evident the addition of this chapter is an afterthought; for the book is brought to a regular epic conclusion, by the promises and denunciations in chap. xxvi., and still more by the formula, "These are the statutes, and judgments, and laws, which Jehovah made between him and the children of Israel in Mount Sinai, by the hand of Moses." Or, what is, perhaps, as probable, the book originally ended with this formula appended to chap. xxv.; for chap. xxvi. 3—45, bears marks of a very recent origin,—even later than the captivity. The threat, verse 34, sqq., "Then shall the land enjoy her Sabbaths as long as it lieth desolate, and ye be in your enemies' land, ... because it did not rest in your Sabbaths when ye dwelt in it," and verse 43, must have been written after Jer. xxv. 11,—where the captivity of seventy years is threatened,—and 2 Ch. xxxvi. 21, which says the captivity lasted "until the land had enjoyed her Sabbaths; for as long as she lay desolate, she kept Sabbath, to fulfil threescore and ten years." Perhaps the book ended originally with chap. xxv., to which the formula, xxvi. 46, was appended. Subsequently, the other laws in chap. xxvii. were added, with their concluding formula; and still later, after the return from exile, chap. xxvi. was inserted in its present place, as the most convenient and appropriate. Verse 45 evidently connects with xxv. 55, and the same reference appears in both. There seems an attempt to imitate the language of the preceding passage.

It would seem that originally the history of the transactions at Sinai ended with Ex. xl. 31, 36—38; but there were still laws and narratives which required a distinct historical occasion, and so they were referred to the period when the nation was at that mountain, though the law of historical probability was violated in so doing. Some of the inconsistencies resulting from this treatment are obvious. Chap. xxv. 32—35, seems to demand, at least, the latter part of the Mosaic age as the period of its composition; for in Num. xxxv. it is said Moses first received the law allotting cities to the Levites when he had come to the banks of Jordan. This law, in Leviticus, which pretends to have been made at Sinai, presupposes the other and later enactment already made.

A part of this book, at least, may be more modern than the Elohistic fragment in Exodus. This appears from the different character of the exhortations in Ex. xxiii. 20—33, and Levit. xxvi. 3—45. In the first, the people are told to obey the national leader,[a] to refrain from idols, and to do all that God commands. Here only *natural* duties are prescribed; there is nothing merely ritual, conventional, or arbitrary, in the admonition. But, in the latter, something *ritual* is demanded; the people are bid to keep the Sabbath, and reverence the sanctuary, as well as to refrain from idols, and obey the voice of God. The religious law, Ex. xx. 21, sqq., is free and liberal, while that of Levit. xvii. is more rigorous. In Ex. xxiii. 16, it is said, "Thou shalt keep the feast of ingathering at the end of the year, when thou hast gathered in thy labors from the field." But in Levit.

---

[a] מלאך יהוה.

xxiii. 33, the month and day are pointed out, the length of the festival determined, the offerings for each day are fixed, and severe labor is forbidden. This may be explained as consistent with the course of events in the history of the national observance of religion.]

§ 153.

D. *Numbers.*

In this book, the earlier Elohistic and Jehovistic fragments again alternate with one another.

The document "Elohim" extends over i. 1—x. 10, and includes the laws and ordinances that were made up to the time when the nation departed from Sinai. These passages are shown to be Elohistic: —

I. Sometimes by the style, and the recurrence of Elohistic forms of speech;[a] by its diffuseness and circumstantiality, as in chap. i. v. 11, sqq., and x. 1—10; and by the formulas of conclusion, "This is *the law.*"[b]

II. Sometimes by an agreement with earlier Elohistic passages, or a reference to them.[c]

---

[a] For example, *Sabaoth* (צבאות) is applied to the *multitude of the people*; i. 3, ii. 3, 9, 10, 16, 18, 23, 25, 32. *Bring to the door of the tabernacle of assembly*, הקריב (הביא) אל פתחא "מ"; v. 15, vi. 10, vii. 3, 11. *To bring a gift*, הקריב קרבן; vi. 14, vii. 12, ix. 7. *A gift*, קרבן; vii. 17, 23, 29, &c., ix. 13. The form of threatening, *that soul shall be cut off*; ix. 13. *To their generations*, לדרתיכם; ix. 10, x. 8. *A perpetual statute*; x. 8. *The stranger, and a native*, הגר ואזרח הארצ; ix. 14.

[b] זאת תורת; v. 29, sqq., vi. 21.

[c] For example, chap. i. 1, refers to Ex. xvi. 1, and xix. 1, and has a chronological connection. Chap. i. connects with Ex. xxx. 11—16, though

DOCUMENT "ELOHIM."	DOCUMENT "JEHOVAH."
Chap. x. 11—28. The departure from Sinai. This presupposes the statement of chap. ii.[a] Here the cloud seems, for the first time, to guide the host, which is contrary to Ex. xiii. 21, 22.[b]	Chap. x. 29—36. It is plain this passage is Jehovistic from verse 33, for the fact of the ark *preceding the main body three days' journey* does not agree with 11—28.

there is a chronological contradiction between i. 1, where Moses is directed to take a census of the people, and Ex. xxxviii. 25, where it is already done; so the action precedes the command. Chap. ii. connects with chap. i.; iii. 14, relates to Levit. x.; [?] iii. 25, 26, 31, 32, 36, 37, and iv. 5, sqq., distributing the several offices of the priests, refer back to Ex. xxv. and following. There is, however, a slight contradiction between iv. 6 — which supposes the staves taken out of the rings of the ark — and Ex. xxv. 15, which forbids their removal. Chap. v. 1—4, relating to the lepers, refers to Levit. xiii.—xv.; v. 5—10, relating to trespasses, connects with Levit. v. 16, 25, (vi. 6;) vi. 15, with Ex. xxix. 2, and Levit. viii. 2, (vi. 20, with Ex. xxix. 27, 28.) Chap. vii. 1, refers, in its chronology, to Ex. xl.; vii. 2, to chap. i.; verses 4—9, to chap. iv.; viii. 1—4, to Ex. xxv. 31, 37, 40; viii. 5—19, to Ex. viii. ix. However, there is a contradiction between Num. viii. 23—26, and Num. iv. 3, 23, 30, 47: the former passage makes the Levites serve from the twenty-fifth to the fiftieth year of their age, the latter from the thirtieth to the fiftieth. Chap. ix. 15, 23, is like Ex. xl. 34—38. Chap. x. 1—10, presupposes the contents of chap. ii.

[a] [Though verse 17 makes Gershom and Merari go before and carry the tabernacle, while Num. ii. 17, commands that it shall be in the midst of all the Levites.]

[b] [This section also has some peculiarities of its own; e. g. an unusual form of conclusion, in which it is said that the command was executed; e. g. i. 54, ii. 34, iii. 42, 51, iv. 34, 49, vii. 6, viii. 20. It occurs, however, elsewhere; e. g. xvii. 11. Some passages seem foisted into this section from some other source, such as iii. 11—13, iv. 17—20. In vii. 89, there is a singular use of the pronoun, *to speak with Him*, (לדבר אתו,) where there is nothing in the context to show the word refers to Jehovah. Indeed, the verse has no connection with what precedes or follows. But see *Glass*, ed. *Dathe*, vol. i. p. 158.

It is not always easy, or, perhaps, possible, to refer all the following passages to their true source. The distinctive marks either fail, or else are mingled with one another, and not easily separated. If here were a place for conjecture, I should suppose the compiler who gave the book its present form had the two documents before him, — and it may be others, — and took from each, and sometimes blended the two, without taking care to preserve

DOCUMENT "ELOHIM."

Ex. xvi. and xviii. 13—27, are similar to this.[a]

Chap. xii. 16—xiv. 45. Spies sent to the land of Canaan. Chap. xiii. 4—16. Here Joshua appears for the first time [in the Elohistic document, though mentioned xi. 28.][c]

DOCUMENT "JEHOVAH."

Chap. xi. The quails and the pestilence. Appointment of the seventy elders. Verse 10 ("Moses heard the people weep, every man in the door of his tent") agrees with Ex. xxxiii. 8. [Verses 24—29 disturb the connection, and seem out of place.]

Chap. xii. Punishment of Miriam. Signs of the Jehovistic document are, the descent of God, (verse 11,) "I will come down and talk with thee;" verse 25, "And Jehovah came down in a cloud and spake unto him;" and xii. 5. The tabernacle is out of the camp, xi. 26, xii. 4. Joshua is the servant of Moses, xi. 28.[b] Chap. xii. 16, makes the camp continue some time at Hazeroth before going to Paran, and in this differs from x. 12.

Chap. xiii. 22. *Hebron* occurs as in Gen. xiii. 18, though it does not agree with xxiii. 2. Chap. xiii. 27, *flowing with milk and honey* occurs. The *Canaanites* are mentioned, verse 29.

---

the distinctive phraseology of each. Many passages, in all parts of the book, have evidently been torn from their connection. In xxi. 14, 17, 21, the compiler seems to have *invented* occasions to account for the origin of certain snatches of popular songs. In xv. 1—31, most dissimilar matters are grouped together, which have not the faintest connection; e. g. a law about sacrifices, story of a man who gathered sticks on the Sabbath, a law relating to the fringes on garments.]

[a] [See above, p. 108, sqq.]

[b] [Still more the character assigned to God — namely, that of a passionate and irritable man — is Jehovistic. See xi. 1, 10, 16—20, 23, 33, xii. 4, 8, 9.]

[c] [The safer arrangement seems to be xiii. 1—xiv. 10, as far as *stone them*

DOCUMENT "JEHOVAH."

Chap. xiv. 8 is like xiii. 28. Verse 11, sqq., is like Ex. xxxii. 10, sqq. [The character assigned to God is Jehovistic.] The *cloud and the pillar* are mentioned in verse 14. Verse 18 is like Ex. xxxiv. 6, sq. Perhaps xiv. 11—25, belongs to the Jehovistic, and verse 26—38 to the Elohistic document. On this supposition the repetition is explained.

DOCUMENT "ELOHIM."

Chap. xiv. 10. The appearance of the glory of Jehovah [is accounted for as above.]

Chap. xiv. 29, relates to chap. i.

Chap. xv. Laws respecting offerings and other things. Elohistic formulas occur in verses 15, 21, 23—31, 41, and other marks. [Here the unusual phrase, "And *it shall be forgiven them*," [a] occurs several times, (verses 25, 26, 28,) as in Levit.; and "I am *Jehovah your God*," in verse 41, as in Levit. xviii., sqq. Verses 32—36, from their rigorous character, seem to belong to the Jehovistic document.]

Chap. xvi. 1—xvii. 15. The rebellion of Korah, Dathan, and Abiram.

Elohim: Verse 2. *Princes* [b] and *chosen men*, [c] as in i. 16.

Jehovah: Verse 2. "*Men of renown*," [d] as in Gen. vi. 4.

---

with stones, with occasional alterations from the Elohistic; e. g. *Hebron*, the *Canaanites*, *flowing with milk and honey*. Then verse 10, and *the glory of Jehovah*, &c., to verse 25, will be Jehovistic, and 26—45 Elohistic, though still the character of God in 26—38 savors of the Jehovistic. The immediate destruction of the ten messengers who reported unfavorably appears, verse 36, 37.]

[a] נסלח להם. [b] נשיאים. [c] אנשי שם. [d] קריאים

DOCUMENT "ELOHIM."

Verses 5—11,[a] as in Ex. xvi. 7.

Verses 16—19 connect with 5—11. *The glory of Jehovah* appears, verse 19, (compare Levit. x. 1, sqq.;) in verse 19, the rebels are before the tabernacle; in verse 24, before their own tent.

Verse 22. Compare xxvii. 16.

Verse 35 connects with 16—19.

Chap. xvii. 1—5, (xvi. 36—40,) connects with the preceding verse. *That no stranger approach* is like i. 51, iii. 10, 38. Verse 6—15 is doubtful; for, verse 7, the *glory of Jehovah appears;* but only Korah is mentioned, verse 14. Moses falls down, verse 10, as in xiv. 5, and xvi. 4.

Chap. xvii. 16—28, (xvii. 1—13.) The story of Aaron's rod that grows green, connects with the account of Korah's insurrection. Verse 4 is like Ex. xxv. 22.[b]

Chap. xviii. Rights of the priesthood.[c]

DOCUMENT "JEHOVAH."

Verses 12—15, 13, 14. *Flowing with milk and honey.*

Verses 24—30. Verse 25, the *elders* are mentioned, as in chap. xi. Verse 27. Compare xi. 10. Verses 29, 30, a miracle to confirm the authority of Moses. Compare Ex. iv. 1, 31, xiv. 13, 31,[d] as in Ex. xxxiv. 10.

Verses 31—34 connect with the preceding. The document Elohim relates only the rebellion of *Korah* and his destruction, while the Jehovist connects with it the rebellion of *Dathan* and *Abiram.* This confusion explains the abruptness of verse 1, and the contradiction between xvi. 35,[e] and xxvi. 11.

[In the former, it is said the children of Korah, and all their possessions, were swallowed up: in the latter, it is expressly stated they *did not die.*]

---

[a] הקריב.

[b] *Prince* (נשיא) occurs often, as in xvi. 2, i. 16, &c.

[c] Verse 6, *a gift* (נתנים) occurs in iii. 9. Verse 8, קרבן, *a gift.* Verse 19, *a perpetual statute.* Verse 23, *your generations.* [Verse 1 answers the question in verse 13 of the previous chapter. There is no historical occasion assigned for this question of the people, in verses 12, 13, in the English Bible; but a better connection is given them if they are placed at the end of xvi. 50. This, xvii. 1—11, may be regarded as another fragment removed from its true connection.] Chap. xix., *water of purification.* Verses 13, 20, *that soul shall be cut off.* Verses 10, 21, *perpetual statute.* Compare verse 5 with xvi. 27; verse 10 with xvi. 28; verse 6 with xiv. 4, 6.

[d] ברא.

[e] Chap. xvi. 36—38, is evidently out of its time and place, and interrupts the connection.

DOCUMENT "ELOHIM."

Chap. xx. 1—13. *Water out of the Rock.*

"Then came the children of Israel, even the whole congregation, into the desert of Zin, in the first month: and the people abode in Kadesh; and Miriam died there, and was buried there. And there was no water for the congregation: and they gathered themselves together against Moses and against Aaron. And the people chode with Moses, and spake, saying, 'Would to God that we had died when our brethren died before Jehovah! And why have ye brought up the congregation of Jehovah into this wilderness, that we and our cattle should die there? And wherefore have ye made us to come up out of Ægypt, to bring us in unto this evil place? it is no place of seed, or of figs, or of vines, or of pomegranates; neither is there any water to drink.' And Moses and Aaron went from the presence of the assembly unto the door of the tabernacle of the congregation, and they fell upon their faces: and the glory of Jehovah appeared unto them.

"And Jehovah spake unto Moses, saying, 'Take the rod, and gather thou the assembly together, thou and Aaron thy brother, and speak ye unto the rock before their eyes; and it

DOCUMENT "JEHOVAH."

Ex. xvii. 1—7. *Water out of the Rock.*

"And all the congregation of the children of Israel journeyed from the wilderness of Sin, after their journeys, according to the commandment of Jehovah, and pitched in Rephidim: and there was no water for the people to drink. Wherefore the people did chide with Moses, and said, 'Give us water, that we may drink.' And Moses said unto them, 'Why chide ye with me? wherefore do ye tempt Jehovah?' And the people thirsted there for water: and the people murmured against Moses, and said, 'Wherefore is this that thou hast brought us up out of Ægypt to kill us and our children and our cattle with thirst?' And Moses cried unto Jehovah, saying, 'What shall I do unto this people? they be almost ready to stone me.' And Jehovah said unto Moses, 'Go on before the people, and take with thee of the elders of Israel: and thy rod, wherewith thou smotest the river, take in thine hand, and go. Behold, I will stand before thee there upon the rock in Horeb; and thou shalt smite the rock, and there shall come water out of it, that the people may drink.' And Moses did so in the sight of the elders of Israel. And he called the name of the place Massah,

DOCUMENT "ELOHIM."

shall give forth his water, and thou shalt bring forth to them water out of the rock: so thou shalt give the congregation and their beasts drink.' And Moses took the rod from before Jehovah, as he commanded him. And Moses and Aaron gathered the congregation together before the rock, and he said unto them, 'Hear, now, ye rebels; must we fetch you water out of this rock?' And Moses lifted up his hand, and with his rod he smote the rock twice: and the water came out abundantly, and the congregation drank, and their beasts also.

"And Jehovah spake unto Moses and Aaron, 'Because ye believed me not, to sanctify me in the eyes of the children of Israel, therefore ye shall not bring this congregation into the land which I have given them.' This is the water of Meribah; because the children of Israel strove with Jehovah, and he was sanctified in them."

Compare verse 6 with xvi. 5, 19.

Verse 8, 9. The rod of Moses seems to be the same which appears xvii. 25, (xvii. 9.)

Chap. xx. 22—29. Aaron's death. Compare verse 24 with verse 10. *Was gathered to his*

DOCUMENT "JEHOVAH."

and Meribah, because of the chiding of the children of Israel, and because they tempted Jehovah, saying, 'Is Jehovah among us, or not?'"

Chap. xx. 14—21. Message to Edom.

Verse 16, the angel occurs, and verse 20, the *strong hand.*[a]

[a] יד חזקה.

DOCUMENT "ELOHIM."

people occurs, as in Gen. xxv. 8, xxxv. 29, xlix. 29.

In xxxi. 8 and 16, we have a very different account of Balaam. "Balaam...... also ...... they slew with the sword....... These caused the children of Israel, *through the counsel of Balaam, to commit trespass*," &c.

Chap. xxv. 1—18. Pestilence on account of the sin at Baal-peor. We have the phrases to *give a covenant*, verse 12, and *the plague was stayed*, verse 8, as in xvii. 12. Verse 13 is like Gen. xvii. 7.

Chap. xxv. 19—xxvi. 65. Second census, like chap. i. [The number is the same in both.]

DOCUMENT "JEHOVAH."

Chap. xxi. Conquest over the king of Arad, the fiery serpents; encampments; message to Sihon, &c.

Compare verse 7 with Ex. viii. 4, x. 17. Odes are inserted, 14—18, 27—30. Compare verse 21, sqq., with xx. 14, though verse 3 conflicts with xiv. 45.

Chap. xxii.—xxiv. Story of Balaam. The *angel of Jehovah* appears, xxii. 22, sqq.[a] On the other hand, Elohim occurs, xxii. 9, 12, and elsewhere. Chap. xxiv. 9, is like Gen. xlix. 9, and is an imitation; and *Shaddai*, not *El-shaddai*, is found, verse 16.

Chap. xxvi. 9, 10. Compare xvi. 31, sqq.

Chap. xxvii.—xxxi. belong to the document "Elohim." Chap. xxvii. 1—11. Story of the daughters of Zelophehad. Verse 3 refers to xvi. 35;[b] xxvii. 12—23, where Joshua becomes the successor of Moses, (verse 13,) agrees with xx. 24; 14 with xx. 12. *Urim*, in verse 21, as in Ex. xxviii. 30. *At his command*,[c] verse 21, as in ix. 20, 23. Chap. xxviii. 1—xxxi. Laws relating to sacri-

---

[a] Compare verse 26 with Gen. iii. 1. נקרה, *to come to meet*, xxiii. 3, 4, like Ex. iii. 18; *to put the word in the mouth*, xxii. 38, xxiii. 5, 6, as in Ex. iv. 15; the power of the blessing and curse, as in Gen. ix. 25, chap. xxvii., &c.

[b] אחזה occurs in 4 and 7, sqq.

[c] על פה.

fice, as in Levit.; xxx. 2—17, to vows; xxx. 16; there is a formula of conclusion, *These are the statutes*, &c.[a]

Chap. xxxi. (the victory over Midian) connects with xxv. 17. Compare, also, verse 6 with x. 9; verses 19, 20, with xix. 11, 16, 18, 19; verse 23 with xix. 13. However, there is a contradiction, as noticed above, between xxxi. 8, 16, and xxii.—xxiv.

DOCUMENT "ELOHIM."	DOCUMENT "JEHOVAH."
Chap. xxxii. The division of the land beyond the Jordan (verse 1—32) is, perhaps, Elohistic, though with the exception, it may be, of verse 8—15.[b]	Chap. xxxii. 33—42. The half tribe of Manasseh appears, and mention is made of Sihon and Og, as in xxi. 21, sqq., and 33, sqq.
Chap. xxxiii. 1—49. List of the journeys of the Israelites.[c]	The *writing by Moses* occurs also in Ex. xvii. 14, xxiv. 4, 7, xxxiv. 27, where the passages are Jehovistic. Verses 10—15, and 17, refer to Jehovistic accounts, though verses 45, sqq., do not agree with xxi. 13, sqq. Chap. xxxiii. 50—56. The command to extirpate the Canaanites. But it is doubtful that this belongs here; for verse 54 seems to be Elohistic.

The following belong to the document "Elohim:" chap. xxxiv., which relates the division and bounds of the land; xxxv., the cities of the Levites, and the free cities;[d] and xxxvi., statute of heiresses. This is connected with xxvii. 1—11.

---

[a] The same formula mentioned above also occurs xxvii. 22, sq., xxix. 40, xxxi. 41.

[b] אחזה recurs, 5, 22, 29, 32.

[c] *Sabaoth* (צבאות) is used verse 1; *according to the command*, (על פה,) verse 2, compare ix. 20, 23; *judgments*, (משפטים,) verse 4, as in Ex. vii. 4.

[d] אחזה occurs, verses 2, 8, 28; לדרתיכם, verse 29; *native and stranger*, האזר והגר, verse 15; שגגה, *by mistake*, verse 11, 15, as in Levit. iv. 2, 13. 22, 27.

§ 154.

E. *Deuteronomy.*

This book consists of the following parts:—

I. Chap. i.—iv. 40. An admonitory harangue of Moses, with an historical notice appended; iv. 41—43.

II. Some new laws of Moses, beginning with a similar admonition; iv. 44—xxvi. 19.

III. Pledge to observe the Law; the blessing and the curse; xxvii.—xxx.

IV. Moses' departure and death; xxxi.—xxxiv.

By far the greater part belongs to one author, and, as it appears, to the Jehovistic, of which it has numerous characteristic marks.[a]

---

[a] The following characteristics of that document occur: יד חזקה, *the strong hand*; iii. 25, iv. 34, vi. 21, vii. 19, ix. 26, xi. 2, xxxiv. 12. *As the stars*; i. 10, x. 22, xxviii. 62. *Flowing with milk and honey*; vi. 3, xi. 9, xxvi. 9, 15, xxvii. 3, xxxi. 20; comp. xxxii. 13, 14. *Judges*, שטרים; i. 15, xvi. 18, xx. 5, 8, 9, xxix. 9, xxxi. 28, Ex. v. 6—10, 14, 15, Num. xi. 16. *House of Jehovah*, בית יהוה; xxiii. 19, as in Ex. xxiii. 19, and xxxiv. 26. *To put in the mouth*; xviii. 8, as Ex. iv. 15, Num. xxii. 38, xxiii. 5. *For a sign on the hand and the frontlet*; vi. 8, xi. 18—20, as in Ex. xiii. 9, 16. *The hornet*; vii. 20, as in Ex. xxiii. 28. *Enumeration of the Canaanites*; xx. 17. *Abib*; xvi. 1, as in Ex. xiii. 4, xxiii. 15, xxxiv. 18: xxxii. 11, is like Ex. xix. 4; vi. 25, and xxiv. 13, are like Gen. xv. 6.

There are some historical marks, viz.: *pillar of cloud*, xxxi. 15. Joshua is the *servant of Moses*, i. 38. The historical references and reminiscences relate chiefly to the Jehovistic documents. Thus i. 22—25, refers to Num. xiii. 21—26; verse 35, and Num. xiv. 23, are almost literally the same.

Deut. i. 22—25, 35. "Surely there shall not one of these men of this evil generation see that good land, which I sware to give unto your fathers, save Caleb," &c. — Ver. 39. "Moreover your little ones which ye said would be a prey," &c.	Num. xiii. 21—26, xiv. 23. "Surely they shall not see the land which I sware unto their fathers," &c. "But my servant Caleb," &c. Ver. 31. "But your little ones," &c.

ויכתו is used in verse 44, as in xiv. 45: i. 33, refers to Num. x. 33; ii. 1—

There are some peculiarities of the Law, similar to those in the Jehovistic documents.[a]

However, the following passages, iv. 41, sqq., and x. 6—9, are perhaps interpolations. The document "Elohim" reappears in a passage in the latter part of the book; xxxii. 48—52.[b]

22, to Num. xxi. xxxii. 33, sqq. *Sihon* and *Og* appear, xxix. 6, xxxi. 4; iv. 9—36, and v. 2—5; 23—31 refers to Ex. xix. xxiv; (compare also xviii. 16, 17, with Ex. xx. 16;) vi. 22, xi. 3, xxix. 1, 2, refer to Ex. vii. 8—xi. 10, ix. 8, sqq., x. 1, sqq., refer to Ex. xxxii.—xxxiv.; ix. 12, is like Ex. xxxii. 7, 8; ix. 22, refers to Ex. xvii. 7, and Num. xi. 8, sqq.; xi. 6, to Num. xvi. 25, sqq.; xi. 4, to Ex. xiv.; xiii. 5, agrees with Num. xxii.—xxiv.; xxix. 9, with Num. xii.; xxix. 22, and xxxii. 32, refer to Gen. xix. and xiv. 2, 3.

[a] Num. xvi. 1—8, law of the passover, is like Ex. xiii. 3—10. Here the *seventh day* of the passover is a feast; the cooking of the passover is contrary to Ex. xii. 9: xvi. 16, the three annual feasts, when they *appear before Jehovah*, are mentioned as in Ex. xxiii. 17, and xxxiv. 20, 23; though the phrase also appears, xxxi. 11: xiv. 21, "Thou shalt not seethe a kid in his mother's milk," is like Ex. xxiii. 19, xxxiv. 26: xv. 12—18, the law of voluntary slaves, is like Ex. xxi. 1—11, and different from Levit. xxv. 39, 40. The command to take care of your neighbor's cattle, xxii. 1—4, is like Ex. xxiii. 4, 5. The law against kidnappers, xxiv. 7, is like Ex. xxi. 16; that about pledges, xxiv. 12, 13, like Ex. xxii. 15. The conduct of Amalek, xxv. 17—19, agrees with Ex. xvii. 14. The contents of Gen. xxxviii. are presupposed in xxv. 5, 6. The altar of *unhewn stones*, xxvii. 5, is like Ex. xx. 22: the Canaanites and their idolatry are spoken of in vii. 5, 19—26, xii. 2, 3, xx. 17, as in Ex. xxiii. 24, sqq., xxxiv. 11, sqq. The Euphrates is mentioned as the border of the land, i. 7, xi. 24. Some civil laws, — that of lease and release, xv. 1, sqq.; of civil action, xvi. 18, sqq. Laws of war, xx.; of female captives, xxi. 11, sqq.; of stray cattle, xxii. 1, sqq.; of illegitimate children, xxiii. 1, sqq., agree with Ex. xxi. 1, sqq.

[b] This is like Num. xxvii. 12—23; though it has the phrase בעצחם הירם הזה, verse 48. However, part of this appears as a repetition. *Ewald*, *Tuch*, and others, consider xxxiii. as Elohistic, of which fact *Urim and Thummim* are signs. But *Massah*, in the same verse, is Jehovistic. Verse 9 refers to Ex. xxiii. 25, sqq.; *the bush*, verse 16, to Ex. iii. 2. The whole passage is an imitation of Gen. xlix. Chap. xxxiv. 1—9, is *Elohistic*. In verse 8, they mourned for Moses *thirty days*, as they had *done for Aaron*: this refers to Num. xx. 29. Verse 9, "And Joshua was full of the spirit of wisdom, for Moses had laid his hands upon him," is like Num. xxvii. 18, 23, "And Jehovah said unto Moses, 'Take thee Joshua, ... a man in whom is the Spirit, and lay thy hand upon him,' . . . . . . and he laid his hands upon him," &c.

§ 155.

Same Subject continued.

If Deuteronomy was written by the author of the Jehovistic fragments in the earlier books, then the Pentateuch, in its present form, has not been produced by compiling and revising, or recasting, various documents, at different times, as some have supposed,[a] but it is the result of a recension or compilation,[b] made all at once. But, in this case, we must admit the use of Jehovistic documents which were written at another time.[c]

The author of the Elohistic fragments also seems to have made use of some foreign documents, and some, likewise, of his own, but written at a previous time. He seems to use the writings of another in Gen. xlix., Num. xxxiii. 1—49, as it might be inferred from verse 2. He seems to use his own earlier compositions in Ex. xxxv. 1—3, Levit. xix. xxvi. 1, sqq. From this cause proceed some of the contradictions and repetitions mentioned above.[d]

But verses 10—12 are Jehovistic. Verse 10 says, Jehovah knew Moses *face to face*, as in Num. xii. 8, " with him will I speak *mouth to mouth*, even apparently, and not in dark speeches; and the similitude of Jehovah shall he behold." Verse 11, all the signs and wonders, refers to Ex. vii. 8—xi. 10; and *the strong hand* (יד חזקה) appears, verse 12.

[a] *Ewald* in Stud. und Krit. for 1831, p. 602. *Bleek*, in *Rosenmüller*, Rep. vol. i. p. 48, sqq. *Stähelin*, Genes. p. 105.

[b] *Stähelin*, Stud. und Krit. 1835, p. 474. *Tuch*, Gen. lxxvii., sqq. *Von Bohlen*, Gen. p. cxc. *Bleek*, Program. for 1836, p. 6.

[c] *Tuch* admits this, in Gen. xiv.; *Bleek*, in ii. 3—iv. 24, which differs too much from chap. i. to be the work of one who wished merely to finish the work. Probably this was the case with Gen. xv. (Compare also xvii.) We see marks of a compilation in Num. xvi. 1, sqq.

[d] § 152, 153.

§ 156.

Same Subject continued.

But if this view of the origin of Deuteronomy is not destroyed, it is at least modified by the following considerations: —

1. In addition to the Jehovistic style, this book has some peculiarities of its own, not only in forms of speech and words. There is a diffuse fulness of words, which can scarcely be explained from the rhetorical design of the author.[a]

---

[a] The following are some of the peculiar phrases of the book: *To put away the evil*, בער הרע, (xiii. 6, xvii. 7, &c.,) occurs seven times; compare Judg. xx. 13. *Take heed to thyself*, השמר לך and השמרו לכם; iv. 9, 23, viii. 11, xi. 16, xii. 19, 30. However, Ex. xxiii. 13, 21, is similar. *Keep to do*, שמר לעשות; v. 1, 29, vi. 3, 12, 25, viii. 1, xi. 32, xii. 1, xiii. 1, xv. 5, xvi. 19, xix. 9, xxiv. 8, xxviii. 1, 15, 18. *The good land*, הארץ הטובה; i. 35, iii. 25, iv. 22, vi. 18, viii. 7, 10, ix. 6, xi. 17. *Cleave to Jehovah*, דבק ביהוה; iv. 4, x. 20, xi. 22, xiii. 5, xxx. 20. *To give before them*, נתן לפנים; i. 8, 21, ii. 31, 33, 36, vii. 2, 23, xxiii. 15, xxxi. 5; compare xxviii. 7, 25. הדף in the sense of *expel*; vi. 19, ix. 4. *Commandments, statutes, and judgments*, המצות, החקים והמשפטים; v. 31, vi. 1, 17, 20, vii. 11, viii. 11, xi. 1, xxvii. 17, xxx. 16. *To put the hand upon business*, משלח ידים; xii. 7, xv. 10, xxiii. 21, xxviii. 8, 20. *Work of the hands*, מעשה ידים; ii. 7, xiv. 29, xxiv. 19, xxviii. 12, xxx. 9. *As it is this day*, כיום הזה; ii. 30, iv. 20, viii. 18, x. 15, xxix. 27 גדל, for כבוד; iii. 24, v. 21, ix. 16, xi. 2, xxxii. 3. היטב, as *infinitive absolute*; ix. 21, xiii. 15, xvii. 4, xix. 8, xxvii. 8. *Loves of the flock*, עשתרות צאן; vii. 13, xxviii. 4, 18, 51. הרפה*, with the *accusative*; iv. 31, xxxi. 6, 8. נדח*, in *Hiphil*; xiii. 6, 11, 14; in *Niphal*; iv. 19, xix. 5, xxx. 17. התגרה*; ii. 5, 9, 19, 24. Feminine forms of the infinitive, not merely אהבה, יראה, but also דבקה; xi. 22, xxx. 20. שנאה; i. 27, ix. 28. *Heaven of heavens, God of gods*, &c. See 1 Kings viii. 27, 2 Ch. ii. 5. — The words marked * seem conformable to the later usage, as well as the forms וַיֵּתֵא, for וַיֶּאֱתֶה, and for this ויבוא; xxxiii. 24. אָזְלַת; xxxii. 36. הַיּוֹצֵת, for היוצאת; xxviii. 57. יוֹלֵךְ יַדְבֵּק; xxviii. 21, 36. תשי (תֶּשִׁי), future Hiphil of נשה; xxxii. 18.

Others agree with the style of Jeremiah, זעוה; xxviii. 25, Jer. xv. 4, xxiv.

2. The author allows himself to make striking alterations, and sometimes contradicts himself, not only in those passages where he has regard to the Elohistic accounts of the earlier history, — and which were more foreign to his manner, — but likewise where he might keep in his own course.

The following are examples of the first kind: —

Chap. i. 6—19, relates the appointment of officers, and so is parallel with Ex. xviii.: —

"So I took the chief of your tribes, wise men and known, and made them heads over you, captains over thousands, and captains over hundreds, and captains over fifties, and captains over tens, and officers among your tribes."

This is in part taken verbally from Ex. xviii. 21: —

"Moreover thou shalt provide out of all the people able men, such as fear God, men of truth, hating covetousness; and place such over them, to be rulers of thousands, and rulers of hundreds, rulers of fifties, and rulers of tens."

The following passage (verses 6—8) is not in the former document, and is put too early in Deuteronomy: —

"Jehovah our God spake unto us in Horeb, saying, 'Ye have dwelt long enough in this mount; turn you, and take your journey and go to the mount of the Amorites, and unto all the places nigh thereunto in the plain, in the hills, and in the vale, and in the south, and by the sea-side, to the land of the Canaanites, and unto Lebanon, unto the great river, the River Euphrates. Behold, I have set the land before you; go in and possess the land which Jehovah sware unto your fathers, Abraham, Isaac, and Jacob, to give unto them, and to their seed after them.'"

9, xxix. 18, xxxiv. 17. דבר סרה על; xiii. 6, as Jer. xxvii. 16, xxix. 32. שִׁכֵּל; xxxii. 25, Jer. xv. 7, Lam. i. 20. שרירות לב; xxix. 18, Jer. iii. 17, vii. 24, ix. 13, xi. 8. *Von Bohlen* (p. clxvii.) makes too much of this agreement. See, on the other hand, *König*, Alt. Test. Stud. vol. ii. p. 12, sqq. *De Wette*, Diss. de Deut.; 1805. Opusc. p. 155. *Gesenius*, l. c. p. 32. *Hartmann*, Hist. Krit. Forsch. p. 660, sqq. But it may be observed that *Engel's* theory fails in the passages related to Ex. xxiii. 30, sqq., namely, i. 30, vii. 20, sqq., xi. 13, sqq.

The following (verses 9—14) does not occur in Exodus:—

"And I spake unto you at that time, saying, 'I am not able to bear you myself alone. Jehovah your God hath multiplied you, and, behold, ye are this day as the stars of heaven for multitude. (Jehovah God of your fathers make you a thousand times so many more as ye are, and bless you as he hath promised you!) How can I myself alone bear your cumbrance, and your burden, and your strife? Take ye wise men and understanding, and known among your tribes, and I will make them rulers over you.' And ye answered me, and said, 'The thing which thou hast spoken is good for us to do.'"

Verse 15 differs somewhat from Ex. xviii. 21, 25. Chap. iii. 23—28 relates to the desire of Moses to enter the land, and the command for him to ascend Pisgah and look at it. But it differs essentially from Num. xxvii. 12. There is an anachronism in the passage which relates the making of the ark, (x. 1, 3;) and in verse 8, which treats of the choice of the Levites; in verse 6 we have *Moserah*, instead of *Mount Hur*, (Num. xx. 23, sqq.) Therefore this whole chapter has been rejected by Cappellus and others.[a]

The following are examples of the second kind:—

Jehovah is angry with Moses on account of the people, (i. 37, iii. 26, iv. 21,) which does not agree with the Elohistic account in Num. xx. 12,—where Jehovah is angry with Moses because the latter did not believe him,—nor does it agree very clearly with the Jehovistic passage (Num. xiv.)—where Jehovah prefers Moses to all the people, whom he designs to destroy entirely and at once. Besides, the mention of Kadesh-barnea does not agree with the Jehovistic account, (Num. xiii. 26,)

---

[a] [Crit. sac. lib. vii. § 11, p. 987.] *Hengstenberg* has a forced defence of this passage, Pent. vol. ii. p. 427, sqq. See, for verse 6, *Von Raumer*, Zug d. Israel, p. 40, sqq.; and, on the other hand, *Winer*, Real. Wort. Buch, vol. ii. p. 815.

but with the Elohistic, (xxxiv. 4.) In Deut. i. 22, the *people* send the messengers; in Num. xiii. 2, *Moses* sends them.[a] Deut. i. 44, we find the "*Amorites*" instead of the "*Amalekites*," (Num. xiv. 45.) Deut. ii. 3—8, is obscure, and differs from Num. xx. 14—21.

Deut. ii. 3—8. "And Jehovah spake unto me, saying, 'Ye have compassed this mountain long enough: turn you northward. And command thou the people, saying, "Ye are to pass through the coast of your brethren the children of Esau, which dwell in Seir, and they shall be afraid of you: take ye good heed unto yourselves, therefore. Meddle not with them; for I will not give you of their land, no, not so much as a foot-breadth; because I have given Mount Seir unto Esau for a possession. Ye shall buy meat of them for money, that ye may eat; and ye shall also buy water of them for money, that ye may drink." For Jehovah thy God hath blessed thee in all the works of thy hand: he knoweth thy walking through this great wilderness: these forty years Jehovah thy God hath been with thee; thou hast lacked nothing.' And when we passed by from our brethren the children of Esau, which dwelt in Seir, through the way of the plain from Elath, and from Ezion-gaber, we turned,

Num. xx. 14—24. "And Moses sent messengers from Kadesh unto the king of Edom, 'Thus saith thy brother Israel: Thou knowest all the travel that hath befallen us: how our fathers went down into Ægypt, and we have dwelt in Ægypt a long time; and the Ægyptians vexed us and our fathers. And when we cried unto Jehovah, he heard our voice, and sent an angel, and hath brought us forth out of Ægypt; and behold, we are in Kadesh, a city in the uttermost of thy border. Let us pass, I pray thee, through thy country: we will not pass through the fields, or through the vineyards, neither will we drink of the water of the wells; we will go by the king's highway, we will not turn to the right hand nor to the left, until we have passed thy borders.' And Edom said unto him, 'Thou shalt not pass by me, lest I come out against thee with the sword.' And the children of Israel said unto him, 'We will go by the highway; and if I and my cattle drink of thy water, then I will

[a] [Here the difference is merely formal.]

and passed by the way of the wilderness of Moab.' "

pay for it: I will only (without doing any thing else) go through on my feet.' And he said, 'Thou shalt not go through.' And Edom came out against him with much people, and with a strong hand.

"Thus Edom refused to give Israel passage through his border: wherefore Israel turned away from him."

Chap. ii. 29, contradicts the other statement, in Num. xx., especially 18—21. *Kedemoth* occurs in ii. 26, but not in the Jehovistic parallel, (Num. xxi. 21.) Chap. ii. 19, 27, differs in the locality from Num. xxi. 24. Chap. v. 23—27, is a very free paraphrase of Ex. xx. 18, 19.

Deut. v. 23—27. "And it came to pass, when ye heard the voice out of the midst of the darkness, (for the mountain did burn with fire,) that ye came near unto me, even all the heads of your tribes, and your elders, and ye said, 'Behold, Jehovah our God hath showed us his glory, and his greatness, and we have heard his voice out of the midst of the fire: we have seen this day that God doth talk with man, and he liveth. Now, therefore, why should we die? For this great fire will consume us. If we hear the voice of Jehovah our God any more, then we shall die. For who is there of all flesh, that hath heard the voice of the living God speaking out of the midst of the fire, as we have, and lived? Go thou near, and hear all that Jehovah

Ex. xx. 18, 19. "And all the people saw the thunderings, and the lightnings, and the noise of the trumpet, and the mountain smoking: and when the people saw it, they removed, and stood afar off. And they said unto Moses, 'Speak thou with us, and we will hear: but let not Elohim speak with us, lest we die.'"

our God shall say; and speak thou unto us all that Jehovah our God shall speak unto thee, and we will hear it, and do it.'"

Chap. ix. 18, is obscure, and differs from the parallel, Ex. xxxii. 31, sqq.

Deut. ix. 18. "And I fell down before Jehovah, as at the first, forty days and forty nights: I did neither eat bread nor drink water, because of all your sins which ye sinned, in doing wickedly in the sight of Jehovah, to provoke him to anger. (For I was afraid of the anger and hot displeasure wherewith Jehovah was wroth against you to destroy you.) But Jehovah hearkened unto me at that time also."

Ex. xxxii. 31—35. "And Moses returned unto Jehovah, and said, 'O, this people have sinned a great sin, and have made them gods of gold. Yet, now, if thou wilt, forgive their sin; and if not, blot me, I pray thee, out of thy book which thou hast written.' And Jehovah said unto Moses, 'Whosoever hath sinned against me, him will I blot out of my book. Therefore now go, lead the people unto the place of which I have spoken unto thee. Behold, mine angel shall go before thee; nevertheless, in the day when I visit I will visit their sin upon them.' And Jehovah plagued the people, because they made the calf, which Aaron made."

The following differ considerably:—

Deut. xxv. 17—19. "Remember what Amalek did unto thee by the way, when ye were come forth out of Ægypt; how he met thee by the way, and smote the hindmost of thee, even all that were feeble behind thee, when thou wast faint and weary; and he feared not Elohim. Therefore it shall be, when Jehovah thy God hath given thee rest from all thine enemies round about in the land which Jehovah thy God

Ex. xvii. 8—10. "Then came Amalek, and fought with Israel in Rephidim. And Moses said unto Joshua, 'Choose us out men, and go out, fight with Amalek: to-morrow I will stand on the top of the hill with the rod of Elohim in mine hand.' So Joshua did as Moses had said to him, and fought with Amalek: and Moses, Aaron, and Hur, went up to the top of the hill."

giveth thee for an inheritance to possess it, that thou shalt blot out the remembrance of Amalek from under heaven; thou shalt not forget it."

Besides, in Deuteronomy, *Horeb* is the central point throughout, i. 6, 19, iv. 10, 15, v. 12, ix. 8, xviii. 16, xxviii. 69, (xxix. 1,) while the Jehovist has not only *Horeb*, in Ex. xiii. 1, and xxxiii. 6, but *Sinai* likewise, in xxxiv. 24.

In general, the Mosaic history seems to be more remote from the author of this book than it would be from one who wrote down an historical narrative, even if, at the same time, he wished to make use of it as an allegory, and for the purpose of admonishing the people. Examples of his method of treatment may be seen in iv. 12, 15, 32, sqq., and 36, where *God appears without form in the fire*. The account does not agree with Ex. xix. 18, 19. Besides, "the fire" is farther removed in verse 11, v. 4, 22, ix. 15. We observe the same method in viii. 3, 4, when compared with Ex. xvi. 35, and also in the following passages: —

Deut. vii. 6—8. "For thou art a holy people unto Jehovah thy God: Jehovah thy God hath chosen thee to be a special people unto himself, above all people that are upon the face of the earth. Jehovah did not set his love upon you, nor choose you, because ye were more in number than any people; for ye were the fewest of all people. But because Jehovah loved you, and because he would keep the oath which he had sworn unto your fathers, hath Jehovah brought you out with a mighty hand, and redeemed you

Deut. xviii. 16—18. "According to all that thou desiredst of Jehovah thy God in Horeb, in the day of the assembly, saying, 'Let me not hear again the voice of Jehovah my God; neither let me see this great fire any more, that I die not.' And Jehovah said unto me, 'They have well spoken that which they have spoken. I will raise them up a Prophet from among their brethren, like unto thee, and will put my words in his mouth; and he shall speak unto them all that I shall command him.'"

out of the house of bondmen, from the hand of Pharaoh king of Ægypt."

Compare Num. xx. 15, 16. The author here makes the same use of the history as is made in the book of Wisdom, (xii. 19, sq., and xvi.—xix.)

The book of Numbers (xxxvi. 13) expressly includes all of the later enactments of Moses, from the time of the residence on the plains of Moab. It also brings the history down to the last point, (xxvii. 12—23;) so that the Elohistic author, at least, knew of nothing beyond the death of Moses, (Deut. xxxiv.) The book of Deuteronomy leaves us at the same point, (i. 1—5, though it is stated indistinctly, iv. 46;) consequently the speeches of Moses — which it has contributed — have since been appended to the Mosaic history.

The laws in this book are new, not only in respect to the time in which they are alleged to have been given, but in respect to their more modern character. Some of them refer to more modern affairs.

1. Some refer to the temple at Jerusalem, as in chap. xii. xvi. 1—7.[a]

2. Some relate to the condition of the Levites, while they dwelt in the cities of the rest of the nation, without possessing the cities allotted them in Num. xxxv., and while they had not the tithes allowed them in Num. xviii. 20, sqq.; but had a place at the tithe-feasts, (xii. 12, 18, 19, xiv. 22—29, xvi. 11, 14, xxvi. 12.)[b] The priests, however, exercised some judicial authority, (xvii. 8—13, 18, xix. 17, xxi. 5, xxxi. 9.)

3. A reference is made to the office of kings and prophets, in the following passage: —

---

[a] *De Wette*, Beiträge, vol. i. p. 226, sqq. Archäol. § 268.

[b] Chap. xviii. 1—8, corresponds to Num. xviii. 8—13.

Deut. xvii. 14—20. "When thou art come unto the land which Jehovah thy God giveth thee, and shalt possess it, and shalt dwell therein, and shalt say, 'I will set a king over me, like as all the nations that are about me;' thou shalt in any wise set him king over thee whom Jehovah thy God shall choose; one from among thy brethren shalt thou set king over thee: thou mayest not set a stranger over thee, which is not thy brother. But he shall not multiply horses to himself, nor cause the people to return to Ægypt, to the end that he should multiply horses: forasmuch as Jehovah hath said unto you, "Ye shall henceforth return no more that way." Neither shall he multiply wives to himself, that his heart turn not away; neither shall he greatly multiply to himself silver and gold. And it shall be, when he sitteth upon the throne of his kingdom, that he shall write him a copy of this law in a book, out of that which is before the priests the Levites: and it shall be with him, and he shall read therein all the days of his life; that he may learn to fear Jehovah his God, to keep all the words of this law, and these statutes, to do them: that his heart be not lifted up above his brethren, and that he turn not aside from the commandment, to the right hand or to the left; to the end that he may prolong his days in his kingdom, he, and his children, in the midst of Israel."

Reference is made to the same thing in chap. xiii. 1—5, xviii. 9—22. The expression *the priests the Levites,*[a] or *priests the children of Levites*, deserves notice, (xxi. 10.)

4. Some refer to a later constitution, and later laws of war.

Deut. xvi. 18—20. "Judges and officers shalt thou make thee in all thy gates, which Jehovah thy God giveth thee, throughout thy tribes: and they shall judge the people with just judgment. Thou shalt not wrest judgment; thou shalt not respect persons, neither take a gift: for a gift doth blind the eyes of the wise, and pervert the words of the righteous. That which is altogether just shalt thou follow, that thou mayest live, and inherit the land which Jehovah thy God giveth thee."

Chap. xvii. 8—13. "If there arise a matter too hard for thee in judgment, between blood and blood, between plea and plea, and

---

[a] Chap. xvii. 9, 18, xviii. 1, xxiv. 8, xxvii. 9. Compare Ezek. xliii. 19, xliv. 15.

between stroke and stroke, being matters of controversy within thy gates; then shalt thou arise, and get thee up into the place which Jehovah thy God shall choose; and thou shalt come unto the priests the Levites, and unto the judge that shall be in those days, and inquire; and they shall show thee the sentence of judgment; and thou shalt do according to the sentence, which they of that place, which Jehovah shall choose, shall show thee; and thou shalt observe to do according to all that they inform thee: according to the sentence of the law which they shall teach thee, and according to the judgment which they shall tell thee, thou shalt do: thou shalt not decline from the sentence which they shall show thee, to the right hand, nor to the left.

"And the man that will do presumptuously, and will not hearken unto the priest that standeth to minister there before Jehovah thy God, or unto the judge, even that man shall die: and thou shalt put away the evil from Israel. And all the people shall hear, and fear, and do no more presumptuously."

In xix. 17, and xxi. 2—6, 19, xxv. 8—20, the *judges and aldermen* are spoken of. Besides, other later peculiarities may be observed, such as the prohibition of *worshipping the sun and moon*, (iv. 19, xvii. 3,) the *punishment of stoning*, (xiii. 11, xvii. 5, xxii. 21, 24, xxi. 21,[a]) which, in the Jehovistic passages, Ex. xxi.— xxiii., is only inflicted on *beasts*, (xxi. 28, 32,) and in the Elohistic, Levit. xx. 2, 27, is only inflicted *on men*. However, it occurs in the doubtful passages, Levit. xxiv. 16, 23, Num. xv. 35.[b] The name *feast of tabernacles* (xvi. 16) belongs to the same class.

Now, since these things are so, it remains the most probable that these laws — contained in Deut. i.—xxxii. 47 — were brought into their present form after the

---

[a] רגם.

[b] *Vatke's* view, (Bib. Theol. vol. i.,) and *George's*, (Die Altern Jüd. Feste,) and *Von Bohlen's*, (l. c.,) — that Deuteronomy contains the most ancient laws, — has been sufficiently answered by the results of the previous criticisms of the language. See Theol. Stud. und Krit. for 1837, p. 933, sqq.

other books of the Pentateuch were finished, and were then inserted between Numbers and Deuteronomy, xxxii. 48.

§ 157

4. Date of these Fragments, and of the whole Pentateuch.

Attempts have been made to prove, from the archaisms and other peculiarities of the language, that Moses composed the Pentateuch.[a] All that can be proved from that argument is, that *some of the fragments of which it*

---

[a] See *Jahn*, in *Bengel*, Archiv. vol. ii. p. 578, sqq., vol. iii. p. 168, sqq. *Fritzsche*, Prüfung, &c., p. 104, sq. *Jahn*, without examining and sifting, has huddled all together, even ἅπαξ λεγόμενα, which could prove little or nothing, (comp. *Pustkuchen*, Hist. Krit. Untersuch, p. 21, sq.,) especially things which do not elsewhere occur, (e. g. צְפַרְדֵּעַ;) technical terms; words which occur in other places, but not often, as שֶׁרֶץ, the favorite word of the document "Elohim:" he likewise assumes arbitrarily that, if a Mosaic word occurs in a later book, it was used from a preference for archaisms, (e. g. יְשֻׁרוּן, Deut. xxxii. 15, xxxiii. 4, 26, Isa. xliv. 2;) finally, he considers *the book of Job* Mosaic. Comp. *Hartmann*, l. c. p. 651.

The following examples have by far the most weight as proof-texts: הוּא is used in the feminine, and הִיא, the proper feminine, only occurs eleven times in the whole Pentateuch; [but הוּא occurs as a feminine in 1 Kings xvii. 15, Job xxxi. 11, and Isa. xxx. 33.] נַעַר [*a boy*] is also used in the feminine, and נַעֲרָה only occurs once, Deut. xxii. 19; but perhaps the same form is used also in Ruth ii. 21, [and Job i. 19.] הַלָּזֶה occurs, Gen. xxiv. 65, xxxvii. 19. The suffix ה־ occurs, Gen. xlix. 11, Ex. xxii. 4, 26, et al., (and later in poetry, and in Kings and Ezekiel.) אֵל and הָאֵל, instead of אֵלֶּה and הָאֵלֶּה; (but comp. 1 Ch. x. 8, Ezra v. 15.) זָכוּר, instead of זָכָר. צָחַק, instead of שָׂחַק; (but comp. Judg. xvi. 25, Ezek. xxiii. 32.) צַדֵּף, which appears in no other place. נֶאֱסַף אֶל עַמָּיו, (only found in 2 Ch. xxxiv. 28, and somewhat altered, 2 Kings xxii. 20,) instead of the usual form. שָׁכַב עִם אֲבוֹתָיו, also in Deut. xxxi. 16. גִּבְלָה, כֶּשֶׂב, מִין, מִסַּת מִינִים, רְגָלִים, עֶרְוָה. Unusual forms: נֵאחֲזוּ; Num. xxxii. 30, (Josh. xxii. 9.) נְתֹן; Gen. xxxviii. 9, Num. xx. 21. יָדוֹן; Gen. vi. 3. יְרֵעוּן; Deut. iii. 7, 16.

is composed, are earlier than others. And, since the book of Joshua, notwithstanding its affinity with Deuteronomy, does not possess, in common with it, certain archaisms, we must admit that a certain uniformity of language was observed and established by the author or compiler.

The real or pretended Ægyptian words,[a] and others, the use of which can be explained at a more recent date, appear as marks of a period later than that of Moses. The Chaldaisms serve the same purpose, for we can scarcely conceive the Hebrews acquainted with them while in Ægypt, or the Arabian desert.[b]

Besides, the subject matter, the whole character of the narrative,[c] and the numerous passages which mark a later age,[d] that have been already adduced, are evidence against so early a date of the composition.

§ 158.

A. *The Document Elohim.*

This document was written after the death of Moses, which is related, Deut. xxxiv. 5, 6; after the expulsion of the Canaanites from the land, for this also is men-

[a] Such as תֵּבָה, אַבְרֵךְ, and others.

[b] See the list of these Chaldaisms in *Hirzel*, De Chaldaismi Bib. Origine et Auctor. crit.; Lips. 1830, 4to. p. 5, sqq. The following are examples: שָׂהֲדוּתָא; Gen. xxxi. 47, (but designedly selected.) הֱוֵה; xxvii. 29. נַשַּׁנִי; xli. 51, (which is chosen on purpose.) הֵא; xlvii. 23. הֵן, *when*; Ex. viii. 22, (26,) Lev. xxv. 20. יִשְׁפּוּטוּ; Ex. xviii. 26. עָשָׂת; Lev. xxv. 21. הִרְצָת; xxvi. 34. תְּמַנִּי; Num. xvii. 28. יַחֵל, for יָחֵל; xxx. 3. The canon laid down by *Movers*, in *Bonner's* Zeitschrift f. Phil. und Kath. Theol. vol. xvi. p. 157, that "Aramaisms in a book are proof either of a very early or very late origin," is derived solely from Judg. v., to which it has a peculiar application. § 175.

[c] § 146. [d] § 147, 148.

tioned, Levit. xviii. 28—"That the land do not vomit you out, *as it vomited out the nations which were before you*;"—after the land was inhabited by the Hebrews, for the country is called *the land of the Hebrews*, (Gen. xl. 15;) and after its cities were built, for *Hebron*, *Beth-el*, and *Dan*, are mentioned, (Gen. xxiii. 2, xxxv. 15, Deut. xxxiv. 1;) at a time when the tribe of Levi was despised, as it appears from the following:—

Gen. xlix. 5—7. "Simeon and Levi are brethren; instruments of cruelty are in their habitations. O my soul, come not thou into their secret; unto their assembly, mine honor, be not thou united: for in their anger they slew a man, and in their self-will they digged down a wall. Cursed be their anger, for it was fierce; and their wrath, for it was cruel: I will divide them in Jacob, and scatter them in Israel."

It was written during the time of the kings, for they are mentioned, Gen. xvii. 6, 16—"Kings shall come out of thee:" xxxv. 11, and xxxvi. 31, it is said, "These are the kings of Edom, before there reigned any king over the children of Israel."

It was written before Jeroboam's time, for *Beth-el* is still a holy place, (Gen. xxxv. 15;) while it was considered "*the sin of Israel*," after Jeroboam had polluted it with idolatrous worship, (Hos. iv. 15, v. 8, x. 5, 8.) It was written before the time of David, for Edom is still independent, (Gen. xxxvi.;) Ephraim has the supremacy, (chap. xlviii.,) and Shilo is still the place where the nation holds its sacred meeting, (xlix. 10?) Consequently, it is probable the *document Elohim was written in the time of Samuel or Saul*, [that is, about 1120, or 1055, B. C., or about four hundred years after Moses.] This is the conclusion of Stähelin, Bleek, and Tuch.

§ 159.

B. *The Jehovistic Documents.*

If these documents are the work of a restorer, then it is superfluous to bring forward the proof—so easily adduced—that they were composed after the death of Moses,—which is mentioned, Deut. xxxiv. 10—12; after the expulsion of the Canaanites, Gen. xii. 6, xiii. 7; after the time of the judges, Num. xxxii. 41, where Jair is mentioned, who, according to Judg. x. 4,[a] was one of the judges.

These fragments are written considerable time after the Elohistic documents; after Saul's victory over the Amalekites,—for, in Num. xxiv. 7, it is said, "Israel's *king shall be higher than Agag*, and his kingdom shall be exalted," &c., which first took place when *Saul conquered Agag*, (1 Sam. xv. 2—8;)—after David's victory over the Edomites and Moabites,—for, in Gen. xxv. 23, it is said "the elder (Edom) shall serve the younger," (Israel;) in xxvii. 29. Israel's portion is to "be lord over thy brethren, and let thy mother's sons (the Edomites) bow down unto thee;" in verse 40, Edom, when he desires it, shall shake off the yoke of his brother; Israel is to rule both Edom and Moab:—

Num. xxiv. 17—19. "I shall see him, but not now: I shall behold him, but not nigh: there shall come a Star out of Jacob, and a Sceptre shall rise out of Israel, and shall smite the corners of Moab, and destroy all the children of Sheth. And Edom shall be a possession; Seir also shall be a possession for his enemies; and Israel shall do valiantly. Out of Jacob shall come he that shall have dominion, and shall destroy him that remaineth of the city."

---

[a] *Studer* (in loc.) thinks the author of the book of Judges has made a chronological mistake.

This could not be till after the event mentioned in 2 Sam. viii. 2—"And he [David] smote the Moabites, and measured them with the line, ... and so the Moabites became the servants of David;" verse 14, "and he put garrisons in Edom, ... and all Edom became subject unto David." They must have been written after the commencement of the trade to Ophir, (for it is mentioned in Gen. x. 29;[a]) after David had extended the limits of the kingdom to the Euphrates, which is mentioned as the border of the empire in Gen. xv. 18, and Ex. xxiii. 31; after the tribe of Simeon was mingled with the tribe of Judah, for *Simeon* does not appear in the blessing pronounced on each of the tribes, in Deut. xxxiii., and he seems to be included with Judah and Benjamin, in 1 Kings xii. 21, 23;[b] after the erection of the temple, for the *house of Jehovah* is mentioned, Ex. xxiii. 19, and xv. 13—*the habitation of thy holiness.*

It was written after the people were so well wonted to the formal worship of Jehovah, that they could not conceive of the ancient time without the same forms, nor without certain central places for this worship, such as *Sichem* and *Beth-el*, (Gen. xii. 7, 8,) *Hebron*, (xiii. 18,) *Beer-sheba*, (xxi. 33.)[c] The reference to Edom's attempt to get free (xxvii. 40) would lead to the time of Joram, in whose reign "Edom revolted from under the hand of

[a] Because *Asher*, *Nineveh*, and *Babel*, are mentioned, some writers place this chapter, and i.—xi., in the Assyrian period; e. g. *Pustkuchen*, Hist. Krit. Untersuch, p. 88, Urgeschichte d. Menscheit, vol. i. 1821; *Hartmann*, l. c. p. 782, sqq. Comp. *Winer*, l. c. vol. i. p. 398; *Von Bohlen*, l. c. On the other side, *Tuch*, l. c. p. xcvi., sqq.

[b] See *De Wette's* Archäol. § 139. *Winer*, l. c. art. *Simeon*. [It appears from Josh. xix. that Simeon had a district containing seventeen cities, in the south-west part of the land. *Josephus*, Ant. v. 1, 26. But two of these cities soon appear in the hands of Judah—*Beer-sheba*, (1 Kings xix. 3,) *Ziklag*, (1 Sam. xxx. 30;) and the Simeonites seem to be wanderers, 1 Ch. iv. 42, 43.]

[c] *Tuch*, l. c. p. xciv., sqq.

Judah, and made a king over themselves." And though he defeated them in a battle, they still preserved their independence, (2 Kings viii. 20—23,) "and broke the yoke from off his neck," (Gen. xxvii. 40.) The reference to the annihilation of Amalek, (Num. xxiv. 20,)—"The head of the nations is Amalek, but his end...... is for destruction,"—would point to Hezekiah's time, for (1 Ch. iv. 43) it is said the Jews smote the remnant of the Amalekites, and possessed the territory, at the date of that passage. But, on the other hand, Num. xxi. 4—9, which commemorates the wonders of the brazen serpent, must have been written before the reformation of Hezekiah took place, in which he destroyed this serpent because the people still burned incense to it, (2 Kings xviii. 4;) and, besides, there are certain historical proofs of the existence of the first four books of the Pentateuch in their present form before that date.[a] Therefore we must refer the Edomites' revolt (Gen. xxvii. 40) to the affair in Solomon's time, 1015—975 B. C., (1 Kings xi. 14, sqq.,)[b] and the destruction of the Amalekites (Num. xxiv. 20) to Saul's conquest of Agag, (1 Sam. xv.) However, Hitzig and Von Bohlen refer Num. xxiv. 24, to the history of Senacherib, while Bertholdt and Bleek regard it as an interpolation.

---

[a] § 162, *b*.

[b] [But this revolt did not give them a lasting independence, for we still find them subject to Judah, 1 Kings xxii. 48, 49, 2 Kings viii. 20: yet the verse, Gen. xxvii. 40, may have been written in the time of Solomon, for to me it does not imply that they had broken the yoke. I would render it—"By thy sword shalt thou live, and serve thy brother, and it shall be that, *when thou desirest*, thou shalt break his yoke from off thy neck." Our English translation has no meaning—"when thou shalt have the dominion...... thou shalt break his yoke."—It may well enough have been written in the time of Solomon, just after the revolt, when the connection seemed so slight that the subject could escape the restraint when he would.]

§ 160.

C. *Deuteronomy*.

Moses cannot have been the author of xxxi.—xxxiv., as it appears in special from xxxi. 24—26, xxxiii. 1, and xxxiv. The anachronisms in ii. 12, iii. 14, xix. 14, and xxxiv. 1, and the general manner in which the Mosaic history is treated, as in i.—iii., carry us to a period after Moses. The references to Jerusalem and its temple transfer us to the time when the Jehovistic documents of the other books were written. The references to the earlier books bring us to a time considerably later than that in which those books originated.[a] The laws respecting the kings, prophets, and Levites, and that respecting the unity of worship, bring us to the period after Solomon, and to the times of Josiah, when the unity of worship was first carried out.[b] In xxxi. 26, is a command to place the law book in the ark; but as it was not there when the temple was consecrated, (1 Kings viii. 9,) this must have been written long after that event. The lamentation, xxxii. 5—33, must have been written in the most unfortunate period of the state. The following predictions may refer to the exile of the ten tribes:—

Chap. iv. 27. "And Jehovah shall scatter you among the nations, and ye shall be left few in number among the heathen, whither Jehovah shall lead you."

---

[a] See *De Wette*, Beitr. vol. ii. p. 393. *Bleek*, in Theol. Stud. und Krit. for 1831, p. 514, sqq. *Eichhorn's* doubts upon these chapters, § 434, and in the old edition, vol. ii. p. 406. *Rosenmüller*, Schol. in Deut. p. 451, sqq.

[b] See *Hoffmann*, Com. in Mosis Benedict. in the Analekten f. d. Stud. d. ex. and Syst. Theol. vol. iv. p. 5, sqq. *De Wette*, Beitr. vol. i. p. 285. Archäol. § 223—227. Comp. *Bleek*, Rep. vol. i. p. 21. *Hoffmann*—following *Gesenius*, Sam. Pent. p. 7—refers xxxiii. 7, to the exile of Judah. On the other hand, see *Bleek*, p. 25.

Chap. xxviii. 25. "Jehovah shall cause thee to be smitten before thine enemies: thou shalt go out one way against them, and flee seven ways before them; and shalt be removed into all the kingdoms of the earth."

Chap. xxviii. 36. "And Jehovah shall bring thee, and thy king which thou shalt set over thee, unto a nation which neither thou nor thy fathers have known; and there shalt thou serve other gods, wood and stone."

Chap. xxviii. 64—68. "And Jehovah shall scatter thee among all people from the one end of the earth even unto the other; and there thou shalt serve other gods, which neither thou nor thy fathers have known, even wood and stone. And among these nations shalt thou find no ease, neither shall the sole of thy foot have rest: but Jehovah shall give thee there a trembling heart, and failing of eyes, and sorrow of mind: and thy life shall hang in doubt before thee; and thou shalt fear day and night, and shalt have none assurance of thy life: in the morning thou shalt say, 'Would God it were even!' and at even thou shalt say, 'Would God it were morning!' for the fear of thy heart wherewith thou shalt fear, and for the sight of thine eyes which thou shalt see. And Jehovah shall bring thee into Ægypt again with ships, by the way whereof I spake unto thee, 'Thou shalt see it no more again:' and there ye shall be sold unto your enemies for bond-men and bond-women, and no man shall buy you."

Chap. xxix. 28. "And Jehovah rooted them out of their land in anger, and in wrath, and in great indignation, and cast them into another land, as it is this day."

§ 161.

HISTORICAL TRACES OF THE EXISTENCE OF THE PENTATEUCH.

In looking for historical evidence in this matter, if we would not be deceived through want of a critical method, as Jahn, Hartmann, Hengstenberg, and Hävernik, have been, we must separate *the allusions to the Pentateuch, or the citations of it*, on the part of the author, and even on the part of the persons he introduces as speaking, —

for the words of the latter will not be free from mixture with the former,[a]—*from the evidence drawn from matters of fact* which exist in the history.

Attention, therefore, must be directed to this question: Whether the allusions or references, which occur in the historical books and other written memorials, refer to *the original documents*, or to the *first four books and Deuteronomy in their present form.* Finally, those books and written memorials, whose credibility or date is contested, must not be referred to for proofs. This is the case with the accounts in Chronicles, and the allusions or citations in the Psalms.[b]

§ 162, *a*.

A. Traces in Matters of Fact.

A law book is mentioned in Josh. xxiv. 26. But it cannot be the Pentateuch in its present form, for the latter does not contain what Joshua wrote in this book. "And Joshua wrote these words [that is, the covenant of the people to serve Jehovah] in the book of the Law of God."[c]

Some have looked for such marks in 1 Sam. xv. 2, 3:—

"Thus saith the Lord of hosts, 'I remember that which Amalek did to Israel, how he laid wait for him in the way when he came up from Ægypt. Now go, and smite Amalek, and utterly destroy all that they have, and spare them not; but slay both man and woman, infant and suckling, ox and sheep, camel and ass.'"

---

[a] This has taken place in 1 Kings ii. 3, Judg. xi. 17, sqq. Comp. Num. xx. 14, sqq., xxi. 21, sqq.

[b] Ps. lxxviii. 13, sqq. (Compare, on the contrary, verses 3, 5, 19, 20, 49.) Comp. Ps. lxxxvi. 15, with Ex. xxxiv. 6; Ps. cv. 8, sqq., and cvi. 7, sqq., 28, sqq., with Num. xxv. 3; Ps. cviii. 14, with Ex. xv. 2; Ps. cx. 4, with Gen xiv. 18, and Ps. xl. 8.

[c] See *Maurer* on Josh. i. 8, and comp. *Hävernik*, l. c. p. 556.

This is supposed to refer to Ex. xvii. 14—"Write this for a memorial in a book, and rehearse it in the ears of Joshua, for I will utterly put out the remembrance of Amalek from under heaven." In 1 Sam. x. 25, it is written, "Then Samuel told the people the manner of the kingdom, and wrote it in a book, and laid it down before Jehovah." Some have supposed there was a reference in this to Deut. xvii. 14, sqq.:—

"When thou art come unto the land which Jehovah thy God giveth thee, and shalt possess it, and shalt dwell therein, and shalt say, 'I will set a king over me, like as all the nations that are about me;' thou shalt in any wise set him king over thee whom Jehovah thy God shall choose: one from among thy brethren shalt thou set king over thee."

So it has been thought there was such a reference in 1 Kings viii. 9,—"There was nothing in the ark save the two tables of stone, which Moses put there at Horeb, when Jehovah made a covenant with the children of Israel, when they came out of the land of Ægypt,"—to Deut. xxxi. 26: "Take this book of the law, and put it in the side of the ark of the covenant of Jehovah, ... that it may be a witness against you." But it is vain to expect such a reference in these passages.

It is probable there is such a trace of it, at the coronation of Jehoash, about 880 B. C., (2 Kings xi. 12:) "And he brought forth the king's son, and put the crown on him, and [gave him] the law."[a] However, this does not necessarily suppose the existence of the whole Pentateuch in its present form.

The discovery of the book of the Law, in the temple, under Josiah's reign, about 624 *B. C.,* related in

[a] עֵדוּת. [But it is difficult to find the Mosaic Law in this.]

2 Kings xxii., *is the first certain trace of the existence of the Pentateuch in its present form.* Here the following passages, (xxii. 16, 17, and 2 Ch. xxxiv. 24,) as well as the reformation occasioned by the discovery, all point to Deuteronomy.

"Thus saith the Lord, 'Behold, I will bring evil upon this place, and upon the inhabitants thereof, even all the words of the book which the king of Judah hath read: because they have forsaken me, and have burned incense unto other gods, that they might provoke me to anger with all the works of their hands; therefore my wrath shall be kindled against this place, and shall not be quenched.'"

This, however, presupposes the existence of the other books. After the exile, we find frequent traces of it. *The Law of Moses*, or *Law of God*, occurs, Ezra iii. 2, vi. 18, vii. 6, 12. Ezra is called *learned in the Law of Moses*, vii. 6, 10, ix. 1, sqq. The *Law of Moses* occurs, Neh. i. 7, sqq., (verse 9 alludes plainly to Deut. xxx. 4, xii. 11,) Neh. viii. 1, sqq., ix. 2, sqq., xiii. 1. These, however, are later accounts.

§ 162, *b*.

B. Traces of its Existence in Writers.

About 790 B. C., we find that Amos (iv. 11) unites the Elohistic and Jehovistic fragments in Gen. xix. 29. Therefore he must have had the book of Genesis in its present form. In ii. 9, he says, "Yet I destroyed the Amorites before them ...... whose height was like the height of the cedars." This refers to Num. xiii. 32, which says, "All the people that we saw" in the land "are men of great stature, and there we saw the giants." Accordingly, he seems to have been acquainted with the book of Numbers.

About 785 B. C., Hosea affords us a trace of its existence; xii. 3—5:—

"He took his brother by the heel in the womb, and by his strength he had power with Elohim. Yea, he had power over the angel, and prevailed: he wept, and made supplication unto him: he found him in Beth-el, and there he spake with us; even Jehovah God of hosts."

Here the allusions are obvious to the story of the birth of Esau and Jacob, in Gen. xxv. 26; to the struggle with the angel, xxxii. 24, sqq.; to the appearance of Jehovah in xxxv. 9, sqq. In the following, (xii. 12, 13,) there is a reference to Gen. xxvii. 43—45, xxix. 18, sqq., which relate Jacob's visit to Laban, and service for his wife:—

"And Jacob fled into the country of Syria, and Israel served for a wife, and for a wife he kept sheep. And by a prophet the Lord brought Israel out of Ægypt, and by a prophet was he preserved."

The mention of Admah and Zeboim (xi. 8) refers to Gen. xix. and xiv. 2, 3. Again, ix. 10:—

"I found Israel like grapes in the wilderness; I saw your fathers as the first ripe in the fig-tree at her first time: but they went to Baal-peor, and separated themselves unto that shame; and their abominations were according as they loved."

This refers to Num. xxv. 3—"Israel joined himself unto Baal-peor." Therefore he must have known the book of Numbers, as well as the original documents and later fragments of Genesis.

About 759 B. C., Isaiah (i. 9, 10) mentions Sodom and Gomorrah, evidently referring to Gen. xix. 5.

About 725 B. C., Micah (in vi. 5) speaks of Balak, king of Moab, and Balaam, the son of Beor, referring, apparently, to Num. xxii. 2, sqq. The mention of Nimrod (v. 6) refers to Gen. x. 9, sqq.[a]

---

[a] See *Tuch*, l. c., p. lxxxix., sq.

In Jeremiah (630 B. C.) the acquaintance with our present Pentateuch is pretty clear, (Jer. xi. 1—8.)

Chap. xi. 3—7. "Thus saith Jehovah God of Israel: 'Cursed be the man that obeyeth not the words of this covenant, which I commanded your fathers in the day that I brought them forth out of the land of Ægypt, from the iron furnace, saying, "Obey my voice, and do them, according to all which I command you: so shall ye be my people, and I will be your God: that I may perform the oath which I have sworn unto your fathers, to give them a land flowing with milk and honey, as it is this day."' Then answered I, and said, 'So be it, O Jehovah.' Then Jehovah said unto me, 'Proclaim all these words in the cities of Judah, and in the streets of Jerusalem, saying, "Hear ye the words of this covenant, and do them. For I earnestly protested unto your fathers in the day that I brought them up out of the land of Ægypt, even unto this day, rising early and protesting, saying, 'Obey my voice.'"'"

Here the reference in verse 4 is pretty direct to Deut. iv. 20 — "Jehovah ...... hath brought you forth out of the iron furnace out of Ægypt." The following refers to Deut. xxviii.: —

Chap. xi. 8. "Yet they obeyed not, nor inclined their ear, but walked every one in the imagination of their evil heart: therefore I will bring upon them all the words of this covenant, which I commanded them to do; but they did them not."

Chap. xxiii. 17, refers to Deut. xxix. 17, 18; xxxiv. 14, the command to release every Hebrew slave at the end of the seventh year, refers to Ex. xxi. 2, and Deut. xv. 12. The following (xlviii. 45, 46) refer to Num. xxi. 27, sqq.: —[a]

"They that fled stood under the shadow of Heshbon because of the force; but a fire shall come forth out of Heshbon, and a flame from the midst of Sihon, and shall devour the corner of Moab, and

[a] See more examples in *Kuerper*, Jerome, Librr. Sac. Interpret. atque Vindex; 1837, p. 1—51. [But see below, p. 420.]

the crown of the head of the tumultuous ones. Woe be unto thee, O Moab! the people of Chemosh perisheth: for thy sons are taken captives, and thy daughters captives."

About 600—570, Ezekiel refers to these books, (xx. 11.) "I gave them my statutes and showed them my judgments, which if a man do he shall even live by them," refers to Levit. xviii. 5; xxii. 26, to Levit. x. 10; xliv. 20, sqq., to xxi. 2, sqq.; verse 28, to Num. xviii. 20.

This acquaintance is still more obvious in the writers who lived during the exile, and collected the books of the Kings. Here are references to the Law. Thus the two following passages refer to Deut. xxiv. 16:—

2 Kings xvii. 36, 37. "But Jehovah, who brought you up out of the land of Ægypt with great power and a stretched-out arm, him shall ye fear, and him shall ye worship, and to him shall ye do sacrifice. And the statutes, and the ordinances, and the law, and the commandment, which he wrote for you, ye shall observe to do forevermore; and ye shall not fear other gods."

Chap. xiv. 6. "But the children of the murderers he slew not: according unto that which is written in the book of the Law of Moses, wherein Jehovah commanded, saying, 'The fathers shall not be put to death for the children, nor the children be put to death for the fathers; but every man shall be put to death for his own sin.'"

So (1 Kings ii. 3) allusions to the Law, and passages somewhat similar to it, also occur. The cloud over the temple (1 Kings viii. 10) alludes to the cloud in Ex. xl. 34, 35; verse 51, speaking of Ægypt as the furnace of iron, alludes to Deut. iv. 20. So ix. 3, xi. 36, xiv. 21, 2 Kings xxi. 4, 7, refer to Deut. xii. 5. The threat, in case of disobedience, (1 Kings ix. 7, 8,) alludes to Deut. xxviii. 37, xxix. 24. The words put into the mouth of Jeroboam when he set up the two calves,

"These are thy gods, O Israel, which brought thee up out of the land of Ægypt," (1 Kings xii. 28,) allude to Ex. xxxii. 4, 8, where the same words occur. So 1 Kings xxii. 17, where Israel is compared to sheep without a shepherd, alludes to Num. xxvii. 17.[a]

§ 162, *c*.

HISTORICAL PROGRESS OF THE OBSERVANCE OF THE MOSAIC LAW.

The observance or non-observance of particular laws, the appearance or non-appearance of particular legal institutions, in a certain period, can prove nothing, either for or against the existence of a written law book.[b] But the internal reasons which tend to show the date of the different legal fragments of the Pentateuch, may be confirmed by the circumstance, that we can find in the history a gradual progress in the observance of the Law. Thus, in the state and development of the formal worship of Jehovah at the time of David and Solomon, we see the result of the influence of the Elohistic document. In the reformation effected by Josiah, (624 B. C.,) we find men are forbidden to worship Jehovah freely, in various sacred places, as had previously been the practice. This is the result of the book of Deuteronomy, which was written about that time.[c]

---

[a] See *Herz*, Sind in die B. B. d. Könige Spuren des Pentateuchs und d. Mos. Geschichtes zu finden, &c.; Alt. 1822.

[b] See *Otmar*, Fragmente, in *Henke*, Magazin, vol. ii. p. 447, sqq. On the other side, *Eckermann*, Theol. Beit. vol. v. p. 5, sqq.

[c] *De Wette*, Beiträge, vol. i. p. 226, sqq. Archäol. § 222. *Bleek*, in Stud. und Krit. 1831, p. 501, sqq. *Tuch*, l. c. p. xci., sqq.

§ 162, *d.*

SOURCES WHICH THE AUTHOR OF THE PENTATEUCH MADE USE OF.

It is incontestable that the Elohistic author had access to the most ancient sources. But the uniformity of his style does not allow us to suppose that he inserted the original documents touching the Mosaic history directly, and without alteration. If such documents were in his hands, he worked them over anew. Besides, he may have drawn from tradition,—for he lived about four hundred years after Moses, and one thousand after Abraham,—and from such of the Mosaic institutions as were in existence at his time.

The Jehovistic author refers to Mosaic documents: Ex. xvii. 14, "Jehovah said unto Moses, '*Write this for a memorial in a book;* repeat it in the ears of Joshua;'" xxiv. 4, "Moses *wrote all the words of Jehovah;*" verse 7, "He took the *book of the covenant*, and read;" xxxiv. 27, "Jehovah said to Moses, '*Write thou these words;*'" and perhaps Num. xxxiii. 2, "Moses *wrote their journeys.*" But the legal passage, Ex. xxi.—xxiii., which he probably would give us as Mosaic, may rather be ascribed to this author himself. There is no trace of ancient sources in his writings, except in Num. xxi.

The author of Deuteronomy, as it appears, would have us regard his whole book as the work of Moses; so he makes Moses speak of "the Book," (xvii. 18, 19, xxviii. 58, 61, xxix. 20, 21, 27, xxxi. 9, 19, 22, 24, 30.) But the obscurity and unfitness of these claims deprive them of all value as proofs.[a] He derived his

---

[a] *Bleek*, l. c. p. 509, sqq. The opinion that these latter passages refer to a short treatise which has been worked over in Deuteronomy, is entirely arbitrary.

historical statements entirely from the first four books, and his *legal* statements from the institutions prevalent at his time. Besides, he treated both with great freedom.

§ 163.

OPINION THAT MOSES WAS THE AUTHOR OF THE PENTATEUCH.

After coming to these results, we find no ground and no evidence to show that the books of the Pentateuch were composed by Moses. But some consider him their author, merely from traditionary custom, because the Jews were of this opinion; though it is not certain the most ancient Jews shared it; for the expressions the "*book of the Law of Moses*," and the "*book of the Law of Jehovah by the hand of Moses*," only designate him as the author or mediator of the *Law*, but not as author of the *book*. The Law is ascribed to the *Prophets* in 2 Kings xvii. 13, and Ezra ix. 11. Others believe Moses was the author of these books, because this opinion is supposed to prevail generally in the New Testament. But such a prejudice should have no weight at all in criticism; for, as Vater has said, "Faith in Christ can set no limits to critical inquiries; otherwise he would hinder the knowledge of the truth."

The opinion that Moses composed these books, is not only opposed by all the signs of a later date, which occur in the book itself,[a] but also by the entire analogy of the history of Hebrew literature and language. But even admitting it was probable, on account of the influence the Pentateuch had on the language of the Hebrews, and

---

[a] § 147, sqq.

on account of the analogy of the Syriac and Arabic languages, that, during a period of nearly a thousand years, the Hebrew language had changed as little as it would appear on this hypothesis, from the slight difference between the style of the Pentateuch and the other books of the Old Testament, even the latest of them,[a]—still, even then, it would be absurd to suppose that one man could have created beforehand the epico-historical, the rhetorical and poetic style, in all their extent and compass, and have perfected these three departments of Hebrew literature, both in form and substance, so far that all subsequent writers found nothing left for them but to follow in his steps.

§ 164.

HISTORY OF THE HISTORICAL CRITICISM OF THE PENTATEUCH.

During the long supremacy of an uncritical belief in tradition from time to time, and even in antiquity, there arose doubts as to the genuineness of the books of Moses.[b]

---

[a] See *Michaelis*, Einleit. in A. T. p. 166, sqq. *Eichhorn*, § 437. *Jahn*, vol. i. p. 266. *Eckermann*, l. c. vol. v. pt. 1, p. 92. On the other hand, *Vater*, vol. iii. p. 611, sqq. *Gesenius*, Gesch. de heb. Spr. p. 19, sqq.

[b] *Celsus* doubted on account of the myths in Genesis. See *Origen*, Cont. *Cels.* iv. 42: *Εἰ μὴ ἄρα οὐδὲ Μωϋσέως οἴεται εἶναι τὴν γραφὴν, ἀλλά τινων πλειόνων.* [He thinks, also, the story of Noah and the flood is borrowed from the *Greek myth of Deucalion.*]

1. *Dogmatic Doubts.*—*Ptolemy*, [a Valentinian Gnostic of the third century,] in his Epist. ad *Floram*, preserved in *Epiphanius*, Hæres. xxxiii. 3, says, "*The entire law embraced in the Pentateuch of Moses. was not given by any one man, I say—it was not given by the only God.* ...... It is, indeed, attributed to Moses, not as if the very God enacted the law through him, but because Moses, incited by his own mind, enacted certain laws. *It is also attributed to the elders of the people*, for the principal men devised certain ordinances, and promulgated their own laws." *Ὁ σύμπας ἐκεῖνος νόμος ὁ*

But these doubts were first confirmed, by the science of historical criticism, in modern times. But this, how-

---

περιεχόμενος τῇ Μωσέως Πεντατεύχῳ οὐ πρὸς ἑνός τινος νομοθέτηται, λέγω δὲ οὐχ ὑπὸ μόνου θεοῦ·—διαιρεῖται δὲ καὶ εἰς τὸν Μωσέα, οὐ καθὰ αὐτὸς δι᾽ αὐτοῦ νομοθετεῖ ὁ θεός, ἀλλὰ καθὰ ἀπὸ τῆς ἰδίας ἐννοίας ὁρμώμενος, καὶ ὁ Μωσῆς ἐνομοθέτησέ τινα· καὶ εἰς τοὺς πρεσβυτέρους τοῦ λαοῦ διαιρεῖται, οἱ πρῶτοι εὑρίσκονται ἐντολάς τινας ἐνθέντες ἰδίας.

The *Nazarenes*, also, had dogmatic doubts, as it appears from *Jo. Damascus*, De Hæres. xix. vol. i. p. 80, ed. *Le Quien*, (see *Neander*, Gnostiche Systeme, p. 386,) and from the Pseudo-Clementine Homilies, [Hom. ii. ch. 41—44, 52, in *Cotelerius*, Pat. Apost. ed. *Clericus;* Amst. 1724, vol. i. p. 632, sqq.] (See *Neander*, l. c. p. 386. *Baur*, Christ. Gnosis, p. 319.) *Jerome*, Cont. Helvid. Opp. vol. iv. pt. 2, p. 134, says, "I will not complain, whether *you call Moses the author of the Pentateuch, or Ezra the restorer of the same work.*"

2. *Critical Doubts* are expressed by the following writers: *Aben Ezra*,—who died A. C. 1167,—in his Comment. on Deut. i. 1. [But since the Pharisees condemn men as heretics who doubt the genuineness of the Pentateuch, he did not dare express himself openly, but only to hint his opinion in obscure words. See *Spinoza*, Tract. Theol. polit. ch. vii. p. 104.] But his doubts related only to some particular passages. *Isaac Ben Jasos*, in the beginning of the eleventh century, did more, as *Maier* has shown, in the Stud. und Kritiken for 1832, p. 634, sqq. *Carlstadt*, De Script. canon., 1521, G. 4, a. b., went farther still, and said, "Defendi potest: *Mosen non fuisse scriptorem quinque librorum:* ista de morte Mosis nemo nisi plane dementissimus Mosi velut autori tribuet." (See Unschuldige Nachrichten for 1707, p. 550.) *And. Masius*, Com. in Jos. 1574, Præf. p. 2, ad cap. x. 13, and xix. 47, [says, "The books of Moses, in their present form, were not composed by him, but by Ezra, or some other divine man, who, instead of the ancient and obsolete names of places, inserted the modern names."] *Thos. Hobbes*, Leviathan, ch. xxxiii. [Works, ed. *Molesworth*, vol. iii. Lond. 1839, p. 369, says, "It is sufficiently evident that the five books of Moses were written after his time." Yet he thinks Moses "wrote all that he is there said to have written."] *Is. Peyrerius*, Syst. Theol. ex Præadamitarum Hypothesi, 1655, lib. iv. c. 1, [supposes that only fragments and extracts from the genuine Mosaic books now remain.] *Benedict Spinoza*, l. c. 1670, ch. viii. ix. [He brings forward most of the modern arguments against the genuineness of the Pentateuch, and adds, that none but Ezra can be suspected of writing these books. For his influence on biblical criticism, see, who will, *Amand Saintes*, Hist. de la Vie, &c., de B. de Spinoza; Paris, 1842; and his Hist. du Rationalisme en Allemagne; Paris, 1841.] *Rich. Simon*, Hist. crit. du V. T., 1678, i. 5, [thinks the Pentateuch was not written by Moses, but by different men at various times.] *Leclerc*, Sentimens de quelques Theologiens de Hollande, &c., 1685, letter vi., [refers it to

ever, was not done satisfactorily, or without mistakes.[a] The investigation was, for the first time, thoroughly made by Vater.[b] Others have pushed the inquiry still further.[c] Those who defend the later origin of the Penta-

---

the priest sent by the Assyrian king to teach the new Gentile settlers in Palestine "the way of the God of the land." (2 Kings xvii. 24—28.) But he expresses a different opinion in the Dissertation (diss. iii. De Script. Pent. Moses, &c.) prefixed to his Commentary on the Pentateuch.] *Ant. Van Dale*, De Origine et Progressu Idololatriæ, 1696; in his Dissertationes, p. 71, sqq.; and his Epist. a *Steph. Morinum*, p. 686. *Hasse*, Aussichten zur künft. Aufklärungen üb. d. A. T., 1785; though he thinks otherwise in his Entdeckungen im Felde der ält. Erd- und Menschengesch. vol. ii.; 1805.

[a] *Fulda*, in *Paulus*, N. Rep. vol. iii.; 1791. His Memor. vol. vii. *Corrodi*, Beleucht. d. jüd. u. christl. Bibelkanons; 1792, vol. i. p. 58, sqq. *Otmar*, (*Nachtigall*,) Fragmente üb. d. allmähl. Bildung der den Israeliten heil. Schr., in *Henke's* Mag. vol. ii.; 1794, p. 433, sqq.; iv. p. 1—36, 329—370; v. p. 291. Comp. *Eckermann*, Theol. Beitr. vol. v. p. 1; 1796. *Bauer*, Einl. 2 Aufl.; 1801, p. 242, sqq., 309, sqq. *E. Chr. Schuster*, Aelt. Sagen d. Bibel nach ihrem hist. u. prakt. Gehalte; 1804. *H. E. G. Paulus*, Comment. üb. d. N. T. vol. iv.; 1804, p. 230, sq.

[b] Abhandlung über Moses und der Verfasser d. Pent., in his Commentary, vol. iii.; 1805, p. 393, sqq.

[c] *De Wette*, Beitr. z. Einl. ins A. T. vol. i., or Krit. Vers. üb. de Glaubwürdigk. d. BB. d. Chron. mit Hins. auf d. Gesch. d. mos. B.B. u. Gesetzgeb. Ein Nachtr. z. d. Vaterschen Unters. üb. d. Pent.; 1806, vol. ii. Kritik d. Israel. Gesch.; 1807. *Augusti*, Einl.; 1806; 2 Aufl. 1827. *Gesenius*, De Pent. Sam.; 1815. Gesch. d. hebr. Spr.; 1815. *Bleek*, Aphorist. Beitr. z. d. Unters. ü. d. Pent. in *Rosenmüller*, Rep. vol. i.; 1822, p. 1, sqq. Beitr. z. d. Forsch. ü. d. Pent. in Theol. Stud. u. Kr.; 1831, vol. iii. p. 488, sqq. *Hartmann*, Hist. kr. Forschungen üb. d. Bildung, d. Zeitalter u. d. Plan d. 5 BB. M. nebst e. beurtheilenden Einl. u. e. genauen Charakteristik d. hebr. Sagen u. Mythen; 1831. Comp. his Aufklärungen üb. Asien; 1806, p. 19, sqq. Die Hebräerin am Putztische, &c.; vol. ii. 1809, p. 5, sqq.; iii. p. 163, sqq. Linguistische Einl. in d. Stud. d. BB. d. A. T.; 1818, p. 311, sqq. *Schumann*, Prolegg. in Pent. p. xxxvi. *Von Bohlen* and *Tuch*, in their Introductions to Genesis. *Bertholdt* (l. c. p. 759, sqq.; 1813) was not so intimately connected with these inquiries. Without reference to these authorities, a similar view was taken by *Volney*, Recherches nouv. sur l'Hist. anc. pt. i.; Paris, 1814. See the Review in *Bertholdt*, Krit. Journal, vol. viii. p. 55, sqq.

The following are some of the modern defenders of the genuineness of the Pentateuch: *Michaelis*, Einleit. *Eichhorn*, Einleit.,—who has con-

teuch, however, are divided among themselves as to the positive date of its composition and compilation. This difference, in part, results from their different views of the history and literature of the Hebrews.

---

ceded a good deal in his last edition. *Jahn*, Einl. u. Beiträge zur Vertheid. der Aechtheit des Pentat. in *Bengel*, Archiv. vol. ii. iii. *Lüderwald*, Untersuch. einiger Zweifel üb. die Aufrichtigkeit u. Göttlichkeit Mosis u. seiner Begebenheiten; 1782. *Jerusalem*, Briefe üb. d. mos. Schriften u. Philosophie, 3 Aufl.; 1783. *Hasse*, in his Entdeckungen, &c.; 1805. *Griesinger*, Ub. d. Pentateuch; 1806. *Kelle*, Vorurtheilsfreie Würdigung der mos. Schriften, als Prüfung d. myth. u. offenbarungsgläubigen Bibelerklärung, vol. i.—iii.; 1811, 1812. *Ch. A. Fritzsche*, Prüfung der Gründe, mit welchen neuerlich d. Aechtheit d. BB. Mosis bestritten worden ist.; 1814. *J. G. Scheibels*, Unters. über Bibel- u. Kirchengesch. vol. i.; 1816. *J. G. Herbst*, Observ. de Pentateuchi IV. Librorum posteriorum Auctore et Editore; 1817, 4to.; imp. in Commentt. theol. ed. *Rosenmüller*, *Fuldner*, et *Maurer*, vol. i. pt. 1; 1825. In a modified form, *Kanne*, Bibl. Untersuch. u. Ausleg. mit. u. ohne Polemik. vol. i. ii.; 1820. *Rosenmüller*, Schol. in Pentateuchum, vol. i. ed. 3; 1821, Prolegg. *Pustkuchen*, Hist. krit. Untersuchung d. bibl. Urgesch. nebst. Untersuchungen über Alter, Verfasser u. Einheit der übrigen Theile des Pentateuchs; 1823. *Ranke*, Untersuch ub. d. Pent. vol. i. 1834; vol. ii. 1840. *Hengstenberg*, Beiträge zur Einleit. in A. T. oder die Authentie d. Pent. erwiesen; 1836—1839. [See, too, his Christology of the O. T., translated by *Reuel Keith;* Alexand. D. C. 1836—1839, 3 vols. 8vo.] *Hävernik*, l. c. *Drechsler*, Einheit und Aechtheit d. Gen.; 1838. *König*, Altest. Stud. vol. ii.; 1839. The following occupy the old position: *Richard Graves*, Lectures on the Four Last Books of the Pentateuch, designed to show the divine Origin of the Jewish Religion; Lond. 1808. *Thomas Hartwell Horne*, l. c. [*Turner*, Companion to the Book of Genesis; New York, 1841. See, too, the peculiar theory of Dr. *Palfrey*, Acad. Lectures, vol. i. and ii.; Boston, 1838, 1840. (See a review of vol. i. in Boston Quarterly Review for July, 1838.) *Laborde*, Commentaire sur l'Exode et les Nombres, &c.; Paris, 1841, folio.]

CHAPTER II.

THE BOOK OF JOSHUA.[a]

§ 165.

CONTENTS OF THE BOOK.

It was forbidden to Moses to conquer the theocratic land, and Joshua, following in his footsteps, and with similar divine assistance, advanced to this work. He contended triumphantly with the Canaanites, and conquered the greatest part of them, though many were still left to possess large parts of the land. Joshua divided it among the ten tribes and a half, but the conquest still remained incomplete; he set apart the cities which Moses had appointed for the Levites, and likewise the cities of refuge. He departed after he had admonished the people, and pledged them to observe the covenant. Thus this attaches itself to the Mosaic books, as a supplementary portion, as well to the history of the establishment of the theocracy, as to the laws relating to it. Now, since the book treats of the di-

---

[a] Josuæ Imperat. Hist. illustr. ab *Andr. Masio*; Antverp. 1574, fol.
Seb. Schmidt, Prælect. in viii. prior. Capp. Lib. Jos.
Jo. Clerici Comment. *Jo. Drusii* Annotat. in loca diff. Jos., &c.
A. J. Osiandri Comm. in Josuam; Tub. 1681.
Jac. Bonfrerii Comm. in Jos., Jud., et Ruth; Par. 1631, fol.
Nic. Serrarii Comm. in Libr. Jos., Jud., Ruth, Regg., et Paralipp.; Mog. 1609, 1610, 2 vols. fol.
Exegetisches Handb. des A. T. 1 and 3 pt.
Paulus, Blicke in d. B. Jos., in his Theol. exeg. Conservator. vol. ii. p. 149, sqq.
F. J. V. D. Maurer, Comm. üb. d. B. Jos.; Stuttg. 1831. *Geddes*, l. c. *Palfrey*, l. c. vol. ii.

vision of the land, which Moses had already conquered and divided; of the portion which Joshua conquered; that which was conquered after him, and that which remained unconquered,—it has the value of a primitive theocratical model. It has a close connection with the Pentateuch, and particularly with Deuteronomy.[a] It is very obviously divided into two parts. The first includes chapters i.—xii., and contains the history of the conquest. The second includes xiii.—xxiv., and contains the history of the division of the land, and the assemblies of the people which Joshua convoked to sanction the theocracy.—[It is further related that, after the death of Moses, Joshua sent secretly two messengers to Jericho. They were discovered, but escaped through the intervention of Rahab.[b] They brought back an account of the fear of the inhabitants. Then the whole nation marched over, through the Jordan, for its waters were stopped miraculously at Zaretan. After this, those were circumcised who, during the last forty years, had not previously received that rite, on account of the inconvenience it would have occasioned on the march. The passover was then celebrated, and the manna ceased. An irrevocable curse was then pronounced upon Jericho, and after the Jews had marched round it seven times, its walls miraculously fell to the ground. These events increased the fear of the Canaanites, and gave the Hebrews new courage, so that, after messengers

---

[a] See chap. i. iii. 7, iv. 23, viii. 30—35, xi. 15, xvi. 5, 6, xx. xxi. 43—45, xxii. xxiii. 6.

[b] [There is a Jewish tradition that Joshua married Rahab, who was twenty years old at the time of the departure from Ægypt. But Jerome (Cont. Jovinian. lib. i. c. 12) says, indignantly, "Ostende mihi Jesum Nave vel uxorem habuisse vel filios, et si potueris monstrare, victum me esse fatebor."]

returned from Ai, they thought they could conquer it with two or three thousand men. But when they were repulsed with the loss of thirty-six men, the whole people fell into the opposite extreme, and lost all courage. On this occasion, it was discovered, by casting lots, that Achan had appropriated to himself a part of the spoil of Jericho, which had been cursed. He was stoned to death, and then Ai was conquered. Upon this, Joshua, in obedience to Deut. xxvii., erected an altar on Mount Ebal, engraved the law on stones, and uttered the blessings and curses.

The Gibeonites fraudulently made a covenant, and when they were threatened with war by the king of Jebus, or Jerusalem, and his confederate kings, — whose allies they were, — Joshua hastened to relieve them. He fell upon the enemy, and, in a single campaign, conquered almost the whole of *southern* Canaan. He next determined to attack the north Canaanites, who, with their kings, united under King Hazor, were encamped on the sea-coast. In this expedition he conquered nearly all of *northern* Canaan. Thirty-one kings were now conquered, without including Sihon and Og. Joshua put them all to the sword, as it was commanded in the Law. Then, in the seventh or eighth year after entering the land, it was divided among the people by lot. In the account of this transaction, the division of the land on the other side of the Jordan is related again, more circumstantially than before. The free cities were then appointed. The Levites received forty-eight cities from all the tribes. Joshua allowed the forty thousand men from the ten tribes and a half to return home. He then held two assemblies, and died.][a]

---

[a] [See *Jahn*, vol. ii. § 24.]

§ 166.

PECULIARITY OF THE NARRATIVE.

In this book, as in the Pentateuch, the narrative is, in many parts, very full, complete, and even diffuse;[a] but in others it is merely summary,[b] or abrupt.[c] In its prevailing character, the narrative here, as in the Pentateuch, is mythical. Jehovah immediately directs and influences affairs; sometimes by his *word* (i. 1):—

"Now after the death of Moses the servant of Jehovah, it came to pass that *Jehovah spake unto Joshua.*"

The same form occurs in iii. 7, iv. 1, and very frequently. Sometimes he directs by the *sacred lot*, (vii. 10—21;) sometimes by an *apparition*, as in the following (verses 13—15):—

"Now it came to pass when Joshua was near Jericho, that he lifted up his eyes and looked, and behold a man was standing beside him, with his sword drawn in his hand. And Joshua went to him, and said unto him, 'Art thou for us, or for our foes?' And he said, 'Neither; for I am come the Prince of Jehovah's host.' And Joshua fell on his face to the earth, and did homage to him, and said unto him, 'What would my Lord say to his servant?' And the Prince of Jehovah's host said to Joshua, 'Loose thy shoe from thy foot, for the place thou standest upon is holy.' And Joshua did so."

Sometimes this is effected by *miracles*, as at the passage of the Jordan, (iii. iv.,) the destruction of Jericho, (vi.,) and the following (x. 11—14):—

"And it came to pass as they fled from before Israel, and were in the going down to Beth-horon, that the Lord cast down great stones from heaven upon them unto Azekah, and they died: they were more which died with hail-stones than they whom the children of Israel slew with the sword.

---

[a] Chap. ii.—iii. iv.—vi. vii.—viii. 1—29 ix. x. 1—27.

[b] Chap. x. 28—39, 40—43, xi. 10—21.

[c] Chap. xviii. 1, xxiii. 1.

"Then spake Joshua to the Lord in the day when the Lord delivered up the Amorites before the children of Israel, and he said, in the sight of Israel, 'Sun, stand thou still upon Gibeon, and thou Moon, in the valley of Ajalon.' And the sun stood still, and the moon stayed, until the people had avenged themselves upon their enemies. Is not this written in the book of Jasher? So the sun stood still in the midst of heaven, and hasted not to go down about a whole day. And there was no day like that before it or after it, that the Lord hearkened unto the voice of a man: for the Lord fought for Israel."

We discover a striking analogy between the mythology of this book and that of the Pentateuch.[a]

A later Levitical spirit, also, is displayed in this book, similar to that in Chronicles. Compare the important office of the priests and Levites, in iii.—vi., with the statement in 2 Ch. xiii., where the greatest offence of the nation seems to be that they have cast out the sons of Aaron and the Levites. But see, also, Num. x. 9, where the Levites are commanded to blow with the trumpets, when the people go to war.

---

a Compare the passage of the Red Sea (Ex. xiv.) with the passage of the Jordan, (Josh. iii. iv.;) the appearance of the Prince of Jehovah's host (Josh. v. 13, sqq.) with the appearance of Jehovah, (Ex. iii. 1, sqq.) Compare the following:—

Josh. v. 12. "And the manna ceased on the morrow after they had eaten of the old corn of the land; neither had the children of Israel manna any more; but they did eat of the fruit of the land of Canaan that year."	Ex. xvi. 35. "And the children of Israel did eat manna forty years, until they came to a land inhabited: they did eat manna until they came unto the borders of the land of Canaan."

Compare, also, the accounts of the murder of the kings, in Josh. x. 17—43, with the similar narratives in Num. xxxi. 8, sqq.

[The mythology of the book of Joshua, however, is peculiar in this respect; namely, *the ark of the covenant is the miracle-worker*, and has the same power as the rod of Moses in the previous books — a power which it has, in some measure, in Judges also. See, e. g., Josh. iii. 6, 11, 13, 17, iv. 9, 11, 18, vi. 7—13, &c.]

Etymologies occur, as in the following cases: v. 9, "This day have *I rolled away*[a] the reproach of Ægypt from you. Therefore the name of the place is called *Gilgal*[b] (*a rolling away*) unto this day;" and vii. 26, "And Joshua said, 'Why hast thou *troubled us?*' ...... Wherefore the name of that place is called *the valley of Achor*[c] (*troubling*) unto this day."

[Besides, the book contains pompous accounts of miracles wrought in favor of the sacred nation, and relations of their victories; sometimes it is rhetorical, sometimes admonitory, like Deuteronomy. The author frequently adds short explanatory passages; for example, (i. 2,) "*Moses my servant is dead;* go over this Jordan, thou and all this people, unto the land which I do give them, *to the children of Israel;*" (iii. 13,) "Ark of Jehovah, ... *the Lord of all the earth,*" (verses 14—16, &c.) These explanations sometimes seem to be the remarks of a later commentator. He frequently makes repetitions, either because he is confused, and relates events both out of their proper connection and in it, or because he wishes to add something to a previous account. Some of the narratives are simple and full of beauty; for example, the journey of the spies to Jericho, their reception and escape, (chap. ii.,)[d] and the story of the Gibeon-

---

[a] גַּלּוֹתִי. [b] גִּלְגָּל. [c] עָכוֹר.

[d] [Dr. *Palfrey* (l. c. vol. ii. p. 145, 146) thinks the author's aim was rather to collect local legends, than to write a history, and very truly says, many of his narratives are connected with some local monument, like the heap of stones at Gilgal, or in the Jordan. "The naming of Achor and Dan, (vii. 26, xix. 47,) the monuments at Ai, (viii. 29,) Makkeda, (x. 27,) and Shechem, (xxiv. 26,) the inheritance in the female line of Caleb, (xv. 19,) the altar on the west of the Jordan, (chap. xxii.,) and the tombs at Gaash. Shechem, and Gabaath, (xxiv. 30, 32, 33,) were facts and objects which tradition had undertaken to explain;" and the writer simply collected the traditionary legends.]

ites, (chap. ix.) There is considerable difference in the style of the various sections, showing they did not all proceed from the same hand.[a]]

§ 167.

HISTORICAL INACCURACY AND CONTRADICTIONS.

Joshua is the hero of all the theocratic conquests and acquisitions, as Moses is the hero of the legislation. Therefore, contrary to historical truth, the triumph over the Canaanites, and the conquest of the entire land, are ascribed to him, as in the following passages:—

Chap. xi. 16—23. "So Joshua took *all that land, the hills, and all the south country, and all the land of Goshen, and the valley, and the plain, and the mountain of Israel, and the valley of the same;* even from the Mount Halak, that goeth up to Seir, even unto Baal-gad, in the valley of Lebanon, under Mount Hermon: and all their kings he took, and smote them, and slew them. Joshua made war a long time with all those kings. There was not *a city that made peace with* the children of Israel, *save the Hivites, the inhabitants of Gibeon:* all other they took in battle. For it was of the Lord to harden their hearts, that they should come against Israel in battle, that he might destroy them utterly, and that they might have no favor, but that he might destroy them, as the Lord commanded Moses.

"And at that time came Joshua, and cut off the Anakims from the mountains, from Hebron, from Debir, from Anab, and from *all the mountains of Judah*, and from *all the mountains of Israel: Joshua destroyed them utterly with their cities.* There was none of the Anakims left in the land of the children of Israel: only in Gaza, in Gath, and in Ashdod, there remained. So Joshua took the whole land, according to all that the Lord said unto Moses, and Joshua gave it for an inheritance unto Israel according to their division by their tribes. And the land rested from war."

---

[a] [See, e. g., chap. vi. and vii. *Maurer*, Einleit. § 3.]

Chap. xii. 7, 8. "And these are the kings of the country which Joshua and the children of Israel smote on this side Jordan on the west, from Baal-gad in the valley of Lebanon, even unto the Mount Halak that goeth up to Seir; which Joshua gave unto the tribes of Israel for a possession according to their divisions; in the mountains, and in the valleys, and in the plains, and in the springs, and in the wilderness, and in the south country; the Hittites, the Amorites, and the Canaanites, the Perizzites, the Hivites, and the Jebusites," &c.

But in this the book contradicts itself; for in xiii. 1, sqq., it is said, "Now Joshua was old and stricken in years, and Jehovah said unto him, 'Thou art old and stricken in years, and *there remaineth yet very much land to be possessed.*'" Then follows a list of the countries still in the hands of the Canaanites.

Again, in xxiii. 4, Joshua says, "I have divided unto you by lot *these nations that remain*, ... and Jehovah, your God, shall expel them for you." The contradiction is striking between the following passages:—

Chap. x. 40. "So Joshua smote all the country of the hills, and of the south, and of the vale, and of the springs, and all their kings: he left none remaining, but utterly destroyed all that breathed, as the Lord God of Israel commanded."

Chap. xi. 16, 17. "So Joshua took all that land, the hills, and all the south country, and all the land of Goshen, and the valley, and the plain, and the mountain of Israel, and the valley of the same; from the Mount Halak, that goeth up to Seir, even unto Baal-gad, in the valley of Lebanon, under Mount

Chap. xiii. 2—6.[a] "This is the land that yet remaineth: all the borders of the Philistines, and all Geshuri, from Sihor, which is before Ægypt, even unto the borders of Ekron northward, which is counted to the Canaanite: five lords of the Philistines; the Gazathites, and the Ashdothithes, the Eshkalonites, the Gittites, and the Ekronites; also the Avites: from the south, all the land of the Canaanites, and Mearah that is beside the Sidonians, unto Aphek, to the borders of the Amorites: and the land of the Giblites, and all Lebanon toward the sunrising,

[a] Especially verse 4.

Hermon: and all their kings he took, and smote them, and slew them."

from Baal-gad, under Mount Hermon, unto the entering into Hamath, all the inhabitants of the hill-country, from Lebanon unto Misrephoth-maim, and all the Sidonians: them will I drive out from before the children of Israel: only divide thou it by lot unto the Israelites for an inheritance, as I have commanded thee."

In reference to single conquests, it contains the most striking contradictions and inaccuracies.

1. Conquest of Hebron.

Chap. x. 36, 37. "And Joshua went up from Eglon, and all Israel with him, unto Hebron; and they fought against it: and they took it, and smote it with the edge of the sword, and the king thereof, and all the cities thereof, and all the souls that were therein; he left none remaining, (according to all that he had done to Eglon,) but destroyed it utterly, and all the souls that were therein."

Here the destruction of the city, the king, and the inhabitants, is declared to be total. But in the next chapter, Joshua conquers Hebron at another date.[a]

Chap. xi. 21. "And at that time came Joshua, and cut off the Anakims from the mountains; from Hebron, from Debir, from Anab, and from all the mountains of Judah, and from all the mountains of Israel: Joshua destroyed them utterly, with their cities."

Nor is this all; for, still later, it remains unconquered, and Caleb, an old man, boasts that he is still strong for war, and says to Joshua, —

---

[a] [This statement may refer to a previous conquest. But it does not affect the general assertion in the text.]

Chap. xiv. 12, 13. "Now therefore give me this mountain, [Hebron,] whereof the Lord spake in that day; for thou heardest, in that day, how the Anakims were there, and that the cities were great and fenced: if so be the Lord will be with me, then I shall be able to drive them out, as the Lord said. And Joshua blessed him, and gave unto Caleb, the son of Jephunneh, Hebron for an inheritance."

Still further, at a subsequent date, Caleb drives out the *three Anakim*, Sheshai, Ahiman, and Talmai, from Hebron. But, again, it is said in Judg. i. 9—11, that, *after the death of Joshua*, the children of Judah went up to Hebron, fought the Canaanites who dwelt there, and slew the *same three Anakim* — Sheshai, Ahiman, and Talmai — whom Caleb had killed before.[a]

2. Conquest of Debir.

Chap. x. 38, 39. "And Joshua returned, and all Israel with him, to Debir; and fought against it: and he took it, and the king thereof, and all the cities thereof, and they smote them with the edge of the sword, and utterly destroyed all the souls that were therein; he left none remaining: as he had done to Hebron, so he did to Debir, and to the king thereof; as he had done also to Libnah, and to her king."

The same event is related above, in xi. 21; and after the conquest of Hebron, Caleb does what is above related.

Chap. xv. 15—17. "And he went up thence to the inhabitants of Debir, and the name of Debir before was Kirjath-sepher......

"And Caleb said, 'He that smiteth Kirjath-sepher, and taketh it, to him will I give Achsah my daughter to wife.' And Othniel the son of Kenaz, the brother of Caleb, took it: and he gave him Achsah his daughter to wife."

---

[a] *König* (Alt. Test. Studien, vol. i. p. 22) thinks two conquests of Hebron are spoken of. *Stähelin*, who reviews König in Stud. und Krit. for 1837, p. 261, thinks the author generalized one, and referred the other to a special occasion. (?)

After the death of Joshua, the same event is said to take place; and it is described in almost the same words, in Judg. i. 11—13.

3. Conquest of the North, South, and West Part of Canaan.

Chap. x. 40—42. "So Joshua smote all the country of the hills, and of the south, and of the vale, and of the springs, and all their kings: he left none remaining, *but utterly destroyed all that breathed,* as the Lord God of Israel commanded. And Joshua smote them from Kadesh-barnea even unto Gaza, and all the country of Goshen even unto Gibeon. And all these kings, and their land, did Joshua take at one time; because the Lord God of Israel fought for Israel."

In xi. 8, he conquers the north part of the land, and "left none remaining;" and in verse 16, sqq., it is related again that he conquered (or had conquered) the south country and the whole land, "the valley, the plain, the mountain of Israel, and the valley of the same," and the entire country, from its northern to its most southern limit. But, in xiii. 2—6, this very tract of country is mainly in the hands of the old possessors.

Chap. xiii. 2—6. "This is the land that yet remaineth: all the borders of the Philistines, and all Geshuri, from Sihor, which is before Ægypt, even unto the borders of Ekron northward, which is counted to the Canaanite: five lords of the Philistines; the Gazathites, and the Ashdothites, the Eshkalonites, the Gittites, and the Ekronites; also the Avites: from the south all the land of the Canaanites, and Mearah that is beside the Sidonians, unto Aphek to the borders of the Amorites: and the land of the Giblites, and all Lebanon toward the sunrising, from Baal-gad under Mount Hermon unto the entering into Hamath. All the inhabitants of the hill-country from Lebanon unto Misrephoth-maim, and all the Sidonians, them will I drive out from before the children of Israel: only divide thou it by lot unto the Israelites for an inheritance, as I have commanded thee." [a]

---

[a] Compare, also, xi. 10, sq., and Judg. iv. 2, sqq.

4. The Conquest of several Kings.

Chap. xii. 12, sq. In the catalogue of the kings conquered by Joshua, we find it related that the king of *Gezer* was overcome. But, in Judg. i. 29, it appears Gezer had never been conquered — "Neither did Ephraim drive out the Canaanites that dwelt in Gezer," &c.

Verse 16, he conquers the king of *Beth-el.* But, Judg. i. 22, sqq., after the death of Joshua, the children of Joseph attacked Beth-el, gained entrance through the treachery of one of its citizens, and "smote the city with the edge of the sword."

In verses 21 and 23, it is said the king of *Taanach*, and the king of *Dor*, were among the conquered monarchs, whose territories were taken possession of by the Hebrews. But in Judg. i. 27, after the death of Joshua, it appears the Israelites had not conquered "Taanach and her towns, nor the inhabitants of Dor and her towns;" for the "Canaanites would dwell in that land."[a]

In xv. 63, it is said, —

> "As for the Jebusites, the inhabitants of Jerusalem, the children of Judah could not drive them out; but the Jebusites dwell with the children of Judah at Jerusalem unto this day."

In Judg. i. 8, we read, —

> "Now the children of Judah had fought against Jerusalem, and had taken it, and smitten it with the edge of the sword, and set the city on fire."

Here is a contradiction between the two, but they contradict both one another and themselves, in mentioning this same place; for in Josh. xviii. 28, it is said, Jebusi,

---

[a] [See, however, *Rosenmüller*, in loc., and *Gesenius*, sub voce יָאַל.]

that is, Jerusalem, is one of the twenty-six cities of Benjamin; and, in Judg. i. 21, it is said the children of Benjamin did not drive out the Jebusites, but dwelt with them.[a]

The uncertainty of the book becomes very striking when we compare xii. 14 — where the king of *Hormah* is reckoned among the kings *Joshua* had conquered — with Num. xxi. 3 — where *Moses* conquers the same place, and calls it *Hormah*, (Destruction,) — and with Judg. i. 17, in which a third account of its conquest is given: "And Judah went up with Simeon his brother, and they slew the Canaanites that inhabited Zephath, and utterly destroyed it; and the name of the city was called *Hormah*."[b]

The account of the destruction of Jericho is exaggerated, vi. 24; for it appears again, Judg. i. 16 — "And the children of the Kenite . . . . . . went up from the city of palm-trees," that is, Jericho. In iii. 13, Eglon conquers it from the Israelites, and in 2 Sam. x. 5, it is an inhabited city.

The same may be said of the destruction of Ai, (viii. 28; compare Gen. xii. 8.) It is still inhabited in Isa. x. 28, Ezra ii. 28, and Neh. vii. 32.[c]

In a similar manner the division of the whole land is ascribed to Joshua: —

Chap. xi. 23. "So Joshua took the whole land, ... and gave it for an inheritance unto Israel."[d] Chap. xiv. 1. "These are the countries which the children of Israel inherited in the land of Canaan, which Eleazar . . . . . . distributed unto them."

---

[a] [Here, however, it is *possible* there is no contradiction between them; for the Jebusites and children of Benjamin may have inhabited the city in common, while it was called one of the cities of the latter.]

[b] [It has been said there were *three* places by this name; but it may be asked, How is this fact known?]

[c] [But it may have been rebuilt in the interval.]

[d] See xii. 7, and xiii. 7, sqq., xix. 51.

Chap. xxi. 43, 44. "And the Lord gave unto Israel all the land which he sware to give unto their fathers: and they possessed it, and dwelt therein. And the Lord gave them rest round about, according to all that he sware unto their fathers: and there stood not a man of all their enemies before them; the Lord delivered all their enemies into their hand."

In these accounts some anachronisms naturally occur. Thus, in xvi. 2, *Luz* is mentioned as one of the boundaries of the tribe of Joseph; but in Judg. i. 26, it appears Luz was not built till after the death of Joshua.[a]

During the life of Joshua, the children of Dan were straitened in their territory: —

Chap. xix. 47. "The children of Dan went up to fight against Leshem, and took it, and smote it with the edge of the sword, and possessed it, and dwelt therein, and called Leshem Dan, after the name of Dan their father. This is the inheritance of the tribe of the children of Dan according to their families, these cities with their villages.

In Judg. xviii. 27—29, it seems this did not take place till after the time of Samson: –

"In those days the tribe of the Danites sought them an inheritance to dwell in, for unto that day inheritance had not fallen unto them among the tribes of Israel, ... and they came unto Laish,[b] unto a people that were at quiet and secure: and they smote them with the edge of the sword, and burnt the city with fire. And there was no deliverer, because it was far from Zidon, and they had no business with any man; and it was in the valley that lieth by Beth-rehob. And they built a city, and dwelt therein. And they called the name of the city Dan, after the name of Dan their father, who was born unto Israel: howbeit the name of the city was Laish at the first."

In xviii. 25, *Beeroth* is enumerated among the cities of Benjamin; but in 2 Sam. iv. this fact does not seem

---

[a] It is entirely arbitrary in *Eichhorn* (§ 447, p. 374) and *Bertholdt* (856) to say this is not the *same* Luz mentioned in Judges. See *Maurer*, in loc.

[b] [*Laish* is the same as *Leshem*.]

to be well known, and the writer mentions it as something new. "For Beeroth also was reckoned to Benjamin." [Chap. xxi. 13—19, *Hebron* and *Debir* are numbered among the cities of the Levites, the sons of Aaron. But in xiv. 11, sqq., xv. 14, sqq., they belong to Caleb. Besides, if Hebron were a Levitical city, it is difficult to conceive how it could be made the capital of the kingdom, as it seems it was in the time of David. 2 Sam. ii. 1—5.]

In order to have all the theocratical statistics put together, not only is the division of the land to the *east* of the Jordan — which was made in Num. xxxii. — repeated in detail, (xiii.,) but the designation of the cities of refuge in that region, which had been made by Moses, is ascribed to Joshua: —

Deut. iv. 41—43. "Then Moses severed three cities on this side Jordan, toward the sun-rising; Bezer in the wilderness, in the plain country, of the Reubenites; and Ramoth in Gilead, of the Gadites; and Golan in Bashan, of the Manassites."	Josh. xx. 8. "And on the other side Jordan, by Jericho eastward, they assigned Bezer in the wilderness upon the plain out of the tribe of Reuben, and Ramoth in Gilead out of the tribe of Gad, and Golan in Bashan out of the tribe of Manasseh."

[To the other historical inaccuracies, the following may be added: It seems improbable that so large a body of human beings as the Israelites could find subsistence in this land, while so many of the former inhabitants remained, and while the whole country was disturbed by war. Taking the calculation of Rosenmüller,[a] the Jewish territory could not exceed 11,625 square miles. Admitting the Hebrews were 2,500,000 in number, there would be a Hebrew population of a

[a] [Alterthumskunde, vol. ii. p. 85, sqq.]

little more than 215 to each square mile, or a little more than one Hebrew to every three acres of land. The country was, no doubt, very fertile; but it is scarcely probable, even in this fertile spot, and in a climate where little is required to support nature, that so dense a population could be sustained while the original population — perhaps equal in numbers — was still there, and the land devastated, in some measure, by a war of extermination; and yet, from Judg. xviii., it would appear the Danites continued to live a nomadic life in the midst of this dense population.][a]

§ 168.

DIFFERENT FRAGMENTS OF THIS BOOK.

The above contradictions may be, in part, explained by the fact that here, as in the first four books of the Pentateuch, we find fragments of the document "Elohim," and also Jehovistic or Deuteronomical fragments.[b] The Elohistic document included the division of the land in its history of the theocracy. The following examination will show the existence of these two documents: —

DOCUMENT "ELOHIM."	DEUTERONOMICAL OR JEHOVISTIC DOCUMENTS.
	The first part of the book (i—xii.) is, for the most part, Deuteronomical. This appears, in part, from the connection of the narrative; from its affinity with

[a] [See *Rosenmüller*, Alterthumskunde, vol. ii. p. 85, sqq. *Michaelis*, Laws of Moses, vol. i. ch. ii. art. 26, 27, p. 98, sqq.]

[b] See *Stähelin*, Stud. und Krit. 1835, p. 472, 1838, p. 270, and in the manuscript used by *De Wette*.

DOCUMENT "ELOHIM."

Chap. iv. 9. The twelve stones set up in Jordan for a memorial. This is, perhaps, Elohistic. The supposition accounts for its not agreeing with verse 8, which puts the monument on the bank of the river. Maurer thinks it an interpolation from a marginal gloss.[a]

Chap. v. 2—12, is, in part, Elohistic, as might be inferred from the mention of circumcis-

DEUTERONOMICAL DOCUMENTS.

the Jehovistic and Deuteronomical passages; and on account of the Jehovistico-Deuteronomical character of the style and manner.[b]

Chap. viii. 30—35, relates that Joshua erected an altar on Mount Ebal; wrote the Law of Moses on the stones of it; arranged the nation, half on Ebal, half on Gerizim; and then read all the words of the Law, the blessings and the cursings. This obviously refers to the command, Deut. xxvii. 2, sqq. But the passage interrupts the course of the nar-

---

[a] [I cannot entirely agree with the author in this division of the documents. I should put iv. 1—8, 20—22, and 23, 24, in the Elohistic document, though they are now out of their place. With this arrangement the Elohist speaks of the monument of twelve stones at Gilgal; the Jehovist, of that in the bed of Jordan. Then the repetition, in iv. 2, of the command in iii. 12—"Take you twelve men out of the tribes of Israel"—is readily explained.

I would thus connect the Jehovistic fragments: iii. 1—17, unites with iv. 9—19, which connects with vi. 1, sqq. Chap. v. seems to disturb the connection between iv. and vi. The fragments of which it is composed may be thus disposed of: Chap. v. 1—7, is evidently Jehovistic, and agrees with ii. 11, &c., in the description of cowardice; and has, besides, the common marks, mentioned above in the note. Chap. v. 8—12, is Elohistic. I incline to the opinion that v. 13—15, is from a source neither Elohistic nor Jehovistic, but different from both. The mythology of these verses is peculiar, and does not recur in the O. T. It seems a very poor imitation of the appearance of Jehovah in the bush, (Ex. iii. 1, sqq.) Verse 15 is a verbal imitation of iii. 5. But in Joshua this celestial appearance produces no result, except that Joshua took off his *shoes*. It seems scarce possible this story could have been from the same source as Ex. iii. 1, sqq.]

[b] For example, Josh. i. 1—9, is similar to Deut. xxxi. 1—8; verse 3, like xi. 24; verse 5—7, 9, like Deut. xxxi. 6—8, 23; verse 15, like Deut. iii. 20; ii. 11, like Deut. iv. 39; iii. 5, like Ex. xix. 10, and Num. xvi. 30; verses 13, 16, like Ex. xv. 8; iv. 6, 21, like Ex. xiii. 14; v. 13, like Num. xxii. 23; verse 15, like Levit. iii. 5. [?]

DOCUMENT "ELOHIM."

ion; but verse 6, which mentions *milk and honey*, is Jehovistic. Verse 10—12 are decidedly Elohistic. Verse 11, *in that selfsame day*, is like Ex. xvi. 35.

Chap. viii. 12, 13, the ambuscade at Ai, is, perhaps, Elohistic, to judge from its contradiction with 3—11. Maurer thinks it an interpolation, like iv. 9.

Chap. xi. 21, 22, does not repeat the narrative, as x. 36, sqq., and has probably come from some other source.

Chap. xii. 9—24. Maurer and others consider this passage as the work of some other hand.[a]

DEUTERONOMICAL DOCUMENTS.

rative, according to which Joshua *had not yet reached Gerizim.*[b]

Chap. ix. 23, 27. *Servants for the altar of Jehovah* are mentioned, as in Deut. xii. 11, xxix. 11. Compare, also, xii. 5, &c.

Chap. x. 8. The phrase, *Fear them not, for I have delivered them into thy hand*, is like Num. xxi. 34. Verses 14, 42, the phrase, *Jehovah fought for Israel*, is like Deut. iii. 22. Verse 21, *to sharpen his tongue*,[c] is like Ex. xi. 7.

Chap. xi. 20. *To harden the heart*,[d] like Ex. ix. 12, and other places.

There are other Jehovistic peculiarities of language, which, for the most part, are often repeated. *Judges;* i. 10, iii. 2. *Strong hand;* iv. 24. *To give before the face;* x. 12. *A possession;*[e] i. 15, xii. 6, 7, as in Deut. ii. 5, 9, 12, 19, 20. *The brave men;*[f] i. 14, iv. 12, as Ex. xiii. 18. *Not let remain;*[g] viii. 22, x. 28, 30, 33, 37, 39, 40, xi. 8, 11, as in Num. xxxi. 35, Deut. iii. 20, and elsewhere. *To keep to do;* i. 7, 8. *House of Jehovah;* vi. 2, ix. 23. *The priests the Levites;* iii. 3,

---

[a] [This also is, perhaps, more safely to be referred to a source different from the Elohistic or Jehovistic.]

[b] See *Meyer*, on the book of Joshua, in *Bertholdt's* Journal, p. 353, sqq. *Maurer*, in loc.; and *König*, l. c. vol. i. p. 29, sq.

[c] חרצ לשון. [d] חזק לב. [e] יְרֻשָּׁה. [f] חֲמֻשִׁים.

[g] לא - השאיר, &c.

DOCUMENT "ELOHIM."

DEUTERONOMICAL DOCUMENTS.

viii. 33. But the *sons of Aaron the priests* occurs, xxi. 19.

Other Jehovistic peculiarities are, Joshua is *the servant of Moses;* i. 1. *Euphrates is the limit of the land;* i. 4. *Joshua is the angel of Jehovah;* v. 13, 14, vi. 2. *The Canaanites and their expulsion;* iii. 10, ix. 1, 24, xi. 3, xii. 8. *An old song;* x. 13, 14. *Giants;* xii. 4, as in Deut. iii. 11. Jehovistic allusions to the *Amorites, Sihon, and Og;* ii. 10, ix. 10.

In some things it differs from the [former] Jehovistic document, and has peculiarities of its own; for example, *Lord of all the earth;*[b] iii. 11, 13. *Treasure of the house of Jehovah;* vi. 19, 24. The descriptions of cowardice, *our hearts melted;* ii. 11, v. 1, and vii. 5.

Chap. xiii. 15—32.[a]

Chap. xiii. 1—14. This appears to be Jehovistic, for verse 12 connects with xii. 4, and verse 14, (sacrifices ...... and the Levites' inheritance) is like Deut. xviii. 1. Verse 33 is like verse 14.

Chap. xiv. 1—5. Verse 1, *heads of the fathers* occurs, as Ex. vi. 14; verse 2 refers to Num. xxvi.

Chap. xiv. 6—15. Verses 7, 8, 14, *returned word;*[c] *entirely followed after,*[d] as in Num. xiii. 26,

[a] Here is מטה, *tribe*, instead of שבט, though not in verse 29; *according to their families*, למשפחותם, verses 15, 23, 24, 28, 31. Verses 21, 22, the princes of Midian, and Balaam, are mentioned as slain by the Israelites, as in Num. xxxi. 8; but yet verse 16 is like xii. 9, and xiii. 9.

[b] אדון כל הארץ. [c] השיב דבר. [d] מלא אחרי.

DOCUMENT "ELOHIM."

55; verse 4, to Gen. xlviii. and Num. xxxv. 1—10.[a]

Chap. xv. 1—12, 20—62. The same manner and style.

Chap. xvi. 1—xvii. 13. The same style and manner. Chap. xvi. 10, is the same as Judg. i. 29, and therefore Maurer thinks it was derived from it. So xvii. 12, sq., is the same as Judg. i. 27.

Chap. xviii. 11—xix. 51. Here occur formulas of conclusion — *This is the inheritance;* xviii. 20, 28, xix. 16, 23, as in Levit. But xix. 47, contains an extract from Judg. xviii.

Chap. xx. xxi. 1—43, like Num. xxxv. 9, sq., and 18, sqq.; the families of the Levites, as in

DEUTERONOMICAL DOCUMENTS.

xiv. 24, Deut. i. 36. On account of the contradiction between it and xi. 21, 22, and x. 36, 37,[b] Maurer derives it from another source. Herwerden thinks here is a different usage in the language. But this is doubtful.

Chap. xv. 13—19, contradicts the other part, but it agrees with Judg. i. 10, sqq., 20, from which cause Maurer thinks it was derived from the document in Judges.

Chap. xvii. 14—18, is doubtful. Compare it with xv. 13—19.

Chap. xviii. 1—10. Here, again, (verses 2, 4,) we have Jehovistic phrases:[c] a *book*, verse 9, as in Ex. xvii. 14, Deut. xxix. 19; *classes*, or *divisions*,[d] verse 10, as in xi. 23.

---

[a] קנין, *a possession*, as in Gen. xxxiv. 23, and Levit. xxii. 11.

[b] [See above, § 167, 1, *Conquest of Hebron.*]

[c] שבט.

[d] מחלקה.

DOCUMENT "ELOHIM."	DEUTERONOMICAL DOCUMENTS.
Num. iii. 4. Chap. xxi. 19, we have *the priests the sons of Aaron;* verse 25, *the half-shekel,*[a] as in Ex. xxx. 13, 15, Num. xxxi. 30, 42, 47. Maurer and others find an ancient document in xv. and following.	Verses 44 and 45 are Jehovistic.

Chap. xxii.—xxiv. are both Elohistic and Jehovistic;[b] xxiv. 1—28, is Jehovistic; verse 1 is like xxiii. 1; verses 5—17 refer to the Jehovistic account of the *plagues in Ægypt;* verses 6, 7, to the account of the *passage of the Red Sea,* in Ex. xiv. xv.; verses 9, 10, to the story of *Balaam,* (Num. xxii. sqq.;) verse 11, to the *Canaanites;* verse 12, to the *hornets,* (Ex. xxxiii. 28;) verse 13, *cities which they did not build,* as in Deut. vi. 10, 11; verse 19, a *jealous God,* as in Ex. xxiii. 21; verse 25, *a statute and ordinance,* as in Ex. xxiv. 18, and xv. 25; verses 29—33 are Elohistic; perhaps, also, verse 28, (see § 174;) verse 29, a statement of Joshua's age; verse 30, mentioning Timnath-serah, as in xix. 50; verse 32, Jacob's burial-place, refers to Gen. xxiii. 19, and l. 24, 25. According to Maurer, verses 29—31 are derived from Judg. ii. 6—9. But verse 28 might as well come from the same source, and 31 is probably Jehovistic.

In opposition to the above view, Van Herwerden, following, for the most part, peculiarities of the language, divides the book of Joshua into ten separate documents. But König maintains the unity of the book.

---

[a] מחצית.

[b] אז, with the future, occurs here, as in viii. 30, x. 12: verse 5, the command to *love Jehovah,* &c., is like Deut. xi. 22, xxx. 20; but verse 14, the Elohistic *Prince,* נשיא, and מטות, *tribes,* occur; verses, 9, 19, נאחז, *to take possession,* as in Gen. xxxiv. 10, xlvii. 27: verse 27, the *witness,* is like Gen. xxxi. 48. The style is often pretty diffuse. Chap. xxiii. is Jehovistic: verse 1, like xiii. 1, represents Joshua as old. *Judges and elders* occurs verse 2; 3 and 10, *Jehovah fights for them,* as in x. 14, 42; *a book of the Law,* verse 6, as in i. 8; 11, *take good heed,* הִשָּׁמֵר לְנֶפֶשׁ, as in Deut. iv. 15; verses 12, 13, like Ex. xxxiv. 16, xxiii. 34 [?], Num. xxxiii. 55, forbid marriage with the Canaanites; verses 13, 15, mention the *good land,* as Deut. often does; verse 14, like xxi. 45, says all the blessings came to pass. The denunciation, verse 16, is like Deut. xi. 17.

§ 169.

DATE OF THE COMPOSITION OF THE BOOK.

We can by no means suppose the whole book is the work of a contemporary author, as König has recently maintained. The communicative style of speaking, in v. 1, where the author uses the first person, — "Until we had passed over," — proves nothing. The same form occurs, Ps. lxvi. 6, and the Psalmist speaks as if he and his contemporaries had passed through the Red Sea — "There did we rejoice in him." The book nowhere contains separate contemporary documents.[a]

According to what has been said above,[b] the passages

---

[a] [It is sometimes said (e. g. by *Rosenmüller*) that these accounts of the boundaries of the separate tribes must be old, and must have been written at the time of the division, for they could not be retained in the memory of the people. But after the lines of each tribe were determinately settled, by actual possession, it would not be difficult for a writer, after the times of David or Josiah, to write down the boundaries of each tribe; and it seems most probable that the narrative originated in this manner. The real and the imaginary are not often separated with great care in Oriental histories, and it would not be unnatural for a Hebrew writer, in a later time, to refer the exact division of the land to the mythological hero Joshua, who conducted the nation into the territory, and conquered it for them.

The catalogues in the second part (xiii., sqq.) cannot be contemporary, as it appears from the later names of places, *Beeroth*, *Luz*, *Dan*, &c., and from the phrase *until this day*. Perhaps the author of the Jehovistic fragments had before him not only popular legends and oral or written traditions, but also fragments of popular songs and ballads, the substance of which he wrote down in historical prose, thus sometimes taking a figure for a fact. In one instance he refers to a written volume of songs or ballads — "Behold, it is written in the book of Jasher." In this way it is possible the accounts of the passage of the Jordan, the destruction of Jericho, the appearance of a divine being, and many others, originated. Sometimes, however, it is evident the original author uses the documents at present contained in the book of Judges; e. g. compare Josh. xvi. 10, with Judg. i. 20; xviii. 12, with i. 27; xix. 47, with xvii.; xxiv. 28—31, with ii. 6—9.]

[b] § 158.

of the document "Elohim" belong to Saul's time. Some passages refer to that period.

Thus, xvi. 10, — "And they drave out the Canaanites that dwelt in Gezer, but the Canaanites dwell among the Ephraimites until this day," (Judg. i. 29,) — refers to 1 Kings ix. 16, where Pharaoh conquers the Canaanites who dwelt in Gezer up to that time, and gives the place to Solomon as a portion for his daughter. In Josh. xviii. 25, Beeroth is mentioned among the cities of Benjamin; and, 2 Sam. iv. 2, it is said that "Beeroth was reckoned to Benjamin."

If the other parts of the book proceeded from the Jehovistic author in the first four books of the Pentateuch, then their age is already determined, (§ 159.) The book of Jasher (mentioned x. 13) points to the time of David; for his lamentation over Saul and Jonathan is contained in it, (2 Sam. i. 18.)[a] The sixty cities of Jair, in Bashan, (xiii. 30,) point to Solomon's time, (1 Kings iv. 13,) though Judg. x. 4, seems to conflict with this.

It is still a matter of doubt whether the names *Jerusalem* (x. 1) and *mountain of Israel* (xi. 16, 21) first originated in David's time.[b] It is doubtful, also, whether the statement respecting the inhabitants of Jerusalem, (xv. 63,) — "As for the Jebusites, the inhabitants of Jerusalem, the children of Judah could not drive them out, but the Jebusites dwell with the children of Judah unto this day," — extends after the time of David's conquest.[c]

If the book of Deuteronomy was written later than

---

[a] [Dr. *Palfrey* (l. c. vol. ii. p. 159, note) thinks the book of Jasher had an earlier date, but, as it was a collection of poems, "was likely to receive accessions from time to time, while it would be quoted at its different stages by the same name;" which, however, appears quite improbable.]

[b] The gloss, xviii. 28, is, perhaps, from a later hand. Comp. verse 16.

[c] Comp. 2 Sam. v. 6, xxiv. 16. *Maurer*, l. c. On the opposite side, *Bertholdt*, *Stähelin*, and others.

the first four books of the Pentateuch, then the book of Joshua, in its present form, belongs to a time far more recent. The curse, (vi. 26,) — "Cursed be the man ...... that riseth up and buildeth Jericho. He shall lay the foundation thereof in his first-born, and in his youngest son shall he set up the gates thereof," — refers to Ahab's time, 923, 922, B. C.; for, in 1 Kings xvi. 34, it is said, in Ahab's time "did Hiel ...... build Jericho; he laid the foundation thereof in Abiram his first-born, and set up the gates thereof in his youngest son Segub, according to the word of Jehovah ...... by Joshua the son of Nun."

But Hosea, about 785 B. C., — in ii. 15, (14,) in the mention of Achor, — seems to allude to Josh. vii. 26.

[I can by no means find the allusion the author refers to. In Josh. vii. 26, a certain spot is called *Achor*, on account of an event alleged to have taken place there. Hosea speaks of Achor. Now, if the place received that name in the time of Joshua, or at any time subsequent, and previous to the age of Hosea, the reference is explained without the unnecessary hypothesis of supposing that Hosea was acquainted with this book. Besides, in Hos. ii. 15, I find an allusion to something not contained in the book of Joshua — "*She shall sing there* (at Achor) *as in the days of her youth, and as in the day when she came up out of the land of Ægypt.*" Now, we do not read in Joshua that the nation *sang for joy* at Achor; it was rather a place of weeping. It seems Hosea alludes to some legend which has not come down to us; but even if he refers to the story in Joshua, it would not follow the book itself was in his hands, for the story might be preserved either orally or in a written form, as an explanation of the name of the place. To me there is one mark which, more than all others, perhaps, shows the late origin of the book; that is, the frequent mention of the "*Law of Moses*," and the "*Book of the Law*." If what has been said above respecting the origin and date of the Pentateuch in its present form, may be relied on as correct, then such appeals to the Law Book of Moses could not have taken place *before* the reformation under Josiah, about 624 B. C. How long after this date they were made, we cannot tell. The Law is appealed to in Joshua, as in the very late books, Ezra and Nehemiah. The reference (viii. 31) to the "Law of Moses," which is contained in Deut. xxvii. 5, 6, could not have been written until after the time of Josiah, at the earliest.[a] The Levitical spirit of the book, and its entire character, taken in connection with the historical circumstances, might lead one to place it after the commencement of the exile.[b]]

§ 170.

AUTHOR OF THE BOOK.

There are but few and feeble arguments to show the book of Joshua was composed by an author who was different from the Jehovist or the Deuteronomist, and who imitated him.[c]

Andrew Masius, Spinoza and Leclerc, Hasse and

---

[a] [*The Babylonian mantle* (אַדֶּרֶת שִׁנְעָר) seems to indicate a late date. But we know too little of the early history of Babylon, and its traffic with other states in remote antiquity, to infer at what time the inhabitants of Palestine became acquainted with the Babylonians. See *Heeren*, Researches, &c.; Oxford, 1833, vol. i. p. 59, sqq.]

[b] [See the combinations of *De Wette*, in the fourth edition of this work.]

[c] These arguments are as follows, to prove the later character of the language: אותכם, for אֶתְכֶם; xxiii. 15. אוֹתִר, for אִתִּי; xiv. 12, xxiii. 19. But see Lev. xv. 15, 24.) The numeral placed after a word; xii. 94, sqq., xv.

Maurer, date the book after the exile. Baba Bathra[a] mentions Joshua as the author. This is also the opinion of König. [The following are the opinions of some of the Christian writers.

Athanasius[b] says the book of Joshua, and those which follow, till the book of Ezra, were not written by the men whose names they bear, and of whom they treat, but by prophets, who lived at various times. Theodoret[c] thinks the whole book an extract from the book of Jasher, and that the author, suspecting men would not credit him when he spoke of the sun and moon standing still, referred to his authority; "whence," he says, "it is plain that some other person, [not Joshua,] of a later date, wrote this, taking the occasion from another book." Dr. Palfrey refers it to the time of Saul.

The opinion of De Wette, that the book was brought into its present form by the Jehovist or Deuteronomist, seems at variance with the fact that he appeals to the Law of Moses, and even to passages in Deuteronomy,[d] as to a well-known and recognized authority. But this difficulty may, perhaps, be avoided on the supposition

---

36, 59, xviii. 28, xix. 30, xxi. 32. (See *Gesenius*, Lehrgebäude, p. 695, sqq.) But it occurs also in document "Elohim." נְכָסִים, *riches*; xxii. 8, as in 2 Ch. i. 11, sqq., Eccl. v. 18. הִשְׂכִּיל, *to be happy*; i. 7, 8. חמסיר; xiv. 8, (Chaldaism for חמסר.) (See, however, *Ewald*, Gram. Krit. p. 422.) The *article* as a *relative*; x. 24. לֹא יכרת; ix. 23. (But comp. 1 Kings ii. 4, et al., Jer. xxxii. 17, et al.) *Hävernik* (l. c. p. 198) cites the abbreviation of the proverb, (x. 21,) as a sign of a later usage.

The following differ from the peculiarities of the Jehovist and Deuteronomist: *Lord of all the earth*, אדון כל הארץ; iii. 11, 13. *Treasure of the house of Jehovah*; vi. 24. Description of cowardice; ii. 11, v. 1. (Comp. vii. 5.) The *sacred lot*; vii. 16, sqq. (See 1 Sam. x. 20, 21, xiv. 41, 42.)

[a] [Fol. xiv. c. 2.]

[b] [Synop. tom. ii. Opp. p. 73.]

[c] [Quæst. xiv. in Jos. Opp. i. pt. i. p. 202. See these and others in *Carpzov*, p. 150.]

[d] [Comp. viii. 31, with Deut. xxvii. 5, 6.]

that the Jehovistic and Elohistic fragments *originated* with the Jehovistic and Elohistic authors in the Pentateuch, but were united together, and reduced to their present form, by a compiler somewhat later, who made archæological explanations, omitted, altered, added, and combined passages according to his own judgment. If such a writer compiled the book of Joshua after Josiah's reformation, and at a time when the Pentateuch was acknowledged and well known, we can account for the manner in which the Law of Moses is appealed to and quoted, as well as for the abruptness of many passages, and the repetitions, glosses, and omissions, which have been noticed above.][a]

§ 171.

THE SAMARITAN BOOK OF JOSHUA.

In the library at Leyden, there is an Arabic version, written in Samaritan characters, of a Samaritan chronicle, bearing the name of the book of Joshua, which contains the history of Joshua, with the addition of the last transactions during the life of Moses accidentally introduced in this connection. Sometimes it employs the same expressions with the Hebrew book, though sometimes with great departures from it, and with large additions, and continues the history down to the time of Alexander Severus, though probably this is a more modern continuation of it.

This book seems to have been composed by uniting the contents of our book of Joshua with Samaritan fables.

---

[a] See vol. i. Appendix, I.

The beginning of it (i.—xii.) is parallel with Num. xxii.—xxxii., and xiii.—xxiv. with the book of Joshua; then follows an account of an embassy, and the magic of the Persian king, Shaubeck, and of Joshua's war with him. After a short abstract of the Mosaic Law, the book concludes with Joshua's last admonition to the people, (Josh. xxiv.)

Hottinger[a] thus speaks of it:—"In the division of the land, the district containing the loftiest mountain fell to Joshua the son of Nun the king, and his associate Caleb, the leader of all the tribes. He held it in common with him, [Caleb.] And when each one went to his own place, he distributed the Levites, each one into that place which was assigned to him exclusively in the distribution of the whole land, ... so that they might oversee the affairs of men, which relate to prayers, judgments, the rendering and giving of tithes, and the offering of sacrifices. To each of the tribes he appointed chief judges, who should relate all events to the pontiff, and should inform him of all that happened in their districts. Then Joshua erected a fortress on the mountain, on the left side of the blessed mount. . . . . . . Moreover he erected a temple on the top of the blessed mount; and in it a sanctuary to the Lord, which, except himself, none but the priests and the Levites ever saw. . . . . . . On that day (Josh. x.) God showed them miracles against their enemies; so that, if any one wished to withdraw and save himself by flight, fire fell upon and consumed him. Also a certain phantom descended among them, so that the very horses charged them, and chased them to death, as long as they heard the voices of the sons of Israel. The hours of the day were prolonged for them, as God

[a] Smegma Orient. p. 476, 512.

promised, so that, in this day alone, they gained as much as would suffice for the space of an entire year."

Another recension of this history is found in the Samaritan chronicle of Abul Phetach.[a]

CHAPTER III.

THE BOOK OF JUDGES.[b]

§ 172.

CONTENTS OF THE BOOK.

AFTER some introductory notices, (chap. i.,) and a denunciatory oracle, (ii. 1—5,) the book of Judges, properly so called, begins, (ii. 6—xvi. 31,) and contains the history of the anarchy and apostasy which ensued after the death of Joshua, and of the subjugation of the people which was occasioned thereby, and was connected with the divine displeasure.

---

[a] See *Schnurrer*, in *Eichhorn's* Rep. vol. ix. p. 54. See a summary of its contents in Actis, Eruditt.; Lips. an. 1691, p. 167; and an essay by *Schnurrer*, in *Paulus*, N. Rep. vol. i. p. 117, sqq. *Reland*, Diss. ii. p. 314; 1706. *Hottinger*, Exercit. Antimorin. p. 105, sqq. Smeg. Or. p. 437. Hist. Or. p. 40, 120. Disp. Lib. V. T. supposititiis, No. 1. Exeg. Handbuch A. T. vol. iii. p. 18, sqq.

[b] *Bonfrerii*, *Serrarii*, *Jo. Clerici*, *Maurer*, Comment. *Jo. Drusii* Annotatt. in Loca diff. Josh., Judg., et Sam. *Rosenmüller*, Schol. above cited.

Victorin. Strigelii Scholia in L. Judg.; Lips. 1586.

Seb. Schmidt, Comment. in Libr. Judg. above cited.

Exeget. Handb. des A. T. 2 and 3 pt.

Ziegler, Bemerkk. über d. B. d. Richt. im Geiste des Heldenalters, in his Theol. Abhandl. vol. i. p. 275, sqq. *Studer*, B. Richter; 1835.

Coleridge, Miscellaneous Dissertations arising from Judg. xvii. and xviii.; Lond. 1768, 8vo.

Paulus, Blicke in d. B. der Richt., theol. ex. Conservat. vol. ii. p. 180, sqq. *Geddes*, Holy Bible, &c. vol. ii. *Palfrey*, l. c. vol. ii.

As often as the Israelites turned from this anarchy and apostasy, they were delivered by heroes[a] divinely inspired, who, so long as they lived and governed, preserved the people from apostasy and subjection; but, after their death, the old game began anew. The author has very clearly set forth this alternation of crime and punishment, of repentance and restoration to favor, according to a plan laid down in ii. 6—23, which he has only interrupted by episodes, and by the history of Samson, but which has, probably, been kept at the expense of historical completeness.[b]

Chap. i. contains notices of the conquest of the land after Joshua's death. A supplement (chap. xvii.—xxi.) contains two narratives, introduced as proofs of the anarchy and licentiousness which prevailed before the regal government was established in Israel. To judge from xx. 27, 28, the history in xix. xxi. belongs in the time shortly after Joshua.[c] But the statement it contains is designed to explain the existence of idolatry at Beth-el, where there was a private and illegal sanctuary without the ark of the covenant. Now, the existence of such a sanctuary supposes that a long time had passed since Joshua.

§ 173.

CHARACTER OF THE NARRATIVE.

Although distinguished by miraculous and mythological features, the narrative not only bears the marks of a

---

[a] שׁוֹפְטִים, i. e. *rulers*, in war or peace, and in a peculiar sense *judges*, (iv. 5, 1 Sam. vii. 15, sq.) *De Wette*, Archäol. § 28. See *Gesenius*, in verb.

[b] Archäol. § 27, sqq. *Jahn*, l. c. § 33. *Eichhorn*, § 456. Since the judges are from several tribes, and follow one another almost in geographical order, *Studer* conjectures that the present is not the original plan. See § 174, below

[c] See *Josephus*, Ant. v. 2, 3, and *Carpzov*, l. c. p. 1[illegible]

genuine, inartificial, popular legend, but, in part, of a true, historical tradition, and gives a lively picture of the condition and morals of the people at that time. The difference between the spirit of this book and that of the book of Joshua is very evident.

There is but one passage which contains, obviously, an etymological and symbolical myth, (ii. 1—5,) where a place is named Bochim, [*weeping*,] because the people wept. Chapters vi. and vii. are highly mythological. The passage xvii.—xxi. is entirely free from mythology. No narratives in the Old Testament are more beautiful and true to nature than the story of Gideon's achievements, in chap. viii.; of the adventures of Abimelech, chap. ix.; of Jephthah, chap. xi.; and the narratives in xvii.—xxi.[a]

[It seems not to have been the design of the compiler of this book to furnish a regular and continuous history of the times from Joshua to Jephthah. He only selects those periods and instances which are suitable to his purpose, and serve to show that suffering follows sin, and obedience to the law of Jehovah always secures tranquillity and national happiness. He passes over

[a] On a correct view of the legends relating to Samson, see *Dieterich*, Zur Gesch. Simsons, pt. 3, 1778, 1789. *Justi*, on Samson's strength, in *Eichhorn*, Rep. vol. vii. p. 78, sqq. Verm. Abhandlungen, vol. i. p. 164, sqq. *Herder*, Spirit of Hebrew Poetry, vol. ii. *Paulus*, l. c. 199, sqq. [Dr. *Palfrey* (l. c. vol. ii. p. 194, sq.) says, the "character of Samson is but a wild compound of the buffoon, the profligate, and the bravo. With a sort of childish cunning, and such physical faculties as a fantastic invention has ascribed to the *ogre*, he is without a common measure of capacity to provide for his own protection," &c. It is amusing to read in *Horne*, l. c. (iv. 37,) "The Vulpinaria, or feast of the foxes, celebrated by the Romans in the month of April, (the time of the Jewish harvest, in which they let loose foxes with torches fastened to their tails,) was derived from the story of Samson, which was conveyed into Italy by the Phœnicians; and to mention no more, in the history of Samson and Delilah, we find the original of Nisus and his daughters, who cut off their fatal hairs upon which the victory depended."]

long periods in the briefest manner. Thus, in x. 1, he says, "After Abimelech there arose . . . . . . Tola; . . . . . . he judged Israel twenty-and-three years, and died;" iii. 30, "And the land had rest fourscore years;" viii. 28, "and the country was in quietness forty years in the days of Gideon."[a] For this reason, it is difficult to determine the chronology of the book.[b]

Portions of the book are *pragmatic;* for example, "The anger of Jehovah was hot against Israel," (ii. 14, 15, 16, 18, 20—23.) The deliverers of the nation are

---

[a] [See, also, x. 3, xii. 7—15, xv. 20, xvi. 31.]

[b] [The following table is taken from *De Wette's* Archæology, § 27:—

From Joshua till the time when the new race fell into idolatry, (Judg. i. ii. Josephus, Ant. vi. 5, 4,)	18	years.
Servitude under Cushan-rishathaim, (iii. 8,)	8	"
Deliverance by Othniel, and 40 years' rest, (iii. 11,)	40	"
Servitude under the Moabites, (iii. 14,)	18	"
Deliverance by Ehud, and 80 years' rest, (iii. 30,)	80	"
——— Shamgar, (no date,) (iii. 31,)	X.	"
Twenty years' servitude under Jabin, (iv. 1, sq.,)	X.+20	"
Deliverance by Barak, and 40 years' rest, (v. 31,)	40	"
Oppression by Midianites, (vi. 1,)	7	"
Rest under Gideon, (viii. 28,)	40	"
Decline of the Jews after Gideon's death, (viii. 33—35,)	X.	"
Abimelech's reign, (ix. 22,)	3	"
Tola, judge, (x. 2,)	23	"
Jair, ——— (x. 3,)	22	"
New decline and oppression of the Jews, (x. 6—9,)	X.+18	"
Jephthah, (xii. 7,)	6	"
Ebzan, (xii. 9,)	7	"
Elon, (xii. 10,)	10	"
Abdon, (xii. 14,)	8	"
Oppression by the Philistines, (xiii. 1,)	40	"
Samson, judge, (xv. 20,)	20	"
In all, (without the 40 doubtful years, marked in *numerals*,)	428	"

But if the temple of Solomon was built 480 years after the departure from Ægypt, as it is said, 1 Kings vi. 1, the above chronology must be wrong. Rosenmüller makes 410 years.]

raised up by a *special* act of omnipotence, (iii. 9, 15, iv. 6, 23, vi. 8—10, 11, sqq. et al.,) Jehovah is said to deliver the people to their conquerors, (iv. 2, vi. 1.) Less important actions, in the spirit of antiquity, are referred directly to the Supreme Being, as in xiii. 25; ix. 23, "God sent an evil spirit between Abimelech and the men of Shechem;" verse 56, "Thus God repaid the wickedness of Abimelech." The story of Gideon is mythical and pragmatic in a high degree. But there are no marks of a theocratic, still less of a Levitical, spirit in the first part of the book.

The mythology of this book is peculiar. In chap. ii. 1, sqq., an *angel* of Jehovah comes up from Gilgal to Bochim to admonish the nation. But he speaks as if he were Jehovah himself, and not simply his angel. "*I* made you go out of Ægypt," &c.; "Ye have not obeyed *my* voice," &c.[a] Again, in vi. 11, sqq., an angel of Jehovah appears to Gideon, sits under the terebinth in Ophrah, and assures the doubtful son of Joash that Jehovah is with him. But as he hesitates to believe the assertion, the angel speaks as if he were Jehovah,— "Have not *I* sent thee?"—and the narrative seems to confound Jehovah and the angel, (verses 14, 16.) Gideon prepares food for the angel, who causes it to be spread on a rock, and touches it with his staff. Fire comes out of the rock, consumes the food, and the angel vanishes. Then Gideon suspects his visitor was celestial, and is frightened. But Jehovah himself bids him fear not. The same night, Jehovah appears to him

---

[a] [Perhaps the original legend taught that Jehovah himself appeared, and some *redactor*, thinking this too gross, ascribed the action to an angel of Jehovah.]

again, and afterwards Gideon consults him by a sort of divination, (verse 36, sqq.) On another occasion, (xiii. 3,) an angel of Jehovah appears to the wife of Manoah, and predicts the birth of Samson. Manoah, who supposes he was but a man, prayed that he might return. The prayer was granted; the visitant repeated his instructions, refused to eat, or to tell his name, and ascended in the smoke of a burnt-offering. Manoah exclaimed, "We shall surely die, because we have seen God." These appearances of divine beings differ remarkably from those in Genesis. The ark appears but once in the book, then in a gloss on the appendix, (xx. 27.)

The story of Samson is very remarkable, and suggests numerous historical parallels. Paulus thinks his feats of strength are not incredible. He compares him with the Rephaim, Anakim, and Goliath; with David and his heroes, who slew lions and bears single-handed; with Ajax, Diomed, Achilles, Hector, and Turnus—not to mention the strong men of the Teutonic nations. But their strength was only extraordinary, while that of Samson is represented as miraculous. We are to compare him, not so much with Hercules and the demigods of other nations, as with their mythological heroes,—with the Argonauts and Theseus, who lived before Homer's time; while David and his heroes are to be compared with the Ajax, and Hector, and Achilles, of Homer.[a]]

---

[a] See *Paulus*, l. c., and *De Lavaur*, Conference de la Fable avec l'Histoire Sainte, (cited by *Clarke*, Com. in loc.) *Justi*, *Bauer*, *De Wette*, 4th ed., and *Palfrey*, l. c.

§ 174.

COMPILATION OF THE BOOK.

The appendix (xvii.—xxi) is clearly distinguished from the proper book of Judges by taking a different point of view, and referring the sins of the land to the want of a king, (xvii. 6, xviii. 1, xix. 1, xxi. 25,) by its want of mythology, but not by its style.[a] It is a later addition, but it does not contradict itself.

There is a contradiction between i. 18 and iii. 1—3. In the former, it is said Judah took Gaza, Askelon, and Ekron, with their coasts; but, in the latter, it is said the people of these places were left—"Five lords of the Philistines, all the Canaanites, and the Zidonians." On this account, and because i. 27—36, seems, at the least, superfluous, if iii. 3, was to be written, it appears the first chapter could hardly have come from the author of the book of Judges. It may have been derived from some other source. Such is the opinion of Eichhorn. Yet verse 16 agrees with iv. 11. Bertholdt and Studer think it is from a later hand. It is a compilation which contradicts itself. Thus, (verse 8,) it is said, the children of Judah fought against Jerusalem, and took it, and smote it with the edge of the sword, and set the city on fire; (verse 21,) "But the children of Benjamin did not drive out the Jebusites that inhabited Jerusalem, but the Jebusites dwell with the children of Benjamin in Jerusalem unto this day." Again, (verse 10,) "Judah conquered the Canaanites who dwelt at Heshbon, and slew Sheshai, and Ahiman,

---

[a] But see *Eichhorn*, § 457, and *Bertholdt*, p. 876, 886.

and Talmai;" but, in verse 20, Caleb expels from Hebron these three Anakim.

The passage, ii. 1—5, seems removed from its true connection; for the book of Joshua proper begins with verse 6; however, it agrees with the idea of the book, and probably originated with the same author.

The book of Judges proper (ii. 6—xvi. 31) has a strong resemblance to the Jehovistic documents and the book of Joshua, and has an internal agreement with it. For this reason it has been ascribed to the same author.[a] But, as in the Pentateuch and the book of Joshua, more ancient fragments lie at the bottom. Monuments of these appear here and there. The plan of the book, laid down in chap. ii., occurs beforehand in Josh. xxiii. xxiv., and even in Ex. xxiii. 20, sqq. The style is like that in the Jehovistic parts of Deuteronomy,[b] though there are Elohistic passages.

---

[a] *Stähelin*, in Stud. und Krit. for 1835, p. 474, sqq.

[b] For example, *to do evil*, עשה הרע; i. 11, and frequently, as in Deut. iv. 25, ix. 18, xvii. 2, 5, and elsewhere. *The land rested*, שקטה הארץ; iii. 11, 30, v. 31, viii. 28, as Josh. xi. 23, xiv. 15. *Miracles*, נפלאות; vi. 13, as Ex. xxxiv. 10. *Armed men*, חמשים; vii. 11, as Josh. i. 14, and frequently. *For a snare*, למוקש; ii. 3, viii. 27, as in Ex. xxiii. 33, and elsewhere. *To put before the face;* xi. 9. There is a resemblance between ii. 2, 3, and Ex. xxiii. 24, 28, 29, 32; between iii. 6, (*they took their daughters to be wives*, &c.,) and Deut. vii. 3, 4; vi. 39, (*I will speak but this once*,) and Gen. xviii. 32; xiii. 17, 18, (where the angel is unwilling to tell his name,) and Gen. xxxii. 28, 29. Chap. ii. 15, — *as Jehovah said*, — refers to Deuteronomy.

There is a similarity in the mythology; for example: Angel of Jehovah; ii. 1, sqq., vi. 11, 14. Miraculous signs; vi. 17, 36, as in Ex. iv., and elsewhere. It is considered fatal to see God; vi. 22, 23, xiii. 22, as in Gen. xvi. 13, 14. Verses are quoted; xiv. xv. Chap. vi. 11, sqq., is like xiii.; vii. 1, sqq., like xii. 1, sqq.; viii. 27, prepares for chap. ix.; xvi. 17, refers to xiii. 5. But in chap. v. I cannot find the work of the Jehovist, nor in several narratives which give a faithful description of ancient manners. Chap. xi. 15, — "Israel took not away the land of Moab, ... of the children of Ammon,"—

[At this time, we cannot ascertain the author's sources of information. Perhaps they were oral, perhaps writ-

---

agrees pretty well with Num. xxi.; but verse 25 differs from it. Chap. x. 4, contradicts Num. xxxii. 41, and Deut. iii. 14. Chap. x. 11, 12, has not a Jehovistic reference.

The following usages are peculiar: נזעק, נצעק, *called together;* vi. 34, 35, vii. 23, 24, x. 17, xii. 1. *To sell into the hand,* מכר ביד; ii. 14, iii. 8, iv. 2, x. 7; but compare Deut. xxxii. 30. *Do what thy hand finds to do;* ix. 33, as in 1 Sam. x. 7. *Shin* prefixed; v. 7, vi. 17, vii. 12, xviii. 26. However, this occurs in the passages which are mostly Jehovistic.

The Elohistic passage, ii. 6, sqq., corresponds to Josh. xxiv. 28, sqq., and seems to be derived from the document "Elohim:" verses 22, 23, and perhaps, also, iii. 1, sqq., seem to belong to it. Verse 22, נִסָּה, *to try,* is like Ex. xvi. 4. Verse 23 says Jehovah left the Canaanites, and did not deliver them into the hand of Joshua, and so contradicts the book of Joshua.

According to Jahn (vol. ii. p. 191) and Bertholdt, (p. 878,) the history of Samson is derived from two different documents. But one cannot end with xv. 20, but with xvi. 31, and chap. xiii. resembles chap. vi.: xvi. 5, is like xiv. 15. The only difference in the style is merely in the use of צָלַח, *to fall suddenly upon;* xiv. 6, 19, xv. 14. Chap. v. is certainly drawn from a peculiar written source, since it contains matter which differs from what was related before, and which could hardly be preserved in the mouth of the people; for example, verses 6, 14, 15, (compare iv. 5, 10,) 23. Likewise chap. vi.—viii. is distinguished by the *shin* prefixed. According to *Studer,* (p. 438,) the author of the present book of Judges made use of an old book of the genealogy of Heroes, which he worked over, following a plan different from the original.

[This view of the author, that the documents "Elohim" and "Jehovah" can be distinguished in Judges, seems very feebly supported by facts. The arguments adduced are, 1. similarity of manner; and, 2. of matter.

1. In the first argument, the examples brought forward do not appear satisfactory. (1.) *To do evil,* עשה הרע, occurs very frequently in Samuel, Kings, Chronicles, and sometimes in the later Prophets. I find nothing peculiar to the Jehovistic books in this usage. (2.) *The land rested,* שקטה הארץ, may, perhaps, have something which is peculiar. (3.) The term *miracles,* מפלאת, is of very frequent occurrence in this same sense in the Psalms, Job, Daniel, Chronicles, and Nehemiah. (4.) The term *armed,* חמשים, occurs even in the Elohistic fragment, Ex. xiii. 18. (5.) *A snare,* למוקש, is, perhaps, Jehovistic; but it occurs, also, 1 Sam. xviii. 21, Ps. lxix. 23, and elsewhere.

2. The alleged similarity of style, mythology, and miracles, seems to me exceedingly faint. Sometimes there is, indeed, a law or usage referred to in Judges which actually occurs in the Pentateuch, (ii. 1—5, 12, 17, 20, iii.

ten. The occurrence of round and exaggerated numbers would lead us to suspect that he relied on oral tradition. Four of the judges ruled just *forty* years each; three either ten, twenty, or eighty years. There were seventy-seven elders at Succoth, (viii. 14.) Ibzan had thirty sons and thirty daughters, and the same number of sons and daughters-in-law, (xii. 9.) Jair, also, had thirty sons who rode on thirty ass-colts, and ruled thirty cities, (x. 4.) Abdon had forty sons and thirty nephews. Numbers are often much exaggerated. The Gileadites killed 42,000 men of Ephraim, (xii. 6;) Samson, 1,000 with an ox-goad; 400,000 of the people of God met at Mizpeh, (xx. 2;) they killed 22,000 Benjamites on the first day, 18,000 on the second, and 25,100 on the third day, (xx. 15, 17, 21, 25, 35, 44, 46.) There were 700 left-handed Benjamites, (xx. 16,) famous slingers.

There is some probability that the song of triumph (chap. v.) came from a written document, for verses 6, 14, 15, 23, 28, differ from the former chapter, (iv. 6, 10,) which also, it may be, rests on a written statement.

But, on the other hand, Jotham's parable (ix. 8, sqq.)

6;) but there is *never a reference to its language.* "Commandments by the hand of Moses" appears once only, (iii. 4.) These may have been oral commands, preserved in the mouth of the people. The *Book of the Law*, or the *Law of Moses*, never once occurs, nor is any passage even cited from it. None of its favorite Jehovistic phases occur. Allusion is made to the deliverance from Ægypt, (ii. 12, vi. 8, x. 11,) but never to any *written account of that deliverance.* On the contrary, there are passages at variance with the Pentateuch, already cited, and others which seem to belong to a tradition that has not come down to us. Such are, vi. 10, x. 11, 12, xi. 25. The difference in the mythology has been mentioned above, (§ 173.) Now, it seems contrary to the principles of criticism to assume the existence of the two documents on such slender evidence, and in the face of such facts. Chap. i. has a marked resemblance with passages in Joshua, before adduced; but this phenomenon is easily explained on the supposition that it was drawn from a document common to the authors of the two books.]

may have been taken from the mouth of the people. The following proverbs have a popular air: xiv. 14, "Out of the eater came forth meat, and out of the strong came forth sweetness;" verse 18, "If ye had not ploughed with my heifer, ye had not found out my riddle;" and xv. 15, "With the jaw-bone of an ass, heaps upon heaps, with the jaw of an ass have I slain a thousand men."[a] Other passages may be found which are connected with popular traditions, or serve to support them. Thus, in vi. 24, we read, "Gideon built an altar there, and called it *Jehovah Shalom.*" In xi. 39, 40, it is said, after Jephthah's offering, "It was a custom in Israel; the daughters of Israel went yearly to lament the daughter of Jephthah;" and in xv. 19, the occasion of the popular name of a place is given — En Hakkora, *the place of calling*, because Samson called on Jehovah there.

It is evident that the history of Gideon and that of Abimelech are derived from at least two separate documents. In the one, (vi. 11—viii. 28,) the son of Joash is called *Gideon*, throughout, with but a single exception, (vii. 1,) though his name is repeated more than thirty times; in viii. 29—35, he is called indifferently *Gideon* and *Jerubbaal;* but in chap. ix. he is always called *Jerubbaal.* The passage, viii. 34, 35, is apparently an interpolation, either by the compiler or some later hand. The gloss, "who is Gideon," (vii. 1, viii. 35,) evidently came from the compiler.[b] The appendix (xvii.—xxi.) evidently contains two separate documents — xvii. xviii. and xix.—xxi. But both have the same author, who is

---

[a] [See Dr. *Palfrey*, l. c. vol. ii. p. 230.]

[b] [The jealousy of the Ephraimites, because they were not asked to fight the Midianites and Ammonites, is remarkable, (viii. 1—3, xii. 1—6.)]

distinguished by his love of a kingly government, (xvii. 6, xix. 1.) The passage, xx. 36—46, appears to be a supplement to the previous account of the battle. Perhaps this was derived from an independent popular legend.[a] There is a slight numerical difference between the two accounts; in one 25,100 perish, in the other 25,000.]

§ 175, *a*.

THE AGE OF THE BOOK OF JUDGES.

It is plain that the author or compiler of the proper book of Judges belongs to a late period. This appears from the affinity between this book and that of Joshua and Deuteronomy, as well as from the use of the phrases "unto this day,"[b] and "it became a custom in Israel."[c] Chap. v. contains marks of a high antiquity, in verses

---

[a] [Compare verses 45, 46, with 35.]

[b] Chap. vi. 24, x. 4, xv. 19, (compare xi. 39,) where he speaks of contemporary matters.

[c] [This resemblance, however, as it has been shown before, is confined to chap. i., which is no part of the proper book of Judges. To me, the most decided mark of the late origin of chap. v. consists in the parallelism between verses 4, 5, Ps. lxviii. 8, 9, and Deut. xxxiii. 2:—

Judg. v. 4, 5. "Lord, when thou wentest out of Seir, when thou marchedst out of the field of Edom, the earth trembled, and the heavens dropped, the clouds also dropped water. The mountains melted from before the Lord, even that Sinai from before the Lord God of Israel."

Ps. lxviii. 7, 8. "O God, when thou wentest forth before thy people, when thou didst march through the wilderness, ... the earth shook, the heavens also dropped at the presence of God: even Sinai itself was moved at the presence of God, the God of Israel."

Deut. xxxiii. 2. "And he said, 'The Lord came from Sinai, and rose up from Seir unto them: he shined forth from Mount Paran, and he came with ten thousands of saints: from his right hand went a fiery law for them.'"

But who shall tell us which is the original?]

6, 8, 14, 15, (compare iv. 6, 10,) 23, 28.[a] The use of the *shin* prefixed serves less to determine the age than the district in which the primitive documents of the book originated. Ewald and Studer[b] refer this usage to north Palestine, and it might be so if chap. vi. vii. had not such strong Jehovistic marks. Aramaisms also have been found in it.[c] The deterioration of Judah is remarkable in the history of the judges.

§ 175, *b*.

THE SAME SUBJECT CONTINUED.

The formula, (xvii. 6,) "*In these days there was no king in Israel, but every man did what was right in his own eyes,*" places the appendix, (xvii.—xxi.,) beyond doubt, in a period when Israel had enjoyed the prosperity of a regal government, and perhaps for a long time. The reference to a date in xviii. 30, "Until the day of the *captivity* of the land," does not agree with the reference in verse 31, "*All the time the house of God was in Shiloh.*" It is therefore suspicious. Were it not for this, however, it would point to the exile of the ten tribes. This is the opinion of Leclerc, Eichhorn, Rosenmüller, and Studer. It could not mean the capture of the ark by the Philistines, as Kimchi and

---

[a] *G. H. Hollmann*, Comment. in Carmen Deboræ; Lips. 1818, p. 6, sq. [See, also, American Bib. Rep. vol. i. *Palfrey*, l. c. vol. ii. p. 226, sqq.]

[b] *Ewald*, Zur Hohelied, p. 20. *Studer*, l. c. p. 439.

[c] Among the Aramaisms, the following have been reckoned: עֲמָמֶיךָ; v. 14. Comp. Neh. ix. 22, 24, Dan. iii. 4, sqq. [May not this be a more *poetical* form?] The plural termination in ין; v. 10. רִבָּה; v. 11, xi. 40 יְבַבֵּ; v. 28. דהר, for דור; v. 22. חרס, for שמש; xiv. 18. מה, for אשר ix. 48, which occurs, also, Num. xxiii. 3.

Hävernik suppose, nor their conquest of the Israelites, as Eckermann understands it.[a]

If the description, xix. 22, is imitated from Gen. xix. 4, sqq., as Tuch supposes, then this book must have been written in the times after the origin of the first four books of the Pentateuch.[b] The Deuteronomical formula, (xx. 13,) *to put away evil from Israel*, refers us to the time after the date of Deuteronomy.[c] But the lively and natural description seems to claim a higher antiquity, at least for the original documents. Chap. i. 21, seems to belong to the time after David: "The children of Benjamin did not drive out the Jebusites that inhabited Jerusalem, but the Jebusites dwell with the children of Benjamin unto this day." The statement, (verse 29,) "Neither did Ephraim drive out the Canaanites that dwelt in Gezer, but the Canaanites dwelt in Gezer among them," seems to belong to the time after Solomon. Studer finds marks in the geographical location of Shiloh (xxi. 12, 19) to show the author did not live in Palestine.

We cannot conjecture, with any certainty, at what time the appendix was added to the book. Augusti and Bertholdt think it was not added much before the time of Nehemiah and the assembly of scribes. Jahn and Paulus think Samuel was the author. [The book itself, however, (ii. 6—xvi. 31,) to judge from its general spirit and character, may be much older; and since it contains

---

[a] *Eckermann*, Theol. Beit. vol. v. pt. 1, p. 259. Exeget. Handbuch, vol. iii. p. 64.

[b] *Tuch*, l. c. p. 365, 366. But the story in Judges is very plain and natural.

[c] *Studer* (p. 455) takes notice of the later phrase, נשא נשים, for לקח נשים, which occurs nowhere else except in the books of Chronicles, Ezra, and Nehemiah. See the opinions of the ancient writers on the author of Judges, in *Carpzov*, l. c. p. 172, sqq., and the passage from Baba Bathra, in § 14, above, vol. i.

no direct reference, or even allusion, to the Pentateuch and book of Joshua, (except the doubtful case of v. 4, 5;) none to the Law Book or Law of Moses; none to the peculiar Mosaic institutions of the Jehovah *cultus*, such as worship in a single place, a Levitical priesthood, and formal rites; since, on the contrary, it alludes to traditions not preserved in the Pentateuch, — there seems reason for supposing this part of the book is older than the Pentateuch itself.]

CHAPTER IV.

THE BOOKS OF SAMUEL.[a]

§ 176.

NAME AND DIVISION.

THESE books — which, among the Jews, were reckoned as but one,[b] and were originally but one — bear the name of Samuel, not because he was their author, but the main subject and principal hero of the history contained in them.

---

[a] *Serrarii, Seb. Schmidii, Jo. Clerici, Maur.* Commentt.
Jo. Drusii Annotatt. in Locos diffic. Jos., Jud., et Sam.
Victorin. Strigelii Comm. in Librr. Sam., Reg., et Paralipp.; Lips. 1591, fol.
Casp. Sanctii Comm. in iv. Libr. Reg. et Paralipp.; 1624, fol.
Hensler, Erläuterungen des 1 B. Sam. u. d. Salom. Denksprüche; Hamb. 1795.
Exeget. Handbuch des A. T. 4 and 5 pt.
[*Geddes,* l. c. vol. ii.
Dr. *Palfrey,* l. c. vol. ii.]

[b] See *Origen,* cited above, vol. i. p. 87, note *b;* *Cyril* of Jerusalem, in vol. i. p. 97, sqq.; and *Jerome,* in vol. i. p. 111, sqq. The division into two

Abarbanel[a] says these books are called by Samuel's name, "because all things that occur in each book may, in a certain sense, be referred to Samuel—even the acts of Saul and David, for each of them was anointed by him, and, as it were, the work of his hands."

The title "Books of Samuel" is not very suitable; neither, indeed, is that which it has in the Vulgate and the Septuagint; namely, "The First and Second Books of the Kings," for that does not indicate the peculiar contents of the book. Bertholdt maintains that both titles are of more modern origin.[b]

§ 177.

CONTENTS OF THE BOOK.

This book contains the history of Samuel's administration as judge, and of the regal government introduced by his mediation, and established in the house of David. The history is divided into three parts:—

1. The history of Samuel's administration as prophet and judge; 1 Sam. i.—xii.

2. The history of Saul's government, and of the early destination of David, prospectively anointed king; 1 Sam. xii.—xxxi.

3. The history of David's government; 2 Sam. i.—xxiv.

There are chasms in the history between this and the previous book.

---

books, which has been general since the time of Bomberg, is made after the LXX. and Vulgate.

[a] Præf. in Lib. Sam. fol. 74, cited in *Carpzov*, l. c. p. 211. Compare the extract from Baba Bathra, fol. 14, col. 2, quoted above, vol. i. p. 31, sq.

[b] L. c. p. 890, sq.

[Jahn considers chap. xxi.—xxiv. of 2 Sam. an appendix, which he arranges in six divisions:—

1. Account of the famine sent in consequence of the unexpiated murder of the Gibeonites by Saul; xxi. 1—14.

2. A supplement to the account of David's wars; xxi. 15—22.

3. A triumphal hymn of David; xxii.

4. The last words of David; xxiii. 1—7.

5. List of his most remarkable heroes; xxiii. 8—39.

6. Census of the people, and its consequences; xxiv.]

§ 178.

CHARACTER OF THE NARRATIVE.

It is striking how little influence mythology has upon the history. There is but a single appearance of angels in the book, namely, 2 Sam. xxiv., where an angel brings the pestilence. The miraculous agency consists solely in the divine direction of affairs, brought about by means of the prophets and the oracle. In one passage, (1 Sam. xxviii.,)—the story of the witch of Endor,—a false prophet makes use of this ideal pragmatism, and the true historical connection remains doubtful. The predictions of later events are evidently inserted after the event has taken place. An example may be seen in the following curses denounced on the sons of Eli and on David:—

1 Sam. ii. 34—36. "And this shall be a sign unto thee, that shall come upon thy two sons, on Hophni and Phinehas: in one day they shall die, both of them. And I will raise me up a faithful priest, that shall do according to that which is in my heart and in my mind: and I will build him a sure house; and he shall walk before mine Anointed forever. And it shall come to pass, that every one that is left in

thy house, shall come and crouch to him for a piece of silver and a morsel of bread, and shall say, 'Put me, I pray thee, into one of the priests' offices, that I may eat a piece of bread.'"

1 Kings ii. 26, 27. "And unto Abiathar the priest said the king, 'Get thee to Anathoth, unto thine own fields; for thou art worthy of death: but I will not at this time put thee to death, because thou barest the ark of the Lord God before David my father, and because thou hast been afflicted in all wherein my father was afflicted.' So Solomon thrust out Abiathar from being priest unto the Lord; that he might fulfil the word of the Lord, which he spake concerning the house of Eli in Shiloh."

2 Sam. xii. 10, sq. "Because thou hast despised me, and hast taken the wife of Uriah the Hittite to be thy wife. Thus saith the Lord, 'Behold, I will raise up evil against thee out of thine own house, and I will take thy wives before thine eyes, and give them unto thy neighbor, ... in the sight of this sun. For thou didst it secretly: but I will do this thing before all Israel, and before the sun.'"

1 Kings xvi. 22. "So they spread Absalom a tent upon the top of the house; and Absalom went in unto his father's concubines in the sight of all Israel."

Elsewhere the narrative bears the marks of a genuine history, and where it is not partly derived from contemporaneous documents,[a] — as it is in some places, — it is yet drawn from an oral tradition, very lively and true, and is only disturbed and confused here and there. This tradition is in part supported by monuments, proverbs, and significant names. 1 Sam. vi. 18, the stone of Joshua, the Bethshemite, is mentioned as a monument of an important affair. Chap. vii. 12, Saul erects a stone, in honor of a victory, and calls it Ebenezer — Stone of Help. In x. 12, and xix. 24, we have the proverb, "Saul also among the prophets?" In 2 Sam. v. 6—9, the occasion of the following proverb is mentioned, "The blind and lame shall not come into the house."[b] A reason

---

[a] *Hensler*, l. c. p. 9.

[b] [The explanation of the matter is, perhaps, as follows: The Jebusites

is given for the name of *Samuel*—Heard by God, (1 Sam. i. 20.) The wife of Phinehas, hearing of the disasters befallen her country and family, calls her child *Ichabod* —Inglorious, (iv. 21.) Chap. xxiii. 28, Saul was pursuing David when a messenger informs him that the Philistines have invaded the land. His mind is divided between the two dangers; so the place is called Sela-hammah-lekoth—Rock of Escapes, (xxiii. 28.)[a]

The book is so rich in lively pictures of character, and descriptions, that, in this respect, it deviates from true history, and sometimes becomes biographical. The connection of affairs is sufficiently natural, though it may not be clearly enough carried out.

However, the chronology is very imperfect and legendary,[b] as it appears from the following examples: 1 Sam. vii. 2, "The time was long, for it was twenty years, and all the house of Israel lamented after the Lord;" xiii. 1, "Saul reigned one year, and when he had reigned two years, ... he chose," &c. 2 Sam. v. 4, "David reigned thirty years . . . . . . and he reigned forty years;"[c] xv. 7, "and it came to pass after forty years that Absa-

---

taunted David, (v. 6,) telling him, substantially, the blind and lame in the city were able to drive him away; so he could not conquer till he took them away. Therefore David offers a reward to him who shall first break into the fortress where the blind and lame were protected. When he had taken the citadel, he forbade such persons ever to enter it, as their presence reminded him of the disgraceful taunt. But see *Geddes*, in loc., and *Kennicott*, Diss. ii. p. 27, sqq.]

[a] See, also, 2 Sam. ii. 16, v. 20, vi. 8.

[b] See *De Wette*, Archäologie, § 27, 30.

[c] [In the first passage, a literal translation is, "*Saul, son of one year in his kingdom*," and of the second, "*David, a son of thirty years in his kingdom*," &c. Our translators, to give a good sense, say, in the last passage, "David was thirty years old when he *began to reign*," for which there is no authority in the Hebrew words. They often, in these books, take strange liberties with the text. See *Palfrey*, l. c. p. 267.]

lom said," &c. We are not told from what point of time the forty years are reckoned.

[These books abound with little natural touches, which constitute one of the chief beauties of the narrative. For example, the relation of Eli's death; of the fate of the wife of Phinehas, (iv. 10—22;) the conversation between David and his brethren, (xvii. 28,) are of this character. In 2 Sam. xiii. 30, is a remarkable instance of this; Absalom had murdered Amnon, his brother, at a feast, and, with the usual exaggerations, tidings came to David, "They have slain all the king's sons, and there is not one of them left." The account of Shimei is distressingly natural; when David was obliged to flee for his life, he assails him with dust, stones, and curses, (2 Sam. xvi. 5, sqq.;) but when he returns in triumph, this same Shimei is the first to supplicate mercy, (xix. 16.) The conduct of Zibah, and the fidelity of Mephibosheth, are highly characteristic, (2 Sam. xvi. 1—3, xix. 24.) It is in perfect fidelity to nature, that a *woman* finds, of a sudden, a hiding-place in the well for David's two friends, and so adroitly conceals them by spreading a cloth over the mouth of the well, and putting meal upon it, (xvii. 19.) The conduct of Ahithophel is characteristic of the statesman and courtier. He was in high repute for wisdom; "his counsel was as if a man inquired at the oracle of God;" but when his really wise plan was rejected for a traitor's scheme, "he gat him home to his house, put his household in order, and hanged himself," (2 Sam. xvii. 23; compare xvi. 23.)

Some passages savor of anthropomorphitic and mean conceptions of God; for example, (1 Sam. xv. 10—35,) God repents of making Saul king. He is represented as advising Samuel to dissemble, and act an untruth,

(xvi. 2, sq.) Samuel feared Saul would kill him, if he went openly to anoint David, as successor to the throne; so Jehovah says, "Take a heifer with you, and say, 'I am come to sacrifice to Jehovah.'" Jehovah refuses to answer Saul, because he had not kept his vow, but appears to be appeased when Saul condemns Jonathan to death for breaking the command, though Jonathan is not executed, and was not the only offender, (xiv. 19, sqq.) David was displeased because Jehovah had made a "breach upon Uzzah," (2 Sam. vi. 7.)

In some passages, unworthy actions are attributed to the Most High. He wished to destroy the sons of Eli; so they did not obey their father's instructions, (1 Sam. ii. 25.) He wished to bring evil upon Absalom, and so excites Hushai to defeat the good counsel of Ahithophel, (2 Sam. xvii. 14.) He moves David to number the people, having resolved to bring evil upon him, (xxiv. 1, sq.) But passages of this character are far from common in these books. In general, a beautiful, childlike, and trusting piety pervades them.

In some few instances, we discover a sacerdotal, though not a Levitical spirit. The Bethshemites are punished for looking into the ark, and fifty thousand and seventy are slain, if the text is correct, (vi. 19.) In 2 Sam. vi. 6, 7, the ark is jostled by the uneasy gait of the cattle which draw it; Uzzah, with the best intentions, puts out his hand to secure it, "and the anger of Jehovah was kindled against him, and God smote him there for his error." Obed-edom is blessed because the ark remains in his house. The evils which befell the Philistines while they kept the sacred ark, are detailed in a Levitical spirit. Dagon falls down before it; a "deadly destruction" consumes the people. The very cows, selected to bear the consecrated ark, — though never yoked before, and separated from their young, — take the road, from their own home, and proceed directly to a Jewish town. (See 1 Sam. v. vi.) A curse is denounced upon Saul, because he offered sacrifice when Samuel delayed to come. But the general spirit of the books is more liberal; there is little that savors of theocratical, still less of hierarchical despotism. Worship is free; men do not assemble at stated periodical festivals. There is no one place of public and national worship. On one occasion, the people offer a sacrifice unknown to the later Mosaic law. They pour water before Jehovah, (1 Sam. vii. 6.)[a] A few miraculous legends are mingled in the story: such are the accounts of David's wonderful preservation, (1 Sam. xix. 20, sqq.,) when three companies of messengers, sent to take him, receive the Spirit of God, and prophesy; Saul himself is overcome in the same manner, and prophesies, lying naked all day and all night. To this class belong the stories of the witch of Endor, (xxviii.,) of the pestilence, (2 Sam. xxiv.,) and of the oracular responses to David, (1 Sam. xxiii. 2—12.) Sometimes he inquires by means of an ephod, (xxx. 7,) but often without it, (2 Sam. ii. 1, v. 19.)]

§ 179, *a*.

TRACES OF DIFFERENT DOCUMENTS.

It is perfectly obvious that the following passages do not agree together: In 1 Sam. xvi. 14—23, David is Saul's musician and armor-bearer, and is greatly beloved by him: in xvii. 31—40, he arms David for the contest

---

[a] [But see *Palfrey*, l. c. p. 261.]

with Goliah; but in xvii. 55—xviii. 5, David is wholly unknown to Saul, and is afterwards placed by him over the soldiers.

1 Sam. xvi. 14—23. "But the Spirit of the Lord departed from Saul, and an evil spirit from the Lord troubled him. And Saul's servants said unto him, 'Behold now, an evil spirit from God troubleth thee. Let our lord now command thy servants, which are before thee, to seek out a man who is a cunning player on a harp: and it shall come to pass, when the evil spirit from God is upon thee, that he shall play with his hand, and thou shalt be well.' And Saul said unto his servants, 'Provide me now a man that can play well, and bring him to me.' Then answered one of the servants, and said, 'Behold, I have seen a son of Jesse the Bethlehemite, that is cunning in playing, and a mighty valiant man, and a man of war, and prudent in matters, and a comely person, and the Lord is with him.'

"Wherefore Saul sent messengers unto Jesse, and said, 'Send me David thy son, which is with the sheep.' And Jesse took an ass laden with bread, and a bottle of wine, and a kid, and sent them by David his son unto Saul. And David came to Saul, and stood before him: and he loved him greatly; and he became his armor-bearer. And Saul sent to Jesse, saying, 'Let David, I pray thee, stand before me; for he hath found favor in my sight.' And it came to pass, when the evil spirit from God was upon Saul, that David took a harp, and played with his hand: so Saul was refreshed, and was well, and the evil spirit departed from him."

Chap. xvii. 55—58. "And when Saul saw David go forth against the Philistine, he said unto Abner, the captain of the host, 'Abner, whose son is this youth?' And Abner said, 'As thy soul liveth, O king, I cannot tell.' And the king said, 'Inquire thou whose son the stripling is.' And as David returned from the slaughter of the Philistine, Abner took him, and brought him before Saul, with the head of the Philistine in his hand. And Saul said to him, 'Whose son art thou, thou young man?' And David answered, 'I am the son of thy servant Jesse the Bethlehemite.'"

Chap. xviii. 5. "And David went out whithersoever Saul sent him, and behaved himself wisely, and Saul set him over the men of war."

Chap. xviii. 12—16. "And Saul was afraid of David, because the Lord was with him, and was departed from Saul. Therefore Saul removed him from him, and made him his captain over a thousand;

and he went out and came in before the people. And David behaved himself wisely in all his ways; and the Lord was with him. Wherefore, when Saul saw that he behaved himself very wisely, he was afraid of him. But all Israel and Judah loved David, because he went out and came in before them."

Here, then, we can distinguish two different accounts, from which, however, we must separate the interpolation, (xvii. 54,) "And David took the head of the Philistine, and brought it to Jerusalem; but he put his armor in his tent." It is evident this does not agree with xxi. 10, sqq., and 2 Sam. v. 6, sqq. Eichhorn thinks the verse an interpolation. Bertholdt thinks the original has been preserved in the Vatican codex of the Septuagint, where 1 Sam. xvii. 12—31, and 55—xviii. 6, is omitted.[a]

Elsewhere in the book two different sources are discovered in the history of David. 1 Sam. xxiii. 19, the Ziphites inform Saul that David is on the hill of Hachilah, on the *south* of the desert. In 1 Sam. xxvi. 1, they tell Saul he hides in the hill of Hachilah on the *east* of the desert. So, 1 Sam. xxiv., David spares Saul's life *in the cave;* 1 Sam. xxvi., he does the same thing *in Saul's camp.* These accounts are so closely similar that we cannot fail to see they are two different legendary stories of the same event.

So the account, 1 Sam. xxi. 10, sqq., where David flees to Achish, and pretends to be mad, because he is suspected by his friends, excludes the later account, xxvii. 2, sqq., where David dwells with Achish, who gives him the command of Ziklag as a reward, and xxix. 1, sqq., where the chiefs of the Philistines are suspicious of him.

If we now turn back to the history of Saul, we see traces of different documents there; for example,

---

[a] *Eichhorn*, § 477. *Bertholdt*, p. 897.

1 Sam. ix. 1—x. 16,—where Samuel, by the divine command, anoints Saul,—differs from 1 Sam. viii. x. 17—27, where Samuel, compelled by the demands of the people, chooses Saul as king, by lot. With the first document (ix. 1—x. 16) agrees 1 Sam. xi., where Saul, in consequence of his victory over the Ammonites, is publicly confirmed in the dignity of king: to the latter (viii. x. 17—27) belongs chap. xii., where Samuel cannot conceal his disapprobation of the appointment of a king. The statement, (xii. 12,) "*Jehovah your God was your King*," agrees perfectly with viii. 6, sqq., where Jehovah says to Samuel, "They have not rejected thee, but...... me." Samuel's death is related twice—xxv. 1, "And Samuel died, and all Israel assembled and lamented him, and buried him in his house at Ramah." This is related in almost the same words in xxviii. 3. The following accounts of Saul's death differ from one another:—

1 Sam. xxxi. 2—6, 8—13. "And the Philistines followed hard upon Saul and upon his sons; and the Philistines slew Jonathan, and Abinadab, and Malchi-shua, Saul's sons. And the battle went sore against Saul, and the archers hit him; and he was sore wounded of the archers. Then said Saul unto his armor-bearer, 'Draw thy sword, and thrust me through therewith; lest these uncircumcised come and thrust me through, and abuse me.' But his armor-bearer would not; for he was sore afraid. Therefore Saul took a sword, and fell upon it. And when his armor-bearer saw that Saul was dead, he fell

2 Sam. i. 2—12. "It came even to pass on the third day, that, behold, a man came out of the camp from Saul with his clothes rent, and earth upon his head: and so it was, when he came to David, that he fell to the earth, and did obeisance. And David said unto him, 'From whence comest thou?' And he said unto him, 'Out of the camp of Israel am I escaped.' And David said unto him, 'How went the matter? I pray thee, tell me.' And he answered, 'That the people are fled from the battle, and many of the people also are fallen, and dead; and Saul and Jonathan his son are dead also.' And David

likewise upon his sword, and died with him. So Saul died, and his three sons, and his armor-bearer, and all his men, that same day together. And it came to pass on the morrow, when the Philistines came to strip the slain, that they found Saul and his three sons fallen in Mount Gilboa. And they cut off his head, and stripped off his armor, and sent into the land of the Philistines round about, to publish it in the house of their idols, and among the people. And they put his armor in the house of Ashtaroth: and they fastened his body to the wall of Beth-shan.

"And when the inhabitants of Jabesh-gilead heard of that which the Philistines had done to Saul, all the valiant men arose, and went all night, and took the body of Saul, and the bodies of his sons, from the wall of Beth-shan, and came to Jabesh, and burnt them there. And they took their bones, and buried them under a tree at Jabesh, and fasted seven days."

said unto the young man that told him, 'How knowest thou that Saul and Jonathan his son be dead?' And the young man that told him said, 'As I happened by chance upon Mount Gilboa, behold, Saul leaned upon his spear; and lo, the chariots and horsemen followed hard after him. And when he looked behind him, he saw me, and called unto me. And I answered, "Here am I." And he said unto me, "Who art thou?" And I answered him, "I am an Amalekite." He said unto me again, "Stand, I pray thee, upon me, and slay me: for anguish is come upon me, because my life is yet whole in me." So I stood upon him, and slew him, because I was sure that he could not live after that he was fallen: and I took the crown that was upon his head, and the bracelet that was on his arm, and have brought them hither unto my lord.' Then David took hold on his clothes, and rent them; and likewise all the men that were with him. And they mourned and wept, and fasted until even, for Saul and for Jonathan his son, and for the people of the Lord, and for the house of Israel; because they were fallen by the sword."

2 Sam. iii. 14, has the number *one hundred*, where 1 Sam. xviii. 27, has *two hundred*.

2 Sam. v. 1—3. "Then came all the tribes of Israel to David

unto Hebron, and spake, saying, 'Behold, we are thy bone and thy flesh. Also in time past, when Saul was king over us, thou wast he that leddest out and broughtest in Israel: and the Lord said to thee, "Thou shalt feed my people Israel, and thou shalt be a captain over Israel."' So all the elders of Israel came to the king to Hebron; and King David made a league with them in Hebron before the Lord: and they anointed David king over Israel."

Here it is not supposed that Samuel had previously anointed David, and consequently this passage does not belong to the same document with 1 Sam. xvi. 1—13, where the anointing is related. 2 Sam. viii. seems to be different from chap. x., for, in the former, not only the Syrians, but the Ammonites also, are conquered by the citizens of Zoba, (verse 12,) though the Syrians might rise again. Besides, chap. viii. is distinguished by the brief style of its narrative, which resembles a chronicle, as in v. 6—25, and xxi. 15—22. In xxi. 8, *Michal* is written by mistake for *Merab*. This, perhaps, is not written by the same author who has given us the other notices of Michal, (1 Sam. xviii. 19, xxv. 44, 2 Sam. iii. 14, 15, vi. 23.)[a]

[a] *Gramberg* (l. c. vol. ii. p. 80, sqq.) thus separates the two accounts:—

Narrative A. 1 Sam. ix. 1—x. 16, xi. 1—15, xiii.—xv. xvi. 1—23, (verse 21 is an interpolation by the compiler,) xvii. 1—53, (verse 54 is likewise an interpolation,) xviii. 6—30, xix.—xxv. 42, xxviii. 3—25, xxxi. 2 Sam. v. 6—12, vi.—viii. xxi. xxiv.

Narrative B. 1 Sam. viii. x. 17—27, xii. xvii. 55—xviii. 5, xxv. 43, 44, xxvi. xxvii. xxviii. 1, 2, xxix. xxx. 2 Sam. i.—iv. v. 1—5, ix.—xx. *Stähelin* (in *Tholuck*, Theol. Anzeig. for 1838, p. 526) partially agrees with him, and admits two accounts. One corresponds to Gramberg's narrative B. To this belong 1 Sam. iii. vii. 2—viii. x. 17—xii. 25, perhaps xiv. 47—52, certainly xv. and part of xvii. xviii., and still farther, xx. xxvi. xxvii. xxix. xxx. The other comprises the rest of the first of Samuel, the whole of the second, and the first book of Kings i. ii.

According to *Bertholdt*, (p. 894, sqq.,) 1 Sam. i.—vii. viii.—xvi. and xvii.—xxx. are independent documents. But this opinion does not agree with that given above. In 2 Samuel, chap. i.—iv., containing the history of David's

§ 179, *b*.

[THE SAME SUBJECT CONTINUED.

There are other numerous inconsistencies in these books, which can be explained only on the supposition that the author drew from various sources, whose testimony was imperfect, and often conflicting; that he sometimes relied upon unwritten tradition, and made use of lyric compositions and popular sayings in constructing his narrative. Sometimes his materials failed him altogether, especially in the history of Samuel, and the early administration of Saul, in which he drew upon his im-

---

government at Hebron, are separated from the other sources, which *Eichhorn* maintains form a short biography of David, (1 Sam. xxxi. 2 Sam. v. vi. 3—11, vii. viii. x. xi. 1, xii. 30, 31, xxi. 18—22, xxiii. 8—39, xxiv.) These passages are all distinguished by a summary character, which they have in common, and are connected together by this, as he thinks. But this is not true of all of them; for example, of 1 Sam. xxxi. 2 Sam. vii. x. xxiv.; and in some passages the obvious similarity fails, (xxi. 1—14, 15—17,) and other passages are, by their statements of facts, necessarily connected with them. Compare 1 Sam. xxxi. with xxviii. 4; 2 Sam. v. 13—16, with iii. 2—5; 2 Sam. vi. 3—11, with verses 12—20, and 1 Sam. vii. 1; 2 Sam. xi. 1, xii. 30, 31, with the verses between them; especially compare the words, "and David remained at Jerusalem," with verse 2, sqq., which relate the story of Uriah, and xii. 27—29, where David takes Rabbah. (See the application of this hypothesis to the Chronicles, in § 192.) Still further, to ascertain the true connection of the book, compare 2 Sam. i. with 1 Sam. xxx.; 2 Sam. iii. 14, with 1 Sam. xxv. 44, where there is a difference in names; 2 Sam. iv. 4, with ix. 1, sqq.; 2 Sam. xii. 11, 12, with xvi. 22; 2 Sam. xxi. 12, with 1 Sam. xxxi. 12, 13.

The author of the critical essay on the second book of Samuel, in *Paulus*, Memorabilien, vol. viii. p. 61, sqq., thinks the books are made up of small, independent pieces. *Hävernik*, (l. c. p. 121, sqq.,) who does not acknowledge any of those discrepancies, maintains there are two principal sources of the book, one, the *sayings of Samuel, Nathan, and Gad*, cited in 1 Ch. xxix. 29, from which the prophetic elements are derived; the other, *the annals of David's reign*, to which the minute biographical and political accounts belong. The existence of the latter is conjectured from 2 Sam. viii. 17. See below, § 192, *b*.

agination, or passed over a period in silence. The writer has a strong leaning towards the sacerdotal interest; though this tendency is by no means so strong as in the Chronicles.

1. *The History of Samuel.*—Though Samuel was a priest, he was not of Levitical descent. His father is called an Ephraimite; and Ramah, the subsequent place of Samuel's residence, is nowhere called a Levitical city. It is true the later writer, in 1 Chron. vi. 18—28, claims a Levitical birth for Samuel, and even descent from Aaron; but this is conformable with the general spirit of that book. Samuel is a mythical character, like Orpheus and Minos, and not the subject of exact historical information. Like them he stands in the period where history and mythology interpenetrate. Thus his birth is a prodigy, like that of Isaac and Samson, (i. 9—11, 17, 19, 20;) his communication with God is peculiar and miraculous, (iii. 1—14, 19, 21, viii. 7—9, 22, ix. 15, sqq.;) even after his death "his body prophesied," (xxviii. 3, 14—16;) he is consecrated before he is born, (i. 11.) If Samuel offers a sacrifice, or admonishes the people, Jehovah thunders to confirm his authority, (vii. 10, xii. 16, sqq.) He makes kings, and unmakes them, in the name of Jehovah. The writer loved the mythical more than the historical element, for he gives a detailed account of what preceded the birth of Samuel; repeats his mother's song of joy at that event, but gives scarce any details of his long administration of forty years. But the song (ii. 1—10) he puts into Hannah's mouth is entirely inappropriate. There is but a single strain which relates to her peculiar circumstances—verse 5, "the barren hath borne seven." To judge from its

character, and from such passages as the following,—"the bows of the mighty men are broken, and they that stumbled are girded with strength;" "he raiseth up the poor out of the dust," &c.,—it might be inferred this was a triumphal song, more properly put into the mouth of some warrior of humble origin and inferior resources, who had gained a victory over some powerful opponent. The mention of the KING and the *Messiah* (verse 10) betrays its recent and spurious birth.

This book, however, may be taken as descriptive of the manners of the Israelites at some period of their history. Here we find no traces of the Mosaic institutions. There is *one annual feast* at Shiloh, (i. 3, 7, 21, ii. 19,) where a *yearly* sacrifice is offered. There is a chasm between chap. iii. and iv., perhaps of many years. In iv. 1, Samuel assembles the people for war, at a time when he had no authority, that is mentioned. But he takes no further concern in the management of affairs, and does not once appear in the history of the next twenty years, (iv. 2—vii. 2.) In the mean time the ark reappears, as the miracle-worker, and 5070 men—if the text is correct—die in a little village because they looked upon it, (vi. 19.) It is said, in vii. 15, Samuel judged Israel all the days of his life, though, in viii. 1, his sons judge wickedly; and he lived some years after the consecration of Saul, and even after that of David, though the latter was not anointed until the son of Saul, born after his coronation, had grown up. Only four places are named in which Samuel judges the nation, and they are all within the limits of the tribe of Benjamin, (vii. 16, 17.) In xv. 35, it is said Samuel did not see Saul again till the day of his death; that is, he *never* saw him again; but, xix. 18—24, Saul prophesied before Samuel, and lay down naked all day and night before him.[a] These statements show very clearly that we have not before us a history of those times, but only a collection of mythical and historical materials, from which, however, it is scarce possible to collect the true course of events.[b]

II. *The History of Saul.*—The first time Samuel sees Saul, he knows he is to be king. Jehovah says, "Behold the man I told thee of," (ix. 17.) The next day he is privately anointed king, (ix. 1—x. 16.) Then follows a passage, (verses 17—27,) apparently from another source, in which Samuel chooses Saul by lot, making no reference to the former choice. The style in ix. 1—x. 16, differs slightly from the rest of the book; *Elohim* is more frequently used for the Deity. The statements respecting the occasion of the change from the government by judges to that by kings are at variance; viii. 5, it is because Samuel is old, and his children are not suitable rulers; xii. 12, because the nation is in distress, for Nahash, the king of Ammon, had invaded Judea; while from xi. 1, we learn this invasion took place *after* the election of Saul, and not *before* it. There is some geographical confusion in x. 2, sqq., where Saul, in going from Zuph to Gibeah, must pass by Rachel's tomb, at Zelzah, near Beth-lehem, thence to the plain of Tabor, and thence home to Gibeah, and actually accomplishes the journey in one day.[c] Saul is

---

[a] But see Dr. *Palfrey*, in loc.

[b] There is little or no reason for the severe strictures sometimes made upon Samuel; e. g. *Schiller*, Neue Thalia, vol. iv. p. 94, sqq.; the Wolfenbüttel Fragmentist, ed. *Schmidt*, p. 200, sq.; and *Vatke*, Bib. Theol. p. 300, sqq. His administration, to judge from the little we know of it, was wise and profitable to the people.

[c] See *Leclerc*, in loc., and *Palfrey*, vol. ii. p. 253.

evidently a *young man* when anointed by Samuel, (ix. 1, 2;) only *a year* old, according to the present text of xiii. 1; and we hear nothing of his exploits, except his assembling the people and receiving their confirmation of his authority, (xi. 1—15,) until he has a son capable of commanding a garrison, (xiii. 2.) When Saul was first anointed, the Spirit of God came upon him, and he prophesied (x. 9):—

"And it was so, that when he had turned his back to go from Samuel, God gave him another heart: and when they came thither to the hill, behold, a company of prophets met him; and the Spirit of God came upon him, and he prophesied among them. And it came to pass when all that knew him beforetime saw, that, behold, he prophesied among the prophets, then the people said one to another, 'What is this that is come unto the son of Kish? Is Saul also among the prophets?' And one of the same place answered and said, 'But who is their father?' Therefore it became a proverb, 'Is Saul also among the prophets?'"

In xix. 20—24, we find a similar account, though later in Saul's life:—

"And Saul sent messengers to take David: and when they saw the company of the prophets prophesying, and Samuel standing as appointed over them, the Spirit of God was upon the messengers of Saul, and they also prophesied. And when it was told Saul, he sent other messengers, and they prophesied likewise. And Saul sent messengers again the third time, and they prophesied also. Then went he also to Ramah, and came to a great well that is in Sechu: and he asked and said, 'Where are Samuel and David?' And one said, 'Behold, they be at Naioth, in Ramah.' And he went thither to Naioth, in Ramah: and the Spirit of God was upon him also, and he went on and prophesied, until he came to Naioth, in Ramah. And he stripped off his clothes also, and prophesied before Samuel in like manner, and lay down naked all that day and all that night. Wherefore they say, 'Is Saul also among the prophets?'"

The statement (xiii. 19) that there was no smith in Israel, seems somewhat at variance with the account in

xi. 8, that Saul assembled 330,000 soldiers, and still more with that of the formidable force the Philistines brought against the nation—30,000 chariots, (xiii. 5.)

The passage, xiv. 47—52, stands isolated, and is evidently out of its proper connection; for in verse 48, Saul conquers the Amalekites, and the next chapter contains an account of the beginning and progress of the expedition which was undertaken at Samuel's command.

This part of the book, also, may, perhaps, contain a fair account of the manners which prevailed, or were supposed to prevail, at some period of Jewish history. We do not find the Levitical customs of the later Mosaic books. Saul builds altars, (xiv. 35,)[a] and asks counsel *directly* of God, (verses 37, 41;) the Mosaic law is never referred to, nor known; at least, no traces of it are left. In general, it may be said of the history of Samuel and Saul, that it is a collection of accounts, mythical and historical, descriptive of the end of the government by judges, and the beginning of the kingdom. But out of such confusion who shall disentangle for us the thread of history? Two facts, however, may be considered as established; namely, that Samuel the Ephraimite was the last of the judges; that Saul, the tall and well-favored son of Kish, was the first king. It is natural to believe that Samuel reluctantly yielded his power, as the nation passed from the theocratical to the regal government, and that he attempted to throw obstacles in the way of his successor, embarrass his proceedings, and even set up a rival who promised greater fidelity to the sacerdotal interest. There seems little reason for the belief that Samuel was instrumental in establishing the royal government of Saul, or that he wrote a constitution

[a] But see *Palfrey*, vol. ii. p. 272.

of the realm, (x. 25.) It is easy to see how such a report might originate at a later period, and be preserved. The solemn address of Samuel at Gilgal (chap. xii.) is probably a rhetorical fiction, as well as the present form of the admonition against a regal government, (viii. 10—18,) which this writer seems to affect as little as a popular government is affected by the author of Judges, (xvii.—xxi.)]

§ 180.

TIME OF THE COMPOSITION OF THIS BOOK.

The references to a later time are indefinite; for example, *unto this day*, (1 Sam. v. 5, vi. 18, xxvii. 6, xxx. 25, 2 Sam. iv. 3, vi. 8.) "Therefore it became a proverb—'Is Saul among the prophets?'" (1 Sam. x. 12, xix. 24.) "Beforetime in Israel, when a man went to inquire of God, thus he spake—'Come, and let us go to the SEER;' for a PROPHET was beforetime called a SEER," (1 Sam. ix. 9, xiii. 18.)

The following prophecy (1 Sam. ii. 35) was probably first written in or after Solomon's time:—

> "And I will raise me up a faithful priest, that shall do according to that which is in mine heart and in my mind; and I will build him a sure house; and he shall walk before mine Anointed forever."

There is a mistake made in the insertion of the following unsuitable and anachronistic passage (1 Sam. ii. 1—10):—

> "And Hannah prayed, and said, 'My heart rejoiceth in the Lord; mine horn is exalted in the Lord; my mouth is enlarged over mine enemies; because I rejoice in thy salvation. There is none holy as the Lord: for there is none beside thee; neither is there any rock like our God. Talk no more so exceeding proudly; let not arrogancy come out of your mouth: for the Lord is a God of knowledge,

and by him actions are weighed. The bows of the mighty men are broken, and they that stumbled are girded with strength. They that were full have hired out themselves for bread; and they that were hungry ceased: so that the barren hath borne seven; and she that hath many children is waxed feeble. The Lord killeth, and maketh alive: he bringeth down to the grave, and bringeth up. The Lord maketh poor, and maketh rich: he bringeth low, and lifteth up. He raiseth up the poor out of the dust, and lifteth up the beggar from the dunghill, to set them among princes, and to make them inherit the throne of glory: for the pillars of the earth are the Lord's, and he hath set the world upon them. He will keep the feet of his saints, and the wicked shall be silent in darkness; for by strength shall no man prevail. The adversaries of the Lord shall be broken to pieces; out of heaven shall he thunder upon them: the Lord shall judge the ends of the earth; and he shall give strength unto his King, and exalt the horn of his Anointed.'"

This brings us down still later; so does the promise relating to the royal family of David, (2 Sam. vii.,) "I will set up thy seed after thee; I will establish his kingdom. My mercy shall not depart away from him. Thine house and thy kingdom shall be established forever."[a] The statistical notice, (1 Sam. xxviii. 6,) "Ziklag pertaineth unto the kings of Judah unto this day," leads us to the time after the separation of the kingdom. The mistake in respect to Jerusalem, in 1 Sam. xvii. 54, —where David brings Goliah's head to that city, as if it were the national capital, while it was still in the hands of the Jebusites, —could not possibly be made till long after David. But the expressions *Israel* and *Judah* belong to the time of David.[b]

From the expression *Jehovah Zebaoth*—Jehovah of

---

[a] Comp. Ps. lxxxix., and see *Otmar*, in *Henke's* Magazin. vol. iv. pt. 2, p. 354. *Bertholdt*, p. 915.

[b] 1 Sam. xviii. 16, 2 Sam. xxiv. 1. Comp. 2 Sam. v. 1—5, xix. 41, xx. 2. David's death is not mentioned, but this does not prove the author wrote soon after it, as *Hävernik* supposes, p. 144.

hosts—(1 Sam. i. 3,) we may conclude it was written later than the book of Judges. But otherwise it is not distinguished by any later usage.[a] The book must have been composed before the time when the Levitical and Deuteronomical spirit became prevalent; for there is no trace of this spirit in the book.[b] [In 1 Ch. xxix. 29, it is said, "The acts of David, first and last, are written in the book of Samuel the seer, and in the book of Nathan the prophet, and in the book of Gad the seer." Here the reference to the books of Samuel appears more certain than the statement of the authorship of the books; for the citations in Chronicles are so uncertain. On the authority of this passage, many Jewish writers, with Theodoret, Procopius, Gregory the Great, Isidore, Eucherius, with the moderns Walther, Calovius, Hugo, De Lyra, Vatablè, Sixtus Sinensis, Cajetan, Cornelius à Lapide, and others, think Samuel wrote the first twenty-four chapters, and Nathan and Gad the rest. But Abarbanel, Jacob, Ben Chajim, and Grotius, make Jeremiah the author. Spinoza, Hobbes, Simon, and Leclerc, dissent from these opinions.] [c]

---

[a] Comp. 1 Sam. i. 1, and xxv. 14, with Judg. xiii. 2.

[b] Comp. 1 Sam. xi. 15, xiii. 8—14, xiv. 35, xvi. 2, 2 Sam. xv. 7, sq., with the passages referred to in § 184, note *a*. Does not the rareness of Chaldaisms in the book compel us to date it earlier than the end of Manasseh's reign? *Bertholdt* (p. 924) thinks that וַיִּשַּׁרְנָה (1 Sam. vi. 12; comp. Gen. xxx. 28, *Ewald*, Kr. Gr. p. 270) is not to be taken for a Chaldaism. But it must be remarked that יַעְשְׁרֶנּוּ occurs, instead of יַעְשִׁירֶנּוּ, 1 Sam. xvii. 25; יְהוֹשִׁיעַ, instead of יוֹשִׁיעַ, verse 47; the infin. with לְ, instead of the finite verb, xiv. 21; יִנָּתֶּן, instead of יֻתַּן, 2 Sam. xxi. 6· תִּתַּבָּר, xxii. 27; וַתַּזְּרֵנִי, verse 40. Comp. *De Wette*, Com. üb. Ps. xviii. 27, 40.

[c] [See *Carpzov*, p. 213, sqq. See, also, vol. i. § 14.]

CHAPTER V.

THE BOOKS OF THE KINGS.[a]

§ 181.

NAME AND DIVISION.

Among the Jews, these books likewise make but one,[b] and the division into two books, which was made in the Alexandrine and Latin versions, and followed in Christian editions, is entirely arbitrary. It is self-evident that the name[c] merely indicates the contents.

§ 182.

THE CONTENTS.

It contains the history of all the kings after David until the exile of the people.

1. First, it contains the history of Solomon's administration, commencing with his ascent to the throne, consequently with the last times of David; 1 Kings i.—xi.

2. Then follows the history of the revolt of the ten tribes, and of the government of the two kingdoms,—placed opposite one another, — with particular notice of

---

[a] *Serrarii, Vict. Strigelii* Comment. *Seb. Schmidii* Annotat. in Libb. Reg. *Io. Clerici, Maur.* Comment.
Seb. Leonhardi, 'Υπομνήματα in Libb. Reg.; Erf. 1606; Lips. 1610, 1614
Franc. de Mendoza, Comm. in Libb. Reg.; Col. 1634, fol.
Exegetisches Handbuch des A. T. 8 and 9 pt.
Geddes, l. c. vol. ii.

[b] See *Origen*, as above, vol. i. p. 89, sqq., and *Jerome*, p. 111, sqq.

[c] ספר מלכים; *Βασιλειῶν τρίτη καὶ τετάρτη*; Regum iii. and iv.

the prophets who were active in the kingdom of Israel. This history comes down to the overthrow of the kingdom of Israel; 1 Kings xii.—2 Kings xvii.

3. Finally, there comes the history of the surviving kingdom of Judah till its destruction, with an account of the fate of the rest of the nation which remained in the land, and of King Jehoiakim, who was retained a prisoner at Babylon; 2 Kings xviii.—xxv.

According to Eichhorn,[a] in this part of the book, the author has only treated of the history of Judah, because it was connected to, and contemporary with, that of the kingdom of Israel, which was his main subject. But this is a false explanation of the relation of the history of the two kingdoms in reference to particulars, — though the relation, as a matter of fact, is not to be denied, — and the true ground lies merely in this, that the history of the kingdom of Israel is more rich in events, and the influence of the prophets upon it is more important.[b]

§ 183.

CHARACTER OF THE NARRATIVE.

Here Hebrew history rather retrogrades than makes any such advance as we should expect from the increase of literature after the time of David. Besides the authentic historical accounts which are similar to those in the books of Samuel,[c] the history of Solomon contains some myths: —

Chap. iii. 5—15. "In Gibeon the Lord appeared to Solomon in a dream by night: and God said, 'Ask what I shall give thee.' And

---

[a] § 481. [b] *De Wette*, Beiträge, vol. i. p. 31.
[c] 1 Kings i. ii. iv. vi. vii. ix. 10—28, &c.

Solomon said, 'Thou hast showed unto thy servant David my father great mercy, according as he walked before thee in truth, and in righteousness, and in uprightness of heart with thee; and thou hast kept for him this great kindness, that thou hast given him a son to sit on his throne, as it is this day. And now, O Lord, my God, thou hast made thy servant king instead of David my father; and I am but a little child: I know not how to go out or come in. And thy servant is in the midst of thy people which thou hast chosen, a great people, that cannot be numbered nor counted for multitude. Give, therefore, thy servant an understanding heart to judge thy people, that I may discern between good and bad: for who is able to judge this thy so great a people?' And the speech pleased the Lord, that Solomon had asked this thing. And God said unto him, 'Because thou hast asked this thing, and hast not asked for thyself long life; neither hast asked riches for thyself, nor hast asked the life of thine enemies; but hast asked for thyself understanding to discern judgment; behold, I have done according to thy words: lo, I have given thee a wise and an understanding heart; so that there was none like thee before thee, neither after thee shall any arise like unto thee. And I have also given thee that which thou hast not asked, both riches and honor: so that there shall not be any among the kings like unto thee all thy days. And if thou wilt walk in my ways, to keep my statutes and my commandments, as thy father David did walk, then I will lengthen thy days.' And Solomon awoke; and behold, it was a dream. And he came to Jerusalem, and stood before the ark of the covenant of the Lord, and offered up burnt-offerings, and offered peace-offerings, and made a feast to all his servants."

Chap. ix. 1—9. "And it came to pass, when Solomon had finished the building of the house of the Lord, and the king's house, and all Solomon's desire which he was pleased to do, that the Lord appeared to Solomon the second time, as he had appeared unto him at Gibeon. And the Lord said unto him, 'I have heard thy prayer and thy supplication that thou hast made before me: I have hallowed this house, which thou hast built, to put my name there forever; and mine eyes and my heart shall be there perpetually. And if thou wilt walk before me, as David thy father walked, in integrity of heart, and in uprightness, to do according to all that I have commanded thee, and wilt keep my statutes and my judgments; then I will establish the throne of thy kingdom upon Israel forever, as I promised to David thy father, saying, "There shall not fail thee a man upon the throne of Israel." But if ye shall at all turn from following me, ye or your children, and will not keep my commandments and my statutes which I have set before you, but go and serve other gods, and worship them; then will I cut off Israel out of the land which I have given them; and this house, which I have hallowed for my name, will I cast out of my sight; and Israel shall be a proverb and a by-word among all people: and at this house, which is high, every one that passeth by it shall be astonished, and shall hiss; and they shall say, "Why hath the Lord done thus unto this land, and to this house?" and they shall answer, "Because they forsook the Lord their God, who brought forth their fathers out of the land of Ægypt, and have taken hold upon other gods, and have worshipped them, and served them: therefore hath the Lord brought upon them all this evil."' "

Chap. viii. also contains mythical accounts; namely, the miraculous smoke which filled the temple, and the immense sacrifices Solomon offered—22,000 oxen, and 120,000 sheep, if the text is authentic. The book also contains exaggerations; for example, v. 1—14, where it appears Solomon had raised 30,000 men to work at Lebanon, 10,000 being there at one time. Besides these, the account gives him 70,000 porters "that bare burdens," and "80,000 hewers in the mountains," with the addition of 3,300 officers to rule the workmen. The same must be said of chap. x. The queen of Sheba gave Solomon one hundred and twenty talents of gold, equal to $2,917,080, besides "very great store" of spices and precious stones, (x. 10.) His annual income was 666 talents of gold, that is, if the weight is intended, 83,250 pounds of gold; and if the talent is the sum of money, $16,189,794. This did not include the profit from his merchant vessels, from the spice merchants, from the kings of Arabia, and the governors of his provinces. The accounts, also, of his furniture are perhaps exaggerated.

Indeed, in the following history, there is no want of credible accounts and lively portraiture; but the greatest part of the narrative consists of prophetic legends, and dry chronicles, interwoven with pragmatic remarks. The author had evidently a prophetic and didactic tendency. The chief object he aimed at was to set forth the efficacy of the prophets.[a] He dwells at length on the sayings and doings of the prophets: In 1 Kings xi. 29—40, the prophet Ahijah excites Jeroboam to stimulate the ten tribes to revolt; xii. 22, Shemaiah, the man of God, forbids Rehoboam to fight the ten tribes, so the army disperses; chap. xiii. contains the mythical story of prophecy against the altar at Beth-el, its wonderful destruction, and the death of the false prophet, with other adventures; in xiv. 1—16, Ahijah foretells the destruction of the posterity of Jeroboam; in xvi. 1—13, is Jehu's prophecy against Baasha, and its fulfilment; chap. xvii.—xix., the story of the prophets Elijah and Elisha; xx. 35—43, the symbolical action of an unknown prophet; xxi. 17—29, the prophecy of Elijah against Ahab; xxii. 5—40, the adventures of Micaiah the prophet, his predictions, and their fulfilment; in 2 Kings i. ii. and iii. 11—viii. 15, ix. 1, sqq., and xiii. 14—21, are the adventures of Elisha the prophet, his predictions, and their fulfilment; xix. 2—7, and 20—37, xx. 1—19, the oracles of Isaiah, and their fulfilment; xxi. 10—15, the oracles of certain unknown prophets; xxii. 14—20, the sayings of Huldah the prophetess. We find pragmatic remarks: In 1 Kings xiii. 33, 34, the house of Jeroboam was cut off because he made priests

[a] See *Kern*, On the Principal Point of View in the Books of Kings, in *Bengel's* Neu. Archiv. vol. ii. p. 2, sqq. *Gesenius*, Com. z. Jes. vol. i. p. 934. *Hävernik*, vol. ii. pt. 1, p. 146.

of the lowest of the people, and not of the Levites; xv. 4, 5, Asa the son of Abijam (a wicked king) is allowed to succeed his father, because David his ancestor "did what was right in the eyes of Jehovah;" verses 29, 30, Asa conquered Jeroboam "because of his sins;" and in xvi. 7, 12, 13, 19. In 2 Kings ii. 17, viii. 19, Jehovah would not destroy Judah on account of David; in ix. 36, x. 10, xv. 12, the predictions of a prophet are fulfilled. National calamities are sent to punish national sins, (xvii. 7, sqq., xviii. 12, xxiii. 26, xxiv. 3, 4.)

In this history, the connection of later events with earlier predictions is carried to the greatest extent, and is not free from arbitrary treatment, as it will appear from the following examples: 1 Kings ii. 26, 27. Compare 1 Sam. ii. 35.

Chap. xi. 30. "Ahijah the Shilonite found him [Jeroboam] in the way, ... and Ahijah caught the new garment that was on him, and rent it in twelve pieces, and said, 'Take the ten pieces, for thus saith the Lord, "I will rend the kingdom out of the hand of Solomon, and will give ten tribes to thee."' "	Chap. xii. 15. "Wherefore the king hearkened not unto the people, for the cause was from the Lord, that he might perform his saying which he spake by Ahijah the Shilonite unto Jeroboam."
Chap. xiii. 1, 2, 31, 32. "And behold, there came a man of God out of Judah by the word of the Lord unto Beth-el: and Jeroboam stood by the altar to burn incense. And he cried against the altar in the word of the Lord, and said, 'O altar, altar! thus saith the Lord, "Behold, a child shall be born unto the house of David, Josiah by name; and upon thee shall he	2 Kings xxiii. 15—18. "Moreover, the altar that was at Beth-el, and the high place which Jeroboam the son of Nebat, who made Israel to sin, had made, both that altar and the high place he brake down, and burned the high place, and stamped it small to powder, and burned the grove. And as Josiah turned himself, he spied the sepulchres that were there in

offer the priests of the high places that burn incense upon thee, and men's bones shall be burnt upon thee."'

"And it came to pass, after he had buried him, that he spake to his sons, saying, 'When I am dead, then bury me in the sepulchre wherein the man of God is buried; lay my bones beside his bones: for the saying which he cried by the word of the Lord against the altar in Beth-el, and against all the houses of the high places which are in the cities of Samaria, shall surely come to pass.'"

the mount, and sent, and took the bones out of the sepulchres, and burned them upon the altar, and polluted it, *according to the word of the Lord which the man of God proclaimed, who proclaimed these words.* Then he said, 'What title is that that I see?' And the men of the city told him, 'It is the sepulchre of the man of God, which came from Judah, and proclaimed these things that thou hast done against the altar of Beth-el.' And he said, 'Let him alone; let no man move his bones.' So they let his bones alone, with the bones of the prophet that came out of Samaria."

Chap. xiv. 10. "And the Lord said unto Ahijah, 'Therefore, behold, I will bring evil upon the house of Jeroboam, and will cut off from Jeroboam him that pisseth against the wall, and him that is shut up and left in Israel, and will take away the remnant of the house of Jeroboam, as a man taketh away dung, till it be all gone.'"

Chap. xv. 29. "And it came to pass, when he reigned, that he smote all the house of Jeroboam; he left not to Jeroboam any that breathed, until he had destroyed him, *according unto the saying of the Lord, which he spake by his servant Ahijah the Shilonite.*"

Chap. xvi. 1, 3. "Then the word of the Lord came to Jehu the son of Hanani against Baasha, saying, 'Behold, I will take away the posterity of Baasha, and the posterity of his house; and will make thy house like the house of Jeroboam the son of Nebat.'"[a]

Chap. xvi. 12. "Thus did Zimri destroy all the house of Baasha, *according to the word of the Lord which he spake against Baasha by Jehu the prophet.*"

[a] Compare, also, Josh. vi. 26, with xvi. 34.

Chap. xxi. 19, 24. "And thou shalt speak unto him, saying, 'Thus saith the Lord, "Hast thou killed, and also taken possession?" And thou shalt speak unto him, saying, 'Thus saith the Lord, "In the place where dogs licked the blood of Naboth shall dogs lick thy blood, even thine. Him that dieth of Ahab in the city the dogs shall eat; and him that dieth in the field shall the fowls of the air eat."'"

Chap. xxii. 37, 38. "So the king died, and was brought to Samaria; and they buried the king in Samaria. And one washed the chariot in the pool of Samaria; and the dogs licked up his blood; and they washed his armor; *according unto the word of the Lord which he spake.*"

Chap. xxi. 23. "And of Jezebel, also, spake the Lord, saying, 'The dogs shall eat Jezebel by the wall of Jezreel;'" and

2 Kings ix. 10. "And the dogs shall eat Jezebel in the portion of Jezreel."

2 Kings ix. 35, sq. "And they went to bury her, [Jezebel,] but they found no more of her than the skull, and the feet, and the palms of her hands. Wherefore they came again and told him. And he said, '*This is the word of the Lord, which he spake by his servant Elijah the Tishbite*, saying, "In the portion of Jezreel shall dogs eat the flesh of Jezebel. And the carcass of Jezebel shall be as dung upon the face of the field in the portion of Jezreel; so that they shall not say, 'This is Jezebel.'"'"

Chap. x. 30. "And the Lord said unto Jehu, 'Because thou hast done well in executing that which is right in mine eyes, and hast done unto the house of Ahab according to all that was in my heart, thy children of the fourth generation shall sit on the throne of Israel.'"

Chap. xv. 12. "*This was the word of the Lord which he spake unto Jehu, saying*, 'Thy sons shall sit on the throne of Israel unto the fourth generation. And so it came to pass."

In xx. 16, sq., a curse is denounced upon the descendants of Hezekiah, and in xxi. 10, sqq., it is repeated, with an application to Manasseh his son: —

Chap. xxiii. 27. "And the Lord said, 'I will remove Judah also out of my sight, as I have removed Israel, and will cast off this city Jerusalem, which I have chosen, and the house of which I said, "My name shall be there."'"	Chap. xxiv. 2, sqq., 20, and chap. xxv. "And the Lord sent against him bands of the Chaldees, and bands of the Syrians, and bands of the Moabites, and bands of the children of Ammon, and sent them against Judah to destroy it, *according to the word of the Lord, which he spake by his servants the prophets.* Surely at the commandment of the Lord came this upon Judah, to remove them out of his sight, for the sins of Manasseh, according to all that he did."

The great carefulness, in respect to dates, is characteristic. In the beginning, it leads to round numbers, (1 Kings ii. 11, xi. 42;) but afterwards it is carried out to definite numbers. Sometimes the book rises to a general view of the whole history,[a] (1 Kings vi. 1.)

---

[a] On the difficulties in the chronology, see *De Wette's* Archäologie, § 34. *Tiele*, Chronol. d. A. T.; Bremen, 1839, p. 58, sqq.

[CHRONOLOGY OF THE BOOKS OF THE KINGS.

From *De Wette's* Archäologie, § 30—34.

I. BEFORE THE KINGDOM WAS DIVIDED.

Saul reigned,	Acts xiii. 21, *Josephus*, Ant. vi. 14, 19,	40 years,	B. C. 1095.
David	1 Kings ii. 11	40 "	" 1055.
Solomon	1 —— xi. 42,	40 "	" 1015.
Sum of the whole period,		120 "	

From 1095 to 975 B. C.

§ 184, *a.*

LITERARY CHARACTER OF THE BOOK.

A certain unity is obvious from beginning to end.[a] We do not any where find certain marks of the inser-

---

[a] 1. In the remarks *relating to sacrifices on the high places,* which are regarded as sinful: 1 Kings iii. 2, 3, xv. 14, xxii. 44, 2 Kings xii. 3, xiv. 4, xv. 4, 35, xviii. 4.

2. In *allusions to the Law:* 1 Kings ii. 3, "Keep the charge of the Lord thy God,...... as it is written in the law of Moses;" iii. 14, "If thou wilt walk in my ways to keep *my* statutes," &c.; vi. 11, 12, viii. 58, 61, ix. 4, 6, xi. 38, 2 Kings x. 31, "Jehu took no heed to walk in the law of the Lord God of Israel;" xiv. 6, "the book of the law of Moses;" xvii. 13, 15, 34, 37, "law of the Lord;" xviii. 6, and xxi. 8, xxiii. 3, 25, "law of Moses."

3. Expressions of *preference for Jerusalem and the temple:* 1 Kings viii 16, 29, ix. 3, xi. 36, xiv. 21, 2 Kings xxi. 4, 7.

4. Of the *duration of David's house:* 1 Kings xi. 36, "That David may have a light always before me in Jerusalem;" xv. 4, 2 Kings viii. 19.

5. Of *fidelity to Jehovah:* 1 Kings viii. 61, xi. 4, xv. 3, 14, 2 Kings xx. 3.

6. A *proverbial expression to denote the male sex:* 1 Kings xiv. 10, xxi. 21, 2 Kings ix. 8, xiv. 26.

7. *Slept with his fathers—to denote death* of a king: 1 Kings xi. 43, xiii. 20, &c., 2 Kings xxiv. 6.

II. After the Kingdom was divided.

1. *Kingdom of Judah till Hezekiah.*

Rehoboam reigned, ...	1 Kings xiv. 21, ...	17	years,	B. C.	975.
Abiam	——— xv. 2, ...	3	"	"	957.
Asa	——— xv. 10, ...	41	"	"	955.
Jehoshaphat	——— xxii. 42, ...	25	"	"	914.
Joram	2 Kings viii. 17, ...	8	"	"	889.
Ahaziah	——— viii. 25, ...	1	"	"	885.
Athaliah	——— xi. 4—xii. 1, ...	6	"	"	884.
Joash	——— xii. 1, ...	40	"	"	878.
Amaziah	——— xiv. 1, ...	29	"	"	838.
Uzziah	——— xv. 2, ...	52	"	"	809.
Jotham	——— xv. 33, ...	16	"	"	758.
Ahaz	——— xvi. 2, ...	16	"	"	741.
Hezekiah, first period of his reign, ...	——— xviii. 2, 10, ...	6	"	"	725.
Sum of all the reigns, ...		260	"		

tion of different narratives, or of a compilation from

2. *Kingdom of Israel.*

Jeroboam reigned, ...	1 Kings xiv. 20, ...	22 years,	B. C.	975.
Nadab	——— xv. 25, ...	2 "	"	954.
Baasha	——— xv. 33, ...	24 "	"	952.
Elah	——— xvi. 8, ...	2 "	"	930.
Zimri	——— x. 15, ...	— 7 days,	"	928.
Omri	——— xvi. 23, ...	12 years,	"	928.
Ahab	——— xvi. 29, ...	22 "	"	917.
Ahaziah	——— xxii. 52, ...	2 "	"	897.
Joram	2 Kings iii. 1, ...	12 "	"	896.
Jehu	——— x. 34, ...	28 "	"	884.
Jehoahaz	——— xiii. 1, ...	17 "	"	856.
Joash	——— xiii. 10, ...	16 "	"	840.
Jeroboam II.	——— xiv. 23, ...	41 "	"	825.
Zachariah	——— xv. 8, ...	— 6 mo.	"	772.
Shallum	——— xv. 13, ...	— 1 "	"	771.
Menahem	——— xv. 17, ...	10 years,	"	771.
Pekaiah	——— xv. 23, ...	2 "	"	760.
Pekah	——— xv. 27, ...	20 "	"	758.
Hosea	——— xvii. 1, ...	9 "	"	729.
		241 y. 7 m. 7 d.		

The chronologists have made various attempts to reconcile the two different series. The most successful method is to suppose imperfect are given for entire years; that there are errors in the numbers; and sometimes that there was an interregnum — e. g. in the kingdom of Israel, between Jeroboam II. and Zachariah, of eleven years, and between Pekah and Hosea of nine years; so that the duration of the kingdom of Israel may be fixed at 253 years.

From 975 to 722 B. C.

3. *Kingdom of Judah to the Exile.*

Hezekiah, rest of his reign, ...	. . . .	23 years,	B. C.	722.
Manasseh reigned, ...	2 Kings xxi. 1, ...	55 "	"	696.
Amon	——— xxi. 19, ...	2 "	"	641.
Josiah	——— xxii. 1, ...	31 "	"	639.
Jehoahaz	——— xxiii. 31, ...	— 3 mos.	"	609.
Jehoiakim	——— xxiii. 36, ...	11 years,	"	608.
Jehoiachin	——— xxiv. 8, ...	— 3 mos.	"	598.
Zedekiah	——— xxiv. 8, ...	11 years,	"	598
Sum of all the reigns, ...	. . . .	133 y. 6 m.	"	

From 722 to 588 B. C.

them.[a] But 1 Kings xix. 15, does not agree with 2 Kings viii. 7—15. In the first passage, Jehovah commands *Elijah* to anoint Hazael as king of Syria. In the latter, *Elisha* informs Hazael that he shall be king over Syria. The thought appears new to both of them.

The whole story of Elijah and Elisha is derived, directly or indirectly, from legends of the people, or of the schools of the prophets. Perhaps it is compiled from two documents. Eichhorn infers this from the difference of the language, and Meyer from the similarity of the two accounts.[b]

---

[a] [To me it seems we may discover such marks, though perhaps it is not easy to say where one document begins and another ends.

1 Kings iii. 5—28, differs in character from the preceding and following chapters. The writer or compiler of these books is hostile to sacrifices; yet in this chapter, after Solomon had sacrificed at the chief high place, Jehovah appears to him in a dream, and offers him whatever he will choose. This tends to encourage such *un-Mosaic* sacrifices. The story of Solomon's judgment in the case of the two harlots, has a legendary character, unlike the rest of this part of the book. The connection is not broken, if this passage (verses 5—28) is removed. One section may have closed with iii. 4, and the next have begun with iv. 1, and the compiler inserted from a different source the verses now intervening.

Chap. iv. 20, 21, seems to be either an interpolation, or else to be misplaced. Perhaps ii. 45, has been added by a later hand, if it did not proceed from the compiler: x. 1—13, story of the queen of Sheba, disturbs the connection: x. 14, connects well with ix. 28. This account of the queen contains an obvious interpolation: verse 10, "There came no more such abundance of spices," &c., to verse 12; this may have been added by the compiler, but it could scarcely have proceeded from the original relater of this anecdote. The whole of chap. xiii. is distinguished from its context by its mythical character. The same may be said of the entire story of Elisha and Elijah, 1 Kings xvii.—xix. (xx. 28—43?), 2 Kings i. ii. iii. 6—20, iv.—viii. 15, xiii. 14—21.—1 Kings xxi. 25, 26, is evidently an interpolation.]

[b] See *Eichhorn*, § 482, p. 554. לְכִי, instead of לָךְ; 2 Kings iv. 2. אַתִּי, instead of אַתְּ; 16, 23. Suffix כִי, for ךְ; verses 3, 7. See § 185. See, also, *Meyer*, Ub. d. Verhaltniss d. Erzählungen von Elia, in *Bertholdt*, Krit. Journal, vol. iv. pt. 3, p. 223, sqq.

The passage, 2 Kings xiv. 25, is abrupt, and separated from its connection; — Jeroboam, son of Joash, "restored the coast of Israel, from the entering of Hamath, unto the Sea of the Plain, according to the word of the Lord God of Israel, which he spake by the hand of his servant Jonah, the son of Amittai."[a]

The following passages have the most documentary character: 1 Kings i. iv. vi. vii. ix. 10, sqq. The passage, 2 Kings xviii.—xx., is not contemporaneous; it is by no means written by Isaiah.[b] Yet the author seems to have made use of written authorities, which he frequently mentions — such as the Book of the Acts of Solomon,[c] the Book of the Chronicles of the Kings of Israel,[d] and of Judah.[e]

The date of the book,[f] and the legendary character of some of the narratives, forbid us to suppose these were the official annals of the realm;[g] but it is difficult to determine whether they were private historical works, as Eichhorn supposes, or extracts from the annals, as Bertholdt and Movers maintain. The latter, however, thinks he used one authority which he has not mentioned; namely, the "Book of the Kings of Israel," which is referred to in 1 Ch. ix. 1, and 2 Ch. xx. 34.[h]

---

[a] [No reference is made elsewhere to this prophecy of Jonah, nor is the prophecy itself now extant.]

[b] Comp. § 212.

[c] 1 Kings xi. 41.

[d] Chap. xiv. 19, xv. 31, xvi. 5, 14, 20, 27, xxii. 39, 2 Kings i. 17, x. 34, xiii. 8, 12, xv. 11, 15, 21, 26, 31.

[e] Chap. xiv. 29, xv. 7, 23, xxii. 46, 2 Kings viii. 23, xii. 20, xiv. 18, 28, xv. 6, 36, xvi. 19, xx. 20, xxi. 17, xxiii. 28, xxiv. 5.

[f] § 185.

[g] *Hävernik*, vol. ii. pt. 1, p. 150, sqq.

[h] [See *Eichhorn's* opinion, § 482, and *Bertholdt's*, p. 947, sqq. With respect to *Eichhorn's* hypothesis upon the affinity of our book and that of Chronicles, it may be remarked that there is no other vestige of the *life of Solomon* — which, it is pretended, lies at its foundation, as collateral with the life of David — than the fact that some passages have a coloring somewhat more

§ 184, *b*.

[FURTHER CHARACTERISTICS OF THESE BOOKS.

1. Numerous passages occur in which natural actions and events are referred to the ultimate, rather than the immediate cause. Thus, in 1 Kings xi. 31, it is Jehovah who puts the threat in Ahijah's mouth. In xii. 15, where Rehoboam refuses to grant the people's request, it is added, "The thing was from the Lord." The phrase "The word of God came," or "Thus saith the Lord," — as in the previous books, — often denotes mere human counsels, as in xiii. 1, 2, 9, 17, 18, 20, 26, 32, and xiv. 5, where it is probable Ahijah knew from other sources that Jeroboam's wife was coming in disguise to inquire respecting her child. In xx. 13, where a prophet assures Ahab of the victory, the counsel is referred to Jehovah, though it apparently originated with the prophet himself. The same must be said of the mythical narrative in verses 35—42. False prophets make use of the authority of Jehovah; for example, "Zedekiah made him horns of iron, and said, 'Thus saith Jehovah, "With these shalt thou push the Syrians, until thou have consumed them,"'" (xxii. 11.) The result was very different, for the Syrians conquered, and the king of Israel was slain. Micaiah — apparently a true prophet — says to Ahab, in the name of Jehovah, "Go, and prosper, for Jehovah shall deliver it into the hand of the king." But when more earnestly adjured, he utters a prediction of an opposite character. Even Rab-shakeh

---

ancient and chronological than others. From Esther x. 2, and the citations of Chronicles, it may be doubted whether the author ever actually used those works. For the anti-Israelitic spirit of the history of Israel, see *Bertholdt*, p. 949.]

appeals to the same authority, in 2 Kings xviii. 25—"Am I come up *without the Lord* against this place? *The Lord* said to me, 'Go up against this land and destroy it.'"

2. The priests seem to exert but little influence. Solomon had but two—Zadok and Abiathar, (1 Kings iv. 4.) They could be removed at the king's pleasure, for the latter had been previously discharged,[a] and was afterwards restored to favor, (ii. 27.) However, their authority was sometimes respected, for Jehoiada would not suffer Athaliah to be slain in the temple when the priest forbade, (2 Kings xi. 15.) A priest and a prophet anointed Solomon king, (i. 34, 39.) The sacerdotal office did not necessarily descend to the sons, for the son of Zadok was a scribe, (iv. 2.) Even at the consecration of the temple, the priests are subordinate to the king. Uriah the priest makes an idolatrous altar at the command of Ahaz, (2 Kings xvi. 10—16;) and, at Hezekiah's command, (2 Kings xix.,) the elders of the priests wear sackcloth, contrary to the Mosaic law.

3. The book contains numerous mythical passages. In some of them the mythical portion is very conspicuous. Such are the two visions of Solomon, in 1 Kings iii. 5—15, and ix. 1—9; the story of the miraculous cloud of smoke at the consecration of the temple, (viii. 10—12;) the prophecy against the altar and Beth-el, with the symbolical action accompanying it, (xiii. 1—10, especially 4—6;) the story of the death of the prophet, (xiii. 11—32;) Ahijah's prophecy against Jeroboam, (xiv. 1—16;) the story of Elijah, (xvii.—xix.,) especially in the account of his miraculous support, (xvii. 6, xix.

[a] But this seems contrary to the spirit of the Mosaic code, which does not deem it possible for a priest to be faulty, or, at least, makes no provision against a faithless priest. See *Gramberg*, l. c. vol. i. p. 220, sqq.

5—8;) the supply of the widow's flour and oil, (xvii. 16,) and the restoration of the child, (verse 22;) the miraculous fire, (xviii. 38, sqq.;) the visit of Jehovah, (xix. 9—18.) The continuation and conclusion of the history of Elijah and his successor are filled with mythical narratives. Such are the accounts of the destruction of the soldiers sent to capture Elijah, (2 Kings i. 5—15;) and that of his ascent to heaven, (ii. 1—11;) Elisha's miraculous passage of the Jordan, his healing the deadly waters, and the destruction of the little children who mocked him, (ii. 19—22, and 23, 24.) The mythical narrative ascribes nearly the same acts to Elisha which had previously been wrought by Elijah; for example, Elisha increases the widow's oil, (iv. 1—7,) as his master had done, (1 Kings xvii. 16;) he restores the life of a child, (iv. 18—37,) and Elijah had done the same, (1 Kings xvii. 17—24.) He renders poisonous pottage wholesome, and feeds one hundred men with twenty barley loaves, (iv. 38—44.) He cures Naaman of the leprosy, (v. 1—27,) causes iron to swim, (vi. 1—7,)[a] and smites with blindness the troops sent to take him, leads them to the wrong place, and then restores their sight, gives them a feast, and sends them home, (vi. 15—23.) After his death, a dead body is accidentally thrust into his tomb, and is restored to life as it touches his bones, (xiii. 14—21.) In all these instances, it is obvious the accounts are mythical.

The story of the shadow on the dial of Hezekiah being made to go backwards ten degrees, (2 Kings xx. 8—11,) is obviously a myth. But these are, perhaps, the only mythical accounts in the book.

---

[a] *Eichhorn* (Allg. Bib. vol. iv. p. 209, 210) thinks he *fished the axe out of the river with a stick.* Naturalistic attempts at explanation seem often more difficult to accept than the original story.

4. References to the ancient history of the Jews, and the Mosaic Law, or the Law of Jehovah, are most frequent in the latter part of the second book, as in 2 Kings xiv. 6, where a Mosaic statute is quoted, (compare Deut. xxiv. 16;) xvi. 3, where the nations cast out of Canaan for their idolatry are alluded to; and also in xvii. 7, 8, 11, 13, 35—39. The brazen serpent is mentioned as an idol, (xviii. 4.) The covenant of Jehovah and Law of Moses are referred to, (verse 12; compare verse 32.) Instances of this sort are numerous in the latter chapters of this book, (xxi. 1—8, xxii. xxiii.) This is one proof of the fidelity of the historian. As the Mosaic laws began to be written and made known, allusions to them occur in the history.

5. These books, like those of Samuel, abound in little natural touches, which show the author's delicate sense of historical fidelity, and prove he sometimes drew from nature. Some of the most striking traits of this character are the following: The threat of Ben-hadad, (in 1 Kings xx. 10,) that he would bring so large an army that the "dust of Samaria should not suffice for handfuls," with the truly laconic reply of Ahab, "Let not him that girdeth on, boast as he that putteth off," his armor.[a] This is told Ben-hadad while he is drinking. He replies in a single word[b]—"Place;" that is, "Bring up the engines of war." Again: it is said, (verse 27,) "The children of Israel pitched before them like two little flocks of kids. But the Syrians filled the country." The conduct of Jezebel—equally infamous as a wife and a queen—is delineated with graphic fidelity, in xxi. 7, sqq., and 2 Kings ix. 30, sqq.: "She painted her eyes, and tired her head, and looked out at

---

[a] אַל־יִתְהַלֵּל חֹגֵר כִּמְפַתֵּחַ.

[b] שִׂימוּ.

a window." Equally natural are the taunts uttered to Micaiah the prophet, who had predicted the defeat of the Israelites—"Which way went the Spirit of the Lord from me to speak to thee?" and Micaiah's reply—"Behold, thou shalt see in that day when thou shalt go into an inner chamber to hide thyself." The king says, "Put this fellow in prison, ... until I come in peace;" and the prophet answers, "If thou return *at all* in peace, the Lord hath not spoken by me," (xxii. 24, sqq.) Such zeal inspired the nation to repair the temple, that "they reckoned not with the men, ... for they dealt faithfully," (2 Kings xii. 15.) The king of Judah challenges the king of Israel, saying, "Come, let us look one another in the face,"[a] (xiv. 8.) The honesty of a man could not be better delineated, than is done in 2 Kings vi. 5. A laborer had lost his axe in the water, and he exclaims to the prophet, "Alas! master! for it was borrowed."[b]

Throughout the book, the prophets of Jehovah usually appear as hostile to the reigning power. Even in the time of Solomon, Ahijah designates Jeroboam as destined to succeed to the throne, and by a symbolic act predicts the separation of the ten tribes, (1 Kings xi. 29—39.) A prophet, in presence of Jeroboam, utters his fierce denunciations against the altar which that idolatrous king had erected, (xiii. 1—10.) Ahijah, who had assisted in elevating Jeroboam, is also ready to denounce and execrate him and his posterity, (xiv. 1—17.) Micaiah the prophet fearlessly opposes Ahab, who says, "I hate

---

[a] לְכָה נִתְרָאֶה פָנִים.

[b] The Seventy render the Hebrew, שָׁאוּל, by *κεκρυμμένον*, though perhaps *κεχρημμένον* is the true reading. The Dutch version quaintly reads —*Ach! mynheere! want het was geleent.*

him, for he doth not prophesy good concerning me, but evil," (xxii. 8—28.) Elisha expresses the greatest contempt for Jehoram, king of Israel—"Were it not that I regard the presence of Jehoshaphat, ... I would not look towards thee, nor see thee," (2 Kings iii. 13, 14.)]

§ 185.

TIME OF THE COMPOSITION.

Here, likewise, the customary references to a later period, such as *unto this day*, (1 Kings viii. 8, ix. 13, 21, x. 12, xii. 19, 2 Kings viii. 22, x. 27, xiv. 7, xvi. 6, xvii. 23, 34, 41,) do not all unite in one point of time.

Probably these references were made in the works from which the author drew his materials. The same reference to a later age appears in the parallel passages in Chronicles: thus the staves of the ark are said to be "there unto this day," in 2 Ch. v. 9, as well as in 1 Kings viii. 8. Compare, also, x. 19.

According to 1 Kings viii. 8, the temple was then standing, and David's family was still on the throne, according to verse 25; and therefore Bertholdt places the date of the document on which this part of the history is founded in the last part of the kingdom of Judah. Jahn and Hävernik place it during Evil-merodach's reign of two years. According to 2 Kings x. 27, Samaria was still standing.[a]

Some of the works referred to bring us far down into the period after the destruction of the kingdom of Israel. In 1 Kings xiii. 2, the birth of Josiah, and his acts, are spoken of, and again in 2 Kings xxii. xxiii., especially 16, 25. To judge from these passages, the author

---

[a] See *Bertholdt*, p. 945.

wrote long after the time of Josiah. "Like unto him," says the writer, "was there no king before him, ... neither after him arose there any like him."

In 1 Kings viii. 47, the return from exile is mentioned; the destruction of the temple, (ix. 7, 8;) the dispersion of the people, (xiv. 15;) the Babylonian exile, in 2 Kings xx. 17. According to these passages and the conclusion of the book, it was written during the Babylonian exile, and towards the end of it.[a]

This date agrees with the whole spirit of the book; with the constant reference to the Mosaic Law; the aversion to sacrifices on the high places; the stiff prophetic pragmatism; the gloomy view of the history; the legends and exaggerations.[b]

§ 186.

DIFFERENCE FROM THE BOOKS OF SAMUEL.

There is much in favor of the identity of the author of the two books; the strongest arguments are the ref-

---

[a] *Bertholdt*, p. 959, against *Jahn*, vol. ii. p. 236. *Hävernik*, vol. ii. pt. 1, p. 170.

[b] There are likewise more modern peculiarities of language, which determine in favor of this period: אַתִּי, for אַתְּ; 1 Kings xiv. 2, 2 Kings viii. 1; see § 184, *a*, p. 238. אוֹתוֹ, for אִתּוֹ; 2 Kings i. 15; comp. iii. 11, sqq., viii. 8. רְשֹׁם, for רָשֹׁם; 1 Kings ix. 8. רָצִין; 2 Kings xi. 13. מְדִינוֹת; 1 Kings xx. 14, sqq. כֹּר, for חֹמֶר; 1 Kings v. 2. חֹרִים; 1 Kings xxi. 8, 11. רַב; 2 Kings xxv. 8. שָׁלֵם; 1 Kings viii. 61, et al. הִשְׂכִּיל; 2 Kings xviii. 7. בִּטָּחוֹן; verse 19. [פֶּחָה; 1 Kings x. 15, xx. 24, 2 Kings xviii. 24.] יְהוּדִית; verse 26; comp. Neh. xiii. 24. דִּבֵּר מִשְׁפָּט אֵת; 2 Kings xxv. 6. To these the names of the months (1 Kings vi. 1, 37, viii. 2) are sometimes erroneously added. From the words עֵבֶר הַנָּהָר, 1 Kings v. 4, (iv. 24,) *Gesenius* concludes it was composed in Babylonia. But see above, § 147, *a*, p. 41, note *a*.

erence of 1 Kings ii. 26, sq., to 1 Sam. ii. 35,[a] of 1 Kings ii. 11,—"seven years reigned he in Hebron, and thirty and three years reigned he in Jerusalem,"—to 2 Sam. v. 5.—"In Hebron he reigned over Judah seven years and six months, and in Jerusalem he reigned thirty and three years over all Israel and Judah."

The following passages refer to the books of Samuel:—

1 Kings ii. 3, 4. "And keep the charge of the Lord thy God, to walk in his ways, to keep his statutes, and his commandments, and his judgments, and his testimonies, as it is written in the law of Moses, that thou mayest prosper in all that thou doest, and whithersoever thou turnest thyself: that the Lord may continue his word which he spake concerning me, saying, 'If thy children take heed to their way, to walk before me in truth with all their heart, and with all their soul, there shall not fail thee (said he) a man on the throne of Israel.'"

Chap. v. 17, 18. "And the king commanded, and they brought great stones, costly stones, and hewed stones, to lay the foundation of the house. And Solomon's builders and Hiram's builders did hew them, and the stone-squarers: so they prepared timber and stones to build the house."

Chap. viii. 18, 19, 25. "And the Lord said unto David my father, 'Whereas it was in thine heart to build a house unto my name, thou didst well that it was in thine heart. Nevertheless thou shalt not build the house; but thy son, that shall come forth out of thy loins, he shall build the house unto my name.' Therefore now, Lord God of Israel, keep with thy servant David my father that thou promisedst him, saying, 'There shall not fail thee a man in my sight to sit on the throne of Israel; so that thy children take heed to their way, that they walk before me as thou hast walked before me.'"

They refer to

2 Sam. vii. 12—16. "And when thy days be fulfilled, and thou shalt sleep with thy fathers, I will set up thy seed after thee, which

---

[a] See above, p. 226.

shall proceed out of thy bowels, and I will establish his kingdom He shall build a house for my name, and I will establish the throne of his kingdom forever. I will be his father, and he shall be my son; if he commit iniquity, I will chasten him with the rod of men, and with the stripes of the children of men: but my mercy shall not depart away from him, as I took it from Saul, whom I put away before thee. And thine house and thy kingdom shall be established forever before thee: thy throne shall be established forever."

But in this parallel there is an important difference between 1 Kings ii. 4, viii. 25, and 2 Sam. vii. 12—16, in respect to conditions of keeping the law annexed to the blessings pronounced upon David. The formula, "*There shall not fail*,"[a] does not occur in the latter. The only striking parallel is between the commands respecting the erection of the temple. But this is not more striking than the reference to Josh. vi. 26, in 1 Kings xvi. 34. Yet from that no one infers Joshua and Kings were both written by the same author.

There is a similarity also between the following passages:—

1 Kings iv. 1—6. "So King Solomon was king over all Israel. And these were the princes which he had. Azariah the son of Zadok the priest; Elihoreph and Ahiah, the sons of Shisha, scribes; Jehoshaphat the son of Ahilud, the recorder. And Benaiah the son of Jehoiada was over the host: and Zadok and Abiathar were the priests: and Azariah the son of Nathan was over the officers: and Zabud the son of Nathan was principal officer, and the king's friend: and Ahishar

2 Kings viii. 15—18. "And David reigned over all Israel; and David executed judgment and justice unto all his people. And Joab the son of Zeruiah was over the host; and Jehoshaphat the son of Ahilud was recorder; and Zadok the son of Ahitub, and Ahimelech the son of Abiathar, were the priests: and Seraiah was the scribe; and Benaiah the son of Jehoiada was over both the Cherethites and the Pelethites; and David's sons were chief rulers."

---

[a] לֹא־יִכָּרֵת.

was over the household: and Adoniram the son of Abda was over the tribute."

It has been said there is no resting-place between 2 Samuel and 1 Kings, and therefore both books proceeded from the same author. But there is a resting-place in the narrative; for 2 Sam. xxi.—xxiv. has all the characteristics of an appendix, [which was subsequently added to connect that to the following book.][a]

However, the essential difference between the two books appears plain, 1. from the traces of the Babylonish period, from beginning to end; 2. from the acquaintance with the Pentateuch; 3. from the disapproval of freedom of worship; 4. from the different spirit of the history; 5. from a reference to the sources of the author; and, 6. from the accuracy of the dates.

[The Talmud makes Jeremiah the author;[b] but this opinion is contradicted, amongst other arguments, by the fact that the history of his own time is treated of but superficially, and by the following passage: —

2 Kings xxv. 27—30. "And it came to pass in the seven and thirtieth year of the captivity of Jehoiachin king of Judah, in the

---

[a] See *Eichhorn*, § 484. *Jahn* (p. 232) defends the opinion that there is but one author. The remark of *Stähelin* (in *Tholuck*, Theol. Anz., 1838, p. 526) is still more important, viz., that there is a close philological affinity between 1 Kings i. ii. and the books of Samuel, and that originally they were united. *Crethites* and *Plethites* occur in 1 Kings i. 38, and nowhere else except in 2 Samuel. מַלֵּט נפש occurs in the books of Kings only once, 1 Kings i. 12; but in Samuel, 1 Sam. xix. 11, 2 Sam. xix. 6. Likewise, פדה נפש, only in 1 Kings i. 29, but in 2 Sam. iv. 9; הכין מלך, only 1 Kings i. ii.—but see 1 Sam. xiii. 13, 2 Sam. v. 12; מריא, in the books of Kings only, 1 Kings i. 9, 19, 25; but 2 Sam. vi. 13; *ark of the Lord Jehovah*, 1 Kings ii. 26, as in the books of Samuel. To follow this hint, we must distinguish between two redactions, or suppose the author of Samuel left something unused in his authorities, which was taken by the author of the books of Kings.

[b] [See above, vol. i. p. 30, sqq.]

twelfth month, on the seven and twentieth day of the month, that Evil-merodach king of Babylon in the year that he began to reign did lift up the head of Jehoiachin king of Judah out of prison; and he spake kindly to him, and set his throne above the throne of the kings that were with him in Babylon; and changed his prison garments: and he did eat bread continually before him all the days of his life. And his allowance was a continual allowance given him of the king, a daily rate for every day, all the days of his life."]

Hävernik and Movers[a] make use of the affinity between the books of Kings, and, in some places, of Jeremiah's writings; for example, between 1 Kings ix. 8, 9, and Jer. xxii. 8; 2 Kings xvii. 13, 14, and Jer. vii. 13, 24; 2 Kings xxi. 12, and Jer. xix. 3; and the identity of Jer. lii. with 2 Kings xxiv. 18, xxv.,[b] to support their different opinions—one, that Jeremiah wrote the books of Kings; the other, that he wrote an older book of Kings, the source of the present books, and that these latter, and the prophecies of Jeremiah, were collected by the same compiler, who also wrote Jer. lii. But this affinity can be explained in another manner, either on the supposition that Jeremiah was used by the author of Kings, or that Jeremiah made use of a more ancient author, who wrote some passages now in the books of Kings. In 2 Kings xxv. 27—30, especially, there is evidence against the opinion that the books were composed by Jeremiah.

---

[a] *Hävernik*, l. c. p. 171. *Movers*, De utriusque Vatic. Jer. Indole, &c., p. 47. *Hävernik*, Comm. z. Daniel, p. 14.

[b] The other passages cited by *Movers* prove nothing.

CHAPTER VI.

BOOKS OF THE CHRONICLES.[a]

§ 187

NAME, DIVISION, AND CONTENTS, OF THE BOOKS OF THE CHRONICLES.

THESE make but one book in the Hebrew canon, and are but one, if we regard their internal character. In the Hebrew, they have this title—דִּבְרֵי הַיָּמִים, WORDS OF THE DAYS, or ANNALS. In the Alexandrine version, they form two books, with the title *Παραλειπόμενα*, that is, SUPPLEMENTS, or THINGS WHICH ARE LEFT. Following Jerome,[b] we call them the *Books of Chronicles.*

I. They contain a register of families, and other lists, (1 Ch. i.—ix.) In this the list of families in the tribe of Benjamin appears *twice*, (vii. 6—12, and viii. 1—40,) and in part a *third time*, (ix. 35—40.) But the tribes of Dan and Zebulon do not appear at all. These accounts are drawn in part from the older historical books, and in part from other sources unknown to us. Single historical notices are interwoven with them, and there are chasms and inaccuracies.[c]

---

[a] *Serrarii, Sanctii, Vict. Strigelii, Jo. Clerici, Lightfootii, Maur.* Commentt. *Lud. Lavateri* Comm. in Paralip.; Heidelb. 1599, sq.

J. H. Michaelis, Annotatt. in Paralip., in Uber. Annotatt. in Hagiogr. ed. *J. H. Michaelis*; Hal. 1719, 1720; 3 vols. 4to. *Geddes*, l. c.

[b] As cited above, vol. i. p. 111, sq.

[c] *A Table of Passages parallel with* 1 Ch. i.—ix.

1 Ch. i. 1—4, compiled.	Gen. v.
—— i. 5—23.	—— x. 2—29.
—— i. 24—27, compiled.	—— xi. 10, sqq.

On account of the alterations and additions in the parallels to chap. ii., Keil and Hävernik[a] maintain that the Chronicler did not use the historical books of the Old Testament as authorities, but resorted to some other family registers. Bertholdt has a similar theory,[b] and the numerous variants favor this opinion. But these very alterations and additions show that the Chronicler, or his authority, referred to, and made use of, these his-

---

1 Ch. i. 29—31.	Gen. xxv. 13—15.
—— i. 32, 33.	—— xxv. 2—4.
—— i. 35—54, compiled.	—— xxxvi. 10—43.
—— ii. 3, 4, compiled.	—— xxxviii. 3—30.
—— ii. 5.	—— xlvi. 12.
—— ii. 10—12.	Ruth iv. 19.
—— ii. 13—17, enlarged.	1 Sam. xvi. 6, sqq.
—— iii. 1—9, enlarged and different.	2 Sam. iii. 3—6, v. 14.
—— iii. 10—16.	Books of Kings.
—— iv. 24.	Num. xxvi. 12.
—— iv. 28—31.	Josh. xix. 2—5.
—— v. 1—10, enlarged and different	Gen. xlvi. 9, Num. xxvi. 5, Josh. xiii. 16, 17.
—— v. 27—29.	Gen. xlvi. 11, Ex. vi. 18, 23, xxviii. 1.
—— v. 30—41, more complete. . . .	Ezra vii. 1—5.
—— vi. 1—4, 7, ...	Ex. vi. 16—29, 23, 24.
—— vi. 39—66, different.	Josh. xxi. 10—39.
—— vii. 1—5, enlarged.	Gen. xlvi. 13, Num. xxvi. 23.
—— vii. 6—12, different.	Gen. xlvi. 21, Num. xxvi. 38—40, 1 Ch. viii. 1, sqq.
—— vii. 13.	Gen. xlvi. 24.
—— vii. 14—19, different.	Num. xxvi. 29, xxvii. 1.
—— vii. 20—29.	Num. xxvi. 34—38.
—— vii. 30—40.	Gen. xlvi. 17, Num. xxvi. 44—47.
—— viii. 1—28, different.	Gen. xlvi. 21, Num. xxvi. 38—40, 1 Ch. vii. 6, sq.
—— viii. 29—40, and ix. 35—44, different, with various readings. . . .	1 Sam. ix. 1, xiv. 49—51.
—— ix. 2—34, enlarged and different.	Neh. xi. 3—24.

[a] *Keil*, Versuch über d. Bucher d. Chronikeln; 1833, p. 163, sqq. *Hävernik*, l. c. vol. ii. pt. i. p. 182. *Movers*, Ub. d. Ch.; 1834, p. 65, sqq.

[b] P. 965, sqq.

torical books. Thus, for example, the remark upon Er, in ii. 3, that "he was wicked in the sight of Jehovah, and he slew him," is taken, word for word, from Gen. xxxviii. 7. The statement about Achar, (Achan) ii. 7, "the troubler of Israel . . . . . . who sinned in the accursed thing," refers to Josh. vii. In ii. 6, there is a false combination from 1 Kings v. 11, (iv. 31, in the English Bible,) for Ethan, Heman, Calcol, and Dara, are enumerated among the sons of Zerah. In iii. 1—6, the sons of David are divided into two classes—such as were born at Hebron, and such as were born at Jerusalem. This division refers to 2 Sam. iii. 2—5, and v. 14—16. Again: the genealogy of the kings (iii. 11—15) is borrowed from the books of Kings, as it appears from the use of the more ancient form of the name, terminating in יָהוּ, which occurs nowhere else but in vi. 24. In vi. 7, (vi. 22, English Bible,) among the sons of Kohath are Amminadab, Korah, Assir, Elkanah, and Ebiasaph, which are incorrectly borrowed from Ex. vi. 23, 24. Keil himself, however, admits that in vi. 39—66, the same original document—though disfigured—lies at the bottom of both this passage and its parallels.

There is a remarkable parallelism between ix. 2—34, and Neh. xi. 3—24.[a]

---

[a] *Keil* entirely denies this, though *Movers* admits a common source. *Keil* thinks this catalogue in the Chronicles of the inhabitants of Jerusalem, was written before the exile. But *Dahler*, (De Lib. Paralip. Auctoritate; 1819,) *Movers*, and others, think both this and that in Nehemiah were written after the exile. But the latter opinion is incorrect, for "the first inhabitants, in their possessions and their cities," mentioned in 1 Ch. ix. 2, are not "those who dwelt in it before Jerusalem was peopled with the inhabitants of the adjoining country," (Neh. xi. 1,) for these latter are not the inhabitants of Jerusalem, but contrasted with them, as it is clear from verse 3—"And at Jerusalem dwelt of the children of Judah," &c. The earlier inhabitants are obviously contrasted with those who had been brought in from the country.

The following are parallel: —

1 Ch. ix. 2, 3. "Now the first inhabitants, that dwelt in their possessions in their cities, were, the Israelites, the priests, Levites, and the Nethinims. And in Jerusalem dwelt of the children of Judah, and of the children of Benjamin, and of the children of Ephraim, and Manasseh."

Neh. xi. 3, 4. "Now these are the chief of the province that dwelt in Jerusalem: but in the cities of Judah dwelt every one in his possession in their cities, Israel, the priests, and the Levites, and the Nethinims, and the children of Solomon's servants. And at Jerusalem dwelt certain of the children of Judah, and of the children of Benjamin."

So that the corruption is clear, especially in the additions of the Chronicler "of the children of Ephraim and Manasseh," who are not mentioned again.

The following are also parallel: —

1 Ch. ix. 4—17. "*Uthai*, the son of Ammihud, the son of Omri, the son of Imri, the son of Bani, of the children of Pharez the son of Judah. And of the Shilonites; *Asaiah* the first-born, and his sons. And of the sons of Benjamin; *Sallu* the son of Meshullam, the son of Hodaviah, the son of Hasenuah, and Ibneiah the son of Jeroham, and Elah the son of Uzzi, the son of Michri, and Meshullam the son of Shephatiah, the son of Reuel, the son of Ibnijah, and their brethren, according to their generations, nine hundred and fifty and six. All these men were chief of the fathers in the house of their fathers.

"And of the priests; *Jedaiah*, and *Jehoiarib*, and *Jachin*, and

Neh. xi. 4—19. "*Athaiah* the son of Uzziah, the son of Zechariah, the son of Amariah, the son of Shephatiah, the son of Mahalaleel, of the children of Perez; and *Maaseiah* the son of Baruch, the son of Colhozeh, the son of Hazaiah, the son of Adaiah, the son of Joiarib, the son of Zechariah, the son of Shiloni. And these are the sons of Benjamin; *Sallu* the son of Meshullam, the son of Joed, the son of Pedaiah, the son of Kolaiah, the son of Maaseiah, the son of Ithiel, the son of Jesaiah. And after him Gabbai, Sallai, nine hundred twenty and eight. And Joel the son of Zichri was their overseer: and Judah the son of Senuah was second over the city. Of the priests; *Jedai-*

Azariah, the son of Hilkiah, the son of Meshullam, the son of Zadok, the son of Meraioth, the son of Ahitub, the ruler of the house of God; and Adaiah the son of Jeroham, the son of Pashur, the son of Malchijah, and *Maasiai* the son of Adiel, the son of Jahzerah, the son of Meshullam, the son of Meshillemith, the son of Immer, and their brethren, heads of the house of their fathers, *a thousand and seven hundred and threescore;* very able men for the work of the service of the house of God. And of the Levites; Shemaiah the son of Hashub, the son of Azrikam, the son of Hashabiah, of the sons of Merari; and Bakbakkar, Heresh, and Galal, and Mattaniah the son of Micah, the son of Zichri, the son of Asaph; and Obadiah the son of *Shemaiah*, the son of Galal, the son of Jeduthun; and Berechiah the son of Asa, the son of Elkanah, that dwelt in the villages of the Netophathites. And the porters were *Shallum*, and *Akkub*, and *Talmon*, and Ahiman, and their brethren: Shallum was the chief."

ah the son of *Joiarib*, *Jachin*. *Seraiah* the son of Hilkiah, the son of Meshullam, the son of Zadok, the son of Meraioth, the son of Ahitub, was the ruler of the house of God. And their brethren that did the work of the house were eight hundred twenty and two: and *Adaiah* the son of Jeroham, the son of Pelaliah, the son of Amzi, the son of Zechariah, the son of Pashur, the son of Malchiah, and his brethren, chief of the fathers, two hundred forty and two: and *Amashai* the son of Azareel, the son of Ahasai, the son of Meshillemoth, the son of Immer, and their brethren, mighty men of valor, *a hundred twenty and eight:* and their overseer was Zabdiel, the son of one of the great men. Also of the Levites; Shemaiah the son of Hashub, the son of Azrikam, the son of Hashabiah, the son of Bunni; and Shabbethai and Jozabad, of the chief of the Levites, had the oversight of the outward business of the house of God.[a] And *Mattaniah* the son of *Micha*, the son of Zabdi, the son of Asaph, was the principal to begin the thanksgiving in prayer: and Bakbukiah the second among his brethren, and Abda the son of Shammua, the son of *Galal*, the son of *Jeduthun*. All the Levites in the holy city were two hundred

[a] [There is no parallel to this verse.]

fourscore and four. Moreover, the porters, *Akkub*, *Talmon*, and their brethren that kept the gates, were a hundred seventy and two."

But ix. 18—34, is entirely different from Neh. xi. 20—36, for Neh. xi. 20, speaks of such as dwelt in the country, each on his own estate; verse 21, of the "peculiar people;" verses 22, 23, treat of the Levites; verse 24, of the royal magistrate; verse 25, sqq., of the inhabitants of the country towns; — and all of this refers to the state of things in Nehemiah's time. But in the Chronicles, on the contrary, every thing is rather Levitical, and extending backwards to the time of Moses. Movers considers verses 18—25 an interpolation by the Chronicler, and that the document is resumed in verse 26. But the whole passage, from verse 18, is a more modern addition. It departs from the main design and purport of this list, which is resumed at verse 34. This passage, (verses 18—25,) like the whole chapter, is a recasting of Neh. xi. But it is not from the age of Nehemiah, as Movers has erroneously concluded from verse 18, which does not relate to the *particular individuals* designated before, but to *the whole class of porters*. A contemporary of Nehemiah could not have disfigured the list so badly, nor have referred to the circumstances of other times.

The following is characteristic: Chap. ix. 34, "These are the heads of families of the Levites according to their families, chiefs; these dwelt at Jerusalem." This is similar to viii. 28, where it is said, in the midst of a register of the Benjamite families, "These are the heads of families, according to their families, chiefs; these dwelt at Jerusalem." It is like verse 32, "These . . . . . . dwelt at Jerusalem." Then, (ix. 34,) after taking occasion from the words "these dwelt at Jerusalem," the author returns to his list of the Benjamite families, (so that ix. 38, is parallel with viii. 32,) and adheres to it throughout the passage, (35—44,) though he makes a few deviations.[a] The words in viii. 32, "These also dwelt at Jerusalem," stand there without any connection, for the same words, which occur in viii. 28, are, in ix. 34, applied to the Levites. Movers explains this confusion as the fault of a transcriber.

These books are not without their chasms and inaccuracies. For example, the list of high priests, (v. 30 —41,) though it is more perfect than that in Ezra, (vii. 1, sqq.,) has its chasms. The number of high priests — twenty-two — is not sufficient for so long a period. The sons of Zerah, Zimri, Ethan, Heman, Calcol, and Dara, (ii. 6,) are probably the same that occur in 1 Kings v. 11, (English Bible, iv. 31.) But in Ps. lxxxviii. 1, Heman and Ethan appear among the Levites of David's time, (vi. 18, 29.)[b]

In ii. 49, Caleb, that is, Calubai, is confounded with the well-known Caleb the son of Jephunneh. Movers thinks the passage is an interpolation. The Caleb, whose children are enumerated in verse 50, is still different, or else there is another and somewhat similar genealogy. Caleb, in verse 50, is the *son* of Hur, and the *first-born* of Ephratah; but in verse 19, he is the son of Hezron, and the *husband* of Ephrath, and *father* of Hur.[c]

---

[a] Compare viii. 29—38.

[b] See *Movers*, p. 237. What *Hävernik* (vol. ii. pt. i. p. 180) says to the contrary is unintelligible.

[c] On iii. 15, see *Hitzig*, Kritik. p. 189, and, on the other hand, *Movers*, p. 157, who, at least, admits the existence of an error in the statement that Shallum — the same as *Johas* — is mentioned as the fourth son of Josiah. In iii. 19, Zerubbabel is the son of *Pedaiah;* in Ezra iii. 2, the son of *Shealtiel.* Here *Movers* and *Hävernik* help themselves out of the difficulty by assuming a *Levirate* marriage had taken place. Chap. vi. 7, sqq., is defective, compared with Ex. vi. 23, 24. So are verses 18—23. See *Movers*, p. 236.

[In iv. 17, 18, something has, perhaps, fallen from the text, for, after the sons of Ezra are named, it is said, "she bare Miriam," &c., while there is no antecedent to the pronoun *she*. The same has, perhaps, taken place after verse 18, for it says, "these are the sons of Bithiah," and no list is given; and likewise after verse 19, where the sons of Hodiah are mentioned in general, but no list of them is given.]

There are some remarkable historical notices: —

Chap. iv. 21—23. "The sons of Shelah the son of Judah were, Er the father of Lecah, and Laadah the father of Mareshah, and the families of the house of them that wrought fine linen, of the house of Ashbea, and Jokim, and the men of Chozeba, and Joash, and Saraph, who had the dominion in Moab, and Jashubi-lehem. And these are ancient things.[a] These were the potters, and those that dwelt among plants and hedges: there they dwelt with the king for his work."

Chap. iv. 38—43. "These mentioned by their names were princes in their families: and the house of their fathers increased greatly. And they went to the entrance of Gedor, even unto the east side of the valley, to seek pasture for their flocks. And they found fat pasture and good, and the land was wide, and quiet, and peaceable; for they of Ham had dwelt there of old. And these written by name came in the days of Hezekiah king of Judah, and smote their tents, and the habitations that were found there, and destroyed them utterly unto this day, and dwelt in their rooms: because there was pasture there for their flocks. And some of them, even of the sons of Simeon, five hundred men, went to Mount Seir, having for their captains Pelatiah, and Neariah, and Rephaiah, and Uzziel, the the sons of Ishi. And they smote the rest of the Amalekites that were escaped, and dwelt there unto this day."

Chap. v. 10. "And in the days of Saul they made war with the

Compare vii. 6, and viii. 1, with Gen. xlvi. 21. See more examples, in *Gramberg*, l. c. p. 51, sqq.

[a] [*Horne* (pt. v. ch. ii. sect. vii. vol. ii. p. 222) thinks these words refer to "old records," which the Chronicler quoted, as a modern historian writes "Gibbon" in the margin as his authority for a fact.]

Hagarites, who fell by their hand: and they dwelt in their tents throughout all the east land of Gilead."

Chap. v. 19—22. "And they made war with the Hagarites, with Jetur, and Nephish, and Nodab. And they were helped against them, and the Hagarites were delivered into their hand, and all that were with them: for they cried to God in the battle, and he was entreated of them; because they put their trust in him. And they took away their cattle; of their camels fifty thousand, and of sheep two hundred and fifty thousand, and of asses two thousand, and of men a hundred thousand. For there fell down many slain, because the war was of God. And they dwelt in their steads until the captivity."

Chap. vii. 21—24. "And Zabad his son, and Shuthelah his son, and Ezer, and Elead, whom the men of Gath that were born in that land slew, because they came down to take away their cattle. And Ephraim their father mourned many days, and his brethren came to comfort him.

"And when he went in to his wife, she conceived and bare a son, and he called his name Beriah, because it went evil with his house. And his daughter was Sherah, who built Beth-horon the nether, and the upper, and Uzzen-sherah."

§ 188.

THE SAME SUBJECT CONTINUED.

II. 1 Ch. x.—xxix. contains the history of David. In some parts, this is entirely consistent with that in the books of Samuel, but it is distinguished from that by having several accounts peculiar to itself, and especially by its Levitical accounts.

III. The history of Solomon; 2 Ch. i.—ix.

IV. 2 Ch. x.—xxviii. The history of the kingdom of Judah while the kingdom of Israel also subsisted. It does not contain the history of Israel.

V. 2 Ch. xxix.—xxxvi. The history of Judah after

the fall of Israel, with particular reference to the state and history of the worship. The three last chapters are like the books of Kings.[a]

---

[a] *Table of Passages parallel with* 1 Ch. x.—2 Ch. xxxvi.

1 Ch. x. 1—12.	1 Sam. xxxxi.
—— xi. 1—9.	2 Sam. v. 1—10.
—— xi. 10—47.	—— xxiii. 8—39.
—— xiii. 1—14.	—— vi. 1—11.
—— xiv. 1—7.	—— v. 11—16.
—— xiv. 8—17.	—— v. 17—25.
—— xv. xvi.	—— vi. 12—23.
—— xvii.	—— vii.
—— xviii.	—— viii.
—— xix.	—— x.
—— xx. 1—3.	—— xi. 1, xii. 26—31.
—— xx. 4—8.	—— xxi. 18—22.
—— xxi.	—— xxiv.
2 Ch. i. 2—13.	1 Kings iii. 4—15.
—— i. 14—17.	—— x. 26—29.
—— ii.	—— v. 15—32.
—— iii. 1—v. 1.	—— vi. vii. 13—51.
—— v. 2—vii. 10.	—— viii.
—— vii. 11—22.	—— ix. 1—9.
—— viii.	—— ix. 10—28.
—— ix. 1—12.	—— x. 1—13.
—— ix. 13—31.	—— x. 14—29.
—— x. 1—xi. 4.	—— xii. 1—24.
—— xii. 2, 9—11, 13—16.	—— xiv. 21—31.
—— xiii. 1, 2, 23.	—— xv. 1, 2, 7, 8.
—— xiv. 1, xv. 16—19.	—— xv. 11—24.
—— xvi. 1—6, 11—14.	
—— xviii.	—— xxii. 2—35.
—— xx. 31—xxi. 1.	—— xxii. 41—51.
—— xxi. 5—10.	2 Kings viii. 17—24.
—— xxii. 1—9.	—— viii. 25—29, ix. 16—28, x. 12—14.
—— xxii. 10—xxiii. 21.	—— xi.
—— xxiv. 1—14, 23—27.	—— xii.
—— xxv. 1—4, 11, 17—28.	—— xiv. 1—14, 17—20.
—— xxvi. 1—4, 21, 23.	—— xiv. 21, 22, xv. 2—5, 7.
—— xxvii. 1—3, 9.	—— xv. 33—35, 38.
—— xxviii. 1—4.	—— xvi. 2—4.

§ 189.

RELATION OF THE CHRONICLES TO THE EARLIER HISTORICAL BOOKS.

1. In Respect to Antiquity.

To decide upon the degree of affinity between the books of Chronicles and those of Samuel and the Kings, is, above all, to determine upon their antiquity. We have the following facts to guide us in this: —

1. The history itself comes down to the end of the exile.

2 Ch. xxxvi. 20—23. "And them that had escaped from the sword carried he away to Babylon; where they were servants to him and his sons until the reign of the kingdom of Persia: to fulfil the word of the Lord by the mouth of Jeremiah, until the land had enjoyed her Sabbaths: for as long as she lay desolate, she kept Sabbath, to fulfil threescore and ten years.

"Now in the first year of Cyrus king of Persia, ... the Lord stirred up the spirit of Cyrus king of Persia, that he made a proclamation throughout all his kingdom, and put it also in writing, saying, 'Thus saith Cyrus king of Persia, " All the kingdoms of the earth

---

2 Ch. xxix. 1, 2.	2 Kings xviii. 2, 3.
—— xxxii. 9—21.	—— xviii. 17—35, xix. 14, 15, 35—37.
—— xxxii. 24, 25, 30—33.	—— xx. 1, 2, 8, 9, 12, sqq., 20, 21.
—— xxxiii. 1—10, 20.	—— xxi. 1—10, 18.
—— xxxiii. 21—25.	—— xxi. 19—24.
—— xxxiv. 1, 2, 8—28.	—— xxii.
—— xxxiv. 29—33.	—— xxiii. 1—20.
—— xxxv. 1, 18, 20—24, xxxvi. 1. .	—— xxiii. 21—23, 28—30.
—— xxxvi. 2—4.	—— xxiii. 31—34.
—— xxxvi. 5, 6, 8.	—— xxiii. 36, 37, xxiv. 1, 6.
—— xxxvi. 9, 10.	—— xxiv. 8—10, 14, 17.
—— xxxvi. 11, 12.	—— xxiv. 18, 19.
—— xxxvi. 22, 23.	Ezra i. 1, 2.

hath the Lord God of heaven given me; and he hath charged me to build him a house in Jerusalem, which is in Judah. Who is there among you of all his people? The Lord his God be with him, and let him go up."'"

2. In that confused passage, 1 Ch. iii. 19—24, the genealogy of the house of David is brought down to the second generation after Zerubbabel, if no further: —

1 Ch. iii. 19—24. "And the sons of Pedaiah were Zerubbabel, and Shimei: and the sons of Zerubbabel; Meshullam, and Hananiah, and Shelomith their sister: and Hashubah, and Ohel, and Berechiah, and Hasadiah, Jushab-hesed, five. And the sons of Hananiah; Pelatiah, and Jesaiah: the sons of Rephaiah, the sons of Arnan, the sons of Obadiah, the sons of Shechaniah. And the sons of Shechaniah; Shemaiah; and the sons of Shemaiah; Hattush, and Igeal, and Bariah, and Neariah, and Shaphat, six. And the sons of Neariah; Elioenai, and Hezekiah, and Azrikam, three. And the sons of Elioneai were, Hodaiah, and Eliashib, and Pelaiah, and Akkub, and Johanan, and Delaiah, and Anani, seven."

R. Benjamin[a] thinks this genealogy contains nine generations from Jesiah to Johanan, (verses 21, 24,) and therefore comes down to 270 B. C.[b] But, according to Movers and Hävernik,[c] it goes no further than the grandchildren of Zerubbabel — Pelatiah and Jesiah; and then, as they think, the author adds some names from David's posterity in general. But Shemaiah is the son of Shechaniah, (verse 22,) a contemporary of Nehemiah, (Neh. iii. 29;) and therefore the genealogy comes down to the third generation after Nehemiah. This passage is commonly regarded as a later addition.[d]

3. Contrary to all historical propriety, the author reckons by *Daricks* in the history of David, (1 Ch. xxix

[a] In Meor Enajim, fol. 123, *a*. [b] *Zunz*, l. c. p. 31.
[c] *Movers*, p. 29, sqq. *Hävernik*, p. 266.
[d] *Eichhorn*, § 490. *Dahler*, l. c. p. 5. *Keil*, p. 45.

7.) It is plain that the name and use of this coin had long been current among the Jews.[a]

4. The document in 1 Ch. ix., from the time of Nehemiah, (chap. xi.,) could not have been so disfigured as it has been shown to be, (§ 187,) except in a time far more modern. Movers thinks the Chronicler was a younger contemporary of Nehemiah, and wrote about 400 B. C. Zunz places him about 260 B. C.

5. Besides the orthography and language,[b] the mythological and Levitical spirit of the book, as well as its place in the canon, is evidence in favor of its late origin.[c]

§ 190, *a*.

2. In Respect to their common Contents.

In the passages which the books of Chronicles have in common with the books of Kings, there are many

---

[a] [אֲדַרְכֹּון. This word does not appear in the English Bible, but is translated *dram*. The origin of the name is doubtful. According to *Suidas*, *Harpocration*, and the *scholiast* on Aristophanes, (Ecclesiazus, verse 741,) it is derived from a *more ancient* Darius; but according to the common opinion, from Darius *Hystaspes*. *Herodotus* (iv. 166) does not say this distinctly. See the etymologies in *Gesenius* and *Winer*. But see, also, *Hengstenberg*, l. c. vol. i. p. 51, sqq., and *Movers*, l. c. p. 26, note *b*, and the authorities there cited.]

[b] דָּוִיד, for דָּוִד; יְרוּשָׁלַיִם, for יְרוּשָׁלִַם; עֻזָּא, 1 Ch. xiii. 7, for עֻזָּה; הֵיךְ, 1 Ch. xiii. 12, for אֵיךְ; אִישַׁי, 1 Ch. ii. 12, for יִשַׁי; אַרְגְּוָן, for אַרְגָּמָן, 2 Ch. ii. 6; בוּץ, 2 Ch. ii. 13; בִּירָה, 1 Ch. xxix. 1; גַּנְזַךְ, 1 Ch. xxviii. 11; הִתְיַחֵשׂ, 1 Ch. v. 17; מִדְרָשׁ, 2 Ch. xiii. 22, xxiv. 27; נָדָן, 1 Ch. xxi. 27; צֹרֶךְ, 2 Ch. ii. 15; קִבֵּל, 2 Ch. xxix. 16; תַּלְמִיד, 1 Ch. xxv. 8; ראמות, for רמות; רִעְמָא, for רעמה. *Jahn*, vol. ii. p. 244, sq. *Gramberg*, p. 5, sqq. According to *Gesenius* (Gesch. Heb. Sprache, p. 157, sq.) and *Gramberg*, (p. 39,) some of the variants of the Chronicles may be explained by the use of the square letter. But this is doubtful.

[c] *Bertholdt* (p. 983, sqq.) derives too much from this circumstance, for the *order* of the book is not chronological. *Keil*, p. 72.

differences between the two. 1. The orthography of the Chronicles is later.[a] 2. The language is frequently altered to suit the grammar, or the usage of a later time, for the sake of clearness or elegance of expression, but from ignorance and carelessness likewise.[b]

---

[a] 1. The *Scriptio Plena frequently occurs in the Kethib*; e. g. לשאול לו, 1 Ch. xviii. 10; אוניות, 2 Ch. viii. 18.

2. *Writing according to the more modern Aramaic Pronunciation.* — הירך, 1 Ch. xiii. 12, for איך; הררי, 1 Ch. xi. 35, for אררי; דרמשק, 1 Ch. xviii. 5, 6, for דַּמֶּשֶׂק; מכרבל, 1 Ch. xv. 27, for מְכֻבָּל. [*Movers*, p. 200, sqq.]

3. *The Correction of inaccurate or irregular Writing.* — סוֹבֵב, 2 Ch. xxi. 9, for סוֹבֵיב: מביא, 1 Ch. xi. 2, for מבי; כסא, 2 Ch. ix. 18, for כסה; ביר, 1 Ch. xi. 17, 18, 22, for באד. Hence the Chronicler often agrees with the Keri in the parallel passages.

[b] 1. *Exchange of the old for the modern Formation.* — ממלכה, with מלכות, 2 Ch. xiv. 2, sqq.; אנכי, with אני, 1 Ch. xvii. 16, and elsewhere. [See *Ewald*, Krit. Gram. p. 194.]

2. *Exchange of the old and irregular Inflection for the modern or regular*; e. g. אריים, for אריות, 2 Ch. ix. 19; הָיְתָה, for הָיָת, 1 Ch. xix. 12; ידעון, for ידעו, 2 Ch. vi. 29; and similar changes, which often occur.

3. *Alteration of the Construction to favor the later Use.* — Omission of the infinitive absolute, 2 Ch. vi. 2, and elsewhere; plural instead of the feminine in the names of countries, 1 Ch. xviii. 2, 5, 6. [?] Elohim in the singular instead of the plural, 1 Ch. xvii. 21. [The same usage, however, occurs in the very first verse of Genesis.] *He local*, or אל, instead of the accusative, after verbs of motion; 1 Ch. xix. 15, העירה; 2 Ch. xviii. 28, אל רמות. [See *Ewald*, l. c. § 311.] The preposition ב, instead of the *accusative of place*. Omission of ל in the construction ———— למן ויעד, 1 Ch. xvii. 5; of כ, where a second כ follows, 1 Ch. xvii. 21. Use of the *apocopated* form of the *future conversive*, for the *not apocopated* form; וירך, ותעל, 2 Ch. xviii. 33, 34, xxi. 9, for ויכה, and ותעלה. Exchange of prepositions; מן השמים, 2 Ch. vi. 21, for אֶל השמים; עמד לפני, 2 Ch. x. 6, for עמד את פני; על, 1 Ch. x. 3, for אל; and the reverse, 1 Ch. xiv. 10.

4. *A later or more common Word for one older and more unusual.* — גופה, 1 Ch. x. 12, for גויה; מרקד ומשחק, 1 Ch. xv. 29, for מפזז ומכרכר; ויסבו, 2 Ch. xviii. 31, for ויסורו; בתץ, 2 Ch. xxxiii. 3, for אבד; לחסיד, 2 Ch. xxxii. 8, for להגיד.

5. *Confusion of Geographical Names.* — אבל מים, *Abel-maim*, 2 Ch. xvi.

§ 190, *b*.

The same Subject continued.

Some of these discrepancies in the language pass over into such as relate to facts themselves; and, accordingly, we find omissions, abridgments, interpolations, and alterations, by which the history is generally changed for the worse, though it may be altered only in minor matters.

4, for *Abel-beth-maacha;* ארם נהרים, *Syria of the two Rivers*, 1 Ch. xix. 6, for *Beth-rehob*. [See other examples in *Movers*, p. 208, sqq.]

6. *Explanations like Glosses.*—כל הבא על לב, 2 Ch. vii. 11, *all that came into the heart*, for כל חשק, *all he wished;* ויבער באש, 2 Ch. xxviii. 3, for העביר באש.

7. *An indefinite is often used for a definite Term.*—האלה, *a tree*, 1 Ch. x. 12, for האשל, *a tamarisk-tree;* תצא במלחמה, 1 Ch. xiv. 15; תחרץ, *go to battle*, for *cut down;* ויצא לפניהם, *went out against them*, 1 Ch. xiv. 8, for וירד אל המצודה, *went down to the fort.*

8. *Euphemisms.*—עד המפשעה, 1 Ch. xix. 4, for עד שתותיהם.

9. *A Mark of Ignorance or Misunderstanding.*—אניות הלכות תרשיש, *ships that go to Tarshish*, 2 Ch. xix. 21, xx. 36, 37, for אני תרשיש, *a Tarshish ship*, 1 Kings x. 21, 2 Kings xxii. 49—a mistake which *Keil* (l. c. p. 303) in vain seeks to justify, but which *Movers* acknowledges, (p. 254;) מלבד אשר הביאה למלך, 2 Ch. ix. 12, *beside what she brought to the king*, which is without meaning in this connection, instead of מלבד אשר נתן לה ביד למלך שלמה, *beside what was given her by the hand of King Solomon* 1 Kings x. 13, where *Movers* himself (l. c. p. 213) acknowledges either a mistake of the copyist, or an oversight of the author; מַלְכֵי עֲרָב, *kings of Arabia*, 2 Ch. ix. 14, for מַלְכֵי הָעֶרֶב, *kings of the allies.*

There may be mistakes by the transcriber, in 2 Ch. iv. 3, 22. Compare 1 Kings vii. 24, 50; see *Movers*, p. 214. The obscure passages, חרשי קיר 1 Ch. xiv. 1, instead of חרשי אבן קיר, 2 Sam. v. 11; מצא, without לבו 1 Ch. xvii. 25, bear marks of carelessness. The Chronicler alters the construction to serve his turn; e. g. by the insertion of הצליח, 2 Ch. vii. 11, (compare 1 Kings ix. 1;) by omitting the superfluous word, אנשים, 1 Ch. x 3, (compare 1 Sam. xxxi. 3; compare also 1 Ch. xiii. 7, with 2 Sam. vi. 3. See *Movers*, p. 213, sq.) את ידו is inserted, 1 Ch. xiii. 9, to make it more clear, as likewise מלאכים, 1 Ch. xix. 2, 16. See *Movers*, p. 222. But

I. Omissions.

1. *In the Names of Places.*—1 Ch. xiv. 13, "And the Philistines spread themselves abroad in the valley"—*Rephaim* is omitted; xviii. 17, the place, "*at Helam*," is omitted; 2 Ch. xxi. 9, "Jehoram went first *with his princes*," instead of "went *even to Zair*," 2 Kings viii. 21. So in 1 Ch. xxi. 4, the population of Judah, by Joab's census, is 470,000 soldiers; of Israel, 1,100,000; in 2 Sam. xxiv. 4—10, by the same census, in Judah, there are 500,000; in Israel, 800,000. Compare also 2 Ch. xvi. 5, 6, with 1 Kings xv. 21, 22.[a]

2. *Omissions of correlative Designations and Circumstances.*

1 Sam. xxxi. 12, 13. "All the valiant men arose, *and went all night*, and took the body of Saul, and the bodies of his sons, *from the wall of Beth-shan*, and came to Jabesh, *and burnt them there.* And they *took* their bones, *and* buried them under Tamarisk at Jabesh, and fasted seven days."	1 Ch. x. 12. "They arose, all the valiant men, and took away the body of Saul, and the bodies of his sons, and brought them to Jabesh, and buried their bones under the tree in Jabesh, and fasted seven days."

---

something is omitted in 2 Ch. viii. 10, (compare 1 Kings ix. 23,) by which the sense is rendered less clear. *Movers*, p. 217.

[An amusing mistake occurs in 1 Ch. xi. 23, as compared with 2 Sam. xxiii. 21.

Samuel.	Chronicles.
וְהוּא [בְּנָיָהוּ] הִכָּה אֶת־אִישׁ מִצְרִי אֲשֶׁר מַרְאֶה &c.	וְהוּא [בְּנָיָה] הִכָּה אֶת־הָאִישׁ הַמִּצְרִי אִישׁ מִדָּה חָמֵשׁ בָּאַמָּה &c.
And he slew an Ægyptian, *a respectable man*, &c.	And he slew *the* Ægyptian, *a man of tall stature, five cubits high*, &c.

See the attempt of *Movers* (p. 58) to explain this.]

[a] [In Josh. xix. 2—6, we find a list of cities and towns belonging to Simeon; verse 6, it is added, "*thirteen cities*," &c., (ערים שלש־עשרה.) The list is copied, though not without alterations, in 1 Ch. iv. 28—31, but the Chronicler has שערים, verse 31,—a city of *Judah*, Josh. xv. 36,—instead of ערים שלש־עשרה. *Movers* (p. 57) thinks the error arose from mistaking some *numeral abbreviations* used in the text.]

1 Ch. xix. 4, Hanun "took David's servants and shaved them;" 2 Sam. x. 4, "*shaved off the one half of their beards*." 2 Ch. v. 3, all the men of Israel "assembled in the feast which is the seventh month;" 1 Kings viii. 2, "in the *month Ethanim*, which is the seventh month."

1 Ch. xx. 3. "And he brought out the people that were in it; and cut them with saws, and with harrows of iron, and with axes. Even so dealt David with all the cities of the children of Ammon."	2 Sam. xii. 31. "And he brought forth the people that were therein, and *put* them under saws, and under harrows of iron, and under axes *of iron, and made them pass through the brick-kiln;* and thus did he unto all the cities of the children of Ammon."
2 Ch. xvi. 2. "Then Asa brought out silver and gold out of the treasures of the house of the Lord and of the king's house, and sent to Ben-hadad king of Syria, that dwelt at Damascus."	1 Kings xv. 18. "Then Asa *took all the* silver and the gold *that were left in the treasures of the house* of the Lord, *and the treasures* of the king's house, *and delivered them into the hand of his servants; and King Asa* sent them to Ben-hadad, *the son of Tabrimon, the son of Hezion*, king of Syria, that dwelt at Damascus."
2 Ch. xxxiii. 20. "So Manasseh slept with his fathers, and they buried him in his own house: and Amon his son reigned in his stead."	2 Kings xxi. 18. "And Manasseh slept with his fathers, and was buried *in the garden of* his own house, *in the garden of Uzza:* and Amon his son reigned in his stead."

II. Abridgments.

1 Ch. xx. 1, the author takes the words, "and *David remained at Rabbah*," from 2 Sam. xi. 1, but he omits *the whole story of Uriah*, (xi. 2—xii. 25,) and even the statement (xii. 29) that David subsequently went to Rabbah himself; so that the whole which is related in 1 Ch. xx. 2, sqq., appears to take place at Jerusalem

There is a discrepancy between the two following passages: —

2 Ch. xxii. 9. "And he sought Ahaziah: and they caught him, (for he was hid in Samaria,) and brought him to Jehu: and when they had slain him, they buried him: 'Because,' said they, 'he is the son of Jehoshaphat, who sought the Lord with all his heart.'"

2 Kings ix. 27. "But when Ahaziah the king of Judah saw this, he fled by the way of the garden-house. And Jehu followed after him, and said, 'Smite him also in the chariot.' And they did so at the going up to Gur, which is by Ibleam. And he fled to Megiddo, and died there. And his servants carried him in a chariot to Jerusalem, and buried him in his sepulchre with his fathers in the city of David."

Movers thinks this may be explained as a corruption of the text, or by some inaccuracy in abridging, or by the use of a different authority, or in some other way! [a]

III. INSERTIONS OF MATTER NOT CONTAINED IN THE PREVIOUS BOOKS.

1. *Edifying Glosses.* — 1 Ch. xi. 3, David is anointed king, "*according to the word of Jehovah*, by the hand of Samuel the prophet." 2 Ch. xxi. 10, the Edomites and Libnah revolted from Jehoram, "*because he had forsaken the Lord God of his fathers.*" In 1 Kings xxii. 31, 32, the soldiers attack Jehoshaphat, mistaking him for Ahab, king of Israel, but, discovering their error, by *his cries*, they desist; but in 2 Ch. xviii. 31, "Jehoshaphat cried out, and the *Lord God helped him, and moved them to depart from him.*" 2 Kings viii. 29, Joram, the son of Ahab, went back to be healed of his wounds, and "Ahaziah went down to see him, because he was sick." In 2 Ch. xxii. 7, "the destruction of Ahaziah *was of God, because he came to Jehoram, ... and went out*

---

[a] *Movers*, p. 258.

against Jehu ...... whom Jehovah anointed to cut off the house of Ahab." In 1 Kings xiv. 11, 19, Amaziah, king of Judah, would not listen to the proposal of Jehoash, but, hazarding a battle, was overcome; he fled to Lachish, and was there cut off. In 2 Ch. xxv. 20, 27, "Amaziah would not hear, *for it came of God that he might deliver them into the hand ...... because they sought after the gods of Edom;*" verse 27, "After the time that *he turned from following Jehovah*, they made a conspiracy against him."

In 1 Kings ix. 24, Solomon builds a palace in Millo for one of his wives, the daughter of Pharaoh; but in 2 Ch. viii. 11, an edifying speech is put into his mouth:—"My wife shall not dwell in the house of David, king of Israel, because *the places are holy, whereunto the ark of Jehovah hath come;*" and she was a strange woman, whose presence might defile the holy city of David and the ark.

2. *The Insertion of Verses of Psalms;* 2 Ch. vi. 41, 42.

"Arise, O Lord God, into thy rest;
Thou and the ark of thy strength;"

from Ps. cxxxii. 8. Other edifying passages are taken from other places and inserted in the text.

2 Ch. vii. 13, 14. "If I shut up heaven, that there be no rain, or if I command the locust to devour the land, or if I send pestilence among my people: if my people, which are called by my name, shall humble themselves, and pray, and seek my face, and turn from their wicked ways; then will I hear from heaven, and will forgive their sins, and will heal their land."

These are taken from 1 Kings viii. 35—37, as are also 2 Ch. vi. 26—28.

IV. ALTERATIONS.

1. *For the Sake of designating with greater Clearness.* — 1 Ch. xiii. 10, "The anger of Jehovah was kindled against Uzzah, ... because he put his hand to the ark; and there he died before God;" while in 2 Sam. vi. 7, it is "for his mistake." Compare 2 Ch. xxxiv 24, with 2 Kings xxii. 16.

2. But these alterations are sometimes made *to perplex and disguise the Sense.* — Compare 1 Ch. xix. 3, with 2 Sam. x. 3. 1 Sam. xxxi. 6, "So Saul died, and his three sons, and his armor-bearer, and all his men that same day together;" but 1 Ch. x. 6, "So Saul died, and his three sons, and *all his house died together*." 2 Ch. ii. 2—5, is an edifying recast of 1 Kings v. 15—18: —

2 Ch. ii. 2—5. "And Solomon told out threescore and ten thousand men to bear burdens, and fourscore thousand to hew in the mountain, and three thousand and six hundred to oversee them. And Solomon sent to Huram the king of Tyre, saying, 'As thou didst deal with David my father, and didst send him cedars to build him a house to dwell therein, even so deal with me. Behold, I build a house to the name of the Lord my God, to dedicate it to him, and to burn before him sweet incense, and for the continual showbread, and for the burnt-offerings morning and evening, on the Sabbaths, and on the new moons, and on the solemn feasts of the Lord our God. This is an ordinance forever to Israel. And the house which I build is great: for great is our God above all gods.'"

1 Kings v. 15—18. "And Solomon had threescore and ten thousand that bare burdens, and fourscore thousand hewers in the mountains; besides the chief of Solomon's officers which were over the work, three thousand and three hundred, which ruled over the people that wrought in the work. And the king commanded, and they brought great stones, costly stones, and hewed stones, to lay the foundation of the house. And Solomon's builders and Hiram's builders did hew them, and the stone-squarers; so they prepared timber and stones to build the house."

It is absurd to suppose, as we must, from 2 Ch. ii. 8, that Hiram sent sandal-wood from Mount Lebanon.[a] Verse 6 also disfigures the original text. Numbers are enlarged; in 1 Ch. xxi. 5, we have 1,100,000, instead of 800,000, in 2 Sam. xxiv. 9; verse 25, 600 shekels of gold, instead of 50 shekels of silver, 2 Sam. xxiv. 24. But the numbers are sometimes made smaller. There is a remarkable contradiction between the following passages: 2 Ch. xiii. 23, "Asa reigned in his stead. In his days the land was quiet ten years," or xv. 19, "there was no more war unto the five and thirtieth year of Asa," and 1 Kings xv. 32, "*and there was war between Asa and Baasha . . . . . . all their days.*"[b]

---

[a] [If this word, אלגומים, means *sandal-wood*, — which may be but one of several substances to which it is applied, — then it may be used correctly in 1 Kings x. 11, 12, and 2 Ch. ix. 10, 11, where it is brought from Ophir. But if it means *only* sandal-wood, the passage now before us is false.] But see 1 Kings v. 20.

[b] *Movers* thinks the list of David's heroes, 1 Ch. xi. 10—47, is independent of that in 2 Sam. xxiii. 8—39, and drawn from a document used in common by the two authors. He draws this opinion from the numerous variants of the proper names; from the greater perfection of the list in Chronicles, as verse 41 to 47 is wanting in Samuel; and from the difficult readings in Chronicles, for which the easier have been substituted in Samuel. But verse 11 agrees with Samuel; verse 8 is obviously a conjecture drawn from 2 Sam. xxiii. 20. I do not find that the readings are more difficult in verses 14, 15. Compare 2 Sam. xxiii. 12, 13. This is rather the case with verse 19, 25. Compare 2 Sam. xxiii. 17, 23. He confirms this by the fact that 1 Ch. xx. 4—8, only repeats verses 18—22 from 2 Sam. xxi. 15—22, and therefore at the end does not enumerate *four* sons of Repha, and from the circumstance that the Chronicler, in verse 8, uses the ancient form אֵל, instead of אֵלֶּה. Even 1 Ch. xi. 1—9, is, he thinks, more original than 2 Sam. v. 1—10, because verses 4, 5, in Samuel, are an interpolation, which disturbs the connection between verse 3 and verse 6. The Chronicler does not disturb this connection, (but the use of *vau conversive* is slender proof,) for, 1 Ch. xi. 4, the expression "which is Jebus," refers to a time when this was the common name. But the explanation was occasioned by the subsequent mention of the Jebusites. Another argument is, that 1 Ch. xi. 6, contains the additional account which is lacking in 2 Sam. xxiii. 8. But this is a very superficial conjecture.

§ 190, *c*.

The same Subject continued.

The inaccuracy which has produced these discrepancies shows itself also in the improper insertion of 1 Ch. xiv.,[a] from which it would appear that, according to 1 Ch. xv. 1, David built houses in three months. It appears, also, in the unsuitable anticipation of the catalogue of Solomon's riches, in 2 Ch. i. 14—17, which should have been put in 2 Ch. ix. 25, sqq. But, in some other, and especially the most important, discrepancies, we discover a peculiar manner of thinking, a certain predilection and partiality, even a certain design, after which, not only the style and manner of the history, but the facts themselves, are altered and falsified. This appears,

I. In the dogmatic and mythological Alterations and Additions.

1 Ch. xxi. 1. "And *Satan* stood up against Israel, and provoked David to number Israel."	2 Sam. xxiv. 1. "And again the anger of *the Lord* was kindled against Israel, and *he* moved David against them to say, 'Go, number Israel and Judah.'"
1 Ch. xxi. 15, sqq. "And God sent an angel unto Jerusalem to destroy it: and as he was destroying, the Lord beheld, and he repented him of the evil; and said to the angel that destroyed, 'It is enough: stay now thine hand.' And the angel of the Lord stood by the threshing-floor of Ornan the Jebusite. And David lifted up his	2 Sam. xxiv. 16, sqq. "And when the angel stretched out his hand upon Jerusalem to destroy it, the Lord repented him of the evil, and said to the angel that destroyed the people, 'It is enough: stay now thine hand.' And the angel of the Lord was by the threshing-place of Araunah the Jebusite. And David

[a] Compare 2 Sam. v. 11—25.

eyes, and saw *the angel of the Lord stand between the earth and the heaven, having a drawn sword in his hand stretched out over Jerusalem.* Then David and the elders, *clothed in sackcloth, fell upon their faces.*"

"*Then the angel of the Lord commanded* Gad to say to David, that David should go up, and set up an altar unto the Lord in the threshing-floor of Ornan the Jebusite. And David went up at the saying of Gad, which he spake in the name of the Lord. And Ornan turned back, *and saw the angel; and his four sons with him hid themselves.* Now Ornan was threshing wheat. And as David came to Ornan, Ornan looked and saw David, and went out of the threshing-floor, and bowed himself to David with his face to the ground. Then David said to Ornan, 'Grant me the place of this threshing-floor, that I may build an altar therein unto the Lord: thou shalt grant it me for the full price: that the plague may be stayed from the people.' And Ornan said unto David, 'Take it to thee, and let my lord the king do that which is good in his eyes: lo, I give thee the oxen also for burnt-offerings, and the threshing instruments for wood, *and the wheat for the meat-offering;* I give it all.' And King David said to Ornan, 'Nay; but I will verily buy it for the full

spake unto the Lord when he saw the angel that smote the people, and said, '*Lo, I have sinned, and I have done wickedly: but these sheep, what have they done? Let thine hand, I pray thee, be against me, and against my father's house.*'

"And Gad came that day to David, and said unto him, 'Go up, rear an altar unto the Lord in the threshing-floor of Araunah the Jebusite.' And David, according to the saying of Gad, went up, as the Lord commanded. And Araunah looked, and saw the king and his servants coming on toward him: and Araunah went out, and bowed himself before the king on his face upon the ground. And Araunah said, 'Wherefore is my lord the king come to his servant?' And David said, 'To buy the threshing-floor of thee, to build an altar unto the Lord, that the plague may be stayed from the people.' And Araunah said unto David, 'Let my lord the king take and offer up what seemeth good unto him: behold oxen for burnt-sacrifice, and threshing instruments and other instruments of the oxen for wood.' *All these things did Araunah, as a king, give unto the king. And Araunah said unto the king, 'The Lord thy God accept thee.'* And the king said unto Araunah, 'Nay: but I will surely buy it of thee at price: for I will not take that which is thine for the Lord, nor offer burnt-offerings without cost.' So David gave to Ornan for the place *six hundred shekels of gold* by weight. And David built there an altar unto the Lord, and offered burnt-offerings and peace-offerings, *and called upon the Lord; and he answered him from heaven by fire upon the altar of burnt-offering. And the Lord commanded the angel, and he put up his sword again into the sheath thereof.*

"At that time when David saw that the Lord had answered him in the threshing-floor of Ornan the Jebusite, then he sacrificed there. For the tabernacle of the Lord, which Moses made in the wilderness, and the altar of the burnt-offering, were at that season in the high place at Gibeon. But David could not go before it to inquire of God: for he was afraid, because of the sword of the angel of the Lord."

a price: neither will I offer burnt-offerings unto the Lord my God of that which doth cost me nothing.' So David bought the threshing-floor and the oxen for *fifty shekels of silver*. And David built there an altar unto the Lord, and offered burnt-offerings and peace-offerings. So the Lord was entreated for the land, and the plague was stayed from Israel."

2 Ch. vii. 1—3. "Now when Solomon had made an end of praying, *the fire came down from heaven, and consumed the burnt-offering and the sacrifice;* and the glory of the Lord filled the house. And the priests could not enter into the house of the Lord, because the glory of the Lord had filled the Lord's house. *And when all the children of Israel saw how the fire came down, and*

1 Kings viii. 54—61. "And it was so, that when Solomon had made an end of praying all this prayer and supplication unto the Lord, he arose from before the altar of the Lord, from kneeling on his knees with his hands spread up to heaven. And he stood and blessed all the congregation of Israel with a loud voice, saying, 'Blessed be the Lord, that hath given rest unto his people Israel,

the glory of the Lord upon the house, they bowed themselves with their faces to the ground upon the pavement, and worshipped, and praised the Lord, saying, 'For he is good; for his mercy endureth forever.' "

according to all that he promised: there hath not failed one word of all his good promise, which he promised by the hand of Moses his servant. The Lord our God be with us, as he was with our fathers: let him not leave us, nor forsake us: that he may incline our hearts unto him, to walk in all his ways, and to keep his commandments, and his statutes, and his judgments, which he commanded our fathers. And let these my words wherewith I have made supplication before the Lord, be nigh unto the Lord our God day and night, that he maintain the cause of his servant, and the cause of his people Israel at all times, as the matter shall require: that all the people of the earth may know that the Lord is God, and that there is none else. Let your heart therefore be perfect with the Lord our God, to walk in his statutes, and to keep his commandments, as at this day.' "

In 2 Ch. xxxii. 31, it is said, "*God left Hezekiah to try him, that he might know all that was in his heart,*" in the negotiation with the Babylonians; but in 2 Kings xx. 12, 13, it is simply said, "The king of Babylon sent letters and a present to Hezekiah, and he hearkened to them."

II. Alteration made out of a Preference for the Levitical Forms of Worship, and the Tribe of Levi.

1. *Amplifications and Embellishments.*

2 Ch. v. 11—14. "And it came to pass, when the priests were come out of the holy place; (for all the priests that were present were sanctified, and did not then wait by course: also the Levites which were the singers, all of them of Asaph, of Heman, of Jeduthun, with their sons and their brethren; being arrayed in white linen, having cymbals, and psalteries, and harps, stood at the east end of the altar, and with them a hundred and twenty priests sounding with trumpets;) it came even to pass, as the trumpeters and singers were as one, to make one sound to be heard in praising and thanking the Lord; and when they lifted up their voice with the trumpets, and cymbals, and instruments of music, and praised the Lord, saying, 'For he is good; for his mercy endureth forever:' that then the house was filled with a cloud, even the house of the Lord; so that the priests could not stand to minister by reason of the cloud: for the glory of the Lord had filled the house of God."	In 1 Kings viii. 10, 11, only this: "And it came to pass, when the priests were come out of the holy place, that the cloud filled the house of the Lord, so that the priests could not stand to minister because of the cloud: for the glory of the Lord had filled the house of the Lord." Here is no mention of the Levitical music.
2 Ch. vii. 5—10. "And King Solomon offered a sacrifice of twenty and two thousand oxen, and a hundred and twenty thousand sheep. So the king and all the people dedicated the house of God. And the priests waited on their offices; the Levites also with instruments of music of the	1 Kings viii. 63—65. "And Solomon offered a sacrifice of peace-offerings, which he offered unto the Lord, two and twenty thousand oxen, and a hundred and twenty thousand sheep. So the king and all the children of Israel dedicated the house of the Lord. The same day did the

Lord, which David the king had made to praise the Lord, because his mercy endureth forever, when David praised by their ministry; and the priests sounded trumpets before them, and all Israel stood. Moreover Solomon hallowed the middle of the court that was before the house of the Lord; for there he offered burnt-offerings, and the fat of the peace-offerings, because the brazen altar which Solomon had made was not able to receive the burnt-offerings, and the meat-offerings, and the fat.

"Also at the same time Solomon kept the feast seven days, and all Israel with him, a very great congregation, from the entering in of Hamath unto the river of Ægypt. And in the eighth day they made a solemn assembly; for they kept the dedication of the altar seven days, and the feast seven days. And on the three and twentieth day of the seventh month he sent the people away into their tents, glad and merry in heart for the goodness that the Lord had showed unto David, and to Solomon, and to Israel his people."

king hallow the middle of the court that was before the house of the Lord; for there he offered burnt-offerings, and meat-offerings, and the fat of the peace-offerings; because the brazen altar that was before the Lord was too little to receive the burnt-offerings, and meat-offerings, and the fat of the peace-offerings. And at that time Solomon held a feast, and all Israel with him, a great congregation, from the entering in of Hamath unto the river of Ægypt, before the Lord our God, seven days and seven days, even fourteen days."

2 Ch. viii. 12, 13. "Then Solomon offered burnt-offerings unto the Lord on the altar of the Lord, which he had built before the porch, even after a certain rate every day, offering according to the commandment of Moses, on the Sabbaths, and on the new-moons, and on the solemn feasts,

1 Kings ix. 25. "And three times in a year did Solomon offer burnt-offerings and peace-offerings upon the altar which he built unto the Lord, and he burnt incense upon the altar that was before the Lord. So he finished the house."

three times in the year, even in the feast of unleavened bread, and in the feast of weeks, and in the feast of tabernacles."

2 Ch. xxiii. 17—20. "Then all the people went to the house of Baal, and brake it down, and brake his altars and his images in pieces, and slew Mattan the priest of Baal before the altars. Also Jehoiada appointed the offices of the house of the Lord, by the hand of the priests the Levites, whom David had distributed in the house of the Lord, to offer the burnt-offerings of the Lord, as it is written in the law of Moses, with rejoicing and singing, after the manner of David. And he set the porters at the gates of the house of the Lord, that none which was unclean in any thing should enter in. And he took the captains of hundreds, and the nobles, and the governors of the people, and all the people of the land, and brought down the king from the house of the Lord; and they came through the high gate into the king's house, and set the king upon the throne of the kingdom."

2 Kings xi. 18, 19. "And all the people of the land went into the house of Baal, and brake it down; his altars and his images brake they in pieces thoroughly, and slew Mattan the priest of Baal before the altars; and the priest appointed officers over the house of the Lord. And he took the rulers over hundreds, and the captains, and the guard, and all the people of the land; and they brought down the king from the house of the Lord, and came by the way of the gate of the guard to the king's house; and he sat on the throne of the kings."

In 2 Ch. xxxv. 1—19, occurs the following minute account of Josiah's passover: —

"Moreover Josiah kept a passover unto the Lord in Jerusalem; and they killed the passover on the fourteenth day of the first month. And he set the priests in their charges, and encouraged them to the service of the house of the Lord, and said unto the Levites that taught all Israel, which were holy unto the Lord, 'Put the holy ark in the house which Solomon the son of David king of Israel did build; it shall not be a burden upon your shoulders; serve now the Lord your God, and his people Israel. And prepare yourselves by the houses of your fathers, after your courses, according to the writing of David king of Israel, and according to the writing of Solomon his son. And stand in the holy place according to the divisions of the families of the fathers of your brethren the people, and after the division of the families of the Levites. So kill the passover, and sanctify yourselves, and prepare your brethren, that they may do according to the word of the Lord by the hand of Moses.' And Josiah gave to the people, of the flock, lambs and kids, all for the passover-offerings, for all that were present, to the number of thirty thousand, and three thousand bullocks; these were of the king's substance. And his princes gave willingly unto the people, to the priests, and to the Levites: Hilkiah and Zechariah and Jehiel, rulers of the house of God, gave unto the priests for the passover-offerings two thousand and six hundred small cattle, and three hundred oxen. Conaniah also, and Shemaiah and Nethaneel his brethren, and Hashabiah, and Jehiel, and Jozabad, chief of the Levites, gave unto the Levites for passover-offerings five thousand small cattle, and five hundred oxen. So the service was prepared, and the priests stood in their place, and the Levites in their courses, according to the king's commandment. And they killed the passover, and the priests sprinkled the blood from their hands, and the Levites flayed them. And they removed the burnt-offerings, that they might give according to the divisions of the families of the people, to offer unto the Lord, as it is written in the book of Moses. And so did they with the oxen. And they roasted the passover with fire according to the ordinance: but the other holy offerings sod they in pots, and in caldrons, and in pans, and divided them speedily among all the people. And afterward they made ready for themselves, and for the priests; because the priests the sons of Aaron were busied in offering of burnt-offerings and the fat until night; therefore the Levites prepared for themselves, and for the priests the sons of Aaron. And the singers the sons of Asaph were in their place, according to the commandment of David, and Asaph, and Heman, and Jeduthun the king's seer; and the porters waited at every gate; they might not depart from their service; for their brethren the Levites prepared for them. So all the service of the Lord was prepared the same day, to keep the passover, and to offer burnt-offerings upon the altar of the Lord, according to the commandment of King Josiah. And the children of Israel that were present kept the passover at that time, and the feast of unleavened bread seven days. And there was no passover like to that kept in Israel from the days of Samuel the prophet; neither did all the kings of Israel keep such a passover as Josiah kept, and the priests and the Levites, and all Judah and Israel that were present, and the inhabitants of Jerusalem. In the eighteenth year of the reign of Josiah was this passover kept."

In the parallel passage, (2 Kings xxiii. 21—23,) there is only this simple narrative: —

"And the king commanded all the people, saying, 'Keep the passover unto the Lord your God, as it is written in the book of this covenant. Surely there was not holden such a passover from the days of the judges that judged Israel, nor in all the days of the kings of Israel, nor of the kings of Judah; but in the eighteenth year of King Josiah, wherein this passover was holden to the Lord in Jerusalem.'"

2. *In the Omission or Modification of unfavorable Accounts.* — In 2 Ch. xii. 1, we have the following brief statement of the idolatry of Judah: —

"And it came to pass, when Rehoboam had established the kingdom, and had strengthened himself, he forsook the law of the Lord, and all Israel with him."

But in 2 Kings xiv. 22—24, we read: —

"And Judah did evil in the sight of the Lord, and they provoked him to jealousy with their sins which they had committed, above all that their fathers had done. For they also built them high places, and images, and groves, on every high hill, and under every green tree. And there were also sodomites in the land: and they did according to all the abominations of the nations which the Lord cast out before the children of Israel."

The following parallels deserve notice: —

2 Ch. xiii. 2. "He [Abijah] reigned three years in Jerusalem. His mother's name also was Michaiah the daughter of Uriel of Gibeah."	1 Kings xv. 2, 3. "Three years reigned he in Jerusalem. And his mother's name was Maachah, the daughter of Abishalom. *And he walked in all the*

	sins of his father, which he had done before him; and his heart was not perfect with the Lord his God, as the heart of David his father."
2 Ch. xxiv. 2. "And Joash did that which was right in the sight of the Lord all the days of Jehoiada the priest."	2 Kings xii. 2, 3. "And Jehoash did that which was right in the sight of the Lord all his days, wherein Jehoiada the priest instructed him. *But the high places were not taken away: the people still sacrificed and burnt incense in the high places.*"
2 Ch. xxv. 2. "And he [Amaziah] did that which was right in the sight of the Lord, but not with a perfect heart."	2 Kings xiv. 3, 4. "And he did that which was right in the sight of the Lord, yet not like David his father: he did according to all things as Joash his father did. *Howbeit the high places were not taken away: as yet the people did sacrifice and burnt incense on the high places.*"
2 Ch. xxvi. 4. "And he [Azariah] did that which was right in the sight of the Lord, according to all that his father Amaziah did."	2 Kings xv. 3, 4. "And he did that which was right in the sight of the Lord, according to all that his father Amaziah had done; *save that the high places were not removed: the people sacrificed and burnt incense still on the high places.*"
2 Ch. xxvii. 2, 3. "And he did that which was right in the sight of the Lord, according to all that his father Uzziah did: howbeit, he entered not into the temple of the Lord. And the people did yet corruptly. He built the high gate of the house of the Lord, and on the wall of Ophel he built much."	2 Kings xv. 35. "*Howbeit the high places were not removed: the people sacrificed and burned incense still in the high places.* He built the higher gate of the house of the Lord."
2 Ch. xxix. 3. "He [Hezekiah] . . . . . . opened the doors of	2 Kings xviii. 4. "He removed the high places, and brake the

the house of the Lord, and repaired them."

images, and cut down the groves, and brake in pieces the brazen serpent that Moses had made: for unto those days the children of Israel did burn incense to it: and he called it Nehushtan."

The Chronicler never mentions the idolatry of the brazen serpent. The following parallels show his design to conceal the sins of Judah:—

2 Ch. xxxiv. 33. "Josiah took away all the abominations out of all the countries that pertained to the children of Israel, and made all that were present in Israel to serve."

2 Kings xxiii. 4—20. "And the king commanded Hilkiah the high priest, and the priests of the second order, and the keepers of the door, to bring forth out of the temple of the Lord all the vessels that were made for Baal, and for the grove, and for all the host of heaven: and he burned them without Jerusalem in the fields of Kidron, and carried the ashes of them unto Beth-el. And he put down the idolatrous priests, whom the kings of Judah had ordained to burn incense in the high places in the cities of Judah, and in the places round about Jerusalem; them also that burned incense unto Baal, to the sun, and to the moon, and to the planets, and to all the host of heaven. And he brought out the grove from the house of the Lord, without Jerusalem, unto the brook Kidron, and burned it at the brook Kidron, and stamped it small to powder, and cast the powder thereof upon the graves of the children of the people. And he brake down the houses of the sodomites that were by the house of the Lord, where the women wove hangings for the grove. And he brought all the priests out of the cities of Judah, and defiled the high places where the priests had burned incense, from Geba to Beer-sheba, and brake down the high places of the gates that were in the entering in of the gate of Joshua the governor of the city, which were on a man's left hand at the gate of the city. Nevertheless, the priests of the high places came not up to the altar of the Lord in Jerusalem, but they did eat of the unleavened bread among their brethren. And he defiled Topheth, which is in the valley of the children of Hinnom, that no man might make his son or his daughter to pass through the fire to Molech. And he took away the horses that the kings of Judah had given to the sun, at the entering in of

the house of the Lord, by the chamber of Nathan-melech the chamberlain, which was in the suburbs, and burned the chariots of the sun with fire. And the altars that were on the top of the upper chamber of Ahaz, which the kings of Judah had made, and the altars which Manasseh had made in the two courts of the house of the Lord, did the king beat down, and brake them down from thence, and cast the dust of them into the brook Kidron. And the high places that were before Jerusalem, which were on the right hand of the Mount of Corruption, which Solomon the king of Israel had builded for Ashtoreth the abomination of the Zidonians, and for Chemosh the abomination of the Moabites, and for Milcom the abomination of the children of Ammon, did the king defile. And he brake in pieces the images, and cut down the groves, and filled their places with the bones of men.

"Moreover, the altar that was at Beth-el, and the high place which Jeroboam the son of Nebat, who made Israel to sin, had made, both that altar and the high place he brake down, and burned the high place, and stamped it small to powder, and burned the grove. And as Josiah turned himself, he spied the sepulchres that were there in the mount, and sent, and took the bones out of the sepulchres, and burned them upon the altar, and polluted it, according to the word of the Lord which the man of God proclaimed, who proclaimed these words. Then he said, 'What title is that that I see?' And the men of the city told him, 'It is the sepulchre of the man of God, which came from Judah, and proclaimed these things that thou hast done against the altar of Beth-el.' And he said, 'Let him alone; let no man move his bones.' So they let his bones alone, with the bones of the prophet that came out of Samaria. And all the houses also of the high places that were in the cities of Samaria, which the kings of Israel had made to provoke the Lord to anger, Josiah took away, and did to them according to all the acts that he had done in Beth-el. And he slew all the priests of the high places that were there upon the altars, and burnt men's bones upon them, and returned to Jerusalem."

Some of these abominations, however, are named by the Chronicler: —

2 Ch. xxxiv. 3—7. "And in the twelfth year he began to purge Judah and Jerusalem from the high places, and the groves, and the carved images, and the molten images. And they brake down the altars of Baalim in his presence; and the images that were on high

above them, he cut down; and the groves, and the carved images, and the molten images, he brake in pieces, and made dust of them, and strewed it upon the graves of them that had sacrificed unto them. And he burnt the bones of the priests upon their altars, and cleansed Judah and Jerusalem. And so did he in the cities of Manasseh, and Ephraim, and Simeon, even unto Naphtali, with their mattocks round about. And when he had broken down the altars and the groves, and had beaten the graven images into powder, and cut down all the idols throughout all the land of Israel, he returned to Jerusalem."

2 Ch. xxviii. 23. "He sacrificed unto the gods of Damascus, ... and said, 'Because the gods of the kings of Syria help them, therefore will I sacrifice to them, that they may help me.' But they were the ruin of him," &c.

2 Kings xvi. 10—12. "And they set them up images and groves in every high hill, and under every green tree: and there they burnt incense in all the high places, as did the heathen whom the Lord carried away before them; and wrought wicked things to provoke the Lord to anger: for they served idols, whereof the Lord had said unto them, 'Ye shall not do this thing.'"

Movers acknowledges the fact that the earlier accounts have been thus modified.

3. *Conflicting Statements and Self-contradictions.* — 2 Ch. xiv. 2—5, it is said, "Asa took away the altars of the strange gods, and brake down the images, and cut down the groves, ... and took away, out of all the cities of Judah, the high places and the images." But, xv. 17, it is said, the high places were *not* taken away out of Israel;[a] and the same appears from 1 Kings xv. 14. So, xvii. 6, Jehoshaphat "took away the high

[a] [It is evident, from the context, that *Israel* does not mean the *ten tribes*, — who are not mentioned in the chapter, — but all the Hebrews governed by Asa. The other passage obviously relates to *Judah*.]

places and groves out of Judah;" but in 1 Kings xxii. 43, and xx. 33, this is contradicted — "*the high places were not taken away.*" The reason is given — "for as yet the people had not prepared their heart unto the God of their fathers." Movers thinks the high places consecrated to idols were destroyed, but those devoted to other purposes were left untouched.[a]

4. *Alteration of similar Accounts.* — 1 Ch. xviii. 17, the sons of David were chief[b] about the king, (the first at the hand of the king,) instead of saying they were *priests*,[c] as is done in 2 Sam. viii. 18, and xx. 26.[d]

Again: 2 Ch. i. 3, "Solomon ...... went to the high place at Gibeon, for there was the tabernacle of the congregation of God, which Moses ...... had made," while in 1 Kings iii. 4, we have only "the king went to sacrifice there, *for that was the great high place.*" Movers denies the fact that there were different holy places; and even Keil and Winer assume that the tabernacle was conveyed from Shiloh to Nob, — where the posterity of Eli appear as priests, in 1 Sam. xxii. 11, — and from thence to Gibeon. But Nob — where there were eighty-five priests, in 1 Sam. xxii. 18 — was one of the *old holy places*, like Beth-el, and Ahimelech might go there without having carried the tabernacle from Shiloh. The fact that David had two priests, — who were not *high priests*, as some maintain, — Zadok and

---

[a] [This is a very poor attempt to escape the obvious conclusion; for if they were not *idolatrous* high places, why would such an excuse be made for their preservation as that above quoted in the text?]

See *Dahler*, p. 99. *Keil*, p. 299.

[b] הראשנים

[c] כהנים.

[d] What *Movers* has said in justification of this change convinces me as little as the remark of *Gesenius*, Heb. Lex. sub. voce כהן, and *Winer*, l. c. vol. ii. p. 387.

Abiathar, (2 Sam. viii. 17, xxi. 25,) and that Zadok took Abiathar's place, (1 Kings ii. 35,) seems to confirm the opinion that the former dwelt at Gibeon, (1 Ch. xvi. 39.) But he might reside there, though there was no tabernacle in the place. However, this fact does not agree well with the twenty-four classes of priests, mentioned in 1 Ch. xxiv.; for this would lead us to suppose there was but one holy place. The passage in 1 Kings iii. 4, where Gibeon is reckoned one of the high places, is directly contrary to the account in Chronicles; for if the old Mosaic tabernacle had been there, it would not have been an unlawful high place. It may have been called the *great high place*, by way of preëminence, perhaps because a *regular priest* resided there. The tabernacle of the congregation, which was brought into the temple with the ark, (1 Kings viii. 3,) can be no other than that mentioned in 2 Sam. vi. 17.

The *apologetic* design of the account in Chronicles appears from the manner in which the statement in 1 Ch. xxi. 29, 30, is connected with the similar narrative in 2 Sam. xxiv. 25. David had offered sacrifice on the threshing-floor of Ornan, and it is said, "But the tabernacle of Jehovah which Moses made in the wilderness, and the altar of burnt-offering, was at that time in the high place at Gibeon. But David could not go there to seek God, *for he was terrified by the sword of the angel of Jehovah*." Then, as if this circumstance was not sufficient to justify the sacrifice at the threshing-floor, it is added in the next verse, (xxii. 1,) that David determined to build a temple on the spot.

The passage, 1 Ch. xiii.—xvi., is a Levitical recasting of 2 Sam. vi., with which 2 Sam. v. 11—25, has been inserted, though it is evidently out of place

The account in Samuel has been altered by the Chronicler. For example, in xiv. 2, he introduces the *priests*, and the *Levites*, who are not mentioned in the parallel account, 2 Sam. vi. 1. In xv. 1, he suppresses the motive assigned in 2 Sam. vi. 12, for the second attempt to remove the ark. On the other hand, he puts this declaration in the mouth of David: "None ought to carry the ark of God but the Levites, for them hath Jehovah chosen ......" Then follows the assembling of the Levites, (4—14;) and David says, (verse 13,) "Jehovah our God made a breach upon us, because ye (the Levites) did not undertake it in the former attempt — because we did not seek him in due fashion." This amplification of 2 Sam. vi. 15, which makes the Levites carry the ark, may be historically correct.

The passage, 1 Ch. xv. 2—27, is an amplification of 2 Sam. vi. 12. The apologetic design appears in the addition of Levitical musicians, and other servants, (verses 13, 14,) in the remark, that "God helped the Levites." But he omits part of the account of David's dancing, to which verse 29 refers. (2 Sam. vi. 16.)

1 Ch. xvi. 4—42. Here the Levites are appointed to minister before the ark; a cento of Psalms is sung; Zadok and others serve before the sanctuary at Gibeon; verse 43 is parallel with the end of 2 Sam. vi. 19, and the beginning of verse 20. The conversation between Michal and David is omitted, and therefore verse 29 stands there without any meaning.[a]

In 2 Ch. xxiii. 1—11, actions are referred to the *Levites*, which, in 2 Kings xi. 4—12, are ascribed to the *body-guard*. This is done apparently to conform to

---

[a] On *Movers's* view of this, see below, § 192, *d*.

verse 6. But it makes complete confusion in the narrative.[a]

In 2 Ch. xxiv. 4—14, we have an account of the restoration of the temple. But no notice is taken of the charge, tacitly implied in 2 Kings xii. 4—16, that the priests had embezzled the money collected for that work. In 2 Kings xii. 7, the king asks Jehoiada the priest, "Why repair ye not the breaches of the house? Now, therefore, receive no more money of your acquaintance, but deliver it up [what you have already received] for the breaches of the house." On account of their defection, a chest was contrived with a hole in the lid to receive the money. Now, this account is much qualified by the Chronicler. The king says (verse 5) to the priests and Levites, "Go out . . . . . . and gather of all Israel money to repair the house of Jehovah, ... and see that ye hasten in the matter. Howbeit the Levites hastened not," in the collection of the money, as it appears from verse 6, where the king asks Jehoiada, "Why hast thou not required of the Levites to bring in . . . . . . the tax of Moses?"[b] . . . . . .

---

[a] *Movers* (p. 310) admits this, but will only explain it as an interpolation. But the only interpolation which can be admitted is the word הרצימ, in xxiii. 12, parallel with 2 Kings xi. 13. See § 192, *d*.

[b] [2 Ch. xxiv. 4--6, 8—14. "And it came to pass after this, that Joash was minded to repair the house of the Lord. And he gathered together the priests and the *Levites*, and said to them, 'Go out unto the cities of Judah, and gather of all Israel money to repair the house of your God from year to year, and see that ye hasten the matter.' Howbeit, the *Levites* hastened it not. And the king called for Jehoiada *the chief*, and said unto

2 Kings xii. 4—16. "And Jehoash said to the priests, 'All the money of the dedicated things that is brought into the house of the Lord, even the money of every one that passeth the account, the money that every man is set at, and all the money that cometh into any man's heart to bring into the house of the Lord, let the priests take it to them, every man of his acquaintance; and let them repair the breaches of the house, wheresoever any

2 Ch. xxxiv. 8—14, is also parallel with 2 Kings xii. 4—8. But a passage has been interpolated with a view

---

him, '*Why hast thou not required of the Levites to bring in out of Judah and out of Jerusalem the collection...... of Moses, the servant of the Lord, and of the congregation of Israel, for the tabernacle of witness?*' And at the king's commandment they made a chest, and set it without at the gate of the house of the Lord. And they made a proclamation through Judah and Jerusalem, to bring in to the Lord *the collection that Moses the servant of God laid upon Israel in the wilderness.* And all the princes and all the people rejoiced, and brought in, and cast into the chest, until they had made an end. Now, it came to pass, that at what time the chest was brought into the king's office by the hand *of the Levites*, and when they saw that there was much money, the king's scribe and the high priest's officer came and emptied the chest, and took it, and carried it to his place again. Thus they did day by day, and gathered money in abundance. And the king and Jehoiada gave it to such as did the work of the service of the house of the Lord, and hired masons and carpenters to repair the house of the Lord, and also such as wrought iron and brass to mend the house of the Lord. So the workmen wrought, and the work was perfected by them, and they set the house of God in his state, and strengthened it. And when they had finished it, they brought the rest of the money before the king and Jehoiada, whereof were made vessels for the house of the Lord, even vessels to minister, and to breach shall be found.' But it was so, that in the three and twentieth year of King Jehoash the priests had not repaired the breaches of the house. Then King Jehoash called for Jehoiada the priest, and the other priests, and said unto them, 'Why repair ye not the breaches of the house? now therefore receive no more money of your acquaintance, but deliver it for the breaches of the house.' And the priests consented to receive no more money of the people, neither to repair the breaches of the house. But Jehoiada the priest took a chest, and bored a hole in the lid of it, and set it beside the altar, on the right side as one cometh into the house of the Lord: and the priests that kept the door put therein all the money that was brought into the house of the Lord. And it was so, when they saw that there was much money in the chest, that the king's scribe and the high priest came up, and they put up in bags, and told the money that was found in the house of the Lord. And they gave the money, being told, into the hands of them that did the work, that had the oversight of the house of the Lord: and they laid it out to the carpenters and builders that wrought upon the house of the Lord, and to masons, and hewers of stone, and to buy timber and hewed stone to repair the breaches of the house of the Lord, and for all that was laid out for the house to repair it. Howbeit, there were not made for the house of the Lord bowls of silver, snuffers, basins, trumpets, any vessels of gold, or ves-

to aggrandize the Levites; for, in verses 12, 13, *they are placed over the work* — to superintend it. Levitical scribes are mentioned, (verse 13,) who were not needed in this business.

We cannot, however, so clearly detect the same motive in the interpolation of 2 Sam. xxiv. 3—9, which has been made in 1 Ch. xxi. 3—6. Here the speech of Joab has been altered, and he is made to say, "Are not all the people servants of my lord?" [David?] (verse 3.) We might suppose, from verse 6, that the tribe of Levi was not included in the enumeration, because the census was made for a warlike purpose, if the Chronicler had not himself given us another reason, that "the king's word was abominable to Joab." We cannot agree with Movers and Keil, who think Benjamin was not included, because the census was interrupted by the pestilence, (1 Ch. xxvii. 24.) Besides, 2 Sam. xxiv. 5—9, — which is an account of the journeys to take the census, — will not allow this hypothesis.[a]

III. Apologetic Omissions and Alterations;

---

offer withal, and spoons, and vessels of gold and silver. And they offered burnt-offerings in the house of the Lord continually all the days of Jehoiada."

Compare xxxiv. 8—14.

sels of silver, of the money that was brought into the house of the Lord; but they gave that to the workmen, and repaired therewith the house of the Lord. Moreover they reckoned not with the men into whose hand they delivered the money to be bestowed on workmen: for they dealt faithfully. The trespass money and sin money was not brought into the house of the Lord: it was the priests'."

The Chronicler seems to have had the earlier account before him, and to have colored it intentionally to suit his purpose.]

[a] Compare 2 Ch. xxiii. 17—20, with 2 Kings xi. 18—20.

PASSAGES TO ENHANCE THE GLORY OF THOSE KINGS WHO SUPPORTED THE PUBLIC WORSHIP OF JEHOVAH.

1. *Omissions.*—In 1 Ch. xiv. 3, the concubines of David are omitted, though they are mentioned in the parallel, (2 Sam. v. 13.) In 1 Ch. xvii. 13, no mention is made of the chastisement which is threatened the posterity of David in 2 Sam. vii. 14—"If he commit iniquity, I will chasten him with the rod of men, and with the stripes of the children of men, but my mercy shall not depart away from him." In 2 Sam. viii. 2, it is said:—

"And he smote Moab, *and measured them with a line, casting them down to the ground; even with two lines measured he to put to death, and with one full line to keep alive:* and so the Moabites became David's servants, and brought gifts."

In the parallel, (1 Ch. xviii. 3,) this cruelty is omitted—"He smote Moab; and the Moabites became David's servants." In 2 Sam. xii. 31, amongst other torments, it is said David made the men of Rabbah "pass through the brick-kiln," which is omitted in 1 Ch. xx. 3.[a] The omission of larger passages may be accounted for in the same way. Thus, for example, the Chronicler makes no mention of Nathan's touching apologue, or of David's adultery with the wife of Uriah, which is dwelt upon at length in 2 Sam. xi. 2—xii. 26. Nothing is said of the murder of Saul's seven sons, whom David gave up to satisfy the vengeance of the Gibeonites, which is related in 2 Sam. xxi. 1—11. Nothing is said of the strange women of Solomon, *his seven hundred wives, his three hundred concubines, or of his idolatry*, so distinctly set forth in 1 Kings xi. It is on the same principle that we

[a] [This omission may be explained on the supposition that the Chronicler did not understand the term מַלְבֵּן, or was not familiar with this method of torture, and omitted to mention what he did not understand.]

may account for the omission of the troubles in David's family, the wickedness of Amnon and Absalom, and, in general, the whole contents of 2 Sam. xiii.—xx.[a]

2. *Alterations.*—In 2 Sam. v. 21, the Philistines left their idols at Baal-perazim, and David, with his men, took them away. In 1 Ch. xiv. 12, *he burns them with fire.*[b]

3. *Passages are added to enhance the Glory of the Kings.*—2 Kings xx. 21, is the plain statement, "and Hezekiah slept with his fathers." In 2 Ch. xxxii. 33, it is said, "Hezekiah slept with his fathers, and they *buried him in the chiefest of the sepulchres of the sons of David, and all Judah and the inhabitants of Jerusalem did him honor at his death.*" Besides, (verses 27—29) there is a detailed statement of his great wealth and honor, which are not particularly mentioned in the parallel account. In 2 Kings xxiii. 30, Josiah died, and "his servants ...... brought him to Jerusalem, and buried him in his own sepulchre." In 2 Ch. xxxv. 24, 25, it is added:—

> "And all Judah and Jerusalem mourned for Josiah. And Jeremiah lamented for Josiah: and all the singing men and the singing women spake of Josiah in their lamentations to this day, and made them an ordinance in Israel: and behold, they are written in the Lamentations."

IV. Hatred against Israel.

This often appears in the peculiar accounts of the Chronicles, and lies at the bottom of the disagreement between the following passages:—

[a] [These omissions are the more striking, since the character of both David and Solomon was so well known, and their offences were so flagrant. An historian who would omit the offences of these kings, the trouble in David's own family, must write with some other design than that of telling the whole truth.] See *Movers*, l. c. p. 220.

[b] [The English Bible has "*burned*" in both cases, though it gives the true meaning in the margin of 2 Sam. v. 21.]

2 Ch. xx. 35—37. "And after this did Jehoshaphat king of Judah join himself with Ahaziah king of Israel, who did very wickedly: and he joined himself with him to make ships to go to Tarshish: and they made the ships in Ezion-geber. Then Eliezer...... prophesied against Jehoshaphat, saying, 'Because thou hast joined thyself with Ahaziah, the Lord hath broken thy works.' And the ships were broken, that they were not able to go to Tarshish."

1 Kings xxii. 48, 49. "Jehoshaphat made ships of Tharshish to go to Ophir for gold: but they went not; for the ships were broken at Ezion-geber. Then said Ahaziah the son of Ahab unto Jehoshaphat, 'Let my servants go with thy servants in the ships.' But Jehoshaphat would not"

[This partiality of the books of Chronicles shows itself in the whole narrative. The books of Kings are perfectly impartial in respect to the kingdom of Israel. There is no indication in them of a political and religious hostility. They only censure the kings of Israel as founders of the false, Israelitish form of worship. Their impartiality shows itself in the circumstance that these books give the history of Israel as minutely as that of Judah, sometimes even more minutely, but with a preference for the latter, which is particularly obvious in the accounts of the achievements of Elijah and Elisha. Now, the Chronicles omit every thing which can add to the honor of Israel. This renders the book suspicious. The whole of 2 Ch. xiii. is a striking instance of this hostility to Israel.]

§ 191.

CHARACTER OF THE PECULIAR ACCOUNTS OF THE CHRONICLES.

The results of this comparative criticism place these books in an unfavorable light, and tend to weaken the credibility of those accounts which have been added to the earlier statements, and even of those which are independent of these statements. Besides, in the contents themselves we find some grounds for suspicion, improbabilities, and exaggerations. Thus the additions relative to the Levites, in 1 Ch. xv. 16, sqq., and xvi. 4, sqq., are suspicious. Obed-edom, who is appointed porter, in the latter part of David's life, seems arbitrarily reckoned with the Levites in xv. 18, 21, 24, xvi. 38, xxvi. 15. This is suspicious, for he is called a *Gittite* in 2 Sam. vi. 10, — though Movers thinks he was a citizen of Gath-rimmon, a Levitical city, — and the ark was not left in his house *because* he was a Levite. His *father*, Jeduthun, was one of David's musicians, (1 Ch. xxv. 3.) His *children* are introduced as Levites in the service of David, (xxvi. 4, 5,) and his *grandchildren*, (verse 6,) so that *four generations* seem to have served under David.[a]

The list of Levites in chap. xxiii. differs from that in chap. vi. Thus, in xxiii. 7, we have *Laadan* for *Libni*, (vi. 2;) in xxiii. 8, the sons of Laadan are *Jehiel*, *Zetham*, and *Joel*; in vi. 3,[b] the sons of Libni are *Jahath*, who is the son of Shimei, (xxiii. 10.) On the other hand, (xxvi. 21, 22,) Zetham and Joel are the sons of Jehieli, and therefore the grandsons of Laadan, and were treasurers in the time of David. In xxiii. 15—17, *Gershom* and *Eliezer* are mentioned as the sons of Moses, *Shebuel* is the son of Gershom, and *Rehabiah* the son of Eliezer. But in xxvi. 24, *Shebuel* appears as chief overseer of David's treasures, and *Shelomith*, a descendant of *Rehabiah* in the fourth degree, has the same office.[c]

---

[a] See *Movers*, p. 239, 339.

[b] Verse 17, English Bible.

[c] [The common solution of this difficulty is, to make the gratuitous

In 2 Sam. xv. 18, David's body-guard consists of six hundred men; in 1 Ch. xxvii. 1—15, *of two hundred and eighty-eight thousand* men. In the list of the twelve captains of this guard, David's heroes reappear, and in the same order as in xi. 10, sqq.[a]

The accounts of David's preparation for building the temple (1 Ch. xxii. xxviii. xxix.) agree with the statement which Solomon — as his successor — made in the assembly of the people, at the time he was anointed king, (xxix. 22.) But these obviously contradict the authentic narrative, (1 Kings i.,) and consequently the course of affairs in chap. xxviii. xxix. is fictitious. Particular passages also favor this conclusion. Thus, for example, xxviii. 11—19, David gives Solomon a plan or model of the temple, *which he had received from Jehovah;*[b] xxix. 4, gold of Ophir is mentioned; there is an admonitory passage in xxix. 15, which is a reminiscence of Psalm xxxix. 13. In the details of the preparation itself, the numbers are obviously exaggerated. In xxii. 14, there are 100,000 talents of gold and 1,000,000 talents of silver. David, in an address to his son, (xxii. 8,) says, "Jehovah forbid him [David] to build a temple, because he had been a man of blood." This contradicts the earlier account of the matter, 2 Sam. vii. 5, sqq., and 1 Ch. xvii. 4, where a different reason is assigned — "Thou shalt not build me a house, for —*I have not dwelt*

---

supposition that the term *son* is used vaguely, to denote *descendants* in general.]

[a] [There is some difference in the names as well as in the order of the two rolls.] See *Movers*, p. 135.

[b] [11—19. The following is perhaps more accurate than the common version: "David gave Solomon . . . . . . the pattern of the porch, &c., ... all in writing from the hand of Jehovah, who informed me [David] of all the work of the model." See the remarks of *Clarke* in explanation.]

in a house since the days that I brought up Israel." The relation in Chronicles contradicts that in 1 Kings v. 17. 20, 27—31, which is certainly the more credible of the two.[a]

The accounts which relate to the worship of Jehovah are suspicious, when they go beyond the earlier narratives in the books of Kings. There is a contradiction, in the history of Asa, between 2 Ch. xiv. 3—5, and xv. 1—15; for in the latter passage he does, at the command of Obed, what he had done before.[b] There is a contradiction in xvii. 7—9.[c]

In xxix.—xxxi. we have an account of an extraordinary celebration of the feast of the passover, under *Hezekiah*, which lasted fourteen days. Here it is said, (xxx. 26,) "Since the time of Solomon, the like was not in Jerusalem." This does not agree with 2 Kings xxiii. 22, and 2 Ch. xxxv. 18: "Surely there was not holden such a passover *from the days* of the judges, ... nor in all the days of the kings," ...... as that of *Josiah*. Movers attempts to explain the contradiction by saying, that "no passover was kept with *so much pomp*." But this does not remove the difficulty; for, according to the Chronicler, that under *Hezekiah* was begun with sufficient pomp.

In 2 Ch. xxxiv. 3—7, the reformation under Josiah takes place in the *twelfth* year of his reign, while in 2

---

[a] The sophisms of *Movers* (p. 319, sqq.) cannot remove the difficulty.

[b] See § 190, *b*.

[c] [The author does not tell in what it consists, and I am at a loss to discover the contradiction.]

Notice, also, the suspicious relationship between *Kish*, the son of *Abdi*, (xxix. 12,) and *Ethan*, one of David's singers, the son of *Kishi*, the son of *Abdi*, (1 Ch. vi. 29, [44.]) Note, also, that of *Joah*, the son of Zimmah, and of *Eden*, the son of *Joah*, with the ancestors of Samuel; namely, *Zimmah*, *Joah*, and *Iddo*, (1 Ch. vi. 5, 6, [20, 21.])

Kings xxiii. 4, sqq., it takes place in the *eighteenth* year. [The attempt of the Chronicler to disguise the idolatry of the inhabitants of Jerusalem is very obvious, in the suppression of many circumstances detailed in the former history: —

2 Kings xxiii. 4—19.	2 Ch. xxxiv. 3—7, 33.
"And the king commanded Hilkiah the high priest, and the priests of the second order, and the keepers of the door, to bring *forth out of the temple of the Lord all the vessels that were made for Baal, and for the grove, and for all the host of heaven:* and he burnt them without Jerusalem in the fields of Kidron, and carried the ashes of them unto Beth-el. And he put down the *idolatrous priests, whom the kings of Judah* had ordained to burn incense in the high places, *in the cities of Judah, and in the places round about Jerusalem;* them also that burnt incense unto Baal, to the sun, and to the moon, and to the planets, and to all the host of heaven. And he *brought out the grove from the house of the Lord,* without Jerusalem, unto the brook Kidron, and burnt it at the brook Kidron, and stamped it small to powder, and cast the powder thereof upon the graves of the children of the people. *And* he brake down the *houses of the sodomites, that were by the house of the Lord,* where the women wove hangings for the grove. And he brought all the priests *out of the cities of Judah,*	"In the twelfth year he [Josiah] began to purge Judah and Jerusalem from the high places, and the groves, and the carved images, and the molten images. And they brake down the altars of Baalim in his presence; and the images that were on high above them he cut down; and the groves, and the carved images, and the molten images, he brake in pieces, and made dust of them, and strowed it upon the graves of them that had sacrificed unto them. And he burnt the bones of the priests upon their altars, and cleansed Judah and Jerusalem. And so did he in the cities of Manasseh, and Ephraim, and Simeon, even unto Naphtali, with their mattocks round about. And when he had broken down the altars and the groves, and had beaten the graven images into powder, and cut down all the idols *throughout all the land of Israel,* he returned to Jerusalem. And Josiah took away all the abominations out of all the countries that pertained to the children of *Israel,* and made all that were present in *Israel* to serve, even to serve the Lord their God. And

and defiled the high places where the priests had burnt incense, *from Geba to Beer-sheba,* and brake down the high places of the gate that were in the entering in of the gate of Joshua the governor of the city, which were on a man's left hand at the gate of the city. Nevertheless the priests of the high places came not up to the altar of the Lord in Jerusalem, but they did eat of the unleavened bread among their brethren. And he defiled *Topheth,* which is in the valley of the children of Hinnom, that no man might make his son or his daughter to pass through the fire to Molech. *And he took away the horses that the kings of Judah had given to the sun, at the entering in of the house of the Lord,* ...... and burnt the chariots of the sun with fire. *And the altars that were on the top of the upper chamber of Ahaz, which the kings of Judah had made, and the altars which Manasseh had made in the two courts of the house of the Lord,* did the king beat down, and brake them down from thence, and cast the dust of them into the brook Kidron. And the *high places that were before Jerusalem,* which were on the right hand of the Mount of Corruption, *which Solomon the king* of Israel *had builded* ...... And all the houses also of the high places that were in the cities of Samaria, all his days they departed not from following the Lord, the God of their fathers."

which the kings of Israel had made to provoke the Lord to anger, Josiah took away, and did to them according to all the acts that he had done in Beth-el."

The Chronicler contradicts himself, (verse 33,) and gives a short notice of this reformation, and, contrary to the fact, does not suppose the reformation was first brought about by the terror which arose on discovering the book of the Law.[a]

The story in 2 Ch. xxvi. 16—21, which relates that Uzziah was punished with a leprosy because he offered incense with his own hands, is a legend written to confirm the prescriptive privileges of the priests.

Some accounts of victories are liable to suspicion. For example, 2 Ch. xiii. 2, sqq., Abijah appears as an orthodox king, and the *sacred trumpets* perform a miracle; for "God smote Jeroboam ...... so there fell down slain of Israel 500,000 chosen men."[b] Of the same class is the story in 2 Ch. xiv. 6—15, of Asa's victory over the Æthiopians, which he obtains *by the help of a prayer*, (verse 11.) In 2 Ch. xx. 1—25, Jehoshaphat's victory over the Moabites and others is related in an admonitory and entirely miraculous manner. It is said the Jews had nothing to do but gather up the spoil, which they were three days in collecting The whole of the hostile army had fallen without a

[a] *Movers* prefers the narrative of the Chronicler to that in 2 Kings, chiefly on the ground that the passover which Josiah celebrated, in the eighteen years of his reign, in consequence of discovering the Law book, must have been celebrated in the first month, and consequently there would be no time for extirpating the idolaters. Here he supposes the eighteenth year of Josiah's reign was coincident with the civil year.

Usher puts this passover in the end of the eighteenth year. See the reply of *Movers* in the Bon. Zeitschrift, vol. xvii. p. 169, to this objection, which *Von Bohlen* has brought against him.

[b] *Keil's* defence (p. 444) does not deserve a refutation.

blow — "dead bodies fallen to the earth." This story is probably made out of Jehoshaphat's campaign, mentioned in 2 Kings iii. 4, sqq.[a]

---

[a] See *Gesenius*, Comm. zu. Jes. vol. i. p. 502. *Winer*, Lexicon, vol. i p. 710. On the other hand, see *Kleinert*, (Aecht. d. Jes. Weis. vol. i. p. 45,) *Keil*, (l. c. p. 241,) *Movers*, (p. 111,) who seek in vain for a support in Ps. xlviii. 83. See *Clarke*, in loc.

[The exaggeration appears plain from the following: —

2 Ch. xvii. 10—12. "And the fear of the Lord fell upon all the kingdoms of the lands that were round about Judah, so that they made no war against Jehoshaphat. Also, some of the Philistines brought Jehoshaphat presents and tribute silver; and the Arabians brought him flocks, seven thousand and seven hundred rams, and seven thousand and seven hundred he-goats.

"And Jehoshaphat waxed great exceedingly; and he built in Judah castles and cities of store."

The army comprised 1,160,000 soldiers, under five generals, besides his garrison-troops in the walled towns! The Moabites, Ammonites, and others, invade this powerful king. "Jehoshaphat feared, and set himself to seek the Lord, and proclaimed a fast." He then offers a public prayer in presence of the multitude assembled before the "new court;" the spirit of the Lord comes upon a Levite, who prophesies.

2 Ch. xx. 15, sqq. "And he said, 'Hearken ye, all Judah, and ye inhabitants of Jerusalem, and thou King Jehoshaphat: Thus saith the Lord unto you, "Be not afraid, nor dismayed by reason of this great multitude; for the battle is not yours, but God's; to-morrow go ye down against them. Ye shall not need to fight in this battle; set yourselves, stand ye still, and see the salvation of the Lord with you, O Judah and Jerusalem; fear not, nor be dismayed; to-morrow go out against them; for the Lord will be with you."' And Jehoshaphat bowed his head with his face to the ground: and all Judah, and the inhabitants of Jerusalem, fell before the Lord, worshipping the Lord. And the Levites, of the children of the Kohathites, and of the children of the Korhites, stood up to praise the Lord God of Israel with a loud voice on high.

"And they rose early in the morning, and went forth into the wilderness of Tekoa: and, as they went forth, Jehoshaphat stood, and said, 'Hear me, O Judah, and ye inhabitants of Jerusalem; believe in the Lord your God, so shall ye be established; believe his prophets, so shall ye prosper.' And when he had consulted with the people, he appointed singers unto the Lord, and that should praise the beauty of holiness, as they went out before the army, and to say, 'Praise the Lord; for his mercy endureth forever.'

"And when they began to sing and to praise, the Lord set ambushments against the children of Ammon, Moab, and Mount Seir, which were come

The relations of the power, wealth, and achievements, of the kings of Judah, (2 Ch. xiv. 6, sqq., xvii. 10, sqq., xxvi. 5, sqq., xxvii. 4, sqq.,) are suspicious, — like the above description of victories, — on account of the exaggeration in the numbers. There is an obvious anachronism in 2 Ch. xx. 12, sqq. There are difficulties in the history of Manasseh, (2 Ch. xxxiii. 11—17.) The accounts in Chronicles of his captivity, his conversion, and especially of his pretended extirpation of idolatry, do not agree with the history in 2 Kings xxi. 1—17; for example, 2 Ch. xxxiii. 15, "He took away the strange gods, and the idol out of the house of Jehovah, and all the altars, ... and cast them out of the city, and repaired the altar of Jehovah." This contradicts the account in Kings, which sums up his whole life in few words: "Now the rest of the acts of Manasseh, and all that he did, and *his sin that he sinned*, are they not written in the book of the Chronicles?" &c. Here no mention is made of his captivity, or his conversion. He lives and dies in sin, and is referred to again as an idolater, in verse 21, and xxiv. 3, where his sin is deemed unpardonable.[a]

As, in the above case, Manasseh's conversion rests on

---

against Judah; and they were smitten. For the children of Ammon and Moab stood up against the inhabitants of Mount Seir, utterly to slay and destroy them: and when they had made an end of the inhabitants of Seir, every one helped to destroy another. And when Judah came towards the watchtower in the wilderness, they looked unto the multitude, and, behold, they were dead bodies fallen to the earth, and none escaped. And when Jehoshaphat and his people came to take away the spoil of them, they found among them in abundance both riches with the dead bodies, and precious jewels, which they stripped off for themselves, more than they could carry away: and they were three days in gathering of the spoil, it was so much."]

[a] See, also, 2 Ch. xxxiii. 22, Jer. xv. 4. *Movers* (p. 327) acknowledges this contradiction, — though *Keil* (p. 425) will not, — and attempts only to show that he was really carried into captivity.

a pious conjecture, so it is probable Amaziah is made out an idolater, in 2 Ch. xxv. 14, sqq., because he was afterwards unfortunate. It is probable, also, that the narrative in 2 Kings xii. 18, 19, is amplified in 2 Ch. xxiv. 23, in order to make out a suitable recompense for the apostasy of Joash. The two accounts speak for themselves:—

2 Kings xii. 17, 18. "Then Hazael king of Syria went up, and fought against Gath, and took it: and Hazael set his face to go up to Jerusalem. And Jehoash king of Judah took all the hallowed things that Jehoshaphat, and Jehoram, and Ahaziah, his fathers, kings of Judah, had dedicated, and his own hallowed things, and all the gold that was found in the treasures of the house of the Lord, and in the king's house, and sent it to Hazael, king of Syria: and he went away from Jerusalem ...... and his servants arose ...... and slew Joash ...... and they buried him with his fathers."	2 Ch. xxiv. 23—25. "And it came to pass at the end of the year, that the host of Syria came up against him, and they came to Judah and Jerusalem, and destroyed all the princes of the people from among the people, and sent all the spoil of them unto the king of Damascus. *For the army of the Syrians came with a small company of men, and the Lord delivered a very great host into their hand, because they had forsaken the Lord God of their fathers. So they executed judgment against Joash. And when they were departed from him, (for they left him in great diseases,) his own servants conspired against him for the blood of the sons of Jehoiada the priest, and slew him on his bed, and he died:* and they buried him in the city of David, *but they buried him not in the sepulchres of the kings.*"

In 2 Kings xvi. 5, "Rezin king of Syria, and Pekah king of Israel, came up to Jerusalem to war, and they besieged Ahaz, but could not overcome him." He made terms with the king of Assyria; and, though an

idolater, suffered no remarkable calamity, as we learn in the books of Kings. But in 2 Ch. xxviii. 5, sqq., "Jehovah ...... delivered him into the hand of the king of Syria, and they smote him, and carried away a great multitude of them captives ...... and he was also delivered into the hand of the king of Israel, who smote him with a great slaughter; for Pekah ...... slew 120,000 in one day, all valiant men, *because they had forsaken Jehovah, God of their fathers.*" He sent to the king of Assyria for help, who "distressed him, and strengthened him not." At his death, he was not buried in "the sepulchre of the kings of Israel." The statement in verse 7, that Maaseiah, his son, was slain in battle, is obviously false; for, at that time, he could not have had a son able to bear arms.[a]

In 2 Kings xxiv. 6, it is said, "Jehoiakim slept with his fathers;" but in 2 Ch. xxxvi. 6, Nebuchadnezzar ...... bound him [Jehoiakim] in fetters to carry him to Babylon." This latter statement is very doubtful.

The speeches put in the mouth of kings and prophets all have the same admonitory tone, and resemble each other, even in particular expressions.[b]

It must be admitted, also, that these books contain some credible narratives.[c]

---

[a] *Movers*, following *Usher*, *Vitringa*, and *Rosenmüller*, attempts to defend the Chronicler, on the ground that there was an earlier invasion of Judah by the united armies of Syria and Israel, (but neither Kings nor Chronicles speaks of two invasions,) and by reference to Isa. i.; but this explanation of Isaiah is unsuitable for other reasons. *Keil* (p. 420) thinks there was but one invasion, and attempts to reconcile the two statements.

[b] See 1 Ch. xv. 12, 13, 2 Ch. xiii. 4, sqq., xiv. 11, xv. 1, sqq., 12, sqq., xix. 2, 3, xx. 6, sqq., xxviii. 9, xxix. 5, sqq., xxxii. 7, 8, xxxv. 3, sq. See *Movers*, p. 180.

[c] *Movers* has shown much acuteness and power of combination in his attempts to prove this. The present is not the place for a thorough examination of this question.

§ 192, *a*.

SOURCES OF THE BOOKS OF CHRONICLES.

The accounts which run parallel with the books of Samuel and Kings were derived from that source. This appears from the following considerations:—

1. The earlier accounts in Samuel and Kings have a natural connection with those other accounts therein, but which are omitted by the Chronicler. Thus, in 1 Sam. xxxi., the death of Saul and his sons is naturally connected with the previous accounts, (xviii.—xxx.) The assembling of the tribes at Hebron, to elect David king, (2 Sam. v. 1,) refers, naturally, to ii. 1, where, by Jehovah's counsel, David has gone up to that place. So the account of his family at Hebron, (2 Sam. v. 13,) connects naturally with the similar account in iii. 2—5. The relation that Michal despised David because he danced naked before the ark, (2 Sam. vi. 16,) connects with verses 20—23, where Michal reproaches David for the act, and he defends himself. So 2 Sam. xi. 1, which says David remained at Jerusalem while his army invested Rabbah, and xii. 24—31, which mentions his departure for that city, and its destruction, connect naturally with the account of his criminal connection with Uriah's wife, for the sake of which he had remained at Jerusalem. Thus the detail of Solomon's trade and wealth (1 Kings x. 26—29, parallel with 2 Ch. i. 14—17) connects with the general statement in verse 14.[a] The extent of Solomon's dominion (1 Kings

[a] According to *Movers*, (p. 186,) 2 Ch. i. 14—17, is derived from another source, namely, 1 Kings ix. 26—28, (for which the Chronicler had chap. x. before him,) and from which he transcribed the same account in the same

v. 1)[a] connects with iv. 1, which is parallel with 2 Ch. ix. 26. The time spent in building his palace and temple, in 1 Kings ix. 10, (2 Ch. viii. 1,) corresponds with 1 Kings vii. 1—12, where the same number of years is mentioned. The fulfilment of the prediction of Ahijah (1 Kings xii. 15, 2 Ch. x. 15) connects with xi. 29, sqq., where the prediction itself is made, which is omitted by the Chronicler.[b]

2. From the original character of these accounts, compared with those in Chronicles.

3. From the certain fact that the Chronicler must have been acquainted with the previous books.

---

words. But this is incorrect; for i. 14—17, is parallel with 1 Kings x. 26—29; and, on the other hand, ix. 25—28, is an abbreviation of it. The Chronicler wished to avoid repeating the *whole*, and therefore abbreviated it. *Movers* contradicts himself, (p. 254,) and admits this.

[a] English Bible, iv. 21.

[b] See *Movers*, p. 100, 101. The relation between 2 Ch. xxxii. and 2 Kings xviii.—xx. is a matter of controversy. In Chronicles, the earlier account is sometimes condensed, sometimes enlarged. In some verses we discern the original narrative. Compare, for example, verse 14 with 2 Kings xviii. 35; verse 15 with xviii. 29; verse 17 with xviii. 12; verse 18 with xviii. 28; verse 21 with xix. 35—37; verse 24 with xx. 1.

The account of Hezekiah's defence against Sennacherib, by cutting off the supplies of water, (2 Ch. xxxii. 3, sqq.,) — which differs from 2 Kings xviii. 14, where he asks for mercy, — is derived from a different source, according to *Keil*, *Movers*, and *Gesenius*, (Jes. vol. ii. pt. ii. p. 936,) and is confirmed by Isa. xxii. 9. Reference is made to the same circumstance in 2 Kings xxii. 20, which, however, refers to a permanent alteration, that is also mentioned in 2 Ch. xxxii. 4. [It seems to me doubtful that 2 Kings xx. 22, relates at all to the attempt to deprive Sennacherib of water, or that 2 Ch. xxxii. 4, refers to the supply of water which Hezekiah brought into the city.]

Movers, though without good reason, thinks 2 Ch. xxxii. 8—31, is an extract, but not from the second book of Kings, though he refers the citation in verse 32 to this book. Verses 7 and 8 are written in the admonitory style of the Chronicler, and the account of Hezekiah's defence, which is inserted to avoid the discreditable statement in 2 Kings xviii. 14, sqq., may have been derived from tradition, or from Isa. xxii.

§ 192, *b*.

THE SAME SUBJECT CONTINUED.

The above statement is apparently confirmed by the fact that the Chronicler seems to refer to the earlier books. The reference, in 1 Ch. xxix. 29, to "the discourses (histories) of Samuel, Nathan, and Gad," applies to our books of Samuel.[a] "The discourses of Nathan and the prophecy of Ahijah," cited in 2 Ch. ix. 29, are found in 1 Kings i.—xi. The discourses of Shemaiah, (2 Ch. xii. 15,) perhaps, refer to 1 Kings xii. 22. "The book of the kings of Judah and Israel," (2 Ch. xvi. 11, xxv. 26, xxviii. 26, xxxii. 32,) or "the book of the kings of Israel and Judah," (2 Ch. xxvii. 7, xxxv. 27, xxxvi. 8,) and likewise "the history of the kings of Israel," (2 Ch. xxxiii. 18,)[b] might be understood as relating to our present books of Kings. "The prophecy of Isaiah" (2 Ch. xxx. 32) is found in 2 Kings xviii. 13—20, and xix.

But, on the other hand, it seems, this conclusion will not stand, because, in company with the discourses of Nathan and Ahijah, (2 Ch. ix. 29,) we find "the vision of Iddo," which does not appear in the parallel, 1 Kings i.—xi. With the discourses of Shemaiah, we have also, (2 Ch. xii. 15,) "the discourses of the prophet Iddo," which do not occur in the parallel, 1 Kings xii. "The book of the kings of Israel and Judah" (2 Ch. xxvii. 7,) contained something not found in 2 Kings xv. 32—38; "a book of the kings of Israel" is cited in 1 Ch. ix. 1,

---

[a] *Movers*, p. 178.

[b] "The discourses of the seer" are found in 2 Kings xxi. 11, sqq. The "prayer" is not found there, but, without violence, this expression may refer to the following work, in verse 19.

and 2 Ch. xx. 34, which contained the genealogies and discourses of the prophet Jehu, and neither appears in our books of Kings. "The explanation of the books of the Kings"[a] (2 Ch. xxiv. 27) is different from our books of the Kings. "The explanation [Midrash] of Iddo the seer," (2 Ch. xiii. 22,) — which, however, may be regarded as a citation of part of the former work, — and "the history of Uzziah, by Isaiah the son of Amoz,"[b] (2 Ch. xxvi. 22,) are referred to, as well as "the discourses of Hosai," (2 Ch. xxxiii. 19,) and do not appear in the former books. Hence some critics have concluded that these were the sources of the peculiar accounts of the Chronicler.

§ 192, *c*.

THE SAME SUBJECT CONTINUED.

There are several hypotheses which rest on the supposition that the Chronicler *did not use or refer to the earlier books*. According to Eichhorn, the Chronicler did not use our books of Samuel and Kings; but in both accounts of the history of David and Solomon, he thinks a short life of these kings lies at the foundation, which has passed through different hands, and has been wrought over in different ways. In the history of the two kingdoms, there were two different imperial histories of the two states, which were compiled from various works. Now, the author of the books of Kings, Eichhorn thinks, adhered closely to these imperial histories,

---

[a] מדרש.

[b] Perhaps here is an error of the text — דברי חזי, instead of דברי החזים. *Movers*, p. 174, 176. [Our English version follows the conjectural reading in the text, and the other in the margin. The Vulgate reads *Hosai*; the LXX. the *Seers*; the Syriac has *Hunan*; and the Arabic *Suphan*.]

while the Chronicler often himself went behind them, back to the original sources, and followed them, and not the historical work compiled from them. However, he used only the history of the kingdom of Judah; and with him the "book of the kings of Israel and Judah" is the same as the "book of the kings of Judah." When both authors follow the larger historical work, they agree; but when the Chronicler goes back to the sources, there is a difference between them.

According to Bertholdt,[a] both authors used merely different extracts from these imperial histories. The Chronicler did not use the particular words, but merely the citations made from them in the compilation.

According to Keil,[b] the Chronicler did not use the books of Samuel and Kings, but, in the history of David, referred to the work cited in 1 Ch. xxix. 29, and in the history of Solomon, to that quoted in 2 Ch. ix. 29, from which latter the history of Solomon, referred to in 1 Kings xi. 41, was compiled. In the history of Judah, he thinks he used the histories of the kingdom of Judah and Israel, — which are quoted under different names, — and the particular sources, such as the discourses of different prophets, which constituted the materials of the larger historical work.

Hävernik[c] assumes the following sources of the Chronicles; namely, in the history of Samuel, the prophetic works cited in 1 Ch. xxix. 29, and the "book of the kings of Israel," mentioned 1 Ch. ix. 1, which was compiled out of the annals of the realm; in the history of Solomon, the prophetic works referred to in 2 Ch. ix. 29, and the same "book of kings;" in the history of

---

[a] P. 972.
[b] P. 206, sqq.
[c] L. c. vol. ii. pt. i. p. 192.

the kingdom of Judah, the "book of kings," which was one and the same with the Midrash, and contained, likewise, the single prophetic discourses that are cited. Besides these, he merely used two separate works, "the discourses of Hosai," (2 Ch. xxxiii. 19,) and "the history of Uzziah by Isaiah," (2 Ch. xxvi. 22.)

But all these hypotheses are so strongly at variance with the obvious character of the Chronicles, that they fail to convince us.

But, on the other hand, the hypothesis of Movers[a] deserves consideration. According to this, besides our books of Samuel and Kings, the Chronicler made use of the Midrash of the "books of kings," which is quoted, and is identical with the "book of the kings of Judah and Israel," otherwise called "book of the kingdom of Israel and Judah," or "of Israel;" and likewise he cites particular parts of this book, as the "Midrash of the prophet Iddo," or as the "discourses" of different prophets, because the latter occurred in it. However, "the history of Uzziah by Isaiah" was a monograph, which he did not use.

This Midrash, or "book of the kings," contains the edifying discourses by which the Chronicles are distinguished from the earlier canonical books,[b] and also the genealogies and registers of names.[c]

---

[a] P. 160, sqq.

[b] For example, 2 Ch. xiii. 4—12. Compare the citation of the Midrash, verse 22.

[c] Compare 1 Ch. ix. 1, and xxi. 6.

§ 192, *d*.

THE SAME SUBJECT CONCLUDED.

But the application of this theory in detail is very uncertain and complicated. It is conceded that the author did not derive the alterations and additions—in which he differs from the earlier books—merely from the Midrash, but that he himself made interpolations. Thus Movers thinks 1 Ch. xvi. 40, is an interpolation by the Chronicler, because it disturbs the connection.[a] But the cases in which he departs from the earlier books, and is supposed to have followed another authority, are almost always doubtful. If there were only additions, and sometimes large ones, we might be satisfied with this theory. But if there are interpolations made in these very earlier accounts, we do not see why the author himself may not have originated them;[b] at

[a] But is he correct in stating the design of placing ten priests before the tabernacle? (verse 39.) He thinks, also, that, in verse 41, the words "to thank Jehovah because his mercy endureth forever," are interpolated. But here the same question may be asked as before. In verse 42, says Movers, with these words, "and with them Heman and Jeduthun," the author proceeds with copying the longer (?) list of names he had begun, but left off in verse 41 But if this were so, he must have left off again, for only two names follow. The senseless repetition, "and with them," &c., (41, 42,) may be ascribed to the Chronicler without such a process.

It is likewise a mistake that he refers to his authority with the words אשר נקבו וג״; for it does not mean that "they (who are mentioned in the hypothetical register) are given with their names," but "they were (expressly) designated by their names." These words are to be connected with the following, "to thank Jehovah," [just as it reads in the English version.] See, also, 1 Ch. xii. 31, 2 Ch. xxi. 19. *Movers*, p. 169. The same is the case with 1 Ch. xxi., where it is difficult to determine what is the Chronicler's amplifying detail and addition from another source, that Movers speaks of in p. 224.

[b] Now, *Movers* admits (p. 224) that small additions, designed to perfect

least, nothing is gained by this hypothesis in favor of the credibility of the book, and the explanation of its origin is removed still farther off. Here I am reminded of a passage in my Beiträge — " It troubles me little to prove that the author of the Chronicles—that is, the man

---

the account, have been derived from other sources, and refers to 1 Ch. xi. 6, 8, compared with 2 Sam. v. 8, 9, 2 Ch. xi. 42—47, compared with 2 Sam. xxiii. 39, and other places. But where is the certainty that such was the origin of these passages? According to him, (p. 186, 187,) the account (2 Ch. vii. 1—3) that fire fell from heaven, and the glory of Jehovah filled the house, is derived from another source, which was a recasting of 1 Kings viii. 1—11, — where Solomon brings the ark into the temple, and the glory of Jehovah fills the house, — because otherwise it is not conceivable that the Chronicler (in verse 2) could repeat the account of the glory of Jehovah, which he had already (in v. 14) copied from 1 Kings viii. 10, 11. But 2 Ch. vii. 1, corresponds with 1 Kings viii. 54. Now, the Chronicler, instead of making Solomon bless the people after his prayer, [as in Kings,] makes fire come down from heaven, *as the result of his prayer.* With this he connects the mention of the glory of Jehovah, partly for the sake of the similarity between them, and partly from analogy with Levit. ix. 23, 24, where the glory of Jehovah appears to the people.

It is very improbable that the Chronicler, on the other hand, in 1 Ch. xiii xv. xvi., observed the earlier accounts, — as *Movers* thinks he did, (p. 166,) — or derived 1 Ch. xiii. 1—5, from the second source, and verses 6—14 from 2 Sam. But why did the Chronicler depart from that, and what did it contain on this point? To judge from the result, it could afford him more than the earlier accounts. *Movers* ascribes the interruption of the account by the insertion of chap. xiv. to the Chronicler; xv. 1—24, he derives from the second source; but verse 25, from 2 Sam.; verse 27, from the second source, verse 27, which speaks of the twofold raiment of David — [an overcoat of *byssus*, and a mantle of linen, מעיל בוץ, and אפוד בד] — is a combination of the different accounts of the two sources. (This is not bad!) Chap. xv. 28—xvi. 3, proceeds in unison with 2 Sam. vi.; in verses 15—19, the agreement is verbal. But is this derived from the second source, or does it contain nothing therefrom? If so, it passes over the chief matters in silence. He thinks that at 2 Sam. vi. 15, the Chronicler inserted the matter derived from the second source, and contained in xv. 16, sqq. But, in the one case, he tells what is to be done, in the other, what is done; therefore there is no repetition. Before the last words of 2 Sam. vi. 19, he inserts from his second source the different account of placing the Levites before the ark, &c., (xvi. 4 —42,) and in verse 43, he comes back to the last words in 2 Sam. vi. 19 and 20. But it remains unexplained why he omits the rest of 2 Sam. vi. 20—23,

who gave them the precise form in which we have them now — in an arbitrary, and therefore deceptive, manner made the alterations, additions, and falsifications, which I shall proceed to detail. It is possible that, in the course of time, several writers have taken a part in disfiguring the accounts which yet remain unfalsified in the books of Samuel and Kings. Who will contend about that? But as the Chronicle lies before us, it makes a whole of the same character throughout. This character, then, without any falsehood, may be ascribed to one author."[a]

It has been unjustly denied, that, in the time of the Chronicler, there were various writings which have not found a place in the canon.[b] But the literary references are not to be trusted, as it appears from the false citation of Jeremiah's Lamentations, in 2 Ch. xxxv. 25, which is made on the erroneous notion that Josiah's death was the subject of Jeremiah's Lamentations. It is doubtful

---

or, at least, verse 22, and therefore there seems no reason for this alleged return to this document.

The departure, in 2 Ch. xxiii. 1—12, from 2 Kings xi., is explained by *Movers* (p. 307, sqq.) from the use of the second source; but the prohibition in verse 6, "Let none but the priests and they that minister of the Levites come into the house of Jehovah," is ascribed to the Chronicler. In 2 Ch. xxiii. 12, the interpolating alteration of הרצים is acknowledged, and it is admitted that the account in Chronicles is unintelligible without the other.

The case is the same with 2 Ch. xxiv. 4—14. Compare 2 Kings xii. 5—16, (p. 312, sqq.) See above, § 190, *c*, p. 287. According to *Movers*, (p. 103,) 2 Ch. xii. 2, was derived verbally from 1 Kings xiv. 25, then verses 3—8 from the second source, and with verse 9 the Chronicler turned to 2 Kings. But verses 3—8, as well as verse 12, are more correctly considered an interpolation, as it appears from the fact that the connection is disturbed. The remark, in verse 12, that Rehoboam humbled himself, — which connects with verse 6, — is too late after what has been said in verses 10, 11. It should follow after verse 9, and be connected with the statement that God gave the promised assistance, and sent away again the king of Ægypt; but the admonitory interpolator did not know this, for it was not in 2 Kings.

[a] Vol. i. p. 61.

[b] *Gramberg*, p. 25. On the other hand, *Movers*, p. 103, *Zunz*, p. 34.

whether the prophet Jehu—whom we find under Baasha, king of Israel, (1 Kings xvi. 1, 7)—could have been active under Jehoshaphat, who was king of Judah, more than thirty years after, (2 Ch. xix. 2,) as it is implied in the reference to his discourses, (2 Ch. xx. 34.) Yet these (false) discourses are found among the authorities of the Chronicler.

§ 192, *e*.

DESIGN AND AUTHOR.

The design of the author was obviously this—to give an account of the theocratic kingdom of David, which was obviously, but slightly, connected by genealogies, and the death of Saul, with the earlier history of the people of Israel,—an account of that kingdom, which at first embraced all the twelve tribes, and afterwards only the tribe of Judah, and the tribes belonging to it,—the kingdom which observed the Mosaic law, and the Mosaic worship,—and to show how, in this, the true worship of God was preserved in all its perfection under pious kings, or restored by them, and how apostasy from this brought on distress and ruin. This he does in such a manner that the light far surpasses the dark side. Every thing is tried by the priestly standard.

The author is unknown; but it is certain he must be sought among the priests. [Carpzov, Eichhorn, and Hävernik, follow Baba Bathra, and consider Ezra the author. Jahn and Bertholdt differ from that opinion.[a]

---

[a] Baba Bathra, fol. 15, c. 1. *Carpzov*, l. c. p. 286. *Eichhorn*, § 494. *Hävernik*, vol. ii. pt. i. p. 268, sqq. *Jahn*, vol. ii. p. 245. *Bertholdt*, p. 987. On the opinion that its author wrote, also, the book of Ezra, see below, § 196, *b*.

Horne, after stating his reasons for the belief that Ezra did not write the books, says, "Their authenticity is abundantly supported by the general mass of external evidence; by which, also, *their divine authority is fully established*, as well as by the direct attestations of our Lord and his apostles." "Independently of the important moral and religious instruction to be derived from the two books of Chronicles, ... the second book is extremely valuable in a *critical* point of view, not only as it contains some historical particulars which are not mentioned in any other part of the Old Testament, but also as it affords us many genuine readings...... The discrepancies between the books of Kings and Chronicles, though very numerous, are not of any great moment, and admit of an easy solution, being partly caused by various lections, and partly arising from the nature of the books, which, being supplementary to those of Samuel and Kings, omit what is there related more at large, and supply what is there wanting."[a] Respecting this opinion nothing need be said.[b]]

---

[a] *Horne*, l. c. pt. v. ch. ii. § vii. vol. ii. p. 222, sqq.

[b] [The spirit of a considerable part of these books resembles that shown in the public prayers offered by authority in England after the troubles of Charles II. See them in *King's* Life of Locke, 2d ed. vol. i. p. 261 sqq.]

CHAPTER VII.

THE BOOK OF RUTH.[a]

§ 193.

CONTENTS AND DESIGN OF THE BOOK.

THIS family history of the royal house of Jesse is placed in the cyclus of the history before the exile It goes back to the time of the judges, i. 1,[b] and therefore, in the Alexandrian version, it is placed between the books of Judges and Samuel.[c]

The book relates the history of the marriage of Boaz, (which was attended with remarkable circumstances,) the great-grandfather of David, with idyllic simplicity and loveliness, and with a faithful delineation of the manners of the time: a genealogy is appended to the end of the book. This genealogy is incomplete, as genealogies often are with the Hebrews and Arabians.[d]

---

[a] *Jo. Drusii, Bonfrerii, Serrarii, Seb. Schmidii, Jo. Clerici, Maur.* Comment.

Rosenmüller, Scholia.

Sanctii Comm. in Ruth, Esr., Nehem., Tob., &c.; Lugd. 1628, fol.

Victorin. Strigelii Schol. in Lib. Ruth; Jen. 1571.

J. B. Carpzov, Colleg. rabbin.-bibl. in Lib. Ruth; Lips. 1703, 4to.

Jo. Jac. Rambachii Annott. (Uberr. annotatt. in Hagiogr. ed. *J. H. Michaelis*, vol. ii.)

[*Geddes*, l. c.

Palfrey, l. c. vol. ii.]

Ueberss. u. Erkll. von *Dereser*, 1806; *Riegler*, 1812.

[b] *Josephus*, Ant. v. 9, 1, erroneously dates this occurrence in the time of Eli. See *Bertholdt*, p. 2349.

[c] See *Origen*, above, vol. i. p. 89, sqq., and *Jerome*, ibid. p. 111, sqq.

[d] See *Eichhorn*, § 465, and his Monumenta Antiquissima Hist. Arab. § 7, p. 18. [In this instance, there are but four generations between Nahshon and David, a period of four hundred and eighty years, according to 1 Kings

The book was composed in honor of the royal house, but not designed to lend it an outward splendor, — for the mother of the family is a poor Moabitish woman, — but, by means of history and genealogy, to place its origin in a clear light. The mention of Nahshon — a prince of the families of Judah, in the time of Moses — among the ancestors, and the favorable moral picture of Ruth and Boaz, tend to honor and exalt the house of David. [But, on the other hand, we must admit that the poverty of the family is not concealed. They are not merely *forced to flee* from the land, on account of poverty, but, after their return, avail themselves of the rights of the poor. Ruth and her mother live on the gleanings from the fields, and design to sell their inheritance, which they were probably unable to keep; but neither the ancient Orientals, nor the modern, who have not forsaken their simplicity, valued noble blood at a high price.]

Umbreit thinks this book was written with a specific moral design; namely, for the sake of showing how even a stranger, and that of the hated Moabitish stock, might be sufficiently noble to become mother of the great King David, because she placed her reliance on the God of Israel.[a] Bertholdt thinks the history is a pure fiction.

---

vi. 1, or of five hundred and ninety-two years, if we accept the reading which is followed by Josephus, (Antiq. i. viii. 3, 1,) and the apostle Paul, (Acts xiii. 21.) But some Hebrew genealogists allow themselves to pass over parts of the scale in their genealogical table. See Gen. v. xi., Ex. vi. 16—20, Matt. i. See, also, *Eichhorn*, Allg. Bib. vol. i. p. 926, iii. p. 183, sqq., v. p. 400, sqq. *Paulus*, Repertorium, vol. iii. p. 395, sqq.]

[a] See his essay Uber Geist und Zweck des Buches Ruths, in Theol. Stud. und Krit. for 1834, p. 308.

See *Hävernik*, vol. ii. pt. i. p. 113. [*Eichhorn* (§ 463) thinks it was obviously written *to honor the house of David*, though it does not conceal the poverty of the family.]

But he decides on insufficient grounds, and misunderstands i. 21, and thinks it is a contradiction of iv. 3—6. He thinks it was designed to recommend the duty of a man to marry his kinswoman. Certainly we do not know the source whence this narrative was drawn, but it was probably tradition.[a]

[The arguments of Bertholdt are merely nugatory. The chief stress is laid on the symbolic meaning of the names,[b] and on the above contradiction, which, if it really exist, is much more likely to occur in a history than a fictitious narrative. He calls it a "romantic family picture." But since it contains nothing impossible, or even improbable, it seems uncritical, at this time, to attempt to decide that it must be a fiction throughout. The most beautiful and splendid robe of virtue, says this writer, is drawn over the whole. The author has taken particular pains to delineate the characters of Naomi, Ruth, and Boaz. In the former we have the finest picture of intelligent resignation, brought into the closest connection with a mother's anxiety. She does not complain, like a weak woman, at the death of her husband and sons, and is not comfortless in her poverty. In the person of Ruth we have a woman who lives entirely in her duties; she does for her mother-in-law what the national myth commanded a faithful wife to do for her husband.

The whole book is a beautiful idyllic piece of composition, descriptive of the ancient simplicity of rural life.[c]

---

[a] *Bertholdt*, p. 2337—2357.

[b] [He mentions the following: Boaz, בֹּוֹעַז, *one in whom is refuge;* Mahlon, מַחְלוֹן, *diseased;* Chilion, כִּלְיוֹן, *pining;* Naomi, נָעֳמִי, *my beauty;* Elimelech, אֱלִימֶלֶךְ, *god-king;* Ruth, רוּת, *beauty.* But the same may be said of almost all Hebrew names.]

[c] [See *Goethe*, West-östliche Divan, p. 249.]

To me it seems that the genealogy (iv. 18—22) is the work of a later hand, and originally formed no part of the book. The relation of Ruth to David is mentioned in verse 17. When Boaz announces in public that he has bought her for his wife, the elders utter a blessing, which seems to have been a popular form of benediction,— "Let thy house be like the house of Pharez, whom Tamar bare unto Judah." Then a later writer, connecting the two facts in verses 12 and 17, supplies some of the links in the genealogical chain, and gives an air of completeness to the whole.

Jahn thinks he discovers a reference to earlier documents, especially in the use of the *second of kin*,[a] (ii. 20.) Eichhorn, though without sufficient evidence, refers it to the author of the books of Samuel.]

§ 194.

ITS AGE AND AUTHOR.

It follows, from the contents and design of the book, that it was written a considerable time after David. The language, though akin to that of the books of Samuel, seems to differ from that in its Chaldaisms[b] and other peculiarities,[c] and to be more modern. Chap. iv. 7, contains an allusion to more ancient times—"In former

---

[a] מְגֹּאֲלֵ.

[b] Chap. i. 17, כֹּה יַעֲשֶׂה יְהוָה לִי. Comp. 1 Sam. iii. 17, xiv. 44. But comp. also 1 Kings ii. 23, 2 Kings vi. 31. Chap. iv. 4, אֶגְלֶה אָזְנְךָ לֵאמֹר. Comp. 1 Sam. ix. 15, xx. 2, 12, [and 2 Sam. vii. 27.]

[c] שִׂבֵּר, עָגַן, i. 13; לָהֵן, for לָכֵן, ibid.; שַׁכַבְתִּי, שַׂמְתִּי, iii. 3, 4; א, for ה, i. 20; ם, suff. for ן, i. 8, 9, 11. According to *Sanct.*, (Comm. in Ruth Prolegg. iv.,) there are in the book Moabitisms; according to *Dereser*, (Vor p. 6,) Bethlehemitisms.

time, ... to confirm all things, a man plucked off his shoe and gave it to his neighbor, and this was a testimony in Israel."

Therefore it is improbable that this is by the same author with the books of Samuel, though it must have been written at a time when marriage with a foreign woman was not unallowed.[a] Now, it is forbidden in Deut. xxiii. 3, Ezra ix. 1, sqq., Neh. xiii. 1—3, 23—27. But we nowhere find any proof that a descent from Ruth was objectionable; nowhere is there the slightest apology for it.

[It is not possible, either from the language or any other circumstances of the book, to determine in what age it was written. Perhaps the narrative circulated some time orally, and was successively enriched with the explanatory passage, iv. 7, and the genealogy of David, (iv. 18—23.) The conjectures of the learned are, as usual in such matters, various, and sometimes absurd. Thus Kimchi considers Boaz the same person with Jozan, a contemporary of Jephthah; Junius refers the events of the book to the time of Deborah; Usher, to that of Shamgar; Patrick, on account of the famine, mentioned i. 1, to the time of Gideon, when a famine also occurred, (Judg. vi. 3—6.) According to Matt. i. 5, 6, Salmon, the father of Boaz, married Rahab the harlot, the contemporary of Joshua; and accordingly the great-grandfather of David lived nearly four hundred years before him. Admitting the genealogy to be true,

---

[a] See *Pareau*, Instit. Interp. p. 144. See the ancient opinions in *Carpzov*, l. c. vol. i. p. 198, sqq. [In Hebrew, this book was perhaps considered a second appendix to that of Judges. Jerome says, Prol. Galeato, subtexunt Hebraii Judicum librum et in eundem compingunt librum Ruth. In the final Masora of a Spanish MS., *Kennicott* finds it called סטר שפט השפטרם. See *Bruns*, in *Kennicott*, Diss. Gen. p. 18, and *Eichhorn*, § 465.]

the difficulty may be solved as indicated above. But Usher concludes that the ancestors of David, and, through him, of the Messiah, were men of extraordinary piety and strength, and were blessed with very long life.][a]

CHAPTER [illegible]

THE BOOKS OF EZRA AND NEHEMIAH.[b]

§ 195.

CONTENTS.

THESE books, which are regarded by the Hebrew and Greek Jews as but one, or as two parts of the same book,[c]—although they were originally separate books,—contain the history of the restoration of the Jewish state after the exile.

---

[a] [See *Junius* and *Patrick* on Ruth i. *Leusden*, Phil. Sac. p. 18, 86. See, also, *Horne*, l. c. pt. v. chap. ii. § iv. vol. ii. p. 218. He follows the date of Patrick, and counts Samuel as its author, and finds in it "reverent observance of the Mosaic law"! *Eichhorn* (§ 464) finds a Chaldaism, or Syriasm, in the use of א, for ה, in מָרָא, i. 20, (but the same form occurs elsewhere; see *Rosenmüller*, in loc.;) in the superfluous י in וְיָרַדְתִּי וְשַׂמְתִּי, iii. 3, and וְשָׁכַבְתִּי, verse 4. The custom of taking off the shoe to confirm a bargain, (iv. 7, 8,) was obsolete when the book was reduced to its present form. The name of the second of kin, מְגֹאָל, was forgotten, it would seem, as it is not mentioned.]

[b] *Jo. Clerici, Sanctii, Maur*

Victorin. Strigelii Schol. in Libr. Esræ; Lips. 1571;—in Libr. Nehem.; ib. 1575.

Jo. H. Michaelis, Annotatt. in Libr. Esr. *J. Jac. Rambachii* Annotatt. in Libr. Nehem. (Uberr. annotatt. in Hagiogr. vol. iii.)

[c] See above, vol. i. § 25, 27, 10. *Buxtorf*, Tib. xi. p. 108.

1. The book of Ezra connects with the Chronicles. The first part (i.—vi.) contains the history of the return from exile, and of the building of the temple. It extends from the first year of Cyrus to the sixth of Darius Hystaspes, that is, from 536 to 515 B. C.

The second part (vii.—x.) contains the history of Ezra's migration with a second company of Jews, and the purification of marriages, effected by him. It begins with the seventh year of Artaxerxes Longimanus,[a] that is, 458 B. C.

[Ezra was descended directly from the high priest Seraiah, who had been executed at the time of the destruction of Jerusalem. His genealogy is twice given in the Old Testament, namely, in Ezra vii. 1, sqq., and 1 Ch. vi. 3, sqq., the latter containing six members not mentioned in the former. While in exile, he busied himself with the Law of Moses, as it seems, for he is called a "ready scribe in the Law of Moses."[b] One of his chief aims was to establish or restore the Mosaic institutions, after his arrival in Palestine. In the time of Nehemiah, he was active in promoting the welfare of the new colony. The time of his death is not known.]

2. The book of Nehemiah relates that Nehemiah received permission and an oral decree from King Artaxerxes Longimanus to return to his native land, and to fortify Jerusalem, which he likewise accomplished in spite of the obstacles which the Samaritans threw in his way, (i. 1—vii. 5.) Then follows a list of the exiles

---

[a] It was in the seventh year of *Xerxes*, according to *Josephus*, *Michaelis*, *Jahn*, and *De Wette's* Archäol. § 50; but of *Artaxerxes*, according to *Bertholdt*, p. 989, sq., *Gesenius*, Thesaurus, *Keil*, Ub. d. Chronik. p. 103, sqq.

[b] [סוֹפֵר מָהִיר בְּתוֹרַת מֹשֶׁה, vii. 6, et al. See the Arabic stories about him in *D'Herbelot*, Bib. Orient. sub voce *Ozair*.]

who returned under Cyrus, (vii. 6—33, of the same tenor with Ezra ii.,) to which is added an account of a religious festival observed under Ezra and Nehemiah, (vii. 73—x. 40.) Chap. xi. treats of the repeopling of Jerusalem. Chap. xii. 1—26, contains more lists; xii. 27—47, the consecration of the walls of the city; and xiii., the reformations introduced by Nehemiah. [The time of the book extends from 444 to about 404 B. C.]

§ 196, *a*.

THE CONSTITUENT PARTS AND AUTHOR OF THE BOOK OF EZRA.

It is quite obvious that this book is not the work of a single author. In the first part (i.—vi.) we find two ancient documents have been used in constructing the narrative.

1. The first document is chapter ii., which Nehemiah found existing as a separate document, as he says, (vii. 5,) "I found a register of the genealogy of them which came up at the first, and found written therein, 'These are the children of the province that went up out of the captivity, of those that had been carried away, whom Nebuchadnezzar the king of Babylon had carried away, and came again to Jerusalem, and to Judah, every one to his city.'" [The quotation is verbatim from Ezra ii. 1.]

2. The second document is iv. 8—vi. 18, which is distinguished from the rest of the book by the use of the Chaldee language, not only in the epistles, as in vii. 12—26, but in the narrative itself, and in the introduction at the beginning. The transition from the Hebrew to the Chaldee language might be explained from

the analogy of Dan. ii. 4, by the fact that a letter is inserted in the Chaldee language; but the introduction to the letter (verses 8—10) is also in that dialect.[a]

The second part (vii.—x.) is connected with the preceding by means of the formula, "Now, after these things," (vii. 1;) but still it is distinguished from it by the style, and makes a whole by itself, though, perhaps, it is not all from the same hand.

The passage, vii. 27—ix. 15, where Ezra speaks in the first person, was evidently written by himself. To this belongs the Chaldee document, vii. 12—26. The tenth chapter speaks of him in the third person, but is a contemporary narrative, and was either written by himself or by one of his assistants. From the use of the expression (vii. 6) Ezra was a "ready scribe," it is doubtful whether the passage, verses 1—11, was written by him.[b]

All these parts were probably added quite late to the

---

[a] This passage, v. 4, leads us to think it was written by an eye-witness, but it is not decisive. (Compare Josh. v. 6.) On the contrary, the mention of Artaxerxes (vi. 14) would refer us to a later origin. However, *Hävernik*, (l. c. p. 293,) and some others, consider this passage an interpolation. *Kleinert* (in Dörpt. Beiträge, vol. i. p. 101) separates iv. 8—23, from v. 1—vi. 18, which is no more to be admitted than *Movers's* theory, which cuts off vi. 16—18, and ascribes it to the redactor. On account of the expression, *king of Assyria*, instead of *king of Persia*, verse 22, *Bertholdt* refers this passage to a later hand than that which wrote i. iii. iv. 1—7. But this is unnecessary. The term "king of *Babylon*" occurs, v. 13. Compare, also, 2 Kings xxiii. 29, Jer. ii. 18, Lam. v. 6. See *Keil*, p. 119, *Hävernik*, vol. ii. pt. i. p. 287.

[b] *Bertholdt* (p. 997, 1000) and *Zunz* (p. 23) derive vii. 1—11, from the redactor.) But *Hävernik* refers them to Ezra. *Movers* (p. 16, 24) considers them interpolated. The honorary appellation סופר מהיר — which is not a mere title, as *Hävernik* thinks — and the similar remark, verse 10, (12,) and the genealogy, (verses 1—5,) could scarcely have been written by Ezra himself. The fact that he speaks in the third person is nothing against his authorship, though, on the other hand, the phrase in verse 7, (9,) כיד אלהים עליו, — which also occurs, Neh. ii. 8, — is not decisive evidence in his favor.

present book of Ezra, as we judge from vi. 22, where the Persian kings are called *Assyrian*. Perhaps the compilation was made by the author of vi. 19—22.[a]

[The singular character of this book, the variety in its language, style, and in the person of the writer, have given rise to several theories and ingenious attempts to account for its peculiarities. Huet supposes the first six chapters are the work of an uncertain author, whom he fancies to be the same with the writer of Chronicles. Leclerc[b] says none can doubt Ezra wrote the three last chapters, for he speaks in the first person, (vii. 27, 28, ix. 1, 5, et al.) From this circumstance, he thinks he wrote the whole book, and thus accounts for some of its peculiarities. At Babylon, Ezra determined to return into Judea with Zerubabel and Joshua; afterwards he went back to Babylon, and returned, a second time, to Judea, under Darius Hystaspes. In the early chapters he does not mention himself, because he was not the leader, as in the second journey. But it is evident that he was in the company of returning exiles, for he is mentioned among them, (vi. 14, 15.) The objections to this theory are so obvious that they need not be mentioned.

Eichhorn[c] thinks Ezra, when he came to Judea, or began to write, found a Chaldee account of the quarrels of the Samaritans with the Jews, about the new temple, written by an eye-witness of and actor in the affairs he described. Ezra wished to incorporate this in his book, and to connect the latter with the book of Chronicles. So he goes back to the time of Cyrus,

---

[a] *Bertholdt's* arguments against chap. x. are erroneous.

[b] [Diss. de Script. V. T. c. viii., and note on Ezra vii. 1.]

[c] [§ 498, sqq.]

and writes, in Hebrew, a short history of the return under Zerubabel, which is now i.—iv. 6, in this book. He then affixed the Chaldee account of the quarrel with the Samaritans, (iv. 7—vi. 18,) and added the history of the second colony,—led thither by himself,—and of the improvements he made, (vi. 19—x. 44.) Here he made use of the Hebrew language, except in the letter of the king, which he gives in its original form. But this theory rests on the supposition that the books of Chronicles were written before the time of Ezra, which cannot be proved. Besides, apart from this consideration, if he had been acquainted with the Chronicles, would he not follow their text in giving his own genealogy? (Compare vii. 1, sqq., and 1 Ch. vi. 3, sqq.) Still further, he would not speak of himself as he does in vii. 6, 10, and x. 3.

Bertholdt's opinion is briefly this—the book consists of three separate and independent pieces: i.—iv. 6, iv. 7—vi. 18, and vii. 1—x. 44. The last of these alone was written by Ezra,—who was acquainted with the others,—though not exactly in their present extent, for he thinks vii. 1—11, is a summary introduction, and x. 1—44, is a supplement. Some man who lived, perhaps, in the time of the Ptolemies, or Seleucidæ, or shortly before Antiochus Epiphanes, reduced them to their present form.

Justin Martyr quotes a passage from Ezra which is now found neither in the Hebrew nor the Greek, namely, "And Ezra said to the people, 'This passover is our Savior and our refuge, and if you consider, and it enters into your heart that we are about to humble him in a figure, and afterwards if we shall put our trust in him, this place shall never be made desolate, says the

God of power. But if you do not believe in him, and will not hear his proclamation, you shall be a laughing-stock to the Gentiles.'"[a]]

§ 196, *b*.

THE SAME SUBJECT CONTINUED.

The opinion that this entire compilation originated with Ezra is wholly untenable.[b] But, on the other hand, it must be admitted, the opinion that the author of the Chronicles was also the compiler of the book of Ezra, is very strongly favored by the affinity between

---

[a] [Dial. cum Tryphone, ch. 72: *Καὶ εἶπεν Ἔσδρας τῷ λαῷ· τοῦτο τὸ πάσχα ὁ σωτὴρ ἡμῶν, καὶ ἡ καταφυγὴ ἡμῶν· καὶ ἐάν διανοήθητε, καὶ ἀνάβῃ ὑμῶν ἐπὶ τὴν καρδίαν, ὅτι μέλλομεν αὐτον ταπεῖνουν ἐν σημείῳ καὶ μετά ταῦτα ἐλπίσωμεν ἐπ' αὐτον ὁ μή ἐρημώθῃ ὁ τόπος οὗτος εἰς τὸν ἁπάντα χρόνον λέγει ὁ Θεός τῶν δυναμεῶν. ἐάν δὲ μή πιστεύσητε αὐτῷ, μηδὲ εἰσακούσητε τοῦ κηρύγματος αὐτου, ἔσεσθε ἐπιχάρμα τοῖς ἔθνεσι.*

It was formerly the custom to ascribe several of the books of the Old Testament to Ezra; but recently the current of opinion has run in another channel, leaving for the "ready scribe" only a few chapters in all. Numerous apocryphal books have been assigned him. Thus, for example, Picus Mirandula says — no one knows on what authority — that, after the return from captivity, Ezra, fearing lest the knowledge of the Law should be lost, assembled all the sages of the land, seventy in number; each of them told all he knew of the mysteries of the Law; scribes recorded the matter, and thus seventy volumes were produced. After forty days were completed, continues Picus, the Most High commanded him to publish these books, — containing the "*vein of intellect*," and "*fountain of wisdom*," that the worthy and unworthy might read them. These books, he says, contain not only the Mosaic, but the Christian religion, the mystery of the Trinity, the incarnation of the Word, the divinity of the Messiah, &c. &c. In the apocryphal book of Ezra, (2 Esd. xiv. 44,) *two hundred and four* books are ascribed to him, seventy of which are reserved for the wise, the rest are published. See *Carpzov*, vol. i. p. 319, sqq.]

[b] Baba Bathra, fol. 15. *Eichhorn*, 3, § 493, 498. *Klein*, l. c. *Hävernik*, ii. 1, p. 285.

the two books.[a] Thus, for example, the last three verses of the Chronicles are almost word for word the same as the first three verses of Ezra: —

2 Ch. xxxvi. 22, 23. "Now in the first year of Cyrus king of Persia, that the word of the Lord by the mouth of Jeremiah might be accomplished, the Lord stirred up the spirit of Cyrus king of Persia, that he made a proclamation throughout all his kingdom, and put it also in writing, saying, 'Thus saith Cyrus king of Persia, "All the kingdoms of the earth hath the Lord God of heaven given me; and he hath charged me to build him a house in Jerusalem, which is in Judah. Who is there among you of all his people? the Lord his God be with him, and let him go up."'"

Ezra i. 1—3. "Now in the first year of Cyrus king of Persia, that the word of the Lord by the mouth of Jeremiah might be accomplished, the Lord stirred up the spirit of Cyrus king of Persia, that he made a proclamation throughout all his kingdom, and put it also in writing, saying, 'Thus saith Cyrus king of Persia, "All the kingdoms of the earth the Lord God of heaven hath given me; and he hath charged me to build him a house in Jerusalem, which is in Judah." Who is there among you of all his people? his God be with him, and let him go up to Jerusalem which is in Judah, and build the house of the Lord God of Israel, (he is the God,) which is in Jerusalem.'"[b]

The whole passage in the Chronicles is out of its proper connection, and therefore we must conclude that

---

[a] So *Eichhorn*, *Hävernik*, and *Movers*, p. 14. *Zunz*, p. 21, sqq.

[b] Attempts have been made to prove that the Chronicler did not borrow these verses: 1. From the use of the *copulative conjunction* with which Ezra begins. But Joshua, Judges, Esther, and Ezekiel, begin in the same manner. See *De Wette*, (Beit. vol. i. p. 47.) 2. From the reference to the prophecy of Jeremiah, for which there is not the same reason in Ezra i. 1, as in 2 Ch. xxxvi. 21 and 22; [?] but this prophecy was sufficiently well known at the time. 3. From the occurrence of easy and explanatory readings in Ezra, for example, מִפִּי, for בְּפִי; but it is doubtful if this reading is of such a character; the verb יְהִי is inserted in verse 3, and omitted in the parallel. See *Keil*, p. 91. *Movers*, p. 12. *Hävernik*, p. 269.

the books of Chronicles were originally united with the book of Ezra; but we cannot properly tell how the two have been separated, or rather torn asunder.

According to Movers, the passages, i. iii. iv. 1—7, and vi. 16—22, have the same Levitical character, the same diffuseness in the accounts of offerings, — though this may be doubted, — and the same favorite phrases, which occur in the Chronicles.[a] The affinity between them is undeniable; but is it any thing more than a conformity with the spirit of the times?

---

[a] E. g. *Favorite Phrases.* — להעלות עליו עלות ככתוב בתורת משה; Ezra iii. 2. Comp. 1 Ch. xvi. 40. Ezra iii. 3, is like 2 Ch. xiii. 11. But iii. 4, 5, has but slight resemblance to 2 Ch. xxxi. 3, and viii. 18, is, in *Movers*, an incorrect citation.

Again: the phrase מתנדב נדבה ליהוה, *to consecrate voluntarily;* Ezra iii. 5. Comp. i. 6, ii. 68, (but not Neh. vii. 70.) Comp. 1 Ch. xxix. 5, 6, 9, 14, 17. But here only the verb occurs without the substantive. On the contrary, it is found, also, in Neh. xi. 2.

לנצח על מלאכת, *to superintend the work;* Ezra iii. 8. Comp. 1 Ch. xxiii. 3, 4. In other respects, there is a difference in regard to the age of the two.

על ידי דויד, *at the hands of David,* i. e. *according to his ordinances;* Ezra iii. 10. Comp. 2 Ch. xxix. 27, and elsewhere. "*Because he is good, his mercy endureth forever;*" Ezra iii. 11. Comp. 1 Ch. xvi. 41, 2 Ch. v. 13, et al.

בשמחה להרים קול, *lifted up their voices for joy;* Ezra iii. 12. Comp. 1 Ch. xv. 16. הוסד, *foundation;* Ezra iii. 11. Comp. 2 Ch. iii. 3. עד למרחוק; iii. 13. Comp. 2 Ch. xxvi. 15.

Chap. vi. 16—18, resembles the previous passages, and yet is written in Chaldee, and by a different author. So, likewise, Neh. viii.—x.; e. g. מבינים, viii. 9, as in 1 Ch. xv. 29, xxv. 8; the exchange of עמד with קום, ix. 2, 3, as in 1 Ch. xx. 4, xxi. 1; the joy of the feast, viii. 12, 17, (of which Neh. xii. 43;) העביר קול, viii. 15, as in Ezra i. 1; the remark, viii. 17, as in 2 Ch. xxx. 26, &c.; therefore *Zunz* (p. 24, 25) refers these chapters to the compiler of Ezra. Finally, the Chronicles never have the formulas כאיש אחד (Ezra iii. 1; see Neh. viii. 1) and כאחד, (ii. 64, iii. 9, vi. 20,) though the latter occurs somewhat differently in 2 Ch. v. 13.

§ 197, *a*.

CONSTITUENT PORTIONS, AND AUTHOR OF THE BOOK OF NEHEMIAH.

The passage, i.—vii. 5, is written by Nehemiah in his own manner, which is quite peculiar.[a] After this, he inserts an old catalogue which he had found, as he says himself, (verse 5,)—"I found a register of the genealogy of them which came up at the first." This is to be found also in Ezra ii. It includes vii. 6—73, as far as the words "*in their cities*." But verses 70—72 have been wrought over with reference to Nehemiah and his time, though scarcely by his hand, but by that which wrote viii.—x.[b] But this passage connected therewith

---

[a] [He has some remarkable phrases: *according to the good hand of my God upon me*, כְּיַד־אֱלֹהַי הַטּוֹבָה עָלָי ; ii. 8, 18. מָה אֱלֹהַי נֹתֵן אֶל־לִבִּי, *which my God put in my heart*; ii. 12. שְׁמַע אֱלֹהֵינוּ, *hear, O our God*; iii. 36, (iv. 4.) כֵּן מִפְּנֵי יִרְאַת אֱלֹהִים, *from fear of God*; v. 15. זָכְרָה־לִּי אֱלֹהַי לְטוֹבָה, *remember me, O my God, for good*; v. 19. See, also, vi. 9, 14, 16, vii. 5.]

[b] [The catalogue agrees in many points with that in Ezra; but some of the numbers are widely different, as will appear from the following, in which the dissimilar numbers are given:—

LIST OF MEN.

	In Ezra.		*In Nehemiah.*
Children of Arah,	775		652
——— Pahath-Moab, &c.,	2,812		2,818
——— Zattu,	945		845
——— *Bani*,	642	*Binnui*,	648
——— Bebai,	623		628
——— Azgad,	1,222		2,322
——— Adonikam,	666		667
——— Bigvai,	2,056		2,067
——— Adin,	454		655
——— Hashum,	273		328
——— Bezai,	323		324
——— *Jorah*,	112	*Hariph*,	112

and extending from vii. 73, — "and when the seventh month came," — to x. 40, is an interpolation.

This appears from the following considerations: —

1. The style is different. The personal character of Nehemiah does not appear; it is Nehemiah the *Tirshatha*, (governor,) viii. 9, x. 2; while elsewhere he is called the *Pachah*, (prefect,) v. 14, 15, 18. The names *Jehovah*, *Adonai*, and *Elohim*, are used promiscuously, viii 1, 6, 8, 9, 10, 14, 16, and elsewhere, while in all other parts of Nehemiah, except i. 5, 11, iv. 8, *Elohim* is the prevalent name.[a] On account of a certain degree of affinity between this and the genuine and spurious books of Ezra, Hävernik ascribes the whole passage to Ezra himself. Kleinert, however, refers only chapters ix. and x. to him, and ascribes viii. to an assist-

	In Ezra.	*In Nehemiah.*
Children of Bethlehem and Netophah,	179	188
———— Bethel and Ai,	223	123
———— Lod, &c.,	725	721
———— Senaah,	3,630	3,930
———— Asaph,	128	148
———— Shallum, &c.,	139	138
———— Delaiah, &c.,	652	642

Yet the sum total is said to be the same in both, though differing widely from the amount of the separate numbers given. There is also a difference in the sums of money contributed for the temple. Ezra says, the chiefs of the fathers gave sixty-one thousand gold daricks, and five thousand pounds of silver, and one hundred priests' garments; while Nehemiah makes the contribution of these chiefs twenty thousand gold daricks and two thousand two hundred pounds of silver. He adds, also, the Tirshatha gave one thousand gold daricks, fifty basins, and five hundred and thirty priests' garments, and makes the rest of the people add twenty thousand gold daricks, two thousand pounds of silver, and sixty-seven garments. Besides this, Nehemiah adds some names omitted in Ezra; e. g. (vs. 7) *Nahamani*, one of the companions of Zerubabel. There is also a slight deviation from the order followed in the previous account. A name mentioned in Ezra is omitted in Nehemiah; e. g. children of *Magbish*, 156, Ezra ii. 30. There is sometimes a difference in the names; e. g. Neh. vii. 54, *Bazlith;* in Ezra, *Bazloth;* Neh. *Pherida;* Ezra, *Pherouda;* and others.]

[a] See *Kleinert*, p. 132, sq.

ant of Ezra and Nehemiah. But the passage could not have been written by a contemporary of Nehemiah, nor by the author of Ezra iii. Indeed, the argument that Ezra died before Nehemiah's time,—which otherwise might be of use,[a]—in spite of Nehemiah's silence respecting him, (i. 1—vii. 5,)—is not tenable; for in that case we should be obliged to regard the mention of him in xii. 36, as an interpolation.

2. The reading of the Law (viii. 1, sqq.) is mentioned here as if it now took place for the first time. In verse 14, the feast of tabernacles, which had already been celebrated, (Ezra iii. 4,) is regarded as something which has just been learned out of the Law, and (verse 17) the celebration is mentioned as the first that has taken place since the time of Joshua. Besides, in Ezra x. 3, sqq., an oath had been taken by the people that they would not marry foreign women; but here the same oath is required anew, (x. 29, 30.) Again: in the mention of the profanation of the Sabbath, and the measures for preventing that (xiii. 15—22) and the marriage of foreign women, (verses 23—31,) no reference is made to the account of the same thing in x. 29, sqq.

3. Again: this passage is shown to be an interpolation, from the verbal affinity between the beginning of it and Ezra iii. 1.

Ezra iii. 1. "And when the seventh month was come, and the children of Israel were in the cities, the people gathered themselves together as one man to Jerusalem."	Neh. vii. 73, viii. 1. "And when the seventh month came, the children of Israel were in their cities, and all the people gathered themselves together as one man," &c.

The same thing also appears from the connection

---

[a] See *Josephus*, Ant. xi. 5. *Augusti*, § 152. *Bertholdt*, p. 1023.

between this and the document interpolated at the end of chap. vii., which is parallel with Ezra ii.[a] Chap. x. has the appearance of a contemporary document, for the author speaks in the first person, (verses 1, 31, 33, 40,) and it contains a list of those who signed the covenant, (verses 2—27.) But the spuriousness of many of the names shows it is a forgery of a later time.[b]

§ 197, *b*.

THE SAME SUBJECT CONTINUED.

Chap. xi. contains a list of the inhabitants of Jerusalem, and is connected in a certain manner with vii. 5. This may have been written by Nehemiah, and is at least from his time. 1 Ch. ix. is, it is well known, a later recast of the same thing. But, according to Bertholdt,[c] the list contains, also, the inhabitants from Zerubabel's time. But this may be doubted.

Chap. xii. 1—26, contains a list of priests and Levites, which comes down to Jaddua, a high priest, who

---

[a] [But it sometimes contradicts Ezra. Comp. viii. 17, with Ezra iii. 4.]

[b] According to this passage, Zerubabel's contemporaries are *Seraiah*, x. 2, mentioned in xii. 1, and Ezra ii. 2; while, instead of him, in Neh. vii. 7, we have *Azariah*, who reappears in this passage. Seraiah, indeed, occurs as a priest in Neh. xi. 11; but the similarity of the name with *Jeremiah*, a contemporary of Zerubabel, (xii. 1,) favors the former opinion. *Hattush* occurs verse 4, as in xii. 2: one of that name occurs, indeed, in Ezra viii. 2, but he is a descendant of David, while this one is a priest. *Shebaniah* (verse 5) is the same with *Shechaniah*, (xii. 3.) *Mallech* (verse 4) occurs in xii. 2; *Harim*, (verses 6, 28,) — in Zerubabel's time, there were only sons of Harim, — Ezra ii. 32, x. 21, 31. *Meremoth* (verse 5) occurs in xii. 3; *Mijamin* (verse 7) as in xii. 5; yet a priest *Minjamin* occurs in xii. 41. *Maaziah* and *Bilgai* (verse 8) are called *Maadiah* and *Bilgah* in xii. 5. *Jeshua* and *Binnui* (verse 9) are found in xii. 8. *Kadmiel* (verse 9) and *Sherebiah* (verse 12) appear in xii. 8; *Bigvai* (verse 16) in Ezra ii. 2.

[c] P. 1027.

is contemporary with Alexander the Great, as Josephus says.[a] This is probably derived from the history of the times referred to, verse 23, and cannot be the work of Nehemiah. In order to ascribe this to Nehemiah, Hävernik, without any reason, assumes that it relates to the consecration of the walls, (xii. 27, sqq.,) and attempts to make it probable that Nehemiah lived to the time of Jaddua. According to xiii. 28, he outlived the sons of Joiada, who was the grandfather of Jaddua.

The passage, xii. 27—43, relating to the consecration of the walls, is from Nehemiah's hand.

The clause, xii. 44—xiii. 3, is an interpolation which fills up a chasm in Nehemiah's memoirs, and is probably from the hand of a later priest, perhaps the compiler of the book. Chap. xii. 47, combines the times of Zerubabel and Nehemiah. The use of the name *Elohim*, in xiii. 1—3, favors the opinion that Nehemiah wrote the passage; but there is nothing else to support it. His memorials commence again with xiii. 4, and continue to the end of the book. It is, therefore, obvious that the whole book did not originate with Nehemiah, but is the work of a compiler who lived considerably later.

[Bertholdt[b] thinks xiii. 28, is an interpolation. His reason is, that it contradicts the well-known passage in Josephus.[c] The verse says, a son of *Joiada*, the high priest, married the daughter of Sanballat, while Josephus, who relates the story more in detail, says it was a son of *John*, the high priest, and therefore a *grandson* of Joiada, who engaged in this alliance. Besides, this

---

[a] *Josephus*, Ant. xi. 7, 8. See, also, *Rambach's* Annot. in hoc loco. *Vitringa*, Observ. sac. L. vi. p. 337. *Leclerc*, in loc. The two last think the passage is an interpolation. *Darius the Persian* (verse 22) may be Darius *Nothus*, as *Hävernik* thinks.

[b] P. 1033. [c] Ant. xi. 8, 2.

verse involves other chronological difficulties, making Nehemiah live in the time of Jaddua, the high priest, in the reign of Darius Codomannus; consequently, he must have lived at least one hundred and fifty years. It may have been on account of this chronological difficulty that Josephus departs from this authority. The next verse must likewise be considered an interpolation, as the two are so closely united.]

CHAPTER IX.

THE BOOK OF ESTHER.

§ 198, *a*.

CONTENTS AND CREDIBILITY OF THE BOOK OF ESTHER.

THIS narrative relates that Esther, a Jewess, without regard to her Jewish origin, was raised to the dignity of queen, by Ahasuerus, the Persian king;[b] that the

---

[a] *Jo. Clerici*, *Jo. Drusii*, *Maur.* Comment.

J. J. Rambach. Annotatt. in Lib. Esth.; (Uberr. Annotatt. in Hagiogr. vol. ii.)

Oliv. Bonart. Comm. litter. et mor. in Lib. Esth.; Col. 1647, fol.

Serrar. Comm. in Tob., Judith, Esth., et Maccab.; Mog. 1610, fol.

Corn. Adami Observatt. theol. philol.; Gron. 1710, 4to. cap. ii.

[b] See the old opinions about *Ahasuerus*, in *Carpzov*, vol. i. p. 356, sqq. *Gesenius*, in *Ersch* and *Gruber's* Encyclop. vol. ii. p. 238. The following authors think he was *Xerxes: Scaliger*, De Emend. Temp. lib. vi., Animadvers. Eusebianæ, p. 101, sqq. *Drusius*, *Pfeiffer*, *Carpzov*, and most of the moderns; e. g. *L. J. C. Justi*, on King Ahasuerus, in *Eichhorn's* Repert. vol. xv., and in his own Vermischte Abhand. No. 2. *Eichhorn*, § 508. *Jahn*, vol. ii. p. 298, sqq. *Bertholdt*, p. 2422, sqq. *Gesenius*, Thesaurus Heb. sub voce. *Hävernik*, vol. ii. pt. i. p. 339. *Mich. Baumgarten*, De Fide Lib. Estheris; 1839, p. 129, sqq.

destruction of the Jews in the Persian kingdom was resolved upon by Haman, but prevented by Esther and Mordecai, her foster-father; that Haman was ruined, and Mordecai elevated to his place, and that permission was given to the Jews to take bloody vengeance upon their enemies; in memory of which, the feast of Purim was instituted. It violates all historical probability, and contains the most striking difficulties, and many errors with regard to Persian manners, as well as just references to them.[a]

The main point on which the authenticity of this book has been rested, namely, that Ahasuerus is the same with Xerxes, is very doubtful. If they are the same, then the expedition against Greece must have taken place between the *third* year of his reign, when Vashti is repudiated, (i. 3,) and the *seventh*, when Esther is made queen, (ii. 16.) Now, no mention of that event is made in this book, which can only be accounted for on the supposition that the author knew nothing of it.[b] But after the seventh year, history speaks of other favorites, and another wife of Xerxes; namely, Amestris,[c] who, it is acknowledged, was not Esther. The hypothesis that he had many wives beside her, — for which the uncertain passage, ii. 17, has been adduced, — is improbable, on account of his fear of Amestris; and, besides, in ii. 17, sqq., Esther is distinctly

---

[a] For the ancient and modern doubts, see *Oeder*, Freie Untersuch. üb. d. Kan. d. A. T. p. 12, sqq. *Michaelis*, Or. Bib. vol. ii. p. 35, sqq. Anmerk. ub. d. B. Esther. *Corrodi*, Beleucht. d. Gesch. d. Jüd. Kanon. vol. i. p. 66, sqq. *Bertholdt*, p. 2425. He considers the whole book a fiction. — See, on the other side, *Eichhorn*, § 510. *Jahn*, p. 305, sqq. *Kelle*, Vindic. Esther; 1820. *Hävernik*, p. 339, sqq. *Baumgarten*, l. c. p. 10, sqq.

[b] *Michaelis*, in loc. On the other side, *Justi*, Verm. Abhand. vol. i. p. 81. *Baumgarten*, p. 140.

[c] *Herodotus*, ix. 108, sqq.

called *the queen.* There would be a most decided argument against this view, if the *twelfth*, and not, as is the common opinion, the *twenty-first*,[a] year of Xerxes, when Haman, and then Mordecai, were his grand viziers, were his last year; for, about this time, Artabanus, chief of his body-guard, who murdered Xerxes, controlled him.

According to the most natural construction of ii. 5, 6, Mordecai must have been carried into exile with Jechoniah; consequently, at the time these events took place, he must have been about one hundred and twenty years old, and Esther must have been a superannuated beauty.[b]

From what we know of Persian manners, it is improbable that the king should invite Vashti, his wife, not to a banquet, but to a Bacchanalian carousal: it would only be possible on account of the advancing corruption in Xerxes' time, and through the folly of Xerxes himself. It is not probable that he would have chosen Esther — a person not descended from one of the seven families from which the queens were exclusively taken — for his queen;[c] nor that he would have granted royal honors to Mordecai, because — we know not how — he had detected a conspiracy.[d] This account of the honor paid Mordecai has affinity with the reward of Joseph, (Gen. xli. 43,) and on that account is suspicious.

From what we know of the base character and despotism of Xerxes, it may perhaps be believed that Haman obtained from him a decree for the extirpation of

---

[a] *Vitringa*, Obs. sac. Lib. vi. 2. *Hengstenberg*, Christol. vol. ii. p. 541, sqq. *Krüger*, in *Seebode*, Archiv. vol. i. pt. ii. p. 205, sqq. *Baumgarten*, p. 146. On the other side, *Kleinert*, in the Dörpt. Beit. vol. ii.

[b] See *Rambach*, in loc.

[c] *Baumgarten*, p. 45. But see *Herodotus*, iii. 88, *Ctesias*, Pers. xx., and *Heeren*, l. c. p. 398.

[d] *Baumgarten*, p. 38—44.

the Jews, and Mordecai, in return, obtained a corresponding counter decree. But it is incredible that the Jews, in consequence of this last decree, went to work so fiercely, and massacred more than seventy-five thousand Persians. It was only the national vanity of the Jews that could induce the author to write this, or that all Shushan was thrown into consternation by Haman's decree, but into joy by that of Mordecai.

The weakest part of the story is this — that Esther concealed her Jewish descent, not only until she was queen, (ii. 20,) but, as it appears, until the catastrophe itself was over, (viii. 1 ;) that Haman suspected nothing of it, or of her relation to Mordecai, though he came every day into the court of the palace, — for if he had known this, he would have done differently, — and also that the king himself knew nothing of it, and therefore is struck with surprise at her petition (vii. 5) for herself and her nation.

§ 198, *b*.

THE SAME SUBJECT CONTINUED.

It is incontestable that the feast of Purim (ix. 20, sqq.) originated in Persia, and was occasioned by an event similar to that related in Esther. But, farther than this, perhaps it is not possible to determine how much of the whole narrative is historically true. Although it is simple in style, and free from declamation, and in this way is advantageously distinguished from the similar stories in the Apocrypha, — in particular from the third book of Maccabees, — yet it breathes the spirit of revenge and haughtiness.[a] The book refers nothing to the opera-

---

[a] See ix. 13. But see how *Baumgarten* (p. 61, sq.) attempts to defend it.

tion and direction of God, and contains no religious element, except in the value put upon the refusal to worship Haman, (iii. 2,) in the fast that was kept, (iv. 16,) and the allusion to the restoration of the Jews, (iv. 14.) Even the name of God is not once mentioned. It is probable these peculiarities are to be explained as belonging to the spirit of the Persian Jews. However, Baumgarten finds in this a proof of the author's historical fidelity, who wished to depict the history of Mordecai and Esther in the light of their religious feeling, which prevented them from publicly displaying their Jewish belief. Hävernik, on the contrary, says, "The author did not wish — in the hypocritical way of the Alexandrian Jews — to conceal the conviction that the Jews were forsaken by God, and thereby lend a false coloring to the facts." But all the books written after the exile prove the falseness of this hypothesis.[a]

§ 198, *c*.

THE SAME SUBJECT CONTINUED.

[For a long time this book was considered a history of actual events. Some writers at this time hold such an opinion, but it is involved in numerous and inexplicable difficulties; for the book does not bear the marks of an historical composition.

1. It is said (i. 4) that Ahasuerus made a feast unto all his princes and officers, which lasted one hundred and eighty days. How could the affairs of any government, especially an Oriental despotism, — where so much

---

[a] See the ancient opinions in *Carpzov*, vol. i. p. 368, sq. *Rambach*, Præf. § 7. See *Luther's* unfavorable judgment, De Servo Arbitrio, tom. iii.; Jena, Lat. p. 182. See the judgment of *Gregory* Nazianz., *Athanasius*, and the Synopsis Scrip. above, vol. i. § 25, 26.

depends upon the magistrate, — be managed, when, for a whole half year, all these magistrates were assembled in Susa? It is sometimes said they went up by turns, each party remaining but a short time, and then giving place to new guests. But of such an arrangement the text says nothing.

2. The king, heated with wine, sends for his queen, Vashti, to appear, unveiled, before his intoxicated guests. She very wisely declines such an invitation. Upon this he issues a decree, apparently dictated at the table, and sends it to all the provinces of his kingdom, "that every man shall bear rule in his own house." It may be said a king "merry with wine" might issue such a decree, and this explanation would perhaps suffice, were this the only passage presenting such a difficulty. But it requires a great extent of credulity to believe the king issued this decree.

3. Haman is offended because Mordecai, a Jew, refuses to do homage to him, and, therefore, scorning to revenge himself on the offender alone, he wishes to satisfy his vengeance by destroying the whole nation of the Jews. Now, at that time, all Judea was a Persian province; besides, Jews were scattered throughout all the other districts, and therefore it is a limited estimate which computes them at two millions, at that time within the Persian territories. Haman, to avenge himself in his own quarrel, obtains permission to destroy all this great number of people. The king consents that all of them should be massacred in a single day. The numerous massacres that defile the page of history, naturally recur to the mind. But amongst them all, among the Sicilian vespers, the St. Bartholomew massacres, the horrors of Roman or Arabian butchery, or the atrocities of the

French revolution, there is nothing which approaches the murder of two millions of human beings in a single day. Nero, wishing all Rome had but one neck, must have shrunk from such murder as this king is said to command for the sake of avenging his grand vizier. The ten thousand talents alleged to be offered as purchase money for such a body of subjects, only increase the difficulty, by showing the writer of this story was at a loss what motive to ascribe to the king for so unnatural and impolitic an act, and could find none more probable than the love of gold.[a]

The murderous decree is published in all the provinces, "to destroy, to kill, and to cause to perish, all Jews, both young and old, little children and women, in one day." This is not done hastily, for the time was fixed upon by casting lots a whole year before the deed was designed to be consummated, (iii. 7.) No attempt was made to conceal the design from the intended victims. The Jews were aware of the plan, yet neither offered to flee nor to resist with arms. Yet the decree for their total destruction was publicly promulgated in all parts of the kingdom a whole year before the day appointed for the massacre. Is it to be credited that this number of men, enjoying the rights of other subjects of the Persian monarch, and possessed of the warlike spirit

[a] Josephus, feeling this difficulty, as it seems, and considering 10,000 talents too small a sum for the lives of 2,000,000 human beings, fixes the sum at 40,000 talents. Josephus differs, also, from the Hebrew text in other particulars. His narrative is more full; the remarks of the monarch more minute, and farther extended; the names are not always the same in the two accounts: Josephus (xi. 6, 1) makes this king Artaxerxes *Longimanus*, and not *Xerxes the Great*. In this he follows the apocryphal addition, contained in the Seventy. But the question, *Who is the Ahasuerus of Esther?* seems to belong to the large list of queries that can never be answered, and need not be asked.

of the Jews, would wait tamely to be slaughtered, "on a set day," like sheep? An edict so unusual and important must have been known to other historians; but none of them mentions it except Josephus, who evidently draws his information entirely from this book itself.

The account of the Jews killing their enemies on the appointed day, is, if possible, more incredible than the preceding narrative. The whole story is this: One night, the monarch, unable to sleep, commanded the chronicles of his kingdom to be read to him. He found Mordecai had formerly done him a good service, previously mentioned in the book, but hitherto had received no recompense. Mordecai is rewarded in public. At a banquet, Esther laments to her royal spouse, that her people are all to be cut off. He seems then alike unacquainted with her descent, and with the design he had so readily sanctioned before, (vii. 5.) He finds, what he had previously known, that Haman is at the bottom of the affair, and, seeing the gallows erected for Mordecai, says, "Hang him thereon." The current now sets in favor of the Jews; and, on the twenty-third day of the third month, public letters are sent, sealed with the king's ring, "to the Jews, and to the lieutenants, and deputies, and rulers of the provinces, who are from India to Æthiopia, unto every province, according to the writing thereof, and unto every people after their language, and to the Jews after their writing, and according to their language." These letters "granted the Jews which were in every city to gather themselves together, and to stand for their life, to destroy, to slay, and to cause to perish, all the power of the people and province that would assault them, both little ones and women, and to take the spoil of them for a prey." They were sent, and "published to all people," eight months and twenty days before the decree was to be executed. Wherever the letters came, the "Jews had joy and gladness, a feast, and a good day, and many of the people became Jews." It would be supposed the Persians, and others, likely to be injured by this decree, with so long a time for preparation, would provide means of defence against the Jews, who were a small minority in the whole kingdom. But nothing of this kind takes place. They wait quietly during the eight months, as the Jews had done in the previous twelve months. On the appointed day, the Jews assemble, "to lay hand on such as sought their hurt," and no man could withstand them. It seems no attack was made upon the Jews, and no resistance offered to the massacre. Even the magistrates, for fear of Mordecai, helped the Jews. Upwards of seventy-five thousand were slain in a single day. It is not mentioned that a single Jew fell in the slaughter. Permission is even granted them to continue the murder on the next day, and three hundred are slain at Shushan. The Jews celebrated the next day as "a day of gladness and feasting, and a good day, and of sending portions one to another." Perhaps no amount of historical evidence would render the above narrative credible to an unprejudiced inquirer. How much less is it to be credited when related by an apocryphal writer, who lived no one knows when, or where, and whose book is encumbered with so many other difficulties! Truly Xerxes was a foolish, but scarcely a bloodthirsty king. The above account would not only represent him as eminently stupid and barbarous with scarce a parallel, but would ascribe first to the Jews, and next to the Persians, a tameness of spirit, and incapacity of self-defence, "which are not paralleled even among the most timid of animals,—sheep and doves,—which at least will flee from danger." It is not necessary to mention other less important historical objections.

It seems most probable the book was written as a patriotic romance, designed to show that the Jews will be delivered out of all troubles, and he that seeks to injure them shall himself be destroyed. The narrative may have some historical facts for its basis, or be purely fictitious. This, at least, is certain—that it is impossible, at this day, to determine where facts begin and fiction ends.]

§ 199.

AGE AND AUTHOR OF THE BOOK.

It seems to be a fact that it was designed the book should be considered as written by Mordecai:—

Chap. ix. 20. "And Mordecai wrote these things, and sent letters unto all the Jews that were in all the provinces of the king Ahasuerus, both nigh and far."

It may be said, the "writing"[a] attributed to Mordecai, in this passage, is limited to the letters he sent. But (ix. 32) it is said, expressly, the command of Esther was written in the book; "and the decree of Esther confirmed these matters of Purim, and *it was written in the book*."[b] The opinion, however, that Mordecai wrote the book, does not deserve to be confuted.

Reference is made to the royal Chronicles of Persia:—

Chap. x. 2. "And all the acts of his power and of his might, and

---

[a] וַיִּכְתֹּב מָרְדֳּכַי אֶת־הַדְּבָרִים הָאֵלֶּה.

[b] Comp. Deut. xxxi.

the declaration of the greatness of Mordecai, whereunto the king advanced him, are they not written in the book of the Chronicles of the kings of Media and Persia ? "

Some passages display an acquaintance with Persian customs. The well-known *one hundred and twenty-seven* provinces of Persia are mentioned; the eunuchs of the seraglio, the absence of females at the feast, the magi, (i. 5, 10, 15, 19 ;) the unchangeableness of the royal edicts, (verse 19, and viii. 8 ;) the use of lots in divination, (iii. 7 ;) the prohibition of all approach to the king without permission; the manner of publishing decrees, (iii. 12—15, viii. 14 ;) and others, (i. 5, ii. 9, iv. 11.) Besides, there is no theocratical spirit, or any fondness for Palestine. All these circumstances would favor the opinion that the author wrote in the Persian empire.

An explanation is sometimes given of Persian customs and history; viii. 8, "seal it with the king's ring," says the monarch; and the writer adds, "for the writing which is written in the king's name, and sealed with the king's ring, may no man reverse."

Chap. i. 13. "Then the king said to the wise men, which knew the times, (for so was the king's manner toward all that knew law and judgment;") and,

Chap. i. 1. "Now it came to pass in the days of Ahasuerus, (this is Ahasuerus which reigned from India even unto Æthiopia, over a hundred and seven and twenty provinces.)"

These explanations would lead us to the time after the destruction of the Persian monarchy. The bloodthirsty spirit of revenge and persecution displayed in the book refers to the time of the Ptolemies and Seleucidæ ; [a]

---

[a] *Bertholdt*, p. 2449, sqq. *Gesenius*, in Allg. Lit. Zeit. for 1818, No. 54, p. 432. *Hävernik* puts it in the time of Artaxerxes.

at all events, the language belongs to a very late period.[a]

[Augustine, Isidore, and Origen, refer the book to Ezra; Mr. Horne inclines to the same opinion; forgetting that he died before the date of the alleged events. Some of the Jewish rabbins, with the Pseudo-Philo, refer it to Jehoiachim, a high priest of the Jews. Other Jewish writers, whom Huetius follows, ascribe it to the men of the *Great Synagogue*. R. Isaac Ben Aramah goes so far as to add, that Esther entreated these worthies of the Great Synagogue to write the book, taking the facts from the Persian records. Aben Ezra, and the greatest part of the Jewish and Christian scholars, refer it to Mordecai. Clement of Alexandria was of this opinion. Spinoza thinks it was written by some Jewish scribe, after the restoration of the temple by Judas the Maccabee. An author in Leclerc's Bibliotheca[b]—supposed to be Leclerc himself—says the book embraces figments collected by Hellenistic Jews; while the grave authorities, Nicolius Serrarius and Oliver Bonartius, consider it the joint work of *Esther* and Mordecai. More modern writers, with better judgment, affirm only their ignorance of the authorship.[c]]

---

[a] The following examples are selected only from chap. i. *Persian words*. [דָּת, verse 8, and often;] פַּרְתְּמִים, 3; פִּתְגָּם, 20.—*Later words, forms, and usages:* בִּירָן, 5; בּוּץ, 6; כֶּתֶר, 11; מַאֲמָר, 15; אָמַר, *with sense of command*, 10, 17; מְדִינָה, 1, and often; גִּנַּת, 5; מַלְכוּת, 2, and often; יְקָר *honor*, 20; שֵׁשׁ, *marble;* רַב, 8; טוֹב עַל, 19.

[b] [Vol. iii. p. 47; an. 1686.]

[c] *Carpzov*, vol. i. p. 360, sqq.

§ 200.

ADDITIONS TO THE BOOK OF ESTHER.

The Alexandrian version and the Itala, besides other less important variations from the Hebrew text, contain some additions to the book of Esther, which Jerome, in his Latin version, has placed at the end of the book, and Luther has placed in the Apocrypha. Josephus, also, is acquainted with these.[a]

From the contradictions between these fragments and the rest of the book, it appears they are not genuine. [In the English version of these passages, (x. 2, xi. 1, sqq.,) it is said Mordecai discovered the conspiracy against the monarch in the *second* year of Artaxerxes. Now, from Esth. ii. 16, it appears Esther became queen in the *seventh* year, and at that time Mordecai sat at the king's gate, and "in these days, while he sat

---

[a] The fragments are as follows: —

1. A dream of Mordecai, which, in the Alexandrian version, is prefixed to i. 1; in the Vulgate and English version, it appears after xi. 1—xii. 6. It is chap. vii. in Luther's Bible.

2. The decree of Haman, referred to in iii. 12, sqq. In the Alexandrian version, this is placed after iii. 13. It is xiii. 1—7 in the Vulgate and English Bible, and chap. i. in Luther.

3. A prayer of Mordecai and Esther, which, in the Seventy, is put after iv. 17; in the Vulgate and English, xiii. 8—xiv. 19; and ii. and iii. in Luther's version.

4. An embellished account of the scene between Esther and the king, v. 1, 2, in the Seventy; xv. 4—19, in the Vulgate and English; and iv. in Luther.

5. The edict of Mordecai, alluded to in viii. 9. In the Septuagint, this occurs after viii. 12; in the Vulgate and English, xvi. 1—15; Luther, vi.

6. An explanation of Mordecai's dream, and an account of the manner in which the feast of Purim was celebrated in Ægypt. In the Alexandrian, Vulgate, and English versions, this is placed after x. 3; and in chap viii. in Luther's version.

at the gate," discovered the conspiracy. The names of the two conspirators differ in the two accounts. In the first, they are Bigthan and Teresh, (ii. 21;) in the second, Gabatha and Tharra, (Apoc. xii. 1.) In one, Haman is angry because Mordecai will not do homage to him, (iii. 5;) in the other, on account of the eunuchs of the king, (xii. 6.) In ix. 20 and 32,[a] Mordecai sends letters commanding the *Jews* to keep the feast of Purim, and Esther confirms these letters; but in xvi. 22, the king himself orders, not merely the Jews, but all his subjects, to keep it, "among their solemn feasts, a high day, with all feasting."]

From its religious tone, it is probable it is of Hellenistic and Alexandrian origin. This appears, also, from the party-colored and bombastic language, and the transformation of Haman into a Macedonian, (xvi. 10 and 14.) Bertholdt thinks the fragments were first added as supplementary notes, and has based this opinion on the incompleteness of these fragments in the Hebrew manuscripts, and in the Syriac and Arabic versions in the London Polyglot.[b]

---

[a] *Eichhorn*, Einl. in die Apocryphen, p. 488, sqq.

[b] *De Rossi* (Specimen Varr. Lectt. sacri Textus et Chaldaica Estheris Additamenta; Tub. 1783) thinks the original book of Esther was a larger work, written in Chaldee by Mordecai, containing the present apocryphal additions, and the present book of Esther has been extracted from it. He founds this opinion upon a Hebrew MS. containing some of these chapters in the Chaldee language. But *Bertholdt* (p. 2457, sqq.) has satisfactorily answered the claims of this hypothesis. See, also, *Usseri*, Syntagmata de Græcæ LXX. Interprett. Vers. cum Libri Esth., Editione Origenica, et vet. Græca altera, in the appendix.

BOOK II.

THE THEOCRATICAL INSPIRED BOOKS.

---

§ 201.

THEIR RELATION TO THE FOREGOING.

While the historical books show in what manner the theocracy originated, and point out its destiny, to warn and admonish later generations, here the present condition of the theocracy, and the future consequences of this condition, are treated of for the warning and admonition of the people. Here, as there, the same religious ideas are applied to the circumstances of the Jewish nation, and the same view of the world is taken. But the spirit and disposition[a] of the theocratic historian and that of the inspired prophet are different in this respect: The former, occupied with quiet contemplation of the past, gives rather the true picture of affairs than his own view of them; but the latter, impelled by his active participation in the present, and in the yet unformed future, living in the fire of inspiration and of holy zeal, expresses his own thoughts, demands, and wishes, cares and hopes, rather than paints the history of his time. This difference displays itself in their style.[b]

Besides, the Hebrew historians pay little regard to

---

[a] Stimmung. [b] § 126, 127.

the history of other nations; but the inspired guardians of the theocracy had so much to fear from them that they could not fail to bring them within the circle of their vision.[a]

§ 202.

NAME AND IDEA OF A PROPHET.

The authors of these books, for the most part, bear the name of *prophets*, *interpreters of God*,[b] (Ex. vii. 1.)

---

[a] See *Knobel*, Der Prophetismus der Hebräer; 1837, 2 vols. 8vo. *Köster*, Die Propheten des A. und N. T. nach ihren Wesen und Wirken; 1838.

[b] נְבִיאִים, προφῆται, not μάντεις, the word by which the LXX. translate קָסַם. *Plato*, Timæus, Opp. ix. p. 391, ed. Bipont, or p. 101, ed. *Bekker*: ...... μαντικὴν ἀφροσύνῃ θεὸς ἀνθρωπίνῃ δέδωκεν· οὐδεὶς γὰρ ἔννους ἐφάπτεται μαντικῆς ἐνθέου καὶ ἀληθοῦς, ἀλλ' ἢ καθ' ὕπνον τὴν τῆς φρονήσεως πεδηθεὶς δύναμιν, ἢ διὰ νόσον ἤ τινα ἐνθουσιασμὸν παραλλάξας. Ἀλλὰ ξυννοῆσαι μὲν ἔμφρονος τά τε ῥηθέντα ἀναμνησθέντα ὄναρ ἢ ὕπαρ ὑπὸ τῆς μαντικῆς τε καὶ ἐνθουσιαστικῆς φύσεως, καὶ ὅσα ἂν φάσματα ὀφθῇ, πάντα λογισμῷ διελέσθαι, ὅπῃ τι σημαίνει καὶ ὅτῳ μέλλοντος ἢ παρελθόντος ἢ παρόντος κακοῦ ἢ ἀγαθοῦ· τοῦ δὲ μανέντος, ἔτι τε ἐν τούτῳ μένοντος, οὐκ ἔργον τὰ φανέντα ἢ φωνηθέντα ὑφ' ἑαυτοῦ κρίνειν, ἀλλ' εὖ καὶ πάλαι λέγεται τὸ πράττειν καὶ γνῶναι τά τε αὑτοῦ καὶ ἑαυτὸν σώφρονι μόνῳ προσήκειν. Ὅθεν δὴ καὶ τὸ τῶν προφητῶν γένος ἐπὶ ταῖς ἐνθέοις μαντείαις κριτὰς ἐπικαθιστάναι νόμος· οὓς μάντεις αὐτοὺς ἐπονομάζουσι τινὲς, τὸ πᾶν ἠγνοηκότες. ὅτι τῆς δι' αἰνιγμῶν οὗτοι φήμης καὶ φαντάσεως ὑποκριταί· καὶ οὔ τι μάντεις, προφῆται δὲ μαντευομένων δικαιότατα ὀνομάζοιντ' ἄν. Comp. *Bardili*, De Significatu primitivo Vocis *Προφήτης*; Gott. 1786. *Chrysost.* Hom. xxix. in Ep. ad Corinth.: Τοῦτο γὰρ μάντεως ἴδιον τὸ ἐξεστηκέναι, τὸ ἀνάγκην ὑπομένειν, τὸ ὠθεῖσθαι, τὸ ἕλκεσθαι, τὸ σύρεσθαι, ὥσπερ μαινόμενον. Ὁ δὲ προφήτης οὐχ οὕτως, ἀλλὰ μετὰ διανοίας νηφούσης καὶ σωφρονούσης καταστάσεως καὶ εἰδὼς ἃ φθέγγεται, φησὶν ἅπαντα. *Neander*, Gnost. Syst. p. 387. *Jerome*, Proœm. in Jes.: Neque vero, ut Montanus cum insanis feminis somniat, Prophetæ in extasi sunt loquuti, ut nescirent, quid loquerentur, et quum alios erudirent, ipsi ignorarent, quid dicerent. See *Epiphanius*, Hæres. xlviii. 3. *Carpzov*, Introd. vol. iii. p. 36, sq.

Yet, on the other hand, *Hengstenberg* (Christologie, vol. i. pt. i. p. 293) maintains the fanatical opinions of *Montanus* respecting the prophets of the O. T. [See *Noyes*, in Christian Examiner for 1833, vol. xvi. p. 321, sq., and

They are also called *men of God*, and *angels*, or *messengers of God*, because, by their inspired discourses, they carried out the divine idea of the theocracy, or the will of God, in the public life of the people.[a]

They were likewise called *seers*,[b] on account of the higher intuition they had of divine truth, and, enlightened by that, of the course of earthly events, both present and future, and by virtue of which they were prophets and foretellers of the future. After Samuel, the common practice of soothsaying seems to have been restricted by the prophethood, or office of prophets.

Other nations of antiquity had their seers also, but they were destitute of the true and moral spirit of monotheism, by which the Hebrew prophecy was purified and made holy.[c] The reason why prophecy in general finds no place in modern times, is to be found in the preponderance of reflection over spontaneity.

[" Samuel committed the direction of the *spirit* of the theocratic government into the hands of the prophets, to whom merely a personal reverence was paid among the people. He left the management of the theocratic *forms* to the priests. By these means he produced a more free development of the Mosaic religion. The

---

vol. v. p. 348, sqq.] *Hendewerk*, Jesaias, vol. i. p. xxxiii., sqq. See, also, 1 Cor. xix. 32. See the use of the word מְשֻׁגָּע in Jer. xxix. 26, Hos. ix. 7, 2 Kings ix. 11. On the use of נָבִיא, see *Hartmann*, Ubers des Mich. 3 Excurs., and *Gesenius*, in Lexicon, sub voce. *Knobel*, vol. i. p. 103.

[a] אַנְשֵׁי אֱלֹהִים and מַלְאֲכֵי אֱלֹהִים. There is a distinction between the prophets, and demagogues, (judges or heroes,) and kings, which is marked by the *idea of the word* of God. *Redslob*, Begriff. d. Nabi; 1839.

[b] רֹאִים and חֹזִים. See 1 Sam. ix. 9.

[c] Jer. xxiii. 22. *De Wette*, Programm. de Prophetarum in V. T. Ecclesia, et Doctorum Theol. in Eccles. evang. Ratione, atque Similitudine, (Ber 1816,) Opusc. theol. p. 169, sqq.

prophets broke through the symbolical forms, rose to a spiritual view of them, and served the cause of truth by proclaiming the word of God, while the priests remained attached to the symbols, and preserved them in their ancient restrictions and narrowness. Thus it was the office of the prophets to purify and extend the influence of religion and morality; they were politicians, naturalists, and workers of wonders. Their action and influence on the public were sustained and promoted by religion, poetry, symbols, and music. The last, perhaps, held an important place in their education at the schools of the prophets."][a]

The writings of Isaiah and Jeremiah — especially Isa. liii., Jer. xx. — contain allusions to the conflict of the prophets with the false prophets, with the priests and rulers of the land, and with the unbelief of the people.

§ 203.

CONTENTS AND OBJECTS OF THE PROPHETIC DISCOURSES.

While the prophets were zealous for the support and perfection of the theocracy, they fixed their eyes upon the outward as well as upon the inward. They censured the false, untheocratical policy which was pursued with respect to foreign nations, and disclosed the abuses in the government and in the administration of justice. This they seem to have done especially under a feeble admin-

[a] *De Wette*, Bib. Dogmatik, § 70. On the relation of the prophets to the priests, their political and scientific tendency, their ascetic life, and the schools of the prophets, see *De Wette*, as above, and Archäol. § 145, 268. *Carpzov*, vol. iii. p. 41, sqq. *Knobel*, l. c. vol. i. p. 39, sqq., 82, sqq., ii. 39, sqq. *Köster*, p. 52, sqq.

istration.[a] They found fault with the corrupt morals, with the degeneracy of the public worship of God, which was defiled with idolatry, and reduced to a mere shadow. In respect to all these subjects, they pointed out the True and the Right, and admonished the public and individuals to reform and amend their lives. They threatened the disobedient and impenitent with the punishments of divine justice; but they restored the downcast by joyful promises, by predicting the humiliation of the enemies of the theocracy, and the approach of prosperous times.[b]

§ 204.

SPIRIT OF THE PROPHETIC PREDICTIONS.

1. The predictions of the future were occasioned by, and founded upon, the idea of retribution, — as we see in Levit. xxvi. and Deut. xxviii., — and on the unshaken confidence in the love of Jehovah towards his people. Consequently their predictions had a moral and religious meaning, and might be recalled. This appears from Jer. xxvi. 13, where it is promised Jehovah will repent of the evil denounced, if the people will mend their ways; and verse 29, where an instance is given of his actually withdrawing a denunciation against Hezekiah.[c]

2. These ideas were applied to the circumstances of the time; and in this manner the predictions were occasioned by the historical phenomena of the age. Thus Isaiah threatened the Jews with an invasion by the

---

[a] *Credner*, Der Prophet Joel, p. 65.

[b] *Knobel*, vol. i. p. 203, sqq., 246, sqq. *Köster*, p. 223, sqq.

[c] See, also, Jonah iii. 10.

Assyrians; Jeremiah, with invasion by the Chaldees. [At first, says Eichhorn, the prophets of the kingdom of Israel only threaten their nation with the *Syrians*, so long as they were the only powerful nation in the neighborhood. Thus Elisha, in his reply to Joash, (2 Kings xiii. 14, sqq.,) speaks of the Syrians. Sometimes they promise victories over them, as Jonah did, under Jeroboam II. (2 Kings xiv. 25.)

In the mean time, the *Assyrians* were becoming a great nation; then the prophets alarm the quiet people with threats of them; but this is done gradually, as a knowledge of this people becomes more clear and distinct. Thus Amos (vi. 14, vii. 10—17) predicts their coming without naming them, probably because in his time they were not entangled in the affairs of Israel. But during the civil troubles that ensued after the death of Jeroboam II., one of the factions into which the state was divided, it is probable, sought aid of the Assyrians, (Hos. ix. 3, xi. 5.) Then Hosea comes out boldly, and prophesies that the Assyrians, sooner or later, will overpower the feeble kingdom of Israel.

The same is true of the prophecies which relate to Judah. In the times of Isaiah, the *Babylonians* were so unimportant that the Hebrew prophets do not mention them. They begin to speak of them when the Chaldees in Babylon took the place of the Assyrians as rulers of Asia.] [a]

---

[a] *Eichhorn*, § 513. See, also, *Justi*, Verm. Abhandl. ub wichtig. Gegenstande d. theol. Gelehrsamkeit, vol. i. p. 266, sqq. [contained also in *Paulus*, Memorab. vol. iv. p. 139, sqq. He thinks it is so certain the prophets spoke only of such nations as had direct intercourse with the Hebrews, that he denies the date of certain oracles, which speak of distant enemies. He says the office of the prophet was to be a counsellor of the king and people in the exigencies of the time, not to satisfy or excite their curiosity by dwelling on the distant future.]

3. Since this idea of retribution prevails in the prophets throughout, their predictions are in part to be regarded as HOPES and WISHES, menaces and expressions of anxiety; and therefore the fundamental rule of giving them an historical explanation, is *to seek the occasion of an oracle in history, rather than its fulfilment.* Particular caution is necessary in respect to predictions against foreign nations.

4. These prophecies are almost always indefinite and fluctuating. The later referred to the oracles of earlier prophets; and thus, for example, the Messianic idea gradually received its form, and became permanent.[a] The definite predictions of Ezekiel (xii. xxiv. 25, 26, xxxiii. 21, 22) seem not to have been fulfilled. The same must be said of those of Jeremiah, (xxii. 18, 19, xxxvi. 30,) as may be seen by comparing 2 Kings xxiv. 6, 2 Ch. xxxvi. 6, for the authority of Josephus (x. 6, 3) can scarcely be decisive in this case. The following, also, are not fulfilled: Amos vii. 11; Hosea's curse of the people, (ix. 3, and xi. 5;) Isaiah's oracle, (xxii. and xxix.;) his curse pronounced upon Moab, (xvi. 14,) and his prophecy of the destruction of Tyre, (xxiii.)—though Hengstenberg is of the contrary opinion;[b]—the prophecy of Obadiah; Jeremiah's curse of Ægypt and Edom, (xliii. 8, xlix. 7, sqq.;) Ezekiel's prophecies against Mount Seir, (xxxv.,) against Ægypt, (xxix.,) and against Gog and Magog, (xxxviii.—xxxix.)

The following are not completely fulfilled: Isa. vii.

[a] See *Eichhorn*, § 515, p. 27. *Credner* (l. c. p. 63, sqq., and 71, sqq.) perhaps carries this reference of the later to the earlier prophets too far. *De Wette*, Bib. Dogmatik, § 116.

[b] See *Hengstenberg*, De Rel. Tyr.; 1832. [But see *Heeren*, Researches into the Intercourse, Policy, Trade, &c., Eng. translation; Oxford, 1833, vol. ii. p. 11, note 2. *Knobel*, vol. i. p. 300, sq.]

17, sqq.; his oracle against Damascus and Samaria, (viii 4;) that against Babylon, (xiv. 23;) against Damascus, (xvii. 1—3;) and that against Idumea, (xxxiv. 9.)

There are also predictions in the historical books which were either put into a more definite form, or were forged, after the event. But it is entirely in opposition to the spirit of the Hebrew prophets to suppose these oracles were only veiled and obscure pictures of the present and of the past.[a]

§ 205.

THE DISCOURSE AND STYLE OF THE PROPHETS.

The prophets expressed themselves spontaneously and directly with the living voice. They sometimes appeared and spoke in public places, and sometimes at home addressed a circle of men that sought advice or edification. This latter appears from 2 Kings iv. 22, 23, whence it appears men were accustomed to seek the prophets, chiefly on the Sabbath, and days of the new moon,[b] (vi. 32, Isa. xxxviii. 5, 21, Jer. xxi. 1, Ezek. viii. 1, xiv. 1, xx. 1.) When they spoke in public, their speeches were, probably, for the most part, artless outbreaks of their zeal and inspiration, short addresses and appeals, which, perhaps, were followed by replies, or a disputation.[c] When they spoke in private, their dis-

---

[a] *Eichhorn*, (Heb. Proph. on Isa. xxix. and elsewhere) takes this false view. See *Gesenius*, Com. ad. Jes. vol. i. p. 828. See, also, on this entire subject, *Griesinger*, Prüfung d. Jem. Begriffs von der übernaturlich, ursprung d. proph. Weissag.; 1818. [But the author of the book of Daniel, at least, seems to have done this continually. See below, § 254—257.]

[b] Perhaps this is the first trace of the synagogue service.

[c] 1 Kings xxii. 6, sqq., 14, sqq., Isa. vii., Am. vii. 10, sqq., Jer. xxviii.

courses may have been more connected, and have entered more into details. Sometimes they spoke after making preparation, and sometimes unpremeditatedly.[a]

Sometimes they confirmed their assertions, particularly such as related to the future, by *signs*,[b] some of which are the appointed tests of a prophet's truth, as in Deut. xiii. 2, sq. Such is the case in 1 Sam. ii. 34, and in Isa. vii. 10, sqq. Sometimes these signs consist in the extraordinary deeds which they performed, (Ex. iv. 1, sqq.,) and which, it is probable, have, for the most part, been enlarged, and misrepresented in the legendary accounts.

To bring their thoughts and instructions before the senses of the people, they made use of *symbolical actions*, and of a certain sort of signs. Thus Zedekiah made horns of iron, and thrust with them, to show that the nation was in like manner to thrust down the Syrians, (1 Kings xxii. 11;) Isaiah walks naked and barefoot for three years, to show that the king of Assyria should lead away the Ægyptians and Æthiopians naked and barefoot, (Is. xx.) So in viii. 1—4, and 18, he says, "Behold, I and the children whom the Lord hath given me are for signs and for wonders." Ezekiel (iv. 1, sqq.) makes a drawing of Jerusalem on a slate, and represents himself as lying beside it four hundred and thirty days, to show the city was to endure a long siege. Again: (xii. 1, sqq.) he carries away his possessions, through an opening he has digged in the wall, in the twilight, and bears them on his shoulders, to show the nation that they likewise shall remove and go into captivity.

In earlier times, perhaps they made use of music, for

---

[a] *Knobel*, vol. i. p. 418.

[b] מוֹפְתִים, אוֹתוֹת.

Elisha plays on an instrument in presence of the kings of Judah and Israel, before he prophesied, (2 Kings iii. 15;) the prophets, mentioned in 1 Sam. x. 5, were preceded by a band of music, and David played before Saul, to drive away the evil spirit from him, (xix. 8, sqq.) But it is certainly incorrect to consider the prophets as singers and improvisators.[a]

If they subsequently wrote down their speeches, or if they preferred to publish their opinions by writing them, they made use of a more artificial, rounded, and even poetic style, and symbolic actions were then added to the true or fictitious narrative. The following belong to the latter class, namely, the story of Jeremiah burying his girdle, (xiii. 1—7;) of Ezekiel lying four hundred and thirty days before a slate, (iv. 1, sqq.;) of his typical removal from Jerusalem, (xii. 1, sqq.;) of Hosea taking an unchaste wife, (i. 2—9, iii. 1—5,) and elsewhere. Many are uncertain, like the account of Isaiah walking barefoot and naked.[b]

These symbolic actions, together with the symbolic revelations and visions, make up the prophetic symbolism,

---

[a] [The use of music, to excite the soothsayers, was not unknown to the heathen. *Jamblichus* (De Mysteriis, iii. 9) says, "Some of the transported, having cymbals or drums, or some other kind of music, *are filled with the Spirit*," &c. So *Cicero*, (Div. i. 50,) "And so they whose minds, scorning their bodies, fly and rush abroad, when inflamed and incited by some ardor, behold these things which they predict. Such minds, which inhere not in their bodies, are inflamed by various causes. *Some are incited by a certain modulation of voices, and Phrygian songs*," &c. &c.

Spinoza (Tract. theol.-polit. p. 19) thinks Elisha, in the above instance, used a musical instrument to *moderate his anger;* but the supposition seems gratuitous.]

[b] See, on these symbolic actions, *Stäudlin*, N. Beiträge zur Erläut. d. Bibl. Propheten, p. 123, sqq., and *Eichhorn*, Einl. § 556, and 603. [See also *Knobel*, Prophetismus, § 38. He thinks the following *may* have been per-

which assumes different forms, to suit the spirit of the times. Without wishing to deny that there was a direct and immediate revelation, — that is, an actual divine excitement, and, in some cases, an actual ecstasy or trance, — I only maintain that it was indirect and mediate also, and that there was something arbitrary in the style of their discourse. This appears, 1. From the circumstance of their speeches being connected with symbols, which, it is obvious, were arbitrary,[a] and at the same time with those symbolic actions. 2. From the variations of taste in respect to this revelation; thus Isaiah (vi.) receives inspiration from seeing Jehovah, sitting on a lofty throne, with a train that fills the temple, and surrounded by the seraphim. Jeremiah (i.) says, simply, "The word of Jehovah came to me;" and Ezekiel sees the heavens opened, and has visions of God, (i.,) which are very common in the later prophets. 3. From the well-known analogy with other symbols, in Ps. xviii. 4, and 1 Kings xviii. 25. And, 4. From the clear spirit of Hebrew prophecy, which did not favor the state of ecstasy,

---

formed, though we are not expressly told that such was the case, viz., that of Zedekiah, mentioned above, (1 Kings xxii. 11;) of Isaiah going naked, though not during the whole period of three years; of Jeremiah breaking an earthen vessel, (xix. 1, sqq., v. 14,) and his putting on a yoke, (xxvii. 1,) — it is not said he wore it; those mentioned in Ezek. xxxvii. 15, sqq., and Jer. xliii. 8. Common actions, performed without any unusual design, he thinks were sometimes made, afterwards, to assume a symbolical character; e. g. Jeremiah's purchase of his deceased kinsman's estate, (xxxii. 5.)

The following, he thinks, *cannot* have been performed, viz., that of Ahijah stripping Jeroboam of his new garment, and rending it into twelve pieces, (1 Kings xi. 29;) that of Hosea, mentioned above, which is peculiarly inconsistent with a character so severely moral as that prophet; that of Jeremiah, (xiii. 1—7,) and Ezekiel, (xii. 1, sqq., iv. v. and xxiv. 3, sqq.)]

[a] Am. vii. 1—9, viii. 1, 2, Jer. i. 11—14, Zach. i. 7, sqq., 18, sqq., ii. iii., 1 Kings xxii. 19, sqq.

though it did not exclude it.[a] This use of symbols degenerated, as it was copied by other prophets, — as may be seen in the instances already given, (Ezek. iv. and xii.,) — so that it became merely an unmeaning phantasmagoria,[b] as in Ezek. i., or a sport with enigmatical language, as in Zachariah's vision of a red horse, (i. 7, sqq.,) of the golden candlestick, (iv.,) or the flying roll, (v.,) and in the accounts in Daniel, (ii. and vii.) The power of the prophetic spirit stands in inverse ratio with the use of symbols. This fact is alluded to in Num. xii., "If there be a prophet among you, I Jehovah will make myself known unto him in a *vision*, and will speak unto him in a *dream*. But not so my servant Moses. He is intrusted with all my house. *Mouth to mouth speak I to him, and suffer him to see plainly, and not in images. He looks on the form of Jehovah;*" and in Jer. xxiii. 25, "I have heard what the prophets said, that prophesy lies in my name, saying, *I have dreamed, I have dreamed* ...... they think to cause the people to forget my name by their dreams."[c]

Since, among the Hebrews, all inspired discourse is accompanied with rhythm, the prophets commonly made

---

[a] See *Knobel*, vol. i. p. 169, sqq. Compare the case of Paul the apostle

[b] *Schilderei.*

[c] See *Carpzov*, l. c. p. 14. *Maimonides*, (More Nevochin ii. c. 45, p. 316,) in his various degrees of inspiration, has anticipated this conclusion, in some measure. [He maintains there are *eleven* degrees of the prophetic spirit. The *first* is the spirit of heroism, as it animated the old judges and warriors to noble deeds, and the *last* is that state of mind in which a man finds himself speaking with an angel in a vision. This happened to Abraham, when he was about to sacrifice Isaac. But Moses, says he, surpassed even this degree of prophetic inspiration, by many a parasang; for, while all the others heard the word through the mediation of an angel, he spoke face to face with God. See also *Knobel*, l. c. § 11, 12.]

use of a certain symmetrical arrangement of the members of their sentences. But since they are rather orators than poets, their rhythm is usually distinguished from lyric poetry by the use of longer periods. When they relate facts, they make use of prose. The later prophets, whose inspiration had grown cold, suffered their rhythmical periods to flow into the prosaic, or, perhaps, wrote wholly in prose.

§ 206.

THE COMPOSITION OF THE PROPHETIC BOOKS

The oldest prophets seem to have written nothing; probably because, in their time, the living speech and action were more efficient, and literature was not sufficiently advanced. A prophetic literature first arose more than two hundred years after the establishment of the schools of the prophets.[a]

In the written prophecies that have come down to us, it is mentioned, sometimes, that the command of God was given to write down *particular words*, as in Isa. viii. 1, xxx. 8; or a *whole prophecy*, as in Hab. ii. 2, 3, Jer. xxx. 2; or a whole collection of prophecies, as in Jer. xxxvi. But sometimes they are written down

---

[a] See the article in *Eichhorn's* Allg. Bib. vol. x. p. 1077, sqq. "Why do the written oracles of the Hebrew prophets begin about 800 B. C.?" [It is evident there were prophets from the commencement of the Hebrew state, and fragments of their oracles appear throughout the early course of Jewish history, from Joshua to Joel; e. g. Judg. ii. 1—3, an anonymous prophet appears, and is called an angel of Jehovah. Deborah, also, is a prophetess. An anonymous prophet appears, also, Judg. vi. 8, sqq. See the other instances collected in *Eichhorn*, l. c.]

without mentioning any such express command of God, as in Jer. li. 60.

But where no such remarks about the reduction of the prophecies to writing occur, we must assume that the genuine works of the prophets, now extant, were all written down by themselves, or their assistants. Some of them were written down after they had been delivered in public, and even long after their first delivery, (Jer. xxxvi.;) and others were written without any such previous delivery.[a] The greater part of the extant prophecies, probably all, whereof the occasion is not mentioned, seem to have originated in this latter way. It can scarcely be true that we possess discourses taken down by others, or sketches of discourses afterwards delivered.

Some prophets, in writing down their oracles, seem to have designed to produce a complete literary work; others, at least, wrote down their separate speeches in a collection. Only a few flying leaves of some other prophets appear to have got into circulation; and these have been badly interpolated, in a course of uncritical treatment, provided with false inscriptions, put in a false connection, or worked over anew.[b] Finally, it has happened that later predictions have been falsely attributed to the old prophets. This has been done, not merely as an idle sport of fancy, but with real prophetic design.[c]

---

[a] [About twenty-three years elapsed between the time he first began to prophesy, (i. 1, sqq.,) and the date of his committing his works to writing. Jeremiah is the only prophet who has given any account of his *writings*.]

[b] See below, § 217—219.

[c] See above, § 147, 159, and below, § 257.

CHAPTER I.

ISAIAH.[a]

§ 207.

HIS LIFE AND TIMES.

WE know nothing of the person of Isaiah, except that he was the son of Amos, (or Amotz,) an unknown man,

---

[a] *Jerome*, Comm. in Proph. maj. in his Opp. iii. *Mart.* iv. v. *Vallars.*
Cyrilli Alex. Ἐξήγησις ὑπομνηματικὴ in Isa. Opp. ii.
Is. Abarbanel, Comm. in Isa.
Dav. Kimchii Comm. in Isa. Lat. Interpr. *Cæs. Malanimeo*; Flor. 1774, 4to.
Jo. Calvini Comm. in Jes.; ed. 3, Genev. 1570, fol.
Victorin. Strigelii Conciones Esaiæ Proph. ad Ebr. Veritatem recogn. et Argumentis atque Scholiis illustratæ; Lips. 1565.
Wolfg. Musculi in Esaiam Comm.; Bas. 1570, fol.
Casp. Sanctii in Comm.; Mogunt. 1616, fol.
Andr. Hyperii in Jes. Oracula Annotatt.; Bas. 1547.
Seb. Schmidii Comm. super Prophet. Isa.; Hamb. 1702, 4to.
Campegii Vitringæ Comm. in Librum Prophet. Isa.; Leov. 1714, 1720, 2 vols. fol. Extracts by *Büsching*; Halle, 1749, 1750, 2 vols. 4to.
Isaiah, a new Translation, with a Dissertation and Notes, by *Robt. Lowth.* The German version, by *Richerz*, with Additions and Remarks, by *J. B. Koppe*; Gött. 1779, 1781, 2 vols. Comp. *D. Köcher*, Vindiciæ Text. Heb. Esaiæ adversus Lowthii Criticam; Berne, 1786.
Esaias ex Rec. Textus Hebr. Latine vertit et Notas subjecit *J. Chr. Döderlein*; ed. 3, 1789.
H. E. G. Paulus, Philol. Clavis über das A. T. Jesaia; Jen. 1793.
Jo. Clerici Comment. *Rosenmülleri* Scholia.
Exeget. Handb. des A. T. 6, 7 pt.
Der Prophet Jesaia, übers., mit e. vollst. philol. krit. u. hist. Comment. begleitet, von D. *Wilh. Gesenius*; Lpz. 1820, 1821, 3 vols.
Der Proph. Esaias., übers, &c., von *Hitzig*; 1833. *Hendewerk*, Des Proph. Jes. Weissagungen, chronolog. giordnet., &c. pt. i. the proto-Esaianic prophecies; 1838; German version, by *J. H. Walther*, 1774, 4to. *G. F. Seiler*, 1785, with notes. *J. D. Cube*, with notes, 1785, 1786, 2 vols. extending to chap. xxxix. *Ch. G. Hensler*, 1788. *G. Krägelius*, 1790, 1791, 2

concerning whom the rabbins have a tradition, which makes him a prophet, and the brother of Amaziah.[a] It is unnecessary, as well as uncertain, to suppose that his standing with Hezekiah depended on any thing except his piety, and vocation as prophet; to say that it depended on his family, and offices at court, is a supposition equally needless and unfounded.[b]

According to vi. 1, he appeared as a prophet in the year of King Uzziah's death, 759 B. C.; and according to i. 1, he prophesied in the reigns of the three following kings—Jotham, Ahaz, and Hezekiah. This is confirmed by the subject and contents of his prophecies,[c] and [with xix., which is of somewhat uncertain authenticity, and belongs to the time of Manasseh] brings us down to the fourteenth year of Hezekiah, 710 B. C.[d] The legendary story that he was put to death by Manasseh, is very uncertain.[e] There is no incontestable reason for extending the period of his action till the time of Manasseh's reign.

---

vols. [See the English works of *White*, 1709; *Stock*, 1804; *Harris*, 1739; *Horsley*, 1801; *Jones*, 1830; *Jenour*, 1831; *Maculloch; Barnes*, Phil. 1840, 3 vols. 8vo.; *Noyes's* New Translation Heb. Proph., Bost. 1833, sqq., 3 vols. 8vo., 2d ed. 1843.] See list of writers in *Rosenmüller*.

[a] Megilla, f. 10, c. 2: "R. Levi said, there is a tradition, received from our fathers, that Amos and Amaziah were brothers." But here אָמוֹץ, the father of Isaiah, is confounded with עָמוֹס. See, on the contrary, *Jerome's* Procœm. to Amos. For the rabbins' opinion that he was a prophet, see *Carpzov*, (l. c. p. 91, sqq.,) who also gives the more ancient literature relating to Isaiah.

[b] See *Augusti*, § 203. *Bertholdt*, p. 1348. *Paulus*, Clavis, p. 62. And on the other side, *Gesenius*, Com. vol. i. p. 14, sqq.

[c] See chap. vii. xiv. 28, xxii. and many other passages. Comp. xxxvi.—xxxviii.

[d] According to *Gesenius*, chap. xix. belongs in Manasseh's time. It is *Möller's* hypothesis that Isaiah composed the second part of his prophecies during the exile of Manasseh. See De Authent. Oracc. Es. c. 40—66, p. 121, sqq. See below, § 210.

[e] Jebamoth, f. 49, c. 2. Sanhedr. f. 103, c. 2. *Justin* Mart. Dial. p. 349,

In Isaiah's time, the powerful kingdom of Assyria arose, and assumed a very threatening aspect. Its lust of conquest was so much favored by the blind policy of the small states of Syria, Israel, and Judah,—which mutually enfeebled one another,—that, after a few years, an Assyrian army stood in the neighborhood of Jerusalem.

§ 208.

SPURIOUSNESS OF THE SECOND PART OF THE PROPHECIES ASCRIBED TO HIM.

The whole of the second part of the collection of oracles under Isaiah's name (xl.—lxvi.) is spurious.[a] It contains discourses designed to console and admonish the people, then in captivity, and promises their return to their native land, and the restoration of the state.

The following are the arguments that support this opinion:—

1. *There is a difference of style.*—The style is more

ed. Col. *H. Michaelis*, Præf. in Jes. c. v. in the Halle Bible. *Stäudlin*, l. c. p. 12, 17, sqq.; and on the design and effects of the death of Jesus, in Gött. Theol. Bibl. vol. i. p. 321. *Gesenius* has examined these legends, (l. c. p. 10, sqq.)

[a] The following works relate to this part of the subject: *L. J. E. Justi*, on the oracles of Isaiah, and the deportation of the Jews in the Babylonian captivity, in *Paulus*, Mem. vol. iv. p. 139, sqq., and enlarged in his Abhandlungen, vol. i. p. 254, sqq., vol. ii. p. 1, sqq. *Eichhorn*, § 525. *Bertholdt*, p. 1374. *Gesenius*, l. c. vol. ii. p. 19, sqq. *Hitzig*, p. 463, sqq. *Knobel*, vol. ii. p. 332, sqq. *Maurer*, p. 386, sqq., and others cited by *Bertholdt*, p. 1356. On the other side are *Hensler*, Uebers. d. Jes. *Beckhaus*, Integrität, d. proph. Schriften d. A. T.; 1796, p. 152, sqq. *Jahn*, l. c. vol. ii. pt. i. p. 458, sqq. *Dereser's* version of Isaiah, in *Brentano's* Bibelwerk, p. 2, sqq. *Greve*, Ultima Capp. Jes.; Amst. 1810, 4to. Proleg. p. 1—21. *J. U. Möller*, l. c. *A. F Kleinert*, Echtheit. sämmtl. in d. B. Jes. enthaltenen Weissag. vol. i.; 1829. *Hengstenberg*, Christologie, d. A. T.; 1829, vol. ii. p. 172. [See, also, a reply to *Gesenius*, in the Biblical Repository, vol. i. p. 700, sqq.]

flowing, perspicuous, and easy, than in the genuine passages of Isaiah; but, at the same time, it is also weaker, and more diffuse. It has many peculiarities, and bears marks of a later age. Some of the chief peculiarities of the style may be seen below.[a]

2. *There is a difference in the political relations of*

---

[a] The phrase "servant of Jehovah," applied to *Israel*, (see *Bertholdt*, p. 1374, sq.; *De Wette*, Com. ub. Psalmos, p. 23; *Gesenius*, vol. iii. p. 16, 23, sqq.,) xli. 8, 9, xlii. 19, xliv. 1, 21, xlv. 4, xlviii. 20; to the *prophets*, and to *himself*, whom he also calls the *messenger* or *angel* of Jehovah; xlii. 1, xliv. 26, xlix. 3, 5, lii. 13, liii. 11, xlii. 18. The word אִיִּים, applied to *distant lands*; xlii. 4, 10, 12, xlix. 1, li. 5, lix. 18. צֶדֶק, for *salvation and victory*; xli. 2, 10, xlii. 6, 21, xlv. 8, 13, li. 5, lviii. 2, lxii. 1, 2. צְדָקָה, used in the same sense; xlv. 8, 24, xlvi. 15, xlviii. 18, li. 6, 8, liv. 17, lvi. 1. (Comp. Jer. xxxiii. 16, and Dan. ix. 24, Ps. cxxxii. 9, for the same, or a similar use of the word.) מִשְׁפָּט, used for *law and religion*; xlii. 1, 3, 4, li. 4. צָמַח, to *sprout*, used in the sense of to *originate*; xlii. 9, xliii. 19. מֵרֹאשׁ, in the sense of *from old time*; xl. 21, xli. 4, 26, xlviii. 16. לְאָחוֹר, *for the future*; xli. 23, xlii. 23. The use of the expression *darkness of prisons*; xlii. 7, xlvii. 5, xlix. 9. Comp. Ps. cvii. 10.

The use of the figure of *a widow*; xlvii. 8, liv. 1, 4, lxii. 4; of *a fruitful mother*; liv. 1, lvi. 7. The use of כְּאַיִן, or מֵאַיִן, כְּאֶפֶס, or מֵאֶפֶס, and תֹּהוּ; xl. 17, xli. 11, 12, 24, 29, xliv. 9. The *relative use of the first and second person*; xli. 8, 9, xlix. 3, 9, 23. *The emphatic reiteration of words*; xli. 27, xliii. 25, li. 12, xlviii. 15, xlviii. 11, xl. 1, lii. 11, lxii. 10, lvii. 14, lxii. 10, li. 9, lii. 1, li. 17, lvii. 6, lvii. 19. *The accumulation of epithets of the person speaking, or the one addressed*; xlii. 5, xliii. 16, 17, xliv. 2, 6, 24, xlv. 11, 18, xlviii. 17, xlix. 5, 7, li. 15, lvi. 8, lvii. 15, xli. 8, 9, xlviii. 1, xlv. 1, and many others. Comp. Jer. xxxi. 35. *Repetition of prepositions*; xlii. 22, xlviii. 9, 14, lviii. 13, lxi. 7. *Synonymes*; xl. 27, xli. 8, 20, xlii. 22, xlviii. 12, 19, 20, xlix. 7, 14, lii. 1, lxvi. 2. The double parallelism is more frequent. *Wanton, and sometimes sportive descriptions*; xli. 18, sqq., xliii. 20, xlix. 23, liv. 11, 12, lv. 12, 13, lx. 4, sqq.

Later Hebraisms and Chaldaisms.—הֵן, for *if*; liv. 15. חֵפֶץ, *an affair* or *business*; xliv. 28, liii. 10, lviii. 2, 13. צָבָא, to *finish*; xl. 2, as in Dan. x. 1 Job vii. 1. יֶתֶר, *exceedingly*; lvi. 12. בָּחַר, to *try*, or to *prove*; xlviii. 10. גָּשַׁשׁ; lix. 10. כֹּהֵן; lxi. 10. מֵאוֹתִי, instead of מֵאִתִּי; liv. 15. אוֹתָם instead of אִתָּם; lix. 21. אֶגְאָלְתִּי, instead of הִגְאַלְתִּי; lxiii. 3. וְגֹאֵל; lix. 3. מְנוֹאָץ; lii. 5.

Hitzig (p. 474) finds Arabisms in the following: צַדִּיק, xli. 26;

the people, which is not merely predicted, but supposed to have actually taken place, and which shows the author wrote in the time of the Babylonian captivity. According to the representations of the writer, Jerusalem, the cities, and the temple, are all destroyed. "Who saith of Jerusalem, 'She shall be inhabited,' and of the cities of Judah, 'They shall be built,' and 'Her desolate places I will restore;' ...... of Cyrus, 'He is my shepherd; he shall perform all my work;' ...... of Jerusalem, 'She shall be built;' and of the temple, 'Her foundation shall be laid.'"[a]

The land is laid waste. "No more shalt thou be called the Desolate, and thy land the Forsaken, but thou shalt be called My-delight-is-in-thee, and thy land the wedded-matron." (lxii. 4.)

The nation is in captivity. "It is a robbed and plundered people; they are all of them bound in prisons, and hid in dungeons; they have become a spoil, and none

---

צְדָקָה, xlv. 23, in the sense of *true* and *truth;* in חָבַר, xlvii. 13; כִּנָּה, xliv. 5, xlv. 5; שָׁרָב, xlix. 10; and many others.

It is true this part has much in common with the genuine portion; e. g. *Holy One of Israel*, קְדוֹשׁ יִשְׂרָאֵל, occurs in almost all the chapters, and elsewhere only in Ps. lxxi. 22, lxxviii. 41, lxxxix. 19, Jer. l. 29, li. 5. (Comp. Hos. xi. 9, "the Holy One *in the midst of thee*.") It has, also, in common, the *figure of speech*, in iv. 3, ix. 5, xix. 18, xxx. 7, xxxv. 8, xliv. 5, xlvii. 1, 4, 5, lvi. 7, lx. 14, lxi. 3, lxii. 4. Yet there is something similar in Hos. i. 10, and Zech. viii. 3. But these peculiarities, which it has in common with the genuine portion, and others adduced by *Jahn* and *Möller*, prove nothing. Their agreement, in this respect, cannot have been accidental, and must be explained as an imitation of the genuine, or in some other way. Thus, e. g. lxv. 25, is borrowed from xi. 9. And still farther, on the other hand, much that is characteristic of the genuine Isaiah is wanting in this latter part; e. g. the word סֹבֶל, *the burden*, ix. 3, x. 27, xiv. 25; מַטֶּה, and שֵׁבֶט, a *branch*, i. e. a *tribe*, ix. 3, x. 5, xiv. 29, xxx. 31, 32; מַעֲשֶׂה; applied *to divine punishments*, v. 12, x. 12, xxviii. 21, xxix. 23; נִשְׁעַן עַל־, to *lean upon*, x. 20, xxx. 12, xxxi. 1, and elsewhere. See *Stähelin*, in Stud. und Krit. for 1830, p. 91, sqq. *Gesenius*, l. c. p. 29.

[a] Chap. xliv. 26, 28, li. 3, lii. 9, lviii. 12, lxiv. 9—11.

delivereth. Who hath given Jacob for a spoil, and Israel to plunderers?" (xlii. 22, 24.) "Shake thyself from the dust, ... O Jerusalem; loose thyself from the bands of thy neck, O captive daughter of Zion." (lii. 2, 3, 5.)

The oppression of the Assyrians is an old affair. "Formerly . . . . . . the Assyrian oppressed them without cause;" but now it is the Chaldeans to whom they are subject. "O daughter of the Chaldeans, ... I was angry with my people, and gave them into thy hand. Thou didst show them no mercy. Even upon the aged thou didst lay a very grievous yoke." (xlvii. 6.) "Come ye forth from Babylon, flee ye from the land of the Chaldeans with the voice of joy." (xlviii. 20.)

But Jehovah will take vengeance upon their enemies. "All who are enraged against thee shall be ashamed and confounded; all that contend with thee shall come to nothing and perish." [a]

He will take vengeance by means of *Cyrus*. "Thus saith Jehovah to his anointed, [Messiah,] to Cyrus, whom I hold by the right hand," &c. (xlv. 1.) "He whom Jehovah loveth will execute his pleasure upon Babylon, and his power upon the Chaldeans." (xlviii. 14, 15.) "I have raised up one from the north, and he cometh, from the rising of the sun, and he calleth upon my name." (xli. 25, xlvi. 11.)

This king will restore the nation. "He (Cyrus) shall build my city and release my captives." (xlv. 13, xliv. 28.)

The nation is to come out of captivity and return to their native land. (xlviii. 20, xlix. 9.) "Thus shall the ransomed of Jehovah return; they shall come to

---

[a] Chap. xli. 11, xlii. 13, xliii. 14, xlvi. 1, xlvii. xlix. 26, li. 23, lix. 17, 18.

Zion with singing." (li. 11, lii. 11, lv. 12, lvii. 14, lxv 9.) They shall rebuild their cities, (xliv. 26.) "The voice of thy watchmen, they shout for joy ...... they behold that Jehovah restoreth Zion." (lii. 8, 9.) "Thy people shall build the ancient desolations." (lviii. 12, lx. 10, lxi. 4.)

They shall enjoy a happy future which will recompense them for all they have suffered. "Comfort ye my people, speak encouragement to Jerusalem, and declare to her that her hard service is ended; that her iniquity is expiated; that she shall receive from the hand of Jehovah double for all her punishment."[a]

However, the apostates shall have no peace, but are to suffer a severe punishment. "The wicked is like the troubled sea, that can have no rest, ... 'there is no peace,' saith my God, 'to the wicked.'" (lvii. 20, 21.) "Ye that have forsaken Jehovah, and have forgotten my holy mountain — yourselves do I destine to the sword." (lv. 6, and 11—15, lxvi. 15, sqq., 24.) "Then shall they go forth and see the dead bodies of the men that rebelled against me, for their worm shall not die, and their fire shall not be quenched."

Now, if we should admit that Isaiah foretold the exile, — and there is something like a prediction of it in xxxix. 6, sqq., and 2 Kings xx. 17, sqq., — yet still such definite and distinct predictions of events that lay beyond the prophet's circle of vision, are themselves contrary to the general analogy of Hebrew prophecies. Still more, it is contrary to all analogy to maintain that he not only predicted the exile, but took his standing point in the time of captivity.

3. *The internal condition of the nation is different.* —

---

[a] Chap. xl. 1, 2, xlix. 19, sqq., liv. 1, sqq., 11, sqq., lx. lxi. 7, sqq., lxii. 1—9, lxv. 17, sqq., lxvi. 10, sqq.

It has only overseers or watchmen to govern it. "His watchmen are all blind; they know nothing; they are all dumb dogs, that cannot bark; dreaming, lying down, loving to slumber; yet are they greedy dogs, that cannot be satisfied," &c. (lvi. 10—12.)

There is no regular offering of sacrifice. "Keep ye justice and practise righteousness. . . . . . Happy the man that doeth this, — that keepeth the Sabbath." (lvi. 1, 2, also lviii. 1—14.)

Chap. lvii. 9, seems to refer to Isaiah's time. "Thou goest to the king with oil, and takest much precious perfume; thou sendest thine ambassadors afar." But verse 12 much more certainly refers to the exile. "But now I announce thy deliverance, and thy works do not profit thee. When thou criest, let their host of idols deliver thee; but the wind shall bear them all away." The idolatry mentioned in lvii. 3, sqq., and especially in lxv. 3, 11, may, very properly, be ascribed to the Babylonian Jews. It is not supposed, in lxvi. 1—3, that there is an actual temple existing, where service is performed.[a]

4. *There are references to earlier prophecies.* — Jehovah says, "Let them come and show us what shall happen. Tell us what ye have predicted in times past, that we may consider and know its fulfilment." (xli. 22.) "Behold, the former things are come to pass. (xlii. 9, xlv. 19.) "Who hath made this known from ancient time? Is it not I, Jehovah?" (verse 21, xlvi. 10.) "I spake not in secret from the beginning." (xlviii. 16.) Chap. lxv. 25, is borrowed from xi. 6, 7.

5. *There are predictions of a splendid future*, uttered with as much distinctness as if it were present, and not

---

[a] See *Stähelin*, Stud. und Krit. for 1831, p. 564.

in harmony with the state of things in Isaiah's time, and the actual result. This may be seen by comparing these descriptions in Isa. lx. lxv. lxvi., with the books of Ezra and Nehemiah, with Zech. i. 12, sqq., and Hag. i. 3, sqq.

Besides, the whole of this second part is the work of one author, as the style, which is the same throughout, and the unity of substance and spirit, prove in a manner not to be mistaken.[a] Although there is not a strict and rigorous unity preserved, and the author falls into repetitions, yet all his predictions refer to one and the same

---

[a] Compare the animating addresses to Israel: xl. 1, 2, 9, xli. 8—10, 13, 14, xliii. 1, 5, xliv. 1, 2, 21—23, xlix. 13—16, li. 1—3, 12, 17, lii. 1, 2, 7—10, liv. 1, 4, 11, lx. 1, lxvi. 10, 13. The grounds of consolation: xl. 2, xliii. 25, xliv. 22, liv. 6—8, l. 1, xlix. 14—16, li. 17—23, lvii. 16—18, lx. 10. The announcement of redemption and restoration: xl. 4, xlii. 16, xliii. 19, lvii. 14, xli. 17—20, xliii. 20, xliv. 3, sq., xlviii. 21, xlix. 9—11, lv. 1, sq., 13, xlviii. 20, lii. 11, lxii. 10. Promise of revenge and reward: l. 10, lix. 18, lx. 4, 9, lxii. 11, lxvi. 15, 16. The restoration of the people: xliii. 5, sq., xlix. 12, 22, sq., lxvi. 19, sq. The reëstablishment of the holy city and state: xlix. 17—23, liv. 1—3, 11—13, lx. lxi. 5—9, lxv. 17—25, lxvi. 6—14. Dominion over the heathen: xlv. 14, xlix. 22, sq., lx. 4—7, 9, sq., lxi. 5, lxvi. 20. Defence of the power and truth of God: xl. 6—11, xliv. 24—28, xlv. 5—7, 12, 18—25, xlvi. 8—13, xlviii. 3—8, 12—16, l. 2, sq., li. 12—16, lii. 9, sq., lv. 10, sq., lix. 16—18, lxiii. 3—6. In opposition to the impotence and nothingness of idols: xl. 12—31, xli. 1—7, 21—29, xlii. 17—21, xliii. 8—13, xliv. 6—20, xlv. 15—25, xlvi. 5—7, xlvii. 12—15, xlviii. 5—8, 14, lvii. 3—13. The threats: xlii. 22—25, xliii. 22—28, xlviii. 1, 4, 8, liii. 4—6, lvi. 10—lix. 15, lxiii. 17—lxiv. 12, lxv. lxvi. 1—5, 15—17, 24. The prophet's apologetic mention of himself: xl. 6, xlii. 1—7, xliv. 26, xlviii. 16, xlix. 1—9, l. 4—10, li. 16, lii. 13—liii. 12, lix. 21, lxi. 1—3. Upon Isa. liii., comp. *Rosenmüller*, Leiden u. Hoffn. d. Propheten in *Gabler's* Neuest. theol. Journ. vol. ii. pt. iv. *De Wette*, Comment. de Morte Jes. Chr. p. 26, sqq., (Opusc. p. 38, sqq.) *Gesenius*, Comm. On the other side, *Rosenmüller*, Schol. *Hengstenberg*, Christol. vol. ii. p. 364, sqq. *Stähelin*, l. c. p. 553. There is a similarity of thought in xl. 12, sqq., xliv. 24, xlv. 5—12, 18, 22, xlviii. 12, sq., li. 6, lv. 8, sq., lvii. 15, lxvi. 1, sq.; xlii. 4, xlv. 23, li. 4, sqq., lvi. 3, sqq., lxvi. 20, sqq.; xli. 8, xliii. 1, 4, 21, xliv. 1, sq., 21, 24, xlv. 4, lxiii. 8, 16, lxiv. 8, sq., lxv. 9. See other peculiarities of style above, with similar applications and images: xli. 28, lix. 16, lxiv. 5; xliii. 3, xlv. 13, lii. 3. Against this view, see *Augusti*, § 206. *Bertholdt*, p. 1375.

historical stand-point; namely, the time of the appearance of Cyrus.[a] In lvi. 9, the author takes a different tone — that of reproof. In the sins of the people he finds the obstacle that has prevented the fulfilment of his inspired promises. This is the cause of the earnest prayers, and the deep and intense anxiety, shown in lxii. 1; "For Zion's sake I will not keep silence, and for Jerusalem's sake I will not rest;" and verse 6, "Upon thy walls, O Jerusalem, have I set watchmen: all the day and all the night shall they not keep silence. O ye that praise Jehovah, keep not silence, and give him no rest, until he establish Jerusalem." So in lxxii. 15, sqq., lxiv. 1, sqq., he says, "O that thou would rend the heaven and come down, that the mountains might tremble at thy presence." Hence comes also the threat of punishment against the ungodly, mentioned above.[b]

§ 209.

SPURIOUS PASSAGES CONTAINED IN THE FIRST PART.

The passage (xiii. 1—xiv. 23) which treats of the destruction of Babel and the Babylonian empire by the Medes, and of the return of the exiles, must be pronounced spurious, and for the same reason as the last part of the book, — which is probably the work of the same author, — because the writer takes his stand-point

---

[a] According to Zech. viii. 7, 8, our author, whom Jeremiah has worked over, (Jer. xxxi.,) prophesied in the time of rebuilding the temple. § 217, *b.*

[b] See *Stähelin*, l. c. 535, sqq. *Bertholdt's* unfounded date, p. 1390. See *Hitzig*, p. 458, sqq. *Gesenius*, p. 33, sqq. *Rückert* and *Hitzig* divide it into three books, each of nine chapters: 1. Chap. xl.—xlviii. 2. Chap. xlix.—lvii. 3. Chap. lviii.—lxvi. But this is erroneous; for, by this division, the point at which the tone of reproof begins (lvi. 9) is made obscure, and the form of conclusion in xlviii and lvii. affords us no true mark of division.

in the exile. Thus he says, "So shall Babylon, the glory of kingdoms, the pride and boast of the Chaldeans, be like Sodom and Gomorrah, which God overthrew." (xiii. 19.) "Then shalt thou utter this song over the king of Babylon, and say, 'How hath the tyrant fallen, the tribute ceased!'" (xiv. 4.) "I will arise against them, ... I will cut off from Babylon the name and the remnant." (verse 22.) "For Jehovah will have compassion upon Jacob, ... the nations shall take them, and bring them to their own place; and the house of Jacob shall possess them in the land of Jehovah, as servants and as handmaids; they shall take captive their captors, and they shall rule over their oppressors." (xiv. 1—4.)

This spurious passage appears to be the work of the author of the last part of the book, from a comparison of the verses last quoted with the following sentences: "The wealth of Ægypt and the merchandise of the Æthiopians and Sabeans, men of stature, shall come over to thee." (xliv. 5.) "I will lift up my hand to the nations, ... and they shall bring thy sons in their arms." (xlv. 14.) "The nation which thou knowest not thou shalt call." (xlix. 22, sqq., and lv. 5, and also lx. 4—7, 9, 10, lxi. 5, lxvi. 20.)

The inscription, (xiii. 1,) "a prophecy concerning Babylon, which was revealed to Isaiah, the son of Amoz," is incorrect, either through design or mistake; and several of the inscriptions in Isaiah seem to be the work of a foreign hand.

We must consider chap. xxxiv. xxxv. as spurious, which treat of the devastation of Edom, and the return of the exiles. We are enabled to fix the date of these by the following considerations: *By the parallel passages* in Obadiah, Jeremiah, (xlix. 7, sqq.,) Ezekiel, (xxv. 12, sqq.,) and Isaiah, (lxiii. 1—6.)

By the affinity between this and previous passages of the book; for example, in xxxiv. 4, we read, "All the host of heaven shall waste away, and the heaven shall be rolled up like a scroll;" and in xiii. 10, "The stars of heaven, and the constellations thereof, shall not give their light; the sun shall be darkened at his going forth." In verse 11, sqq., we read, "From generation to generation it shall lie waste; none shall pass through it forever and ever; the pelican and the hedgehog shall possess it, and the heron and the raven shall dwell in it;" and in xiii. 20, sqq., "It shall not be inhabited forever, nor shall it be dwelt in from generation to generation; . . . . . . there shall the wild beasts of the desert lodge," &c.

By its affinity with the second part of Isaiah; thus, in xxxiv. 1, 2, we find, "The wilderness and the parched land shall be glad, and the desert rejoice, and blossom as the rose;" and in lv. 12, "For ye shall go out with joy; . . . . . . the mountains and the hills shall break forth before you into singing, and all the trees of the field shall clap their hands. Instead of the thorn shall grow up the cypress-tree." (xl. 5, lx. 1, lxii. 11.) In verses 3, 4, we read, "Strengthen ye the weak hands, and confirm the tottering knees; say to the faint-hearted, 'Be strong; fear ye not; behold your God;'" and in xl. 1, sq., "Comfort ye, comfort ye my people, saith your God; speak ye encouragement to Jerusalem, and declare to her that her hard service is ended;" in verse 9, "Say to the cities of Judah, 'Behold your God;'" in verses 5, 6, "Then shall the eyes of the blind be unstopped," &c.; and in xl. 16, "Then will I lead the blind in an unknown way; . . . . . . I will make darkness light before them."[a] We read, in verse 8, "And a path shall be there, and a highway, and it shall be called the holy way;" and in xl. 3, 4, "Prepare ye in the wilderness the way of Jehovah;"[b] in verse 10, "Yea, the ransomed of Jehovah shall return; they shall come to Zion with songs; everlasting joy shall be upon their heads; they shall obtain joy and gladness, and sorrow and sighing shall flee away;" and in li. 11, the selfsame words occur.

The passage, xxi. 1—10, where the conquest of Babylon by the Medes and Persians is predicted with graphic minuteness, belongs to the same period.[c] It is, however, remarkably distinguished from the other spurious passages of the book.

We can also, with considerable certainty, refer to the same period the passage, xxiv.—xxvii. This speaks of the devastation of the land of Judea, the deliverance of the Jews from their masters, (xxvi. 13,) of their return, (xxvii. 12, 13,) and the destruction of the enemy's capital, (xxv. 2, xxvi. 5.) We are led to refer it to this date, *By the nature of the contents of the passage:* It

---

[a] Comp. verses 6, 7, with xliii. 19, 20, xlviii. 21, xlix. 10, 11.

[b] Comp. also xlix. 11, and lxii. 10.

[c] Comp. verse 5, "The table is prepared; the watch set; they eat, they drink; arise, princes, anoint the shield," with the well-known account in *Herodotus*, (i. 191,) "There happened to be a feast;" with *Xenophon*, Cyrop. vii. 5, 15, sqq.; verse 7, with *Xenophon*, vii. 1, 14, 27. *Strabo*, xx. p. 727. See *Michaelis*, and *Rosenmüller*, in loc. [The last author says there is no doubt that the poet himself was present at the capture of the city, and, full of those things he had seen and heard, uttered this oracle. *Gesenius* (Com. in loc.) is of a different opinion. See, also, *Maurer*, in loc.]

teaches some doctrines which belong to a later age of Jewish history, such as the resurrection of the dead, contained in the following passages: "The dead shall live again;" "The dead bodies of thy people shall arise," (xxvi. 19;) "In that day will Jehovah punish the high ones, and the kings of the earth," (xxiv. 21;) "He will destroy death forever," (xxv. 8.)

By the style,[a] which admits of a play upon words, (xxiv. 3, 4, 16—19, 21;) of reminiscences, or allusions to earlier poets, as in xxiv. 7, and 11, "The new wine mourneth, ... there is a cry for wine in the streets," which refers to Joel i. 10, 5, "The new wine is dried up;" and the figure of an olive-tree, (verse 13,) referring to xvii. 6; of reiterations, "My wretchedness, my wretchedness," (verse 16, and xxvi. 3, 15;) of tautological parallels;[b] "Peace, peace," for constant peace; and of "painful efforts after beautiful expressions," as Bertholdt remarks.

By the parallel passages: (xxiv. 17, 18,) "The terror, the pit, and the snare, are upon thee, O inhabitant of Moab. Whoso fleeth from the terror shall fall into the pit, and whoso escapeth from the pit be taken in the snare." Nearly the same words occur in Jer. xlviii. 43.[c] In xxvi. 16, we read, "In affliction they sought thee;" and xxvii. 9, "By this shall the iniquity of Jacob be expiated;" and in xl. 2, "Declare to her that her hard service is ended, that her iniquity is expiated;"—in xxiv. 16, "The plunderers plunder;"

[a] The stand-point of the prophet in xxiv. 1—13, is doubtful. *Gesenius* and others suppose it refers to the desolation of the land of Judah; *Hitzig*, to the desolation of the enemy's country. The antithesis in verse 14, sqq., and the parallels, verses 17—20, favor this opinion.

[b] Chap. xxiv. 3, 5, 22, xxv. 7, 9, 12, xxvi. 5, xxvii. 5.

[c] Comp. also xxiv. 15, with xlii. 10—12; xxvi. 13, with lxiii. 19.

and the same words occur in xxi. 2;—in verse 19, "The earth is violently moved from her place;" and in xiii. 13, "And the earth shall be shaken out of her place."

On the other hand, there is a difference in the following particulars: in the use of the figure of an *olive-tree*, in xxiv. 13, and in the use of the same figure in xvii. 6. In xxv. 4, it is said, "Thou hast been...... a refuge from the storm, a shadow from the heat;" and in iv. 6, "He shall be a tent by day, for a shadow from the heat, and for a refuge and shelter from the storm and rain." The nation is compared to a vineyard in xxvii. 2, and v. 2.[a]

§ 210.

DOUBTFUL PASSAGES IN THE FIRST PART.

But if those passages above named are later than Isaiah's time, on the contrary, it is wrong to place the oracle concerning Moab, contained in chap. xv. xvi., in the time of Jeremiah,[b] as some have done, on the ground that they contain an imitation of one of that prophet's oracles, in Jer. xlviii.[c] No sufficient argument for rejecting them is found in the circumstance that their historical fulfilment did not take place in the time

[a] See *Gesenius*, in loc. p. 756, sqq. *Rosenmüller*, in the first edition, denied the genuineness of the passages, but admits it in the second. See his edition of *Arndt*, De Loco Jes. xxiv.—xxvii. vindicando et explicando; Hamb. 1826. *Knobel*, vol. ii. p. 319.

[b] The relation which the kindred verses bear to the whole passage, and also the character of the various readings in Jeremiah, are against the opposite opinion of *Bertholdt*, p. 1440. Comp. Isa. xvi. 6—9, with Jer. xlviii. 31, 32. See § 225.

[c] *Koppe*, l. c. in loc. *Bertholdt*, p. 1389.

of Isaiah.[a] But yet, from the difference in language and style, we must decide that they do not belong to Isaiah. Hitzig and Knobel think Jonah is the author, (2 Kings xiv. 25,) and that the oracle originally related to an invasion by the Israelites under Jeroboam II.[b] It is probable the epilogue (xiii. 13, 14) belongs to Isaiah — "This is the word which Jehovah spake concerning Moab *of old:* 'But *now* — within three years, like the years of a hireling — the glory of Moab shall be put to shame, with all his great multitude. The remnant shall be very small, and without strength.'" This is probable, from its affinity with other passages, admitted to be genuine; for example, with xxi. 16, "Within one year, according to the years of a hireling, shall all the glory of Kedar be consumed," and x. 25, and xxix. 17, "yet a very little while."

[The following account, says Gesenius, appears the most probable: The oracle was first uttered without the epilogue, by a prophet contemporary with Isaiah, or somewhat older than he. It was designed as a general prediction of adversity that was to fall upon Moab, and, like most of the oracles against foreign nations, is to be considered as the production of national zeal, and national hatred against the Moabites, — a wish and hope for their destruction, uttered as a prophecy. Such oracles would be most often uttered at a time when the national hatred had received new nourishment from the

---

[a] According to Jer. xlviii. 11, the Moabites appear to have suffered nothing from the Assyrians, in the time of Isaiah.

[b] *Hitzig*, Der Prop. Jonas Orakel üb. Moab; Heidel. 1834, 4to. *Knobel*, l. c. vol. ii. p. 125, sqq. On the other side, see *Credner*, in Stud. und Krit. for 1833, p. 780. He refers it to the expedition of Tiglath-pileser, in the time of Ahaz. *Hendewerk* (l. c.) puts it in the early part of Hezekiah's reign. Both think it a genuine production of Isaiah.

injustice experienced in one war or another, or when some foreign conqueror afforded a hope of its fulfilment, either sooner or later. In this particular case, the occasion may be found in the war waged against the Hebrews because they had not paid the tribute, about 896 B. C.; or in the incursion of the Moabites, about 849 B. C.; or in the seizure of the domains of Reuben and Gad,—though a special occasion is not needed. In foretelling the enemy that is to lay waste Moab, the prophet certainly had the Assyrians before his eyes, who had ruined so many of the enemies of Judah, and might be expected to destroy Moab also. The oracle was not immediately fulfilled, and therefore Isaiah repeats it at a time when the Assyrians threatened soon to swallow up all small states. He added an epilogue, fixing the time, which, as usual, is done by the use of a round and poetic number.] [a]

Chap. xix. The prophecy respecting Ægypt would be subject to doubt if it relates—as Rosenmüller and Gesenius suppose—to the Ægyptian dodecharchy and Psammeticus. Then we must place it in Manasseh's time, (696—641 B. C.,) though chap. i. 1, would be against such an hypothesis, as that does not make Isaiah's prophetic office extend beyond the time of Hezekiah. But this oracle may be placed earlier,—as it has been shown by Hitzig and Hendewerk,—and may be referred to the invasion of Ægypt by the Assyrians. The genuineness of this prophecy, therefore, need not be doubted.[b]

---

[a] *Gesenius*, p. 508, sq. See *Hitzig*, p. 16.

[b] *Koppe*, *Eichhorn*, and *Künöl*, (in *Gabler's* Theol. Journal, vol. i. p. 564,) consider verses 18—25 spurious. *Hitzig* thinks 16—25 spurious, while *Gesenius* expresses doubts against only 18—20. *Hendewerk* (p. 422, sqq.) de-

The genuineness of the prophecy against Tyre (chap. xxiii.) has been denied on account of its mention of the Chaldeans, (verse 13;) on account of its alleged reference to Nebuchadnezzar's siege of Tyre, and the later style in which it is alleged to be written.[a]

---

fends the genuineness of the whole. But the hopes expressed in verses 17—25 seem too fanatical for Isaiah:—

["In that day shall there be five cities in the land of Ægypt, speaking the language of Canaan, ... one of them shall be called 'the city of Deliverance.' In that day shall there be an altar to Jehovah, in the midst of the land of Ægypt, which shall be a sign and a witness . . . . . . that they cried to Jehovah, on account of their oppressors, and he sent them a Savior," &c. . . . . . . "And the Ægyptians shall know Jehovah in that day, and shall offer him sacrifices and oblations. . . . . . . In that day shall Israel be the third in a covenant with Ægypt and Assyria." Compare these expressions with iv. 5, 6, "Then shall Jehovah create upon the whole extent of Mount Zion, ... a cloud and smoke by day, and the brightness of a flaming fire by night. . . . . . . He shall be a tent by day, for a shadow from the heat, and for a refuge and shelter from the storm and rain."

Now, in some similar passages of Isaiah, (ix. 5, 6, xxx. 19—26, xxxii. 1—8, 15—20, and xxxiii. 17—24,) there is a modest picture of the happiness the people are to expect. The greatest blessing promised is, not that Judah shall conquer Assyria and Ægypt, or that the latter country shall adopt the worship of Jehovah, but the Jews shall have peace. "Thou shalt see no more a fierce people, ... of a dark language, which thou couldst not hear. . . . . . . Thine eyes shall behold Jerusalem as a quiet habitation, a tent that shall never be moved." However, xxiii. 18, contains similar predictions respecting the glory of Judah; for he says the gain of Tyre "shall be holy to Jehovah; it shall not be treasured nor laid up in store, but it shall be for them that dwell before Jehovah, for abundant food and for splendid clothing."

Gesenius thinks verses 18—20 may have been inserted in the text in Jeremiah's time, by the party who considered the nation's flight to Ægypt—which Jeremiah opposed—was not contrary to the spirit of the theocracy At that time the Jews possessed Migdol, Tahpanes, Noph, and Patros, which may be the cities mentioned, as the number *five* is probably a poetical rather than an *exact* number; or, perhaps, the place they first visited in coming to Ægypt—well enough called "city of Deliverance"—is to be added to the list, and the number *five* taken in its proper sense. The entire chapter, with the exception of 18—20, he thinks closely resembles the genuine portions of Isaiah, in style and sentiment.]

[a] See *Eichhorn*, § 525, p. 106, sq.; Hebr. Propheten, vol. ii. p. 574. *Bertholdt*, p. 1389. *Rosenmüller* and *Hitzig*, in loc. *Movers* (in Theol. quartal-

But these arguments, to say the least, are not sufficient to prove the passage spurious.[a]

[An historical occasion for Isaiah uttering this prophecy against Tyre can easily be found. After Shalmaneser had taken Samaria, — in the year 717 B. C., according to Calmet, — he invaded Syria and Phœnicia. Josephus cites Menander's account of the invasion, which that historian had translated out of the archives of Tyre into Greek, as follows: "One whose name was Eluleus reigned thirty-six years. This king, on the revolt of the Citteans, (Chittin,) sailed to them, and reduced them again to submission. Against these did the king of Assyria (Shalmaneser) send an army, and in a hostile manner overran all Phœnicia, but soon made peace with them all, and returned back. But Sidon, and Ace, (Arke,) and old Tyre, — which was built on the continent, the chief city at that time being on a neighboring island, — revolted; and many other cities there were which delivered themselves up to the king of Assyria. Accordingly, when the Tyrians (inhabitants of the great city on the island) would not submit to him, the king returned, and fell upon them again, while the Phœnicians had furnished him with threescore ships, and eight hundred men to row them; and when the Tyrians had come upon them in twelve ships, and the enemy's ships were dis-

schrift for 1836) ascribes it to Jeremiah. *Hitzig* thinks the following particulars are not like Isaiah: the slow movement of the discourse, (verses 2—4;) the return of the thought of verse 6, in verse 12; the dulness of verses 6, 12; the grammatical inaccuracy in verse 13; שחרר, verse 3; the agreement of verse 7 with Zeph. ii. 15; *virgin, daughter of Sidon,* verse 12; זנה, *to drive a trade,* comp. Nah. iii. 4, Ezek. xxiii. 11, 29;) מְכַסֶּה, verse 18. Compare xiv. 11, the 70 years, verse 17, Jer. xxix. 10.

[a] *Gesenius, Hendewerk,* and *Hengstenberg,* (De Rebus Tyr.) But the latter makes the oracle refer to Nebuchadnezzar, as *Jerome, Vitringa,* and *J. D. Michaelis,* have done.

persed, they took five hundred prisoners; and the reputation of all the citizens of Tyre was thereby increased. But the king of Assyria returned, and placed guards at their river and aqueducts, who should hinder the Tyrians from drawing water. This continued for five years, and still the Tyrians bore the siege, and drank the water they had out of the wells they dug." The Jews had good reason for their aversion to the Tyrians, for they had trafficked in Jewish slaves, taken in war, and sold them to the Greeks; and when the Assyrian king invaded Tyre, Isaiah very naturally expresses the indignation of his countrymen against their oppressors, and predicts their ruin. But it has been alleged that the Chaldeans mentioned in verse 13, as composing the army of Shalmaneser, were not at that time known to the Jews. But this is a statement, in our present knowledge of the history of Asia at that period, we are by no means justified in hazarding. The oracle mentions them as a new nation, "who not long ago were not a people." This was their first appearance in history, and here they are represented as a nomadic people whom the Assyrians had introduced to their armies, and assigned them possessions and fixed habitations. We may suppose, with Gesenius, they first came into the dominions of the Assyrians about 747, not long before the date of this oracle. Soon after, they became a powerful nation, their might increasing as the Assyrians degenerated under the influence of wealth and luxury. They seem to have run the same course with the Medes and Persians; that is, were first a rude and nomadic people, were admitted to the armies and territories of a neighboring and superior nation, and at length became their masters. In the beginning of the next century, the

Chaldeans were masters of Assyria, and the Babylonian-Chaldean empire was founded, which Nebuchadnezzar exalted to such a degree of wealth and power. This, in its turn, shared the fate of its predecessor, and Cyrus founded the Median empire on its ruins.

The question may now be asked, Was the prophecy against Tyre ever fulfilled? The Bible does not say it was, and Menander, cited above, says, expressly, that the city was not taken, though *old Tyre*, with other cities, had surrendered. Some have referred the oracle to the time of Nebuchadnezzar's invasion of Tyre; but the prophecy does not suit the historical relations of the Chaldeans, at that time well known, and the most powerful nation in Western Asia; nor, indeed, is it fulfilled, for Nebuchadnezzar, after wasting thirteen[a] years in a siege, retired without effecting his purpose, as it is evident from Ezek. xxix. 17, sqq., "Son of man, Nebuchadnezzar, the king of Babylon, caused his army to serve a great service against Tyre. Every head was made bald, and every shoulder peeled, (with carrying burdens:) yet neither he nor his army had wages from Tyre for the service which he served against it."][b]

Nothing important can be urged against the genuineness of the short passages, xxi. 11, 12, and verses 13—17, the oracle concerning Dumah, and the oracle against the Arabians. In the latter, we find, on the contrary, marks of Isaiah's style. On account of the

---

[a] See *Josephus*, Ant. x. 11, § 1, who quotes *Diocles's* accounts of Persia, and *Philostratus's* of India and Phœnicia, for the fact. See, also, *Joseph.* against Ap. i. § 21.

[b] See *Gesenius*, l. c. Also, *Heeren*, Researches, vol. ii. p. 11, note 3, and p. 146, sqq., and *Knobel*, l. c. § 22.

threats against Arabia in Jer. xlix. 28—33, this oracle has been incorrectly referred to his time.[a]

[The short passage, (vii. 8,) "And within threescore and five years shall Ephraim be broken, that he be no more a people," is evidently an interpolation, as it interrupts the sense completely. Besides, it is contrary to the custom of Isaiah to give definite numbers, as in this place. It contains great chronological difficulties.]

§ 211.

GENUINE PASSAGES OF ISAIAH.

I. From the time of Uzziah, (chap. vi.;) the prophet's consecration in the year of Uzziah's death, (758 B. C.) However, Hitzig thinks this is a prediction after the event, and was written in Hezekiah's time.

II. From the time of Jotham, (758—741.) Here, perhaps, belong chap. ii.—iv. However, these are placed by some in the first part of the reign of Ahaz. Gesenius hesitates between Ahaz and Jotham; Hitzig refers it to the former, Hendewerk and Knobel to the latter. Chap. ii. 1—3, is parallel with Micah iv. 1—3, though it is more complete.

Isa. ii. 1—4. "It shall come to pass, in future times, that the mountain of the house of Jehovah shall be established above all the mountains, and exalted above the hills, and all nations shall flow to it, and many kingdoms shall go, and shall say, 'Come, let us go up to the mountain of	Mic. iv. 1—3. "But it shall come to pass, in future times, that the mountain of the house of Jehovah shall be established above all the mountains, and exalted above the hills, and the nations shall flow to it: and many nations shall go, saying, 'Come, let us go up to the moun-

[a] *Gesenius*, in loc.

Jehovah, to the house of the God of Jacob, that he may teach us his ways, and that we may walk in his paths; for from Zion shall go forth a law, and the word of Jehovah from Jerusalem. He shall be a judge of the nations, and an umpire of many kingdoms; and they shall beat their swords into ploughshares, and their spears into pruning-hooks; nation shall not lift up sword against nation, neither shall they learn war any more.' "	tain of Jehovah, to the house of the God of Jacob; that he may teach us his ways, and that we may walk in his paths. For from Zion shall go forth a law, and the word of Jehovah from Jerusalem; he shall be a judge of the nations, and an umpire of many kingdoms afar off. They shall beat their swords into ploughshares, and their spears into pruning-hooks; nation shall not lift up sword against nation, neither shall they learn war any more."

Judging from the state of the times, and the Messianic idea in this passage, it is not probable Micah was its author, but that both he and Isaiah borrowed it from an old prophet,—perhaps, as Hitzig thinks, from Joel.[a]

III. It is expressly stated the following are from the time of Ahaz, (741—725 B. C.,) namely, 1. Chap. vii. 1, x. 4; and, 2. Chap. xvii. 1—11; both relating to the hostile kingdoms of Israel and Damascus. 3. Chap. xiv. 28—32, an oracle against the Philistines. Perhaps, 4. Chap. i., as Gesenius thinks. Vitringa, Eichhorn, and Hitzig, refer it to Hezekiah's time; Hendewerk to Jotham's, and Rosenmüller to Uzziah's. 5. Chap. v.

IV. The following belong to Hezekiah's time, (725—696 B. C.) 1. Chap. xxviii.—xxxiii., announcing the destruction of the kingdom of Ephraim by the Assyrians; the peril of Judah; the siege and deliverance of Jerusalem, (xxix. 1—8;) the desolation of the land,

---

[a] See *Michaelis*, *Gesenius*, and *Hendewerk*. *Hitzig* (in Stud. und Kritik. for 1829, p. 349, sqq.) ascribes it to *Joel*; but *Hendewerk* and *Credner* (l. c. p. 72, sqq.) do not agree with him.

(xxxii. 10—14, xxxiii. 8, 9;) the humiliation of the enemy, (xxx. 27—33, xxxiii. 10—12;) reproof for disbelieving prophecies, (xxix. 9, sqq.;) reproof of a wanton reliance on the friendship and help of Ægypt, (xxx. xxxi.;) and the promise of happier times after their misfortunes, (xxxii. 1, sqq., xxxiii. 17, sqq.)[a] 2. Chap. x. 3, xii. 6, and perhaps the fragment, xix. 24—27, should be inserted after x. 34. It speaks of the arrogance of the Assyrians, the chastisement they inflict on Judah, their humiliation, and a Messianic prophecy, from the time after the fall of Samaria. (x. 9.) 3. Chap. xx., threat against Ægypt, from the time of Sargon, the predecessor of Sennacherib, and therefore before the fourteenth year of Hezekiah. 4. Chap. xxii. 16—25, the fall of Shebna, the elevation of Eliakim. This is from the time before Sennacherib's invasion.[b] 5. Chap. xxii. 1—14, the siege of Jerusalem by the Assyrians. It was probably written during this invasion. 6. Chap. xvii. 12—14, the extirpation of the Assyrians. 7. Chap. xviii. an enigmatical passage, relating to the embassy to Ægypt.

§ 212.

ON ISAIAH XXXVI.—XXXIX.

This historical passage is not the work of Isaiah.[c] Its spuriousness is proved by its relating the murder of Sennacherib, and the succession of Esar-haddon, events

---

[a] These chapters seem to belong together, and to the period before the time when Samaria was taken by Shalmaneser. *Hitzig* and *Hendewerk* try to determine the date of the separate chapters. *Hitzig* erroneously places chap. xxviii. after this event.

[b] Comp. 2 Kings xviii. 18, xix. 2.

[c] Comp. 2 Chron. xxxii. 32.

much later than Isaiah's time, (xxxvii. 38,) and by its mythical contents, and more modern language.[a] With the exception of Hezekiah's song of thanksgiving, (xxxviii. 9, sqq.,) it may be found in 2 Kings xviii. 13—xx. 19. The passage, xxxvi. 1, 2, is made more intelligible by referring to 2 King's xviii. 7, 13—16:—

Isa. xxxvi. 1—3. "Now it came to pass in the fourteenth year of King Hezekiah, that Sennacherib king of Assyria came up against all the defenced cities of Judah, and took them. And the king of Assyria sent Rabshakeh from Lachish to Jerusalem unto King Hezekiah with a great army. And he stood by the conduit of the upper pool in the highway of the fuller's field. Then came forth unto him Eliakim, Hilkiah's son, which was over the house, and Shebna the scribe, and Joah, Asaph's son, the recorder."[b]

2 Kings xviii. 7, 13—16. "And the Lord was with him; and he prospered whithersoever he went forth: and he rebelled against the king of Assyria, and served him not.

"Now in the fourteenth year of King Hezekiah did Sennacherib king of Assyria come up against all the fenced cities of Judah, and took them. And Hezekiah king of Judah sent to the king of Assyria to Lachish, saying, 'I have offended; return from me; that which thou puttest on me I will bear.' And the king of Assyria appointed unto Hezekiah king of Judah three hundred talents of silver, and thirty talents of gold. And Hezekiah gave him all the silver that was found in the house of the Lord, and in the treasures of the king's house. At that time did Hezekiah cut off the gold from the doors of the temple of the Lord, and from the pillars which Hezekiah king of Judah had overlaid, and gave it to the king of Assyria."

---

[a] פֶּחָה, xxxvi. 9; יְהוּדִית, verse 11.

[b] Verse 3 is imperfect. Comp. 2 Kings xviii. 18.

2 Kings xx. 4, 5. "And it came to pass, afore Isaiah was gone out into the middle court, that the word of the Lord came to him, saying, 'Turn again, and tell Hezekiah the captain of my people, "Thus saith the Lord, the God of David thy father, 'I have heard thy prayer, I have seen thy tears: behold, I will heal thee: on the third day thou shalt go up unto the house of the Lord.' "' "[a]

Isa. xxxviii. 4, 5. "Then came the word of the Lord to Isaiah, saying, 'Go and say to Hezekiah, "Thus saith the Lord, the God of David thy father, 'I have heard thy prayer, I have seen thy tears: behold, I will add unto thy days fifteen years.' "' "

The following passage from Kings is more complete than that from Isaiah, and perhaps its author was more fond of the marvellous: —

2 Kings xx. 9—11. "And Isaiah said, 'This sign shalt thou have of the Lord, that the Lord will do the thing that he hath spoken: shall the shadow go forward ten degrees, or go back ten degrees?' And Hezekiah answered, 'It is a light thing for the shadow to go down ten degrees: nay, but let the shadow return backward ten degrees.' And Isaiah the prophet cried unto the Lord, and he brought the shadow ten degrees backward, by which it had gone down in the dial of Ahaz."

Isa. xxxviii. 7, 8. "And this shall be a sign unto thee from the Lord, that the Lord will do this thing that he hath spoken; 'Behold, I will bring again the shadow of the degrees, which is gone down in the sun-dial of Ahaz, ten degrees backward.' So the sun returned ten degrees, by which degrees it was gone down."

Now, since the text of the passage in Kings in many

---

[a] Comp. Isa. xxxviii. 22. Verses 21, 22, are misplaced. Comp. 2 Kings xviii. 7, 8. Comp. Isa. xxxvi. 21, with 2 Kings xviii. 36, (הָעָם is wanting;) and xxxvii. 25, with 2 Kings xix. 24, זרים. Explanatory readings occur in Isaiah: אֲמַרְתִּי, for אָמַרְתָּ; xxxvi. 5. מָרַדְתָּ is omitted. Verse 14, עָרֵיךָ is more regular than עֲרֵיךְ. ברב רכבי; xxxvii. 17. Verse 24 is like the Keri in 2 Kings. לַחְשְׁאוֹת, for לְהַשְׁאוֹת, (a more difficult form;) verse 26, and many others.

places seems to be more correct and original than that in Isaiah,[a] and since the collection of the Isaianic prophecies was made at a later date than the books of Kings, therefore some have maintained that the passage in Isaiah was derived from that in Kings. Such was the opinion of Gesenius, and expressed in former editions of this work. But, on the other hand, it has been observed that the text in Isaiah, also, has, sometimes, an original character,[b] and that the song of thanksgiving, (xxxviii. 9, sqq.,) and the whole chapter, must have been derived from one and the same source. Accordingly, it has been maintained that both collectors drew from a larger historical work.[c] But the analogy of Jer. lii. is not favorable to this hypothesis; for that chapter is derived from the second book of Kings, and its text has been subsequently revised and enlarged.[d]

§ 213.

ORIGIN OF THIS MISCELLANEOUS COLLECTION.

Since in chap. i. xii. there are combined passages that are certainly genuine, all of which relate to the kingdom of Judah, this is, perhaps, the original collection, to which the inscription (chap. li.) belongs. Bertholdt makes use of the account in Baba Bathra to support the opinion that Hezekiah caused this collection to be made.

---

[a] See last note.

[b] בָּנָיו (Isa. xxxvii. 38) is lacking in 2 Kings xix. 37. וַיִּקְרָאֵהוּ (Isa. xxxvii. 14) is more difficult than וַיִּקְרָאֵם, (2 Kings xix. 14.) But compare the following: אֶת כָּל־הָאֲרָצוֹת, (xxxvii. 18,) which is more difficult than הַגּוֹיִם, (2 Kings xix. 17.) [?]

[c] *Hitzig*, l. c. p. 411, sq. *Keil*, Chronik. p. 229, sqq.

[d] See below, § 219, *b*, &c.

However, he also, on this account, separates i. 1—ii. 4, from it, which is too hazardous.

The prophecies, (xiii.—xxiii.,) with the exception of xiv. 24—27, xvii. 12—xviii. 7, and xx., relate to foreign nations, and bear the title "oracle."[a] Perhaps the miscellaneous collection (xxviii.—xxxiii.) is a separate, small collection of passages that are certainly genuine.

The *first part* (i.—xxxix.) originated from the combination of these independent collections, to which xxiv. —xxvii. xxxiv. xxxv. were added. Then xxxvi.—xxxix. were appended, with the design of collecting together all that related to Isaiah.[b]

Finally, the *second part* (xl.—lxvi.) was added; but it is not clear for what reason. All this was done after the exile, and probably after the redaction of the older historical books.[c]

§ 214.

LITERARY CHARACTER OF ISAIAH.

The genuine passages of Isaiah, both in form and substance, are to be ranked with the noblest productions of the golden age of prophetic literature.

The discourse is, for the most part, oratorical; it rarely contains symbols or parables. The style is noble, powerful, concise, rich in images and thoughts, and rarely indulging in enumerations or antitheses, as in ii. 12—17, and iii. 1—4, 18—24. It makes

---

[a] מַשָּׂא.

[b] Compare Jer. lii.

[c] *Gesenius*, vol. i. p. 19, sqq. See the opinions of *Eichhorn*, § 526, sqq., and *Bertholdt*, p. 1393, sqq. [Also, *Knobel*, l. c. § 19, 28, 31, 32.] *Gesenius* divides Isaiah into four books, viz., i.—xii., xiii. xxiii., xxiv.—xxxv., and xl.—lxvi. He makes the third consist of supplementary matter.

moderate use of a play upon words;[a] but it is not without hardness, and sudden transitions, which appear in the following passages: —

"Yea, in that day shall they roar against them like the roaring of the sea; and if one look to the land, behold, darkness and sorrow, and the light is darkened in the heavens." (v. 30.) "But the darkness shall not remain, where now is distress. Of old he brought the land of Zebulun and the land of Naphtali into distress, into contempt. In future times shall he bring the land of the sea beyond Jordan, the circle of the Gentiles, into honor." (viii. 23, and xxviii. 15.)

The rhythm is strong and full, often running out into beautiful periods. One passage (ix. 7—x. 4) consists of strophes. The thoughts are earnest, natural, and free: —

"What to me is the multitude of your sacrifices? I am satiated with the burnt-offerings of rams, and the fat of fed beasts: in the blood of bullocks, and of lambs, and of goats, I have no delight. ...... Incense is an abomination to me; the new moon, also, and the Sabbath, and the solemn assembly, iniquity, and festivals I cannot endure. Your new moons and your feasts my soul hateth. They are a burden to me. I am weary of bearing them," &c. (i. 11, sqq.) "Since this people draweth near to me with their mouth, and honoreth me with their lips, while their heart is far from me, and their worship of me is according to the commandments of men, therefore, behold, I will proceed to deal marvellously with this people." (xxviii. 13.)

Sometimes the style is sublime: —

"Go into the rock; hide yourselves in the dust; from the terror of Jehovah, and the glory of his majesty." (ii. 10.) "At that time shall men cast away their idols of silver, and their idols of gold, which they have made to worship, to the moles and the bats; fleeing into the caves of the rocks, and the clefts of the craggy rocks, from the terror of Jehovah, and the glory of his majesty. Trust, then, no more in man, whose breath is in his nostrils; for what account is to be made of him?" (ii. 20—22.)[b]

---

[a] See examples in i. 23, ii. 19, x. 18, xvii. 1, xxix. 9, xxxii. 18.

[b] See, also, v. 15, 16, x. 5—15.

Sometimes it is full of a high inspiration, but without fanaticism, as in iv. 2—6.[a]

There is but one parable in the book, and that is successful, (v. 1—6.)

There is but one vision, (chap. vi.,) and that is simple and sublime. It contains but few symbolical actions, and these are performed without any pretension, (viii. 1—3, xx.) The somewhat enigmatical sign (vii. 14) was probably suited to the circumstances of the time—"Behold, the damsel shall conceive and bear a son, and she shall call his name Immanuel," &c.

The spurious passages also — in particular, xiii. xiv. xl.—lxvi. — deserve great praise on account of their lively and flowing style, — which is sometimes lyric, — (lxiii. 7—lxiv. 12,) and of their beautiful and often sublime thoughts, (xl. 15—17, lv. 8, 9, and lxvi. 1, 2.)

Sometimes the thoughts are free and bold, as in lviii. 3—17, where *real* and not *formal* holiness is commended; but verse 13 enjoins the *formal* observance of the Sabbath. In lxvi. 21, the poet says, priests and Levites shall be taken, not from one tribe, but from all nations. But, in general, the spurious parts are destitute of the powerful dignity of the genuine Isaiah, and the depraved, sunken taste they display cannot be denied.[b]

---

[a] See i. 27, sq., and xxviii. 16, sqq., xi. 1—16, and xxxii. 16—18.

[b] There is an apocryphal book of Isaiah, published with the title Ascensio Jesaiæ Vatis, Opusculum Pseudepigraphum, multis abhinc Seculis, ut videtur, deperditum, nunc autem apud Æthiopes repertum, cum Versione Lat. Anglicanaque publici Juris, factum a *Ricardo Laurence*; Oxon. 1819, 8vo. See *Gesenius*, l. c. vol. i. p. 47. *Nitzsch*, Examination of two Fragments of an old Latin Version of the *Ἀναβάτικον Ἡσαΐου*, in Stud. und Krit. for 1830, p. 209, sqq.

CHAPTER II.

JEREMIAH.[a]

§ 215.

HIS LIFE AND TIMES.

JEREMIAH of Anathoth (i. 1) was the son of Hilkiah the priest, who, as Eichhorn thinks, is mentioned in 2 Kings xxii. 4, though Jahn maintains another Hilkiah is there spoken of.[b] He prophesied from the thirteenth year of Josiah (i. 2, 3) to the destruction of the kingdom of Judah, — from 629 to 588 B. C., — and even after that event, or nearly half a century. (xl.—xlv.)

He lived in that eventful period when the feeble

---

[a] *Sanctii* Comm. in Jerem. Proph. et Thren.; Lug. Bat. 1618, fol.
Joa. Œcolampadii Comm. in Jerem. et Thren.; Arg. 1530, fol.
Joa. Piscatoris Comm. in Jerem.; Herb. 1614.
Seb. Schmid. Comm. in Jerem.; Frcf. 1685, 2 vols. 4to.
Jo. Clerici Comment. in Proph.
Herm. Venemæ Comment. in Librum Prophet. Jerem.; Leov. 1765, 2 vols. 4to.
Benj. Blayney's Jeremiah and Lamentations; a new Translation, with Notes, critical, phil. and explanatory; Lond. 1784, 4to.
J. D. Michaelis, Observatt. philol. et crit. in Jerem. Vaticinia et Thren. Ed. *J. F. Schleusner*; Gott. 1793, 4to.
Chr. F. Schnurrer, Observatt. ad Vatic. Jeremiæ, 4 Dissert.; Tüb. 1793—1797, 4to. in Commentatt. theol., ed. *Velthusen* et al. vol. iii.
Hensler, Bemerkk. üb. Stellen in Jerem. Weissagg.; Lpz. 1805.
Rosenmülleri Scholia in Jerem. *Maurer*, l. c.
Spohn, Jeremias Vates e Vers. Jud. Alexandr. ac Reliqu. Interpr. Græc. emendatus Notisque crit. illustratus; Lips. 1794, 1824, 2 vols.
F. C. Movers, De utriusque Recensionis Vet. Jeremiæ, Græcæ Alexand. et Heb. Masoret. Indole et Origine, Com. Crit.; 1837. [*Hitzig*, Der Prophet Jeremia; Lpz. 1841, (pt. iii. of Exegetische Handbuch, zur. A. T.)]

[b] *Eichhorn*, § 535. *Jahn*, vol. ii. p. 540. [See *Knobel*, vol. ii. p. 253, sqq.]

kingdom of Judah, torn asunder by inward disorders, must necessarily fall a sacrifice in the collision of the two prevailing powers, Babylon and Ægypt. His efforts, by wise counsel, to retard the destruction of his earnestly-beloved country, were rewarded by his corrupt contemporaries with ingratitude, and even with a prison, and attempts to murder. He himself complains touchingly of his treatment.

Chap. xv. 10.

"Alas for me, my mother, that thou hast borne me,
To live in strife and contention with all the land!
I have neither borrowed nor lent money,
Yet doth every one curse me."

Chap. xi. 19.

"I...... knew not that they had formed plots against me,
[Saying,] 'Let us destroy the tree with its fruit,
Let us cut him off from the land of the living,
That his name may no more be remembered.'"[a]

When he was set free by Nebuchadnezzar, he preferred to dwell among the ruins of his native land, (xxxix. 11, sqq., xl. 1, sqq.,) but followed the relics of the people in their flight to Ægypt, though he had spoken against it. (xlii. xliii.) Here he probably ended his life.

§ 216.

CONTENTS OF THE BOOK.

Besides prophecies, this book contains also historical accounts, and may be divided into two parts:—

[a] See, also, xii. 5, 6, xvi. 18, sqq., xviii. 18, sqq., xix. 7, sqq., xx. xxvi. 7, sqq., xxxii. 2, xxxvi. 26, xxxvii. 13, sq., xxxviii. See the stories about Jeremiah, in 2 Maccabees, ii. 1—7. *Fabricius*, Cod. Pseudepigraphus, V. T p. 1111. *Carpzov*, l. c. p. 130. *Bertholdt*, p. 1415, sq.

I. *Domestic Prophecies and History.*—1. Till the destruction of Jerusalem, (i.—xxxix.)—2. After that event, before and after the flight to Ægypt, (xl.—xlv.)

II. *Prophecies relating to Foreign Nations*, (xlvi.—li.) An appendix (lii.) relates the history of the last king, Zedekiah.

The prophecies of the first part (i.—xxxix.) relate mostly to the destruction of Judah, then threatened by Babylon. The prophet sees this continually approaching, and admonishes the people to avert it, by a penitent and humble submission to the will of Jehovah, who gives the dominion to the Chaldeans.

The prophet's reproaches, lamentations, and threats, are rarely interrupted by more cheerful views, but such occur in xxx. xxxi. and xxxiii. The prophecies of the second part (xl—xlv.) are directed against the flight to Ægypt, against Ægypt itself, and the Jews who dwelt there. The foreign prophecies in xlvi.—xlix. relate mostly to the victories of Nebuchadnezzar. But in l.—li. the destruction of the haughty Babylon itself is threatened.

§ 217, *a*.

SPURIOUSNESS OF PARTS OF THE BOOK.

Since some larger and smaller paragraphs have been inserted in the text,[a] so likewise some false inscriptions have been added. Thus, for example, to judge from xxvi. 1, the inscription in xxvii. 1, is false—"In the beginning of the reign of *Jehoiakim*, ... came this word unto Jeremiah." It should be Zedekiah.[b]

---

[a] § 218.

[b] [Verses 3, 12, 20, are against the time of Jehoiakim. *Leclerc* would

In xlvii. 1, the date — "before Pharaoh smote Gaza" — is false; for in this chapter the author predicts the destruction of the Philistines by a people from the north, (verse 2,) and not by the Ægyptians.[a]

The hard construction — "The word of Jehovah, that came to Jeremiah"[b] — which occurs in xiv. 1, xlvi. 1, and xlix. 34, but never in the Septuagint — seems to be the work of some foreign hand. Since the oracle, (xlix. 34—39,) to judge from the analogy of the others, against the same people, seems to belong to the fourth year of Jehoiakim, therefore it appears that the date is false in verse 34 — "in the beginning of the reign of Zedekiah." It seems the original inscription was "concerning Elam,"[c] which is still preserved in the Septuagint.[d] The date (i. 2, 3) — from the thirteenth of Josiah to the eleventh of Zedekiah — does not include the oracles in xl.—xliv., but belongs to an earlier collection; or else it originated in a mistake. Perhaps it was interpolated, because it applies to the last chapter of Jeremiah.

Jeremiah cannot be the author of lii.; for in verse 31, sqq., events are related which took place after Jeremiah's

---

insert צדקיהו אָחִי before Jehoiakim. The contents of the chapter hardly agree with the *first* year of Zedekiah. *Hitzig*, in loc.] The Seventy have merely *οὕτως εἶπε κύριος.*

[a] Here the Seventy have simply *ἐπὶ τοὺς ἀλλοφύλους τάδε λέγει κύριος.*

[b] אשר היה דבר יי״.

[c] לעילם, *τὰ Αἰλάμ.*

[d] *Movers* (l. c. p. 35) explains the circumstance that the masoretic inscription of xlix. 34—39, is in the Seventy found at the end of the oracle, by the hypothesis that some one added the collection in xxvii.—xxix. to the original collection of oracles against foreign parts, [xlvi.—xlviii.,] but that another man afterwards separated these three chapters (xxvii.—xxix.) therefrom, and left the inscription of xxvii. remaining. On other inscriptions, probably added later, see *Movers*, l. c. p. 24.

time.[a] The whole passage, with the exception of verses 28—30, — which are not in the Septuagint, — is borrowed from 2 Kings xxiv. 18—xxv. 30, and interpolated here.

There are two interpolations in l. li., namely, l. 39—46, and li. 15—19. The first is borrowed from Isaiah, and other parts of Jeremiah : —

Jer. l. 39—46. "Therefore the wild beasts of the desert, with the wild beasts of the islands, shall dwell there, and the owls shall dwell therein : and it shall be no more inhabited forever ; neither shall it be dwelt in from generation to generation. As God overthrew Sodom and Gomorrah and the neighbor cities thereof, saith the Lord, so shall no man abide there, neither shall any son of man dwell therein.

"Behold, a people shall come from the north, and a great nation, and many kings shall be raised up from the coasts of the earth. They shall hold the bow and the lance : they are cruel, and will not show mercy : their voice shall roar like the sea, and they shall ride upon horses, every one put in array, like a man to the battle, against

Isa. xxxiv. 14. "The wild beasts of the desert shall also meet with the wild beasts of the island, and the satyr shall cry to his fellow ; the screech-owl also shall rest there, and find for herself a place of rest."

Chap. xiii. 19—21. "And Babylon, the glory of kingdoms, the beauty of the Chaldees' excellency, shall be as when God overthrew Sodom and Gomorrah. It shall never be inhabited, neither shall it be dwelt in from generation to generation : neither shall the Arabian pitch tent there ; neither shall the shepherds make their fold there : but wild beasts of the desert shall lie there ; and their houses shall be full of doleful creatures ; and owls shall dwell there, and satyrs shall dance there."

Jer. xlix. 18. "As in the overthrow of Sodom and Gomorrah

---

[a] [It relates, in part, what Jeremiah had treated of elsewhere, (xxxix. xl. ;) in part, what took place at Babylon, while Jeremiah was in Ægypt, whence he never returned ; and, in part, what took place in the time of Evil-merodach, when, it is probable, Jeremiah was not alive. The subscription (li. 64) — "Thus far the words of Jeremiah" — shows that his genuine books were supposed to end there. See also *Hitzig*, l. c. p. 415, sqq.]

thee, O daughter of Babylon. The king of Babylon hath heard the report of them, and his hands waxed feeble: anguish took hold of him, and pangs as of a woman in travail. Behold, he shall come up like a lion from the swelling of Jordan unto the habitation of the strong: but I will make them suddenly run away from her: and who is a chosen man, that I may appoint over her? for who is like me? and who will appoint me the time? and who is that shepherd that will stand before me? Therefore hear ye the counsel of the Lord, that he hath taken against Babylon; and his purposes, that he hath purposed against the land of the Chaldeans: Surely the least of the flock shall draw them out: surely he shall make their habitation desolate with them. At the noise of the taking of Babylon the earth is moved, and the cry is heard among the nations."

and the neighbor cities thereof, saith the Lord, no man shall abide there, neither shall a son of man dwell in it."

Jer. vi. 22—24. "Thus saith the Lord, 'Behold, a people cometh from the north country, and a great nation shall be raised from the sides of the earth. They shall lay hold on bow and spear; they are cruel, and have no mercy; their voice roareth like the sea, and they ride upon horses, set in array as men for war against thee, O daughter of Zion. We have heard the fame thereof: our hands wax feeble: anguish hath taken hold of us, and pain, as of a woman in travail."

Chap. xlix. 19—21. "Behold, he shall come up like a lion from the swelling of Jordan against the habitation of the strong: but I will suddenly make him run away from her: and who is a chosen man, that I may appoint over her? for who is like me? and who will appoint me the time? and who is that shepherd that will stand before me? therefore hear the counsel of the Lord that he hath taken against Edom; and his purposes that he hath purposed against the inhabitants of Teman: Surely the least of the flock shall draw them out: surely he shall make their habitations desolate with them. The earth is moved at the noise of their fall; at the cry, the noise thereof was heard in the Red Sea."

The second is borrowed from earlier passages in Jeremiah:—[a]

Jer. li. 15—19. "He hath made the earth by his power, he hath established the world by his wisdom, and hath stretched out the heaven by his understanding. When he uttereth his voice, there is a multitude of waters in the heavens; and he causeth the vapors to ascend from the ends of the earth: he maketh lightnings with rain, and bringeth forth the wind out of his treasures. Every man is brutish by his knowledge; every founder is confounded by the graven image: for his molten image is falsehood, and there is no breath in them. They are vanity, the work of errors: in the time of their visitation they shall perish. The Portion of Jacob is not like them: for he is the former of all things: and Israel is the rod of his inheritance: The Lord of hosts is his name."	Jer. x. 12—16. "He hath made the earth by his power, he hath established the world by his wisdom, and hath stretched out the heavens by his discretion. When he uttereth his voice, there is a multitude of waters in the heavens, and he causeth the vapors to ascend from the ends of the earth; he maketh lightnings with rain, and bringeth forth the wind out of his treasures. Every man is brutish in his knowledge: every founder is confounded by the graven image: for his molten image is falsehood, and there is no breath in them. They are vanity, and the work of errors: in the time of their visitation they shall perish. The Portion of Jacob is not like them: for he is the former of all things; and Israel is the rod of his inheritance: The Lord of hosts is his name."

The passage, li. 44—48,[b] which is omitted by the Seventy, is probably spurious; for the supposition in l. 28, li. 11, 51, that the temple is destroyed, and the long duration of the Babylonian exile, in l. 33, do not agree with the date given in li. 59, 63, 64, although we find

---

[a] *Movers*, l. c. p. 16. See doubts on the genuineness of this passage in *Eichhorn*, § 542, *a*. *Von Cöllen*, in A. L. Z. Erganz. Blat. for 1828, xvi. p. 118. *Gramberg*, l. c. vol. ii. p. 396, sqq., and the 4th edition of this work. *Knobel* (vol. ii. p. 353, sqq.) ascribes it to Baruch.

[b] From גַּם־, in verse 44, to 48

obviously the expressions and turns of the prophet Jeremiah;[a] yet there are, likewise, the peculiarities of the pseudo Isaiah.[b] Therefore it may be conjectured that this portion of the prophet has been wrought over by some later hand.

§ 217, *b*.

THE SAME SUBJECT CONTINUED.

The following chapters (xxx. xxxi. and xxxiii.) have been wrought over by the pseudo Isaiah, as it appears from the following considerations: —

1. The following passage, in Zech. viii. 7, 8, refers to Jer. xxxi. 7, 8, 33.

Zech. viii. 7, 8. "Thus saith the Lord of hosts, 'Behold, I will save my people from the east country and from the west country; and I will bring them, and they shall dwell in the midst of Jerusalem: and they shall be my people, and I will be their God, in truth and in righteousness.'"

Jer. xxxi. 7, 8, 33. "For thus saith the Lord, 'Sing with gladness for Jacob, and shout among the chief of the nations: publish ye, praise ye, and say, "O Lord, save thy people, the remnant of Israel."

---

[a] Jer. l. 3 = ix. 9; l. 4 = iii. 18, 21; l. 5 = xxiii. 1, sqq.; l. 7 = ii. 3; l. 13 = xlix. 17, xix. 8, xviii. 15; l. 16 = xlvi. 16; l. 19 = xxiii. 3; l. 20 = xlix. 26; l. 32 = xlix. 27, xxi. 14, xvii. 27; li. 7 = xxv. 16; li. 8 = xlvi. 11, viii. 22; li. 14, 27 = xlvi. 23; li. 25 = xxi. 13, xxiii. 30, 31; li. 24, 27 = ii. 15, &c.; li. 43 = xlix. 33.

[b] קדש ישראל; l. 29, li. 5. גאל; l. 34. (Comp. Isa. xli. 14, xlvii. 4.) נשבע בזרוע, ὤμοσε κατὰ τοῦ βραχίονος; li. 14. Comp. Isa. lxii. 8; l. 17, 33. Comp. Isa. lii. 4, l. 8, li. 69. Comp. Isa. lii. 11; xlviii. 20, li. 5. Comp. Isa. liv. 4; l. 33. Comp. Isa. xiv. 17. See *Movers*, p. 45. He has not cited all these passages, but some which he has adduced seem unsatisfactory to me. In xlviii., especially verses 24—38, 40, 43, 44—47, he finds additions from Isa. xv. xvi., and burdens that prophet with the mistakes in verse 32. [See *Hitzig*, l. c. p. 375, sqq.]

Behold, I will bring them from the north country, and gather them from the coasts of the earth, and with them the blind and the lame, the woman with child and her that travaileth with child together: a great company shall return thither....... But this shall be the covenant that I will make with the house of Israel; after those days, saith the Lord, I will put my law in their inward parts, and write it in their hearts, and will be their God, and they shall be my people.'"

Now, the former passage appears as an exclamation of the prophets who prophesied at the founding of the temple. Zechariah did not regard it as a prophecy of Jeremiah.[a]

2. The style is like that of the pseudo Isaiah.[b]

3. Chap. xxxiii. is connected to chap. xxx. xxxi. by the similarity of its contents; it carries out what is said in xxxi. 31. Zechariah (viii. 16—19) alludes to "Peace and Truth,"[c] in Jer. xxxiii. 6, and therefore must have read this chapter in connection with the others. (xxx. xxxi.)

4. Here (xxxiii.) we find the style of the pseudo Isaiah.[d]

---

[a] [This argument has little force in itself. The later prophet may have borrowed from the other without acknowledgment, or even without remembering he had borrowed at all.]

[b] Comp. Jer. xxx. 10, 11, with Isa. xli. 8, 10, 14, xliii. 1, xliv. 1, sq. Since xxx. 10, 11, is wanting in the LXX., and xlvi. 27, 28, — containing the same words, — occurs in both masoretic and Alexandrian text, *Movers* (p. 44) has concluded that it was an interpolation in xxx. 10, 11. (Comp. Jer. xxx. 17, with Isa. lx. 15, and lxii. 4; xxxi. 13, with Isa. xlix. 13, and elsewhere; xxxi. 3, with Isa. xliii. 4; xxxi. 8, with Isa. xliii. 5, xlix. 12, lix. 19; xxxi. 9, with Isa. lxiii. 16, lxiv. 7, lv. 12, xlix. 10, lxiii. 13; xxxi. 10, with Isa. xl. 11; xxxi. 10, sq., with Isa. xlix. 1, xliv. 23, xlviii. 20, &c.) The use of ארים and גאל deserves particular notice. Comp. xxxi. 12, with Isa. lviii. 11; xxxi. 21, with Isa. lxii. 10; xxxi. 33, with Isa. li. 7; verse 34 with Isa. liv. 13, xliii. 25; verses 35, 36, with Isa. lxi. 8; verses 35, 37, with Isa. xlii. 5, xlv. 7, li. 15.

[c] שלום ואמת.

[d] Comp. xxxiii. 2, with Isa. xlvi. 11, xliii. 7, 8; verse 3 with Isa. xlviii. 6.

5. The introduction of the Levites (xxxiii. 18, 21) is unsuitable,[a] and does not correspond with the views of Jeremiah. In fine, xxxiii. 24, seems to apply to the Samaritans

However, the stand-point of the writer (xxx. 5—7, xxxiii. 4, 5) agrees with Jeremiah's time. I cannot, with Movers, find the condition of the returning exiles depicted in xxx. 5—7; and in xxxiii. 4, 5 I find no trace of the pseudo Isaiah. His rejection of the inscription of these two chapters seems, also, too hasty. In many passages, the style of Jeremiah is so obvious that it cannot be mistaken.[b]

§ 217, *c*.

THE SAME SUBJECT CONTINUED.

Chap. x. 1—16, when purified from the additions made to the masoretic text, which are not in the Septuagint, (x. 6—8, 10,) is entirely the work of the pseudo Isaiah. This appears from the following considerations: —

1. There are warnings against the soothsaying and idolatry of the heathens.

---

[a] The expression לֹא יכרת איש (verse 18) is imitated from the earlier passages. In verse 21, the construction is forced, and the parallelism disturbed.

[I must confess that I cannot see the force of the above arguments, either to prove the authorship upon the pseudo Isaiah, or to sustain the spuriousness of the passage.]

[b] Comp. xxx. 6, with xlvi. 5, ii. 14; verse 11 with v. 10, 18; verse 12 with xv. 18, x. 19; verse 13 with xlvi. 11; verse 17, and xxxiii. 6, with viii. 22; xxxi. 4, 21, with xviii. 13; verse 28 with l. 10, 11; xxxiii. 4, with xix. 12; verse 11 with vii. 34, xxv. 10, xvi. 11; verse 15 with xxii. 15, xxiii. 5.

Chap. x. 2—5.

2 "Thus saith Jehovah,
'Conform ye not to the way of the heathen,
And be not dismayed at the signs of the heavens,
Because the heathen are dismayed at them!
3 The customs of the nations are vanity.
For a tree of the wood is cut down,
It is wrought by the hands of the artificer with the axe,
4 It is decked with silver and gold,
And with nails and with hammers is it fastened,
That it may not totter.
5 They are like a pillar, and cannot speak;
They must be borne by men, for they cannot walk.
Be not afraid of them, for they cannot hurt,
Nor is it in their power to do good.'"

Verse 11 is in Chaldee.[a] These circumstances show that the writer lived during the exile.

2. The style is that of the pseudo Isaiah.[b]

According to Movers, chap. xxvii.—xxix. have been wrought over anew by some later hand. This appears from the later form of some names,[c] the frequent addition of the term *the prophet*, before proper names, (xxviii. 5, 6, 10—12, 15, xxix. 1, [xxviii. 17,]) which is wanting in the Septuagint, and, above all, from the following interpolations:—

---

[a] According to *Houbigant*, *Venema*, *Rosenmüller*, *Maurer*, this is spurious. This opinion is necessary on the supposition that Jeremiah is the author, and that verses 6—8, 10, belong in the text. But, on the above hypothesis, it agrees well with the connection, and is required by verse 15.

[b] Comp. verse 2 with Isa. xlvii. 13; verse 3 with Isa. xliv. 12; verse 4 with Isa. xl. 19, 20, xli. 7, xliv. 12, xlvi. 7; verse 5 with Isa. xlvi. 1, xli. 23, xliv. 9; verse 11 with Isa. lx. 12; verses 12, 13, with xlii. 5, xliv. 24, li. 13; verse 14 with Isa. xliv. 11, xlv. 16, xlii. 17, xli. 29, xliv. 21. In verse 16, יצר is like Isa. xlv. 7. Comp. also Isa. lxiii. 17, xlvii. 4, xlviii. 2, li. 15, liv. 5. However, בעת פקדתם is Jeremianic. (viii. 12.) Comp. vi. 18 [See *Hitzig*, l. c. p. 80, sqq., and 238, sqq., who favors the above view of *De Wette* and *Movers*.]

[c] ירמיה, צדקיה, יכניה, and others.

Chap. xxvii. 7, 16—22. "And all nations shall serve him, [Nebuchadnezzar,] and his son, and his son's son, until the very time of his land come: and then many nations and great kings shall serve themselves of him. Also I spake to the priests and to all this people, saying, 'Thus saith the Lord, "Hearken not to the words of your prophets, that prophesy unto you, saying, 'Behold, the vessels of the Lord's house shall now shortly be brought again from Babylon; for they prophesy a lie unto you.' Hearken not unto them; serve the king of Babylon, and live: wherefore should this city be laid waste?" But if they be prophets, and if the word of the Lord be with them, let them now make intercession to the Lord of hosts, that the vessels which are left in the house of the Lord, and in the house of the king of Judah, and at Jerusalem, go not to Babylon.

"'For thus saith the Lord of hosts concerning the pillars, and concerning the sea, and concerning the bases, and concerning the residue of the vessels that remain in this city, which Nebuchadnezzar king of Babylon took not, when he carried away captive Jeconiah the son of Jehoiakim king of Judah from Jerusalem to Babylon, and all the nobles of Judah and Jerusalem; yea, thus saith the Lord of hosts, the God of Israel, concerning the vessels that remain in the house of the Lord, and in the house of the king of Judah and of Jerusalem, "They shall be carried to Babylon, and there shall they be until the day that I visit them, saith the Lord; then will I bring them up, and restore them to this place."'"

Verse 7 is entirely wanting in the Septuagint. It is obviously a later addition, for it is designed to show that the Babylonian captivity should continue under the son and grandson of Nebuchadnezzar, and the Chaldeans are threatened with subjugation by the Persians. But this is done also in xxv. 14. In xxvii. 16—22, according to the Seventy, Jeremiah contradicts the false prophets, who predict that the vessels of the temple, which had been carried away, should be brought back, and adds that the remaining vessels should, likewise, be carried away. According to the masoretic text, the false prophets predict that these vessels should *now*, *immediately*, be returned; and Jeremiah says, on the contrary, that the remaining vessels should also be carried away, but, *at some time*, should be restored. Thus the masoretic text preserves the veracity of the prophet, who, according to the Alexandrian text, seemed more in error than the false prophets.[a]

§ 218, *a*.

MASORETIC AND ALEXANDRIAN RECENSION.

In the Alexandrian version, the prophecies against foreign nations have a place by themselves, and are collected together after xxv. 13. But their order is different from that of the masoretic text, as may be seen in the table below.[b]

---

[a] *Movers* considers the prolixity of verse 18 a mark of its spuriousness. The masoretic certainly seems not the genuine text; but the Alexandrian also seems imperfect. What does this mean, in verse 18, — *ἀπαντησάτωσάν μοι?* Even if this be a poor translation, instead of *απαντ, τῷ κυρίῳ* = יפגעו ביהוה, still it is, in this connection, without a proper sense.

[b]

Alexandrian Version.	Masoretic Text.
Chap. xxv. 34—39,	xlix. 34—39.
—— xxvi. 1—11,	xlvi. 2—12.
—— xxvi. 12—26,	xlvi. 13—28.
—— xxvii. xxviii.,	l. li.
—— xxix. 1—7,	xlvii. 1—7.
—— xxix. 8—22,	xlix. 7—22.
—— xxx. 1—5,	xlix. 1—6.
—— xxx. 6—11,	xlix. 28—33.
—— xxx. 12—16,	xlix. 23—27.
—— xxxi.,	xlviii.
—— xxxii.,	xxv. 15—38.
—— xxxiii.—li.,	xxvi.—xlv.
—— lii.,	lii.

§ 218, *b*.

THE SAME SUBJECT CONTINUED.

The two texts stand in the following relation to one another: —

1. The Alexandrian version has short passages, that are taken from the context, near or remote, or from parallel passages, and which have been added to explain the text, or make it complete. They are not in the masoretic text. Examples of this may be seen below.[a]

2. The masoretic text has yet more numerous additions of this sort, which are not in the Septuagint.[b]

---

[a] Chap. xxiv. 6, *εἰς ἀγαθά*, is repeated; xxix. 22, *ἐποίησε*, from the preceding. Chap. i. 17, *ὅτι μετὰ σοῦ εἰμι*, taken from verses 8, 19. Chap. xxviii. 10, *ἐν ὀφθαλμοῖς παντὸς τοῦ λαοῦ*, from verse 1, 5, 11. Chap. xlvii. 12, *καὶ ἔλαιον*, from verse 10. Chap. xxxii. 25, *καὶ ἔγραψα*, &c., from verse 10, 12. Chap. ix. 14, *τῆς κακῆς*, from iii. 17, vii. 14, &c. Chap. iii. 18, *καὶ ἀπὸ πασῶν τῶν χωρῶν*, from xvi. 15. Chap. ii. 28, *καὶ κατ' ἀριθμὸν*, &c., from xi. 13, et al.

[b] Chap. i. 13, אני ראה, from verse 11. Chap. iii. 10, אחותה, from verse 7. Chap. iii. 11, משבה, from verses 6, 8, 12. Chap. vii. 10, חזה, from verse 11. Chap. vii. 27, ולא ישמעו······יענוכה, from verses 13, 26. Chap. xi. 22, לכן כה אמר וג״, from verse 21. Chap. xiii. 4, אשר קנית, from verses 1, 2. Chap. xxviii. 11, "within two years," from verse 3. Chap. xxviii. 15, "hear now, Hananiah," from verse 7. [?] Chap. xxviii. 17, "the same year," from verse 16. Chap. xxxii. 7, הגאלה, from verse 8. Verse 9, "in Anathoth," from verses 7, 8. Chap. xxxvi. 22, "in the ninth month," from verse 9. Verse 25, "Gemariah," from verse 12. Verse 28, "the king of Judah," from verse 30. Chap. xxxviii. 6, 11, "with cords," from verse 12. [?] Verse 11, בידו, from verse 10. [?] Verse 17, "princes of the king of Babylon," from verse 17, et al. Very often the Hebrew text has "sword, famine, and pestilence," where the LXX. have only "sword and famine," xxi. 9, xxvii. 8, 13, et al.; often it has the epithet הנביא, which is omitted by the LXX., except in xlii. 2, xliii. 6, xlv. 1, li. 59; it adds the epithet מבקשי נפשם to אויבים, xix. 9, xxxiv. 20, 21. This occurs three times in xix. 7, et al.; and the phrase "whereunto I have driven them," or "whereunto they are

3. Both texts have additions of this character, but in different places.[a]

4. The masoretic text has large additions that are spurious. Among these Movers reckons xxxix. 4—13, which, he thinks, has been taken from lii. 7—16.[b]

---

driven," in xxiii. 8, and three times in viii. 3, et al. We find, also, דרכיכם ומעלליכם, "*your ways and your deeds*," xviii. 11, xxiii. 22, xxxii. 20; here an addition has been made from xxvi. 13, et al. So, in xxxi. 28, an addition is made from i. 10, &c. &c. However, I am not convinced that all which the Hebrew has more than the LXX. is a spurious addition. Sometimes the reading of the masoretic text seems necessary; sometimes suitable, in the following examples: xiv. 3, xxv. 3, xxvii. 10, xxviii. 19, xxxvi. 6, (here הקראם demands אשר כתבת ...... דברי יהוה, which is omitted by the LXX.) xxxvi. 9, (where the LXX. have οἶκος Ἰούδα,) 15, 28, xlii. 22, xliv. 12. The same may be said of the repetition of standing phrases, such as "sword, famine, and pestilence."

[a] Thus, in xxix. 21, the Hebrew has, in addition, "who prophesy lies to you in my name," and verse 23, "lies;" the LXX., in xiv. 15, have ψευδῆ. In xlix. 24, the Hebrew has, "anguish and sorrow have seized her as a travailing woman;" the LXX., viii. 21, ὠδῖνες ὡς τικτούσης. In xxiv. 10, the Hebrew has, "and their fathers;" the LXX. have a similar addition in xvii. 23. In xliii. 2, the Hebrew has "proud" men, הזדים; the LXX., in xlii. 17, have πάντες οἱ ἀλλογενεῖς; (here they read זרים, for זדים.) נאם יהוה often occurs in the Hebrew, where it is omitted by the LXX.; sometimes they add it, as in ii. 2, and frequently. Instances like the above are numerous.

[b] His reasons, which are not satisfactory, are as follows: —

1. The connection between xxxix. 3, and 14, is disturbed by this insertion of 4—13. (But this is true only of the text of the LXX.)

2. It is false that Zedekiah fled as soon as he saw the Chaldee princes "in the middle gate," for, according to verse 1, they went there after they had taken the city. (But the sense of the Hebrew text is, they had previously *taken post* in the middle court.)

3. It is not true that Nebuzar-adan took Jeremiah out of the prison after the capture of the city, (excidium?) for Nebuzar-adan arrived later. (lii. 3. Comp. xl. 2.) (But xxxix. 8—10, parallel with lii. 12—16, places the arrival of Nebuzar-adan before that.)

4. This addition is derived from the later recension of chap. lii., and belongs to the time of Nehemiah, as it appears from the more modern readings; e. g. חרי, (verse 6,) for שרי, (lii. 10,) and רבי, (verse 13,) for שרי, (verse 3;) for the expression חרים was there used; (but it occurs also in 1 Kings xxi. 8, 11.) [However, see *Hitzig*, l. c. p. 318, sqq.]

Chap. xxxix. 4—13. "And it came to pass, that when Zedekiah the king of Judah saw them, and all the men of war, then they fled, and went forth out of the city by night, by the way of the king's garden, by the gate betwixt the two walls: and he went out the way of the plain. But the Chaldeans' army pursued after them, and overtook Zedekiah in the plains of Jericho; and when they had taken him, they brought him up to Nebuchadnezzar king of Babylon to Riblah in the land of Hamath, where he gave judgment upon him. Then the king of Babylon slew the sons of Zedekiah in Riblah before his eyes: also the king of Babylon slew all the nobles of Judah. Moreover he put out Zedekiah's eyes, and bound him with chains, to carry him to Babylon.

"And the Chaldeans burned the king's house, and the houses of the people, with fire, and brake down the walls of Jerusalem. Then Nebuzar-adan the captain of the guard carried away captive into Babylon the remnant of the people that remained in the city, and those that fell away, that fell to him, with the rest of the people that remained. But Nebuzar-adan the captain of the guard left of the poor of the people, which had nothing, in the land of Judah, and gave them vineyards and fields at the same time.

"Now Nebuchadrezzar king

Chap. lii. 7—16. "Then the city was broken up, and all the men of war fled, and went forth out of the city by night, by the way of the gate between the two walls, which was by the king's garden; (now the Chaldeans were by the city round about:) and they went by the way of the plain.

"But the army of the Chaldeans pursued after the king, and overtook Zedekiah in the plains of Jericho; and all his army was scattered from him. Then they took the king, and carried him up unto the king of Babylon to Riblah, in the land of Hamath; where he gave judgment upon him. And the king of Babylon slew the sons of Zedekiah before his eyes: he slew also all the princes of Judah, in Riblah. Then he put out the eyes of Zedekiah; and the king of Babylon bound him in chains, and carried him to Babylon, and put him in prison till the day of his death.

"Now, in the fifth month, in the tenth day of the month, which was the nineteenth year of Nebuchadrezzar king of Babylon, came Nebuzar-adan, captain of the guard, which served the king of Babylon, into Jerusalem, and burned the house of the Lord, and the king's house; and all the houses of Jerusalem, and all the houses of the great men, burned he with fire: and all the army of

of Babylon gave charge concerning Jeremiah to Nebuzar-adan the captain of the guard, saying, 'Take him, and look well to him, and do him no harm; but do unto him even as he shall say unto thee.'"

the Chaldeans, that were with the captain of the guard, brake down all the walls of Jerusalem round about. Then Nebuzar-adan the captain of the guard carried away captive certain of the poor of the people, and the residue of the people that remained in the city, and those that fell away, that fell to the king of Babylon, and the rest of the multitude. But Nebuzar-adan the captain of the guard left certain of the poor of the land for vine-dressers and for husbandmen."

Chap. viii. 10—12, he thinks, is derived from vi. 13—15; perhaps xi. 7, 8, from vii. 24, 25; xvii. 1—4, in part from xv. 13, 14, though this is doubtful; xxx. 10, 11, and xlviii. 45, sq., from Num. xxi. 28, xxiv. 17, and xxi. 29.[a]

§ 218, *c*.

THE SAME SUBJECT CONTINUED.

5. Both texts have additions designed to complete and embellish the sentence, which are not derived from any known source. They are more numerous in the masoretic text.[b] Some of these contain historical errors.[c]

---

[a] See § 217, *b*, p. 402, note *b*.

[b] E. g. xiv. 15, *ἀποθανοῦνται*; xvi. 4, *πεσοῦνται*; viii. 21, השברתי; xx. 9, בלבי; xxxv. 7, לא תטעו; v. 15, 16, "a mighty nation, an ancient nation …… their quiver an open sepulchre."

[c] E. g. xxxiv. 1, "all the kingdoms of the land of his dominion," instead of *καὶ πᾶσα ἡ γῆ τῆς ἀρχῆς αὐτοῦ*; xlvi. 5, "its kings," while Ægypt at that time had but *one* king. In x. 16, li. 19, the LXX. have the text, *οὐκ ἔστι τοι αὐτη μερὶς τῷ 'Ιακὼβ, ὅτι ὁ πλάσας τὰ παντα, αὐτὸς κληρονομία αὐτοῦ* —more correct than the Hebrew לא כאלה חלק יעקוב כי יוצר הכל הוא וישראל שבט נחלתו

6. Additions are sometimes found in the Hebrew text, and more rarely in the Alexandrian, which make the sense clear, or explain the matters of fact.[a] Some historical passages are furnished with such additions;[b] their late origin is shown by the use of such phrases as "king of Babylon," and "Nebuchadnezzar." (xxxvii. 1, xxvii. 20, and elsewhere.) Perhaps the names of the priests, *Seraiah* and *Zephaniah*, in lii. 24, are erroneous.[c] In xxv. 1, the addition, "The first year of Nebuchadnezzar," is of later origin.[d] Here belong the false inscriptions mentioned above.[e] In xxv. 9—14, the Hebrew text is furnished with many additions which are not in the Septuagint. They came from a later author, who wrought over the text, designing to make the prediction more clear.[f]

---

[a] E. g. xxxv. 5, אמר - אלהים; ix. 13, xix. 1, *εἶπε ...... πρός με*; xlviii. 4, השמיעו - זעקה, (here the later orthography is observable;) xliii. 2, מדבר שקר - אתה; the LXX. have merely *ψευδῆ*, as in xxxvii. 14.

[b] Chap. xl. 2—9, 11, 12, xli. 1—3, 6, 7, 9, 10, 13, 15, 16, xxxviii. 6—12, 14, 18, xxix. 2, הסריסים - שרי יהודה וירוש.

[c] Comp. 1 Ch. v. 41, Jer. xxix. 26. The names interpolated in xxvi. 22, betray themselves by the repetition of "to Ægypt," למצרים.

[d] The same may be said of lii. 12, xxxii. 1, where the LXX. have the same. In xlvii. 4, the additions כפתור and פלשתים disturb the sense: the simpler text of the LXX. gives a suitable sense — "Jehovah destroys the relics of the sea-coast." Comp. xxviii. 16, xxix. 32, v. 13, xxiii. 36.

[e] § 217, *a*.

[f] Verse 9, "Behold, I will send and take *all* the families of the north, *saith Jehovah, and to Nebuchadnezzar, the king of Babylon, my servant;*" verse 11, "*the king of Babylon;*" verse 12, "*to the king of Babylon, ... and the land of the Chaldeans;*" verse 14 is added entire, and is like the interpolation in xxvii. 7. (See § 217, *c*.) So, verse 26, מלך ששך וג״ is wanting in the LXX., and, indeed, the name *Sheshach* actually seems to be not *Jeremianic*. *Venema* has justly observed — though *Movers* has not — that verse 13, כל הכתוב בספר הזה, cannot have come from the hand of Baruch. In verse 18, הזה היום belongs also to the later additions.

§ 218, *d*.

THE SAME SUBJECT CONCLUDED.

7. In both the masoretic and Alexandrian text, we find in different places different readings, for the most part easier, or of an explanatory character.[a] Sometimes the Alexandrian readings are older than the masoretic.[b]

8. In both we find common variants, which arose from the repetition of a word or a letter, and the misconception of the sense, occasioned by that repetition,[c] or from the admission of glosses into the text.[d]

9. In chap. lii., the Seventy follow the text of 2 Kings xxv., which appears to be older than the masoretic text of Jer. lii.

These discrepances between the Hebrew and Greek text of Jeremiah may be traced at an early date. They are mentioned by Origen and Jerome.[e] From the char-

---

[a] E. g. xxii. 5, the LXX. have *ποιήσητε*, as if it were in Hebrew תעשר, according to verse 4, instead of תשמער; xxii. 22, עבדיך ועמך, as in iv. 21; xxi. 7, the LXX. have *ὁ οἶκος σου καὶ ὁ λαός σου.*

[b] E. g. ii. 18, *Γηῶν*, for שיחר [?]; li. 14, *ὤμοσε κύριος κάτα τοῦ βραχίονος αὐτοῦ*, instead of בנפשו; xliii. 13, *καὶ συντρίψει τοὺς στύλους Ἡλιουπόλεως*, (a mistranslation for *temple of the sun*,) *τοὺς ἐν Ὤν*, instead of ושבר את מצבות בית שמש אשר בארץ מצרים.

[c] There is such a mistake of the LXX. in ii. 2, 3. In xli. 9, בור גדול הוא, the letters הו were accidentally repeated, and the LXX. translated *φρέαρ μέγα τοῦτό ἐστιν*; from a misunderstanding of בור arose the masoretic reading, ביד גדליהו הוא.

[d] In this way, in xi. 13, מזבחות לקטר לבעל is added to מזבחות לבשת the LXX. have only *Βωμοὺς θυμιᾶν τῇ Βάαλ.* Comp. xliv. 3, vii. 24.

[e] *Origen*, Ep. ad Africanum: *Πολλὰ δὲ τοιαῦτα καὶ ἐν τῷ Ἰερεμίᾳ κα-*

acter of the variations above described, and from the literal fidelity of the version, it is plain these discrepances are not to be charged to the transcriber, as Grabe maintains,[a] nor to the translator, as others have thought.[b]

§ 219, *a.*

DIFFERENT EDITIONS AND COLLECTIONS OF THESE PROPHECIES.

According to Jer. xxxvi., — written in the fourth year of Jehoiakim,[c] — the previous oracles of the prophet were written down by Baruch,[d] and, when the first copy was burnt, they were written anew, and enlarged. The several parts of this collection are not arranged in chron-

---

τενοήσαμεν, ἐν ᾧ τὴν πολλὴν μετάθεσιν καὶ ἐναλλαγὴν τῆς λέξεως τῶν προφετευομένων εὕρομεν. *Jerome*, Procem. ad Com. in Jer.: Jeremiæ ordinem *librariorum errore* confusum, multaque quæ desunt, ex Hebraiis fontibus digerere, ordinare, deducere, et complere (censui,) ut novum ex veteri, verumque pro corrupto atque falsato prophetam teneas. Præf. in Jer.: Præterea ordinem visionum, qui apud Græcos et Latinos omnino confusus est, correximus.

[a] De Vitiis LXX. Interpret. p. 12, sqq.

[b] *Spohn*, Præf. ad Jerem. p. 7, sqq. *De Wette*, in the 4th edition of this work. For an example of the fidelity of the LXX., see xlii. 7. According to *Movers*, the translator has only made omissions from *ὁμοιοτέλευτον*, and misunderstanding. He gives no explanation of the difference between the Hebrew and Greek text in xlvi. 15, (Heb. xxvi. 15,) *διατί ἔφυγεν ἀπὸ σοῦ ὁ Ἄπις; ὁ μόσχος ὁ ἐκλεκτός σοῦ οὐκ ἔμεινεν.* I should rather ascribe these differences, and some others, to the translator. (See above, § 218, *a.* p. 406.)

[c] *Movers* (p. 34, note) thinks in verse 9 we must read *fifth* year, and not *fourth.*

[d] *Eichhorn* (§ 537) rightly maintains that Jeremiah dictated to Baruch from memory. *Bertholdt* (p. 1421) erroneously explains קרא (verse 18) by *reading* from what was written down before. It is contrary to verse 32 to suppose, as *Eichhorn* does, that Baruch wrote on separate leaves.

ological order, either in the masoretic or Alexandrian text.[a]

The following chapters seem to belong to the first collection: i.—xx.[b] xxvi. xxxv. xxxvi. xlv. xxv. 1—13. Here, the words "which Jeremiah hath prophesied against all the nations" seem to have made the transition to the oracles against foreign nations, (xxv. 15—38, xlvi.—xlix.,—in the Septuagint xxv. 34—xxxii. 38,)[c]

[a] TABLE OF THE PROPHECIES, WITH THEIR DATE.

Under Josiah.	*Under Jehoiakim.*	*Under Zedekiah.*	*After the Capture of the City.*
iii. 6—vi. 30.	xxv. 4th year of J.	xxi.	
		xxiv. beginning of Z.	xl.—xlii.
		xxvii. id., according to the true reading.	(xlvii.—xlix.)
	xxvi. beginning of J.	(xxxiv. in LXX.)	
	(xxxiii. in LXX.)	xxviii. 4th year of Z.	
	xxxv. 4th year of J.	(xxxv. in LXX.)	xliii. 8.
	(xlii. in LXX.)	xxix. beginning of Z.	(l. 8.)
	xxxvi. 4th year of J.	(xxxvi.)	In Ægypt.
	(xliii. in LXX.)	xxxii. 10th yr. of Z.	
	xlv. 4th year of J.	(xxxix.)	xliv.
	(li. in LXX.)	xxxiii.	(li.)
		(xl.)	
		xxxiv.	
		(xli.)	
		xxxvii.	
		(xliv.)	
		xxxviii.	
		(xlv.)	
		xxxix. 15.	
		(xlvi. 15.)	
		xlix. 34, (false.)	
		l. li. 4th year of Z.	
		(xxvii. sq.)	

[b] According to *Movers*, (Bonner Zeit. vol. xii. p. 98, sqq.) chap. i.—ix. belong in the time of Josiah; x. 17—xx. in that of the Ægyptian invasion. *Maurer* places ii. 1—iii. 5, vii.—ix. x. 17—25, xi. 1—17, xvi. 1—xvii. 18, xviii., in Jehoiakim's time; xiii., in Jehoiachin's; and xix. 1—13, in Zedekiah's time. See *Knobel*, vol. ii. p. 270, sqq.

[c] According to *Movers*, Isa. xxiii. belongs to Jeremiah, and to this date.

which likewise were uttered before that time — the fourth year of Jehoiakim.[a] The position of these prophecies against foreign nations in the book, is given more correctly in the Septuagint, but the arrangement in the masoretic text is the best; for, as the Ægyptians are mentioned first, (xxv. 19,) and Elam last, (verse 25,) so the oracle upon Ægypt should come first, (chap. xlvi.,) and that on Elam last. (chap. xlix.) The Alexandrian text places the oracle on Elam first, because that was of the greater interest when that version was made.

Chap. xxii.—xxiv. were written at the beginning of Zedekiah's reign, (xxiv. 1,) and published;[b] for Ezekiel was acquainted with chap. xxiii., and had reference to it in his similar prophecy, (chap. xxxiv.,) — though this may be questioned, — which was written after the destruction of the city. He was acquainted with Baruch's collection, as Movers concludes from the numerous parallels between that and Ezekiel.[c]

Chap. xxvii.—xxix. were written at the beginning of Zedekiah's reign; and, since they have passed through the hands of the redactor, it appears they were published separately.

Chap. xxx. xxxi. xxxiii. (according to xxx. 2) and l. li. (according to li. 60) form, likewise, separate books.

But if we remove the spurious additions from chap. xxv., (see above, § 218, *c*,) and leave verse 13, אשר דברתי עליה, remaining, then, according to his hypothesis, the logical connection would be lost; for these words would relate to chap. l. li., which do not belong to this collection, for they are of later origin, and belong to the 4th year of Zedekiah.

[a] Comp. xlvi. 2, xlv. 1, xxxvi. 32.

[b] But xxii. 1—19, must have been written in Jehoiakim's time, and xxii. 20—30, in Jehoiachin's. See *Maurer*, *Knobel*, and *Hitzig*, in locc.

[c] The most certain are Ezek. v. 12, vi. 11, 12, vii. 15, xii. 16, xiv. 21, (comp. Jer. xiv. 12, et al.,) xiii. 10, 16, (comp. Jer. vi. 14,) xvi. 51, (comp. Jer iii. 11,) xxiii. 11, (comp. Jer. iii. 7,) xxxiii. 4, (comp. Jer. vi. 17.)

Chap. xxi. xxxiv. xxxvii. xxxii. xxxviii.—xliv. were written before and after the destruction of Jerusalem, and published by Jeremiah in Ægypt.

It appears, then, that originally the Jeremianic prophecies were in six books.[a]

§ 219, *b*.

THE SAME SUBJECT CONTINUED.

According to Movers, these six different books of prophecies previously extant — with the exception of xxvii.—xxix. xxxi. xxxiii., which were unknown to Zechariah — were first collected into one book, soon after the exile, by the same author who compiled the books of Kings. This author wrote 2 Kings xxv. at the end of Jer. lii. Since the Talmud[b] declares that "Jeremiah wrote his book, the book of Kings, — that is, an ancient book of Kings, the source of our present books of Kings — and his Lamentations, and since there is a certain affinity between Kings and Jeremiah,[c] therefore it is probable that the same author compiled the Prophecies and Lamentations of Jeremiah, as well as the books of Kings;[d] that he originally placed the latter between the Prophecies and the Lamentations of Jeremiah; that afterwards the passages mentioned in Baba Bathra[e] were, for the first time, put between Jeremiah and Kings,[f] and, when the others were separated from the Prophecies, 2

---

[a] [1. Chap. i.—xx. xxvi. xxxv. xxxvi. xlv. xxv. 1—13. 2. Chap. xxv. 15—38, xlvi.—xlix. 3. Chap. xxii.—xxiv. 4. Chap. xxvii.—xxix. 5. Chap. xxx. xxxi. xxxiii. l. li. 6. Chap. xxi. xxxiv. xxxvii. xxxii. xxxviii.—xliv.]

[b] Baba Bathra, fol. 14, c. 1, vol. i. p. 31.

[c] See above, § 186, p. 251, sqq.

[d] "Fragmenta ספר מלכים."

[e] Fol. 14, c. 2, vol. i. p. 31.

[f] [*De Wette* says, "between *Samuel* and Jeremiah;" but this appears to be a misprint for *Kings*.]

Kings xxv. was allowed to remain at the end of Jeremiah. (lii.)[a]

§ 219, *c.*

THE SAME SUBJECT CONTINUED.

A second and complete collection of these Prophecies was afterwards made, distinguished by the insertion of xxxix. 4—13, which is derived from a later recension of lii.;[b] by the later recension of xxvii.—xxix. xxx. xxxi. xxxiii., which were then first added to the collection; and by numerous additions to the text, such as xlvi. 25, xlvii. 1, l. 28.[c] Nehemiah was the author of this collection, for xxxiii. 18, 23, refers to his time. 2 Macc. ii. 13, ascribes the collection of the Prophets to him, and the writer of the book of Chronicles—which Movers thinks was composed in his time—is actually acquainted with Jer. xxvii., with its present additions.[d]

He, or the previous compiler, used Baruch's collection as the basis of his work, but separated the predictions against foreign nations from chap. xxv., placed them at the end, and added thereto chap. l. li. He then inserted the other prophecies in chronological order, and according to a certain similarity of their contents, so that, in his arrangement, the domestic prophecies were together, (i.—xlvi.,) and foreign prophecies came afterwards. (xlv. —li.) At the same time, he made a recension of the text. For this purpose, he made use of an old copy of the

[a] The opinion of *Movers* is still obscure to me. Sometimes he says this passage (lii.) is added to Jeremiah from the books of Kings, (p. 64;) sometimes (p. 47) he seems to regard the passage in Jeremiah as original.

[b] See § 218, *b*, note *b*, p. 407.

[c] It would be more consistent to maintain that chap. l. and li. were also first added at this time. [?]

[d] Comp. 2 Ch. xxxvi. 20, 21, with Jer. xxvii. 7, and xxv. 13, 14.

Jeremianic writings, free from additions, and took from other manuscripts sometimes different readings, and marginal notes likewise, and sometimes such additions as l. 45—48. He found others, but did not insert them.

The author of the Alexandrian recension, which is not much later than the masoretic, adhered to the unchronological arrangement of this compiler, but left the prophecies against foreign nations in their former place. In the recension of the text, he pursued a similar plan; he also adopted some later additions into the text, but rejected many, and, for the most part, adhered to the old text.

§ 219, *d*.

THE SAME SUBJECT CONCLUDED.

The above hypotheses are far less admissible than the results of the preceding critical inquiries. There is but a feeble argument for supposing that the books of Kings and the prophecies of Jeremiah were collected by the same compiler. The use made of the statement in the Talmud is arbitrary; there is but a feeble reason for assuming that the compiler of Jeremiah's prophecies did not take chap. lii. from a contemporary work. The above conjectures do not explain why the Seventy, who left the prophecies against foreign nations in their former place, transposed xxv. 15, sqq.; nor why, if they had the old edition before them, they followed the masoretic recension in its false arrangement of the domestic prophecies.

There are other hypotheses, but they are still more improbable.[a]

---

[a] *Eichhorn* (§ 540) supposes there was an *old* collection of Jeremiah's

§ 220.

LITERARY CHARACTER OF THE PROPHECIES OF JEREMIAH.

In Jeremiah's prophecies, the spirit of his time and the condition of his people are faithfully reflected. His humor is sad, melancholy, and depressed. His thoughts

---

oracles, written on separate sheets, or leaves, which was circulated in Ægypt, and another and *later* edition — enlarged in some parts — that came into circulation in Babylon and Palestine. This hypothesis in an easy manner explains many variations from the Hebrew text; such, for example, as vii. 1, 2, xxv. 1, xxix. 1, xxv. 18, and others. But it does not account for the additions made in this version. The position of the oracles against foreign nations, considered as a whole, might have been changed by the caprice of some critic, who took occasion to make this change, from xxv. 13, and Ezek. xxv. sqq. This change would involve the omission of xxv. 14. The different arrangement of the separate chapters in this portion of the book might have been caused by an accidental confusion of the separate leaves on which it was written. But this whole hypothesis rests on the false supposition that the oracles were written on loose and separate sheets. And, besides, it is improbable for other reasons.

Bertholdt (p. 1457, sqq.) maintains that the book of Jeremiah originated out of *three compilations*, and *two loose* LEAVES. Chap. i.—xxiv. he calls Codex A. Chap. xlvi.—li. (in the Greek, xxv. 14—xxxii.) he supposes was compiled twice, a different arrangement being followed each time. These he calls Codex B. 1, and B. 2. Chap. xxvi.—xlvi., (with the omission of xxiii. 14—19,) and xxxix. 4—13, he calls Codex C. 1, but with these passages Codex C. 2. Chap. xxv. 15—38 (in Greek, xxxii.) he calls Codex D.; xxv. 1—13, with an amplification of verses 1—13, Codex E.; or the last two united, Codex F. In Palestine he supposes Codex A., F., C. 2, and B. 1, were united together in the order, A. F. C. 2, B. 1. And in Ægypt Codex A., E., B. 2, D., C. 1, were united in their order. At the same time, abbreviations and omissions were allowed to be made.

But this hypothesis is too artificial, and is, in part, very improbable also. It divides chap. xxv., which makes a whole by itself. It is improbable that chap. xxvi.—xlv. ever constituted an independent collection, since there is no inscription to this portion, which lends it the appearance of probability. This theory does not show why both of the collections, independently of one another, should contain the supplementary chapter lii. For it is an arbitrary supposition to maintain that it was first added to the Greek Jeremiah, after a comparison had been made with the Hebrew text. Besides, too much stress is laid on the statement of *Josephus*, Ant. x. 5, 1.

have no great elevation, and only attempt short, single flights. But he is not destitute of noble and liberal ideas, as in the following passages: —

> "And when ye shall have multiplied, and have increased in the land,
> Then shall ye no more speak of the ark of the covenant of Jehovah,
> Nor shall it come into your mind.
> None shall remember it;
> None shall care for it." (iii. 16.)

> "Thus saith Jehovah of hosts, the God of Israel,
> 'Add your burnt-offerings to your sacrifices,
> And eat ye flesh.
> For I spake not to your fathers, nor commanded them
> Concerning burnt-offerings and sacrifices,
> At the time when I brought them out of the land of Ægypt.
> But this command gave I unto them:
> "Hearken ...... to my voice,
> And I will be your God,
> And ye shall be my people;
> And walk ye in all the ways which I command you,
> That it may be well with you."'" (vii. 22, 23.)

> "This is the covenant I will make with the house of Israel:
> .... I will put my law into their inward parts,
> And upon their hearts will I write it ......
> And they shall teach no more
> Every man his neighbor and every man his brother,
> Saying, 'Know ye Jehovah;'
> For they shall all know me,
> From the least of them, even to the greatest of them, saith Jehovah." (xxxi. 31, sqq.)

But xxxiii. 18, differs from this: —

> "Neither from the priests and Levites
> Shall a man fail before me,
> To offer burnt-offerings, and to kindle meat-offerings,
> And to perform sacrifice continually."

He does not lack deep feeling: —

"For the wound of the daughter of my people is my heart wounded;
I mourn; amazement hath taken hold of me;
Is there no balm in Gilead?
Is there no physician there?
Why, then, are not the wounds of my people healed?
O that my head were waters,
And mine eyes a fountain of tears,
That I might weep day and night
For the slain of the daughter of my people." (viii. 21, sqq.)

Other instances may be seen in xiii. 17, and xxxi. 20.

His style is without uniformity or consistency in regard to expression and rhythm. It is unequal, frequently energetic and concise, especially in the first twelve chapters; but more frequently it is tedious, running out into flatness. It is full of repetitions, and fixed thoughts and expressions. But it is not without certain charms of its own. Jerome says of him, "As he is simple ...... and easy in his language, so is he the most profound in the majesty of his thoughts. ...... In language, he seems to be more rustic than Isaiah and Hosea, and some other prophets among the Hebrews, but in thought he is equal to them."[a] The style, with its alternations, now rising to rhythm, then sinking to prose, is attractive. It is like the flickering of a flame which finds not sufficient fuel. Sometimes whole passages are repeated;[b] sometimes images, thoughts, and

---

[a] *Jerome*, Com. in Jer. Proœm. ad lib. iv. [Some writers deny this alleged rusticity. See in *Carpzov*, l. c. p. 159, sqq. *Lowth*, De sac. Poes. Heb. Prælect. xxi.]

[b] Chap. viii. 10, sqq., (comp. vi. 13, sqq.,) ix. 8, (comp. v. 9,) xi. 12, sq., (comp. ii. 28,) xx. 12, (comp. ii. 20,) xxii. 4, (comp. xvii. 25,) xxiii. 7, sq., (comp. xvi. 14, sq.,) xxvi. 6, (comp. vii. 14,) xxx. 23, sq., (comp. xxiii. 19, sq.,) xxxiii. 25, sq., (comp. xxxi. 35, sq.,) xliii. 11, (comp. xv. 2,) xlvi. 28, (comp. xxx. 11.)

expressions.[a] Some of his expressions are circumlocutory, and some passages are so prolix as to become wearisome.[b]

The passages relating to foreign nations are distinguished by a more energetic tone, and by a more animated style, which has a tendency to rhythm, but also by borrowed passages, as the following parallels will show: —

Jer. xlviii. "CONCERNING MOAB."	Isa. xv. xvi. "CONCERNING MOAB."
3 "A cry is heard from Horonaim.	5 "In the way of Horonaim they raise a cry of despair,
4 At the ascent of Luhith, Weeping goeth up after weeping.	4 For they ascend the heights of Luhith weeping.
37 Every head is bald, And every beard shorn, And upon the loins sackcloth.	2 On every head is baldness, And every beard is shorn. In their streets they gird themselves with sackcloth;
38 Upon all the house-tops of Moab, and in her streets, All is lamentation.	On the tops of their houses, and in their public walks, Every one howleth.
34 From wailing Heshbon to Elealeh, Even to Jahaz, is their voice heard, From Zoar even to Horonaim, As of a heifer three years old;	4 Heshbon and Elealeh utter a cry; Even to Jahaz is their voice heard. Fugitives wander to Zoar, Like a heifer of three years old;

[a] Chap. xxv. 10, (comp. xvi. 9, vii. 34;) xxiii. 15, (comp. viii. 14, ix. 14;) xlix. 22, 24, (comp. xxx. 6, xxii. 23, xiii. 21, vi. 24, iv. 31;) xxxii. 33, vii. 24, ii. 27; xliv. 4, xxxv. 15, xxix. 19, xxvi. 5, xxv. 4, vii. 25; xliv. 13, 18, xlii. 16, sq., xxxviii. 2, xxxiv. 17, xxxii. 36, xxix. 17, xxvii. 13, xxi. 7, 9, xviii. 21, xv. 2, xiv. 12, xliv. 22, xxvi. 3, xxv. 5, xxiii. 2, 21, xxi. 12, iv. 4; xxiii. 17, xviii. 12, xvi. 12, xi. 8, ix. 13, vii. 24, iii. 17; xlix. 37, xliv. 30, xxxiv. 20, xxi. 7. Comp. § 216, *b*.

[b] Chap. viii. 3, xxiv. 8, xxxix. 9; v. 17, viii. 1, sq., xvii. 25, sq., xxi. 5, 7, xxii. 25, xxiii. 37, sq., xxiv. 9, xxv. 18, xxvii. 9, xxix. 18, xxxi. 27, xxxii. 32, 44, xxxiii. 10, 13, xlii. 18, xliv. 9, 12. Comp. § 218, *b*.

For even the waters of Nimrim are desolate.
36 Therefore doth my heart sound like a flute for Moab,
And for the men of Kir-haresh ......
45 A fire is gone forth from Heshbon,
And a flame from the midst of Sihon,
Which devoureth the region of Moab,
And the heads of the sons of tumult.
Woe to thee, O Moab.
Undone is the people of Chemosh,
For thy sons are taken captives,
And thy daughters are captives."

6 For the waters of Nimrim are desolate.
11 Therefore shall my bowels sound like a harp for Moab,
And my heart for Kir-haresh."

Num. xxi. 28, sq.

"For there is a fire gone out of Heshbon,
A flame from the city of Sihon.
It hath consumed Ar of Moab,
And the lords of the high places of Arnon.
Woe to thee, Moab.
Thou art undone, O people of Chemosh.
He hath given his sons that escaped,
And his daughters into captivity."

Jer. xlix. 7—17.

"CONCERNING EDOM."

9 "If grape-gatherers had come upon thee,
Would they not have left some gleanings?
If thieves by night,
They would have destroyed only till they had enough.
14 I have heard a proclamation from Jehovah,
And an ambassador hath been sent among the nations,
[Saying,] 'Assemble yourselves and come against her,
And arise to battle.'

Obad. verses 1—6.

"CONCERNING EDOM."

"Have grape-gatherers come upon thee?
But would they not leave gleanings of the grapes?
Have thieves come upon thee? ......
Would they not cease stealing when they had enough?
We have heard a message from Jehovah,
And an ambassador hath been sent among the nations, [saying,]
'Arise ye, and let us arise against her to war.'

15 Behold, I will make thee small among the nations, Despised among men," &c.	Behold, I will make thee small among the nations; Thou shalt be greatly despised," &c.

Eichhorn[a] thinks the higher rhythmical tone which so strikingly pervades the oracles against foreign nations, arises from the prophet's copying the words of other writers. But perhaps it is better to explain it from the greater elevation of spirit which the subject brought with it. Besides, the discourse elsewhere rises to the same height, whenever he threatens in a decided manner. (v. vi.) His admonitions, on the contrary, usually sink down to prose. There are other imitations or reminiscences of older writers, — of Isaiah, Job, and the Psalms.[b]

In his visions, Jeremiah's use of symbols is poor and weak, and also in his frequent symbolical actions, (xiii. xviii. xix. 1—13, xxvii. xxxii. xxxv.,) which, for the most part, are fictitious. The last two alone are emphatic. The language bears the marks of its age, and is very much degenerated.[c]

---

[a] § 536.

[b] See *Jahn*, l. c. p. 559.

Comp. x. 12, with . . . . Ps. cxxxv. 7. [?]
—— x. 25, with . . . . Ps. lxxix. 6. [?]
—— ii. 21, with . . . . Isa. v. 2.
—— xv. 10, and xx. 14, with . . . . Job iii.
—— xlviii. 43, 44, with . . . . Isa. xxiv. 17, 18. [?]

[c] חֲמוּלָּה, for הֲמֻלָּה; xi. 16. כְּלִימָה, for כְּלִמָּה; li. 51. לוֹא, for לֹא. אוֹתְךָ, אוֹתָם, for אִתְּךָ, אִתָּם; i. 16, xix. 10, xx. 11. אַתְּי, for אַתְּ; iv. 30. לִמַּדְתְּי; ii. 33, (comp. iii. 4, 5, iv. 19, et al.) כִי, for ךְ; xi. 15. הָגְלָת; xiii. 19. אַשְׁכֵּים; xxv. 3. אוֹבִידָה; xlvi. 8. נִבֵּית, for נִבֵּאתָ; xxvi. 9. אֶתְנוּ, for אֶתִינוּ; iii. 22. Substantives in וּת, and ִית, as שְׁרִירוּת, תַּרְמִית. לְ sign of acc.; xl. 2. בָּרַר, גָּאַל, דָּאַב, כָּתַם, דָּיֵק, צְוָחָה, תִּפְלָה, &c. See *Aug. Knobel*, Jeremias Chaldaizans; Vratisl. 1831, 8vo. [*Knobel*, Heb. Proph. vol. ii. p. 264, sqq.]

CHAPTER III.

EZEKIEL.[a]

§ 221.

CIRCUMSTANCES OF HIS LIFE AND TIMES.

Ezekiel, son of the priest Buzi, and a younger contemporary of Jeremiah, was carried into exile by the Chaldeans, with King Jehoiachin, or Jechoniah, and a portion of the people. This took place eleven years before the destruction of Jerusalem. He was carried to Mesopotamia, to the River Chaboras.[b] According to i. 2, he was carried away in the first captivity, mentioned in 2 Kings xxiv. 14, sqq., and Jer. xxix. 2. Josephus erroneously says Ezekiel was carried away in the time of Jehoiakim.[c]

In the fifth year of his residence there, seven years

---

[a] *Joa. Œcolampadii* Comment. in Ezech.; Bas. 1543, fol.

Victorin. Strigelii Ezech. Proph. ad Hebr. Veritat. recogn. et Argumentis et Scholiis illustr.; Lips. 1564, 1575, 1579.

Casp. Sanctii Comm. in Ezech. et Dan.; Lug. Bat. 1619, fol.

Hieron. Pradi et *Jo. Bapt. Villalpandi* in Ezech. Explanatt. et Apparatus Urbis ac Templi Hieros. Commentariis illustratus; Rom. 1596—1604, 3 vols. fol.

Jo. Fr. Starkii Comm. in Ezech.; Frcf. 1731, 4to.

Herm. Venemæ Lectiones acad. ad Ezech. pt. i. c. i.—xxi. Præf. *Verschuir;* Leov. 1790, 4to.

Will. Newcome, An Attempt toward an Improved Version, a Metrical Arrangement, and an Explanation of the Prophet Ezekiel; Dubl. 1788, 4to.

Rosenmülleri Schol. in Ezech. *Maurer*, l. c. See the Elenchus Interprett. in *Rosenm.* Schol. in Ezech.

[b] [Here *Clemens* Alex. thinks he was visited by Pythagoras. Strom. i. p. 304, ed. *Sylburg*. See also *Huetius*, Demons. Ev.; Amst. 1680, Prop. iv vol. i. p. 131, sq., p. 78, sqq.]

[c] Ant. x. 6, 3.

before the destruction of Jerusalem, he appeared as a prophet, as he says in i. 1: "Now it came to pass in the thirtieth year [of Nabopolassar, 595 B. C.] . . . . . . I saw visions of God." So far as we know, he prophesied until about the twenty-seventh year of his captivity, that is, until the sixteenth year after the destruction of Jerusalem, (572 B. C.;) for this is the last date he mentions. (xxix. 17.)[a] It is not known whether he prophesied later or not, or when he closed his life.[b] He was held in much respect by the exiles, and afforded them a point of union. (vii. 1, xiv. 1, xx. 1.)

§ 222.

CONTENTS OF THE BOOK.

Ezekiel amongst the exiles, as Jeremiah at home, had to contend with the spirit of obstinacy and impatience, and vain hopes, which were nourished by the false prophets. (Jer. xxvii. xxix. Ezek. xiii.) His chief theme, (i.—xxiv.,) as well as that of Jeremiah, is the unavoidable destruction of Jerusalem, and the captivity of the people, which he represents as the well-merited punishment of the apostasy of Israel, and in particular of the idolatry which he so bitterly reproaches, (vi. viii. 9—18, xiv. 1—8, xx. xxiii.:) only once (xxi. 33—37) there is a threat against the Ammonites.

After several prophecies — some of which belong to a later period — against foreign nations, and respecting Nebuchadnezzar's victories, (xxv.—xxxii.,) the prophet continually applies himself to the circumstances of his

---

[a] *Rosenmüller*, in loc.

[b] See the apocryphal accounts respecting him in *Carpzov*, p. 200, and *Bertholdt*, p. 1479, sqq.

own nation; for the destruction of Jerusalem had taken place at that time. At first he threatens and punishes them, (xxxiii. xxxiv.;) afterwards he promises restoration and prosperity, (xxxvi. xxxvii.,) victory and vengeance upon their enemies. (xxxv. xxxviii. xxxix.) In a vision he sees the new temple, the new metropolis, and the establishment of the new state. (xl.—xlviii.) The book may, perhaps, be divided into three parts: —

1. Domestic prophecies before the destruction of Jerusalem. (i.—xxiv.)

2. Prophecies respecting foreign nations. (xxv.—xxxii.)

3. Domestic prophecies after the destruction of Jerusalem. (xxxiii.—xlviii.)

It is true the oracle against Edom (xxxv.) ought to stand in connection with chap. xxvi.; but it has a suitable place here where it stands, very much like that of Isaiah. (lxiii. 1—6.) Chapters xxxviii. and xxxix. have rather a reference to domestic than to foreign affairs, and therefore are properly connected with chap. xxxviii.

§ 223, *a*.

THE LITERARY AND PROPHETIC CHARACTER OF EZEKIEL.

Ezekiel's striking peculiarities are impressed upon the work from beginning to end. Oeder and Vogel have raised doubts respecting the genuineness of chap. xl.—xlviii., Corrodi against chap. xxxviii. xxxix., and an anonymous writer against the oracles relating to foreign nations.[a] But Eichhorn, Jahn, and Bertholdt, have replied

---

[a] Monthly Magazine for March, 1798. See *Gabler*, Neu. Theol. Journal,

satisfactorily to all these objections. The latter oracles, — those respecting foreign nations, — it is true, have this peculiarity, that they are without symbolism, and are written in a more poetical and learned style. Chap. xxvii., especially, is very learned.[a]

The most striking peculiarity is his Levitical spirit, which leads him to set a high value on religious ceremonies, as the following passages show:—

"Behold, I have never been polluted; for, from my youth until now, have I not eaten that which died of itself, or was torn in pieces, neither hath unclean food come into my mouth." (iv. 14.)

"I [Jehovah] would not bring them into the land flowing with milk and honey, the glory of all lands, because they despised my laws, and walked not in my statutes, but polluted my Sabbaths." (xx. 16.)

"I would scatter them among the nations, because they did not observe mine ordinances, but despised my statutes and polluted my Sabbaths, ... therefore I gave them statutes that were not good," &c. (verse 24.)

"Her priests . . . . . . make no distinction between the holy and profane, and show not the difference between the clean and the unclean, and they hide their eyes from my Sabbaths, and I am profaned among them." (xxii. 8, 26.)

Even in the formation of his ideals he cannot rise above these ceremonies, (xliii. 13, sqq., xliv.—xlvi.,) but insists strongly on the old ritual observances. But in xlvii. 22, he allows strangers to have an inheritance, as well as native Jews.[b] This adherence to the ritual and Levitical forms and ceremonies, is the cause of his want of depth and richness of mind, and his deficiency in great thoughts. However, there are ex-

---

vol. ii. p. 322, sqq. *Eichhorn*, § 548, sqq. *Jahn*, p. 594, sqq. *Bertholdt* p. 1491, sqq.

[a] See *Vogel*, Freie Untersuch, Büch. A. T. p. 344. *Corrodi*, Beleucht. d Gesch. d. Kanon, i. 95, sqq. *Gabler's* Neuest Theol. Journal, vol. ii. p. 322.

[b] See *Gramberg*, l. c. § 10, 27, 44.

ceptions to this rule, as may be seen in what follows: —

"Have I any pleasure at all that the wicked should die, saith Jehovah, and not that he should turn from his ways and live?" (xviii. 23.)

"I have no pleasure in the death of the wicked, but that the wicked turn from his way and live. Turn ye, turn ye, from your evil ways, for why will ye die?" (xxxiii. 11, and xxxvi. 26.)

His sense of duty is very deep and clear: —

"Speak thou my words to them, whether they will hear, or whether they will forbear." (ii. 7.)

"If the watchman see the sword coming, and blow not the trumpet, and the people be not warned, and the sword come and take away any person from among them, he is taken away for his iniquity, but his blood will I require at the watchman's hand."

"I [Jehovah] have set thee [Ezekiel] for a watchman to the house of Israel, ... when I say to the wicked, 'O wicked man, thou shalt surely die,' and thou speakest not to warn the wicked, — that wicked man shall die for his iniquity, but his blood will I require at thy hand." (xxxiii. 2—9.)

His policy is wise. (xvii. 11, sqq.)

The prophetic style, with him, is sunk down to low, tedious, and dull prose.[a] It is only in symbolical and allegorical fictions that he rises above the common; but then he usually falls down again to what is exaggerated,

---

[a] Amplification; ii. 3—8, iii. 4—11, vi. 3—6, 13, xxxix. 11—16. Great minuteness; xviii. (Comp. Jer. xxxi. 29.) Repetition of thoughts and forms of expression; v. 12, 16, vi. 11, 12, vii. 15, xiv. 21; v. 11, vii. 4, viii. 18, ix. 10; vii. 3, 4. The formula וִידְעוּ (*and they shall know*) occurs more than forty times. Strophes occur in xxv., and something similar in xxxii. 22—30. See *Knobel*, vol. ii. p. 308, sqq.

[His obscurity was confessed by the Jews themselves. *Jerome*, Præf. ad Ezek., says, Aggrediar Ezek. prophetam cujus difficultatem Hebræorum probat traditio. Nam nisi quis apud eos ætatem sacerdotalis ministerii (i. e. tricesimum annum) impleverit, nec principia Geneseos, nec Canticum Canticorum, nec hujus voluminis exordium et finem legere permittitur, &c.]

far-fetched, and confused. He uses the supernatural to excess, as in the remarkable account of his call to the prophetic office, (i.—iii. 14;) in the visions respecting the punishment of Jerusalem, where the same imagery occurs; and in chap. xl.—xlviii. He is the first among all the prophets who introduces *angels*. He repeats the formula, "thus saith Jehovah," to satiety. He even uses it in the proper speeches of Jehovah, as in vi. 3, and repeats it more than eighty times. The allegories could not be understood unless he explained them, as in xvii. xix.; at other times they are a medium between allegory and personification, as chap. xvi. xxiii. Some of the symbolical actions are too minute in their similitude. Instances of this fault may be seen in the account of his lying down and besieging a tile for four hundred and thirty days, (iv.;) of his cutting his hair and dividing it into three parts, to represent the different fate that awaited different portions of the people, (v.;) and that of his eating his food, trembling while he ate. (xii. 18.) Some of them are not sufficiently striking to the eye, as the account of his boiling flesh in a caldron, (xxiv. 3, sqq.;) of taking two sticks, one representing Judah, the other Israel, and uniting them, to show that the two nations should be united. (xxxvii. 16, sqq.) The symbolic account of the dry bones restored to life (xxxvii. 1—14) is the only one that can be considered successful. The language is still more degenerate than that of Jeremiah.[a]

---

[a] Besides the forms אַתְּי; קָטַלְתִּי; כִי, for ךְ; אוֹתִי, for אִתִּי, as in Jeremiah: נִבְהָא, for נִבְהָה; xxxi. 5. אַתִּרְקֵי הָא, for יהָ —; xli. 15. בְּשׁוּבֵנִי, for בְּשׁוּבִי; xlvii. 7. מִשְׁתַּחֲוִיתֶם; viii. 16. Infinitive *Hophel*; xxxii. 19. בֶּן־אָדָם; ii. 1, and very often. [See *Gesenius*, Thesaurus, sub voce.] See other examples in *Eichhorn*, § 548, and *Gesenius*, Gesch. d.

In his writings the literary art predominates over all, and the greater part of his prophecies are to be considered simply as literary productions. (i.—vii. viii.—xi. xl. —xlviii.) In none of the old prophets do we find such definite predictions as in Ezekiel. Thus, in the following, he predicts the flight of the Jews and the captivity of Zedekiah: —

"I will bring him to Babylon, ... yet he shall not see it, though he shall die there." (xii. 13.)

"Moreover the word of Jehovah came to me in the ninth year, in the tenth month, in the tenth day of the month, ... 'Write the name of the day, even of this same day.'" (verse 1.)

"In the day when I take from them their strength, ... in that day shall one that is escaped come to thee, to cause thee to hear it with thine ears." (verse 26.) This is fulfilled in xxxiii. 21. "In the twelfth year of our captivity, in the tenth month, on the fifth day of the month, one who had escaped from Jerusalem came to me, saying, 'The city is smitten.'"

§ 223, b.

THE SAME SUBJECT CONTINUED.

["One characteristic of Ezekiel, universally acknowledged, is this, — that he explains every thing minutely, down to its smallest parts. He unfolds and develops formally, and places before us in all possible lights, what the old prophets would touch upon in a metaphor, or allude to with a glance, or, at most, present in a very few words, or exhibit in one only of its phases. Another characteristic, which distinguishes his oracles from all

---

Heb. Sprache, p. 33, sqq., above, vol. i. Appendix, D. *Hävernik*, vol. i. p. 239. *Zunz*, l. c. p. 159, sqq. He makes the observation that Ezekiel, still more than Jeremiah, uses the language of the Pentateuch. In this he resembles the latest writers of the Hagiographa.

others of whatever age, is *fiction*. To use the word in its noblest sense, — all the prophets of all times have made use of fiction; without it oracles cannot be. But no other prophet has given so free course to his fancy, nor produced so many fictions of such various character. We find scarcely any prophetic discourses in Ezekiel worked out and rounded off like those of the other prophets. Almost all is clothed in symbolical actions, fables, narratives, allegories, or in the yet higher kind of fiction, — in visions. Since these are, for the most part, very complicated, so great labyrinths of fictions occur in his writings; and since but very few commentators have the skill of Theseus, so complaints resound, from all quarters, on the obscurity of the prophet. What belongs in the spiritual he brings over into the material world; introduces long trains of ideas in a single picture, and, as they are represented by objects purely sensual, so there arise great and sometimes dazzling compositions. He who can embrace all these in an eagle-glance, and is not distracted from the main piece by the subordinate parts, all of which concur only to produce the chief figure, — he alone can understand the meaning of the whole picture, and can scarcely fancy how any one can accuse the artist of obscurity."] . . . . .

§ 224.

MANNER IN WHICH THE BOOK ORIGINATED.

There is no doubt that Ezekiel, who commonly speaks of himself in the first person, wrote the whole book. Some of the rabbins expressed doubts respecting the authority of the book, but merely on account of its doctrines.[a] Ezekiel himself may have compiled the separate prophecies, for they are arranged according to a certain plan. The first part (i.—xxiv.) is arranged in perfect chronological order, as the table in the note will show.[b]

In the compilation of the prophecies against foreign nations, (xxvi.—xxxii. 17,) the order of events alone is followed. The following table, in the note, shows the chronology of the chapters.[c]

This collection of prophecies relating to foreign nations may have been inserted as a supplement, or episode, since a resting-place is afforded at the end of the first part of the book, (xxiv. 27 ;) or because some of these prophecies actually belong between xxiv. 27, and xxxiii. 21 : others may have been connected with them on account of the similarity of their subject. Jahn's supposition that these oracles were misplaced at a later period, is unnecessary. Chap. xxxiii. 1—20, a passage of a general character, has been inserted in its present place, without regard to chronology. The prophecy goes regularly on in verse 21, and all that follows belongs in the period after the destruction of the city. Chap. xl. belongs to the twenty-fifth year of the exile.

---

[a] See *Carpzov*, vol. iii. p. 214, sqq. [*Spinoza*, Tractatus Theol. polit. ch. ii.] The statement in Baba Bathra (in § 14, above, p. 31) is striking. *Zunz* (l. c. p. 158, sqq.) makes use of that, the peculiarities of the language, and some other arguments, and dates the composition in the Persian era. [But see *Knobel*, vol. ii. p. 314, sqq.]

[b] Year of the exile, 5, chap. i. 1.
———— 6, —— viii. 1.
———— 7, —— xx. 1.
———— 9, —— xxiv. 1.

[c] Year of the exile, 11, chap. xxvi. 1. Year of exile, 11, chap. xxxi. 1.
———— 10, —— xxix. 1. ———— 12, —— xxxii. 1.
———— 27, —— xxix. 17. ———— 12, —— xxxii. 17.

Eichhorn explains the arrangement of the book by his favorite theory, that it was written on several separate rolls. Bertholdt thinks there were several independent collections made, namely, chap. xxv.—xxxii. xxxiii. 21—xxxix. But xxxiii. 21, is necessarily connected with xxiv. 27.

CHAPTER IV.

THE TWELVE MINOR PROPHETS.[a]

§ 225.

COLLECTION OF THE TWELVE MINOR PROPHETS

THESE twelve prophetic works formerly composed but one book in the canon. In the Wisdom of Sirach it

---

[a] *Jerome*, Comm. in Proph. min., Opp. iii. *Mart.*, vi. *Vallars.*

Theophylacti Comment. in Hos., Habac., Jon., Nah., et Mich., in Opp.; Venet. 1754—1763, vol. iv.

Victorin. Strigelii Argumenta et Scholia in XII. Proph. minores; 1561.

Joa. Merceri Comm. in Prophetas quinque priores inter eos, qui minores vocantur. *Joa. Drusii* Comment. in Proph. min.

Casp. Sanctii Comm. in XII. Proph. min.; Lugd. 1621, fol.

Joa. Schmidii in Proph. min. Comm.; Lips. 1685, 1687, 1689, 4to.

Joa. Tarnovii Comment. in Proph. min., c. Præf. *J. B. Carpzovii;* Frcf. et Lips. 1688, 1706, 4to.

Ed. Pococke, Commentaries on Hosea, Joel, Micha, and Malachi, Oxf. 1685, fol., and in his Works, Lond. 1740, fol.

Joa. Markii in Proph. min. Comm.; Amst. 1696—1701, 4 vols. 4to.

Apparatus crit. ad formandum V. T. Interpretem congestus a D. *C. Fr. Bahrdt.* Vol. i.; Lips. 1775, 8vo. (Hos., Jo., Hab., Hagg.)

Will. Newcome, An Attempt towards an Improved Version, a Metrical Arrangement, and an Explication of the twelve minor Prophets; Lond. 1785, 4to.

G. L. Bauer, Die kleinen Proph. übers. u. m. Comm. erl.; Lpz. 1786, 1790, 2 pts.

is said, (xlix. 10,) "And of the *twelve prophets* let the memorial be blessed, and let their bones flourish again out of their place; for they comforted Jacob, and delivered them by assured hope." But this passage is probably spurious. However, Gregory of Nazianzen says, "The twelve, indeed, are one scripture," and enumerates our present minor Prophets.[a] The Jewish writers make four books of the prophets—Isaiah, Jeremiah, Ezekiel, and the Twelve.

It is probable, therefore, after each of these had, for some time, been in circulation by itself, that they were all collected together, and written on the same roll. Kimchi says, "Our teachers of pious memory say that they were collected into one volume, lest, if they remained separate, one or the other of them, on account of its smallness, would be lost."

They seem to be arranged in a chronological order, though differently in the Hebrew and Greek manu-

---

C. F. Stäudlin, Beit. z. Erläut. d. bibl. Propheten u. z. Gesch. ihrer Auslegung; als Versuche Hoseas, Nahum, Habakuk neu übers. u. exeg. krit. erl.; Stuttg. 1786.

Chr. G. Hensler, Animadverss. in quædam XII. Prophet. min. Loca; Kilon. 1786.

J. Ch. Dahl, Observatt. philol. atque crit. ad quædam Prophet. min. Loca, subjecta vernacula Chabacuci Interpretatione; Neostrelitiæ, 1798.

Rosenmüller, *Hitzig*, and *Maurer*, l. c.

Translated into German, by *Struense*, 1770; *Vollborth*, 1783; *Moldenhauer*, 1787. A translation of Nahum, Habakkuk, Zephaniah, Haggai, and Obadiah, with remarks, 1791; by *Theiner*, with remarks, 1828. *Noyes*, l. c. See the Elenchus Interprett. in *Rosenmüller's* Scholia on the minor Prophets. [Exeget. Handbuch d. A. T. pt. i.; 1838.]

[a] [*Μίαν μέν εἰσιν ἐς γραφὴν οἱ Δώδεκα·*
'Ωσηὲ κ' Ἀμὼς, καὶ Μιχαίας ὁ τρίτος,
'Επεῖθ' Ἰωὴλ, εἶτ' Ἰωνᾶς, Ἀβδίας,
Ναούμ τε, Ἀββακοὺκ τε καὶ Σοφονίας,
'Αγγαῖος, εἶτα Ζαχαρίας, Μαλαχίας,
Μία μὲν οἶδε.] *Greg.* Naz. Carm. xxxiii.

See *Carpzov*, vol. iii. p. 270, sqq.

scripts, and not with perfect accuracy, as the table beneath will show.[a]

This collection may have been commenced earlier, but it cannot have been completed until a long time after the exile.[b]

I. HOSEA.[c]

§ 226.

HIS LIFE AND TIMES.

Hosea, the son of Beeri, was, perhaps, a citizen of the kingdom of Ephraim. But this does not follow from

---

[a] ORDER OF THE TWELVE HEBREW PROPHETS.

According to Hebrew Text.	*Greek Text.*	*According to the Chronology.*
1. Hosea.	1. Hosea.	1. Joel, about 810 B. C.
2. Joel.	2. Amos.	2. Jonah, . . . 810 "
3. Amos.	3. Micah.	3. Amos, . . . 790 "
4. Obadiah.	4. Joel.	4. Hosea, . . . 785 "
5. Jonah.	5. Obadiah.	5. Micah, . . 725 "
6. Micah.	6. Jonah.	6. Nahum, . . 710 "
7. Nahum.	7. Nahum.	7. Zephaniah, 640 "
8. Habakkuk.	8. Habakkuk.	8. Habakkuk, 605 "
9. Zephaniah.	9. Zephaniah.	9. Obadiah, . 570 "
10. Haggai.	10. Haggai.	10. Haggai, . . 520 "
11. Zechariah.	11. Zechariah.	11. Zechariah, 520 "
12. Malachi.	12. Malachi.	12. Malachi, . 440 "

[b] See *Jäger*, De Ordine Prophetarum minorum chronolog. in the Tübingen Zeitschrift, pt. ii. 1828. [But see, also, *Newcome's* chronological table, prefixed to his minor Prophets.]

[c] Hoseas cum Targ. et Comment. Rabb. ed. *Herm. von der Hardt.* See above, § 59.

Is. Abarbanelis Comm. in Hoseam, Latinitate donatus, una cum Notis suis ab *Francisc.* ab *Huysen;* Lug. Bat. 1687, 4to.

Capitonis Comm. in Hoseam; Argent. 1528, 8vo.

Joa. Brentii Comm. in Hoseam Prophetam; Hagenoæ, 1560, 4to.; Tüb. 1580, fol. [*Burroughs*, Exposition of Hos.; Lond. 1643, ed. *Sherman*, 1840.]

Seb. Schmidii Comm. in Hoseam; Frcf. ad M. 1687, 4to.

the contents of his prophecies, so certainly as it is commonly supposed. Amos furnishes us with an example to prove that Jewish prophets sometimes prophesied in Israel, and concerning Israel. The pseudo Epiphanius, in his lives of the prophets, says he was born at Belemoth, in the tribe of Issachar. Dorotheus of Tyre confirms this statement. But they prove nothing. Maurer, judging from the analogy between Amos i. 1, and Hosea i. 1, concludes he was descended from Judah, and appeared as a prophet among the Ephraimites. But Credner and Hitzig disagree with him upon this point.[a] It is said, in i. 1, that he prophesied in the days of Uzziah, Jotham, Ahaz, and Hezekiah, kings of Judah, and in the days of Jeroboam II., king of Israel.

But this statement is very incorrect. If he first appeared as a prophet in the last years of Jeroboam, and prophesied till the beginning of Hezekiah's reign, the time of his active life would extend to almost sixty years, which is quite too much. Hitzig thinks the first date, in the time of the kings of Judah, is spurious.

Jo. Henr. Manger, Comm. in Hos.; Campis, 1782, 4to.

Der Proph. Hosea aus der bibl. u. weltl. Historie erl. u. m. krit., phil. u. theol. Anmerkk. versehen von *J. G. Schröer*; 1782, 8vo.

Annotatt. hist. exeg. in Hos., auctore *L. J. Uhland*, pt. i.—xii.; Tüb. 1785—1797, 4to.

Der Prophet Hos. erkl. von *J. Chr. Vaupel*; Dresd. 1793, 8vo.

F. J. V. Dom. Maurer, Observatt. in Hos., in Comment. theol. ed. *Rosenmüller* et *Maurer*, vol. ii. pt. ii.; Lips. 1827, p. 275.

Hoseas Propheta. Introductionem præmisit, vertit et commentatus est *Joh. Christ. Stuck*; Lips. 1828, 8vo.

Schröder, Die Propheten Hoschea, Joel, u. Amos; Lpz. 1829.

Translated by *Struense*, 1769; *A. Fr. Pfeiffer*, 1785; *Kuinöl*, 1789; *Böckel*, 1801; into English by *Horsley*, and *Noyes*, l. c.

[a] Pseudo *Epiphanius*, De Vitis Prophet. ch. xi. *Dorotheus* Tyr. De Prophetis, ch. i. *Maurer*, l. c. p. 295, sqq. *Credner*, Joel, p. 66, sqq.—*Hitzig*, (l. c. p. 73,) to support his opinion, makes use of the passage, "*our* king," vii. 5; "*the* land," i. 2; and the fact that Judah is not mentioned in the promise, xiv. 2, sqq.

The prophecies of Hosea presuppose the kingdom of Israel to be in that condition in which we know it was under Jeroboam II. and his successors; that is, rent by factions at home, and threatened by dangers from abroad.[a]

§ 227.

CONTENTS OF THE PROPHECIES.

Hosea's prophetic zeal was excited by the kingdom of Ephraim. The corruption and distraction of the

---

[a] Chap. i. 4, refers plainly to 2 Kings xv. 10, and, therefore, belongs in the last time of Jeroboam II. So ii. 4, the prophecy of an interregnum after Jeroboam II., belongs in 785 B. C., though *Hitzig* refers it to the interregnum. Chap. vii. 7, and xiii. 11, refer to the same event; and the death of Shallum, Pekahiah, and Pekah, 2 Kings xv. 10, 24, (perhaps 25, 30.) Chap. vii. 11, "They call upon Ægypt, [but they shall] go to Assyria," and xii. 1, 2, refer to 2 Kings xvii. 4. Shalman, that is, Shalman-ezer, is mentioned, (x. 14;) yet the final catastrophe is not clear to the prophet. It lies in the obscurity of the future, as we see from the prophecies that were not fulfilled; for example, ix. 3, "To Ægypt shall Ephraim go back, and eat unclean things in Assyria;" verse 6, "Ægypt shall gather them; Memphis shall bring them;" and xi. 5.

It is probable he wrote chap. iv.—xiv. in the time of Hoshea, 731—722 B. C. But, according to Maurer, chap. i.—iii. ix. xii. 8, sqq., belong in the time of Jeroboam II., 825—784 B. C. Chap. iv. belongs in the first interregnum, 786—774 B. C.; chap. viii. in the time of Menahem, 771—761 B. C.; chap. v. and vi. in Pekah's time, 761—759 B. C.; chap. xiii. xiv. in the second interregnum, 739—730 B. C.; and vii. x.—xii. 7, in the time of Hoshea, 731—722. But most of these combinations are uncertain; the division into these portions is only effected with violence.

Knobel (p. 158, sqq.) makes Pekah's death (740 B. C.) the *terminus a quo*. *Hitzig* places chap. iv.—xiv. within this period. From the first interregnum till the reign of Menahem he sets Shalman aside entirely, while *Knobel* thinks he is mentioned as Tiglath-pileser's marshal. Chap. iv.—xiv. form a whole, in which the order of time cannot be determined. If the prophet lived under the last king, Hosea, his active life lasted but about fifty years; and this is not so very improbable.

See on Hosea's prophetic discourses in the Theol. Stud. und Krit. for 1831, p. 807. *Stuck* differs from the above, both in the division and in the references to the history of the times.

nation, their apostasy and approaching destruction, are the principal subjects of his discourse. Idolatry,[a] and the meretricious desire of foreign alliances,[b] in particular excite his indignation. He likewise looks upon Judah with a threatening and chiding countenance,[c] yet still with a preponderance of hope for her reformation and deliverance.[d]

The book is divided into two parts, namely, chap. i.—iii. and chap. iv.—xiv. The former contains two symbolical actions, and their explanation: we are not, however, to suppose the actions were ever actually performed.[e] The latter contains a prophetic discourse suited to punish and admonish. It is divided into several sections, with resting-places between them. Probably they were written down from memory, without reference to the order of time.

It is probable the second part is not to be divided into separate chapters, relating to different times, but that old and recent events are united in one picture of the times, with a visible progress from wrath and threatenings to compassion and promises. But the remark of Eichhorn is just: "The prophet followed his subject up to a certain point, until his heart was too deeply moved, or his enthusiasm had reached a certain height. He there stopped for a short time, and after a pause proceeded. In this case, the separate clauses and parts of the same discourse would naturally assume the form of short, independent discourses."[f]

---

[a] Chap. ii. 4—6, iv. 12, sqq., v. 1, sqq., viii. 4, sqq., ix. 10, x. 1, 5, xi. 2, xii. 12, xiii. 1.

[b] Chap. v. 13, vii. 11, viii. 9, xii. 2, xiv. 4.

[c] Chap. v. 5, 12—14, vi. 4—11, viii. 14, xii. 1—3.

[d] Chap. i. 7, iv. 15.

[e] As *Stuck* (l. c. p. 53) maintains.

[f] *Eichhorn's*, *Bertholdt's*, and *Maurer's* divisions do not seem to be just

§ 228.

THEIR LITERARY CHARACTER.

Hosea relates his symbolical actions (i. iii.) in prose; but as soon as he gives free course to the emotions of his heart, he writes in rhythm. But as his style is abrupt, unrounded, and ebullient, so his rhythm is hard, leaping, and violent.[a] Eichhorn says, "His discourse is like a garland woven up of the most manifold flowers; images are woven over images; similitude is wound upon similitude, and metaphor connected with metaphor. He breaks off one flower and throws it away, that he may likewise break off another. Like a bee, he flies from flower-bed to flower-bed, to suck his honey from the most various juices."[b]

The language is peculiar and difficult.[c] His thoughts disclose rather a warm and beating heart, than a mind that sees clearly and soars sublime. Yet in matters of religion and politics he discerns the truth. (vi. 4, sqq.,

---

and necessary. *Hitzig* adheres to the present division into chapters, but puts chap. iv. in the interregnum; chap. v. under Zechariah. He finds Zechariah's murder in vi. 8; Shallum on the throne, in vii. 3, 5; his murder, vii. 7; Menahem's elevation to the throne, ("They chose kings without me,") viii. 4; the Assyrians, in verse 10, x. 4, xii. 2, and dependence upon them, xi. 5.

[a] *Jerome*, Præf. ad XII. Proph.: Commaticus est et quasi per sententias loquens.

[b] *Eichhorn*, § 555. Comp. the different images, v. 9, sqq., vi. 1, sqq., vii. 8, sqq., x. 11, sqq., xiii. 3, 7, 8, 13.

[c] In respect to the *connection:* vii. 16, לֹא עָל; ix. 8, צֹפֶה עִם; xiv. 3, נְשַׁלְּמָה פָרִים שְׂפָתֵינוּ;—to the *vocabulary:* viii. 13, הַבְהָבַי; xiii. 5, תַּלְאֻבוֹת; x. 2, עָרַף; xi. 7, תְּלוּא; v. 13, x. 6, מֶלֶךְ יָרֵב; xi. 4, the form אוֹכִיל, for אַאֲכִיל. *Hitzig* finds a use of Amos in many passages of Hosea. This is most probable in viii. 14, (comp. Amos ii. 5;) less probable in iv. 3, (comp. Amos viii. 8,) and iv. 15, (comp. Amos v. 5.)

vii. 9.) He soon passes from indignation to reconciliation, and from threats to promises. (ii. 16, sqq., and xi. 8.) He is poor and unimaginative in his symbols.

§ 229.

THE COLLECTION OF HIS PROPHECIES.

Since the prophecies of the first part are the earliest; since the second part does not consist of separable portions, and contains a reproof which would apply to the whole period of corruption and misery, extending to the reign of Hosea,—therefore we cannot reasonably doubt that this book, in its present form, and, perhaps, with its present inscription, proceeded from the hands of Hosea himself.

II. JOEL.[a]

§ 230.

HIS LIFE AND TIMES.

Joel, the son of Pethuel, was a Jew, as we learn from

[a] Joel cum Adnotatt. et Vers. trium Rabbinorum expositus per *Gilb. Genebrardum ;* Par. 1563, 4to.

Joel explicatus, in quo Textus Ebr. variis Modis per Paraphrasin Chald., Masoram magn. et parv., perque trium præstantiss. Rabb., R. Sal. Jarchi, R. Aben Esræ, et R. Dav. Kimchi, Comm., nec non per Notas philol. illustratur, cui in Fine adjectus est Obadias eodem fere modo illustratus. Auctore *Joa. Leusden ;* Ultraj. 1657.

Corn. Hasæi Prophetia Joelis, Analysi et Positionibus theol.-philol. illustrata ; Brem. 1697.

A Paraphrase and critical Commentary on the Prophecy of Joel. By *Sam. Chandlor ;* Lond. 1735, 4to.

several distinct allusions to the kingdom of Judah.[a] The pseudo Epiphanius says he was of the tribe of Reuben.[b] We know nothing further respecting him. Even his age is uncertain. Jahn and others place him in the time of Manasseh; Eckermann, under Josiah; and Schröder, with others, after the destruction of the Jewish state.

We cannot determine his age from the plague of locusts and the drought of which he prophesies. The language proves nothing.[c] The age can be determined only by his references to the political state of the nation. These lead us to a time when neither the Syrians nor the Assyrians were hostile to Judah; but the Phœnicians and the Philistines, (iv. 4,) the Ægyptians and the Edomites, alone (iv. 19) had shown themselves their enemies. Consequently, Joel seems to have been an elder contemporary of Amos. This appears from the similarity of their language. (Compare iv. 4, 19, with

---

Interpretatio Joelis in *Turretini* Tract. de sac. Script. Interpret. ed. a *Guil. A. Teller*, p. 307—343.

Sigm. Jac. Baumgarten, Auslegung des Propheten Joel; Hal. 1756, 4to.

C. F. Cramer, Scythische Denkmäler in Palästina; Kiel, 1777, p. 143—245.

C. Ph. Conz, Diss. de Charactere poetico Joelis, cum Animadverss. philol. crit.; Tub. 1783, 4to.

Joel Vates olim Hebræus, Cura *Joa. Büttneri;* Cob. 1784.

Joel Latine versus et Notis philol. illustratus ab *A. Svanborg* in sex Dissertatt.; Upsal. 1806, 4to.

Translated, with explanations, by *Eckermann*, 1786; *Justi*, 1792; *Holzhausen*, 1829; *Credner*, 1831.

[a] Chap. i. 14, ii. 1, 15, iii. 5, iv. 1, 2, 6, 16, 17, 20, 21.

[b] De Vit. Proph. c. xiv.

[c] *Kimchi* supposes the famine alluded to is that mentioned in 2 Kings viii. 1. See *Eckermann's* version, p. 49, and compare Jer. xiv. 1. See *Carpzov*, p. 310, and *Bertholdt*, p. 1604, *Knobel*, p. 135, sqq., *Credner* p. 55, sq.

Amos i. 9, 11.) He seems to have prophesied under Uzziah,[a] about 810 B. C.

§ 231.

CONTENTS AND SPIRIT OF THE PROPHECY.

The distress produced by the extraordinary devastations of swarms of locusts, accompanied with a drought, gave Joel occasion to admonish his nation to repent. By their repentance, he says, not only will abundance return, but a golden age will be introduced, in which the theocracy shall be triumphant, and exert a more inspiring influence.

The Chaldee interpreter, Ephraim Syrus, Jerome,

---

[a] *Abarbanel*, *Vitringa*, (Typus Doct. Proph. c. iv. p. 35, sqq.,) *Rosenmüller*, *Von Cölln*, (De Joel. Ætate; 1811,) *Holzhausen*, (l. c. p. 17,) *Eichhorn*, (§ 559,) and *Knobel*, (§ 15,) are of this opinion. On the other hand, *Credner* (l. c. p. 41, sqq.) places him in the first period of Jehoash, 870—865 B. C. He is led to this conclusion by the fact that the pretended incursion of the Syrians, mentioned in 1 Kings xii. 17, is not spoken of in Joel; (but this was only a feint, which has been exaggerated in 2 Ch. xxiv. 23, sqq. Amos i. 3, does not mention it. *Knobel*, vol. ii. p. 139;) by the hostile positions of the Edomites, which is presupposed in iv. 19, (but see Amos i. 11, sqq.;) and on account of the condition of the law here presupposed. Such is the opinion of *Winer*, (Lexicon,) *Krahmer*, (De Joel. Ætate; 1837,) *Movers*, (Chronik, p. 119, sqq.,) and *Hitzig*. In support of this, some maintain there is in iv. 4—6, 17, a reference to the pretended conquest of Jerusalem, by the Philistines, under Jehoram. (2 Ch. xxi. 16.) Others place him still lower — *Hengstenberg*, (Christol. vol. i. pt. i. p. 209,) in the time of Micah; *Bertholdt* and *Steudel*, (*Bengel*, Archiv. vol. ii. p. 234,) in that of Hezekiah; *Eckermann*, in that of Josiah; *Jahn*, under Manasseh; and *Schröder*, at the end of the Jewish state. Chap. iv. 1, 2, taken by itself, speaks in favor of the Assyrian, or rather Chaldee period, (*Eckermann*, p. 44, *Bertholdt*, p. 1604,) but not in connection with the rest.

Jerome's maxim is false. Prol. in XII. Proph. min.: In quibus (Proph. script.) tempus non profertur in titulo, sub illis eos regibus prophetasse, sub quibus et hi, qui ante eos habent titulos, prophetarunt.

Abarbanel, Grotius, and others, — whom Bertholdt and Theiner have recently followed, — maintain that the book must be explained as an allegory, [the locusts representing hostile armies.][a] But this view is contrary to all the analogy of Hebrew prophecy. It has been opposed by Justi and Rosenmüller, while Holzhausen takes a middle course. There are some passages which refer to political events, (ii. 17, 20, iii. iv.,) but they agree very well with the common method of interpreting them. Credner thinks Joel prophesied *after* this plague of the locusts had taken place. He supposes (ii. 10) "The earth quaketh before them, the heavens tremble," refers to a thunder-storm, and puts verse 18, "Then will Jehovah be zealous for his land, and pity his people," in the preterit tense. But all this is contrary to analogy, and not demanded by the rules of grammar.[b] Chap. ii. 20, which predicts the removal and destruction of the locusts, must, with his view, be treated contrary to the spirit of the parallelism, and rendered highly artificial.

The prophet's discourse is to be praised as much on account of his classic language, as for his blooming, rich, and yet finished style, and his regular, measured rhythm. Notwithstanding his national and sacerdotal limitations, his thoughts are liberal and magnanimous. The prophecy, ii. 28—32, has become important from the fulfilment in Acts ii. 16.

---

[a] See *Eichhorn*, Allg. Bib. vol. iv. p. 3, and *Justi's* version of Joel, p. 39, sqq

[b] *Gesenius*, Gram. p. 228. *Hitzig* and *Knobel* put it in the preterit. [But yet Joel is cautious in his use of tenses, and if these passages are read in the future, they appear hard and unsuitable.]

III. AMOS.[a]

§ 232.

HIS LIFE AND TIMES.

Amos was a shepherd of Tekoah. But we are not on this account to suppose he was a poor and rude man, though he was simple and unlearned. (vii. 14.) The historical information he sometimes affords (ii. 9, v. 26, vi. 2, viii. 8, ix. 7) does not prove him a learned man. He prophesied in the time of Uzziah and Jeroboam II., in the latter part of Jeroboam's reign, (i. 1, vii. 10—14; compare 2 Kings xiv. 25,) about 790 B. C. The contents of his oracles agree with this date.[b]

The kingdom of Israel under Jeroboam regained its

---

[a] *Jo. Gerhardi* Adnotatt. posth. in Proph. Amos. et Jon. (with his Adnotatt. in Psalm. quinque priores ;) Jen. 1663, and 1676, 4to.

Amos Proph. expositus, interpret. Latina...... ampliss. Commentario...... illustratus, &c. Cur. atque Stud. *J. Chr. Harenberg ;* Lug. Bat. 1763, 4to.

L. Jos. Uhland, Annotatt. ad Loca quædam Amosi imprimis historica; Tub. 1779, 1780, 4to.

Amos übers. u. erl., mit Beifüg. d. hebr. Textes u. d. griech. der Septuaginta, nebst Anmerkk. zu letzterem, herausgeg. von *J. S. Vater ;* Halle, 1810, 4to.; also with title, Oracula Amosi. Textum et Hebr. et Gr. Versionis Alexandrinæ Notis crit. et exeg. instruxit adjunctaque Vers. vern. edidit......

Translated and explained by *J. E. W. Dahl,* Gött. 1795, and *Justi,* 1799.

[b] The date of the earthquake refers indefinitely to Uzziah's time; Zechariah (xiv. 5) mentions it. *Credner* (p. 85) has combined i. 6—8, with 2 Ch. xxvi. 6; but this combination is very uncertain. The date in *Joseph.* (Ant. ix. 10, 4,) and in *Jerome,* (ad Am. i. 1,) is fictitious. Chap. vi. 2, refers to the fall of Gath, (comp. 2 Ch. xxvi. 6, or 2 Kings xii. 18 :) this city is not mentioned in i. 6—8. Chap. i. 3, (see *Hitzig,* in loc.,) refers to the depopulation of Gilead by the Syrians. (2 Kings x. 32.) In respect to the contemporaneity of Uzziah and Jeroboam II., there is a difference of 12 years between 2 Kings xv. 1, and xiv. 23, 17. The latter is probably correct, and Uzziah came to the throne in the 15th year of Jeroboam II. See *Dahl's* translation, p. 6, 7.

ancient limits; for, in vi. 13, the Israelites say, "Have we not acquired dominion?" (Comp. 2 Kings xiv. 25.) But yet their careless arrogance, (vi. 1, 13,) their luxury, (iii. 12, 15, vi. 4, sqq.,) and their injustice, (ii. 6, sqq., iii. 9, sqq., iv. 1, v. 7, 10,) led to the destruction of the kingdom, which the prophet had foretold. (viii. 2.)

The prophet only alludes obscurely to the supremacy of Assyria—"Therefore will I cause you to go into captivity beyond Damascus, saith Jehovah." (v. 27, vi. 14.)

He appeared at Beth-el in his character of prophet, and was opposed by the priests of that place.[a] (vii. 10, sqq.)

§ 233.

CONTENTS OF HIS PROPHECIES.

In the first two chapters Amos chides and menaces all nations and kingdoms that were known to him. In the following chapters he applies himself to Israel alone, and speaks boldly of its transgressions and approaching destruction. Chap. i. ii. and iii.—vi. form each a whole, and are all purely rhetorical. Chap. vii.—ix. is symbolical, but it contains explanations, and an historical account that has been interpolated. (vii. 10—17.) All the single passages probably belong to the same period, and were written by the prophet in their present order, according to a plan he had devised. An artificial arrangement is obvious in vii.—ix.[b]

---

[a] See the apocryphal account of his death in pseudo *Epiphanius*, ch. xii., and *Carpzov*, p. 319.

[b] This is *Eichhorn's* and *Hitzig's* opinion; but *Dahl* and *Bertholdt* differ therefrom, and think part of these prophecies were *impromptus*, and the rest had been meditated before they were uttered. It is more just to consider them all as oracles, at first uttered orally, and afterwards written down

§ 234.

THEIR LITERARY CHARACTER.

In the style of his discourse, Amos is, perhaps, the most regular of all the prophets. He loves what is uniform and measured. (i. 2, ii. 16, iv. 6—11, vii. 1—6, ix. 2—4.) He loves detail. (iii. 3—6, vi. 4—6, 9, 10.) He is not without force and elevation. (iv. 13, v. 8, viii. 7, sqq., ix. 5, 6.) His figures are original and fresh. Jerome says, "Amos the prophet was a shepherd of the shepherds; a shepherd not in cultivated places set with trees and vines, nor indeed among groves and green meadows, but in the wide wilderness of the desert, where lions display their fierceness, and the flocks are devoured, and he uses the language derived from his occupation."[a] His rhythm is finished and periodical. Sometimes he writes in regular strophes. (i. ii.) He makes use of symbols with moderation and good taste. His language, with a few departures from the usual orthography, is pure and elegant.[b]

---

and carried out with more art. According to *Credner*, Amos refers to Joel: i. 2, is borrowed from Joel iv. 16. Chap. i. 3, 6, 9, sqq., confirm Joel's threats.

[a] Jerome on Amos, i. 2. Comp. ii. 13, iii. 4, 5, 12, iv. 1, vi. 12, vii. 1, 2.

[b] מְתָאֵב, instead of מְתָעֵב; vi. 8. בּוֹשַׁסְכֶם, for בּוֹסַסְכֶם; v. 11. *Jerome*, Com. in Am., says, Imperitus sermone, [?] sed non scientia. [*Eichhorn* says, his chief merit, as a writer, is great power of delineation. His painting often speaks so clearly to the senses, that little groups proceed from his hands. Many passages seem as if selected from a collection of miniatures; and, if a painter were to copy them, the loveliest scenes would be produced:—

> "As if a man fled from a lion,
> And a bear met him," &c. (v. 19, iv. 8, vi. 10, &c.)

He is the first among the old prophets who clothed his oracles in visions. The same power of painting individual scenes led to this choice. His imagination is sufficiently rich to enable him to paint several sides of the same object, and each time with naturalness and fidelity, and thereby he is always new. Under what manifold forms does he represent tyranny, and the omnipotence of God! When he paints the golden age, how does one figure vie with the others in his delineation! In his hands every thing becomes local and individual; nothing is expressed generally, but all in the individual form. Many of his images and similes are derived from rural scenes; fields and vineyards, herds and droves, are ever present before him. His vocation of herdsman probably led him to use images derived from a dry and parched land, and proverbial expressions. He is not unhappy in the invention of new figures, though he commonly uses those of his predecessors. He makes a new application of the figure of the sun,—in the day of adversity, delaying to rise, and first appearing at noon. His graphic account of the extreme fertility of the land is new:—

> "The plougher shall draw near to the reaper,
> And the treader of grapes to the sower of the seed." (ix. 13.)

Since the fulfilment of his prophecies was near at hand, they have a peculiar definiteness. He mentions the place to which the Syrians are to be transferred, namely, the River Kir. He describes the destiny of the Israelites definitely. All shall not be destroyed, but the best part of them shall return to their native land. Yet, here and there, he leaves obscurity still hanging over his oracles. The children of Israel shall go into a land beyond Damascus; but he leaves it indefinite what land it shall be. It is undecided whether the wanton woman of Israel shall be carried into Armenia, or into the harem of a foreign king. (iv. 3.) *Eichhorn*, § 566. Jerome has accused him of inexpertness in the use of language; but this only arises from the supposition that he was merely a shepherd, and a man of no literary education. But the same objections brought against him on account of his grammar and orthography, might be urged against the author of every book in the Old Testament. The opinion of Bishop Lowth seems to be more correct—"Let any person who has candor and perspicuity enough to judge, not from the man, but from his writings, open the volume of his predictions, and he will, I think, agree that our shepherd is not a whit behind the very chief of the prophets. He will agree that as in sublimity and magnificence he is almost equal to the greatest, so in splendor of diction and elegance of expression he is scarcely inferior to any. The same celestial Spirit, indeed, actuated Isaiah and Daniel in the court, and Amos in the sheepfold, constantly selecting such interpreters as were best adapted to the occasion, and sometimes from the mouth of babes and sucklings perfecting praise."—See *Lowth*, lect. xxi. Also, *Knobel*, l. c. vol. ii. p. 143—153.]

IV. OBADIAH.[a]

§ 235.

CONTENTS, AND DATE OF HIS PROPHECY.

False combinations of 1 Kings xviii. 3, and 2 Ch. xvii. 7, have been made, in order to show that our prophet was mentioned in these passages. But his history is wholly unknown to us. Only a single oracle has come down from him, and that contains a censure and menace directed against the Edomites, who had been malicious and hostile to the Jews, at the destruction of Jerusalem. Compare Lam. iv. 21, 22, Ezek. xxxv. Ps. cxxxvii. 7.

The date of the composition of this book must be placed after the destruction of Jerusalem, and the captivity of the Jews; for "the captives of Israel" and "Jerusalem" are mentioned in verse 20.[b]

This prophecy is related to that in Jer. xlix. 7, sqq., and it is still matter of controversy which is the

---

[a] Obad. Ebr. et Chald., &c. Auct. *Joa. Leusden.*

Aug. Pfeifferi Comm. in Obad....... exhibens Vers. Lat. et Examen Commentarii Is. Abarbanelis, &c.; Viteb. 1666; ed. 2, 1670, 4to.

Der Prophet Obad. aus. d. bibl. u. weltl. Hist. erl. u. m. theol. Anmerkk. vers., von *J. G. Schröer;* Bresl. 1766.

J. B. Köhler, Anmerkk. ü. ein. St. im Obad. in Rep. vol. xv. p. 250, sqq.

Chr. Fr. Schnurrer, Dissertatt. philol. in Obadiam, Tub. 1787, 4to., and Dissertatt., Goth. 1790, p. 383, sqq.

H. Venemæ Lectt. in Obad., mit Zusätzen von *Verschuir* u. *Lohze*, in *Verschuir*, Opusc. ed. *Lohze;* Ultraj. 1810.

Translated by *Happach*, Cob. 1779; *Holzapfel*, Rint. 1798.

[b] See *Jerome*, ad Obad. 1. *Carpzov*, p. 332. [See *C. L. Hendewerk*, Obadjæ Prophetæ Oraculum in Idumæos, &c., (Regiomonti Program. 1836,) reviewed in Jahrbücher für wiss. Kritik. for 1836, vol. ii. p. 852, sqq.]

original and independent production.[a] Obadiah mentions the captivity of the Jews, (verse 20,) and the malicious joy of the Edomites at the destruction of Jerusalem. (verses 11—14.) On the contrary, Jeremiah wrote his oracle in the fourth year of Jehoiakim.[b] Jeremiah seems to have a definite expectation of the punishment of the Edomites by Nebuchadnezzar, (xlix. 19, sqq.,) which, it seems, never took place, while

---

[a] The following writers believe that Jeremiah is the original author: *Bertholdt*, p. 1631; *Von Cölln*, A. L. Z. 1828; Erg. Blat. xvi. p. 122; Bib. Theol. vol. i. p. 55; *Credner*, Joel, p. 81; *Knobel*, vol. ii. p. 327; *Hitzig*, p. 341, sqq. The following favor the originality of Obadiah: *Eichhorn*, § 512, sqq.; *Schnurrer*, p. 427; *Rosenmüller; Jäger*, Ub. die Zeit. Obadjah, 1837; and *Hendewerk.*

Arguments may be found on both sides. Thus the difficult תפלצתיך (Jer. verse 16) is omitted in Obad. verse 3. On the other hand, the unsuitable שמענו (Obad. verse 1) is exchanged for שמעתי, (Jer. verse 14,) which may be an easier substitute. In Obad. verse 2, בזוי אתה is obscurer than בזוי, sc. נתתיך, (Jer. verse 15;) so in Obad. verse 5, compared with Jer. verse 9. Obad. verse 17 is dependent on Joel iii. 5.

It is probable this, like the similar oracles of Jeremiah and Ezekiel, was never fulfilled. *Josephus* (Ant. x. 9, 7) says nothing of Edom's destruction, as *Bertholdt* maintains. (See *Gesenius's* introduction to chap. xxxiv., sq., of Isaiah, [and the valuable article of Dr. *Robinson*, on Ancient Idumea, or Edom, in Bib. Repository, vol. iii. p. 247, sqq.) Dr. R. differs from *De Wette* in regard to the fulfilment of this oracle, and says, (l. c. p. 258,) "The opinion that the Edomites, notwithstanding their alliance with the Chaldeans, escaped the lot of the Jews, and other surrounding nations, so as not to be brought under subjection to the proud monarch of Babylon, is not in itself probable; and there would seem, indeed, to be a direct allusion to such an event in Mal. i. 2, 3. But, however this may be," he adds, "they were, at least, not carried away captive." *Gesenius* (l. c. p. 906) justly thinks Edom was spared by Nebuchadnezzar; indeed, there seems to be no reason why he should make war with the Edomites, who had taken his side, and furnished him forces so early. (Obad. 11—15.)] *Eichhorn's conjecture* — that Nebuchadnezzar conquered Edom a few years after the destruction of Jerusalem — is merely conjecture. [He thinks, also, the five last verses were interpolated into the text, in the time of Alexander Jannæus. But there appears no reason for the suspicion.]

[b] See § 219, *a*. Verse 12 is to be judged according to xxv. 17, sqq.

Obadiah hopes only in general for a day of judgment from Jehovah, and the return of the exiles. (verses 15, 20.) Accordingly, Obadiah wrote later, and made use of Jeremiah from recollection. It is probable the book received its present place in the canon, on account of the reference to Edom, in Amos ix. 12.[a]

[It is difficult to determine the literary character of a prophet who has left us so few lines. However, he is not wanting in strength or vivacity. His language is pure, and his thoughts noble. Theocratic arrogance, and national antipathy towards foreign nations, are too obvious to be denied. Yet his hatred towards other nations is not so deep and deadly as that of some of his younger contemporaries. In style, he resembles the better and more elevated passages of Jeremiah and Zephaniah. Sometimes his figures are bold and striking. (verses 4, 18.) He is fond of questions; and, for the sake of emphasis, repeats a thought in a different form. (verses 12—14.)]

V. JONAH.[b]

§ 236.

CHARACTER OF THE BOOK, JUDGING FROM ITS CONTENTS.

Among works which are prophecies, in the proper sense of the word, there is one small book in the collec-

---

[a] See *Schnurrer*, l. c. p. 432.

[b] *Jo. Gerhardi* Annotatt. in Proph. Am. et Jon.

Jonas illustratus per paraph. Chald., Masoram m. et p. et per trium præ-

tion of the twelve minor Prophets, which is a mere narrative. The hero of the book is Jonah, the son of Amittai, and is probably the same who is mentioned in 2 Kings xiv. 25. This narrative is certainly not a true history; but, on the other hand, it is not a mere fiction.[a] It is probable the materials were derived from popular

---

stantiss. Rabb., S. Jarchi, Abr. Aben Esræ, Dav. Kimchi, Textum punctat., ut et per Michlal Jophi Textum non punctat. nec non per varias Notas philol., Auct. *Joa. Leusden;* Traj. 1692.

Jo. Theoph. Lessing, Observatt. in Vatic. Jonæ et Nahumi; Chemn. 1780.

Curarum crit. et exeg. in LXX-viralem Vers. Vaticiniorum Jonæ Spec. i. ii. iii. Auct. *Jo. G. Chr. Hoepfner;* Lips. 1787, 1788, 4to.

Der Proph. Jonas übers. u. mit erklär. Anmerkk. herausgeg. von *H. A. Grimm;* Düsseld. 1798.

Ex Michlal Jophi ...... part. complect. Prophet. Jonæ.

[a] The following authorities favor the opinion that it is a real history: 3 Macc. vi. 8. [?] *Josephus*, Ant. ix. 10, 2. *Buddeus*, Hist. Eccles. V. T. vol. ii. p. 589, sqq. *J. B. Lüderwald*, Uber Allegorie und Mythologie in d. Bibel; 1787, 8vo. *Griesdorf*, Diss. i. ii. de verosimillima Libr. Jonæ interpretandi Ratione; Viteb. 1794, 4to. *Th. C. Piper*, Diss. Historiam Jonæ a recentiorum Conatibus vindicatam sistens; Gryph. 1786, 4to. *J. H. Verschuir*, Diss. de Argumento Lib. Jonæ ejusque Veritate hist., in his Opuscula, ed. *Lohze;* Ultraj. 1811, 8vo. *Steudel*, in *Bengel's* Archiv. vol. ii. p. 401, sqq. *Reindl*, Sendung d. Proph. Jonas; Bamb. 1826. *Sack*, Apologetik, p. 345, sqq. *Hengstenberg*, Kirchenzeitung; 1834, No. 27, sqq. *Laberenz*, De Vera Lib. Jonæ, Interp.; Fulda, 1836. (See *Jäger*, On the Moral and Religious Design of Jonas, in Tub. Theol. Zeitschrift; 1840, vol. i. p. 62, sqq.) Some explain it as a history, and maintain,

1. *That it has taken a mythical form: Thaddeus*, Sendungsgeschichte der Proph. Jonae; Bonn, 1786, 4to. *Goldhorn*, Excurse z. B. Jona; 1803, p. 28, sqq. *Bauer*, Einleit. 3d ed. p. 489, sqq.; his Hebrew Mythology, vol. ii. p. 213. *Friedrichsen*, Krit. Uberblick. der merkwürdigsten Ansichten d. B. Jona; 1817, 8vo. 219, sqq., 238, sqq.

2. *The supposition that it contains a dream: Grimm*, Uebersetz, p. 61, sqq.

3. *The supposition that the language has been perverted: Anton*, Von der alten Tonkunst Hebraer. in *Paulus*, N. Rep. vol. iii. p. 36, sqq.

4. *The opinion it is an allegory: Less*, on the historical style of antiquity, in his Vermischte Schriften, vol. i. p. 161, sqq. *Palmer*, On Jonah in the Whale, in *Scheerer's* Archiv. vol. i. pt. i. p. 93, sqq. See *Bertholdt*, p. 2364, sqq., and *Rosenmüller*, Prol. in Jon. p. 346, sqq.

legends, and wrought over, with the design of making a didactic work.[a] However, it cannot be proved from Ps. ii. 3, sqq., and Tob. xiv. 4, that facts from the actual history of Jonah lie at the foundation of the work, as some maintain.[b] This fact remains certain, that the book was written for a moral end. We must not, however, insist on a rigorous unity in the means which the author uses to attain this end. The most prominent doctrine of it lies, incontestably, in the fact that God

---

[a] Some consider the narrative as historical allegory: *Hermann von der Hardt*, Ænigmata prisci Orbis. Jonas in Luce in Hist. Manassis et Josiæ; Helmstadt, 1723, fol.; and in his work, Jonas in Carcharia, Israel in Carcathio Kerta; 1718. (Comp. *Rosenmüller*, l. c. p. 388, sqq.) Some take it as a moral fiction: *Semler*, Apparat. ad Lib. V. T. Interpret. p. 271. *Michaelis*, Uebersetz d. A. T. pt. xi. Anmerk. p. 101. *Herder*, Briefe, vol. i. p. 136, 2d ed. *Niemeyer*, Characteristik d. B. vol. v. *Eichhorn*, § 577, *a*. *Stäudlin*, N. Beiträge, p. 224, sqq. *Hezel*, Bibel. d. A. und N. T. vol. vii. p. 129, sqq. *Paulus*, Memorab. vol vi. p. 32, sqq. *G. A. Müller*, in *Paulus*, ibid. vol. vi. p. 124, sqq. *Augusti*, Einleit. § 223, 1st ed. (Comp. § 224, 2d ed.) *Meyer*, Hermeneutik. d. A. T. vol. ii. p. 574, sqq. *Böhme*, in *Illgen's* Zeitschrift; 1836, vol. i. p. 195, sqq.

[b] There is a mythus of *Hesione*, the daughter of Laomedon, whom Hercules delivered from a sea-monster, in *Diodorus* Sic. iv. 42, *Apollodorus*, ii. 5, § 9—12, and, with later additions, by *Tzetzes* ad *Lycophron*, Cassand., verse 33: *Στὰς ὡπλισμένος παρὰ τὸ στομίον, ὡς κεχηνὸς ἐπῄει τὸ κῆτος, ἀθρόως τῷ τούτου ἐμπεπήδηκε στόματι. Τρισὶ δὲ ἡμέραις ἔνδοθεν κατακόπτων αὐτὸ ἐξῆλθεν, ἀποβεβληκὼς τὴν τῆς ἑαυτοῦ κεφαλῆς τρίχωσιν.* See, also, *Cyrill.* Alexand. in Jon. c. ii. *Isaac Porphyrogenitus*, in Posthomeric. in *Allat.* Excerpta var. p. 274. *Eudocia*, p. 344.

A mythus of *Andromeda*, Plin. v. 13. *Bochart*, Hieroz. ii. 743. *Rosenmüller*, p. 354. *Gesenius*, A. L. Z. 1813, xxiii. p. 177, sqq. *Friedrichsen*, p. 237. *Forbiger*, Comment. de Lycophron. Cassand. verse 31—37. Cum Epimetro de Jona; Lips. 1827. *Anton*, Comp. Libb. sac. V. T. et Script. profan. pt. x.; 1831, p. 7. *Krahmer*, Das Buch Jonas; 1839, p. 47, sqq. The story of Jonah has a certain resemblance to the legends of Elijah, especially with 1 Kings xix. *Goldhorn* refers to this. The combination of the history of Jonah with the mythus of *Oannes*, — which *Baur* has made in his "The Prophet Jonas an Assyrio-Babylonian Symbol," in *Illgen's* Zeitschrift for 1837, p. 101, sqq., is peculiar to him. Comp. *Jäger*, l. c. p. 145.

forgave a heathen people, and remitted the punishment intended, in consequence of their repentance. Therefore this is distinguished from the other theocratical books by its universal religious character. "This prophecy is written," says Kimchi, on i. 1, "that it may be a lesson to the Jews; for a foreign nation, which was not of Israelitish descent, was inclined to repent, as soon as the prophet had accused and convinced them of their sin; and with perfect penitence they turned from their wickedness, while the Israelites had not repented, and turned from their impiety, though the prophets had accused them, both early and late. Accordingly, the book is designed to teach, also, that God—to whom be glory—will spare the penitent, of whatsoever nation they are, and will pardon them, especially if they are numerous."[a]

§ 237.

ITS LITERARY CHARACTER.

The opinion that the book is composed of several distinct pieces, cannot be maintained.[b] However, the hymn (ii. 3—10) is very improperly borrowed from some other source.[c] Taken by itself, it must be ex-

---

[a] According to *Jäger*, the author had also this special design,—to justify the policy of God in sparing Nineveh, (Babylon.) See *Knobel*, vol. ii. p. 375, sqq. *Böhme* thinks it teaches the hatefulness of the Hebrews before God, and other nations. *Krahmer* (p. 65, sqq.) thinks it refers to the Jewish colony, and its relation to the Samaritans. But these conjectures cannot find much favor.

[b] See *Müller*, in *Paulus*, Mem. vol. vi. p. 167, sqq., and *Nachtigall*, on the book of Jonah, in *Eichhorn*, Allg. Bib. vol. ix. p. 221, sqq.

[c] The following are the principal peculiarities of the language: רַב; i. 6.

plained in the same manner as Ps. lxix. 1, 2, and 15, which is borrowed from Ps. xviii. 5, and xlii. 7.[a] The

בְּשֶׁלְּמִי; i. 7. בְּשֶׁלִּי; i. 12. הֶעֱבִיר, *deposuit;* iii. 6. קְרָא; i. 2, iii. 2. (Comp. Isa. xl. 6.) וַיְמַן; ii. 1, iii. 6, sqq. טַעַם; iii. 7. רִבּוֹ; iv. 11. עֶשְׁת; i. 6. [חִשֵּׁב; i. 4.] Chap. iii. 9, is an imitation of Joel ii. 14; and iv. 8, of 1 Kings xix. 4.

[a] [The hymn is placed below, with its parallel passages:—

2 "I cried in my distress to Jehovah, And he heard me.	"To Jehovah in my distress I cried, And he heard me." Ps. cxx. 1.
3 "Thou didst cast me into the deep, Into the heart of the sea, And the flood compassed me about;	
All thy billows and thy waves passed over me.	"All thy waves and thy billows are passed over me." Ps. xlii. 7.
4 "Then I said, 'I am cast out from before thine eyes.	"Then I said, ... 'I am cast out from before thine eyes.'" Ps. xxxi. 22.
O, might I once more look to thy holy temple!'	See 1 Kings viii. 38.
5 "The waters compassed me about, even to my life.	"The waters come even to my life." Ps. lxix. 1.
The deep enclosed me.	"The cords of Sheol enclosed me." Ps. xviii. 5.
6 "I went down to the foundation of the mountains, Yet hast thou brought up my life from the pit.	"Thou wilt not leave my soul in Sheol." Ps. xvi. 10.
7 "When my soul fainted within me,	"When my spirit fainted within me." Ps. cxlii. 4.
I remembered Jehovah,	"I cried unto thee, Jehovah." Ps. cxlii. 5.
And my prayer came to thee,	"Let my prayer come unto thee." Ps. lxxxviii. 3.
To thine holy temple.	"He heard my voice out of his temple." Ps. xviii. 6.
8 "They that honor lying vanities Forsake their mercy.	"I have hated those Who honor lying vanities." Ps. xxxi. 6.
9 "I will sacrifice to thee With the voice of thanksgiving. I will pay what I have vowed.	"I will sacrifice to thee The sacrifice of thanksgiving. I will pay my vows." Ps. cxvi. 17, 18.
Salvation is from Jehovah."	"From Jehovah is salvation." Ps. iii. 8.]

ninth verse is to be compared with Ps. xxxi. 7; but it does not suit the circumstances and condition of Jonah.[a]

VI. MICAH.[b]

§ 238.

HIS LIFE AND TIMES.

According to the inscription of the book, (i. 1,) Micah prophesied under Jotham, Ahaz, and Hezekiah. He belonged to the town of Moresheth, and hence is called the *Morasthite*, which appellation some have erroneously considered as a patronymic. Jerome says

---

[a] To judge from the language, the book is one of the latest of the Old Testament; but it is still a matter of controversy whether it was written before, after, or in the exile. *Krahmer* (p. 55) is mistaken in the opinion that the restoration of the temple is presupposed in ii. 5, 8. (See *Gesenius*, l. c. p. 180.) The statement respecting the size of Nineveh (iii. 3) is of no importance in determining its date; for the destruction of this city is not necessarily the *terminus ad quem*, as *Rosenmüller* maintains, Prolegomena ad Jon. p. 358. He, with *Gesenius*, *Goldhorn*, and *Bertholdt*, places it before the exile; *Jäger*, during the exile; *Jahn*, *Knobel*, and *Köster*, place it after that event; and *Hitzig* refers it to the time of the Maccabees, and, on account of קִיקָיוֹן, gives it an Ægyptian author. *Vatke* (Bib. Theol. vol. i. p. 597) places it in the time of the *Ptolemies*. *Jäger* finds in it a resemblance to Ezekiel. [The same fondness for the *grotesque* appears in Ezekiel, Jonah, Daniel, and some of the apocryphal books.]

[b] *Theod. Bibliandri* Comm. in Micham; Tigur. 1534.

Dav. Chytræi Explicatio Michæ et Nahum Proph.; Viteb. 1565, 8vo. Also, in *Chytræi* Opp. ii. p. 2183.

Animadverss. philol.-crit. ad Vatic. Michæ ex Collatione Versionum Græc. reliquarumque in Polyglottis Lond. editarum, præs. *Ch. F. Schnurrer*, Auct. resp. *J. Guil. Andler*; Tub. 1783, 4to.

G. L. Bauer, Animadverss. crit. in duo priora Proph. Michæ Capp.; Altorf. 1790, 4to.

Ueberss. von *Grossschopf*, 1798; *Justi*, 1799; *A. Th. Hartmann*, 1800.

Moresheth is a small village of Palestine, near the city of Eleutheropolis. Others think it is the Maresah, mentioned in Josh. xv. 44, which Eusebius says is a place, now in ruins, in the tribe of Judah, two miles from Eleutheropolis.[a]

But Micah distinguishes his Moresheth from that, by calling it *Moresheth of Gath.* (i. 14.) The Micah [or Micaiah] who occurs in 1 Kings xxii. 8, is a different man from this.

The above date is but partially confirmed. Since Micah presupposes the perilous situation of the two kingdoms with regard to Assyria and Ægypt, which were soon to destroy the kingdom of Israel, and that of Judah, at a later date;[b] since Jeremiah (xvi. 18) expressly places one oracle of Micah (iii. 12) in the time of Hezekiah; and since the other prophecies contain no reference to any different time,—we have the best reason for regarding the last years of Ahaz, and the first of Hezekiah, as the period of his prophetic glory.

The mention of Babylon (iv. 10) makes little difference in the political relations of Israel and Judah; for Babylon also belonged to the kingdom of Assyria. Some think this passage refers to the captivity of Manasseh at Babylon, (2 Ch. xxxiii. 11;) but this opinion is contrary to the prophetic spirit of the passage, and is also uncertain, considered as a matter of history.[c] Hart-

---

[a] See *Cyrill.* Alex. Com. in loc.; *Jerome*, Proll. in Mic.; *Eusebius*, De Locis Hebraicis; *Hitzig*, in loc.; *Bellermann*, Handbuch d. bib. Litt. vol. iii. p. 139; [and *Robinson's* Calmet, art. *Mareshah.*]

[b] Chap. i. 6—16, iii. 12, iv. 9—14, v. 4, 5, vii. 12.

[c] *Justi*, Theol. Abhand. vol. ii. p. 300. *Bertholdt*, p. 1635. *Eichhorn*, Heb. Proph. vol. i. p. 381, sqq. Einleit. § 580, p. 371. See above, § 191. *Hartmann*, p. 16. *Rosenmüller*, in loc. According to *Hartmann*, (p. 8, sqq.,)

mann's opinion is still more uncertain and venturesome. He regards iv. 10, as a later interpolation. Bertholdt supposes that vii. 13, — "Therefore will I sorely smite thee, and make thee desolate on account of thy sins," — implies that the ten tribes were already carried into captivity. But the supposition is unnecessary, at the least; for idolatry still prevailed in Hezekiah's time, as it appears from 2 Kings xxiii.[a]

§ 239.

CONTENTS AND SPIRIT OF HIS PROPHECIES.

Micah prophesied against Israel and Judah, especially against the latter. The moral corruption, apostasy, and false prophecy, and not political mistakes, are the objects of his indignation. He utters bold threats, which he may have lived to see partly fulfilled. (i. 12, sqq., ii. 3, sqq., 10, 12, iv. 9, 10, 14.) Lofty promises are mingled with these threats. (ii. 12, 13, iv. 1, sqq., 8, 13, vi. 1—8, vii. 11, 12, 17.)

He resembles Hosea in his rapid transition from threats of punishment to promises of prosperity, as well as in his style. But he has more roundness, fulness, and clearness, in his style and in his rhythm. He frequently indulges in play upon words in i. 10—15. In vi. 1—8, and vii. 1—20, he makes a successful use of

---

with whom *Eichhorn* agrees, Micah prophesied from the fourteenth year of Hezekiah to some period in Manasseh's time. Against this view, see *Rosenmüller*, Procem. in Mic.

[a] *Hitzig* places iii. 12, iv. 9, 11, 14, in the time after the fall of Samaria. But this date is doubtful.

the form of a dialogue. He is full of feeling, (i. 8, and vii. 1): —

" Woe is me! I live when the summer fruits are gathered,
And the vintage is gleaned;
There is no cluster to eat:
I long for the first ripe fig." [a]

His prophecies are penetrated by the purest spirit of morality and piety, (vi. 6—8): —

" Wherewith shall I come before Jehovah,
And bow myself before the most high God?
Shall I come before him with burnt-offerings,
With calves of a year old?
Will Jehovah be pleased with thousands of rams,
Or with ten thousands of rivers of oil?
Shall I give my first-born for my sin,
The fruit of my body for my transgression?" .....
" He hath showed thee, O man, what is good:
What doth Jehovah require of thee,
But to do justly, and to love mercy,
And to walk humbly before thy God?"

Also, vii. 1—10.

" I will look to Jehovah;
I will hope in the God of my salvation;
My God will hear me.
Rejoice not over me, O my enemy!
Though I have fallen, I shall arise;
Though I sit in darkness,
Jehovah shall be my light.
I will bear the indignation of Jehovah,
Because I have sinned against him;
Until he maintain my cause, and execute judgment for me;
Until he bring me to the light,
And I behold his mercy."

---

[a] It is hardly possible to make an accurate distinction between the separate prophecies. Probably they were all written one after the other. But see *Bertholdt*, p. 1638, sqq. *Eichhorn*, Heb. Proph. p. 360, sqq. *Hitzig*, p. 164.

VII. NAHUM.[a]

§ 240.

HIS LIFE AND TIMES.

Nahum of Elkos[b]—to follow the contents of his oracles—prophesied after the unsuccessful irruption of Senna-

---

[a] *Theod. Bibliandri* Proph. Nahum, juxta Veritatem Ebr. Latine redditus cum Exegesi, &c.; Tigur. 1534.

J. H. Ursini Hypomnemata in Obad. et Nah.; Frcf. 1652.

Matth. Hafenrefferi Comm. in Nah. et Habac.; Stutg. 1663, 4to.

R. Abarbanelis Rabbinicus in Nahum Comm. Latio donatus a *J. Did. Sprechero;* Helmst. 1703, 4to.

Petri von Höke, Zergliedernde Auslegung üb. d. sechs letztern kl. Proph. Nah., Hab., Zeph., Hagg., Zachar., u. Malach. u. s. w.; Holl. Leid. 1709, 4to. Deutsch Frkf. 1710, 4to.

Vaticc. Chabac. et Nah. itemque nonnulla Jes., Mich. et Ezech. Oracula, Observatt. hist. phil. illustr., &c. Auct. *J. Gottl. Kalinsky;* Vratisl. 1748, 4to.

Vaticc. Nah. Observatt. phil. illustratum. Diss. præs. *M. C. M. Agrell,* resp. *N. S. Colliander;* Ups. 1788, 4to.

Vaticc. Nah. et Habac. Interpret. et Notas adjecit *E. J. Greve.* Edit. metrica; Amst. 1793, 4to.

Nahum Latine Vers. et Notis philol. illustratus, pt. i. Diss. Præs. *Andr. Svanborg,* resp. *J. Boden;* Ups. 1806, 4to.

Chr. M. Frähn, Curarum exeg. crit. in Nah. Proph. Spec.; Rost. 1806, 4to.

Nahumi Vatic. phil. et crit. expositum. Spec. acad., præs. *J. H. Pareau,* resp. *Ever. Kreenen;* Harderv. 1808, 4to.

Translated into German, by *Wahl,* in his Mag. 1790; *Grimm,* 1790; *Neumann,* 1808; *Middeldorpf,* 1808; *Justi,* 1820, and in his Blumen althebr. Dichtk. vol. ii. p. 577.

[b] *Jerome,* in the Proem to his Commentary on this prophet, says, "Some think Helkeseus was the father of Nahum, and, according to the Hebrew tradition, he was a prophet also. But, at this day, Elkos (Helkesei) is a village in Galilee, small, indeed, and scarcely disclosing the remnants of some ancient edifices, in ruins, yet it is well known to the Jews, and was pointed out to me by my guide."

Some have conjectured that *Capernaum,* כְּפַר נַחוּם, derived its name from *Nahum,* נַחוּם. (See *Hitzig* and *Knobel.*) Pseudo *Epiphanius* (De Vit. Proph. c. xvii.) says, *Οὗτος ἦν ἀπὸ Ἐλκεσεὶ (υἱὸς Ἐλκεσαίου ἀπὸ Ἰεσβεὶ) πέραν τοῦ Ἰορδάνου εἰς Βήγεβαρ ἐκ φυλῆς Συμεών.* *Cyrill.* Alex. ad Nah.

cherib into Judea, and consequently after the fourteenth year of Hezekiah.[a] Sennacherib's ill-success led Nahum to hope for the deliverance and restoration of his countrymen, (i. 13, ii. 3,) and the destruction of the hostile kingdom. (i. 14, ii. 2, 4, sqq., iii. 1, sqq.)[b]

The destruction of Thebes is mentioned in iii. 8—"Art thou better than No-ammon, that was situated among the rivers?" &c. But this is an uncertain date. However, it leads us to Hezekiah's time. [It is uncertain when Thebes was conquered, or to what conquest of it the prophet alludes; but we may reasonably conjecture it was near the beginning of Hezekiah's reign, for in Isaiah's time, Sargon, one of the Assyrian monarchs, invaded Ægypt, conquered Ashdod, and for three years

---

i. 1: *"Ορασις Ναοὺμ, τοῦ ἀπὸ τῆς 'Ελκεσέ· κώμη δὲ αὕτη πάντως που τῆς 'Ιουδαίων χώρας.* *Asseman* (Bib. Or. vol. i. p. 525, and iii. pt. i. p. 352) and *Niebuhr* (Reise, vol. ii. p. 352) think *Elkos* was in Assyria. *Michaelis*, (Uebers. A. T. vol. xi. Anmerk. p. 138,) *Eichhorn*, (§ 585,) *Hezel*, (Bibelwerk, vol. vii. p. 175,) and *Grimm*, (Ubers. p. 1, sqq.,) think Nahum was born there. See the well-founded objections of *Jahn*, (p. 509, sqq.,) *Kreenen*, (Nah. Vatic. p. 28,) *Bertholdt*, (p. 1652, sq.,) and *Knobel*, to this view.

[a] i. 11, 12, ii. 1, 3, 14. Comp. 2 Kings xix. 22, 23.

[b] *Jerome*, l. c.: Post Micheam sequitur Nahum, qui interpretatur consolator. Jam enim decem tribus ab Assyriis deductæ fuerant in captivitatem sub Ezechia rege Juda, sub quo etiam nunc in consolationem populi transmigrati adversum Niniven visio cernitur. Nec erat parva consolatio tam his, qui jam Assyriis serviebant, quam reliquis, qui sub Ezechia de tribubus Juda et Benjamin ab iisdem hostibus obsidebantur, ut audirent Assyrios quoque a Chaldæis esse capiendos. And yet *Jerome* makes him the first to prophesy the defeat of Sennacherib.

The above view is taken by *Vitringa*, (Typ. Doct. Proph. p. 37,) *Rosenmüller*, (Procœm. in Nah.,) *Bertholdt*, and *Knobel*. On the other hand, *Hitzig* places him somewhat later. See the erroneous opinions of *Josephus*, (Ant. x. 11, 3,) *Jarchi*, *Abarbanel*, *Grotius*, and *Grimm*.

Nahum could not have alluded to the historical circumstances under which Nineveh was taken by Cyaxares, king of the Medes, with the help of Nabopolassar the Chaldean, (625, 603, or 600, B. C.,) for at that time Babylon, and not Assyria, was formidable to the Hebrews. Perhaps, however, he was led to prophesy by the liberation of the Medes (from the Assyrians,) and their election of a king, in the person of Dejoces.

waged a successful war against the Ægyptians and their allies. The history is silent respecting the particular events of this war, and of its date. But it must have taken place soon after the commencement of Hezekiah's reign; and the capture of Thebes, to which Nahum alludes, may have taken place at that time, — perhaps between 720 and 716 B. C.][a]

§ 241.

CONTENTS AND SPIRIT OF HIS PROPHECY.

Aroused by a holy indignation at the ruin brought by the Assyrians upon the land of Judea, and confiding in the retributive justice of God, Nahum looks upon it as already at work, and so paints the destruction of Nineveh with lively colors. But he only speaks of it with the inspiration of the prophet, without mentioning the political combinations by which it was to be effected. The style is classic in all respects.[b] It is marked by clearness, by its finished elegance, as well as by fire, richness, and originality. The rhythm is very regular, and peculiarly lively. The whole book holds together well, and makes but one poem. The prophet only holds his breath, as it were, in the last chapter.[c] [" The most

---

[a] See *Eichhorn*, (§ 584,) *Rosenmüller*, and *Gesenius*, on Isa. xx.

[b] *Hitzig* (p. 214) finds peculiarities in the language; impure and later usages; the pronunciation of שְׂעָרָה, for סערה, i. 3, (Job ix. 17;) קַנּוֹא, i. 2, (Josh. xxiv. 19;) נִפֹּשׁוּ, for נָפֹצוּ, iii. 18; the form of the suffixes of the *second* person, ii. 14, and of the *third*, i. 13, ii. 4, (comp. Hab. iii. 10;) the *un-Shemitish* טפסר, iii. 17, and נהג, ii. 8, in the Syriac sense; דהר, iii. 2, (Judg. v. 23.) Chap. ii. 11, betrays a late writer. (Comp. Isa. xxiv. 1, xxi. 3, Ezek. xxx. 4, 9.) Nahum often agrees with Jeremiah. (ii. 5, 14, iii. 5, 13, 17.)

[c] *Eichhorn*, § 586. *Bertholdt*, to the contrary, p. 1661. *Kalinsky* and others erroneously think there were two conquests of Nineveh. The single

striking characteristic of Nahum's style is the power of representing several phases of an idea in the briefest sentences. Examples of this are his description of God, (i. 2—6,) the conquest of Nineveh, (ii. 4,) and the destruction of No-ammon, (iii. 8, sqq.) The variety in his manner of presenting his ideas discovers much poetic talent in the prophet. The reader of taste and sensibility will be affected by the entire structure of the poem, by the agreeable manner in which the ideas are brought forward, by the flexibility of his expressions, the roundness of his turns, the delicate outline of his figures; by the strength and delicacy, and the expression of sympathy and greatness, which diffuse themselves over the whole subject. He does not come upon you roaring and violent, nor yet softly and lightly. Here, there is something sonorous in his language; there, is something murmuring; and with both there alternates somewhat that is soft, delicate, and melting — as the subject demands. This is not possible for a poet of art, but only for the poet of nature."][a]

VIII. HABAKKUK.[b]

§ 242

HIS LIFE AND TIMES.

We have only apocryphal accounts of the person of Habakkuk.

---

inscription, מַשָּׂא נִינְוֵה, seems to have been added later. *Bertholdt,* p. 1659, sq.

[a] *Eichhorn,* § 587.

[b] *R. Abarbanelis* rabbinicus, in Habac. Comm. Latine redditus a *J. Didr Sprechero;* Helmst. 1790.

Habakkuk lived and prophesied in the Chaldee period; but it is doubtful, and contested, in what part of this period we are to place him.[a] Chap. i. 5, sqq., certainly refers to the beginning of it, and belongs to the reign of Jehoiakim, 610—599 B. C. (Compare 2 Kings xxiv. 1.) Even the last chapter does not seem to demand a later

---

W. F. Capitonis Enarratt. in Proph. Hab.; Arg. 1526.

Dav. Chytræi Lectiones in Proph. Hab., in his Opp. t. ii.

Anton Agelli Comm. in Proph. Hab.; Antverp. 1597.

Habac., Vates olim Hebr., imprimis ipsius Hymnus denuo illustratus (Auct. *Chr. Gottl. Perschke;*) Frcf. 1777.

Chabac. Vatic., Comm. crit. atque exeg. illustratum, ed. *B. P. Kofod;* Havn. 1792.

J. Ad. Tingstadii Animadverss. philol. et crit. ad Vaticc. Hab.; Ups. 1795, 4to.

Hänlein, Symbola crit. ad interpret. Vatic. Hab.; Erl. 1795.

G. A. Ruperti Explicatio Cap. i. et ii. Chab. in the Commentatt. theol. ed. *Velthusen*, *Kuinöl*, et *Ruperti*, vol. iii. p. 405, sqq.

Guil. Ad. Schröderi Dissert. in Cant. Chab.; Gron. 1781, 4to.

Ch. F. Schnurreri Diss. phil. ad Carm. Chab. Cap. iii., (Tub. 1786, 4to.,) in his Dissertatt. phil. crit. p. 342, sqq.

Hymnus Hab. Vers. ac Notis phil. et crit. illustr. auct. *Mœrner;* Ups. 1791, 4to.

Translated and explained in German, by *B. Ludwig*, 1779; *Wahl*, (mit Einl. und Abhandll.,) 1790; an anonymous writer, Lpz. 1796; *Horst*, 1798; *Justi*, 1821; *Wolf*, 1822.

[a] [Pseudo *Epiphanius* (l. c., c. xviii.) says he was of the city of Bethzochar, or Bidzechar, in the tribe of Simeon; that, when Nebuchadnezzar came to lay waste Jerusalem, he fled to Ostrakine, — a city on the borders of Ægypt, Arabia, and Palestine, — and remained there, a dweller in the land of Ishmael. But when the Chaldeans withdrew from Jerusalem to their own territories, he returned to his native place, betook himself to agriculture, and died two years before the return from the Babylonian exile. *Isidore* and *Dorotheus* of Tyre agree, substantially, with this account. In the apocryphal fable of Bel and the Dragon, *Habakkuk* is made to carry food to Daniel in the lions' den, (verse 33, sqq.;) but that story contains its own refutation. Some of the rabbins have, in their tasteless method, combined his name, חֲבַקּוּק, with the words אַתְּ חֹבֶקֶת בֵּן, (i. e. thou shalt embrace a son,) which the prophet Elisha addresses to the Shunammitish woman, and have attempted to show that Habakkuk was the son of this woman.] *Abarbanel*, in Hab. i. 1. *Carpzov*, p. 398. *Knobel*, p. 291.

date, for he has no misgivings of the destruction of Judah, (iii. 16, 17;) consequently he was a younger contemporary of Jeremiah. Rosenmüller, in his Proem to this prophet, thinks chap. ii. belongs to a later period; but it obviously agrees with chap. i., and the last chapter agrees with both. Stickel says that in chap. iii. only "the day of trouble, the approach of the destroyer, and the devastation of the land," are in sight. Jahn, misunderstanding i. 2—4, and the purity of Habakkuk's language, places him in the time of Manasseh.[a]

§ 243.

CONTENTS AND SPIRIT OF HIS PROPHECY.

When the prophet, in the spirit, saw the formidable power of the Chaldees approaching and menacing his land, and saw the great evils they would cause in Judea, he bore his complaints and doubts before Jehovah, the JUST and the PURE. (i. 2—17.) And on this occasion the future punishment of the Chaldees was revealed to him. (ii.) In chap. iii. a presentiment of the destruction of his country, and acquiescence in Jehovah's will, contend, in the inspired breast of the prophet, with his hope that the enemy would be chastised.

If Habakkuk is to be compared with the most excel-

---

[a] *Stickel*, Prol. ad interpret. Tent. Cap. Heb. pt. i.; Neostad, 1827, p. 22, 27. See *Hirzel*, in *Winer's* Zeitschrift. vol. vii. p. 393. The opinions of *Bertholdt*, (p. 1667,) and of *Friederich*, (in *Eichhorn's* Allg. Bib. vol. x. p. 400,) that Habakkuk lived in the time of the destruction of Jerusalem, are not tenable. The Chaldees appear, in iii. 14, 17, et al., in hostility with the Jews.

See *Jahn*, vol. ii. p. 513, and *Wahl's* version, p. 16. *Rosenmüller* explains these verses correctly. *Perschke*, *Ranitz*, (Introd. in Hab. Vatic.; Lips. 1808, p. 24,) and *Stickel*, (l. c. p. 47,) justly suppose Habakkuk prophesied before the invasion of the Chaldees. [*Noyes* (l. c. vol. ii. p. 245, sq.) and *Knobel* (l. c. 293) are of this opinion.]

lent prophets — with Joel, Amos, Nahum, and Isaiah — in point of prophetic style, so, in the lyric passage, chap. iii., he surpasses all which Hebrew poesy can offer in this department. In his sublimest flights, he unites the greatest strength and fulness with moderation, clearness, and beauty. His rhythm is at once the purest and the most regular. His language is fresh and pure.

[" The two first chapters are written in the form of a dialogue between the prophet and Jehovah. Habakkuk complains of the sad state of his nation, opposed by their enemies. (i. 2—4.) Jehovah replies that he is doing a great work in raising up the Chaldeans, " a fierce and swift people," for his purposes. They are to gather captives like the sand, and to scoff at kings ; to mock at fortresses, and take them. (i. 5—11.) The prophet rejoins, and confesses that he knows the Chaldeans have been sent to judge and punish the Jews, — but the Jews are less wicked than their proud oppressors, who regard them as but fish and worthless reptiles, whom no man protects or cares for. Shall these, he inquires, continually slay the nations without mercy ? (i. 12—ii. 1.) Jehovah answers again, that the Chaldeans also are to be punished, and the time is hastening to approach, when the proud Chaldeans shall not be at ease, and the just Jews shall be saved by their faithfulness. The violence done to the Jews shall return upon the perpetrator, and his graven images shall not save him. (ii. 2—20.) The last chapter is a lyric prayer.

" The theme of this poem was the most interesting and inspiring to a Jew. He saw the foe invade his native land ; he saw equity and justice lying prostrate ; he saw independence and the dignity of the nation — what once was dearest and best to a Jew — now lost. This prospect must depress every feeling heart into deep sorrow; but a heart warm as the prophet's it must quite rend asunder. It was not natural that, with such a thought in his mind, Habakkuk should waken the soft lute over the ruins of his wicked nation. He must hear the war-trumpet sound.

"He has all the attributes of a great poet united—an imagination full of creative power; just judgment, which, in almost every case, gives correctness and the most delicate outline to the creations of his glowing fancy; an unlimited power over language, to give it, at will, harmony and loveliness, or sonorous strength. O that greedy time, and the Babylonian exile, which have devoured so many monuments of the Hebrews, had left us more of this sublime poet's works! He begins with a living portraiture, and ends with the same. Did poet ever paint a powerful and haughty conqueror in finer colors than he has depicted the Chaldeans? (i. 6—11.) Did a poet ever mock with more biting taunts than he, when he makes the abused people triumph over their haughty tyrants, after they have themselves lain at their feet? (ii. 6—17.) Did ever a poet represent the solemnity of universal nature at the arrival of God with more strength and sublimity? (ii. 3—15.) The entire ancient history of the Jews, with all its great and wonderful scenes, lends him ideas and images; all that is grand and terrible in nature flows together into one stream. He contends with words; he struggles with images; and who is not seized with a holy shudder as he reads,—like that of the sacred prophet, as he saw the sublime and terrible appearance of the Indescribable? Paint it better, ye who can."] [a]

---

[a] *Eichhorn*, § 591. A sort of strophe occurs in ii. 6—20. Chap. iii. contends for originality with Ps. xviii. and lxviii. Chap. ii. 1, 2, is symbolical.

IX. ZEPHANIAH.[a]

§ 244.

HIS LIFE AND TIMES.

Zephaniah was a descendant of Hezekiah, though it is scarcely probable he was descended from the *king* of that name, as Eichhorn seems inclined to suppose, while Jahn and Rosenmüller are of a different opinion. He prophesied under King Josiah, (642—611 B. C.,) and since he zealously opposes idolatry, (i. 4—6,)[b] and is the first

---

The formation of קִרְקָלוֹן (ii. 16) is peculiar. (See *Gesenius* and *Rosenmüller.*) What *Eichhorn* says (p. 412) of the peculiar language of Habakkuk, requires examination.

[The inscription and the subscription of chap. iii. were occasioned by the use of this passage in public worship. In the latter there is a mistake in the text — בִּנְגִינוֹתָי, instead of בִּנְגִינוֹת.

It is very improbable that ii. 19, is an interpolation, arising from the same cause, as *Bertholdt* maintains, p. 1669. *Hanlein's* attempt at a critical emendation of chap. iii. is unsuccessful. See *Bertholdt*, p. 1675.]

[a] *Mart. Buceri* Sophonias ad Veritatem Ebr. versus et Comm. explicatus; Arg. 1528.

Jo. Arn. Noltenii Diss. exeg. prælim. in Proph. Zeph.; Traj. ad Viadr. 1719.

C. F. Cramer, Scyth. Denkmäler in Palästina; 1777.

Dan. a Cölln, Spicileg. Observat. exeget. crit. in Zephan.; Vratisl. 1818, 4to.

F. A. Herwig, Beit. z. d. Erläut. des Proph. Zeph., in *Bengel*, Arch. vol. i. pt. iii.

Translated into German, with Remarks, by *E. Ewald;* 1827.

[b] The phrase שְׁאָר הַבַּעַל, *remnant of Baal*, cannot support the opposite conclusion, — viz. that he wrote in the latter part of Josiah's reign, after the extirpation of idolatry, — as *Eichhorn, Bertholdt, Rosenmüller*, and *Jäger*, maintain. *Hitzig* places him between the 12th and 18th of Josiah, following 2 Ch. xxxiv. 3, 8, xxxv. 19. *Movers*, Chron. p. 334, sq. See above, § 191, p. 298, sqq. *Knobel*, p. 247.

to expect the destruction of Nineveh, (ii. 13,) it appears that he prophesied in the first years of Josiah.[a]

§ 245.

CONTENTS AND SPIRIT OF HIS PROPHECIES.

Zephaniah has left us two prophecies, (i.—ii. and iii.,) in which he treats the same thoughts in different manners. In chap. i. he predicts the destruction of the idolatrous and corrupt nation,[b] and in chap. ii. exhorts them to reformation, but promises that all the enemies of the land shall be punished. (ii. 4, 15.) In chap. iii., after reproving anew the sins of the nation, he foresees the restoration of the people after they have reformed themselves.

In respect to style, Zephaniah is by no means equal to the best prophets. He is often heavy and tedious. His rhythm frequently sinks down to prose; however, his language is pure.[c]

---

[a] The *king's sons*, (i. 8,) on which *Bertholdt* lays so much stress, are not necessarily the sons of Josiah.

[b] According to the common view, he speaks of its conquest by the *Chaldeans*. *Knobel*, p. 248. *Cramer*, *Eichhorn*, and *Hitzig*, understand the *Scythians* to be referred to, who, in the time of Psammeticus, made an incursion as far as Ægypt. *Herodotus*, i. 103, sq.

[c] [*Eichhorn* and *Jahn* accuse him of imitating the earlier prophets. The former selects the following instances: Zeph. ii. 14, "Flocks shall lie down in her; the pelican and the hedgehog shall lodge in the capitals of her pillars," compared with Isa. xiii. 21, and xxxiv. 11, "The pelican and the hedgehog shall possess it," &c.; and also ii. 15, "That said in her heart, 'I, and none beside me,'" compared with Isa. xlvii. 8, "And sayest in thy heart, 'I am, and there is none beside me,'" &c. But, unfortunately for this hypothesis, each of these parallels belongs to the spurious portion of Isaiah, which was written after the time of Zephaniah. But yet, though his want of originality has been exaggerated, it cannot be denied. He borrows both figures and thoughts from his predecessors. Chap. i. 13.

X. *HAGGAI.*[a]

§ 246.

HIS LIFE AND TIMES.

Haggai prophesied at the time of Zerubbabel and Joshua, in the second year of Darius Hystaspes, 520 B.C., (i. 1,) at a time when the temple, which had been begun by the young colony, had for some time been impeded by outward hinderances and the indolence of the Jews, and when a favorable opportunity presented itself for finishing the work. See Ezra iv. 24, v. 1.[b]

"They also shall build houses, but not inhabit them,
And shall plant vineyards, but not drink the wine thereof."

Compare with Amos v. 11: —

"Though ye build houses of hewn stone, ye shall not dwell in them;
Though ye plant pleasant vineyards, ye shall not drink the wine of them."

Compare also ii. 8, with Isa. xvi. 6; iii. 10, with xviii. 1, sqq. He is fond of a certain kind of repetition. Chap. ii. 15,

"A day of distress and anguish,
A day of destruction and desolation,
A day of darkness and gloominess," &c.

And iii. 2, 17.

He furnishes more proofs of a poor and low taste than we could reasonably expect in so short a book. He sometimes indulges in paronomasia and play upon words; e. g. i. 15, ii. 1, 4.] See *Eichhorn*, § 595. *Knobel*, ii. p. 246, sqq.

[a] *J. Merceri* Scholia et Vers. ad Proph. Hagg.; Par. 1551.

Jo. Jac. Grynæi Comm. in Hagg.; Genev. 1581.

Frid. Balduini Comm. in Hagg., Zach., et Malach.; Viteb. 1610, 8vo. Published in *Joa. Schmid.* Comm. in Proph. minor.

Balth. Willii Prophetæ Hagg., Zach., Malach., Comment. illustrati; Brem. 1638.

Aug. Varenii Trifolium Prophet., s. tres poster. Prophetæ, scil. Hagg., Zach., et Malach., explicati; Rost. 1662, 4to. His Exercitatt. duæ in Hagg. ib. 1648, 1650, 4to.

Andr. Reinbeck, Exercitatt. in Proph. Hagg.; Brunsv. 1692, 4to.

Dan. Pfeffinger, Notæ in Proph. Hagg.; Arg. 1703, 4to.

Franc. Woken, Annotatt. exeg. in Proph. Hagg.; Lips. 1719.

Vaticc. Haggæi vers. et illustr. a *Nic. Hesslen*; Lund. 1799, 4to.

[b] *Jerome*, commenting on Hag. i. 13, says some think that John the Bap-

§ 247.

CONTENTS AND SPIRIT OF THE PROPHECY.

Haggai has left us four short prophecies on the subject of the erection of the temple, which was then at a stand. They are carefully furnished with historical statements. Eichhorn thinks that these are only summaries of the real discourses he delivered. The discourses themselves, then, must have been more meagre than even these tedious productions. The last four verses compose a supplementary explanation of ii. 6—9. Without any inspiration, and following the principles of the common doctrine of retribution, and at the suggestion of a vulgar patriotism, (ii. 6—9,) he chides, admonishes, and promises, with an unprophetic zeal for the restoration of the ancient worship. He uses frequent interrogations. (i. 4, 9, ii. 2, 3, 12, 13, 19.) The style is devoid of all spirit and energy; yet he sometimes attempts rhythm. See also i. 5, 7, ii. 15, 18.

[High religious and moral views nowhere occur in the book. He has a few favorite formulas, which he uses to excess; for example, "Consider how it goeth with you;" "Saith Jehovah of hosts," (which occurs ten times in this short book;) and, "Zerubbabel, the son of Shealtiel, governor of Judah, and Joshua, the son of Josedech, the high priest, and all the people." Parallelisms

---

tist, Malachi, — whose name is interpreted *angel of the Lord*, — and Haggai, whom we have now before us, were angels, who took human bodies, at God's command, and dwelt among men. However, both he and *Cyril* of Alex. (ad loc.) take the phrase, מַלְאַךְ יְהוָה, in the sense of *prophet*. See also pseudo *Epiphanius*, ch. xx. He is said to have been a member of the Great Synagogue. See *Carpzov*, l. c. p. 426.

sometimes occur. (i. 6, 9, 10, &c.) The language is somewhat Chaldaic, and poor.] [a]

XI. ZECHARIAH.[b]

§ 248.

HIS LIFE AND TIMES.

Zechariah was the son of Barachiah, the son of Iddo. (i. 1, 7.) According to Ezra v. 1, and vi. 14, he was the son of Iddo; but here the term *son* is used in the sense of *descendant*, and requires no further explanation. In Matt. xxiii. 35, this Zechariah is confounded with another Zechariah, the son of Jehoiada the priest, who is mentioned in 2 Ch. xxiv. 20, sqq. He was contemporary with Haggai, and entered upon the office of a prophet only a few months later than Haggai. His taste

---

[a] See *Hitzig* and *Knobel.*

[b] *Ph. Melanchthonis* Comm. in Proph. Zachar. Opp. ii. p. 531.
Jo. Jac. Grynæi Comm. in Zachar.; Genev. 1581, 4to.
Casp. Sanctii Comm. in Zachar.; Lugd. 1616, 4to.
Jo. Henr. Ursini Comment. in Proph. Zachar.; Frcf. 1652.
Sam. Bohlii Analys. et Exeg. Proph. Zachar.; Rost. 1711.
C. Vitringæ Comm. ad Libr. Prophetiarum Zachar. quæ supersunt; Leovard. 1734, 4to.
(*B. G. Flügge*) Die Weissagungen, welche den Schriften des Zacharias beigebogen sind; Hamb. 1788.
H. Venemæ Sermones acad. vice Comm. in Libr. Proph. Zach.; Leov. 1789, 4to.
B. Blayney, A new Translation, with Notes; Oxf. 1797, 4to.
Köster, Meletemata crit. et ex. in Zachar. pars poster. c. ix.—xiv.; Gott. 1818.
Ed. Forberg, Comment. crit. et exeg. in Zachar. Vatic. pars post. pt. i.; Cob. 1824, 4to.
Translated into German (by *Trinius*;) Quedlinb. 1780.

and fondness for symbols, and the Chaldaic doctrine of angels and spirits, which he has adopted, show that he had received his education in Chaldea.[a]

§ 249.

CONTENTS AND SPIRIT OF THE FIRST PART OF HIS PROPHECY.

The oracles contained in chap. i.—viii. constitute a whole, by themselves, and all relate to the restoration of the Jewish state and temple. After exhorting the people to obedience in general, (i. 1—6,) the prophet, in a series of symbolical visions, (i. 7—vi. 8,) and accompanied by one symbolical action, (vi. 9—15,) gives many admonitions, encouragements, and promises. In a later prophecy, he answers the question which is put to him respecting the days of fasting, hitherto observed, and promises a joyful future. (vii. and viii.)

Zechariah writes almost entirely without rhythm, without energy, and without effect. Like Ezekiel, he loves

[a] [Pseudo *Epiphanius* (l. c. cap. xxi.) says he came from the land of the Chaldees in old age, and when he was there he taught the people many things, and performed many miracles, to confirm their faith in him, (εἰς ἀπόδειξιν.) He foretold that Josedech should have a son, who should discharge the office of priest at Jerusalem. He also blessed Salathiel, announcing that he should beget a son, and call his name Zerubbabel. Besides this, he performed a miracle under Cyrus, king of the Persians, promoting the victory over Crœsus, king of the Lydians, and over Astyages, king of the Medes. Besides, he predicted the service which Cyrus should perform for Jerusalem, and blessed him with great blessings. ...... He died in Judea, in extreme old age, and was buried near Haggai, the prophet. But another codex of Epiphanius adds, that he was slain by *Joash*, king of Judah, between the temple and the altar, while he was exhorting both king and people to desist from impiety, and return to God, &c. &c. The author of this sentence did not reflect that Joash, and Zechariah, son of Barachiah, were separated by a period of 320 years. See *Carpzov*, l. c. p. 439, sq.]

to repeat his favorite formulas; as, for example, "Thus saith Jehovah of hosts," (i. 3, &c.,) [a phrase which occurs no less than forty-one times in these eight chapters;] "Ye shall know that Jehovah of hosts sent me." (ii. 9, 11, iv. 8, vi. 15.)

His language bears marks of a late age.[a] His manner of using symbols is obscure, and displays no power of invention. His symbols require the explanations, which he gives himself. The substance and contents of his writings by no means compensate for these defects of style, for there is nothing original or living in his admonitions, or his prophetic visions. He refers to the earlier prophets.[b] Hengstenberg adduces many other instances of imitation, or acquaintance with the earlier prophets; but all the rest are too uncertain.[c]

The arrangement of the prophecies is, incontestably, to be ascribed to the prophet himself. [A Jewish and Levitical spirit pervades the book. It relates, almost

---

[a] ה art. before the stat. constr.; iv. 7, 10. אֵסָּעֲרֵם, Syriasm. for אֲסַעֲרֵם; vii. 14. עָזַר with לְ; i. 15. (Comp. 2 Sam. viii. 5.) בָּבַת עֵינוֹ; ii. 12. הֶעֱבִיר, *abstulit*; iii. 4. מַהְלְכִים; iii. 7. גֻּלָּה, גֻּל; iv. 2, 3. (Comp. Eccl. xii. 6.) שָׁמִיר; vii. 12. (Ezek. iii. 9. Jer. xvii. 1.) Hard constructions. פְּרָזוֹת, cas. absol.; ii. 8. זֶרַע הַשָּׁלוֹם; viii. 12. תְּשֻׁאוֹת, cas. abs. or supp. תִּחְיֶרְנָה; iv. 7. אֶת־כָּל־אֵלֶּה; viii. 17. הֲלֹא אֶת־הַדְּבָרִים; vii. 7. כְּפִי אִישׁ ii. 4. אַחַר כָּבוֹד; ii. 12, vi. 6, 13. Omission of כִּי; vii. 23. Comp *Köster*, l. c. p. 27, sqq., 38, sqq.

[b] Chap. i. 4—6, and vii. 7, sqq., iii. 8, and vi. 12. Comp. with Jer. xxiii 5, xxxiii. 15, vi. 13. Comp. Ps. cx. 4, (?) viii. 20—23. Comp. Isa. ii. 3.

[c] [The resemblance in these instances, except the last, is exceedingly slight. *Hengstenberg* (l. c. vol. i. p. 367, sq.) considers an acquaintance with the old prophets, and an imitation of them, as one of the characteristics of Zechariah. He mentions the following instances: Chap. ii. 8, an imitation of Isa. xlix. 19, 20; iii. 10, of Mich. iv. 4; iii. 8, and vi. 12, from Jer. xxiii. 5, and xxxiii. 15, and Isa. iv. 2. The fundamental thought of chap. v. he takes from Ezek. ii. 9, 10; viii. 4, from Isa. lxv. 20.]

exclusively, to the temple and the form of worship; yet some general ethical maxims occur, which the prophet applies. He is fired with revengeful hatred against the heathen nations, and, on account of their ancient oppressions, he predicts their ruin and subjugation to the Jews, for whom he entertains high and rash hopes. He often reminds the people of the fruitless prophecies and admonitions of the earlier prophets. For the most part, he makes use of visions, to set forth his thoughts. They are almost always symbolical, and often very obscure, so that he usually explains them. Simple comparisons and images do not occur in his writings, as in those of the elder prophets. Instead of these, he has symbols, and in this respect resembles Daniel and Ezekiel, with whom he has in common the frequent introduction of higher spiritual beings. He alone, of all the prophets, mentions Satan, who occurs in a similar manner in the later apocalyptical writers. In general, he writes without inspiration, energy, or effect; abounds in repetitions, and therefore is diffuse and uniform. He closely resembles Ezekiel, but is to be placed below him in rank. The style is prosaic, and the language slightly Chaldaic.] [a]

§ 250, *a*.

ON THE SECOND PART, IX.—XIV.

The contents of these chapters are in part enigmatical. Chap. ix. contains threats against Hadrach,—which is, perhaps, Persia,—Damascus, Tyre and Sidon, Philistia, and a promise that Judah shall be powerful, victorious, and happy, under its conquering and peaceful

---

[a] *Knobel*, l. c. p. 384, sq.

kings. Chap. x., in like manner, predicts that the house of Judah — notwithstanding its present condition — shall be warlike and triumphant; the exiles shall return, (x. 6,) and no foreigners — neither Assyrians nor Ægyptians — shall rule over them any more. Chap. xi. 1—3, relates the humiliation of the proud. Lebanon is taken as an image of Persia, or of all the enemies of Judah. The enigmatical part of the picture now begins, — though there was an allusion to it in chap. x. 2, 3. Israel will be corrupted by bad shepherds; the harmony will be disturbed; God will punish them, (chap. xi. 4—xiv.;) Judah must pass through a great purification, for she has forsaken God; all nations shall besiege Jerusalem; the herdsman shall be slain; two thirds of the inhabitants shall perish, and the remaining third must be purified yet more. But Jehovah, appearing in terrible majesty, contends against the foreign nations, and smites them with plagues. Then Jerusalem will be quietly inhabited; a living water will proceed from it; sin and unrighteousness will be abolished, and all nations shall come up to Jerusalem to worship.

§ 250, *b*.

THE SAME SUBJECT CONTINUED.

Here, with the single exception of chap. xi. 14—17, the style is not symbolical; sometimes it is not devoid of poetical elevation and rhythm. (ix. 3, sqq., and xi. 1—3.)

The form of introducing his oracles, used in the first part, (i. 1, iv. 8, vi. 9, vii. 1, 8, viii. 1, 18,) is omitted, and others occur, in which the name of Zechariah is not mentioned. (ix. 1, xi. 4, xii. 1.) The historical circumstances seem to be different, for Damascus, Tyre, Philistia, (ix. 1—6,) Javan, (ix. 13,) Assyria, and Ægypt, (x. 11,) are the enemies of Judah. The separation of the tribes is mentioned, (xi. 14, ix. 13, x. 6, 7;) the kingdom itself, (xi. 6, xiii. 7; comp. xii. 7, 8, 12;) idolatry and false prophets, (x. 2, sqq., xiii. 2, sqq.; but compare Nehemiah vi. 10—14;) and these do not belong to the time when Zechariah actually lived. Thus there seem sufficient grounds for denying that these chapters belong to Zechariah, and for referring them to some earlier prophet.[a]

But, on the other hand, it must be said that these

---

[a] [Doubts respecting the authenticity of the latter part of the book were first suggested, it is believed, by Mr. Mede, in his remarks on Matt. xxvii. 9, 10. He says, "It may seem the evangelists would inform us that these latter chapters, (ix. x. xi.,) ascribed to Zachary, are indeed the prophecies of Jeremy, and that the Jews had not rightly attributed them. Certainly, if a man weigh the contents of some of these, they should, of a likelihood, be of an elder date than the time of Zachary; namely, before the captivity, for the subjects of some of them were scarce in being after that time....... As for their being joined to the prophecies of Zachary, that proves no more they are his, than the like adjoining of Agur's proverbs to Solomon's, proves they are therefore Solomon's; or that all the psalms are David's, because joined in one volume with David's psalms."]

J. Mede's Works, fol.; Lond. 1678. He was followed by *Joh. Bridge, Hammond, Rich, Kidder*, (Demonstration of the Messiah,) *Will. Whiston, Newcome*, and *Döderlein*, who doubted the genuineness of these chapters, after making a regular investigation. See the literature in *Köster*, (l. c. p. 10, sqq.,) *Flügge, J. D. Michaelis, Bauer, Eichhorn*, (in 4th edition,) *Corrodi*, and *Augusti, Bertholdt, De Wette*, (in the first three editions of this Introduction,) *Forberg*, (l. c.) *Rosenmüller*, (2d ed. of his Schol. on Minor Proph.,) *Hitzig*, (in Studien und Kritiken for 1830, p. 25,) *Credner*, (Joel, p. 67.) The genuineness has been defended by *Carpzov*, (Crit. Sac. p. 808,) *Beckhaus*, (Integrität d. Proph. p. 337,) *Jahn*, (l. c. vol. ii. p. 675,) *Rosenmüller*, (1st ed.,) *Köster*, (l. c.,) and by *Hengstenberg*, (Beit. vol. i. p. 361, sqq.) [*Blayney* also attempted a defence of the genuineness in the preliminary discourse to his translation of Zechariah, p. xii., sq., and notes on chap. ix. p. 35, sqq. See, also, *Hennell*, Inquiry into the Origin of Christianity; Lond. 1841, p. 333, note. He refers ix.—xiv. to Jeremiah.]

chapters have some affinity with the former part in language and style,[a] and also in the reference to other and sometimes quite late prophets.[b] These circumstances show it could not have been written before the exile. It is clearly presupposed that the nation, and not merely the ten tribes, are in exile. (ix. 12, x. 6, 9, 10.)[c] The

---

[a] רַאֲמָה, for רָמָה; xiv. 10. צָבָה, for צָבָא; ix. 8. דָּוִיד, for דָּוִד; xii. 7, and often, as in Chronicles. הֶעֱבִיר; xiii. 2, (iii. 4.) זָוִיּוֹת; ix. 15. (Comp. Ps. cxliv. 12.) חָזִיז; x. 1, (Job xxviii. 26, xxxviii. 25.) בָּחַל; xi. 8. Hard constructions: עֵין אָדָם; ix. 1. אֲסִירֵי הַתִּקְוָה; ix. 12. וְלֹא עֲלֵיהֶם; xiv. 18. צָרָה, perhaps cas. absol.; x. 11. (Comp. *Köster*, p. 44.) Omission of כִּי; ix. 12. (Comp. viii. 23.) עֹבֵר וָשָׁב; ix. 8, vi. 14. (Comp. Ex. xxxii. 27, Ez. xxxv. 7.) For the formula, "Ye shall know that Jehovah of hosts hath sent me," which occurs in ii. 9, 11, iv. 8, vi. 15, a corresponding expression occurs but once, (xi. 11,) they "knew it was the word of Jehovah." The formula, "God said," is more rare. (x. 12, xi. 6, xii. 4, xiii. 2, 7, 8, ix. 9.) "Rejoice greatly, O daughter of Zion! Shout, O daughter of Jerusalem!" &c., is similar to ii. 14, (10 in our version and *Noyes*,) "Sing and rejoice, O daughter of Zion!" [The phrase, "Jehovah of hosts," occurs but 7 times in the latter, and 41 in the former portion.] The prolixity of xii. 10—14, and xiv. 15, reminds one of viii. 19; but comp. vii. 5. [The resemblance is much less striking than with many passages of more ancient prophets; e. g. Jer. xxxi. 9, vi. 26, Amos viii. 8—12. It would perhaps be difficult to equal the prolixity of i. 2—6, — to mention but a single instance, — with any passage in the second part.] The parallelism of many members (ix. 5, 7, 9, 10, 13, 15, xii. 4, et al.) reminds us of vi. 13, and both belong to the taste of later times. [But examples of this kind of parallelism are common even in so old a writer as Hosea, or Joel; e. g. Joel ii. 6, 9, 10, 20, Hos. ii. 14, iv. 3, v. 1, &c.] The symbol in xi. 4, sqq., is equally obscure with any symbol in the first part of the book, and in general much in this part is obscure.

[b] Chap. ix. 5, comp. Zeph. ii. 4; ix. 10, comp. Ps. lxxii. 8, Mich. v. 9; ix. 13, comp. Joel iv. 6; ix. 12, comp. Isa. xl. 2; x. 3, comp. Ez. xxxiv. 17; xi. 3, comp. Jer. xii. 5, xlix. 19; xi. 6, comp. Jer. l. 7; xi. 16, comp. Ez. xxxiv. 4; xii. 1, comp. Isa. xliv. 24, li. 13; xiii. 2, comp. Hos. ii. 19; xiii. 8, sq., comp. Ez. v. 12; xiii. 9, comp. Hos. ii. 25; xiv. 5, comp. Deut. xxxiii. 3; xiv. 8, comp. Joel iv. 18, Ez. xlvii. 1, sqq.; xiv. 16, comp. Isa. lxvi. 23. [This proves nothing, for the references to old prophets are rare in the first part of the book. See above.]

[c] It is not a *future*, but a *present* thing. וְאֶזְרָעֵם is in the past time, as it appears from vii. 14.

Levitical spirit, (xiv. 16, 20,) and the fantastic expectations, agree with the times after the exile. There are also some other marks which point to this period.[a]

Now, since it is not possible to combine all the allusions to the time into one point, and make them all harmonize with the condition of the land at any one period of its history,[b] therefore it may be the most ad-

---

[a] Uzziah, *king of Judah*, is mentioned, xiv. 5; but comp. Jer. xxvi. 18, 19. [The inference the author would draw from this mention of Uzziah is probably this: If the oracle were written before the exile, the time of Uzziah would not be referred to as time long past, nor would it have been added that he was king of Judah. Uzziah came to the throne about 811 B. C., while the exile commenced 588. But in Jeremiah, (l. c.,) the days of Hezekiah, *king of Judah*, are referred to, and in Haggai, his contemporary Zerubbabel is called "*the son of Shealtiel, the governor of Judah.*"] The *former gate* (שַׁעַר הָרִאשׁוֹן) is mentioned, xiv. 10—as the *old* gate is mentioned, Neh. iii. 6. A drought is alluded to, x. 1, which also is mentioned in viii. 10, sqq., and in Hag. i. 6, 10, sqq.; and the jealousy between Judah and Jerusalem, alluded to in xii. 7, seems to have been caused by the state of affairs at that time. The addition of the term "oracle" (מַשָּׂא) to the "word of Jehovah," (דברי יהוה,) ix. 1, which also occurs in Mal. i. 1, seems to be caused by Jer. xxiii. 33, sqq., where the same word occurs. *Hadrach* is probably a mystical name for *Persia*. Chap. x. 4, seems to imply that Judah was not warlike at that time. *Jahn*, Append. Hermeneut. vol. i. p. 175. *Köster*, p. 77.

[b] *Newcome* separates ix.—xi. from xii.—xiv. The former he places before the overthrow of the kingdom of Israel, and the latter after Josiah, and before the destruction of Jerusalem. *Flügge* divides it into nine sections, which he ascribes to different authors and ages, and refers chap. ix. to that Zechariah who is mentioned in 2 Ch. xxvi. 5. *Bertholdt* places ix. x. in the time of Ahaz; xi. a little earlier; xii. 1—xiii. 6, under one of the last kings of Judah; xiii. 7—xiv. 21, and the first two passages, he refers to the Zechariah mentioned in Isa. viii. 2. The author of this Introduction took a view slightly different in the three first editions. *Hitzig* once placed the whole in the time of Uzziah,—but is now compelled to place it after that time,—and *Credner* puts it in that of Ahaz. [But in the passages, xiv. 5, (x. 6, ?) ix. 9, where a personal Messiah is mentioned, the style, language, and expression, and in particular the acquaintance with later writers, show it must not be referred to the time of Uzziah.]

Knobel (p. 172) places ix.—xi. about 770—740 B. C., and xii.—xiv. he ascribes to a different author, (p. 280, sqq.,) for he finds a difference in style

visable to suppose that these parts, which seem to belong to an earlier period, were written with reference to the future, and that the form of a prediction was adopted in part. This view agrees well with the unconnected, inconsistent, and obscure character of these prophecies.[a]

---

viz. והיה ; xii. 3, 9, xiii. 2—4, 8, xiv. 6, 8, 14, 16, 21. ביום ההוא ; xii. 3, 4, 6, 8, 9, 11, xiii. 1, 2, 4, xiv. 8, 9, 13, 20, 21. נְאֻם יהוה ; xii. 1, 4, xiii. 2, 7, 8; (but the 2d occurs in ix. 16; the 3d only x. 12, xi. 16.) "All nations," "all nations around," "all nations of the earth;" xii. 2, 3, 6, 9, xiv. 2, 12, 14, 16, 19. "The inhabitants of Jerusalem;" xii. 5, 7, 8, 10, xiii. 1. "The house of David;" xii. 7, 8, 10, 12, xiii. 1. *Family* for *people;* xiv. 17, 18. The sacerdotal and Mosaic words, נִדָּה, xiii. 1; כִּיּוֹר, xii. 6. *Saints*, i. e. angels; xiv. 5. The *scriptio plena;* xii. 7, 8, 10, 12, xiii. 1.

Hitzig thinks the style of these chapters more uniform and dull; he explains this by their composition at a period somewhat later, and reminds us of the affinity of ix. 7, and xii. 5, 6, (governors in Judah;) ix. 15, xii. 8, גנן ; x. 5, xii. 4, (riders upon horses.) He compares xii. 8, and x. 7, 5 (?); xiii. 7, and ix. 16, sq.; xiv. 17, and x. 1; and appeals to the similar use that is made of Joel.

The supposition that both houses of Israel are rejected and dispersed, (x. 6, sqq.,) and the idea of a Messiah, (ix. 9,) which has become positive, are not in favor of the times of Uzziah, Jotham, and Ahaz. *Knobel* erroneously finds a special hatred of Ægypt in xiv. 18, sqq.; but there is no definite historical relation with foreign nations at the bottom of xii.—xiv. Something seems to waver before the prophet's mind, like the campaign of Gog, in Ezek. xxxviii. However, not only xiv. 4, sqq., but the whole, is fantastic.

[a] In this manner we can explain the reference to political affairs. (ix. 1—6, 13, x. 11.) Zechariah would not wish to prophesy against Persia, at least not publicly. (See vi. 8, and Hag. ii. 22.) Therefore he transferred himself to an earlier time, and then directed his predictions to the future. The expressions, ix. 13, x. 6, sqq., are archaisms, and are based on the expected restoration of the nation, as also is x. 10, where Gilead and Lebanon are put for the extreme limits of the land; xi. 6, and xiii. 7, belong to the future. It seems that he expected tyrants, or false Messiahs, to precede the Messianic kingdom. The house of David is mentioned in connection with the Messiah, (xii. 7, 12.) Chap. x. 2, and xii. 2, may have been designed as warnings for the future, or for the present time; for it seems, from Neh. vi. 10—14, they were needed, and who knows that idolatry had not at that time secret supporters? I cannot, with *Köster*, (p. 166, sq.,) understand xiii. 2—6, as applying to the extirpation of the prophecy. Every thing is indeed taken from fancy; but this was conformable to the spirit of the later prophets. [See *Knobel's* arguments against the passage, l. c. § 18, 25.]

XII. MALACHI.[a]

§ 251.

We know nothing of the person of Malachi. [Origen supposed he was an angel incarnate; and in this opinion he has been followed by many, both ancient and modern. Others think the name *Malachi* is only a title of Ezra, and that he is the author of these oracles.][b] He prophesied, it is probable, in the time of Nehemiah. Vitringa and Bertholdt place him in the time of Nehemiah's second coming to Jerusalem. He seems to have aided Nehemiah in his efforts to induce the people to repudiate "the outlandish women" they had married, and to give the tithes to the Levites, and offerings to the Lord. Compare ii. 10—16, with Neh. xiii. 23, sqq., and iii. 7—12, with xiii. 10.[c]

---

[a] *Dav. Chytræi* Explic. Malach. Proph.; Rost. 1568, Opp. ii. p. 455.

J. Jac. Grynæi Hypomnemata in Malach.; Genev. 1582, 8vo.; Bas. 1583, 1612, 4to.

Sam. Bohlii Malach. Proph. cum Commentariis Rabbinorum, Disputationibus Ebr. et Explicatione; Rost. 1637, 4to.

J. H. Ursini Comment. in Malach.; Frcf. 1652.

Sal. van Til, Malach. illustratus; Lug. Bat. 1701, 4to.

Joa. Wesselii Malachias enucleatus; Lubec. 1729, 4to.

Malachiæ Proph. c. Targum Jonath. et Radaki, Raschii et Aben Esræ Commentariis Interpretatio a *J. Chr. Hebenstreit* (xvii. Diss. et Progr.;) Lips. 1731—1746, 4to.

H. Venem. Comment. ad Librum Malach.; Leov. 1759, 4to.

C. F. Bahrdt, Comment. in Malachiam c. Examine crit. Verss. Vet. et Lectionum var. Hubigantii; accedit Spec. Bibliorum polygl.; Lips. 1768.

J. M. Faber, Comm. in Malach. Proph.; Onold. 1779, 4to.

[b] *Jonathan Ben Uzziel* (ad Mal. i. 1) says, Malachi, whose name is called Ezra the scribe; and *Jerome* (l. c.) thinks he was the same person. (See, also, § 246, sup.) The LXX. translate the title of the book, *Λῆμμα λόγου κυρίου ἐπὶ τὸν Ἰσραὴλ ἐν χειρὶ ἀγγέλου αὐτοῦ.* See other trifling speculations in *Carpzov*, l. c. p. 454, sqq.

[c] *Vitringa*, Ob. sac. L. vi. p. 331, sqq.; Typ. Doctr. prophet. p. 42. *Carp-*

He prophesied later than Haggai and Zechariah, as it appears from the position which this book holds in the canon, and also from the fact that the temple was finished when he wrote, as we see, i. 10, and iii. 1: —

"O that some one would close the doors,
That ye might not kindle the fire upon mine altar in vain;
The Lord, whom ye seek, shall suddenly come to his temple."

The mention of the Jewish governor (i. 8) forbids us to place the time after the death of Nehemiah, as Rosenmüller observes. But Hitzig thinks this governor preceded or followed Nehemiah.

§ 252.

CONTENTS AND SPIRIT OF THE PROPHECY.

After the destruction of the theocracy, and the loss of true prophetic inspiration, Malachi, in his six prophetic discourses, undertakes to reprove the nation for transgressing the rules relating to public worship, and other precepts of the law; in particular, that which prohibited marriage with foreign women. (i. 6—ii. 9, ii. 10—16, iii. 7—12.) The dissatisfaction which the people express with these restrictions, only leads him to make the comforting comparison of their condition with the harder lot of other nations, (i. 2—5,) and the promises of a Messiah. (ii. 17—iii. 9, iii. 13—24.) These are not devoid of the moral spirit of ancient prophecy, and are not destitute of peculiar and original ideas. (iii. 2, 23.)

In style, rhythm, and imagery, Malachi imitates the

---

zov, p. 463. Pseudo *Epiphanius* says he was of the tribe of Zebulon, and was highly honored by the people for his gentleness and sanctity. *Hitzig* refers to differences in these parallels, and observes that Malachi not only reproves the Jews for marrying heathen women, but for deserting their former wives.

old prophets, and not without success. Yet we are continually sensible of the dull, exhausted spirit, which attempts, but cannot perform, for the thought is not sufficiently vigorous.[a]

CHAPTER V.

DANIEL.[b]

§ 253.

ACCOUNTS OF DANIEL.

DANIEL, a young Hebrew, of noble birth, according

---

[a] See *Eichhorn*, § 609, sq., and *Knobel*, l. c. p. 388. He repeatedly uses the same turn of words. (i. 2, 6, 7, ii. 14, 17, iii. 7, 8, 13.)

[b] *Ephraim*, Expos. Proph. Daniel, Opp. ii. p. 203, sqq.

Hieron. Comment. in Dan., Opp. iii. p. 1071, sqq. *Martianay.*

Theodoreti Comment. in Visiones Danielis Prophetæ, Opp. ed. *Schulz*, ii. p. 1053, sqq.

Paraphrasis Dni *Josephi Jachiadæ* in Danielem c. Vers. et Annotatt. *Const. L'Empereur ab Oppyk;* Amst. 1633, 4to.

Ph. Melanchthonis Comm. in Danielem; 1543, 8vo.

Prælectt. *Jo. Calvini* in Libr. Prophetiarum Danielis, *Jo. Budæi* et *Car. Jonuillæi* Lab. et Industr. exceptæ; 1571, fol.

Prælectt. acad. in Dan. Proph., habitæ antehac Lipsiæ a *Mart. Geiero;* Lips. 1767, ed. 2, corr. 1684, 4to.

Is. Newton, Observatt. upon the Prophecies of Dan. and the Apoc. of St. John; Lond. 1733, 4to. Latin, by *W. Sudermann;* Amst. 1737, 4to. Deutsch mit Anmerkk. von *Chr. Fr. Grohmann;* Lpz. 1765, 8vo.

Herm. Venemæ Dissertatt. ad Vaticc. Danielis, c. ii. vii. et viii.; Leov. 1745, 4to. Comment. ad Dan. xi. 4—xii.; ib. 1752, 4to.

Chr. B. Michaelis, Annotatt. in Dan. in *J. H. Michaelis*, Uberr. Annotatt. in Hagiogr. vol. iii. p. 1, sqq.

Bertholdt, Dan. aus dem Hebräisch-Aramäischen neu übers. und erkl. mit e. vollst. Einleit. u. einigen hist. u. exeg. Excursen; Erl. 1806, 1808.

Hävernik, Comment. üb. d. B. Daniel; Hamb. 1832.

Rosenmüller, Schol. See his Elenchus Interprett.

[*Wintle*, Daniel, Improved Version, with Notes; Lond. 1807, 4to. *Amner*,

to the narrative in this book,[a] was brought to the court of Nebuchadnezzar, with other Jewish youths, in the third year of King Jehoiakim, (about 605,) and, under the name of Belteshazzar, was educated in the wisdom of the Chaldeans, for the service of the court.[b]

Essay towards Interpret. Dan.; Lond. 1776, 1798, 8vo. *Girdlestone*, Observations on the Visions of Dan.; Oxf. 1820, 8vo. *Wilson*, Dissertations on the Proph. Dan.; Oundle, 1824, 8vo. Dissertations on Dan. by *Blayney*, *Faber*, *Stonard*, and *Atwood*. *Folsom*, Proph. of Dan.; Bost. 1842.]

[a] According to i. 3, the captive youths were "of the king's seed, and the princes." *Josephus* (Ant. x. 10, 1) says he was of the race of Zedekiah, and pseudo *Epiphanius* (chap. x.) makes him descended from some of the chief officers in the kingdom — *τῶν ἐξόχων τῆς βασιλικῆς ὑπηρεσίας, — ἐγγενήθη ἐν Βεθεβορῷ τῇ ἀνωτέρᾳ, πλησίον Ἱερουσαλήμ.*

[b] It is obviously false that he was carried thither at that date, for, according to Jer. xxv. 1, and xlvi. 2, the *fourth* year of Jehoiakim is the *first* of Nebuchadnezzar; and according to xxv. 9, in the *fourth* year of Jehoiakim, yea, according to xxxvi. 9, even in his *fifth* year, the Chaldeans had not yet come to Jerusalem. [Besides, in the third year of Jehoiakim, the *Ægyptians* were the masters of Judea. If he had said in the third *month* of *Jehoiachin*, the date would have been more correct. (2 Ch. xxxvi. 9.)] Excepting the captivity under Zedekiah, none is known to history, save that under Jehoiachin, in the *eighth* year of Nebuchadnezzar. (2 Kings xxiv. 12, sqq. According to Jer. lii. 28, this was in the *seventh* year of Nebuchadnezzar.) The Chronicles alone (2 Ch. xxxvi. 6, 7) mention the captivity under Jehoiakim, [but make this take place after Jehoiakim had reigned *eleven* years.] Perhaps the author made use of this passage, and took the date, the *third* year of Jehoiakim, from 2 Kings xxiv. 1. *Chr. B. Michaelis* (Præf. in Dan. § 8) and *Bertholdt* (Daniel, p. 172) have attempted to explain the difficulty by showing that the *third* year of Jehoiakim may, by a different enumeration, be the *eleventh* year, when *Josephus* (Ant. x. 6, 3) says Jerusalem was taken and the people carried off. *Hengstenberg* (Beit. vol. i. p. 5) and *Hävernik* (on Dan. chap. i.) have made artful and plausible combinations to show that the capture of Jerusalem, mentioned in Dan. i. 1, was accomplished in Nebuchadnezzar's expedition, undertaken during the last years of his father, and mentioned by *Berosus*, in *Josephus*, Ant. x. 11, 1, — the expedition in which Phœnicia and Syria were brought under the dominion of the Babylonians. They maintain that this expedition commenced in the third year of Jehoiakim; that after the battle of Carchemish, (which Jeremiah places in the *fourth* year, xlvi. 2,) and in the same year, Nebuchadnezzar came to Jerusalem, as Jeremiah had predicted. (xxv. 9.) Here they rely upon Jer. xxxvi. 9, and, following the analogy of Zech. viii. 9

While Daniel is at the court, he commends himself to the king by a felicitous explanation of a dream, and is raised to the office of chief governor of the wise men of Babylon. (ii. 48.) He seems to have held this office to the end of the Chaldee monarchy. (v. 11.) After the conquest of Babylon, he is elevated by Darius the Mede — Cyaxares II. — to one of the three highest offices of the state. (vi. 1.) This he held till the first time of Cyrus. (i. 21, vi. 29, x. 1.)

Ezekiel mentions Daniel as a model of righteousness and wisdom.[a] But the Daniel of this book must, at that time, have been very young. Therefore it is not improbable that the author of this book has falsely transferred an old mythical or poetical character to the times and circumstances of this work, and, at the same time, has made use of the statements of Nehemiah (x. 3, 7, 24, and viii. 4) for the same purpose.[b] The false

---

refer the *fast*, which is mentioned, to the invasion of the Chaldeans, which had taken place the *previous* year, and refer the threat denounced in verse 29 to a *future* and *total annihilation* of the state. The words, (Dan. i. 1,) "Nebuchadnezzar came unto Jerusalem," (בָּא יְרוּשָׁלַם,) refer only to the undertaking of the expedition, as if it meant he *drew towards* Jerusalem. (Comp. Jon. i. 3.) They make the first year of Nebuchadnezzar fall part in the *third* and part in the *fourth* of Jehoiakim, and consequently there is, then, only an apparent, and not a real, contradiction between Dan. i. 1, and Jer. xxv. 1. But if we admit the accuracy of *Berosus's* statement, — which does not mention the battle of Carchemish, and which even *Josephus* (x. 6, 1) does not follow, — then, if we rightly balance these passages of Jeremiah, and the circumstances, the warlike expedition of Nebuchadnezzar against Jehoiakim could not have taken place before the *fifth* year of the latter; and besides, no captivity is mentioned. *Hitzig*, Begriff der Kritik. p. 183, 185, sqq. *Von Lengerke*, Daniel, Einleit. to chap. i. *Schmeidler*, Unters. Jud. p. 84.

[a] "Though these three men, Noah, Daniel, and Job, were in it, they should deliver only themselves by their righteousness." (xiv. 14, 18, 20.) "Thou art wiser than Daniel." (xxviii. 3.)

[b] See *Bleek*, in the Berlin Theol. Zeitschrift, vol. iii. p. 283, sqq.

statement, in i. 1, renders the historical existence of Daniel exceedingly doubtful.

Afterwards, the fiction was continued still farther. The stories of Susannah, of Bel and the Dragon at Babylon, were added in the Septuagint, and later legends have been written respecting him.[a]

§ 254.

CONTENTS OF THE BOOK OF DANIEL.

After an account of the circumstances of Daniel's life, written in Hebrew, (chap. i.,) there follows (chap. ii., which is in Chaldee from verse 4) the story of Nebuchadnezzar's dream, of a figure composed of various materials, and of a stone which broke it in pieces. Daniel interpreted this dream, and, according to his explanation, four kingdoms were symbolically represented in it, the last of which was the Messianic kingdom. Chap. iii., written in Chaldee, relates the miracle of the three men in the fiery furnace. Chap. iii. 31—iv. 34, in Chaldee, purports to be a narrative by Nebuchadnezzar himself, in which he relates that, in accordance with Daniel's explanation of the dream, he fell into an insane and brutal state,[b] and was delivered from it. Chap. v., in Chaldee, contains an account of a writing which appeared to Belshazzar at a feast on the night of the conquest of Babylon, and which was explained by Daniel as relating to that event. In chap. vi., also in Chaldee, under Darius the Mede, Daniel is cast into the lions' den, and is miraculously preserved

[a] See them in *Carpzov*, l. c. p. 231. *Bertholdt*, Dan. i. 9, sq.

[b] *Wahnsinnigen viehischen Zustand.*

therein. Chap. vii., in Chaldee, contains Daniel's vision of the four beasts,[a] which signify so many kingdoms. They are the same as in chap. ii., but their meaning is contested. This same chapter treats also of the judgment of the world, and the kingdom of God, in which all former kingdoms are to come to an end.

---

[a] *Jahn* incorrectly gives different explanations of the term. By the golden head, (ii. 32,) and the FIRST BEAST, (vii. 4,) all the interpreters understand the *Babylonian empire*, except *Hitzig* (Heidelberg Jahrbuch; 1832, vol. ii. p. 132) and *Redepenning*, who refer it to Nebuchadnezzar himself. By the breast and arms of silver, (ii. 32,) and the SECOND BEAST, (vii. 5,) some understand the *Medo-Persian empire*, (*Theodoret*, *Jerome*, *Chrysostom*, *Polychron*, *Grotius*, *C. B. Michaelis*, *Bertholdt*, *Jahn*, on chap. vii., *Rosenmüller*, *Hengstenberg*, and *Hävernik*.) Others understand the *Median empire*, (*Ephraim* Syrus, *Eichhorn*, *Jahn*, on chap. ii., and *Von Lengerke*.) The writer actually seems to have thought of that kingdom (vi. 1) as the one which was to succeed the Babylonian, while, in v. 28, the Medes and Persians are named together. Doubtless the beast (viii. 3) denotes the Medo-Persian empire; but it may be said the author here places himself in the period when the two kingdoms of which it is composed — represented by two horns — are united. According to this view, the *three ribs* (vii. 5) — which *Jerome*, *Rosenmüller*, and others, refer to the three kingdoms of the Medes, Persians, and Babylonians, which *Jahn* refers to the Lydian, Babylonian, and Ægyptian, and which *Bertholdt*, *Hävernik*, and others, refer to the Median, Babylonian, and Lydian, — are only emblems of frailty. By the belly and the loins of brass, (ii. 32,) and the THIRD BEAST, (vii. 6,) *Jerome*, *Polychron*, *C. B. Michaelis*, *Hengstenberg*, and *Hävernik*, understand the *kingdom of Alexander and his successors*; while *Cosma's* Indicopleustes, *Grotius*, *J. C. Becmann*, (De Monarch. quarta, in his Meditatt. Polit.; 1679,) *Bertholdt*, *Rosenmüller*, and *Jahn*, on chap. vii., understand the *kingdom of Alexander* alone; and *Ephraim* Syrus, *Eichhorn*, and *Von Lengerke*, understand the *Persian kingdom*. The first refer the four heads of the beast to the four chief Macedonian empires; the second, to the four chief generals of Alexander; and the third refer them to the four Persian kings. By the legs of iron and the feet of iron and clay, (ii. 33,) and the FOURTH BEAST, (vii. 7,) *Theodoret*, *Jerome*, *Chrysostom*, *C. B. Michaelis*, *Hengstenberg*, and *Hävernik*, understand the *Roman empire*; while *Grotius*, *Becmann*, *Bertholdt*, and *Rosenmüller*, understand that of *Alexander's successors*; but *Ephraim* Syrus, *Eichhorn*, and *Von Lengerke*, refer it to that of *Alexander and his successors*. Since the last explanation is necessary in vii. 7, therefore those which harmonize with it are the true ones.

Chap. viii., in Hebrew, contains another vision of two beasts, which, according to Daniel's explanations, denote the *Medo-Persian* and the *Macedonian* kingdom, with that which grew out of it, especially the Macedonico-Syriac, for King Antiochus Epiphanes is very distinctly described.

Chap. ix., in Hebrew, contains a revelation made to Daniel respecting the seventy years of exile, predicted by Jeremiah, which he here enlarges to seventy weeks of years, so that they may include the time to Antiochus Epiphanes.

Chap. x.—xii. contain an unsymbolic, but very clear and perspicuous revelation of the Persian and Macedonian monarchies, with the Asiatic monarchies which arose out of them, down to the death of Antiochus Epiphanes. After this, the resurrection of the dead, and the kingdom of God, are to follow.

§ 255.

SPURIOUSNESS OF THE BOOK.

It appears Daniel is not the author of this book,—

I. From its legendary contents. It is full of improbabilities. Nebuchadnezzar demands that the wise men should tell him the dream he had forgotten, and threatens to put them to death in case of their inability to obey his command. (ii. 3, sq.) He gives the greatest rewards to Daniel for restoring his lost dream, and explaining it. (ii. 46, sq.) He makes an image of gold, sixty cubits high, and six cubits in diameter, (iii. 1,) and commands men to worship it. (iii. 5.) He commands the mightiest men in his army to bind Shadrach, Meshach, and Abed-nego, (verse 20,) and cast them into the furnace, which was so hot as to destroy these mighty men, as they cast in their victims. (verse 22.) He blesses the God of these three men, and makes a decree, that "every people, nation, and language," which speaks any thing reproachful of this God, "shall be cut to pieces, and its houses made a dunghill." (verse 28, sq. iii. 31, and iv. 31; al. iv. 1, and 34.)[a] Other im probable circumstances are mentioned: v. 11, sqq., the mention of Daniel; verse 18, sqq., his remarks to Belshazzar, and the honors bestowed upon him by that king, (verse 29,) on account of his explanation of the words written on the wall. The prohibition to ask any

[a] *Hengstenberg* (l. c. p. 105, sq.) attempts to justify the account of Nebuchadnezzar's peculiar madness, by the statements of *Berosus* in *Josephus*, Cont. Apion, i. 20: "Nebuchadnezzar, after he had commenced the forementioned undertaking, *falling into a sickness*, died." But *Berosus* merely says, Nebuchadnezzar fell sick and died. He also uses the passage of *Abydenus*, in *Eusebius*, Præp. Ev. ix. 41, and Chron. Comm. Lat. p. 151, for the same purpose: "I found these narrations in the writing of Abydenus upon the Assyrians, and upon Nebuchadnezzar. Megasthenes said that Nebuchadnezzar was more valiant than Hercules, and waged war against Lybia and Iberia; and, having conquered both, transplanted a colony from thence to the right side (εἰς τὰ δεξία) of Pontus. It is said by the Chaldeans that, after this, when he had returned to his palace, he was suddenly struck by some god, so that he cried out, and said, 'I, Nebuchadnezzar, O ye Babylonians, foretell the fate that is coming upon you, which neither Belus, my ancestor, nor Queen Beltis, can persuade the Fates to avert. There will come a Persian mule, who, using the aid of our deities assisting him, will force you into subjection. A certain Mede — the former boast of Assyria — will be his coadjutor in this. O that, before he had thus afflicted my citizens, some Charybdis, or deep gulf of the sea, had received and destroyed him; or that, destroyed by other methods, he had been borne through the wilderness, where there are no cities, nor any vestige of man, but where wild beasts have their dwelling, and birds fly at large, that he might perish alone, among rocks and clefts of the earth. O that I had found a happier end, before these things came into my mind.'" Having uttered these oracles, he immediately vanished. But there is, at the most, only a traditional connection between them, as *Bertholdt*, *Bleek*, and *Kirms*, maintain. *Jahn* (p. 214) and *Lengerke* (p. 151) find a later forgery in this story of Abydenus.

thing of God, or man, except from the king, (vi. 8, sqq.,) and the subsequent decree, that all men "should tremble and fear before the God of Daniel," (verse 26, sqq.,) are of this character.[a] It is full of grotesque miracles — Daniel recalling the dream which the king had forgotten, (ii. 28;) the preservation of the three men in the furnace, (iii. 23, sqq.;) the apparition of a hand on the wall, writing an oracular sentence, (v. 5;) and the preservation of Daniel in the lions' den. (vi. 23—25.) It abounds, also, in historical inaccuracies.[b]

II. This appears from its prophetic contents, which differ in a striking manner from all the other prophetic books, —

1. In its apocalyptic character, or the fact that the future

---

[a] See *Bertholdt's* introduction to chap. v. and vi., and *Eichhorn*, § 614, p. 501.

[b] Inaccurate accounts of the wise men of Babylon, and the inconceivable reception of Daniel among them. (ii. 2, iv. 4, v. 7, 14.) *Von Lengerke*, p. 74. On the other side, *Hävernik*, Neu. Unters. p. 66. Darius the Mede, instead of Cyaxares II. (vi. 1, ix. 1, xi. 1.) See *Bertholdt*, 4th Excurs. on Dan. p. 841. *Rosenmüller*, Alt. vol. i. pt. i. p. 369, Proœm. in Dan. p. 13. *Hengstenberg* (p. 49, sq.) attempts to justify the use of the names as *surnames*, and *Knobel* agrees with him. For this purpose he quotes the Chron. Armen. of *Eusebius*, (ed. Ven. vol. i. p. 61,) *A Dario rege eadem provincia pulsus est*, (but here Darius Hystaspes is meant,) and, also, the etymology of the word Δαρεικός, *Darick*, in *Suidas* and *Harpocration*, who say it was not named "from Darius the *father of Xerxes*, but from another and *more ancient king*." *Hitzig* (p. 141, sq.) and *Lengerke* (p. 219, sqq.) doubt his existence; but see *Hävernik*, l. c. p. 74, sqq., *Knobel*, p. 359, and *Gesenius*, Thes. 349, sqq. Mention is made of the government by one hundred and twenty satraps under *Nebuchadnezzar*, (iii. 3,) and *Darius the Mede*. (vi. 2.) [This seems to be an exaggeration of what *Herodotus* ascribes to *Darius Hystaspes*.] — *Ahasuerus* is called the father of Darius the Mede, (Cyaxares II.,) when *Astyages* was his father, (ix. 1;) but *Hengstenberg* (p. 52) makes them identical. On the other side, see *Lengerke*, p. 234, sqq. — Belshazzar, the last king of Babylon, is made a son of Nebuchadnezzar, (v. 11, 13, 18, 22, 30,) in opposition to *Berosus*, in *Josephus*, Cont. Ap. i. 20. (See *Lengerke*, p. 204, and *Hitzig*, in Heidel. Jahrbuch; 1832, p. 137.) *Hävernik*, to remove the difficulty, makes Belshazzar and Evil-merodach the same person; and, after his downfall and the capture of Babylon, he puts *Nabonned* between v. 1, and vi. 1. The den of lions is represented as if it were a cistern, or pit. (vi. 18.) See *Knobel*, p. 401, on the legends in Daniel.

splendor of the Messianic kingdom is conceived of and described, and its historical circumstances related. This is done in a manner unusually symbolical, with a great outlay of visions, and the like.[a] 2. The events of a distant future, and the fate of kingdoms not then existing,—though extending only to the time of Antiochus Epiphanes,—are related with great distinctness and accuracy, even with the addition of the dates. (viii. 14, ix. 25, sqq., xii. 11, 12.)[b] This was evidently done after the event. 3. The moral spirit of admonition appears with less prominence than usual in the prophets. If Daniel were a prophet, it must have been in the spirit of Ezekiel and Zechariah; but although the symbolical style of this book is not wholly foreign to them, yet they are very far from the apocalyptical style of this book. This later shoot of the Old Testament prophecy belongs to a time long after them.[c] Through the apocalyptic spirit of the later Jews, prophecies were forged, and made to apply to the events of actual history, and then dated back to ancient times. This is shown by the Sibylline oracles, which are strongly analogous to the book of Daniel.[d]

---

[a] See *Lücke*, Offenbar. Joh. p. 24.

[b] *Hengstenberg* (p. 195) attempts to remove this objection, by supposing that the author extends his prophecies beyond the time of Antiochus Epiphanes. He thinks the fourth monarchy is the Roman empire, and the eleventh horn (vii. 8) is Antichrist. But it is evident that this, as well as the horn, (viii. 9,) refers to Antiochus Epiphanes, who is clearly described in xi. 21, sqq. The double sense which *Hengstenberg* adopts is only a help he has snatched at in extremity.

[c] In Jer. xxv. 12, 13, xxix. 10, we see an occasion for the explanation of the seventy years, in Dan. ix. 2.

[d] [See the fourth book of Ezra, as it is called. The apocryphal writings of Isaiah are also analogous with the book of Daniel. Its resemblance to the third book of the Sibylline oracles (156—271, and 319—746) is striking. The latter, like the former, announce the destruction of all the kingdoms of the world, especially the Ægyptian and Roman; they threaten Antiochus

III. It appears Daniel is not the author, from the fact that honorable mention is made of Daniel himself—"Daniel had understanding in all visions and dreams," (i. 17;) "Among them all was found none like Daniel, Hananiah," &c., (verse 19;) "He found them ten times better than all the scribes," &c., (verse 20;) "In whom is the spirit of the holy gods,—light, and understanding, and wisdom, like the wisdom of the gods," (verse 11, 12;) "He was faithful, and no error or fault was found in him." (vi. 4, ix. 23, x. 11.)

IV. This appears, also, from the corrupt language,[a] both

Epiphanes with destruction. The order of nature is to be changed; the people of God, under the guidance of kings sent by him, are to extend his dominion over the whole world. See *Bleek*, l. c. p. 253, sq. See, also, his article on the origin and compilation of the Sibylline oracles, in vol. i. of the same work, where he shows this *third book* was written by an Alexandrian Jew, in the second century B. C. See, also, *Schoel*, Geschichte der Griechischen Literatur, &c., translated from the French, by *J. F. J. Schwarze*; Berlin, 1828, vol. i. p. 33, sqq. See *Laurence's* translation of the book of Enoch, Oxford, 1821, 8vo., or *Hoffman*, Das Buch Henoch, Jena, 1833 and 1838.] The book of Enoch is an imitation. See above, § 50.

[a] Besides the later Chaldee and Persian words which occur in the other recent books of the Old Testament, (such as בִּזָּה, xi. 24, 33, מַדָּע, i. 4, 17, כְּתָב, x. 21, מַרְעִיד, x. 11, פַּרְתְּמִים, i. 3,) the following occur: אַפֶּדֶן; xi. 45. אַשָּׁפ; i. 20, ii. 2. גִּיל, *age, race;* i. 10. זֵרֹעִים, זֵרְעֹנִים; i. 12, 16. מִכְמַנִּים; xi. 43. הַתָּמִיד, without עֹלַת or מִנְחַת; viii. 11—13, xi. 31, xii. 11. הֶחֱנִיפ, *to lead to revolt;* xi. 32. הָרַךְ; ix. 24. רָשַׁם; x. 21. פַּלְמֹנִי; viii. 13. קְדֹשִׁים, applied to the Jews; viii. 24. The Syriac infinitive, התחברות; xi. 23. Persian words: כְּרַז; v. 29. כָּרוֹז; iii. 4. נְבִזְבָּה; (?) ii. 6, v. 17. Sometimes the style is negligent, indefinite, [?] and obscure; i. 2, 21, viii. 8. חָזוּת, for ח" קְרְנֵי; ix. 2, 13, 26, x. 7, 20, xi. 2, 6, 17. The article is often omitted; viii. 13, 14, ix. 24, (?) 25, 27. Sometimes the style is well studied and elegant; הִגִּיעַ; x. 10. נִרְדַּם עַל פָּנִים; viii. 18, x. 19. עָמְדִי; xi. 1, (Job ix. 27.) זְרוֹעִים, זְעוֹעוֹת, *an army;* xi. 15, 22, 31. The poetic use of the apocopate form, xi. 16, and the abbreviated form of the future, xi. 10, 17, sqq., 25, 28, 3, 30. Use of the archaism שנאר, i. 2, and of the Pentateuch, ii. 1, viii. 14, x. 14, חר טמים רכוש. Daniel makes use of Ezekiel, who lived near his time, if the book is genuine, (viii. 26. Comp. Ezek. xii.

Hebrew and Chaldee, and from the Greek words that are found in it.[a]

V. The doctrine of angels, (*angelologie*,) the christology and asceticism, form, at least, an auxiliary to this argument.[b]

VI. The position of the book in the canon — in the Hagiographa — seems to prove it was written after the collection of the Prophets was closed.[c]

VII. Finally, the silence of Jesus Siracides (xlix.)

27, and also Hab. ii. 3, x. 8, Ezek. ix. 2, x. 6, Ezek. i. 7,) and also Neh. ix. (Dan. ix.)

[a] קִיתָרוֹס, *κίθαρις*; סַבְּכָא, *σαμβύκη*; סוּמְפֹּנְיָה, *συμφωνία*; פְּסַנְתֵּרִין, *ψαλτήριον*; iii. 5, 7, 10. But it is certainly possible that Greek instruments, and their names, may have been known to the Babylonians at this time.

The Greek origin of the last word may, at least, be placed in doubt. *Hengstenberg* (p. 15, 16) refers to the use of the word (in Midr. Kohel, i. 3) in the sense of "*olla*," "*lebes*;" but this is against him, for, in the passage referred to, פְּסַנְטְרָא is probably a false reading for פְּכַכְתְּרָא, which is the Greek *ψυκτὴρ*. See *Rosenmüller*, Prooem. p. 14, note.

[b] The author recognizes orders, or classes of angels, and introduces *Gabriel* (viii. 19, ix. 21) and *Michael* (x. 13, 21, xii. 1) by name. This has no parallel in the Old Testament. He sees, also, a *watcher* (עִיר) coming down from heaven. (iv. 14.) He mentions the Messiah as a mysterious being, that comes in the clouds of heaven; is to rule forever, over all people, nations, and languages. (vii. 13, 14.) He foretells a general resurrection from the dead, and final retribution of the good and the bad. (xii. 1—3.) He thinks sins may be expiated by alms-deeds. (iv. 24, or 27.) A similar doctrine is taught in Tobit xii. 9 — "Alms doth deliver from death, and shall purge away all sin." (iv. 11.) He takes an ascetic view of the use of food, and rejects flesh and wine, (i. 8—16,) similar to that in 2 Macc. v. 27, and the apocryphal Esther, iv. 17, in the LXX. He commends prayer three times a day. (vi. 11.) (Comp. Acts ii. 15, iii. 1, x. 9, 12.) All of this has its parallel only in the degenerate spirit of the times in which Esther, the Chronicles, and some of the apocryphal books, were written, and is quite foreign to the true Hebrew spirit. (See *Knobel*, l. c. p. 402, sq.) According to *Hävernik*, only abstinence from flesh and drink *offered to idols* is spoken of. (i. 5.)

[c] *Hengstenberg* revives the old view that the book was placed there on account of the lower degree of inspiration ascribed to it. *Hävernik* (p. 62) differs from him in this.

respecting Daniel — who must have appeared to him a very important prophet, if he had lived at the time and place alleged — deserves to be taken into consideration.[a]

[a] [Some writers lay but little stress on this argument. *Eichhorn* does not mention it. *Bertholdt* only mentions it in passing. *Bretschneider* and *Kirms* deny that it has any value; while *Bleek* assigns a high importance to this argument. *Hengstenberg*, (p. 21,) in reply to his remarks, maintains this argument would prove too much, for Ezra and Mordecai are omitted as well as the minor Prophets; for he considers xlix. 10, not genuine. But this consideration does not weaken the value of the argument to any considerable degree; for the writer does not pretend to give an *exhaustive* catalogue of "famous men," and there was less reason for naming those prophets, or Ezra and Mordecai, than for mentioning so remarkable a person as Daniel, if this book is genuine and authentic.]

The following is a summary of the history of objections to the genuineness of the book. *Porphyry* made objections to it, which have been preserved by *Jerome*, in the Procem. ad Comm. in Dan., who says, "*Porphyry* wrote his twelfth book against Daniel the prophet, wishing to prove the book was not written by him with whose name it is inscribed, but by some one who had been in Judæa, in the times of Antiochus Epiphanes, and that the book of Daniel did not so much foretell things which were to come, as relate events that had taken place; and, finally, that whatever was related of the times before Antiochus was true history, but when he attempted to go beyond this, his remarks were false, because he was ignorant of the future. *Eusebius*, *Apollinaris*, and *Methodius*, replied to these arguments."

After this, the genuineness of Daniel remained undisputed until quite recent times. *Spinoza* (Tr. theol. pol. c. x. p. 130) merely conjectured that a later writer had taken the first seven chapters from the Chaldean annals, and *Isaac Newton* and *Beausobre* (Remarques sur le N. T., vol. i. p. 70) ascribe only the last six chapters to Daniel himself. [*Newton* says, he that would reject Daniel's prophecies would undermine the Christian religion, which was based upon them by Christ himself. *Bertholdt* thinks that some Christian teachers doubted, in silence, its genuineness. *Hobbes* (Leviathan, c. 33) also denied it.] *Uriel Akosta* and *Anthony Collins* actually denied its genuineness. [*Akosta* did this in a tract in the Spanish language, called An Examination and Comparison of the Tradition of the Pharisees, with the Written Law touching the Immortality of the Soul; Amst. 1624, 4to. (See *Wolf*, Bib. Heb. vol. ii. p. 161.) *Collins* (in a treatise, Scheme of literal Prophecy considered; Lond. 1727) made but a feeble attack, through his want of the requisite learning. *Sam. Chandler* has replied — after his manner — to his arguments, and with no great courtesy pointed out his numerous mistakes, in his Vindication of the Antiquity and Authority of Daniel's Prophecies, &c.; Lond. 1728, 8vo.] *Semler*, in his Inquiry on the Canon, (vol. iii.

§ 256.

UNITY OF THE BOOK.

Single passages have a relation and connection with one another. Shadrach, Meshech, and Abed-nego, are mentioned as "set over the affairs" of Babylon. (ii. 49,

---

p. 505,) denied its inspiration. *J. D. Michaelis*, in his remarks on ii. 40, rejected chap. iii.—vi., and *Eichhorn*, in the second edition of his Introduction, rejected the first six chapters. *Hezel* (l. c. vol. vi.) has followed him.

The following writers have declared against the genuineness of the whole book, namely, *Corrodi*, Freim. Vers. üb. Versch. in Theol., &c.; 1783, p. 1. Beleuchtung d. Gesch. d. Kanon, vol. i. p. 75. *Eichhorn*, in his third and fourth edition. *Bertholdt*. *Griesinger*, N. Ansicht d. Aufsätze in B. Dan.; 1815. *Bleek* and *Kirms*, Com. Hist. crit. de Dan. Libro Opinionum; Jena, 1828, 4to. *Luderwald*, Die vi. ersten ch. Dan.; 1787. *Städudlin*, N. Beit. zur Erlaut. d. Proph. p. 95, sqq. *Beckhaus*, Integ. Proph. Schriften, p. 197, sqq. *Jahn*, l. c. p. 624. *Dereser*, Die Proph. Ezek. und Daniel, p. 228, sq. *Sack*, Apologetik, p. 276, sqq. *Ackermann*, Introduct. in V. T. *Hävernik*, l. c. *Hengstenberg*, Beit. vol. i.; 1831. The arguments of these critics, and especially of the latter, are as follows: —

I. *The External Arguments.*

1. Daniel announces himself the author, at least of the second part— "Daniel spake and said," (vii. 2;) "I Daniel." (15, 28, viii. 2, ix. 2, x. 2.) The inscriptions betray no other hand—"In the first year of Belshazzar ..... Daniel had a dream; then he wrote the dream and related the sum of the matters," &c., (vii. 1, 2;) "In the third year of Cyrus was a revelation to Daniel....... In these days I Daniel," &c. (x. 1, 2.) Compare this with Ezra i. 1—3.

The fact that Daniel is always spoken of in the third person (i.—vi.) does not prove that Daniel did not write the passage, as it appears from a comparison with Hos. i.—iii., Isa. vii., xx., Amos vii., and other examples.

The first and second part are written by the same hand, (§ 256,) and this circumstance renders it difficult to suppose it was written at a later date in Daniel's name. But yet it must be observed, that such is the fact with respect to Deuteronomy, Ecclesiasticus, and the apocryphal books of Wisdom and Tobit.

2. The alleged late composition of this book is not consistent with the history of the canon, which, according to *Josephus*, and the Jewish and Christian tradition, was closed in the time of Ezra and Nehemiah. But *Josephus's* statement (Cont. Apion, i. 8) is indefinite, and depends on the alleged date of the book of Esther. It is *certain* that the books of Ezra,

and iii. 12.) In i. 2, it is said Nebuchadnezzar brought from Jerusalem part of the vessels of the temple, and

---

Nehemiah, Esther, Chronicles, and Ecclesiasticus, were written and received into the canon after the time of Ezra and Nehemiah. See § 189, 197, *b*, 199, 284.

3. There is direct and indirect testimony of Christ; e. g. "the abomination of desolation, spoken of by Daniel the prophet." (Matt. xxiv. 15, Mark xiii. 14.) The appearance of the *Son of man*, (Matt. x. 23, xvi. 27, xxvi. 64,) as it is used in Dan. vii. 13: and the testimony of the apostles, also, (1 Peter i. 10, sqq.;) but here the reference to Daniel (xii. 8) is doubtful. The *apostasy*, and the *man of sin*, mentioned by Paul, (2 Thess. ii. 3,) have only a doubtful reference to the predictions in Dan. vii. 8, 25. The passage, "We know that the saints shall judge the world," (1 Cor. vi. 2,) is supposed to refer to the sentence, "Judgment was given to the saints of the Most High," (Dan. vii. p. 22;) and that Heb. xi. 33, "stopped the mouths of lions, quenched the violence of fire," is supposed to refer to circumstances mentioned in this book. (chap. vi.) But if all this were admitted, still, from the nature of things, Christ neither *would* nor *could* be a critical authority.

4. The narrative of *Josephus* shows the book was in existence in Alexander's time. But this narrative is not credible in each of its circumstances.

Jesus Siracides refers to Daniel; xvii. 17, "He set a ruler over every people, but Israel is the Lord's portion." This is said to relate to Dan. x. 21, and xii. 1, "No one aideth me but Michael your prince," and x. 20, where the angelic princes of Persia and Greece are mentioned. But the passage of Siracides is well explained by verses 14 and 15, "He gave every man commandment concerning his neighbor," &c. The following passage is thought to refer to Daniel's kingdoms: "Because of unrighteous dealings, injuries and riches got by deceit, the kingdom is translated from one people to another." (x. 8.) See *Hävernik*, p. xl.

The writer of the first book of the *Maccabees* presupposes an acquaintance with the book of Daniel, and even with the Alexandrian version of it. The *abomination of desolation*, mentioned in Dan. ix. 27, is spoken of in i. 54 — "Ananias, Azariah, Mishael, by believing, were saved out of the flames. Daniel . . . . . . was delivered from the mouth of lions." (ii. 59, 60.) Here the reference is evident to Dan. iii. and vi. But it is a sectarian assumption to suppose the book of Maccabees was originally written in Hebrew, and at the time of John Hyrcanus, as *Hengstenberg* maintains, (134—105 B. C.,) for it appears from xvi. 23, sq., that it was written later. It cannot be determined at what time the Greek version of Daniel was made, but from its character we might suppose it was a considerable time after the book was written. (§ 258.)

II. *Internal Arguments.*

1. The alternate use of Hebrew and Chaldee would point to the time of the exile, when both languages were currently spoken by the Jews. But

in verse 2, we find them used at a feast; ii. 48, Daniel is set over the province and the "wise men" of Babylon; and in v. 11, he is alluded to as holding that office.

---

this was the case at a date still later, at least among the learned, who still used the Hebrew language. The books of Chronicles, Ecclesiastes, and others, are a proof of this.

The agreement of the Chaldaisms in Daniel with those in the book of Ezra, in opposition to those of the Targums, is sometimes used as an argument; but its force is weakened by the consideration that probably the Chaldaizing popular language of the Jews in exile — like every *patois* — fluctuated very much. But this agreement is more easily explained on the supposition that the book is spurious, than on the supposition of its genuineness. The comparison with the Targums can lead to no certain results, on account of our ignorance of the time when they were composed. There is, however, some difference. In Daniel we always find לְהֵן, לְכֵן, but in Ezra, לְהֹם and לְכֹם. But see *Hengstenberg*, p. 303, sqq.

2. In the book we find numerous proofs of an actual acquaintance with the history of that time. (See *Bertholdt*, Daniel, p. 68, 817, sq. *Gesenius*, in *Ersch* and *Grüber's* Encyclopädie, vol. xvi. p. 188, sq. *Bleek*, 221, sqq.) [The latter writer has shown that it is common to overrate the historical fidelity of this book; but he goes too far in assuming the author's ignorance of the subject. The common method has been to assume the correctness of such passages as ii. 2, where the conjurers are mentioned by classes, חַרְטֻמִּים, אַשָּׁפִים, מְכַשְּׁפִים, and כַּשְׂדִּים, and iii. 2, where the magistrates are mentioned by classes, אֲחַשְׁדַּרְפְּנַיָּא, סִגְבַיָּא, פַּחֲוָתָא, אֲדַרְגָּזְרַיָּא, גְּדָבְרַיָּא, דְּתָבְרַיָּא, תִּפְתָּיֵא, and all the שִׁלְטֹבֵר, and then, reasoning in a circle, infer that such minute and accurate information could only be obtained by a resident at Babylon. But, granting the accuracy, a writer in the time of Antiochus Epiphanes could have easily obtained the information; and, besides, he may have lived at Babylon, or at least have visited that city, and thus have become familiar with institutions both ancient and modern. Some curious information respecting the Chaldee magic, &c., may be seen in *Brucker*, Hist. Phil. vol. i. p. 113; but, on the other hand, see *Hengstenberg*, l. c. p. 343, sqq. See a good account of the Babylonians in *Heeren*, Researches, &c., vol. ii. p. 130—399, in the English translation.] But the book also contains inaccuracies and improbabilities, which show the author could not have been eye-witness or contemporary with the events he relates. These arguments, therefore, only show that he derived much that is correct from the tradition, and perhaps from his own acquaintance with the Babylonians. See § 149.

3. The spirit and taste displayed in this book — especially its peculiar

The remarks upon Nebuchadnezzar (v. 18, sqq.) agree with the oracle in a former passage. (iv. 22, sqq.) The successor of Belshazzar is called Darius. (v. 30, and vi. 1.) In viii. 1, reference is made to the vision of the preceding chapter, and in ix. 21, mention is made of the man Gabriel, spoken of in the previous chapter, and again in x. 5. So x. 12, refers to ix. 23.

The historical and prophetic passages are similar, and related to one another. Nebuchadnezzar honors Jehovah—"Your God is the God of gods," (ii. 47;) and in iii. 28, he commands all men to worship him. He is spoken of in the same honorary manner in iii. 31—33, iv. 34, vi. 27, 28. Chap. iii. and vi. have a general resemblance. (Compare, for example, iii. 30, and vi. 29.) Similar visions occur in chap. ii. vii. and viii. In viii. 26, it is said, "Shut up the vision, for it relates to distant days;" and the same opinion is repeated, (xii. 4,) "Shut up these words, and seal the book even to the time of the end. Many shall run eagerly through it, and much knowledge shall be gained;" and again verses 8, 9. Compare, also, ix. 3, with x. 2, 3; and viii. 18, with x. 10.

The oracles are written in a regular series, ascending

---

use of symbols—could only belong to an author who lived in Chaldea, and are, besides, different from those which prevailed in the times of the Maccabees. These are very vague statements, but we are still at liberty to suppose the real author of the book lived at Babylon.

Finally, it is said the immediate appearance of the kingdom of God after the death of Antiochus Epiphanes, as predicted in this book, could only occur in the prospective vision of an ancient prophet, but is not consistent with the hopes of a contemporary of this king. But we find such an instance in Matt. xvi. 28, "There be some standing here which shall not taste of death till they see the Son of man coming in his kingdom," and in 1 Thess. iv. 17, "Then we which are alive and remain shall be caught up together with them into the clouds, to meet the Lord in the air." See *De Wette's* article on *Daniel*, in *Ersch* and *Gruber's* Encycl., and *Hitzig*, l. c. p. 133, sqq.

from the indefinite to the definite, and following a chronological order. The same style not only pervades each of the separate (Chaldee or Hebrew) portions, but extends throughout both.[a]

Now, if any one takes all these facts into consideration, he cannot maintain this book is the work of different authors, either on account of the use of different languages, — which he used with equal facility, as it is probable,[b] — or on account of the contradictions which occur in the first part, but yet make no claim to be independent documents. Such passages are the following: i. 5, 18, 21.[c]

---

[a] The same threats of punishment occur, ii. 5, iii. 29. הֶזְוֵי רֵאשׁ, *visions of thy head;* ii. 28, iv. 2, 7, 10, vii. 1, 15. קָרָא בְחַיִל, *cried with strength;* iii. 4, v. 7, iv. 11. זִיוֹ שְׁנָא, *his bright looks were changed;* v. 6, 9, vii. 28. (Comp. the equivalent Hebrew expression, x. 8.) הוֹד נֶהְפַּךְ; iii. 8, vi. 25. אֲכַל קַרְצֵי דִי, *to accuse,* (literally, *to eat up the pieces of any one;*) iv. 16, v. 6, 10, vii. 28. רַעְיוֹנֹהִי יְבַהֲלֻנֵּהּ, *his thoughts grew sick;* iii. 4, 7, 31, v. 19, vi. 26, vii. 14. עַמְמַיָּא, אֻמַּיָּא, וְלִשָּׁנַיָּא, *people, nations, and languages;* vii. 25, xii. 7. The same length of time, viii. 26, x. 11. לְיָמִים, *future* time viii. 19, xi. 27, 35. לַמּוֹעֵד; viii. 18, x. 9. נִרְדָּם, *stunned;* ix. 27, xi. 31, xii 11. שִׁקּוּץ שֹׁמֵם, *the abominations of the destroyer;* viii. 9, xi. 16, 41. צְבִי; &c.

Daniel is mentioned and commended in the same manner, ii. 26, iv. 5, 16, x. 1, iv. 15, v. 11, ix. 23, x. 10, 19. Repetitions: iv. 17, sq., 29, sq., iii. 7, 10, 15. The dissimilarities of style mentioned by *Bertholdt* can scarcely be shown to exist.

[b] Observe the easy transition from Hebrew to Chaldee, ii. 4.

[c] Where it is said Nebuchadnezzar nourished the young Jews, of noble birth, *three years,* with his meat and wine, that they might be brought before the king at the end of that time. In ii. 1—13, it appears that Daniel was wont to stand, with the other magicians, before the king, in the *second year of his reign.* In i. 21, it is said Daniel lived until the *first year of King Cyrus,* and in x. 1, that he had a vision in the *third year* of that monarch. *Hengstenberg* (p. 66, sq.) has explained this latter contradiction pretty well, by maintaining that the first year of Cyrus is not mentioned as the *ultimate terminus;* but he attempts to remove the former, and the difficulty in i. 1, by supposing Nebuchadnezzar had a partner on the throne, and was sole king

§ 257.

AGE AND DESIGN OF THE BOOK.

At the time of Antiochus Epiphanes, when prophecy had long been extinct, a Jewish patriot wished to excite his suffering and struggling countrymen, and to strengthen them by predictions of the approaching triumph of the theocracy. For the sake of obtaining the more ready belief, as well as to compensate for the want of credibility in the predictions themselves, he ascribes them to the old prophet, Daniel, of whom, perhaps, some legends were still in circulation. He very wisely makes his promises come to fulfilment gradually, and at a distant time, so that he may speak with the more certainty. After the manner of the old works of the prophets, he in-

---

again in ii. 1; but admitting the fact, — which is not proved, — still the capture of Jehoiakim (i. 2, sqq.) took place during the same period, after Nebuchadnezzar's restoration to the throne.

Eichhorn (§ 615, *c*) divides the book into two parts, which he ascribes to two different authors. They are vii.—xii. and ii.—vi., with the introductory passage, i.—ii. 3. But this seems to be arbitrary, especially if we compare ii. 4, sqq., with the preceding verses.

The difference between the first and second of his divisions is, that in the first, Daniel is spoken of in the third person, while in the second, he speaks in the first person. But this manner of speaking agrees well with the subject It is true there is a recension of vii.—xii. ii.—vi. differing from the original; but this is likewise to be explained from the peculiar character of this passage. According to *Eichhorn's* hypothesis, we could not explain why chap. vii. was written in Chaldee. *Bertholdt* maintains there were as many authors as there are passages or sections, viz. *nine*, of whom the later connected their writings with the earlier; but this has not the smallest probability. *Bertholdt* divides the book as follows, (p. 1549, sqq.:) 1. Chap. i. 2. Chap. ii. 3. Chap. iii. 1—30. 4. Chap. iii. 31—iv. 34; (according to another arrangement of the verses, chap. iv. 1—37.) 5. Chap. v. vi. 6. Chap. vii. 7. Chap. viii. 8. Chap. ix. 9. Chap. x.—xii. (See *Bleek*, l. c. p. 242.) [The same spirit, aim, and style of expression, are manifest in all parts of the book, so that its unity is almost perfect. Chap. vi. 29, has the aspect of an interpolation.]

terweaves history with his predictions, but especially such accounts as are applicable to the history of his own times, and are suitable to nourish the spirit of martyrdom among his people.

Nebuchadnezzar and *Belshazzar* are used to signify Antiochus Epiphanes. The source of the historical statements was, perhaps, traditionary legends; but still more the author's fancy, quickened by his zeal. Chap. iii. and vi. may be an entire fiction; for there was no occasion for making such legends of martyrs before the time of Antiochus Epiphanes. The legends which are parallel with chap. iv. have already been mentioned, (§ 255,) and there is an historical foundation for chap. v. But there is reason for suspecting chap. i. is an entire fiction. Composed in this manner, the book might receive such an historical value and importance as the predictions of the old prophets enjoyed.

[Taking into consideration these facts, and the peculiar character of the book itself, there seems abundant reason for placing the date of the book in the time of Antiochus Epiphanes, (175—160 B. C.,) and towards the latter part of his reign; certainly after the Jews had experienced many calamities from him. The Jewish nation, oppressed with adversity from without; distracted by their fondness for foreign customs, introduced by the Greeks; torn by dissension among themselves, and becoming, each day, more indifferent to the Law of Moses, and the ancient institutions of the theocracy, — certainly needed both instruction and encouragement. And both would be peculiarly welcome and useful at the time when the temple worship had been forcibly suspended. The author seems to have written with the design to arouse whatever patriotism and religious feeling was left in their hearts. But, at the same time, he must veil his words of reproof and encouragement in obscure and dark symbols, lest his meaning should be too obvious, and his work be suppressed. To accomplish this object, he assumes the position and historical circumstances of Daniel, — an old sage, of whom little was known. Perhaps tradition had related something respecting his fidelity to Jehovah, while a captive at Babylon; but perhaps the reference to him and his three companions, in 1 Macc. ii. 39, 60, is to be traced to the book of Daniel itself. Going back to that age, he could speak with an authority which did not belong to his own times, when there was no longer open vision, but men waited "till a prophet should come." (1 Macc. iv. 46.) Taking his stand in the time of Daniel, he introduces into his work enough that is historical and local to give it the appearance of a real historical statement, and yet composes it so skilfully that none could fail to see the application to his own times. He showed how his countrymen, even under heathen kings, like Nebuchadnezzar and Belshazzar, had been faithful to Jehovah, who had rewarded them for their fidelity; that these kings had violated the law of God, and were punished, the one with madness, the other with a violent death. The inference to be drawn was obvious; the application to the Jews and their persecutors was plain. If the former were faithful, they should be blessed, while the latter would soon be destroyed.

If we read carefully the first and second books of Maccabees, we shall see that our author has taken his coloring from his own fancy, but his facts from the history of his times, and has copied and altered events that took place under his own eyes.

1. After the destruction of Jerusalem, Antiochus issues

a decree, that all nations in his kingdom should be one people, and that each should have its own peculiar laws. He sent letters to Judea, commanding the people to follow his new and strange laws. He forbids the accustomed sacrifice, the observance of the Sabbath, and holy days; pollutes the sanctuary and the saints; sets up altars and shrines to idol deities, and "sacrifices swine's flesh and unclean beasts, to the end that they might forget the law and change all the ordinances." He commands that all who disobey shall be put to death. (1 Macc. i. 41—50, 2 Macc. vi. 1.) In like manner, the writer makes his idealized Darius the Mede, after conquering Babylon, issue a decree forbidding all men from asking any thing of man or God, except from himself, under penalty of death. This imaginary decree is a refinement and caricature upon that of Antiochus. But Daniel refuses to obey the decree of the Persian despot, suffers the extreme rigor of the monarch's wrath, and is saved by a miracle, while the tyrant confesses the greatness of God, permits Daniel to enjoy his religion in peace, and commands all men to worship the God of Daniel. Those who had accused the faithful man are themselves put to the same death they had designed for him. The lesson to be learned from this is very plain; and the satire upon Antiochus is not contemptible.

2. Antiochus, after defiling the temple at Jerusalem, consecrated it to Olympian Jove; and that on Gerizim, to Jupiter Hospitalis. In the former, he erects an altar on the high altar of Jehovah, and commands the Jews to worship and sacrifice there, and eat the unclean and forbidden food. This was the *abomination of the destroyer.*[a]

[a] [*Βδέλυγμα ἐρημώσεως*. (1 Macc. i. 54, 2 Macc. vi. 1, sqq.) Such as disobeyed the command were put to death. (1 Macc. i. lx.—lxiii.) Eleazar and the seven brothers, with their mother, suffered nobly. (2 Macc. vi. vii.)]

This also is repeated, with some refinements, in the book of Daniel. There it is said that Nebuchadnezzar erected a statue, and commanded men to worship it, at the time when all the instruments of music sounded.[a] Three Jews are faithful to the law of Jehovah, and refuse, — three, who hitherto had refused to eat the idolater's meat or to drink his wine. They, for their disobedience, suffer all which the angry despot can inflict — are cast into a furnace heated seven times hotter than usual. The result is, that their persecutors perish, while they escape without the smell of fire on their garments. They are permitted to worship Jehovah as they wish, are exalted to high offices, and all the people are forbidden to speak reproachfully of the living God, "because there is no other God that can deliver after this sort." The application of this, also, is obvious.

3. When these brothers and their mother are about to suffer death, they denounce curses upon Antiochus, and predict his downfall — "Be not lifted up without cause, nor puffed up with uncertain hopes; for thou hast not yet escaped the judgment of Almighty God — thou shalt receive just punishment for thy pride." (2 Macc. vii. 31, sqq.) Daniel, in explaining Nebuchadnezzar's dream, utters oracles foretelling his fate, all of which are executed; and at the end of his punishment he confesses the greatness and justice of God. (chap. iv.) Again: Daniel predicts the ruin which is to fall upon Belshazzar, and, wonderful to tell, receives a recompense from the tyrant, whom he denounces in the name of God. (chap. v.)

---

[a] [Sir *Thomas Brown* long ago remarked on the strangeness of the proportions ascribed to this image, — *sixty* cubits high, and *six* cubits in breadth, — thinking that the Babylonians had strange ideas respecting symmetry. *Hengstenberg* attempts to show צֶלֶם and צַלְמָא may mean an obelisk as wel. as a statue; and *if this is true*, the proportions are symmetrical.]

4. Antiochus "Epiphanes" was called, also, and with perfect propriety, "Epimanes"—"*the mad.*" This may have given the author a hint to represent the old and idealized persecutor of his nation as bereft of reason, and reduced to the form and character of a beast. Here the historical fact is idealized, and an exquisite piece of sarcasm on the folly and brutality of Antiochus is produced, (Dan. iv. 14, 22—24, 29, 31, 32, 34,) and his future disgrace and penitence are foreshadowed.[a]

5. Antiochus had penetrated into the temple, and plundered it of the sacred vessels, including all the furniture of the altar. (1 Macc. i. 21—24, 2 Macc. v. 15, 16.) In the prophetic book, Nebuchadnezzar also had plundered the sacred vessels, and brought them to Babylon. (i, 1.) Belshazzar used them in a scene of great debauchery and riot; and forthwith there appeared a miraculous hand to write the words of doom against his kingdom and himself, which were executed that very night, and a deliverer of the Jews possessed his empire. Here was a very plain prophecy of the approaching fate of Antiochus, and the delivery of the Jews. Viewed in this light, the whole book appears as a very ingenious, and, judging by the Oriental standard, a very beautiful work, suitable to encourage the desponding Jews.][b]

---

[a] [It is vain to attempt to prove Nebuchadnezzar actually suffered the *kind of transformation* mentioned in this book. *Origen* and *Jerome* could find no authority for the story. The latter admits this fact, but says, "Who does not see that mad men live like brute beasts in the fields and woody places? and in what is it wonderful that this punishment should be inflicted by God's judgment to show the power of God, and to humble the pride of kings? Greek and Roman histories relate that much more incredible things have happened to men. Their stories (*fabulæ*) relate that men were changed into *Scylla*, the *Chimæra*, the *Hydra*, and the *Centaurs*, into *birds* and *beasts*, *flowers* and *trees*, *stars* and *stones*." Note on iv. 1. See *Ovid's* Metamorphoses, passim.]

[b] See *Bleek*, 259, sqq. *Gesenius*, Esaias, vol. i. p. 52.

Griesinger maintains that it has a parenetic or moral relation to the times, but denies that it has any prophetic tendency. Gesenius and Bleek admit its prophetic character, while Eichhorn and Bertholdt think it contains only history, in the guise of prophecy.[a]

§ 258.

ALEXANDRIAN VERSION OF DANIEL.

The Alexandrian version, although in general adhering pretty accurately to the original text, differs from it

---

[a] *Griesinger*, N. Ansicht der Aufsätze in B. Daniel. *Gesenius*, A. L. Z. for 1816, Nos. 57 and 80. *Bleek*, l. c. p. 246, sqq. The dates which *Bertholdt* assigns to the separate portions of the book have no certain ground, except the gradual progress of the work. (See *Gesenius*, l. c. p. 635.) According to x. 6, 17, the passage (ii. 43) relates to the marriage of the Macedonian kings in general, and not merely to that of Antiochus Theos with Berenice.

The account in the Talmud, Baba Bathra, fol. 15, c. i., (see above, § 14,) is not to be regarded in this place, for it is false in respect to Ezekiel. See *Stäudlin*, l. c. p. 98. *Bertholdt*, Dan. p. 87.

[*Bleek* attempts to fix the time when the several portions of the book were written. He supposes the first six chapters were written at the same time, while the Hebrew worship was suspended, and shortly after the altar of Jehovah had been consecrated to idols. The prophetic passages were written soon after the restoration of the Jewish worship by Judas the Maccabee, which took place 164 B. C., (1 Macc. iv. 52, 2 Macc. x. 5,) and shortly before, or immediately after, the death of Antiochus himself, which occurred the next year. (1 Macc. vi. 16.) They were probably written in the order they now stand, for viii. 1, refers to the previous vision; ix. 21, to chap viii.; and xi. 1, alludes to chap. ix. In chap. vii. the prophecy is brought down to the time of Antiochus, " who is to harass the saints of the Most High, and resolves to change times and laws," (verse 25,) for *three and a half* times, or years, when the kingdom is to be taken from him, and given forever to the people of God. This period, perhaps, is to be dated *from* the time when Apollonius took Jerusalem, *to* the time when the worship of Jehovah was restored. (1 Macc. i. 29, 2 Macc. v. 24.) The eighth and ninth chapters were probably written a little before Antiochus's death. The last passage (10—12) was written immediately after that event, which is accurately described, with all its circumstances — " But [while he is in Ægypt] tidings out of the east, [Persia,]

in many passages, (i. ii. vii. ix.,) and in particular expressions and sentences.[a]

In several passages, as chap. iii.—vi., almost the whole form of the text is different. Sometimes impor-

---

and out of the north, [Judea,] shall trouble him, and he shall go forth with great fury to destroy, and utterly to make away many. And he shall pitch his palace-tents [shall encamp] between the sea [the Nile, so called in Nah. iii. 8, Isa. xix. 5, Ezek. xxxii. 2] and the glorious holy mountain, [Zion. In his march out of Ægypt into Judea and Persia, he will encamp between Judea and Ægypt.] And he shall come to his end, and none shall help him." (xi. 44, 45.) This passage involves many difficulties, and has led to very various interpretations, as any one will see from *Rosenmüller*, and to many absurd conjectures; such appear in *Newton* on the Prophecies. *A. Clarke* observes, "From the beginning of the chapter to verse 30, all is very clear and plain, relative to the Grecian, Syrian, and Ægyptian histories. From the 31st verse to the end, the mode of interpretation is not so satisfactory in its application to the times since Christ. *Yet possibly these alone may be intended, though the whole might be,* with considerable ease, *applied to the remaining part of the Syrian and Ægyptian history.* It is a wonderful piece of prophecy, and of great utility to the cause of divine revelation." Jerome, and many others, consider the word אפדנו (*a palace*) as the name of a place, *Apadno*, which *Porphyry* places between the Tigris and Euphrates. See *Jerome*, in loc.]

[a] Chap. i. 3, 11, and 16, where *Abiesdri* is read, instead of *Ashpenaz.* [The Syriac follows both *Ashpenaz* and *Abiezer.*] Chap. ii. 8, there is an addition — " But as I have commanded, so shall it be;" in verse 11, "The thing is hard," and "*illustrious*," (ἐπίδοξος,) adds the LXX.; in verses 28, 29, "There is a God in heaven that revealeth secrets ...... he has shown King Nebuchadnezzar what is to come to pass in the last days ...... yea, he that revealeth secrets has shown thee what is to come to pass." Again: in vii. 6, the following passage is omitted: "And dominion was given to it;" while in verse 8 there is an addition — "And it made war against the saints." In ix. 25, the reading is different from the Hebrew, viz. "Thou shalt know, and understand, and rejoice, and shalt find commandments to keep them, and shalt build Jerusalem a city to the Lord;" verse 27, "and the covenant (διαθήκη) shall prevail over many; and again it shall return, and be restored, in its length and breadth, even till the consummation of the times, and after seventy and seven times, and sixty-two years, until the time of the consummation of war, and the desolation shall be taken away in the establishment of the covenant for many weeks; and in the end of the week the sacrifice shall be taken away, and the libation; and in the temple the abomination of desolations shall continue until the consummation, and consummation shall be made of the desolation."

tant additions are made: such are, the prayer of Azariah, (iii. 24, sqq.,) and the song of the three men.[a] (iii. 51.) Sometimes the text is abridged. (v. 17—25, 26—28.) Sometimes there are additions and abridgments both. (iii. 31—33.) The passage, iv. 3—6, is omitted. Chap. iv. 15, 33, sqq., contain additions. Other variations from the original are found in iv. 10, sqq., 28, sqq., v. 69, and chap. vi.

We find the addition to chap. iii. in Theodotion's version, in the Syriac, and the Vulgate, but it is probable they use interpolations. In the Codex Chisianus — which contains the Septuagint version of Daniel — there is a short recension of the fifth chapter, as well as a translation of that chapter itself.[b]

Some critics have thought they found traces of a Chaldee original in these additions.[c] Hence it has been

---

[a] [The song of the Three Holy Children of our Apocrypha.]

[b] [The recension or abstract of the chapter consists of only three verses, corresponding in sense to 1, 4, 5, 26, and 27, of the original. Some have thought this addition was an independent fragment. But see *Bertholdt*, Dan. p. 131 and 113.]

For the opinion of the primitive church on this version, see *Jerome's* Præf., as cited in § 44, above.

[c] Chap. iii. 32, *ἀποσταιῶν* = מָרְדִין (?); verse 35, *Ἀβραάμ, τὸν ἠγαπημένον ὑπό σου* = רְחִימָךְ, (?) (comp. LXX. 2 Ch. xx. 7, *τῷ ἠγαπημένῳ σου*;) verse 37, *ταπεινοὶ ἐν πάσῃ τῇ γῇ* = בְּכָל־אַרְעָא, instead of מִכָּל־א (?); verse 40, *ἐξιλᾶσαι ὄπισθεν, τελειῶσαι ὄπισθεν* = אִתְכַּפָּרָא אֲחוֹרֵי, אִתְגַּמָּרָא אֲחוֹרֵי, (?) (comp. Heb. ix. 9;) verse 44, *οἱ ἐνδεικνύμενοι* = מַחְמַיִן, or מַרְאַיִן, (?) (comp. 2 Tim. iv. 14;) verse 48, *πνεῦμα δρόσου διασυρίζον* = רוּחַ טַל שָׁרֵק (?); verse 51, *ἀναλαβόντες* = וּנְטַלוּ, (?) (comp. Jer. vii. 29, Targ. 1 Makk. i. 27. *Bertholdt*: "They arose;") verse 65, *πνεύματα*, instead of *ἄνεμοι* = רוּחוֹת (?); iv. 25, *τούτους τοὺς λόγους ἀγάπησον* = רְחַם (?); verse 31, *ἔδωκα τὴν ψυχήν μου εἰς δέησιν* = נִתְנֵת נַפְשִׁי לִצְלוֹ (?); verse 8, *ἦν ἐν αὐτῷ ᾤκουν* = הֲוָה בֵּיהּ דָּאֵר (?); verse 28, *ἐξουσία* = שָׁלְטָן (?); v. 4, *τὸν*

conjectured that the Chaldee text has been rewrought and altered by later and different hands. It appears, indeed, as Bertholdt has shown, that the prayer of Azariah and the song of the three men are the work of different authors. (Compare iii. 38, with verses 53, 55, 84, 85.) Perhaps they were originally composed to be used in public worship, in a liturgy.

It appears the prayer of Azariah is an interpolation, from the Hebrew names of the three men, that are used instead of the Persian titles, by which they are mentioned in other places. Compare iii. 24, 49, 88, with verses 19, 93, 95, 97.

[Bertholdt maintains, though with small probability, that, after the collection of the fragments of the canonical Daniel, there were some other pieces relating to him still in circulation, and that a second collection was made, which comprised them.

But, on the other hand, we see that the Jewish text is the original, from the efforts of the Alexandrian writer to introduce a better connection into the narrative. There is no connection between iii. 23, in the Hebrew, where the three men fall down into the fire, and the next verse, where the astonished king rises up with exclamations at a great wonder he appears to have seen. The Greek makes the connection plain by inserting between these passages the following clause, (iii. 49, sqq.:) "The angel of the Lord descended at the same time with these men who were with Azariah in the furnace, and drove out the flame of fire from the furnace,

---

ἔχοντα τὴν ἐξουσίαν τοῦ πνεύματος αὐτῶν = דִּי לֵהּ שׁוּלְטַן נַפְשְׁהוֹן (?); verse 6, *ἐκαυχῶντο* = חֲדַרוּ, an error for חֲדַדוּ; vi. 5, *νεανίσκοι*, עַבְדִין, (?) &c. *Bertholdt*, Dan. p. 130, sq., 138, sqq. *Michaelis*, Or. Bib. vol. iv. p. 118, sqq. *Eichhorn*, Einl. § 617.

and made the midst of the furnace like the gently-breathing spirit of dew,[a] and the fire touched them not;" "They, arising, sang a hymn, as it were with one voice;" and (verse 91,) "And it came to pass, that, when the king heard them praising God, he stood up, and saw them alive."

They attempt, also, to remove whatever is inappropriate, though without perfect success. Therefore they omit the first three verses of Nebuchadnezzar's epistle, (iii. 31—33, or iv. 1—3,) and add a long confession of the king at the end of chap. iv. An attempt, also, is made to moderate exaggerations. Chap. ii. 5, where the Hebrew reads, "If ye will not make known to me the dream, and the interpretation thereof, ye shall be cut in pieces," &c., the Seventy read, "You shall be made an example of, and all your property shall be confiscated." Again: in iii. 1, instead of the famous statue, sixty cubits high, and six in breadth, the Seventy read, "its height was six cubits."]

But the alleged errors of translation do not hold; and so, perhaps, we may come to this conclusion, that the translator allowed himself to recast the passages, which gave an opportunity for such treatment. This only is certain, that the prayer of Azariah and the song of the three men are the work of different authors.[b]

§ 259.

THE APOCRYPHAL ADDITIONS TO DANIEL.

Besides the additions to the third chapter, in the Alexandrian and the other versions, there are found two

[a] *Πνεῦμα δρόσου διασυρίζον.*

[b] See *Hävernik*, p. xlix.

additions to the book of Daniel. One is the history of Susannah. In the Codex Chisianus, and in the Complutensian edition of Theodotion, this forms chap. xiii. But in the Vatican Codex and Roman edition of the Seventy, it precedes chap. i. The other is the history of Bel and the Dragon, at Babylon. (chap. xiv.) Both were written originally in Greek. There are some Hebraisms in it, (xiii. 1, 7, 14, 15, 19, 28, 52, xiv. 4, 9, 13, 26,) but they do not prove there was a Hebrew or Chaldee original. Neither is it proved by the fact that they are admitted into the version of Theodotion, Symmachus, and Aquila. In Theodotion's version, they appear after having undergone a different recension.[a] The play upon words proves there was a Greek original.[b]

---

[a] See *Bertholdt*, Daniel, p. 149, in opposition to the editor of the Codex Chisianus. See *De Magistris*, ad cap. xiii. 1. *Dereser*, Ubers. des Ezech. and Dan. p. 227, sqq. *Eichhorn*, Allg. Bib. vol. ii. p. 1, sqq.; Einleit. § 617, in Die Apok. p. 431. *Bertholdt*, Dan. p. 145, sqq., and Einleit. p. 1576, sqq.

[b] *Jerome* was aware of this, and says, in the Procem. ad Comm. on Daniel, "We ought to know that, amongst others, Porphyry made this objection to the book of Daniel, viz., that it appeared to be a forgery; that it was not extant among the Hebrews, but was a false story written in the Greek language; for, in the fable of Susannah, where Daniel is speaking to the elders, it is said, Ἀπὸ τοῦ σχίνου σχίσαι, καὶ ἀπὸ τοῦ πρίνου πρίσαι, an etymology which agrees rather with the Greek than with the Hebrew language. *Eusebius* and *Apollinaris* agree with him in this, and reply that the stories of Susannah, and Bel and the Dragon, are not contained in the Hebrew, but are a part of the prophecy of Habakkuk, the son of Joshua, (Jesu,) of the tribe of Levi, as it is said in the title of the story of Bel and the Dragon, according to the LLX.

"Accordingly, when I translated Daniel, many years ago, I marked these visions with an *obelus*, to indicate that they were not in the Hebrew. And I wonder that some censorious fellows (μεμψιμοίρους) were offended at me, as if I had curtailed the book, when *Origen*, *Eusebius*, *Apollinaris*, and other ecclesiastical men and teachers of Greece, confess, as I have said, that these visions are not extant among the Hebrews." Again: commenting on xiii. 59, he says, "If this etymology does not hold good in Hebrew, the passage must be rejected; but if it can be shown to belong to the Hebrew, then it may be received"

These additions are later and supposititious offsets from the original Danielitic stock of traditions and legends. Chap. xiv. 31, 32, has a resemblance with vi. 15, 16, namely, in representing Daniel as cast into the lions' den. The author may have been a certain Habakkuk, to judge from the title of chap. xiv.[a] At any rate, they did not originate with the Alexandrian translators, but have an independent origin.[b]

---

[a] *'Εκ προφητείας 'Αμβακοὺμ υἱοῦ 'Ιησου ἐκ τῆς φυλῆς Λευί.*

[b] See *Bertholdt,* Dan. p. 150, Einleit. p. 1581, 1589, on the Syriac and Arabic versions of these passages.

BOOK III.

POETICAL BOOKS.

---

§ 260.

CHARACTER AND KINDS OF HEBREW POETRY—ITS RELATION TO PROPHECY.

["The promise made to Abraham was never perfectly fulfilled, by reason of the disobedience of the people: the land of Canaan was not entirely conquered, and thus an occasion was left for the apostasy and misery of the nation. History presents us only the alternative—apostasy and repentance, punishment and reconciliation. In vain God sent new messengers and heralds of his word, with threats and promises. Only once, under David, did the empire flourish, through obedience to its sovereign, Jehovah. Soon after his death, the greater part of the nation rebelled from the covenant of God, and were destroyed. Afterwards Judea, which, for a time, remained more faithful, revolted, and suffered the consequences of her apostasy. But, under this imperfect realization of the promise, the pious worshipper consoled himself only with the hope, that at some time, after their sin had been expiated, and God's wrath mitigated, the divine Spirit would appear in a more perfect form on the earth, through the mediation of a descendant of David, on whom all divine gifts would rest; that the divine Spirit would be diffused over the whole nation, (Joel iii. 1,) and a new and more perfect covenant would be made. (Jer. xxxi. 31.) Accordingly, the nation was governed by the sense of a higher power in history, and of a benefit which surpassed their own powers, and was conferred on them by their worshipping the invisible God, and fulfilling his holy will. But, at the same time, there arose the feeling that they were the objects of God's choice, and that his word was continually imparted to some consecrated men in the midst of them. In the better part of public opinion, there was a reverence for the Spirit of God, which was continually working in the human mind, though the expression of this Spirit was often perplexed and disturbed by the intrusions of a false spirit. There was left, therefore, a free right of judging between what was divine and true, and what was human and false. The primitive revelation by Moses was only authenticated by the law of the two tables and the institutes of the theocracy. It therefore remained the object of free inquiry, and of further and more perfect development. Yea, the thought of rendering it more perfect might be entertained.

"The Hebrew conceived of God as continually active in preserving the material universe he had created. He produces the common phenomena of nature, and by his immediate action. In particular he was conceived of as the God of thunder. He causes physical evils, to punish and correct mankind. It was the will of God, and not any natural necessity, which governed all things. In these conceptions, the idea of the eternal duration of all things, through the power of God, shows itself rather in feeling than in thoughts."]

This being the case, we find the sentiment of devotion prevails in the institutions of the Hebrews. Lyric poetry corresponds to this sentiment, and therefore it prevailed among the Hebrews to such a degree, that whatever poetry there is in the prophetic writings, it is of this kind. The theocratic, moral, and religious subjects of the prophetic discourses, must have often led to lyric flights, while the general course of thought and style continued to be rhetorical and more quiet, by reason of its intelligible application to the details of actual public life. But, on the other hand, the prophets themselves at other moments, or some other pious poets, treated the same subjects, or more especially the particular state of the religious life, in the higher tone, and with the higher vision of lyric poetry.[a]

§ 261.

THE SAME SUBJECT CONTINUED.

As the lyric element of prophecy was particularly developed, so likewise was the didactic. Not only the religious doctrine of retribution, which lies at the foundation of all the prophecies, and constitutes the fundamental thought in all their lyrico-elegiac effusions of the heart, but likewise religious ethics, which the prophets brought within their sphere, are treated of in independent productions, in a general or universal manner, and free from all particular applications. But both of these depart-

[a] The difference between the prophetic and lyric manner of treating the same or similar subjects, may be seen by comparing Psalms xlvi. and xlviii. with Isa. xxxii. and xxxiii. The affinity of prophetic and lyric poetry is indicated by the names נָבִיא and חֹזֶה, which are common to both. See Ex. xv. 20, Judg. iv. 4, 1 Ch. xxv. 5, 2 Ch. xix. 30. *De Wette*, Dogm. § 94, 105.

ments, the doctrine of retribution and of ethics, always remain with them, to a certain extent, under the dominion of lyric poetry, and can never obtain an entire independence. The form of a proverb, which these subjects sometimes take, is the only one which appears peculiar to them; but this form was highly favored by the symmetry of the members in Hebrew poetry.

§ 262.

LYRIC POETRY.

Agreeably to its nature, this kind of poetry, — the handmaid of song, — in its simple form, at first sprang from the mouths of the people, particularly of the women. Thus Miriam sings, Ex. xv. 20; a woman in Psalms lxviii. 12, Judg. v. 1, xi. 34, xxi. 19, 21, 1 Sam. xviii. 6. It continued with them until David, the master of the *chinnor*, and perhaps other contemporaries of the prophetic schools, brought it to perfection.[a] It was found in the sanctuary and at the court of Jerusalem, in connection with more highly finished songs. (2 Sam. vi. 16, 21, xix. 35, Eccl. ii. 8, Ps. lxviii. 26.) Here it received further attention from the Levites and prophets. Since it did not, like prophecy, derive its support from public life, it lived through the exile in all the vigor of its youth; and the collection of Psalms contains some beautiful specimens produced at that period. Although it was consecrated to holy uses, agreeably to its main purpose and religious tendency, yet, in the time when it flourished most, among the Hebrews it embellished

---

[a] See *De Wette*, On the Origin and Cultivation of Lyric Poetry among the Hebrews, p. 5; and in Biblical Repository, vol. iii. p. 445, sqq.

common life also, and served the purposes of wine and love. (Amos vi. 5.) But only a few specimens of the amatory poetry have come down to us.

§ 263.

LYRIC LITERATURE.

As *prophecy* was divorced from the living speech by means of the increasing use of writing, and was artificially expressed in books, so, likewise, there are many *lyrical* productions which had not their origin in living song, and which never were actually sung. In this class must be reckoned the greater part of the Psalms, for they contain prayers, lamentations, contemplations, and the like, and belong to didactic poetry. The free use of the *chinnor* seems in general to have been lost among the people at a subsequent date.

§ 264.

DIDACTIC POETRY.

Among all nations, common sense, wit, and practical wisdom, first express themselves in *proverbs*.[a] The Hebrew parallelism is its natural form. The Proverb and the Ode were originally distinguished only as Discourse and Song.[b] (Compare Judg. xv. 16, with 1 Sam. xviii. 6.) As the ode was winged by instrumental music, and

---

[a] מָשָׁל, חִידָה.

[b] See the parallels among the Arabs, Persians, and Greeks, collected in *Ziegler*, Uebers d. Denksprache Salomos, p. 1, sqq. *Rhode*, De vet. Poetarum Sapientia gnomica, Hebræorum imprimis Græcorum; Havniæ, 1800, 8vo.

thus attained a higher development, so, by the conversation of sages,[a] and by the use of writing, the proverb increased, and became a didactic discourse, or didactic poem. Subsequently it became again the companion of lyric poetry, now expressed in writing.

The wisdom of proverbs found its master in Solomon.[b] "And Jehovah gave Solomon wisdom," and "he spake three thousand proverbs, and his songs were a thousand and five." (1 Kings v. 12, iv. 32.) Proverbs found a genial home at his court. So long as the religious spirit of devotion animated them, they preserved their peculiar beauty; but this was destroyed by the spirit of skepticism, which, however, never passed into philosophy. Afterwards it threw out a vigorous shoot in the proverbs of Jesus the Son of Sirach.

§ 265.

CLASSIFICATION OF THE POETIC BOOKS.

The most purely *lyrical* productions, such as hymns, odes, and prayers, are found in the Psalms. But many of these belong to the class of *lyrical elegies*. The Lamentations of Jeremiah must be reckoned with these. The Song of Solomon is of the *amatory idyllic* character. The book of Psalms contains also *didactic* and *gnomological* passages. The religious doctrine of retribution

---

[a] The conduct of the book of Job justifies this assumption. (Comp. Prov. xxv. 1.) Perhaps the prophet-schools had an influence in producing this effect. See *Nachtigall*, on Samuel's company of singers, in *Henke's* Magazin, vol. vi., and in *Nachtigall's* Koheleth, p. 25, sqq.

[b] *Ewald* (Poet. Büch. A. T. vol. i. p. 34, sq.) thinks Solomon was the author thereof, for proverbs do not occur before his time. But this is doubtful.

is the most fully developed in Job; that of morals, in Proverbs. The book of Ecclesiastes stands midway between the two, but it is the product of uninspired reflection.[a]

§ 266.

RHYTHMICAL PECULIARITIES.

The rhythm of lyric poetry is less periodic, and more bold and easy in its movement, than the prophetic. A peculiar limitation of the verse appears in the Songs of Degrees, as they are called.[b] In the Proverbs, the symmetry of numbers is almost always simple, rigid, and exact. The Lamentations have this peculiarity, that the symmetry, which is merely rhythmical, and not logical, is, in part, regularly formed and uniform. Ecclesiastes is almost entirely prosaic.[c]

---

[a] *Ewald* (l. c. p. 38, sqq.) treats of a dramatic poetry of the Hebrews. But there is only a distant approach to it in the alternate songs of Solomon's Song, and speeches in Job, and in the sort of dialogue in Hos. vi. and Mic. vi.

[b] שִׁירֵי הַמַּעֲלוֹת. See *Gesenius*, in A. L. Z. for 1813, No. 205. *De Wette*, in Bib. Repos. l. c. For other opinions on these names, see *Rosenmüller*, Proleg. in Psalm. *Bertholdt* (p. 1932) on the strophes. See above, § 134. The musical execution of the Psalms lies in great obscurity, but it is probable they were merely cantillated. *Bertholdt* compares it to the sacred song of the primitive Christians. The favorite opinion of *choruses* in the Psalms, — which *Bertholdt* favors, — can neither be proved to exist from the rhythm nor from exegesis, except, perhaps, in Ps. cxxxvi.

[c] See *Lowth*, Prælect. xxii. p. 453, and *De Wette*, l. c.

CHAPTER I.

THE PSALMS.[a]

§ 267.

THE TITLE, CONTENTS, AND DIVISION, OF THE BOOK.

UNDER the title תְּהִלִּים, תִּלִּים, תִּלִּין, (*ψαλμοὶ, ψαλτήριον,*) which was probably introduced by their liturgical use,

---

[a] Psalmorum LL. V. ad Ebr. Veritatem versi et familiari Explanat. elucidati per *Aretium Felinum* (*Mart. Bucerum ;*) Arg. 1526, fol., 1529, 4to., and under the author's real name.

M. Ant. Flaminii in Libr. Pss. brevis Explanatio; Ven. 1548. Recudi curavit *S. Th. Wald;* Hal. 1785.

Fr. Vatabli Annotatt. in Pss. (in Bibl. R. Stephan.; Par. 1557, fol.) subjunctis H. Grotii Notis, quibus Observatt. adspersit *G. J. L. Vogel ;* Hal. 1767.

Libri Psalmorum Paraph. Lat., quæ Oratione soluta breviter exponit Sententias singulorum, ex opt. Interpretum vet. et recent. Rationibus. Addita sunt Argumenta singulorum Pss., et redduntur Rationes Paraphraseos, adspersis alicubi cert. Locorum Explanatiunculis. Excepta omnia e scholis *Esromi Rudingeri* in Ludo litter. Fratrum Boëm. Evanzizi in Moravis; Gorl. 1580, 1581, 4to.

Anton. Agellii Comment. in Psalmos; Par. 1611, fol.

Mos. Amyraldi, Paraphrasis in Pss. Davidis una cum Annotatt. et Argg.; Salmur. 1662, ed. 2; Traj. ad Rh. 1769, 4to.

Mart. Geieri Comm. in Pss. Dav.; Dresd. 1668, 2 vols. 4to., 1709, fol.

Herm. Venemæ Comm. in Pss.; Leov. 1762—1767, 6 vols. 4to.

J. Chr. Döderlein, Scholia in Librr. V. T. poeticos, Job., Pss. et tres Salom.; Hal. 1779, 4to.

Philol. Clavis über das A. T. Die Psalmen. Von *H. E. G. Paulus;* Jen. 1791, 2 Ausg. Heidelb. 1815.

Psalmi ex Rec. Textus Hebr. et Verss. antt. Latine versi Notisque crit. et philol. illustrati (a *N. M. Berlin ;*) Ups. 1805.

Commentar über die Psalmen von *W. M. L. de Wette:* Heidelb. 1811, 4th ed. 1836.

J. B. Köhler, Krit. Anmerkk. üb. d. Pss., in *Eichhorn's* Rep. vol. iii. p. 1, sqq., vol. iv. p. 96, sqq., vol. v. p. 1, sqq., vol. vi. p. 1, sqq., vol. vii. p. 240, sqq., vol. viii. p. 227, sqq., vol. ix. p. 47, sqq., vol. x. p. 110, sqq., vol. xiii. p. 95, sqq., vol. xviii. p. 95, sqq., p. 117, sqq.

we have a collection of miscellaneous, though for the most part religious, odes and poems. They are one hundred and fifty in number.[a]

Th. F. Stange, Anticritica in Locos quosd. Psalmorum a Criticis solicitatos; Lips. 1791, 1794, 2 Thle.

G. Ph. Chr. Kaiser, Zusammenhäng. hist. Erklärung der fünf Psalmen-BB. als National-Gesang-B. auf die Zeit von David bis zu Simon d. Maccab.; Nürnb. 1827.

Rosenm. Schol. *J. A. Cramer*, (poet.) mit Abhandll. 2 A. 1763, fol. 4 vols. *J. Chr. Fr. Schulz*, m. Comm. 1 Th. (Ps. i.—l.) 1772. *G. T. Zachariä*, (frei. u. erklär.) 1773. *Knapp*, mit Anmerkk. 1773, 3 A. 1789. *Struense*, 1783. *Mos. Mendelssohn*, 1783, 2 A. 1788. *Thenius*, m. Anmerkk. 1788. *Seiler*, 1784, 2 A. 1788. *Briegleb*, 1789, 1790, 2 vols. *Zobel*, metr. mit Anmerkk. 1790. *G. Ringeltaube*, 1 vol. (Ps. i.—l.) 1790. *Herm. Muntinghe*, a. d. Holländ. von *Scholl*, m. Anmerkk. 1792, 1793, 3 vols. *Wobeser*, 1793. *J. A. Jacobi*, mit Anmerkk. 1796, 2 vols. *Nachtigall*, 1796, fol. 2 vols. *Künöl*, m. Anmerkk. 1799. *Hezel*, 1800. *Vollbeding*, 1806. *Stuhlmann*, 1812. *Schärer*, 1812. *Lindemann*, 1812. *F. V. Reinhard*, 1814. *Stolz*, 1814. *Goldwitzer*, 1827. *Krahmer*, 1837. *Köster*, 1837. [A New Translation of the Book of Psalms, by *G. R. Noyes;* Boston, 1831, 1 vol. 12mo. There are, also, translations of the Psalms into English, by *Z. Mudge*, Lond. 1774, 4to. *Thos. Edwards*, Lond. 1755, 8vo. *Wm. Green*, Lond. 1763, 8vo. *J. Merrick*, 1765, 4to.; his Annotations, in 1768, 4to. *Steph. Street*, 1790, 2 vols. 8vo. *W. Wake*, 1793, 2 vols. 8vo. *Alex. Geddes*, 1807, 8vo. *Wm. Goode*, 1811, 2 vols. 8vo. Bishop *Horsley*, 1815, 2 vols. 8vo. There are, also, commentaries, and notes, and applications, by *Hammond*, 1659, fol. Bishop *Nicholson*, 1662, fol. *Fenwick*, 1759, 8vo. Bishop *Horne*, 1771, 2 vols. 4to. *Dimmock*, 1761, 4to. *Travell*, 1794, 8vo.]

[a] The number and the division of the same psalms differ in the Hebrew MSS. from the LXX. and Vulgate.

Hebrew.	*LXX.*
Psalms ix. x.	Psalms ix.
——— xi.—cxiii.	——— x.—cxii.
——— cxiv. cxv.	——— cxiii.
——— cxvi.	——— cxiv. cxv.
——— cxvii.—cxlvi.	——— cxvi.—cxlv.
——— cxlvii.	——— cxlvi. cxlvii.
——— cxlviii.—cl.	——— cxlviii.—cl.
	——— cli. apocryphal.

According to the MSS., it is certain that Ps. xlii. and xliii. are to be united; perhaps, also, ix. and x. See *Eichhorn's* Allg. Bib. vol. ii. p. 944. *Anton*,

They are divided into five books, separated by doxologies: 1. Ps. i.—xli. 2. Ps. xlii.—lxxii. 3. Ps. lxxiii.—lxxxix. 4. Ps. xc.—cvi. 5. Ps. cvii.—cl.

A sharp classification of the Psalms cannot be made, but they may be divided according to their contents, as in the note.[a]

Carmen alphabet. integrum, Ps. ix. et x. conjuncto restituit; Viteb. 1805. *Bellermann*, Metrik. p. 140, sqq. *Stuhlmann*, in *Keil* and *Tzschirner's* Annal. vol. iii. pt. iii. p. 1, sqq. [These writers maintain that these two originally formed one alphabetical psalm, which they attempt to reconstruct, by changing the position of some verses, and amending the text according to conjecture. There are traces of an alphabetical psalm; e. g. the letters ד, ז, ח, ט, follow one another in regular order. But כ occurs three times, and מ not at all. Not to mention other objections of this character, the tone of the two psalms is entirely distinct.]

On the other hand, Ps. xix. is to be divided into two parts, viz. i.—vii. viii.—xv.

[a] I. *Hymns in Honor of God.* — Ps. viii. civ. cxlv.; xix. xxix. xxxiii. lxv. xciii. xc. cxxxv. cxxxvi. cxxxix. cxlvii.; xlvii. lxvi. lxvii. lxxv.; xlvi. xlviii. lxxvi.; xviii. xxx. cxxxviii.

II. *National Psalms.* — Ps. lxxviii. cv. cvi. cxiv.

III. *Psalms of Zion and the Temple.* — Ps. xv. xxiv. lxviii. lxxxi. lxxxvii. cxxxii. cxxxiv. cxxxv.

IV. *Psalms respecting the King.* — Ps. ii. xx. xxi. xlv. lxxii. cx. The Messianic signification, sometimes ascribed to many of these psalms, is not consistent with the spirit of lyric poetry, nor even with the Messianic idea itself.

V. *Supplicating and plaintive Psalms* of pious men in distress. — These often relate, also, to the misfortunes of the nation. Ps. vii. xi. xxii. lv. lvi. cix.; x. xliv. lxxiv. lxxix. lxxx. cxxxvii.; lxix. lxxvii. cii.; xii. xiv. xxxvi. To this class belong the *songs of thanksgiving*, Ps. xxxiv. xl., &c., and the *teleological didactic Psalms*, like Ps. xxxvii. xlix. lxxiii. See *De Wette's* remarks in *Daub* and *Kreuzer's* Studien, vol. iii. pt. ii. p. 252, sqq. *Gesenius* (in A. L. Z. for 1816, No. 81, p. 643) confirmed some of *De Wette's* opinions, and corrected others. He has made a profound comparison of this kind of psalms with such passages of the prophets as Jer. xi. 19, 20, xii. 1, sqq., xv. 10, sqq., xvii. 14, sqq. xviii. 18, sqq., xx. 7, sqq., Lam. iii., Isa. xlix., 1, sqq., lii. 13, liii. Yet such passages as Isa. xiv. 28, sq., xxix. 18, sqq., Hab. i. 2, sqq., are also to be regarded. See *De Wette's* Com. in Ps. ix. x. xiv.

VI. *Religious Odes.* — Ps. xxiii. xci. cxxi. cxxvii. cxxviii.; xlii. xliii. ci.

§ 268.

INSCRIPTIONS OF THE PSALMS.

With the exception of thirty-four, all the psalms are furnished with inscriptions.[a] 1. Sometimes the inscription designates the kind of compositions to which the psalm belongs.[b] 2. Sometimes the titles designate the author.[c] 3. Sometimes they mention the occasion of the psalm.[d] 4. Sometimes they contain directions for the musical or liturgical use to be made of the psalm.[e]

---

cxxxi.; i. cxxxiii., and the *religious didactic Poems*, Ps. xxxii. l. cxix. With regard to the degree of inspiration and the tone of each, these may be divided into, 1. Hymns and Odes. Ps. xviii. lxix. xc. cxxxix., &c. 2. Songs. Ps. xxiii. cxiv. cxx., &c. 3. Elegies. Ps. xlii. xliii. lxxxiv., &c. And, 4. into didactic Poems. Ps. xxxix. lxxiii., and others. *De Wette*, l. c. *Augusti*, § 159, and Einleit. in Ps. p. 11.

[a] Namely, i. ii. x. xxxiii. xliii. lxxi. xci. xciii. xciv. xcvii. xcix. civ.—cvii. cxi.—cxix. cxxxv.—cxxxvii. cxlvi.—cl. According to *Carpzov* and *Rosenmüller*, there were formerly only twenty-five destitute of inscriptions. But *Bertholdt* has corrected this mistake.

See *Chr. Sonntag*, ראשי תלין; i. e. Tituli Psalmorum, &c.; Silus. 1687, 4to. *Ol. Celsius*, De Titl. Pss.; Holm. 1718, 4to. *Guil. Irhov*, Conjectan. in Pss. Titulos; Lug. Bat. 1728, 4to. *Calmet*, Bibl. Untersuch. vol. vi. p. 259, sqq.

[b] Such are the titles מִזְמוֹר, שִׁיר, מַשְׂכִּיל, שִׁגָּיוֹן, תְּהִלָּה, מִכְתָּם, הַמַּעֲלוֹת, which may originally have been characteristic appellations, in most cases; but now they are not.

[c] For example, לְדָוִד לְאָסָף, לִבְנֵי קֹרַח. (?) Comp. Hab. iii. 1.

[d] Ps. iii. vii. xviii. xxxiv. li. lii. liv.—lvii. lix. lx. lxiii. cii. cxlii. This can scarcely be the case in Ps. lxxii. and cx. *De Wette*, l. c. p. 13.

[e] Directions to the *music-master*, לַמְנַצֵּחַ, which occurs in 53 psalms, and in Hab. iii. 19, at the end. *Andros* calls it the Syriac infinitive Paël, which means *to be sung*. But *Gesenius* conjectures it is a symbolical name of David, — as *Koheleth* is of Solomon, — and denotes that he is the author. To the *choir*, יְדִיתוּן; Ps. xxxix. lxii. lxxvii. (1 Ch. xxv. 1, 2 Ch. xxxv. 15.) The *sons of Korah;* Ps. xlii.—xlvii. lxxxiv. lxxxv. lxxxvii. lxxxviii., though it is better to suppose this term denotes the authors. The proba-

The inscriptions of the second and third class are, for the most part, false; and their character, also, refers us to a later period, and therefore they may justly be rejected as not genuine.[a] They originated with the compilers of the Psalms, who followed inaccurate conjectures and traditions, as they did in regard to the prophecies that were scattered.

§ 269.

THE AUTHORS OF THE PSALMS.

In the titles, the following authors are mentioned. Moses,[b] David, Solomon, Asaph, Heman, Ethan, the sons of Korah.

---

bility of this is not destroyed by the fact that a different author is mentioned besides the *sons of Korah.* Probably this inscription is composed of two, or the author considered Heman the Ezrahite as one of the sons of Korah, which is not impossible, since the Chronicles are very uncertain respecting the genealogy of this singer. (1 Ch. ii. 6. Comp. 1 Kings v. 11, 1 Ch. vi. 18, xv. 17, 18. See *Bertholdt*, p. 1774. *Gesenius*, ubi sup. p. 646, sq.) The *instrument* with which it was to be accompanied; Ps. viii. vi. v. lxxxviii., &c. The *manner* in which it was to be sung; Ps. lvi.—lix. lxx., &c. The *liturgical* use to be made of it; e. g. לְתוֹדָה, Ps. c. [*for praise, or thanks;*] לְהַזְכִּיר, Ps. xxxviii. lxx. cii., &c. [*to bring to remembrance.*]

[a] See *De Wette*, Introduction to the Psalms, mentioned in No. 3, (in his Commentary,) and § 269, infra.

Such is the opinion of *Theodore Mopsuestius*, cited in *Leontius* Byzant. lib. iii. cont. Nestor. et Eutych. n. 15. *G. J. L Vogel*, Diss. inscript. Pss. serius demum additas videri; Hal. 1767. *Eichhorn*, § 627, and *De Wette*, Com. p. 26, and *Bertholdt*, who brings forward some new arguments, (p. 1978, sqq.,) and yet defends the genuineness of some of these. But this must be proved of each one. It may be doubted that the directions as to the manner of singing originated with the author. But see *Bertholdt*, p. 1995. [*De Wette*, Introd. to the Psalms, chap. vi.]

[b] *Moses* is made the author of Ps. xc., but this can hardly be correct; *David*, of Ps. iii.—ix. xi.—xxxii. xxxiv.—xli. li.—lxv. lxviii.—lxx. lxxxvi. ci. ciii. cviii.—cx. cxxii. cxxiv. cxxxi. cxxxiii. cxxxviii.—cxlv., in all seventy-

It is surprising that none are ascribed to the old prophets, who certainly wrote a great part of the

---

four. To these the LXX. add Ps. xxxiii. xliii. xci. xciv.—xcix. civ. But it is certain many of these do not belong to David; e. g. v. ix. xii. xiv. xx. xxi., (which probably were written *concerning* David;) xxv.—xxvii. xxxiv. xxxv. xxxviii. li. lix.—lxi. lxiii. lxv. lxix. ciii. cviii.—cx., (the last is probably written concerning David,) cxxii. cxxiv. cxxviii. cxxix. cxliv. Others are more or less doubtful; iii. iv. vii. xi. xiii. xvi. xvii. xix. xxii. xxiv., which probably belong to the time of Solomon; as also xxviii. xxxi. xxxvi. xxxvii. xxxix. xl. xli. lii. lviii. lxii. lxiv. lxviii. lxxxvi. cxxxi. cxxxiii. cxl.—cxliii. cxlv. To judge from the psalms that are undoubtedly genuine, (vi. viii. xv. xviii. xxiii. xxix. xxx. xxxii. ci., 2 Sam. i. 18, sqq., and others,) David is equally excellent and successful in the hymn, the song, the elegy, and the didactic poem. See *Eichhorn*, § 622.

The following are the positive results of the latest criticism on the Psalms ascribed to David:—

		According to Ewald.	*According to Hitzig.*
Psalms	iii. iv.,	by David,	by David.
———	v.,	from the 2d period, from the 7th century B. C. till the exile,	by Jeremiah.
———	vi.,	from the age after David,	by Jeremiah.
———	vii. viii.,	by David,	by David.
———	ix. x.,	after the exile.	
———	xi.,	by David,	by David.
———	xii.,	2d period,	by David.
———	xiii.,	1st period,	by David.
———	xiv.,	time of the exile,	by Jeremiah.
———	xv.,	time of David,	by David.
———	xvi. xvii.,	2d period,	by David.
———	xviii.,	by David,	by David.
———	xix.,	by David,	by David.
———	xx. xxi.,	1st period,	time after David.
———	xxii.,	2d period,	by Jeremiah.
———	xxiii.,	1st period,	by Jeremiah.
———	xxiv.,	by David,	by Jeremiah.
———	xxv.,	after the exile,	by Jeremiah.
———	xxvi.—xxviii.,	2d period,	by Jeremiah.
———	xxix.,	from David,	by Jeremiah.
———	xxx.,	1st period,	by Jeremiah.
———	xxxi.,	2d period,	by Jeremiah.
———	xxxii.,	by David,	by Jeremiah.

Psalms, and in general belonged to the first golden age of Hebrew poetry. This circumstance would not produce a prejudice in favor of the correctness of the tradition. It is surprising also that the songs which occur in 1 Sam. i. 19—27, and xxiii. 1—7, are omitted.[a]

A false rule has sometimes been given, that all the psalms, whose author is not mentioned in the title, should be ascribed to the author of the last psalm preceding.[b]

	According to Ewald.	*According to Hitzig.*
Psalms xxxiii., sq.,	after the exile,	by Jeremiah.
——— xxxv, sq.,	2d period,	by Jeremiah.
——— xxxvii.,	after the exile,	by Jeremiah.
——— xxxviii.—xli.,	2d period,	by Jeremiah.
——— ci.,	David,	Maccabaic.
——— cx.,	David,	Maccabaic.

Solomon is mentioned as the author of lxxii. cxxvii. The first may have been written concerning him, and the second has been ascribed to him by an erroneous conjecture. On the other hand, Ps. cxxxii. belongs to his time, and perhaps was written by him.

Asaph, David's chorister according to 1 Ch. vi. 24, xv. 17, xvi. 5, is called the author of l. lxxiii.—lxxxiii. Only the first, with perhaps some part of lxxiii. and lxxv., can be ascribed to him.

Heman, one of David's singers, (1 Ch. xv. 17, 19,) is mentioned as the author of Ps. lxxxviii.

Ethan, also, one of David's singers, is called the author of Ps. lxxxix. But both incorrectly.

The sons of Korah. (See above, § 168, No. 4.) Some of the nameless psalms may belong to David, or to his contemporaries; but this cannot be proved with certainty.

[a] On the inscriptions peculiar to the old versions, in which prophets are mentioned, see *Bertholdt*, p. 1963. He thinks they had merely a liturgical meaning. *Hitzig* ascribes too many psalms to Jeremiah.

[b] *Jerome*, (ad Cyp. Opp. ii. p. 695,) *Augustine*, (Civ. Dei, xvii. 14,) [see the curious note of *Vives*,] *Chrysostom*, (Prol. in Psalm.) *Euthymius Zigabenus*, (Præf. in Pss. Tr. Pesach, fol. 117, c. 1,) support the opinion that David wrote all the psalms. Baba Bathra, fol. 14, c. 2. David scripsit librum Psalmorum, ad modum (על ידי) decem seniorum, ad modum primi hominis, ad modum Melchisedeki. According to Ezra iii. 10, we must refer this to a reproduction, or writing over anew. See *Bertholdt*, p. 1971.

§ 270.

AGE AND ORIGINALITY OF THE PSALMS.

In respect to the spurious and anonymous psalms, there are questions to be asked, not only relating to their authors, but more especially to their age, and the historical circumstances to which they refer. It is pretty certain that a great part of them, in particular the plaintive psalms, are to be placed in the later times, not far from the exile. A great many belong to the time of the exile.[a] Some are to be placed after it.

There are strong exegetical arguments for referring some psalms to the time of the Maccabees, such as xliv. lx. lxxiv. But on account of the difficulties arising from the history of the canon and of the Septuagint version, this becomes doubtful.[b]

Besides, the critic must distinguish, by means of the language and æsthetical considerations, the ancient from

---

[a] Psalm xiv. li. lxxvii. lxxxv. cvi. cvii. cxxvi. cxxix. cxxxvii. cxlvii., and others.

[b] The following authors believe there are psalms from the Maccabaic age: *Rudinger*, *Herman von der Hardt*, *Venema*, *Rosenmüller*, *E. G. Bengel*, (Diss. in Psal.; Tub. 1806,) *Bertholdt*, *Kaiser*, and *Hesse*, (De Psal. Macc.; 1838.) *Hitzig* finds none before the time of the Maccabees, after Ps. lxxiii. [?] [*Eichhorn*, (§ 621,)] *Gesenius*, (A. L. Z. for 1816, xvi. No. 81, p. 643,) and *Hassler*, (Com. crit. de Ps. Maccab.; Ulm, 1727—1732, 4to.,) think it is doubtful that there are Maccabaic psalms. Certainly it is not necessary, on account of the late composition of the book of Daniel, to assume that the canon was finally closed, and the Alexandrian version complete, in all parts, at the time when the Wisdom of Sirach was translated; but yet it is difficult to believe the collection of Psalms remained open till that time, for the later books of the Psalms were needed for liturgical purposes. Yet it is still more difficult to explain how Maccabaic psalms came in the first books of Psalms. Finally, it is not easy to see how false opinions on the origin of such recent works could, in so few years, become current, and be preserved in the inscriptions of the psalms.

the more modern, and the originals from the imitations. Imitations occur most frequently among the temple hymns, the psalms of entreaty and complaint.[a]

§ 271.

ORIGIN OF THE COLLECTION OF PSALMS.

This collection was gradually made from several smaller collections. This appears, 1. From the dissimilarity of the titles. 2. From the repetition of a psalm; thus, Ps. liii. is the same as Ps. xiv. The recurrence, however, of parts of psalms, is not so strong an argument.[b] 3. From the fact that the psalms of the same author are not all collected together, but are in part scattered about, here and there, (Psalms of David, iii.—xli.; of the Korahites,[c] xlii.—xlix.; of Asaph, lxxiii.—lxxxiii.) Sometimes those hymns of a similar character are placed together, (the plaintive psalms, lvi.—lix.; the songs of degrees, so called, cxx.—cxxxv.; and the songs of praise, cxlvi.—cl.) 4. From the doxologies at the end of the books, and the formula at the end of the second book, "The prayers of David, the son of Jesse, are ended." (lxxii. 20.)

It is certain we are to regard the first book (i.—xli.) as the original collection. The second book, it is probable, was made up from several separate compilations

---

[a] Psalm xxv. xxxv. lxix. lxxxviii. cxix., and others; xcvii. c. cxxxvi., and others. *De Wette*, Com. in Ps. p. 15, sqq.

[b] Ps. lxx. is the same as xl. 13—17; Ps. cviii. 1—5, as lvii. 8—12; and Ps. cviii. 6—13, as lxx. 7—14. The difference in the text of these reiterated pieces, and also between Ps. xviii. and 2 Sam. xxii., does not arise from different recensions of the poet, but only from the free treatment it received in being copied, or in passing from mouth to mouth.

[c] [Psalm xliii., however, is anonymous.]

(xliii.—l. and li. lxv.) and supplementary additions, and afterwards appended to the first book. A third collection was made, in the same manner, from separate collections, (lxxiii.—lxxxiii. lxxxiv.—lxxxix.) This formed the third book, and was distinguished from the two preceding by the formula. Here Ps. lxxxvi., standing among psalms that certainly are not David's, is ascribed to him, by the title; but this title has, perhaps, been interpolated, through force of a conjecture founded on verses 2, 4, 16. It is the only psalm in the book ascribed to David; all the rest are referred to Asaph, the sons of Korah, and Ethan the Ezrahite.

The two last books, which contain most of the liturgical pieces, were added in the same manner.[a]

Judging from Ps. xiv., the first collection was made about the time of the exile, or after it. The completion of the whole must be referred to a much later period. The collection was designed, incontestably, for religious, ascetical, and liturgical uses. Bertholdt has examined the various opinions of ancient and modern writers, respecting the age of the collections, but he has himself gone the farthest in this analysis, and certainly too far.[b]

---

[a] *Ewald* (vol. i. p. 194) thinks Ps. xcii.—c., which closely resemble each other, form a collection by themselves. The connection between the psalms of degrees (cxx.—cxxxiv.) is obvious. The hallelujah psalms begin with civ., and *Ewald* thinks they also form an independent collection. Book i. is mostly *Davidic*; book ii. mostly *Koraitic* (xlii.—l.) and *Davidic*. (li.—lxv.)

[b] *Bertholdt*, p. 2009, sqq. *Ewald* (p. 188) thinks the division into five books was subsequently made; and *Hitzig* divides them into three larger books, which were originally independent collections: 1. Ps. i.—xli., for the most part Davidic, and perhaps older odes. 2. Ps. xlii.—lxxxix., odes of the middle period. 3. Ps. xc.—ci., modern and very modern odes. He makes the interesting remark, that *Elohim* is the prevalent name of God in xlii.—lxxxiii., which he sets down to the account of the collector, but we to that of the age when they were composed. See below, § 284.

CHAPTER II.

THE LAMENTATIONS.[a]

§ 272.

THE KIND OF COMPOSITION.

On the one side, these Lamentations are connected with the psalms of entreaty and complaint. They have the same occasion and the same subject. They are national songs, — of true patriotism. But on the other side, they are connected with the lamentations for the dead, which occur in 2 Sam. i. 19, sqq., iii. 33, and 2 Ch. xxxv. 25. Perhaps they have the same tone and rhythm as these. The literary notices in these passages, in Samuel and Chronicles, must certainly refer to our book of Lamentations: this is plain, since the writer of the Chronicles thought that Josiah was

---

[a] *Tarnovii* in Threnos Jer. Comm.; Hamb. 1707, 4to.

J. Theoph. Lessing; Observatt. in Tristia Jer.; Lips. 1770.

Threni Jer. philol. et. crit. illustrati a *J. H. Pareau;* Lug. Bat. 1790.

Curæ exeg. et crit. in Thren. Jer., Auctore *Jo. Fr. Schleusner*, in *Eichhorn's* Rep. vol. xii.

Beit. z. Erkl. des sogen. hohen Liedes, Koheleths und der Klaglieder, von *Gaab;* Tüb. 1795.

Diss. ad Thren. Jer. Auct. *J. Otto*, præs. *Schnurrer;* Tüb. 1795, 4to.

Rosenmüller, Schol.

Translated by *Börmel*, m. e. Vorr. v. *Herder*, 1781; *Horrer*, 1784; *Joel Löwe* and *Aaron Wolfssohn*, 1790; *M. Hartmann*, in *Justi's* Blumen althebr. Dichtk.; (*Welcker*,) in griech. Versmaas. 1810; *Riegler*, 1814; *Goldwitzer* mit Vergl. der LXX. u. Vulg. u. krit. Anmerkk. 1828; *Wiedenfeld*, Elberf 1830; *Ewald*, l. c. vol. i.

[Translated into English by *Broughton* and *Blayney*.]

celebrated in both, and at his time it is scarcely probable there were other lamentations extant.[a]

§ 273.

TITLE AND CONTENTS OF THE BOOK.

Under the title אֵיכָה, which is the characteristic word for beginning a complaint — in 2 Sam. i. 19, 27 — and also with the title קִינוֹת, (or θρῆνοι among the Greeks,) we have five songs relating to the conquest and destruction of the city of Jerusalem, and the temple, (i. ii. iv. v.,) and to the unfortunate lot of the poet himself. (iii.) The historical relation of the whole cannot be doubted; but yet there seems to be a gradual ascent in describing the condition of the city.[b]

---

[a] See § 273.

[b] See *Josephus*, x. 5, 1; *Jerome*, Com. in Zech. xii. 11; *J. D. Michaelis*, in his Uebers.; note on *Lowth*, Sac. Poet. Heb. xxii. (p. 565, *Rosenmüller's* ed.,) though he afterwards changed his opinion in N. Or. Bib. vol. i. p. 106; and *Dathe*, Proph. Maj. ed. 1, (different in ed. 2.) See, on the other side, *Eichhorn*, § 652. —*Horrer* and *Jahn* (p. 572) think the final chapter refers to the events related in 2 Kings xxiv. 8, sqq. *Bertholdt* (p. 2314—2322) takes the opposite view; but, even if this is not correct, *Eichhorn's* explanation is forced. He says, "The first lamentation bewails chiefly the deathlike stillness about Jerusalem; and the second, the destruction of the city and temple." Perhaps chap. i. is written in the interval between 2 Kings xxv. 4 and 8. This is the opinion of *Riegler*, (Uebers, p. 4;) but *Bertholdt* (p. 2318) dissents from it. *Pareau* refers chap. i. to Jer. xxxvii. 5, sqq.; chap. iii. to Jer. xxxviii. 2, sqq.; chap. iv. to Jer. xxxix. 1, sqq., and 2 Kings xxv. 1, sqq.; chap. ii. to the destruction of the city and temple. Chap. v. appears to be the latest, and is referred to the time after it. *Ewald* (p. 145, sq.) says the situation is the same, only the time is different. "In chap. i. and ii. we find sorrow without consolation; in chap. iii., consolation for the poet himself; in chap. iv., the lamentation is renewed with greater violence; but soon the whole people, as if urged by their own spontaneous impulse, fall to weeping and hoping, (17 —21;) (?) and in chap. v., nothing remains but the simple prayer of the whole community for deliverance — a prayer, which, though full of anguish, is yet composed and hopeful."

§ 274.

THE AUTHOR.

An old tradition mentions Jeremiah as the author. It is contained in the beginning of the first chapter of the Septuagint version—"And it came to pass after that Israel was taken captive, and Jerusalem was laid waste, that Jeremiah sat weeping, and lamented this lamentation over Jerusalem, and said"[a] . . . . . .

The contents, spirit, tone, and language, of the book agree with this tradition.[b] The elegiac humor of the sufferer has here expressed itself with a certain completeness.[c]

---

[a] Compare *Josephus*, Ant. x. 5, 1.

[b] Comp. i. 8, sqq., with Jer. iv. 30, xiii. 21, 22, 26; i. 20, and iv. 13, sqq., with Jer. xiv. 7, 18; ii. 14, with Jer. xiv. 13; i. 16, and ii. 11, iii. 48, 49, with Jer. viii. 21, sqq., ix. 16, sqq., x. 19, sqq., xiii. 17, xiv. 17; iii. 52, with Jer. xv. 26, 27; iii. with Jer. xv. 10, sqq., 15, sqq., xvii. 5, sqq., 14, sqq., xx. 7, sqq., 14, sqq.

בְּתוּלַת בַּת עַמִּי; i. 15, ii. 13. (Compare Jer. xiv. 17, xlvi. 11.) מָגוֹר; ii. 22. (Compare Jer. iv. 25, x. 3, 10.) זוֹלֵלָ; i. 11. (Compare Jer. xv. 19.) מַחֲמוּדֵּים, for מַחֲמַדִּים; i. 11. נִידָה, for נִדָּה; i. 8. לוֹא, for לֹא; אֲבַל לְ; iv. 5. גֹּאַל; iv. 14. מְדִינָה; i. 1. תָּפֵל; ii. 14. Chaldaisms: שׁוֹמֵמִין; i. 4. יִשְׁנֶא, for יִשְׁנֶה; iv. 1. מַטָּרָא; iii. 12. הֵעִיב; ii. 1. שָׂרַג; i. 14. Peculiarities: שֹׁמֵמִם, applied to men; i. 13, 16, iii. 11, iv. 5. שׁ prefixed; ii. 15, iv. 9.

[c] [Each chapter, or elegy, is divided into twenty-two periods, to correspond to the letters in the Hebrew alphabet. The first four chapters are in the form of acrostics. In the first three chapters, each verse contains three lines, and the initial letters are, with a slight variation, in the order of the letters in the alphabet. In the fourth chapter, each verse consists of four lines. In the third, the alphabet is repeated three times.]

CHAPTER III.

THE SONG OF SOLOMON.[a]

§ 275.

THE KIND OF COMPOSITION TO WHICH THE BOOK BELONGS.

In the Song of Songs, we possess the only relic of the amatory poetry of the Hebrews. This, from its

---

[a] *J. H. Michaelis* Annotatt. uberr. in Hagiogr. vol. ii.

See the other numerous authors in *Rosenmüller*, Schol. p. 283, sqq.

Eclogæ Regis Salom. interpr. *Jo. Th. Lessing;* 1777.

Döderlein, Auctar. ad Hug. Grot. adnotatt.; 1779, 4to.

Materialien z. e. n. Erklär. d. h. Liedes vom Verf. der Beobacht. üb. d. Orient, (*Harmar.*) Aus d. Engl. 1778, 1779, 2 Thle, 4to.

G. A. Ruperti Symbolæ ad interpret. S. Cod. vol. i. Fasc. 1, 2; Gott. 1792.

Nic. Schyth, Cant. Cantic. recens versum, comment. exeget. atq. crit. illustratum; Havn. 1797.

Gaab, Beiträge z. Erklär. d. sogen. h. L. u. d.; Klagl. 1795.

Salom. Regis et Sap. quæ supersunt ejusque esse perhibentur omnia ex Hebr. Lat. vertit Notasque adj. *Jos. Fr. Schelling;* 1806.

Kistemaker, Cant. Canticorum illustratum ex Hierographia Orientalium; 1818.

J. Chr. C. Döpke, Philol. krit. Comm. z. h. L. Sal. 1829.

Ueberss. u. Erkll. von (*J. F. Jacobi*) d. . . . . . gerett. h. L. 1771; *Hezel*, 1777; *Herder*, 1778; *J. F. Kleuker*, 1780; *J. F. Schlez*, 1782; *Döderlein*, (m. d. Pred.) 1784; *Hufnagel*, 1784; *Velthusen*, 1786; (comp. his Amethyst, 1786; Cantilena Cantilenarum in Sal. 1786;) (*Ammon*,) Sal. verschm. Liebe, 1790; *Beyer*, 1792; *Briegleb*, 1798; *Justi*, Blumen alt-hebr. Dichtk. 1807; *Umbreit*, 1820, 2 A. 1828; *G. H. A. Ewald*, 1826.

[See *Robinson's* ed. of *Calmet*, and *Michaelis* in *Lowth*, p. 609.

It has been translated into English by Bishop *Percy*, 1764, 12mo.; *Hodgson*, 1785, 4to.; *Thos. Williams*, 1801, 8vo.; *J. M. Good*, 1803, 8vo.; *Fry*, 1811, 8vo. The following authors have written commentaries or explanations upon it: *Ainsworth*, Annotation on Pent., Ps., and Cant.; 1627, fol. *Gill*, 1728, fol., (often republished.) *Harmer*, Outlines of a Com. on Sol. Song, 1768, 8vo. *Durell*, 1772. An anonymous Scotch author, 1775. (See in Critical Review, vol. xv. for 1795.) *Thos. James*, D. D., Oxford, 1607. Other writers in Eng-

nature, must fluctuate between lyric and epic poetry, and therefore it often becomes descriptive and pictorial, (or idyllic,) and willingly makes use of the form of dialogue. This kind of poetry must have existed in the form of song; but there are only slight indications thereof—ii. 12, "the time of song has come," and Lam. v. 14, "The young men have ceased from their music." The relation of the amatory idyl to the Psalms cannot be determined more accurately. The rhythm is more periodic than that of the Psalms.[a]

§ 276.

TITLE AND CONTENTS.

The title (שִׁיר הַשִּׁירִים) signifies the *most beautiful song*. This is the only explanation which is conformable to the usage of the language, and the rules of grammar.[b] Under this title are included several songs, and fragments of songs, which treat of love. For the most part, the subject is rural and pastoral love, which is treated of with the glowing passion of the East, and without the degen-

---

lish, on this book, are, *Durham*, Bishops *Hall* and *Patrick*, Messrs. *Dove*, *Trapp*, *Jackson*, *Collings*. Dr. *Owen* "has given one of the best spiritual explications of the most interesting passages," in his "Communion with Father, Son, &c." See also *Croxall*, Fair Circassian; Lond. 1720. *Davidson*, Brief Outline, &c.; 1817, 8vo. See the translation and explanation of Mr. *Taylor*, in *Calmet's* Dictionary, and the remarks of Dr. *Robinson*, its American editor, article *Canticles*.]

[a] See a comparison of the Canticles and Theocritus's Idyls, by *Stäudlin*, in *Paulus*, Mem. vol. ii. p. 161, and an explanation of these songs, p. 171, sqq.

[b] See other significations in *Gesenius*, Lexicon, and *Bertholdt*, p. 2580. *Ewald* (Hohesleid, p. 25, and Poet. Buch. A. T. vol. i. p. 184) connects אשר לשלמה more intimately with the inscription, and translates it, *Das schönste Lied, welches von Salomo ist*; i. e. which Solomon composed.

erate bashfulness of modern times, but still in conformity with the moral spirit of the Hebrews.[a]

> "But *one* is my Dove, my chaste one." (vi. 9.)
> "Apply me, like a seal, to thine heart,
> Like a seal to thine arm;
> For love is strong as death;
> Fixed as the grave is its zeal;
> Great waters cannot quench love,
> And streams cannot wash it away.
> Let a man offer all the wealth of his house for love,
> It will be despised." (viii. 6, 7.)

It has been explained as an allegory by the writer of the Targum, Jarchi, Aben Ezra, Origen, Epiphanius, Theodoret, and many others, among the ancients.[b] The latest attempts of this kind are by Rosenmüller, Hug, and Kaiser.[c] But this method of explaining it derives no probable support from the exegesis of the book; and, besides, it is by no means necessary for the honor of the Bible.[d]

---

[a] This is *Herder's* opinion, which has been followed by most of the moderns, who only differ in their modifications of this view. *Carpzov*, p. 348.

[b] See the different exegetical hypotheses in *Kleuker*, l. c. 41, and a criticism of this kind of explanation in *Döpke*, p. 41, *Umbreit*, p. 6, and *Hassler*, Tub. Zeitschrift, vol. iii. p. 172.

[c] *Rosenmüller*, in *Keil*, and *Tzschirner*, Anal. vol. i. p. 138, sqq., though differently in his Prolegg. p. 271, sqq. *Hug*, Das Hoheslied, &c.; 1813, 4to. Schutzschrift, &c.; 1815, 4to. *Kaiser*, Das Hoheslied, ein Collectiv-Gesang, &c.; 1825.

A similar mystical explanation has been made of some of the amatory poetry of the Orientals. See *Herbelot*, Bibl. Orient., art. *Jussuf*, and *William Jones*, On the Mystical Poetry of the Persians and Hindoos, in Asiatic Researches, vol. iii. p. 165, sqq. [in his Works, vol. iv. p. 227, sqq. 8vo.]

[d] *Herder*, l. c. p. 120, sqq. *Ewald*, Hoheslied, p. 355.

Some of the Jews had their doubts upon this book. R. *Nathan* says, "Formerly they determined that the Proverbs, Canticles, and Ecclesiastes, were apocryphal books, written after the manner of parables, and therefore were not to be reckoned with the Hagiographa. For this reason, they concealed them until the time of the men of the Great Synagogue, who at last explained them." Capitula, c. i. *Jerome*, in his Preface to Ezekiel, says

Equally improbable is the opinion that the book is a whole, and is founded upon a true history.[a]

There is a connection between the following passages: i. 2—8, the maiden's anxiety for her lover; i. 9—ii. 7, the lover's conversation when they come together; ii. 8—17, the lover's visit to the maiden, in the vineyard; iii. 1—5, the maiden seeking her lover by night, and finding him; iv. 1—v. 1, the dialogue between the young man, excited with love, and the complying maiden; v. 2—vi. 3, the maiden seeking her lover by night, and praising him; vi. 4—9, the faithful lover's praises of his beloved; vii. 2—viii. 4, the conversation of the pair, now intoxicated with love, and united therein; (compare i. 9—ii. 7, with this;) viii. 5—7, the love of the faithful wedded pair.

If these passages are treated rigorously, it cannot be shown that they constitute one whole, for the scene and the costume change somewhat; thus, in i. 5, ii. 7,

---

no one who has not completed his thirtieth year, is permitted to read the beginning of Genesis, or Canticles, or the beginning and end of Ezekiel, so that he may come to perfect knowledge and to the mystical sense of these books, when his mind is in its greatest vigor. See *Origen*, Prol. ad Cant. *Bartolocci*, Bib. Rab. vol. iv. p. 373.

[a] This is the theory of *Jacobi*, *Velthusen*, *Ammon*, and others. *Umbreit* maintains there is a certain unity in the book, and succeeds without forcing the matter much, though not without arbitrary interpretation. In particular, he gives a false explanation of the slumber song. (ii. 7, iii. 5, and viii. 4.) *Ewald* maintains it is a drama, and is still more guilty of arbitrary treatment, especially in separating the dialogue, (i. 9—ii. 6, vi. 2—4, vii. 2—viii. 4,) and thereby separating the terms which clearly are connected with one another—"*My Beloved*," (רַעְיָתִי,) and "*My Love*," (דּוֹדִי,) which latter term is applied to the absent lover. (i. 15, 16.)

Both *Ewald* and *Umbreit* make the heroine a country maiden, shut up in Solomon's harem. But this opinion is favored only by i. 4—6, and vi. 8. But the intervening passages, (i. 7, sqq.,) where the scene presents us flocks and pastures, &c., as well as those which follow, (vii. 12, sqq.,) lead us away from the court. See *A. T. Hartmann*, On the Character and Explanation of the Song of Songs, in *Winer's* Zeitschrift, vol. iii. p. 412.

iii. 1, v. 1, sqq., the scene is in *Jerusalem;* but it is in the *country* in i. 7, sq., ii. 8, sqq., vii. 12, sqq., and viii. 13, 14. But yet all seems to relate to one and the same pair of lovers, and to bear the impress of one single author.

There are yet other passages which are insulated, abrupt, and perhaps stand in a false connection: iii. 6—11, the bridal song of Solomon, if verse 6 could otherwise belong to it; viii. 8—10, innocence protecting itself; viii. 11, 12, the lover's self-complacency; (?) viii. 13, 14, the lover alarmed.

The passage, vi. 10—vii. 1, is extremely obscure: —

> "Who is this that shines forth like the dawn,
> Beautiful as the moon,
> Pure as the sun,
> And terrible as an army?
> "I went down to the nut-garden
> To see the green things of the valley,
> To see if the vine sprouted,
> And the pomegranates bloomed.
> I did not know, — my soul made me a chariot of my noble people.
> Return, return, Shulamith,
> Return, return, that we may look upon thee.
> What shall you see in the Shulamith,
> [Who is] Like the dancing of angel-choirs?"

Perhaps the fragments, ii. 15, iii. 6, and viii. 5, are inserted in the wrong place. Chap. iii. 6, vi. 10, and viii. 5, have a suspicious affinity with one another, as likewise have ii. 16, 17, iv. 5, 6, [?] vi. 2, 3.[a]

---

[a] *Herder, Kleuker, Döderlein, Döpke, Hufnagel, Paulus,* (*Eichhorn,* Rep. vol. vii. and xvii.) think the book consists of fragments. See *Umbreit,* Erinnerung an das Hoheslied.

§ 277.

AGE AND AUTHOR.

In respect to their language, these songs are to be classed with the latest productions of Hebrew literature, in particular with the book of Ecclesiastes.[a] For this reason, some, like Eichhorn, Bertholdt, and Rosenmüller, place their composition in a very late period. Hartmann places it the lowest.

But the whole circle of images, and historical relations, and the freshness of life it describes, belong to the age of Solomon; for example, i. 4, 5:—

"To the horses in Pharaoh's chariot
I compare thee, my friend." (verse 9.)
"While the king is at his table,
My nard gives its fragrance;
A bunch of myrrh is my friend." (verse 12.)
"Behold the bed of Solomon;
Sixty strong men around it,
Of Israel's strong;
All grasping the sword,
Ready for war," &c. (iii. 7, sqq., iv. 4, vi. 4, 8, 9,
viii. 11, 12.)

Bertholdt thinks the author transferred himself back to the age of Solomon. But this is certainly very improbable, for, as Herder says, "Nothing in the world

---

[a] פַּרְדֵּס (iv. 13) is *Persian*, (a *park*, παραδεισος.) Comp. Eccl. ii. 5, Neh. ii. 8. The following are *Aramæan:* ברוֹת, i. 17; קִפֵּץ, ii. 8; כֹּתֶל, ii. 9; סְתָו, ii. 11; טִנֵּף, v. 3; אַפִּרְיוֹן, (= φορεῖον αμφόρειον,) iii. 9; לְבַר, for לְךָ, ii. 13. The following belong to the *later Hebrew usage:* לְ, as *nota accusat.*, iii. 11; אֵרָכָה, v. 3, (Esth. viii. 6;) הִגִּיעַ, ii. 12, (Ezra vii. 12, Eccl. xii. 1;) שׁ, prefixed, i. 7, iii. 1, sqq.; שֶׁל, iii. 7, i. 6, sqq.; דָּוִיד, iv. 4. *Eichhorn*, § 646, sq. *Hartmann*, l. c. p. 420, sqq., from whose statements much is to be abated. *Köster*, p. 31. On the other hand, see *Döpke*, l. c. p 29, sqq.

demands so entire and intimate a presence as love...... You can do no greater injustice to expressions of love than to rob them of their individuality."

The passage, iii. 6—11, follows the course which Solomon's nuptial song must take. It cannot be shown — as it has been contended — that Thirza (vi. 4) was not a chief town in Solomon's time. It is mentioned in Josh. xii. 24, and the mention of this city proves an earlier age than the Persian.

Herder and Döpke rely on the freshness of the composition, as an argument for its early date. Religious lyrics could not flourish after the exile, and the amatory idyl could scarcely thrive. But Hartmann takes the other side.[a]

Perhaps the riddle may be solved by maintaining that these songs were preserved orally, — in the mouth of the people, — and in some degree transformed. This also will explain the fragmentary compilation of them. A similar opinion has been maintained by Scyth, Ewald, and others, who seek the cause of the peculiarity of the language in the idiom of the province where the songs were composed.

The opinion that Solomon was the author, is but poorly supported by the inscriptions of the book, and is in itself improbable. Such passages as i. 4, 5, 12, iii. 6—11, vii. 6, viii. 11, 12, show that Solomon is not the author. Yet the opinion that he was the author, and the age of the songs, seem to have led to their reception into the canon, which was probably excused by the allegorical interpretation put upon them.

---

[a] *Köster* (p. 32) thinks the book is of late origin, on account of its allegorical character, its far-fetched images, and its learned allusions to other books of the Old Testament, some of them quite recent; e. g. i. 3, 4, iii. 8, iv. 11, 14, vii. 5, comp. Ps. xlv. 15, 4, 9, 8; vi. 12, comp. Ps. cx. 2; viii. 11, comp. Isa. v 1; ii. 14, comp. Obad. 3; vii. 10, comp. Prov. xxiii. 31.

CHAPTER IV.

THE PROVERBS OF SOLOMON.[a]

§ 278.

CONTENTS OF THE BOOK.

HERE, not only short, disconnected proverbs and enigmas, but likewise longer, connected sententious

---

[a] *Phil. Melanchthonis* Explicatio Provv.; 1555. Opp. t. ii.

Jo. Merceri Comm. in Provv. Salom., with his Comment. on Job.

Provv. Salom. c. Cura enucleata a *Mart. Geiero;* Lips. 1669; 1725, 4to.

Chr. B. Michaelis, Annotatt. in Provv. in *J. H. Michaelis* Uberr. annotatt. in Hagiogr.

Proverbia Salom.: Versionem integram ad Hebræum Fontem expressit atque Comment. adjecit *Alb. Schultens;* Lug. Bat. 1748, 4to.; in compend. redegit et Observatt. crit. auxit *G. J. L. Vogel,* cum Auctario per *G. A. Teller;* Hal. 1769.

J. F. Hirts, Vollst. Erklär. der Sprüche Salomos; Jen. 1768, 4to.

Chr. Fr. Schnurrer, Observatt. ad quædam Loca Prov. Salom.; Tub. 1776, 4to. Dissertt. phil. crit. vol. i.

J. J. Reiske, Conjecturæ in Jobum et Provv. Salom.; Lips. 1779.

Zur Exegetik u. Kritik des A. T. von *A. J. Arnoldi;* Frkf. u. Lpz. 1781.

J. G. Jäger, Observatt. in Provv. Salom. Versionem Alex.; Lips. 1788, 8vo.

Hensler, Erläuterungen des 1 B. Sam. u. der Salom. Denkspr.; Hamb. 1796.

F. W. C. Umbreit, Philol. krit. u. philosoph. Comm. ü. d. Sprüche Sal., nebst e. neuen Uebers. u. e. Einleit. in die morgenl. Weisheit überh. u. in d. hebr. salomonische insbesondere; Heidelb. 1826.

Rosenmüller, Schol.

Paraphrase by *G. J. L. Vogel,* 1767; *Ch. A. Bode,* 1791.

Translated by *J. D. Michaelis,* (n. d. Pred. m. Anmerkk. f. Ungel.) 1778, 4to.; *Döderlein,* 3 A. 1786; *Struensee,* 1783; *Kleuker,* 1786; *R. Ch. Reinhard,* 1790; *W. C. Ziegler,* m. Einl. u. Anm. 1791; *Muntinghe,* n. Anmerkk. aus d. Holländ. von *Scholl,* 2 Bde, 1800, 1802; *J. G. Dahler,* n. d. Abweichungen d. alexandr. Uebers., 1810; *C. P. W. Gramberg,* Systemat. geordnet. m. Anm. u. Parall., 1828; *E. G. A. Böckel,* 1829; *Ewald,* l. c. vol. iv.

[*Hunt,* Observations on the Book of Proverbs; Oxford, 1775, 4to. *Hodg-*

discourses, are collected together. These are the manifold productions of Hebrew wisdom, expressing itself in the formation of proverbs. This wisdom rests chiefly on a practical shrewdness, — the result of experience, — and on the religious doctrine of retribution, conceived of in a very positive form. The two mutually support one another. Yet it is not wanting in ideas of a pure, living morality and religion. The style is various, often ingenious, witty, sportive, and enigmatical; but, for the most part, it is simply proverbial, abounding in antitheses, comparisons, and images.

§ 279.

COMPOSITION OF THE BOOK.

After the inscription, (i. 1,) "Proverbs of Solomon, son of David, king of Israel," and the preface, (i. 2—6,) there follows, —

I. 1. Chap. i. 7—ix. 18, — a connected discourse, exhorting men to chastity and wisdom, and extolling the excellency of the latter.

2. Under the title *Proverbs of Solomon*,[a] are single proverbs, (chap. x. 1—xxii. 16.) A better connection, and an admonitory tone, — like that in the beginning of the book, — prevail in the next passage, which is not separated from this by any inscription, (xxii. 17—xxiv. 22.) After this, other single proverbs follow, with the inscription, *These also from the wise.*[b]

II. 1. A new inscription, (xxv. 1,) "These also

are proverbs of Solomon, which the men of Hezekiah, king of Judah, collected."[a] This connects the collection of Proverbs (xxv. 2—xxix. 27) together, and separates it from the preceding collection.

2. The following are supplements to the book: —

(1.) Chap. xxx., containing several proverbs and enigmas, with the inscription, "The words of Agur the son of Jakeh, the prophecy: The saying of the man to Ithiel, to Ithiel and Ucal."[b]

(2.) Chap. xxxi. 1—9, containing precepts for kings, with the inscription, "Words spoken to Lemuel the king, a proverb which his mother taught him."[c]

(3.) Chap. xxxi. 10—31, containing the praise of a virtuous woman.

§ 280.

ORIGIN OF THIS COLLECTION.

The inscription and preface, (i. 1—6,) it is certain, do not relate merely to the first section, (i. 7—ix.,) but to a collection of proverbs. Chap. xxii. 17—xxiv. 22, is, indeed, like i. 7—ix. in its design and contents, but yet is not from the same author.[d] Chap. xxiv. 23—xxv. 1, appears to be a supplementary addition. There-

---

[a] גַּם־אֵלֶּה מִשְׁלֵי, שְׁלֹמֹה אֲשֶׁר הֶעְתִּיקוּ אַנְשֵׁי חִזְקִיָּה מֶלֶךְ יְהוּדָה.

[b] דִּבְרֵי אָגוּר, בִּן־יָקֶה הַמַּשָּׂא נְאֻם הַגֶּבֶר לְאִיתִיאֵל לְאִיתִיאֵל וְאֻכָל.

[c] דִּבְרֵי לְמוּאֵל מֶלֶךְ מַשָּׂא אֲשֶׁר יִסְּרַתּוּ אִמּוֹ.

[d] The peculiarities of the first section (i. 9, iii. 3, 22, iv. 9, vi. 21, vii. 3) do not reappear, and even where a similar thought occurs, (xxiii. 27, 28,) the form of speech is different. (ii. 16, sqq., v. 3, sqq., et al.) Other peculiarities appear, as (xxii. 19, xxiii. 15) the emphatic pronouns, (xxii. 18, xxiii. 8, et al.,) נְעָרִם, and many others. The tone of admonition is not preserved long at a time. *Ewald*, p. 42.

fore we must consider i.—xxii. 16, as an independent whole, forming the first collection, to which xxii. 17—xxiv. 22, was afterwards added by way of supplement.[a]

It is difficult to determine whether the admonition (i. 7—ix.) was composed by the collector of this book, or was of earlier date, and previously in circulation.[b]

The later collection, (xxv.—xxix.,)[c] which originated in Hezekiah's time, was either discovered by the same author who compiled i.—xxii. 16, and with the supplements, xxii. 17—xxiv. 22, added it to that collection, or, which is more probable, it was added at a later period.

The supplements, (xxx. xxxi.,) which in different

---

[a] Most critics are of this opinion. (See *Bertholdt*, p. 2181, sqq.) *Ziegler* (Uebers. p. 273, sq.) finds marks of a later composition in the first passages, and the use of earlier forms of speech in the second. (Comp. xxiv. 24, with xi. 26, and xvii. 15; xxiv. 29, with xx. 23; xxiv. 33, sq., with vi. 10, 11.) *Ewald* (p. 41) thinks the inscription to the supplement (xxiv. 23) came from the same author as that in xxv. 1, who likewise added xxii. 17—xxiv. 22. But if this were the case, xxii. 17, would also have an inscription. To me, xxii. 17—xxiv. 22, seems to be a later epilogue, written in imitation of i.—ix. Chap. xxiv. 23, sqq., may have been added at the same time with xxv. 1, sq.

[b] *Ewald* (p. 36, sqq.) favors the first opinion, and regards this passage as an introduction to the whole collection. But, excepting i. 1—6, no reference is made to the whole collection, as, perhaps, it is done in xxii. 17. The author continually admonishes us to strive after wisdom, to observe and follow *his* doctrine, and that of father and mother. In particular, he dwells on the subject of chastity. *Ewald* thinks the language is more modern, and finds some imitations. (מַרְפֵּא, iv. 22, vi. 15, and "tree of life," iii. 18. ?) He finds an imitation of Job. (iii. 13, sq. viii. Job xxviii.) He maintains that such connected discourses are more characteristic of a later time than the short maxims of the older collection.

[c] For the different character of the language in the second part, see *Ziegler*, p. 25, sq. *Bertholdt*, p. 2187. *Ewald*, p. 31, sqq. The latter adduces the following proofs: 1. *Different style:* the interrogative or conditional preterit; xxv. 12, 16, xxix. 20. Fact and figure connected merely by *and;* xxv. 3, 20, 25, xxvi. 3, 7, 9, 10, 21. Cases of *asyndeton;* xxv. 11—14, 18, 19, 26, 28, xxvi. 23. (But comp. xi. 22, xxi. 1.) 2. We do not find the simple, rigorous parallelism, the condensed fulness and strength of expression, but the thought is extended to two or more verses; xv. 4—10. Longer proverbs; xxvi. 23—28, (?) xxvii. 23—27. (But compare x. 4, 5, 16,

ways transgress the limits of the ancient proverbs, were probably added still later.[a]

§ 281.

AGE AND AUTHOR.

It is highly probable in itself that many proverbs have been ascribed to Solomon — as well as many lyric poems to David — which he never wrote.

These proverbs, judging from their number and variety, seem rather the productions of a whole nation than of a single man. Many of them relate to private and rustic life; with one of which Solomon was not sufficiently acquainted, and in the other he could not participate.[b]

17, 31, 32, xv. 16, 17, xxi. 25, 26.) 3. Signs of a party-colored, complicated, and perilous state of society, where one portion was hostile to another; xxviii. 2, 3, 15—22, 28, xxix. 2, 16, (only xi. 10, is like this; but see xi. 11, 14, xvi. 10—23,) xxv. 3—5, xxix. 12. — Some other peculiarities are not characteristic — the maxims on modesty in the presence of great men, (xxv. 6, sq.;) on being troublesome or importunate in visits and desire of success, (xxv. 16, 17, xxvii. 14;) on love of glory, (xxv. 10, xxvii. 1, 2;) on quarrelsomeness, (xxv. 8—10,) &c. To these I will add, the obvious effort to be witty in comparisons, (xxv. 11, sqq., 20, xxvi. 2, 8, 17, 23, et al.;) and the love of paradox, (xxvi. 4, 5.) — To this may be added the repetition of many proverbs already given before, (xxv. 24, comp. xxi. 9; xxvi. 15, comp. xix. 24; xxvi. 22, comp. xviii. 8; xxvii. 12, comp. xxii. 3; xxvii. 13, comp. xx. 16,) from which we may conclude, not only that these were collected later, but that they originated later.

[a] מַשָּׂא, in the inscription of xxx. and xxxi., means, elsewhere, a *prophetic oracle*; and here the tone sometimes rises to lyrical elevation. (xxx. 2, sq., xxxi. 2, sqq.) There are "spiteful descriptions" in xxx. 11, sqq., 18, 19, 21, sqq., as *Ewald* says. Chap. xxxi. 10, sqq., is simple in sense, though artificial in form. In xxxi. 2, we find the word בַּר, [but see Ps. ii. 12,] and מְלָכִין in verse 3.

[b] See, in particular, xii. 10, 11, xiii. 23, xiv. 4, xxiv. 27, 30—34, xxvii. 23, sqq.; xiii. 7, 11, xiv. 1, xv. 15—17, xvi. 8, 26, xvii. 1, 2, xviii. 9, 22, xix. 14, 15, xx. 13, 14, xxi. 9, 17, xxiii. 1, sqq., 20, sqq., 29, 30, xxv. 17, xxi. 1, xxii.

Chap. i.—ix., with their didactic and admonitory tone, and their strict injunction of chastity, agree rather with the character of a teacher of youth, a prophet, or priest, than a king like Solomon.[a]

We know for a certainty that he did not write xxv.—xxix.; but, three centuries after him, many proverbs might easily be taken for Solomon's which did not really belong to him.

It may at least be doubted that the first collection was made by Solomon; and there is nothing to prove it.[b]

29, xxv. 6, 7, xxviii. 15, 16. See *Bertholdt*, p. 2180, 2186. [It is probable, from the well-known passage, 1 Kings v. 12, that Solomon wrote proverbs; succeeding ages very naturally ascribed to him most of the proverbs which came into general circulation. In the same manner, the Greeks ascribed many of their gnomic sentences to Pythagoras, as the Arabians referred theirs to Locman, Abu-Obeid Mophaddel, and Meidani, and as the northern nations referred their wise sayings to Odin, or as the Oriental fables are ascribed to Pilpay. Part of these sayings may, doubtless, belong to Solomon; yet it is not possible for the critic to lay his finger on any one with the absolute certainty that it is his. Negative criticism is here more safe than positive affirmation, for many passages bear internal marks which show conclusively they could not have proceeded from him.]

[a] *Bertholdt*, p. 2176. Chap. v. 10, vi. 26—31, seem to have proceeded from a private man.

[b] [*Jahn* (p. 731) has a different hypothesis. He thinks, since Solomon uttered 3000 proverbs, and this book has been commonly ascribed to him, that we have no adequate reason for denying that he was the author. He supposes that the chancellor (הַמַּזְכִּיר) wrote in the annals all the remarkable sayings of the king, with the occasion which gave birth to them, and at Solomon's command collected them into a book, to which the king himself wrote the introduction. (i.—ix.) Various readers made extracts from this book, to suit their own taste; the whole was copied more rarely. Thus it happened that much, especially from the end of the book, was lost. Afterwards attempts were made to restore it, and the later additions were made. This explains the reiteration of some proverbs.]

Ewald (p. 30) thinks there is a Salomonic book of proverbs at the basis, which was much abridged, in the two first centuries after its publication, (?) transformed, and gradually enlarged with new additions. In i.—v. he thinks the greater part is old and Salomonic; but additions have been made in the

But it is certain they come from the most flourishing period of Hebrew literature. A large share in the composition of the Proverbs may therefore be reasonably allotted to Solomon, especially in the first part. (i.—xxii. 16.)

The authors of the first two of the latter appendices are mentioned—Agur, and the mother of King Lemuel; but their age is unknown to us.[a]

CHAPTER V.

ECCLESIASTES, OR THE PREACHER.[b]

§ 282.

STYLE AND SPIRIT OF THE BOOK.

In all respects, this book belongs to the gnomological and didactic compositions of the Hebrews. It not only contains, in some parts, actual proverbs, while a connected and prosaic style prevails from beginning to end, but

---

maxims relative to correcting a son, and the proverb about a fair woman without discretion, (xi. 22, sq.,) and some others, have been added.

[a] See the opinions about *Agur* and King *Lemuel*, in *Gesenius's* Lexicon, *Bertholdt*, p. 2193, sq., and *Rosenmüller*, l. c. [*Michaelis* "explains away" Agur, and changes the pointing in xxx. 1, and reads דִּבְרֵי אֱגוֹר בְּנִי קַח הַמַּשָּׂא, i. e. *collect my words, my son; receive the proverb.*]

[b] *Hieronym.* Comm. in Ecclesiast., Opp. iii. *Vallars.*
Merceri Comm. in Eccles., in his Comm. on Job.
Mart. Geieri Comm. in Koheleth; Lips. 1668.
J. J. Rambach, Annotatt. in Eccles. in *J. H. Michaelis*, Uberr. annotatt. in Hagiographa.
Ecclesiast. philol. et crit. illustratus a *Van der Palm*; Lug. Bat. 1784.
Der Pred. Sal. mit e. Erkl. nach dem Wortverstande, vom Verf. des

in its entire character and spirit it seems to be the result of the same practical wisdom of the Hebrews, seen in another point of view. The doctrine of retribution on earth, elevated by no hope of a future state, which constitutes the religious principle of the book, had to contend with powerful doubts, which the sad experience of life suggested, and which show themselves, here and there, perhaps in Proverbs, (xxiv. 19,) but more clearly in the Psalms, (xxxvii. and lxxiii.,) as the times became more disastrous and hopeless. As Faith and Inspiration became more cool, so these doubts became more powerful, and at last took the form of a practical system, inclined to skepticism, fatalism, and Epicureanism. To this the author of the book professes to adhere.[a]

Bergst thinks he finds a foreign influence in the book.[b]

Phädon. Aus dem Hebr. übers. vom Uebers. der Mischnah (*Rabe*); Ansb. 1771, 4to.

G. Zirkel, Unterss. üb. d. Pred. n. krit. u. phil. Bemerkk.; Würzb. 1792. His Uebers; ibid.

G. Ph. Chr. Kaiser, Koheleth das Collectivum der davidischen Könige zu Jerusalem; Erl. 1823, 8vo. *Knobel*, Com. üb. Kohel; 1836. *Ewald*, l. c.

Ueberss. und Erkll. von *Kleuker*, 1777; *Struensee*, 1780; *Döderlein*, 2 A. 1791; *G. L. Spohn*, 1785; *Friedländer*, 1788; *Ch. A. Bode*, 1788; *J. E. Chr. Schmidt*, 1794; *Nachtigall*, 1798; *B. H. Bergst*, 1799; *Umbreit*, 1818; *Köster*, (n. Hiob,) 1831.

[*Des Vœux*, A Philosophical and Critical Essay on Ecclesiastes, &c.; Lond. 1762, 4to. *Greenaway*, Ecclesiastes translated, with a Paraphrase and Notes; 1781, 8vo. *Hodgson*, A New Translation; 1791, 4to. An Exposition of the Book of Eccl. by Bishop *Reynolds;* 1811, 8vo. *Wardlaw's* Lectures on Eccl.; 1821, 2 vols. 8vo. *Holden*, Attempt to illustrate Eccl.; 1822, 8vo. The Philosophy of Ecclesiastes, by Dr. *I. Nordheimer*, in the Biblical Repository for 1838, vol. xii. p. 197, sqq.]

[a] See *De Wette*, Characteristik der Hebraismus, in *Daub* und *Creutzer*, Studien, vol. iii. pt. ii. p. 287, sqq.

[b] In *Eichhorn*, Allg. Bib. vol. x. p. 963, sqq. [He discovers a Grecian influence in the book, and calls its author an "Oriental sophist." *Luther*, in his Table-Talk, says the author of Ecclesiastes rides without boots or spurs, and only in his stockings.]

Here the prosaic style is as natural as in the later prophets; but Köster thinks he has discovered a regular rhythmical strophe in it.

§ 283.

TITLE AND CONTENTS.

The meaning of the word קֹהֶלֶת, the Hebrew title of the book, has long been contested; but the most satisfactory explanation of it is still ἐκκλησιαστής, *concionator*, that is, *speaker in the assembly*, (קָהָל.) This agrees with xii. 9.[a]

At any rate, if the text is correct, the word is a title of King Solomon.[b] Indeed, it is probable that the name

---

[a] [The word, though *masculine* in sense, has the *feminine* form; but *Jahn* (p. 828) shows that in Arabic many appellatives were used with a ة at the end, which corresponds with the Hebrew ת, and were then used indifferently in a masculine or feminine sense. Even in the Hebrew, names of men sometimes occur in a feminine form; e. g. סֹפֶרֶת, Ezra ii. 55, and פֹּכֶרֶת, verse 57. Some suppose the word means *Collector of sentences*, or proverbs; others, *Old man*, *Life-weary*, *Penitent*, a man *gathered* to his fathers, as if it were מְקֹהֶלֶת.] Comp. פֶּחָה בִּנַת, adduced by *Eichhorn*, *Gesenius*, and *Knobel*, to which *Ewald* and *Köster* add חָכְמָה. See *Bertholdt*, p. 2202. *Umbreit*, Coheleth Scepticus de summo Bono, p. 76; 1820. *Dindorf*, Quomodo nomen Koheleth Salomoni tribuatur; 1791, 4to. *Carpzov*, p. 200, sqq.

[b] [*Bertholdt* (p. 2208) conjectures that only the first two words of the inscription, viz. דִּבְרֵי קֹהֶלֶת, are genuine, and the rest of the inscription, as well as the word קֹהֶלֶת, every time it subsequently recurs, is interpolated. See *Gesenius*, sub voce.] *Umbreit*, p. 95, l. c.

[Dr. *Peters*, Crit. Diss. on Book of Job, (2d ed. Lond. 1757,) says, "The book is a sermon, preached by Solomon, but long after his death. I mean that it is composed out of Solomon's remains...... by those that were appointed [by law ?] to revise and publish them; amongst whom, Isaiah...... hath left us a little mark of his own hand-writing, at the end of the book, for those who are capable judges of it...... The sermon ends with a repetition of the text, 'Vanity of vanities,'" &c. (xii. 8.)]

Solomon itself is but a title or *surname*, as well as *Jedidiah*, in 2 Sam. xii. 25. Symbolical and mythical names were not uncommon among the Hebrews, as other passages can prove.[a]

[By a fiction, Solomon is introduced here as speaking. Augusti maintains that he appears in the character of a *man deceased*, or a ghost. But there is no clear intimation of this in the book, and the whole agrees very well together, if we suppose that the author wished to make him appear to speak at the end of his life, but did not adhere rigidly to this plan in his composition.]

The doctrine of the uselessness and nothingness of all things, and the reality of enjoyment alone, would make a deeper impression from the mouth of this wise king, who was surfeited with enjoyment and success, than from any other. Such is the doctrine of wisdom which this later teacher chiefly propounds, in the name of Solomon, and which, with much regularity, he has uttered from the beginning of the book. Since, in general, he lays down the results of his reflection in this book, and from them proceeds to the more thorough treatment of his principal theme, he introduces likewise many other observations and rules of life, which, however, are almost always tinged with skepticism. Though they sometimes contradict the doubts he has elsewhere expressed, (viii. 12, 13, xii. 14,) this only shows the want of clearness and certainty in his reflections. Thus, beneath the interrupted and broken unity of the book, there appears a deeper unity.[b]

---

[a] Isa. xxix. 1, Jer. xxv. 26, Ezek. xxiii. 4. Perhaps *Agur* (Prov. xxx. 1) is a name of Solomon.

[b] The following is a sketch of the contents. The main point of the book is this: *All is vain and fruitless.* The arguments in support of it are, —

1. The aimless course of things. (i. 4—11.)

Since the style of the book, as well as its contents, lies clearly obvious to the eye, it is wonderful that hitherto the interpreters have not agreed respecting it.[a]

---

2. The vanity of attempts to gain wisdom. (i. 12—18.)

3. The vanity of earthly enjoyment, and all attempts to reach it, in comparison with wisdom, although the gratification of desire has still the highest value. (ii.)

4. The transitoriness and change of all things, for which reason gratification of desire is again commended, as the most valuable. (iii. 1—15.)

5. The dominion of injustice and death among men, for which cause death is more to be desired than life, though life is still to be enjoyed cheerfully. (iii. 16—iv. 3.)

6. The vain troubles and strivings of men. (iv. 4—12.)

7. Vanity of royal honors. (iv. 13—16.) Separate maxims respecting idolatry and injustice. (iv. 17—v. 8.)

8. Vanity of the struggle after wealth and honor. Commendation of an enjoyment of life. (v. 9—vi. 9.) Subjection to destiny by the vanity of all things. (vi. 10—12.) Single maxims, mostly of a skeptical character. (vii. 1—viii. 13.)

9. Fruitless striving after wisdom. (vii. 23, 24.)

10. Death is unavoidable. (viii. 8.)

11. Success of the wicked. Adversity of the pious. The government of the world incomprehensible. (viii. 14—ix. 6.) Commendation of pleasure. (ix. 7—10.) The superiority of wisdom, which often is of no avail. (ix. 11—x. 1.) Single maxims, of a skeptical nature. (x. 2—xi. 6.) An exhortation to enjoy life, before old age approaches. (xi. 7—xii. 8.) Conclusion and summary of the book, with an account of *Koheleth* himself. (xii. 9—14.)

[a] The following writers think it is written in the form of a dialogue: *Herder*, Briefe, vol. i. p. 180, sq. *Clericus*, Sentimens de quelques Theol. de Holland, p. 272. The third edition of *Eichhorn*, vol. iii. p. 650, sqq. *Bergst*, in *Eichhorn's* Allg. Bib. vol. x. p. 963, sqq. *Rhode*, De Vet. Poet. Sap gnom. p. 213, sqq. *Kelle*, Die Heil. Schriften in ihrer Urgestalt. vol. i. p. 279. And on the other side, *Döderlein*, Pref. to his translation, p. x. sqq. and *Rosenmüller*, Prolegg. p. 13. See the similar views of *Paulus*, in his new version of the book in his Repert. vol. i. p. 201. *Nachtigall*, Kohel. p. 36, sqq. He finds no plan in it. *J. E. Chr. Schmidt* found in this book a work not fully completed and ready for the people. Others have sought to prove there were in it an orderly plan and division. *Rosenmüller* and *J. D. Michaelis* think it is divided into two parts — i. 1—iv. 16, and iv. 17—xii. 8. *Van der Palm* divides it thus: i.—vi. vii.—xii. The following is *Köster's* arrangement: i. 2—11, the introduction; i. 11—iii. 22, the first chapter, nothing permanent, or the absolute good; iv.—vi., the second chapter, the relative good; vii. 1—ix 16, the third chapter, of true wisdom; ix. 17—xii. 8,

The objectionable character of the book is not to be denied. To do this were to mistake its peculiar meaning, as Köster has done, who finds too much in it that is positive, and maintains that the book "teaches us what is permanent in nothingness;" or as Ewald, who thinks the happiness it recommends is an ideal of life. But Jerome, in his commentary on Eccl. xii. 13, says, "The Hebrews say, that this book ought to be obliterated, — as well as other writings of Solomon, which have become obsolete, and have been lost, — and for this reason, that he asserts the creatures of God are all vain, and thinks the whole of no value, and because he prefers food and drink, and transient pleasures, before all things. But the book deserves to be placed among the divine volumes for that sentence alone, in which he condenses the whole contents and meaning of the book, and says that the end of his discourses is very easy to be heard, and contains nothing difficult, namely, that we should fear God and keep his commandments."[a] The book denies the im-

---

the fourth chapter, of wisdom in its application to the affairs of life. *Umbreit*, (Uebers. p. 13, sqq., Coheleth script. p. 44, sqq.,) to verify his arrangement, makes use of arbitrary transpositions. *Herder*, *Eichhorn*, *Friedländer*, and *Knobel*, justly maintain there is a free course of ideas in it, [not restricted by a formal plan.] *Herder* (l. c. p. 178) and *Eichhorn* (§ 661) give the contents and design of the book correctly, yet *Knobel's* modification thereof may be accepted. "Koheleth wished to prove the nothingness of human life, and then to lead a life conformable thereto." The following give the design of the book erroneously or one-sidedly, and too definitely: *Des Vœux*, Critical Essay of Ecclesiastes. *J. F. Jacobi*, Vorwürfen gerettete Prediger Buch; 1779. *J. D. Michaelis*, Poet. Entwurf. d. Pred. Buch; 2d ed. 1762. *Kleuker*, Salomon. Denkwürdigkeit; 1785. *Döderlein*, l. c. p. viii. *Zirkel*, Untersuch. p. 76. *Schmidt*, Sal. Pred. p. 23. *Paulus*, l. c. p. 209. *Gaab*, Beiträge, &c. p. 48. *Hanlein*, On the Traces of a Belief in Immortality in Ecclesiastes, in his Theol. Journal, vol. iv. pt. iv. p. 278, sq. *Bertholdt*, p. 2248. *Rhode*, l. c. p. 223, sqq. *Umbreit*, l. c. p. 35. *Ewald*, Hoheslied. p. 153, sq. *Köster*, l. c. 105, sqq., and particularly *Kaiser*, l. c.

[a] See Pesikta Rabbati, fol. 33, c. 1. Midrash, Cohel. fol. 311, c. 1. Vajikra Rab. sect. 28, fol. 161, c. 2: Voluerunt sapientes, ἀποκρύπτειν,

mortality of the soul, and this denial is not affected by the passage, (xii. 7,) "And the dust returns to the earth as it was, but the breath of life to God, who gave it." This denial is not mere poetry.

§ 284.

ITS AGE AND AUTHOR.

To follow the letter of the book, it is ascribed to Solomon. Tradition and common opinion favor this hypothesis. The statement in Baba Bathra and Shalsheleth Hakkabala, that Isaiah wrote his own book, the Proverbs, Canticles, and Ecclesiastes, does not deny that Solomon was the author.[a]

But if it is probable that Solomon wrote some of the Proverbs, and that their spirit is conformable to that of his age, then this book can neither belong to the same author, nor the same age, for its spirit is entirely different. This hypothesis is favored by the obvious fiction, and the introduction of Solomon saying, "I the preacher was king over Israel at Jerusalem. I did great things. I builded me houses, and planted me vineyards," &c.; "Besides this, since the preacher was wise, he taught the people knowledge, investigated, and inquired, and set in order many proverbs," &c. (i. 12, ii. 4, xii. 9.)[b]

---

librum Coheleth, quod deprehenderunt in eo verba quæ ad hæresin vergant. Compare *Carpzov*, p. 222. Tr. Schab. fol. 30. On the silence of the New Testament and the Fathers respecting it, see *Knobel*, p. 101, sqq.

[a] Baba Bathra, fol. 15, c. 1. (See above, § 14, and Hakkabala, fol. 66, c. 2.) *Grotius* (on xii. 11) was the first to deny that Solomon was the author. Even *Jahn* does the same, p. 849. But the following defend the genuineness of the book: *Carpzov*, p. 207; *Schelling*, Salomon quæ supersunt, Præf. p. 10; *Van der Palm*, p. 34; and others.

[b] *Döderlein*, (Schol. in Libr. V. T. poet. p. 187; Uebers. p. 161,) *Schmidt*,

This theory is favored, also, by the later character of the language, which is strongly Aramæan.[a] Besides, it bears other marks of a recent and unfortunate age, which had made some advance in religious and literary cultivation.[b]

We shall not be far out of the way, if, with Rosenmüller, Knobel, and Ewald, we date the composition of the book in the last time of the Persian period, or the beginning of the Macedonian, when literary fictions of this kind were common.[c]

(Sal. Pred. p. 204,) *Bertholdt*, (p. 2250, sq.,) and *Umbreit*, (Coheleth, p. 94,) consider the epilogue (xii. 9—14) spurious, but on grounds perfectly worthless. Here the author appears very properly, and speaks of the sage whom he has introduced in the fiction. Besides, he is spoken of in the third person. (vii. 27.) The language of this part does not differ from the rest of the book, as *Schmidt* maintains, who finds Græcisms in it, but only by misunderstanding יוֹתֵר מִן. (verse 9.) Comp. *Van der Palm*, p. 83, sqq.

[a] חֲבַל, for חֶבֶל; i. 2. חֲסוּרִים for הָאֲסוּרִים; iv. 14. כְּבָר; i. 10, ii. 12, 16, iii. 15, iv. 2, et al. כִּשְׁרוֹן; ii. 21, iv. 4, v. 10. כָּשֵׁר; xi. 6, x. 21. זְמָן; iii. 1. פֵּשֶׁר; viii. 1. בָּטֵל; xii. 3. גּוּמָץ; x. 8. פִּתְגָּם; viii. 11. עוֹלָם, *world*; iii. 11. שׁ, prefix, perhaps fifty times. מַה־שֶׁ; i. 9, iii. 15, 22, vi. 10, vii. 24. אֲנִי, with finite verb; ii. 12, 13, 15, 20, iii. 18, iv. 4, et al. The use of *Elohim*. Many things approach the Talmudic usage: עִנְיָן; i. 3, ii. 26, iv. 8, v. 13, et al. חוּץ מִן; ii. 25. חוּשׁ; ii. 25, et al. See *Gesenius*, in vol. i., Appendix, D. *Hartmann*, Linguistische Einleit. in d. B. Koheleth, in *Winer's* Zeitschrift, vol. i. p. 29, sqq. *Knobel*, p. 70, sqq.

[b] *Ewald* (p. 181) adduces some passages in proof of the political condition of the age, which prove nothing. What has been brought forward by *Schmidt* (p. 299, sq.) and *Jahn* (p. 853) from viii. 2, x. 4—7, 16, 17, 20, iv. 13—16, in proof of an earlier age, from Manasseh to Hezekiah, (725—696 B. C.) is of little assistance. See *Berlholdt*, p. 2218, sq.

[c] *Bertholdt* and *Zirkel* bring it down still later. The latter finds allusion to the Sadducees and Pharisees in the book; but see, against this, *Eichhorn*, Allg. Bib. vol. iv. p. 904, sqq. *J. E. C. Schmidt*, p. 278, sqq., and 306, sqq. *Bertholdt*, p. 2221, sqq. But *Knobel* thinks the views of the Pharisees and Sadducees began to develop themselves in the time when this was written.

CHAPTER VI.

THE BOOK OF JOB.[a]

§ 285.

STYLE AND SPIRIT OF THE BOOK.

THIS book is closely connected in character with Ps. xxxvii. and lxxiii. Its subject is the common Hebrew

[a] Catena Græc. Patrum in b. Job., collectore *Niceta*, Heracleæ Metropolita, ex duobus MSS. Biblioth. Bodlejanæ codd., Græce nunc primum in lucem edita et Latine versa op. et st. *Patricii Junii.* Accessit ad calcem textus Jobi στιχηρῶς, justa veram et germanam LXX. Seniorum interpretat., ex Biblioth. Reg. MS. cod.; Lond. 1637, fol.

Mart. Buceri Comment. in Libr. Job.; Arg. 1528, fol.

Jo. Œcolampadii Exegem. in Job. et Dan.; Bas. 1532, 4to., and often.

Victorin. Strigelii Liber Jobi, ad Ebr. Veritatem recogn. et Argumentis atque Schol. illustr.; Lips. 1566; Neostad. 1571.

Joa. Merceri Comm. in Job., Genev. 1573, fol., cum Comm. in Librr. Sal., Lug. Bat. 1651, fol.

C. Sanctii Commentarius in Jobum; Lug. Bat. 1625, fol.

Jo. Drusii Nova Versio et Scholia in Job.; Amst. 1636, 4to.

Seb. Schmidii in Libr. Job., Comm.; Arg. 1670, 4to.

Jo. Henr. Michaelis, Notæ uberr. in Libr. Jobi, Uberr. Annotatt. in Hagiogr. vol. ii.

Animadverss. philol. in Jobum, &c., Auct. *Alb. Schultens;* Traj. ad Rh. 1708, 8vo. Opp. min.; Lug. Bat. 1769, 4to.

Liber Jobi cum nova Vers. ad Hebr. Fontem et Comment. perpetuo. Cur. et ed. *Alb. Schultens;* Lug. Bat. 1737, 2 vols. 4to.

Liber Jobi in versiculos metrice divisus, cum vers. Alb. Schultens notisque ex ejus comm. excerptis. Ed. atque annotatt. suas ad metrum præc. spectantes adj. *Ricard. Grey;* Lond. 1741.

Alb. Schultensii Comm. in Jobum. In Comp. redegit, Observatt. crit. atque exeg. adspersit *G. J. L. Vogel.* Tom. i. ii.; Hal. 1773, 1774.

Observatt. miscell. in libr. Job., quibus verss. et interprett. passim epicrisis instituitur, &c. Præmissa est crit. disquisitio, ubi operis totius indoles et scriptoris consilium expenditur. Cum examine oraculi celebratiss. de Goële. (Auct. *Dav. Renat. Boullier;*) Amst. 1758, 8vo. *Ewald,* l. c. vol. iii.

E. F. C. Rosenmülleri Schol. in V. T. pt. v.

doctrine of final causes, contending with doubts. The inspired soul of the poet must triumph over these doubts, to which the author of Ecclesiastes had yielded. He conquers them, not by rationalism,[a] but by resignation and faith. This spirit of the book, and its form,—that of a dialogue,—borrowed from the assemblies of sages, render it closely similar to the Greek tragedies; and it may be called the Hebrew tragedy. It is characteristic of the Hebrews, that they represent the tragic idea by words and thoughts, rather than by action.[b]

Ueberss. und Erkll. von *S. Grynäus*, 1767; *J. D. Cube*, 1769—1771, vol. iii.; *Eckermann*, 1778; *Moldenhauer*, 1780, 1781, 2 vols. 4to.; *Hufnagel*, 1781; *Kessler*, 1784; *H. A. Schultens* und *H. Muntinghe.* Aus d. Holländ. m. Zuss. u. Anmerkk.; *J. P. Bergs* von *K. F. Weidenbach*, 1797; *Pape*, 1797; *Block*, (metrical,) 1797; *Eichhorn*, 1800, A. Bibl. vol. x. p. 579, sqq., 2 A. 1824; *Stuhlmann*, 1804; *Gaab*, 1809; *J. R. Schärer*, 1818, 2 vols.; *E. G. A. Böckel*, 1821; *L. F. Melsheimer*, 1823; *Umbreit*, 1824, 2 A. 1832; *Gerh. Lange*, (metrical,) 1831; *Köster*, (strophic,) 1832.

See Elench. Interprett. vor *Rosenmüller's* Schol. vol. i. und *Umbreit's* Uebers.

[A Translation of the Book of Job, &c., in *Broughton's* Works, vol. ii. p. 246, sqq. *Heath's* Essay towards a new English Version, &c.; 1756, 4to. The Book of Job in English Verse, by *T. Scott;* Lond. 1773, 8vo. An Improved Version, with Notes, by *Gardner;* Lond. 1796, 8vo. The Book of Job metrically arranged ...... and newly translated, &c., by Bishop *Stock;* Bath, 1805, 4to. The Book of Job, translated by *Elizabeth Smith;* Lond. 1810, 8vo. The Book of Job, literally translated, by *John Mason Good;* Lond. 1812, 8vo. An Exposition, &c., by *J. Caryl;* Lond. 1669, 2 vols. fol. Elihu, or an Inquiry into the principal Scope, &c., of the Book of Job, by *Walter Hodges;* Lond. 1750, 4to. A Dissertation on the Book of Job, its Nature, &c., by *J. Garnett*, 2d ed.; Lond. 1751, 4to. A Commentary on the Book of Job, by *Chappelow;* 1752, 2 vols. 4to. A critical Dissertation on the Book of Job, by *Peters;* Lond. 1757, 4to. See, also, *Warburton*, Divine Legation, b. vi. sect. ii. A New Translation of the Book of Job, by *G. R. Noyes*, 2d ed.; Boston, 1838, 1 vol. 12mo.]

[a] *Vernunftelei.*

[b] The ancients compared it, too closely, to a *tragedy;* e. g. *Beza*, Observatt. in Job. Procem. p. 2, sq. *Jo. Gerhard*, Exogos. Loci i. de SS. § 140. *Mer-*

§ 286.

THE CONTENTS, SUBJECT, AND UNITY, OF THE POEM.

It is pretty clear that the poet writes to disclose the weakness of the common doctrine of retribution. 1. In the prologue, (i. ii.,) he relates the history of Job's misfortunes, and the design of God to try him. 2. Then follows Job's discussion with his friends, (iii.—xxxi.,) beginning, (1.) with a monologue by Job, (iii.,) expressing his despair and weariness of life. This discussion is carried on throughout three acts of the dialogue, namely, (2.) in chap. iv.—xiv.; (3.) xv.—xxi.; and, (4.) xxii.—xxviii. In this controversy, Job's friends set forth and defend the common doctrine of retribution, making it more and more apparent thereby that Job is a transgressor, and deserves what he suffers. Job denies this doctrine, and defends his own innocence. In this way the problem is stated. (5.) Then follows the monologue of Job, (xxix.—xxxi.,) which closes the discussion, but without solving the problem. There is a confusion in this part of the poem, occasioned by Job's conceding to his adversary (xxvii. 13—22)[a] what he

---

cerus, Præf. in Job. But see *Carpzov*, p. 76, sq., and *Lowth*, Prælect. xxxiii., who says this poem is not a proper drama.

The comparison with an *epic poem* is altogether absurd. *J. H. Stuss*, De Epopœia Jobæa Comment. iii.; Goth. 1753, 4to. *Lichtenstein*, Num Lib. Job. cum Odyssea Homeri comparari possit; Helmst. 1773, 4to. *Illgen*, Jobi antiquissimi Carminis Hebræorum Natura atque Virtus; Lips. 1789. *Augusti*, Einleit. § 106.

[a] [*Eichhorn* gives a solution of the difficulty, Allg. Bib. vol. ii. p. 614. It is that of *Kennicott*, Diss. Gen. § 165, viz. that it is not *Job*, but *Zophar*, who speaks in this passage. *Bildad* and *Eliphaz* had each spoken *three* times, and it was therefore necessary, for the sake of symmetry, that Zophar also should speak a third time. He thus arranges the discourses: Bildad, chap. xxv.; Job's reply, xxvi. 1—xxvii. 10; Zophar, xxvii. 11—23; Job, xxviii.

had previously denied, (xii. 6, xxi. xxiv. 22, sqq.,) namely, that the transgressor receives his just recompense, and by his praising the unfathomable wisdom of God, (xxviii.,) and consequent hint at an answer of the question. 3. The progress of the poem is still more disturbed by the solution given in the third part, (the speech of Elihu, xxxii.—xxxvii.,) and the argument that suffering is an instrument, in the hand of the Allwise and Just, for the correction of the wicked. By this, violence is done to the true solution. 4. This is given in the fourth part, in the speeches of God, who makes his appearance, xxxviii.—xlii. 6. These describe the power and wisdom of God, and reduce Job to silence and submission. 5. The book concludes with an epilogue, (xlii. 7—17,) in which God approves Job, but

---

1, sqq. But he passes over the most difficult verses, 7—10, and leaves them as the words of Job. *Ewald* says in his defence, "These chapters contain the chief theme of the book, the solution of the riddle." But it is in this that the difficulty consists. Dr. *Noyes* (l. c. note in loc. p. 165, sq.) denies the fact of inconsistency in Job's language. He does not concede his position that the innocent often suffer, and does not admit that human suffering implies guilt; but as the virtuous do suffer, there is some mysterious cause of it, besides the vices of men. This apparent inconsistency he takes for a necessary part of the plan of the book. But there seems to be an essential discrepancy between this and Job's former speeches. (Compare, in particular, xxi. 6—21, xxiv. 21—25.) But in xxvii. 7—23, the wicked *universally*, at least *generally*, meet with just punishment. But, to me, this and other inconsistencies of Job seem perfectly natural, and show the exquisite art with which the poem was written. What more natural than this, that a man deprived of all, reduced to the last stage of physical suffering, tempted by his wife, and tortured by his friends, should affirm what he just denied! At one time he seems to believe a sort of immortality of the soul, (iii. 13—19;) then, when exasperated still more, he positively denies it. (xiv. 10, 14, et al.)]

Kern (in *Bengel's* Archiv. vol. iv. pt. ii. p. 362) maintains that the poet wished to introduce a *higher view*, in the contested speeches of Job, and those of Elihu, for the purpose of mitigating the severity of Job's conclusions, and also to impede the progress of the poem!

disapproves of his friends. It relates, also, that a twofold restoration of all that was lost, was made to the sufferer. The first of these narrative passages (i. ii.) informs us, that Job's sufferings were designed for a trial of his character, and the second (xlii. 7—17) confirms the common belief in retribution. The two disturb the sublime idea of a trusting and humble submission under the ordinances of divine omnipotence and wisdom, which is given in the speeches of God.[a]

§ 287.

SPURIOUSNESS OF ELIHU'S SPEECHES.

These speeches (xxxii.—xxxviii.) are a later interpolation. This fact is shown by the following considerations:—

1. By the matter and the style, which is far-fetched, dull, tedious, and obscure; as appears in the language itself, and in its peculiar expressions.[b]

2. Elihu's speeches weaken the force of those of Job, and of God, and obscure the antithetic relation between the two. They, in part, anticipate the remarks of God, and make them superfluous, for they give the solution of the difficulty in the way of knowledge, which, according to God's declaration, is only to be found out by sub-

---

[a] See *De Wette*, art. *Hiob*, Allg. Encylop. vol. ii. sect. viii. p. 293.

[b] דֵּעַ; xxxii. 6, 10, 17, xxxvi. 3. חִוָּה; xxxii. 6, 10, 17, xxxvi. 2. חַיָּה; xxxiii. 18, 20, 22, 28. (Comp. xxxviii. 39.) נֹעַר; xxxiii. 25, xxxvi. 14. עָבַר בַּשֶּׁלַח; xxxiii. 18, xxxvi. 12. סָפַק; xxxiv. 26. שֶׂפֶק; xxxvi. 18. (Comp. xxvii. 23.) הֵסִירוֹת; xxvi. 16, 18, et al. Reminiscences from former parts of the book; xxxiv. 3, 7. Comp. xii. 11, xv. 16; xxxiii. 15, comp. iv. 13; xxxvii. 4, 10, 22, comp. xl. 9, xxxviii. 29, 30, xxviii. 1, 12. See *Michaelis*, Einleit. in A. B. vol. i. p. 113, sqq. *Hirzel*, Hiob, p. 190.

mission.[a] Stäudlin is right in saying that the controversy is decided in Elihu's speeches, while the succeeding discourses of God only confirm the decision, for Elihu says more than God.

3. The opinions of Job are misunderstood or perverted. He is made to say, "A man hath no advantage when he is in friendship with God." (xxxiv. 9.) "I am more righteous than God. . . . . . What advantage have I? What have I gained more than if I had sinned?" (xxxv. 2, 3.) This error could only be committed by a writer who was not the author of the rest of the book.[b]

4. Job makes no reply to Elihu.

5. Job is mentioned by name in Elihu's speeches, and not in those of the other speakers.

6. The prologue and epilogue do not mention Elihu.

Stuhlmann, Bernstein, and Ewald, deny the authenticity; Bertholdt, Jahn, Umbreit, and others, defend it. Umbreit thinks the difference in the style arises from the poet's artistic skill, and denies the impropriety of these discourses.[c] But in this matter every thing depends on

---

[a] Comp. xxxvi. 22, xxxvii. 24, with xxxviii.—xl.; in special, xxxvi. 27—32, and xxxvii. 6—8, with xxxviii. 12—30. *Stäudlin*, Beit. zur Gesch. Phil. und Rel. vol. ii. p. 137, sq. *Kern* (in *Bengel*, Archiv. vol. iv. pt. ii. p. 362) thinks the poet aims to give the higher view in these speeches of Elihu.

[b] See *Eichhorn*, § 644, *b*, p. 205, 206.

[c] *Stuhlmann*, Ubers. p. 20. *Bernstein*, in *Keil*, and *Tzschirner's* Anal. vol. i. pt. iii. p. 150, sq. *Ewald*, in Stud. und Krit. for 1829, xv. p. 767, pt. iii.; A. T. p. 247, sq. *Hirzel*, p. 189. *Bertholdt*, (p. 2158,) *Jahn*, (xi. p. 776,) *Umbreit*, (p. 25, sqq.,) defend it. [Dr. *Noyes* contends against *De Wette*, and defends the genuineness of Elihu's speeches. 1. The difference in style was designed; the author did not wish to "give the most respectable appearance to a young man appearing on such an occasion." The "favorite expressions" and "reminiscences" are "circumstances of little importance." 2. The speech of Elihu sets off that of God by the contrast, and if the omission of Elihu's speech would render the poem more perfect, we are not, therefore, to reject it. "The author does give one view of the cause of human suffer-

the critic's taste and judgment; yet I cannot understand how any one can contend that the beauty of the poem would be injured by the omission of Elihu's speeches, on the ground that there would not be then sufficient preparation for the appearance of God; and that it would be a *Deus ex machina* in that case, while it must be a *Deus ex machina* at any rate.[a]

§ 288.

SUSPICIONS AGAINST XXVII. 11—XXVIII. 28.

It is certain that this passage is unsuitable and contradictory in the mouth of Job. This has long been felt. Kennicott and Eichhorn,[b] therefore, refer xxvii. 13—23, to Zophar; Stuhlmann allots verses 11—23 to him,

---

ing in this discourse, not distinctly stated elsewhere. (chap. xxxiii. 14—28.)" (What is it?) 3. Elihu does not pervert Job's speeches to any great extent, and a young man would naturally misunderstand and pervert his opponent in some measure. (?) (But to me the perversion seems great and unnatural.) 4. It was in accordance with Eastern feelings to give this youth no answer. (?) 5. The mention of Job's name is unimportant. (True, if this were the *only* objection; but combined with others, it has some force.) 6. Elihu is not mentioned in the prologue, because the author thought best to have but three speakers in the chief part of the poem; and if he did not judge so wisely as the German professors, still we should not alter his plan. (Here Dr. *Noyes* assumes that the "German professors" would *alter*, and not *restore*, the author's plan.) Elihu is not mentioned in the epilogue, "because nothing occurred to the author which was particularly appropriate to be said to him." But this judgment is somewhat arbitrary. On the whole, Dr. *Noyes* thinks there is a strong presumption against a Jew tampering with such a work. But to me there seems a presumption on the other side; for, as we have seen, they did tamper with the prophecies of Isaiah, and perhaps Zechariah, with the names of David and Solomon.]

[a] Besides, it may still be doubted whether the passage, (xxxviii. 1, sqq.,) alleged to be introductory, refers to the following appearance of God.

[b] See *Kennicott*, Remarks on select Passages in the O. T. p. 169. Diss. Gen. ed. *Bruns*, p. 539. *Eichhorn*, Allg. Bib. vol. ii. p. 613.

but refers chap. xxviii. to Bildad. Bernstein considers the whole as a later interpolation, while Rosenmüller and Umbreit consider it genuine.[a]

But it cannot, with propriety, be assigned to either of Job's adversaries; for, though Zophar has spoken but *twice*, this is obviously by the author's design.[b]

A good deal has been said in defence of this passage, by Kern, Rosenmüller, Umbreit, and Ewald. Hirzel says well, "While Job's opponents wished to prove this proposition against him, that 'the transgressor did not escape punishment in his life,' and charged it upon Job himself, that, since every transgressor was miserable, therefore every miserable man was a transgressor; to stave off this argument, Job had hitherto, though against his better judgment, denied the entire proposition; and, since his opponents laid it down as a permanent and universal rule, he had confirmed this denial, by adducing numerous examples where the contrary was true. But now he goes on to explain the matter to his friends, and admits that they have rightly apprehended the law by which the transgressor's lot is determined. (verse 12.) He gives a description which agrees with their proposition, (13—23,) as a sort of supplement to his remarks, and then calls their attention to this fact, that, in spite of the justice of their general view, they had yet fallen into an error. (verse 12.) He then adds chap. xxviii., designing to show his opponents how great were the depths of divine wisdom, and how narrow the limits of human knowledge." Still, after all, we must charge

---

[a] *Stuhlmann*, Anmerk. zur Uebers. p. 68—76. *Bernstein*, l. c. p. 134. *Rosenmüller*, and *Umbreit*, on xxvii. 13. [*Noyes*, in loc.]

[b] How could Zophar utter verses 11 and 12?—"I will teach *you*," &c., "*Ye yourselves* have *all* seen it," &c. Elsewhere the opponents of Job speak only to him.

the poet with obscurity, at the least, if not with inconsistency; for, in spite of his sublime aspirations, he cannot wholly free himself from the common doctrine of retribution. It is scarcely right to maintain that here is an interpolation, though the bombastic passage, (xli. 4—26,) which disturbs the connection between God's speech (xli. 1—3) and Job's reply, (xlii. 2—6,) is suspicious.[a]

[It is plain xxxi. 38—40, is out of its place. The speech of Job would end finely with verse 37.[b] Chap. xxxi. 38—40, would suit the connection if inserted after verse 25. Chap. xxxviii. 36, disturbs the connection as it now stands, but the sense is preserved if this is placed after verse 38.][c]

---

[a] [Dr. *Noyes* (l. c. p. xxiii.) admits the inconsistency of Job's statements, in xxvii. 7, sqq., with his former assertions, but thinks this not incompatible with the author's design, which was "to throw all possible light upon a moral subject." The object of the poem is advanced by this course, and Job's admission is not inconsistent with his assertions in xxix. 30 and 31, but it is inconsistent with his assertions in xii. 6, 7, xxi. 6—21, xxiv. 2—8, 21—25.]

[b] *Eichhorn*, Allg. Bib. vol. ii. p. 619. On the other hand, see *Hirzel*, in loc.

[c] *Stuhlmann*, *Bernstein*, and *Eichhorn*, insert xli. 12—34, immediately after xl. 7, so that the following order prevails: xli. 1—7, xli. 12—34, ... xli. 8—11. *Ewald* considers the whole passage, xl. 15—xli. 26, as spurious, and chiefly for this reason: The sole design of Jehovah's second speech (xl. 6, sqq.) is to answer Job's doubts respecting the justice of the government of the world, and the description of Behemoth and Leviathan is not suited to this end. But the design of xl. 6, sqq., cannot be determined so sharply, (comp. verse 9,) for sharpness of distinction does not belong to the character of our poet. (See *Umbreit*, Theol. Stud. und Kritiken for 1831, p. 833, sqq. *Hirzel*, in loc.) *Eichhorn* connects xxxix. 30, with xl. 15—24, and places xl. 1—14, between verses 6 and 7 of chap. xlii. [The passages which involve difficulties in their present order will then stand thus: xxxix. 30, xl. 15—24, xl. 1—7, xli. 12—34, xli. 8—11, xlii. 1—6, xl. 1—14, xlii. 7, sqq., and then all these difficulties vanish. *Heath* inserts xl. 1—14, between xlii. 6 and 7.]

§ 289.

SUSPICIONS AGAINST THE PROLOGUE AND EPILOGUE.

For the sake of the perfection of the poem, we could wish these historical passages were away. Accordingly they have been rejected by Hasse, Stuhlmann, and Bernstein.[a] But the prosaic style, the occurrence of Satan therein,[b] the use of the name *Jehovah*, — while *Eloah*[c] is elsewhere used in the book for its poetic effect, — prove nothing against the genuineness of these passages. There is a contradiction between i. 19, where it appears all Job's children were killed, and xix. 17, where he says, —

> "My breath is become loathsome to my wife,
> And my supplication to the children of my own body."[d]

Compare, also, viii. 4: —

---

[a] *Hasse*, Conjectures on the B. Job, in the Magazin für d. bibl. or. Litt. vol. i. p. 162, sqq.

[b] *Herder*, *Eichhorn*, *Stuhlmann*, and *Bertholdt*, think the Satan mentioned here is not the common Satan. But this is contrary to all analogy. *De Wette*, Bib. Dogmat. § 171, and the authors there cited. *Hirzel* defends the prologue and epilogue, and says, "Neither belongs to the didactic part of the book. The prologue initiates the reader into divine mysteries, but in the poem itself he must see that all the attempts of Job and his friends are unable to disclose the causes of his affliction. This would give him a hint to abandon inquiry into what was resolved upon in the counsel of God. In the epilogue, the poet restores Job to prosperity, and thus performs a duty to the reader's feelings, which will clearly appear if we consider the opposite case — had he left Job in endless misery. If Job is repaid for unmerited suffering and loss, the reader goes away satisfied with the divine order of things." But I think he would be confirmed in the common doctrine of retribution, for here a case occurs in actual life where an innocent man suffers to the last, and is not, as in the epilogue, finally restored to happiness. The reader then would be dissatisfied with the divine order of things.

[c] See *Eichhorn*, § 644, *a.* By the use of this word he avoided all the popular and theocratic notions of God.

[d] [*Noyes* translates בְּנֵי בִטְנִי, "*children of my mother.*" The LXX. render it υἱοὺς παλλακίδων μου, but the Vulgate literally, *filios ventris mei.*

"As thy children sinned against him,
He hath given them up to their transgression."

But this contradiction proves little.[a]

More stress is to be laid on the contradiction between xlii. 7, 8, and xxxviii. 2, xl. 2, xlii. 3, in the judgment pronounced on the expressions of Job.[b] The submissiveness of Job (i. 21, 22, and ii. 10) does not agree with what is said here. But still all these considerations are not sufficient to justify us in rejecting the passage.

§ 290.

THE IDEA AND DESIGN OF THE POEM.

Now, if all the contested passages are spurious, then the author carried out the sublime idea, that man can pass no judgment upon the government of the world, and the allotment of human destiny; only a confession of his ignorance and humble submission are left for him. But since the critic can venture to reject only the speech of Elihu, then the poem is an attempt to rise above the common doctrine of retribution. But this

---

So *Schultens.* But *Gesenius* (Lex. Heb.) renders it "*my brethren.*"] I cannot agree with *Ewald* and *Hirzel*, that the word means *grandsons.*

[a] According to *Hirzel*, Job merely defended his innocence, which his friends had attacked; but the word אָכֵן is against this view. At least, the poet has expressed himself very obscurely.

[b] [Jehovah said to Eliphaz...... "My wrath is kindled against thee and thy two friends: for ye have not spoken concerning me that which is right, *as hath my servant Job.* Take ye therefore, &c...... *my servant Job shall pray for you,* (for to him will I have regard,) *lest I deal with you according to your folly; for ye have not spoken concerning me that which is right, as hath my servant Job;*" and xlii. 3, [Thou Job sayest,] "Who is it that darkeneth counsel without understanding?" "I [Job] mentioned what I did not understand, because — what I did not see into was incomprehensible to me." Dr. *Noyes* translates differently.]

attempt is successful only in this,—it teaches, 1. that an innocent man may suffer; and, 2. that he must not murmur, but confide in the wisdom of God, who may have good designs in the infliction of suffering, and turn all to the best result. The poet presents this comforting doctrine to his countrymen, when misfortunes and doubts of Providence were wavering before his eyes.[a]

The application of this poem to the condition of the Jewish people,[b] is not to be disguised by the fable, and the scene on which the events take place. Job is a patriarchal character, and the scene is laid in the east, and in the nomadic period of history.[c] Now, if the whole is not a poetic fiction,—and there are many reasons to favor that opinion,—but if the poet made use of traditional materials,[d] yet his intention in working

---

[a] § 285.

[b] *Bernstein* has placed this in a favorable light, p. 190, sqq. See *De Wette*, On the Characteristics of Hebrew Spirit, in *Daub* and *Creutzer*, l. c. p. 278. Similar opinions may be found in *Herman von der Hardt*, Com. in Jobum, sive Historia Populi Israelis in Assyr. Exilio, tom. i.; Helmst. 1728, fol. *Leclerc*, on Job, i. 1. *Warburton*, Divine Legation, pt. iii. b. vi. § 2, ch. 3. [*Peters* (l. c.) attempts to rebut the statements of *Warburton*, respecting the age, &c., of Job.] *J. Garnett*, Dissertation on the Book of Job, &c.; 2d ed. Lond. 1751.

[c] See chap. i. 3, 5, xlii. 11. Comp. Gen. xxxiii. 15, xlii. 16. Some writers find too much of the *patriarchal* and *nomadic* in the poem. *Eichhorn*, § 614, p. 164. Against this, see *Bernstein*, p. 27, sqq., p. 79, sqq. Numerous passages are opposed to this—v. 4, xv. 28, xxiv. 12, xxix. 7, xxxix. 7, xii. 18, 19, xxxi. 35. Others are in its favor—xxi. 10, sqq., xxix. 6, xxx. 1, sqq. According to i. 3, we must seek the land of *Uz* (עוּץ) in the north of Arabia, and not in the neighborhood of Damascus. See Jer. xxv. 20, Lam. iv. 21, Gen. xxxvi. 28, xxii. 21, x. 23. See *Spanheim*, Hist. Jobi, cap. iii. p. 35, sqq. *Rosenmüller*, Prol. in Job. § 5. *Gesenius*, Lexicon. *Bertholdt*, p. 205, sqq.

[d] Baba Bathra (p. 15, c. 1) says, "Job never existed, nor was created." So says *Maimonides*, Mar. Nevoch. iii. 22, p. 395, sqq. *Junil.*, De Partibus div. Legis, lib. i. *Clericus*, Sentimens de quelques Theologiens, p. 274, sqq.

it over is so obvious, that no one can fail to see the didactic object he had in view.

The addition of the Seventy favors the opinion that Job was an historical person:—[a]

See others in *Carpzov*, vol. ii. p. 34. *Michaelis*, Einleit. p. 1, sqq. The hypothesis that the book is a fiction, is favored by the fact, that the ideal is mingled with the narrative, (i. 2, 3, xlii. 13, 14, 16,) and by the significant name of Job, אִיּוֹב = אָיוּב, *the persecuted.* See *Gesenius*, Lexicon, and *Hirzel*, p. 8. On the other side, *Ewald.*

[a] The following passages in Ezekiel are not certain proofs that the poet made use of traditionary materials: xiv. 16, 20; though *Luther*, (Tischreden, p. 318,) *Eichhorn*, *Rosenmüller*, and *Hirzel*, are of this opinion, as well as the addition of the Seventy: *Οὗτος ἑρμηνεύεται ἐκ τῆς Συριακῆς βίβλου, ἐν μὲν γῇ κατοικῶν τῇ Αὐσίτιδι, ἐπὶ τοῖς ὁρίοις τῆς Ἰδουμαίας καὶ Ἀραβίας· προϋπῆρχε δὲ αὐτῷ ὄνομα Ἰωβάβ. Λαβὼν δὲ γυναῖκα Ἀράβισσαν, γεννᾷ υἱὸν, ᾧ ὄνομα Ἐννών. Ἦν δὲ αὐτὸς πατρὸς μὲν Ζαρὲ ἐκ τῶν Ἡσαῦ υἱῶν υἱὸς, μητρὸς δὲ Βοσόῤῥας, ὥστε εἶναι αὐτὸν πέμπτον ἀπὸ Ἀβραάμ, καὶ οὗτοι οἱ βασιλεῖς οἱ βασιλεύσαντες ἐν Ἐδὼμ, ἧς καὶ αὐτὸς ἦρξε χώρας· πρῶτος Βαλὰκ ὁ τοῦ Βεώρ . . . . . . μετὰ δὲ Βαλὰκ, Ἰωβὰβ ὁ καλούμενος Ἰώβ. Μετὰ δὲ τοῦτον, Ἀσὼμ ὁ ὑπάρχων ἡγεμὼν ἐκ τῆς Θαιμανίτιδος χώρας· μετὰ δὲ τοῦτον, Ἀδὰδ υἱὸς Βαράδ . . . . . . Οἱ δὲ ἐλθόντες πρὸς αὐτὸν φίλοι, Ἐλιφὰζ τῶν Ἡσαῦ υἱῶν, Θαιμανῶν βασιλεὺς, Βαλδὰδ ὁ Σαυχαίων τύραννος, Σωφὰρ ὁ Μιναίων βασιλεύς.* (Comp. *Jahn*, § 758, sqq. *Carpzov*, p. 36, sqq.) ["The book of Job," says Dr. *Hodges* (l. c.) "has suffered as much as Job himself, from critics. Mr. *Horne* (l. c. vol. iii. p. 63, sqq.) maintains the book is a real history. "There is every possible evidence that the book . . . . . . contains a *literal history*," &c. The arguments are, 1. "*Ezekiel and Daniel mention him.*" So Christ mentions Lazarus: does this prove him an historical person? 2. The book of Job "*specifies the names of persons, places, and facts, ... usually related in other true histories.*" So does every work of fiction, e. g. the Arabian Nights' Entertainment, and Paradise Lost. It were impossible to write an intelligible poem without "persons, places, and facts." 3. *Job is mentioned in Eastern tradition*, in the book of Tobit, by Mohammed. Noble Arabians boast of descent from him. And, at the "end of the fourth century (A. C.) . . . . . . many persons . . . . . . went into Arabia to see Job's dunghill;" therefore, "The book of Job contains the history of a real character." Dr. *Hales* (cited in *Horne*, p. 69) forces the *stars* to tell the very date of Job's trial; for, *assuming* that "*Chimah* and *Chesil*, or *Taurus* and *Scorpio*, were the cardinal constellations of spring and autumn," and knowing their present longitude, and the usual rate of the

"This is translated from the Syriac book, for he dwelt in Ausitis, on the borders of Idumea and Arabia. His first name was Jobab, and, marrying an Arabian woman, he had a son, whose name was Ennon. He himself was the son of Zare, of the children of Esau; his mother was Bosorrah, so that he was the fifth from Abraham. Now these are the kings that reigned in Edom, which country he also governed: First, Balak, the son of Beor, and the name of his city was Dennaba; and after Balak, Jobab, who is called Job; after him Asom, who was governor of the country of Thaimanites, [Teman;] after him, Arad, the son of Barad, who cut off Madiam in the plain of Moab. The name of his city was Gethaim. The friends who came to Job were Eliphaz, of the children of Esau, king of the Thaimanites, [Temanites,] Baldad, the sovereign of the Sauchæans, [Shuhites,] and Zophar, the king of the Minæans, [Naamathites.]"

§ 291.

THE COUNTRY AND AGE IN WHICH IT WAS WRITTEN.

The prologue has led to several mistakes, in particular points. The book has been taken for a *foreign production*, though it is Hebrew throughout, both in form

---

precession of the equinoxes, we can, by the rule of three, determine the *time* when these constellations were the cardinals of spring and autumn, namely, 2130 years B. C. This, then, is the date of Job's trial; the confirmation of the book. Unfortunately there is reason to believe *Orion* and the *Pleiades* are the stars mentioned, and the whole theory falls to the ground, and we are driven from the sky to philology to determine the age of the work. See very different reasoning in *Warburton*, l. c.; *Heath*, l. c. p. viii., sqq., xi. xix., sqq., xxxv.; and *Noyes*, l. c. p. xx., sq.]

and substance. It has been referred to the most ancient times.[a]

---

[a] Some think it is of foreign origin. *Aben Ezra*, Com. in Jobum, ii. 1.

1. *That it is of Aramæan origin* is maintained by the pseudo *Origen*, and the addition to the LXX. given above; but *Stark*, (Davidis Carmina, i. 198, sq.,) *Eichhorn*, (§ 645,) and *Bertholdt*, (p. 2045, note 4,) erroneously explain these words of the above addition οὗτος ἑρμηνεύεται ἐκ τῆς συριακῆς βιβλου, as if they related only to the addition itself. See *Carpzov*, l. c. p. 52, and the pseudo *Origen*, Com. in Job.

2. The theory of an *Arabian original* is defended by *Spanheim*, (Hist. Jobi, c. xiii. sqq. p. 221,) *J. Gerhard*, (Exeges. lib. ii. de Script. s. § 137,) *Calov*, (Bibl. illustr. ad Job. Præf.) *Kromayer*, (Filia Matri obstetricans, i. e. De Usu Linguæ Arab. in addiscenda Ebræa, p. 72.) *Jerome* (Præf. in Dan.) says, "Job has a strong resemblance to the Arabic language." On the other hand, see *Gesenius*, Gesch. Heb. Sprach. p. 33, quoted above, vol. i. Appendix, D.

3. The theory of an *Idumean origin* is defended by *Herder* (Spirit of Hebrew Poetry, vol. i. p. 125, sqq.) and *Illgen*, (Jobi antiq. Carm. Hebr. Virtus, p. 28.)

4. The theory of a *Nahoritic author* is advanced by *Niemeyer*, (Charakter d. Bib. vol. ii. p. 480, sqq.) *Eichhorn* (§ 642) adopts the modified opinion that it was written before the time of Moses, by a Hebrew, who resided in Idumea, and was familiar with the appearance and manners of Ægypt. But, on the other hand, see *Richter*, (Prog. de Ætate Libri Jobi definienda; Lips. 1799, 4to. § 11, p. 23,) *Rosenmüller*, (Prol. in Job. p. 31, sq.,) *Stäudlin*, (l. c. p. 238, sqq.,) *Bernstein*, *Bertholdt*, and *Umbreit*.

The absence of geographical, historical, and theocratic notions in the poem, which conform to the opinions of the Hebrews, can be explained only on the supposition that the work is a fiction. (Comp. *Michaelis*, l. c. p. 47, sqq.) But see xxii. 15, 16, where the *deluge* seems to be referred to, and xl. 23, where the *Jordan* is put for a great river.

But, on the other hand, the book is not destitute of peculiar conceptions of another kind; for example, ix. 5—9, xii. 10, xv. 7, xxvi. 5, sqq., xxxviii. 4, sqq.; iv. 19, x. 9, xxvii. 3; iv. 17, sqq., viii. 9, ix. 2, xiii. 26, xiv. 4, xv. 14, xxv. 4, and 6; iv. 18, v. 1, xv. 15, xxi. 22, xxxviii. 7; xxxi. 26, 27; vii. 7, sqq., x. 21, sq., xiv. 10, sqq., xvi. 22, xxx. 23, xxxviii. 17.

To this must be added the affinity between the book and the Proverbs and Psalms; e. g. xxviii. 18, "Wisdom is more precious than pearls;" and Prov. viii. 11, "Wisdom is better than pearls:" xxviii. 28, "The fear of the Lord, that is wisdom;" and, Prov. i. 7, "The fear of the Lord is the beginning of wisdom." (Compare, also, xxvi. 6, with Prov. xv. 11; xv. 16, and xxxiv. 7, with Prov. xxvi. 6; xiii. 5, with Prov. xvii. 28; xxvi. 5, with Prov. ii. 18, and xxi. 16; xxvii. 16, 17, with Prov. xxviii. 8; xxii. 29, with

In respect to the language,[a] to the contents and entire spirit,[b] the book belongs not at all to the golden age,[c] but to the later period of Hebrew literature.

Prov. xvi. 18, xviii. 12, and xxix. 23.) תּוּשִׁיָּה; v. 12, vi. 13, xi. 6, xii. 16, xxvi. 3, xxx. 22. (Comp. Prov. ii. 7, iii. 21, viii. 14, xviii. 1.) הַוָּה; vi. 2, xxx. 13. (Comp. Prov. xix. 13.) תַּחְבֻּלוֹת; xxxvii. 12. (Comp. Prov. i. 5, xi. 14, and elsewhere. Chap. xii. 21, 24, comp. with Ps. cvii. 40; v. 16, and xxii. 14, with Ps. cvii. 42.) (See others, in *Michaelis*, l. c. p. 93; *Rosenmüller*, l. c. p. 32; and *Gesenius*, l. c. p. 33.) The tendency of the whole book speaks still more strongly in favor of its Hebrew origin.

Carpzov, (p. 53, sqq.,) and several ancients adduced by him, suppose it was written before Moses. This is the opinion, also, of *Eichhorn*, (§ 641, sqq.,) *Jahn*, (p. 799, sqq.,) *Stuhlmann*, (p. 55,) and *Bertholdt*, (p. 2132, sqq.) But some of the arguments of the latter, though sought out with great pains, are refuted by the supposition that the work is a fiction, and others are themselves of no value, — such as this, that after Moses, there was no belief in the appearance of God, which is contradicted by Ps. xviii. l., and Hab. iii.; that כֹּהֵן (xii. 19) does not mean *priest*, to support which he gives a wrong interpretation of Gen. xiv. 18; and that צֶדֶק is used differently in the books written after Moses. Baba Bathra and the rabbins considered Moses the author, (see *Hottinger*, Thes. Phil. p. 499; *Wolf*, Bib. Heb. ii. 102; *Michaelis*, § 11—17;) and this is the opinion, also, of pseudo *Origen*, *Ephraim* the *Syrian*, *Huetius*, (Dem. Ev. Pr. iv. § 2,) and *Michaelis*, (p. 89,) while *Eichhorn* (§ 643) and *Stäudlin* (p. 256) refer it to some other writer of great antiquity.

[a] *Gesenius*, l. c. p. 33. *Bernstein*, p. 49, sqq. (But the latter puts here what belongs to the *poetic* style.) Besides its affinity with the usage of the Psalms and Proverbs, the language has a strong tendency to the later Chaldean Hebrew; e. g. קְדשִׁים, *angels*. שָׂהֵד; xvi. 19. תְּקֵף; xiv. 20, xv. 14. קִבֵּל; ii. 10. גָּזַר, *to determine*; xxii. 28. אָחַז, *to shut up*; xxvi. 9. חֵפֶץ; xxi. 21, xxii. 3. מִנִּי; vii. 3. קִנְצֵי, for קִצֵּי; xviii. 2. חִין, for חֵן; xli. 4. לְ, (as *not. accus.*;) v. 2, xxi. 22.

[b] *Later Religious Notions.* — i. 6, ii. 1, iv. 18, v. 1, xv. 15, xxi. 22, xxxiii. 33, 34, xxxviii. 7. *Later Manners and Customs.* — xiii. 26, xix. 23, 24, xxxi. 35; v. 4, xv. 28, xxiv. 12, xxix. 7, xxxix. 7; iii. 14, sq., xii. 18, sq., xv. 19, ix. 24, xii. 6. *Bernstein*, p. 79, sqq. A still stronger proof is furnished by its relation to the sufferings of the Hebrews, to their doctrine of final causes, and the advance in this kind of philosophy, in comparison with the kindred Psalms and Proverbs. [See *Warburton*, Div. Legat. vol. ii. p. 389; Lond. 1837.]

[c] The following writers refer it to *Solomon*, or an author of his times: R. *Nathan*, in Talmud, l. c. *Gregory*, Naz. Orat. ix. *Luther*, Table-Talk. *Harduin*, Chronol. vol. i. p. 533. *Reimarus*, Einleit. zur *Hoffmann*, N. Erk-

Since Ezekiel was acquainted with the character of Job, (xiv. 14, 16, 20,) and it is probable that Jeremiah had read the book,[a] we cannot place its date so low as the Chaldee period,[b] but near it, in the time when the kingdom of Judah was sinking to ruin. Ewald places it at the beginning of the seventh century B. C., and Hirzel at the end of it. The latter critic conjectures that the author of Job was carried to Ægypt by Pharaoh Necho, with King Jehoahaz, 611 B. C., and in this way acquired that familiarity with Ægypt and its remarkable things, which strikes us in his descriptions.[c]

---

lär. d. B. Hiob; 1734, 4to. *Döderlein*, Schol. in Lib. poet. vol. i. p. 2. *Stäudlin*, p. 260. *Richter*, l. c. *Rosenmüller*, p. 35.

[a] Comp. Jer. xx. 14—18, with Job iii. 3—10, x. 18; xvii. 1, with Job xix. 24; xxxi. 29, 30, with Job xxi. 19; but comp. also Deut. xxiv. 16. But the resemblance is too slight to warrant the conclusion that one author had seen the work of the other. [There is, indeed, a very obvious affinity between Job iii. 3—10, x. 18, and Jer. xx. 14—18. But perhaps the thought was original with neither; and, besides, it is quite as probable that the author of Job borrowed from Jeremiah, as Jeremiah from Job. Ezekiel's reference to Job is easily explained on the hypothesis that there was a tradition, oral or written, respecting such a person. At the most, it could only prove there once lived *a* Job, remarkable for piety and virtue — not that the *hero of this poem* ever lived, still less that it is a grave narration of facts. The same may be said of the reference to Job, in James v. 11, and Tobit ii. 12. "Quis, quæso," says *Michaelis*, (Epimetron de Lib. Jobi, p. 648,) "ægre feret, Lazari aut Samaritani exempli moneri ecclesiam, licet utrumque nuspiam fuisse credat?" and, alluding to the passage of Ezekiel, "nec inauditum aut absurdum veras personas et fictas in proponendo exemplo conjungi. Fac patrem, Lucretiæ et Pamelæ castitatem commendare filiæ, quis tam rigidus censor sit, ut id reprehendat?"]

[b] *Bernstein*, *Gesenius*, *Umbreit*, and the former editions of this Introduction, placed the date in the Chaldee period. *Herman von der Hardt*, *Leclerc*, *Warburton*, *Thomas Heath*, *J. Garnet*, Rabbi *Johannan*, (Baba Bath. fol. 15, c. 2, Hier. Sota, fol. 20, c. 4,) and others, were of the same opinion.

[c] See *Hitzig*, Esaias, p. 285, sq.

THE END.